Young Children with Special Needs

FOURTH EDITION

Young Children with Special Needs

Stephen R. Hooper

University of North Carolina School of Medicine
Chapel Hill, North Carolina

Warren Umansky

Children's Clinic
Augusta, Georgia

PEARSON

Merrill
Prentice Hall

Upper Saddle River, New Jersey
Columbus, Ohio

Library of Congress Cataloging-in-Publication Data

Hooper, Stephen R.
  Young children with special needs / Stephen R. Hooper, Warren
Umansky,—4th ed.
    p. cm.
Prev. ed. lists Warren Umansky as first author.
Includes bibliographical references and indexes.
  ISBN 0-13-111340-2
  1. Children with disabilities—Education—United States.
2. Perceptual-motor learning.   3. Child development—United States.
I. Umansky, Warren. II. Title.
  LC4031.U425 2004
  371.91'0973—dc21

                                                        2003010371

Vice President and Executive Publisher: Jeffery W. Johnston
Acquisitions Editor: Allyson P. Sharp
Editorial Assistants: Penny Burleson and Kathleen S. Burk
Production Editor: Linda Hillis Bayma
Production Coordination and Text Design: Carlisle Publishers Services
Design Coordinator: Diane C. Lorenzo
Photo Coordinator: Cynthia Cassidy
Cover Designer: Ali Mohrman
Cover image: Corbis
Production Manager: Laura Messerly
Director of Marketing: Ann Castel Davis
Marketing Manager: Amy June
Marketing Coordinator: Tyra Poole

This book was set in Garamond by Carlisle Communications, Ltd. It was printed and bound by R.R. Donnelley & Sons
Company. The cover was printed by The Lehigh Press, Inc.

Photo Credits: Scott Cunningham/Merrill, pp. 93, 332; Courtesy of Carole Dennis, pp. 229, 238; Courtesy of Carole Dennis
and Kathleen A Schlough, pp. 226, 233; Courtesy of Lisa Harris, pp. 38, 74, 101, 456; Courtesy of Steven Hooper, pp. 55,
120, 448, 452; Courtesy of Intellitools, pp. 210, 214; Courtesy of Lekotek of Georgia, Inc., p. 188; Courtesy of Jean Patz, pp.
249, 276, 292, 294, 295, 296, 312, 336, 421, 439; Courtesy of Prentke Romich Company, p. 204; Courtesy of Rebecca Pretzel,
p. 54; Courtesy of Rebecca Edmondson Pretzel and Jennifer Heimenz, p. 132; Barbara Schwartz/Merrill, pp. 23, 364, 410;
Courtesy of Tina Smith, p. 175; Anne Vega/Merrill, pp. 42, 90, 148, 172, 224, 268, 338, 372; Todd Yarrington/Merrill, pp. 2, 167.

Pearson Education Ltd.
Pearson Education Singapore Pte. Ltd.
Pearson Education Canada, Ltd.
Pearson Education—Japan

Pearson Education Australia Pty. Limited
Pearson Education North Asia Ltd.
Pearson Educación de Mexico, S.A. de C.V.
Pearson Education Malaysia Pte. Ltd.

10 9 8 7 6 5 4 3 2 1
ISBN: 0-13-111340-2

To all of the young children with special needs and their families who have inspired me to work on this project. To my children, Lindsay Rae and Madeline Grace, and to my wife, Mary Anne, who provided constant support for me during this process and many others! I also would like to dedicate this book to the memory of my parents, Virginia Rebecca and Ralph Carr. Mom, your strength continues to drive me forward. Dad, thanks for allowing me the opportunities to become resilient.

Stephen R. Hooper

This book is dedicated to the memory of my parents, Dorothy and George. I also dedicate this book to my wife and children and to the many children and their families who have taught me so very much over the years.

Warren Umansky

Foreword

After more than 30 years, the field of early intervention for young children with special needs has a distinguished history. The most humanistic attributes of professionals in education, human services, and government have been evident as we have collaborated with families to help our most vulnerable children. We have forged groundbreaking social compacts through government regulations and laws to institutionalize our commitments.

The field, itself, draws optimistic and creative people who are convinced of the enduring benefits of expert help given early and continuously for infants, preschool children, and their families. Teamwork among parents and interdisciplinary professionals is the documented foundation for effective early intervention.

Within early intervention, "necessity is the mother of invention." Our field has forged the best synergy among recommended professional practices, evidence-based research, and practical applications. We are known for designing field-validated solutions to difficult problems involving both assessment and intervention, and research in the field.

Yet, helping young children with complex and chronic needs is also an expensive proposition that tests our "best practice" assumptions. The recurrent debate among policy makers and researchers regularly tests our commitment. So far, our humanistic instincts have prevailed in the face of fiscal reforms in government and health care. Nevertheless, vigilance and advocacy are necessary to protect our investment in our most vulnerable young people.

University preparation of new professionals for this interdisciplinary field also requires commitment and unusual expertise. Few individuals and even fewer resources have accomplished this better than Umansky and Hooper in their previous editions of *Young Children with Special Needs*. The current edition of their text also continues a long, distinguished legacy of presenting practical knowledge buttressed by authoritative research. The fourth edition of *Young Children with Special Needs* is strengthened by its contributed nature, comprehensive coverage of the whole child, focus on the family in partnership with professionals, and an authoritative presentation of assessment, intervention, and technology. The liberal use of vignettes of children and families effectively translates the content of each chapter into "best practices." It exudes the optimism of the field while presenting complex information in a practical manner. This text will take its place as a premier resource for new and seasoned professionals.

Stephen J. Bagnato, Ed.D., NCSP
Professor of Pediatrics & Psychology
Director, Early Childhood Partnerships
Faculty Director, Developmental Psychology
*   Interdisciplinary Training*
*   Children's Hospital of Pittsburgh*
The UCLID Center at the University of Pittsburgh
University of Pittsburgh School of Medicine
http://www.uclid.org

Contributors

Carole W. Dennis, Sc.D., OTR/L, BCP
Assistant Professor
Occupational Therapy Department
Ithaca College
Ithaca, New York

Tashawna Duncan
School Psychology Program
Department of Educational Psychology
University of Florida
Gainesville, Florida

Susan R. Easterbrooks, Ed.D.
Associate Professor
Department of Educational Psychology
    and Special Education
Georgia State University
Atlanta, Georgia

Kathryn Wolff Heller, Ph.D.
Associate Professor
Educational Psychology and Special Education
Georgia State University
Atlanta, Georgia

Jennifer Hiemenz, Ph.D.
Assistant Professor
Department of Psychiatry
Clinical Center for the Study of Development
    and Learning
University of North Carolina School of Medicine
Chapel Hill, North Carolina

Joan Lieber, Ph.D.
Professor
Department of Special Education
University of Maryland–College Park
College Park, Maryland

Carrie Mills
School of Education
University of North Carolina–Chapel Hill
Chapel Hill, North Carolina

Jean Ann Patz, M.S., OTR/L
Adjunct Faculty
Occupational Therapy and Occupational Science
    Department
Towson University
Baltimore, Maryland

Rebecca Edmondson Pretzel, Ph.D.
Assistant Professor
Department of Psychiatry
Psychology Section Head
Clinical Center for the Study of Development
    and Learning
University of North Carolina School of Medicine
Chapel Hill, North Carolina

Mary E. Rugg
Institute on Human Development and Disability
University of Georgia
Athens, Georgia

Kathleen A. Schlough
Occupational Therapy Department
Ithaca College
Ithaca, New York

Tina M. Smith, Ph.D.
Associate Professor and Director
School Psychology Program
Department of Educational Psychology
University of Florida
Gainesville, Florida

Zolinda Stoneman, Ph.D.
Director, Institute on Human Development
    and Disability
University of Georgia
Athens, Georgia

Preface

It has been approximately 25 years since the first edition of *Young Children with Special Needs* was published, and there was little history to present about the field at that time. We remarked about that in the preface of the third edition, and now comment on it again in the fourth edition. This remains an important point in that the growth in the field of early childhood special education has been extraordinary. From the first few experimental personnel preparation programs, there have grown dozens—with more contemporary programs evolving at a rapid rate even since the last edition in 1998. From a few demonstration early intervention programs for preschoolers in each state, there have grown thousands of programs, and early intervention is mandatory in every state for eligible children beginning at birth. From a few experimental curricula and homemade materials, there has grown an industry geared to serving the needs of young children with disabilities and their families.

This growth has been unprecedented, and it is likely to continue—even in the face of difficult financial times. There has been a true commitment to early childhood special education on the part of state and federal governments, university training programs, and local communities, and this commitment likely will be rewarded with better services and evidence-based interventions for young children with special needs, better trained personnel, more informed and more involved families and communities, and increasingly more child-friendly public policies. In turn, we should gain increased respect for young children with special needs and their families and, ultimately, there should be valuable contributions to our society as a whole from this population.

The fourth edition of *Young Children with Special Needs* maintains a number of similarities with the third edition. This edition continues to be driven by a developmental theoretical perspective. We have built that perspective into most of the chapters in the latter half of the text, and all of the contributors have done an exceptional job in perpetuating this developmental perspective. We also have continued to put emphasis on some key content areas in early childhood special education such as historical foundations, basic growth and development, families, assessment and intervention, and technology. At the center of successful early intervention are competent professionals who are knowledgeable about children, families, and the tools of assessment and intervention, and who apply that knowledge in a sensitive and skillful way. Many of the chapters in this text provide the reader with an introductory knowledge base about the field and about factors that influence development, and we have made a great effort to present the very latest information and to challenge the reader to think beyond the facts. In this revision, we also continue to emphasize the importance of gaining a broad, yet deep perspective of how children develop as they do and what can go wrong. We have remained consistent in our use of terminology (e.g., we use the term *early interventionist* to refer to the many different professionals, including and most specifically the early childhood special educator, who provide early intervention services), and we have given the instructor in early childhood or special education a clear approach from which to work; that is, a knowledge-content-application approach. We believe this approach is more logical and more conducive to incremental learning by the student.

The fourth edition of *Young Children with Special Needs* also maintains a number of differences when compared to the third edition. The text has a more user-friendly appearance, with a number of instructional aids being added. Specifically, each chapter begins with an outline of the chapter-specific topics, and ends with questions and discussion points. In addition, each chapter provides a number of recommended resources for additional reading, research, and projects. All chapters have additional instructional technologies, including introductory case vignettes, key points listed in a sidebar format, text boxes highlighting a topic directly or indirectly related to the chapter, and boldfaced key words. It is hoped that these new instructional features will facilitate the teaching and learning of this material.

Another subtle difference between the third and fourth editions lies in how the text is organized. Based on peer reviewer comments, we have subdivided the chapters a bit differently from the previous edition via four separate sections. Most chapters have been realigned to emphasize the information that is most important for early interventionists and to provide as broad a perspective as possible to the reader. Philosophically, we see development as the basis of assessment and diagnosis; it is the foundation upon which interventions are built. The early interventionist who knows child development can feel confident and be supportive of children's and parents' needs.

Specifically, **Part I** delves into basic foundational issues in early childhood special education and comprises three chapters. Chapter 1, "Introduction to Young Children with Special Needs," provides an overview of the history of special education, with a key focus on special education classification and research support for early intervention. Chapter 2, "Developmental Processes and Factors Affecting Development," details growth and development, including definitional issues, and provides a current, research-based discussion of the numerous factors that can impact on development. Chapter 3, "Partnerships with Families," continues to emphasize the importance of families in the early years, particularly with respect to programmatic intervention for children.

Part II addresses principles of assessment and intervention and comprises three chapters. Chapter 4, "Assessment of Young Children: Standards, Stages, and Approaches," provides a state-of-the-art discussion of the assessment process and procedures necessary for evaluating young children with special needs, whereas Chapter 5, "Intervention," continues to provide an evidence-based discussion of a wonderful array of contemporary approaches to programmatic treatment in early childhood special education. The discussion on cultural diversity and intervention also is quite noteworthy. Chapter 6, "Technology for Assessment and Intervention," has been thoroughly revised and now has a clearer focus on the use of technology for assessment and treatment. In particular, the various types of technology are discussed and their importance to nearly every developmental domain is asserted. This expansion of the types of technology clearly reflects advances in the field of early childhood special education since the last edition was published.

Part III addresses the core components of this text—developmental domains—and comprises five chapters. Chapter 7, "Gross Motor Development," and Chapter 8, "Fine Motor, Oral Motor, and Self-Care Development," provide exquisite details with respect to these two motor domains. These chapters represent some of the material contained in the third edition of this text when this information was combined into a single chapter, but the content was subdivided for the fourth edition to provide more expansive coverage of these key developmental domains. Chapter 9, "Cognitive Development," and Chapter 10, "Communication," have been updated to reflect contemporary literature in each of these developmental domains. Chapter 11, "Social and Emotional Development," also has been updated to reflect current research, but there is increased focus on peers, friendships, and social play. These latter topics reflect current trends in research in early childhood, with the application of these findings to young children with special needs only beginning to be understood.

The final section, **Part IV**, consists of Chapter 12, "Issues and Directions." In this chapter we comment on some of the more critical and controversial issues that are raised in the other chapters, and have extended topics raised in the third edition of this text. We hope these discussion points will become the basis for reflection and further investigation by the reader. Although perhaps a bit atypical for an epilogue, we also added a case study to provide a clinical framework from which many of the key points and issues could be discussed.

The modifications in this edition either reflect what early interventionists have said about the importance of a specific issue and their need for more comprehensive knowledge, or they reflect our own impressions of what early interventionists need to know. But mastery of the information will lead to mastery on the job. Any redundancy in information among chapters is intentional because it reflects both the natural overlap in material from one developmental area to another, and that repetition facilitates learning.

Acknowledgments

We are indebted to our contributors, whose hard work, knowledge, and judgment have resulted in a comprehensive, relevant, and concise text. We also would like to express appreciation to the professionals who reviewed our manuscript: Barbara A. Beakley, Millersville University; Maureen R. Norris, Bellarmine University; Michael A. Rettig, Washburn University. Special thanks to our editor Allyson Sharp, editorial assistant Penny Burleson, and production editor Linda Bayma, of Merrill/Prentice Hall. We all have worked to produce an edition that will continue to be helpful to those who work with young children with special needs and those who want to know more about them.

Stephen R. Hooper

Warren Umansky

Discover the Companion Website Accompanying This Book

The Prentice Hall Companion Website: A Virtual Learning Environment

Technology is a constantly growing and changing aspect of our field that is creating a need for content and resources. To address this emerging need, Prentice Hall has developed an online learning environment for students and professors alike—Companion Websites—to support our textbooks.

In creating a Companion Website, our goal is to build on and enhance what the textbook already offers. For this reason, the content for each user-friendly web-site is organized by topic and provides the professor and student with a variety of meaningful resources. Common features of a Companion Website include:

For the Professor—

Every Companion Website integrates **Syllabus Manager**™, an online syllabus creation and management utility.

- **Syllabus Manager**™ provides you, the instructor, with an easy, step-by-step process to create and revise syllabi, with direct links into the Companion Website and other online content without having to learn HTML.
- Students may logon to your syllabus during any study session. All they need to know is the web address for the Companion Website and the password you've assigned to your syllabus.
- After you have created a syllabus using **Syllabus Manager**™, students may enter the syllabus for their course section from any point in the Companion Website.
- Clicking on a date, the student is shown the list of activities for the assignment. The activities for each assignment are linked directly to actual content, saving time for students.
- Adding assignments consists of clicking on the desired due date, then filling in the details of the assignment—name of the assignment, instructions, and whether it is a one-time or repeating assignment.
- In addition, links to other activities can be created easily. If the activity is online, a URL can be entered in the space provided, and it will be linked automatically in the final syllabus.
- Your completed syllabus is hosted on our servers, allowing convenient updates from any computer on the Internet. Changes you make to your syllabus are immediately available to your students at their next logon.

For the Student—

- **Overview and General Information**—General information about the topic and how it will be covered in the website.
- **Web Links**—A variety of websites related to topic areas.
- **Content Methods and Strategies**—Resources that help to put theories into practice in the special education classroom.
- **Reflective Questions and Case-Based Activities**—Put concepts into action, participate in activities, examine strategies, and more.
- **National and State Laws**—An online guide to how federal and state laws affect your special education classroom.
- **Behavior Management**—An online guide to help you manage behaviors in the special education classroom.
- **Message Board**—Virtual bulletin board to post and respond to questions and comments from a national audience.

To take advantage of these and other resources, please visit the *Young Children with Special Needs,* Fourth Edition, Companion Website at

www.prenhall.com/hooper

Educator Learning Center: An Invaluable Online Resource

Merrill Education and the Association for Supervision and Curriculum Development (ASCD) invite you to take advantage of a new online resource, one that provides access to the top research and proven strategies associated with ASCD and Merrill—the Educator Learning Center. At **www.EducatorLearningCenter.com** you will find resources that will enhance your students' understanding of course topics and of current educational issues, in addition to being invaluable for further research.

How the Educator Learning Center Will Help Your Students Become Better Teachers

With the combined resources of Merrill Education and ASCD, you and your students will find a wealth of tools and materials to better prepare them for the classroom.

Research

- More than 600 articles from the ASCD journal *Educational Leadership* discuss everyday issues faced by practicing teachers.
- A direct link on the site to Research Navigator™ gives students access to many of the leading education journals, as well as extensive content detailing the research process.
- Excerpts from Merrill Education texts give your students insights on important topics of instructional methods, diverse populations, assessment, classroom management, technology, and refining classroom practice.

Classroom Practice

- Hundreds of lesson plans and teaching strategies are categorized by content area and age range.
- Case studies and classroom video footage provide virtual field experience for student reflection.
- Computer simulations and other electronic tools keep your students abreast of today's classrooms and current technologies.

Look into the Value of Educator Learning Center Yourself

Preview the value of this educational environment by visiting **www.EducatorLearningCenter.com** and clicking on "Demo." For a free 4-month subscription to the Educator Learning Center in conjunction with this text, simply contact your Merrill/Prentice Hall sales representative.

Brief Contents

Contents

5 *Intervention*   *148*

Tina M. Smith and Tashawna Duncan

6 *Technology for Assessment and Intervention*   *188*

Kathryn Wolff Heller

PART III   Developmental Domains

7 *Gross Motor Development* 224

Carole W. Dennis and Kathleen A. Schlough

8 Fine Motor, Oral Motor, and Self-Care Development   *268*

Jean A. Patz and Carole W. Dennis

11 *Social and Emotional Development* 410

Joan Lieber and Warren Umansky

PART IV   Epilogue

12   *Issues and Directions*   *448*
Stephen R. Hooper and Warren Umansky

Note: Every effort has been made to provide accurate and current Internet information in this book. However, the Internet and information posted on it are constantly changing, and it is inevitable that some of the Internet addresses listed in this textbook will change.

PART I

Foundations

CHAPTER 1
*Introduction to Young Children
with Special Needs*

CHAPTER 2
*Developmental Processes
and Factors Affecting Development*

CHAPTER 3
Partnerships with Families

1

Introduction to Young Children with Special Needs

Warren Umansky

Chapter Outline

Alex and Margie

Alex and Margie got married in their mid-30s. Soon afterward, they tried to satisfy one of their mutual goals in life—that of having a child. After several years of marriage, Margie finally became pregnant. Joy was mixed with apprehension. Had they waited too long? They had heard that the chances of problems occurring increased with the age of the parents. Did their family history doom their chances of having a typical child? After all, Margie's older brother had Down syndrome, two of her nephews were being treated for Attention Deficit Hyperactivity Disorder, and an elderly uncle had what probably was a mild case of cerebral palsy. Alex's family also had its share of problems, from autism in his sister's youngest son to his father's congenital deafness in one ear. Maybe they shouldn't have tried to have kids after all, Margie and Alex thought to themselves.

Margie was in good health and she was committed to taking excellent care of herself during pregnancy. They also planned to have prenatal testing done that would alert them to any suspected problems. Although Margie and Alex wanted desperately to envision a healthy and perfect baby, they knew there were no guarantees. They so looked forward to the first sonogram that would allow them to see the fetus in the uterus. They were looking forward to quickening, when Margie would begin to feel the baby moving. They would be more comfortable when they saw a healthy-looking image on the sonogram and felt the baby's movements. They tried hard to concentrate on positive thoughts of a wonderful baby and happy family experiences; yet, they were aware that resources in their community provided early intervention services to their nephew with autism and would be available to them if the need arose. They hoped that need would not arise.

There is mounting evidence that early intervention can have a markedly positive effect on the development of infants and preschoolers with some types of disabilities. Partly because of the influence of professional and advocacy organizations, such as the Council for Exceptional Children, the United Cerebral Palsy Association, the Autism Society of America, and the Epilepsy Foundation of America, decision makers have become more responsive to the needs of children with disabilities and children who are at risk for disabilities. In addition, the experiences of agencies that offer early intervention programs, such as the community resources referred to in the vignette, have contributed to an atmosphere of urgency. These experiences have revealed such benefits of early intervention as long-term savings in program costs as children's needs for complex and expensive services decrease with time.

Not everyone is convinced that early education is successful or necessary, however. Certainly the goal of early childhood special education is an ambitious one: to intervene during the early years to prevent or lessen the effects of harmful biological or environmental influences on a child's development and learning. It is the broad scope of early education efforts that has provided fuel for the fires of both proponents and skeptics.

The idea of early education did not develop overnight; rather, it evolved slowly and on many fronts simultaneously. For example, animal research conducted by Harlow (1974) with monkeys and by Denenberg and his colleagues (Denenberg, 1981; Denenberg et al., 1981) with rats and rabbits related characteristics of early experience to the animals' subsequent behavior and development. Rats that were raised in a complex environment with visual stimulation were found to have brains that were different from those of rats raised in an impoverished environment (Rosenzweig et al., 1969). The preponderance of evidence from psychological research supports the significant impact of early experience on development (Haddad & Garralda, 1992; Lizardi, Klein, Ouimette, & Riso, 1995). Enriched experiences can maintain or accelerate development, and deprivation and abusive experiences can contribute to retarded or deviant development.

Medical research has contributed further evidence of the effects of early experiences on development. The generalized influence of poverty on development is profound, but can be mitigated by early intervention (Brooks-Gunn & Duncan, 1997; Devaney, Ellwood, & Love, 1997). The specific effects of nutrition on brain growth and mental development have been found to be significant (Leibowitz, 1991; Read, 1982), as well. Malnourished children tend to develop at a retarded rate and exhibit learning and behavioral deficits as they get older (Galler, Ramsey, Solimano, & Lowell, 1983a; Galler, Ramsey, Solimano, Lowell, & Mason, 1983b; Ricciuti, 1993). Prenatal malnutrition may have a particularly negative impact on the later development of children (Morgane, Austin, Borzino, & Tonkiss, 1993); however, many of the adverse effects of malnutrition may be overcome by sensory stimulation. Several studies (Winick, Meyer, & Harris, 1975; Yatkin, McLaren, Kanawati, & Sabbach, 1971) revealed that the rate of development and intelligence of severely malnourished children improved to typical ranges when social stimulation was supplemented by individual attention.

In theory, as in practice, attention has focused on early experiences. The works of Freud (1965), Erikson (1963), and Piaget and Inhelder (1969) portray a building-block concept in which development is viewed as a structure made up of different levels. The strength and integrity of the lower levels of the structure—the early

---

The goal of early intervention is to prevent or reduce negative environmental and biological influences on the child.

One basis for early childhood special education is found in animal research.

Children who are malnourished may achieve typical ranges of development with comprehensive early intervention.

years—are necessary for stability as more levels are added. Similarly, this chapter lays the foundation for a logical and supportable approach to the education of young children with special needs. Subsequent chapters focus on characteristics of these children and the process for providing high-quality services to them (and their families) to maximize their development and independence.

A Rationale for Early Childhood Special Education

Particularly during times of economic hardship and competition for limited resources, programs that remain and grow are often those with advocates who present the most logical and compelling arguments. Many arguments can be made for committing resources to the education of young children with special needs. Programs throughout the country that have served these children provide firsthand evidence of the benefits of doing so.

> Garnering support for early childhood special education programs requires that the professional can make clear and compelling arguments that justify its benefits.

Legislation

Until the last half of this century, education for children with disabilities was primarily a local and state concern. The federal government made few specific commitments to children with special needs. Its first commitment to special education was the establishment in 1864 of Gallaudet College for the Deaf in Washington, DC, but it was not until 1930 that the federal government directly addressed the issue of special education and established a Section on Exceptional Children and Youth in the Office of Education of the Department of Health, Education, and Welfare. The needs of young children were also addressed through the Children's Bureau of the same department.

The federal government's role in special education remained limited, however, until the 1960s. It did support programs for children with special needs by (1) supplying matching funds to state and local agencies, (2) granting funds for research in all areas of exceptionality, (3) disseminating information, (4) providing consultative services to state and local groups, and (5) distributing fellowships for the training of professionals in all areas related to special education (Kirk & Gallagher, 1983). A major turning point for federal support of education came in 1965, when Congress passed the Elementary and Secondary Education Act (ESEA). This act and its subsequent amendments (1) made available to schools large amounts of money with which to serve children from 3 to 21 years of age who were educationally disadvantaged and who were disabled, (2) created the Bureau of Education for the Handicapped, and (3) funded research and demonstration projects to improve special education services.

The Handicapped Children's Early Education Assistance Act of 1968 represented the first major federal recognition of the specific importance of early education. The purpose of this legislation was to support model programs throughout the nation that would demonstrate exemplary practices and share their information with others. The act established the Handicapped Children's Early Education Program (HCEEP) to administer and provide technical support for 3-year demonstration programs, called *First Chance* projects. Over the years, this act also funded outreach programs and a Technical Assistance and Development System (TADS) to assist these projects. Called *NECTAS* for many years, the name was changed in 2002 when it was refunded as the **National Early Childhood Technical Assistance Center (NECTAC).** The center still is engaged in technical assistance, publication, and other support activities and continues to be located at the University of North Carolina at Chapel Hill. HCEEP, now called the *Early Education Program for Children with Disabilities* (EEPCD), continues to fund exemplary model programs.

Several hundred demonstration programs have been funded over the years since 1968. Many former demonstration programs still receive funds to help other agencies adopt their documented models for delivering services to young children with special needs in other geographical areas. Two large studies of demonstration projects have evaluated the projects' efforts in meeting their goals. A Battelle Institute report (1976), although criticized for lack of stringent research procedures, cited developmental gains in children beyond those that would have been expected had intervention not been provided. Subsequent to that study, Littlejohn & Associates (1982) followed up on programs and children who once had been part of the First Chance network and found that 84% of the programs continued to serve children when eligibility for federal funding expired. The outcomes for the children who had been served in the programs also appeared to be favorable. The legislative incentive offered in 1968, then, recognized the importance of the early years, and it appears that mandate has been exercised prudently and effectively. The continued growth of early childhood programs and their benefits to children affirms the logic of this incentive.

Other federal legislation has acknowledged the need for early intervention as well. The Economic Opportunity and Community Partnership Act of 1974 and subsequent amendments to the law required Head Start programs in each state to serve a minimum of 10% children with disabilities. In addition, 14 Resource Access Projects were funded to provide training and technical assistance for improved services to children with disabilities in Head Start programs. In 2000 and 2001, more than 858,000 children and their families were served in Head Start programs of which more than 10% were disabled. The Early Head Start Program provided services to 45,000 children under 3 years of age and their families during the same period.

In 1974, Amendments to the Education of the Handicapped Act required states without conflicting laws to establish a plan to identify and serve all children with disabilities from birth to 21 years of age. The same philosophy and a similar age range were included in Public Law (P.L.) 94–142, the Education for All Handicapped Children Act of 1975. (Unfortunately, few states fell within this act's mandate because of state laws that defined an older mandatory school age.) In addition, priorities for serving children were established such that states first had to serve school-aged children who were receiving no education, then children with severe disabilities who were in inappropriate placement, and, finally, preschool children. Nevertheless, several states passed local legislation to serve young children with special needs. Texas, for example, made programs available from birth to children who needed special services. California offered state funds to any school system that served preschool-aged children with disabilities. Virginia maintained a statewide technical assistance system for preschool teachers of children with disabilities and reimbursed the school system for a large portion of the teachers' salaries. P.L. 94-142 is viewed by some as one of the major pieces of legislation ever passed that has motivated states to provide high-quality education to children with special needs. Amendments to the original law have further expanded and refined services.

P.L. 94-142 contains numerous provisions that apply to children with disabilities of all ages and some that apply to preschool-aged children specifically. Some of the requirements of the original law follow (Kirk & Gallagher, 1983):

1. Public education agencies must ensure that all children who need special education and related services are identified and evaluated.
2. Parents have numerous procedural safeguards that protect the rights of each child with a disability to receive a free and appropriate education. These safeguards include the rights of parents to do the following:
   a. Review the child's educational records.
   b. Obtain an independent evaluation of the child.
   c. Receive written notice before the school begins the special education placement process.
   d. Request a hearing before an impartial hearing officer to challenge placement or program decisions.
3. The child must receive a comprehensive multidisciplinary educational assessment. Various types of intellectual, social, and cultural information must be considered in the assessment. The process must be repeated at least every 3 years.
4. An individualized education plan (IEP) must be written for every child in special education. Development of the document is a joint effort of school personnel and the parent. The IEP must be reviewed at least annually.
5. To the maximum extent possible, children with disabilities must be educated with their nondisabled peers. Special classes and separate schools can be used only when the nature or severity of the child's disability prohibits education in a more typical setting.

P.L. 94-142 also provided Preschool Incentive Grants to states that identified preschool children in need of special education services. The act allowed states to receive up to $300 for each 3- to 5-year-old child in addition to the funds the act already made available to all children with disabilities. In actuality, considerably less than that amount was available for each child with disabilities when the law was first implemented; initially, only about an additional $100 was provided by the federal government to states for each identified 3- to 5-year-old in need of special education services.

Legislative action during the past 25 years has left little doubt about the federal commitment to young children with special needs. Congress took a major step in 1986 with the passage of **P.L. 99-457.** In addition to continuing authorization for services to preschool children with disabilities from age 3 under Section 619 of Title B of the law (the Preschool Grants Program), Title H of the law provided incentives to states to serve children from birth who had special needs or were at risk for later problems. The law specified an increased role for families in services to children from birth through 2 years of age and introduced the individualized family service plan (IFSP), which is the equivalent of the IEP but must consider the needs of the whole family relative to the child. States had 5 years to implement a comprehensive, coordinated interagency system of services and resources, including an emphasis on serving infants and toddlers. States that

P.L. 99-457 was a major turning point for services to infants, toddlers, and preschoolers with disabilities.

BOX 1.1	The 16 Minimum Components of Public Law 99-457 (Part C)*

1. A definition of "developmentally delayed" to be used by the state in carrying out the program.
2. A timetable for making appropriate services available to all eligible children in the state.
3. Performance of comprehensive multidisciplinary evaluations to determine the needs of children and families.
4. Development of individualized family service plans and the provision of case management services.
5. A comprehensive child find and referral system.
6. A public awareness program.
7. A central directory of services, experts, research, and demonstration projects.
8. A comprehensive system of personnel development.
9. A single line of authority in a lead agency designated or established by the governor.
10. A policy pertaining to contracting or making arrangements with local service providers.
11. A procedure for timely reimbursement of funds.
12. Procedural safeguards.
13. Policies and procedures for personnel standards.
14. A system for compiling data regarding the early intervention programs.
15. A state interagency coordinating council.
16. Policies and procedures to ensure that early intervention services are provided in a natural environment to the maximum extent appropriate.

*http://www.nectac.org/partc/componen.asp

adopted this initiative were required to have 14 components in place based on a time line specified by the law wherein states had to be prepared to provide full services to infants and toddlers by the fifth year of funding. By the 1993–1994 school year, all states were required to ensure full implementation. There are now 16 components required by P.L. 99-457 as a consequence of subsequent amendments to the law (P.L. 105-17). These components are presented in Box 1.1.

In 1991, Congress reauthorized funds for special education programs as the Individuals with Disabilities Education Act (IDEA). This revision of the original law made services for the 3- to 5-year-old population mandatory for states rather than optional. A subsequent authorization changed the funding formula to increase the amount of money that states received for each identified child. The 1997 Amendments to IDEA (P.L. 105-17) further solidified the funding of services. Figure 1.1 presents funding levels and the number of children served under Part B of IDEA for the 20-year period 1977 to 1998. The amendments also moved provisions for services to infants and toddlers from Part H to Part C.

The specific wording of the law formalized a philosophy of **inclusiveness** promoted by early intervention professionals for many years. According to Odom et al. (2000), "*inclusion* is the active participation of young children with disabilities and typically developing children in the same classroom . . . and community settings" (p. 1).

Inclusiveness is the participation of children with disabilities in settings with typically developing children.

Key:

Dollars (millions) appropriated for distribution to states for Section 619

Children (thousands) receiving FAPE on December 1 of each federal fiscal year, U.S., D.C. & P.R.

$ Per child allocation of 619 dollars

Federal fiscal year For example, in FFY 1986, 261,000 children were reported to be receiving services as of December 1, 1985.

FFY	'77	'86	'87	'88	'89	'90	'91	'92	'93	'94	'95	'96	'97	'98	'99	'00	'01	'02
Dollars (millions)	12	28	180	201	247	251	292	320	326	339	360	360	360	374	374	390	390	390
Children (thousands)	197	261	265	288	323	352	369	398	430	479	528	549	562	572	573	587	599	619
$ Per Child	63	110	679	697	769	713	797	803	750	707	683	656	641	654	653	664	650	630

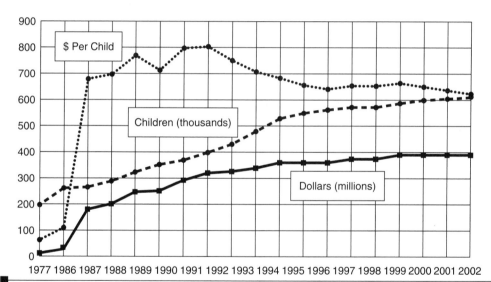

FIGURE 1.1   Number of children served, total appropriations, and allocation per child from 1977 to 2002 under Part B, Section 619 (Preschool Programs) of the Individuals with Disabilities Education Act

Reproduced with permission of the National Early Childhood Technical Assistance Center from Danaher, J., Kraus, R., Hipps, C., & Armijo, C. (Eds.). (2003). *Section 619 profile* (12th ed.). Chapel Hill: The University of North Carolina, FPG Child Development Institute, National Early Childhood Technical Assistance Center.

The purpose of inclusion is to expose children with disabilities to typical settings, activities, and peers, allowing typically developing children to interact with their peers with disabilities. The IDEA also promoted the principle of **natural environments,** which means that the child should receive early intervention services where the child naturally would be—in the home or at a child care center, for example. With increasing numbers

Natural environments enable delivery of services to young children with special needs in settings that are typical for other children of that age.

of children receiving early intervention, programs are being challenged to develop new service delivery models.

The number of children served by early intervention programs and the amount of money spent for services are significant. About 600,000 children with disabilities aged 3 through 5 were served by preschool programs supported by IDEA (Part B, Section 619) during the 2000–2001 school year. Table 1.1 shows the number of infants and toddlers through age 2 served from 1991 to 2002 under Part C of IDEA and the amount of money appropriated. In the following year (2000–2001), over 230,000 infants and toddlers and their families received early intervention services. This represents an increase of 80,000 since the last edition of this book was published in 1998. These children are served in many different settings (see Table 1.2).

IDEA provides other programs that indirectly benefit young children with special needs and their families. For example, the law provides continued funding for demonstration service projects (formerly First Chance projects), for replication of successful demonstration projects (called *outreach*), for research projects and demonstration personnel training projects, for research institutes and other research activities, and for technical assistance. During the 2000–2001 school year, the following activities were funded through IDEA: 39 model demonstration projects including six Child Find projects; 35 outreach projects; 51 research projects; 7 research institutes and studies, and 1 national technical assistance center.

Finally, IDEA provides funds to states for personnel training programs and specifies that each state must have a Comprehensive System of Personnel Development (CSPD) plan to prepare its personnel. Ninety-one training projects were funded for 2000–2001. Recipients of demonstration and outreach grants are encouraged to coordinate activities with the state agency responsible for administering early

TABLE 1.1   Summary of the Infant and Toddler Program (Part C) of the Individuals with Disabilities Education Act

Fiscal Year	Appropriation (in millions of dollars)	Number of Children Served
1991	117	194,363
1992	175	166,634
1993	213	143,392
1994	253	154,065
1995	316	165,253
1996	316	177,634
1997	316	186,859
1998	350	197,376
1999	370	186,819
2000	375	205,769
2001	383.6	230,853
2002	417	247,433

Source: Reproduced with permission of the National Early Childhood Technical Assistance Center from Danaher, J. (Ed.). (2003). *Part C updates*. Chapel Hill: The University of North Carolina, FPG Child Development Institute, National Early Childhood Technical Assistance Center.

Setting	Number of Children
Developmental delay programs	30,248
Home	108,778
Hospital (inpatient)	1,446
Service provider location	21,813
Typically developing programs	6,746
Residential facility	233
Other setting	3,722

TABLE 1.2 Number of Infants and Toddlers in Different Settings Receiving Services Under Part C of the Individuals with Disabilities Education Act as of December 1, 1998

Source: From the *Twenty-Third Annual Report to Congress on the Implementation of the Individuals with Disabilities Education Act (IDEA),* by the U.S. Department of Education, 2001, Washington, DC: U.S. Government Printing Office.

intervention programs. The law gave the governor of each state authority to appoint the state agency to oversee the infant and toddler (Part C) program in the state. The responsible agencies in each state are listed in Table 1.3. The successful application of other federal laws to young children with special needs offers further support for the rights of these children to early education opportunities.

Section 504 of the Rehabilitation Act of 1973 prohibits discrimination on the basis of disability in any state or local government program or activity that receives federal funds. A regulation added in 1977 specifies the applicability of Section 504 to public school districts and other recipients of federal funds in education, health, and social services. These agencies, including schools, must ensure that children with disabilities are not excluded from services or denied benefits. However, whereas the law ensures the participation of children with disabilities in school programs, it does not require that the school provide expensive or extensive services. Rather, the law refers to "reasonable accommodations." These may include a special aide providing assistance, modifications to the class program, monitoring of medications, counseling, using assistive technology, or a behavior management plan. Under Section 504, children may receive related services, such as speech therapy, occupational therapy, or physical therapy, even if the child does not receive services through IDEA. Again, no funds are provided to schools for these services.

The **Americans with Disabilities Act of 1990 (ADA),** like Section 504, is an antidiscrimination law. Whereas mostly aimed at employment settings, two provisions affect students. The first applies protections in nonsectarian private schools, including preschools. Furthermore, ADA requires that public schools make accommodations for students with disabilities. These may include accessibility to facilities, program modifications, and use of assistive technology. The law provides no funds to fulfill these requirements.

Through legislative authority, the U.S. Department of Health and Human Services's Administration for Children and Families and the Administration on Developmental Disabilities also provide specialized funds for some early intervention activities. Funds are allotted through state developmental disabilities councils which may support a variety of child development activities, such as training programs and

Section 504 of the Rehabilitation Act of 1973 requires that "reasonable accommodations" be made in school for children with disabilities.

The Americans with Disabilities Act of 1990 states that public schools must provide accessible accommodations for students with disabilities, including modified programs and adaptive technology.

TABLE 1.3   Lead State Agencies for IDEA, Part C (Infant and Toddler Program)

State/Jurisdiction	Agency
Alabama	Rehabilitation Services
Alaska	Health and Social Services
American Samoa	Health
Arizona	Economic Security
Arkansas	Human Services/Developmental Disabilities
California	Developmental Services
Colorado	Education
Commonwealth of N. Mariana Islands	Education
Connecticut	Mental Retardation
Delaware	Health and Social Services
District of Columbia	Human Services
Florida	Health (Children's Medical Services)
Georgia	Human Resources/Division of Health
Guam	Education
Hawaii	Health
Idaho	Health and Welfare/Developmental Disabilities
Illinois	Human Services
Indiana	Family and Social Services
Iowa	Education
Kansas	Health and Environment
Kentucky	Human Resources/Mental Health-Mental Retardation
Louisiana	Education
Maine	Education
Maryland	Education
Massachusetts	Public Health
Michigan	Education
Minnesota	Education
Mississippi	Health
Missouri	Education
Montana	Public Health and Human Services
Nebraska	Education/Health and Human Services
Nevada	Human Resources
New Hampshire	Health and Human Services
New Jersey	Health and Senior Services
New Mexico	Health/Developmental Disabilities
New York	Health
North Carolina	Public Health
North Dakota	Human Services
Ohio	Health
Oklahoma	Education
Oregon	Education
Palau	Education
Pennsylvania	Public Welfare
Puerto Rico	Health
Rhode Island	Health
South Carolina	Health and Environmental Control

Continued

TABLE 1.3 *Continued*

State/Jurisdiction	Agency
South Dakota	Education
Tennessee	Education
Texas	Interagency Council on Early Childhood Intervention
Utah	Health
Vermont	Education and Human Services
Virgin Islands	Health
Virginia	Mental Health/Mental Retardation/Substance Abuse Services
Washington	Social and Health Services
West Virginia	Health and Human Services
Wisconsin	Health and Social Services
Wyoming	Health

Source: National Early Childhood Technical Assistance System (NECTAS), Chapel Hill, NC. Retrieved from http://www.nectac.org/partc/ext ptclead.asp

workshops. University Centers for Excellence in Developmental Disabilities Education, Research, and Service (UCEDDs), of which there are 61 in the United States, provide interdisciplinary training, exemplary services, technical assistance, and information and dissemination activities for a population beginning at birth. Finally, Projects of National Significance (PNS) are funded annually to address critical needs in the area of developmental disabilities. Among these are projects that develop training and ongoing programs for inclusion of children with developmental disabilities in child care settings.

Clearly, there is now tangible evidence to support the prudence of government involvement in early childhood intervention. Although government action initially was a response to pressure from advocacy groups and legislators with family members or friends with disabilities, federal and state legislative and regulatory activities currently reflect growing acceptance of early education.

Review the legislative actions that had a significant impact on early intervention. What would be the status of early childhood special education without legislation?

Empirical Evidence

Factors that cause impairment in a child are present even before birth. The gene pool of the mother and father, as well as the level and extent of prenatal care, contribute to the outcome of pregnancy. As will be seen in chapter 2, research literature continues to identify specific factors that have an impact during pregnancy and influence the subsequent health and well-being of the child. Intervention in the areas of maternal nutrition and child-rearing attitudes have yielded optimistic results (Badger, 1981; Ginsburg et al., 2002; Ramey & Bryant, 1982). Further, revelations from the Human Genome Project offer hope of prenatal identification and even prenatal treatment for many genetically based disorders. The Human Genome Project is a 15-year, federally funded program whose goal has been to identify the functions of each of the human genes. The findings from the project already have provided revolutionary changes in the search for prevention and treatment of broad-based diseases and disorders.

Once a child is born with a disabling condition, of course, a different set of factors must be addressed. The accumulating evidence indicates that results of efforts to remediate or attenuate children's deficits also can be successful.

Investigations of early intervention have focused on two major groups of children: those who exhibit developmental deficits as a result of environmental factors and those who are disabled as a result of biological factors. These two groups of children comprise the majority of the special education population in public school programs. A question that must be asked is: If these children had been identified and served earlier, could something have been done to make special education placement less likely or, at least, to reduce the severity of the children's problems? Although more evidence exists to support the benefits of early intervention for children at environmental risk (Ramey & Ramey, 1994), research that supports services for young children with biological impairments also is growing. This body of research is riddled with procedural problems such as small sample size, lack of comparison groups, a short period of intervention, and poorly defined intervention procedures (Gallagher, 1991). Even when these problems are considered, however, early intervention with children with biological impairments appears to be effective for maintaining or accelerating their rate of development (Blair, Ramey, & Hardin, 1995; Boyce, Smith, Immel, & Casto, 1993; Fewell & Oelwein, 1991).

Even with procedural problems with the research, the evidence tends to support the benefits of early intervention with a variety of young children with special needs.

Some components of early intervention may have greater impact than others (Shonkoff, Hauser, Krauss, & Upshur, 1992). For example, the impact of child–family interaction (Keogh, Garnier, Bernheimer, & Gallimore, 2000) and biological traits (Hauser-Cram, Warfield, Shonkoff, & Kraus, 2001) was examined in various groups of infants, toddlers, and preschoolers with developmental disabilities in early intervention programs. In general, biological characteristics of the child with disabilities are the best predictors of development during the infant and toddler years. Family factors, which are influenced dramatically by sound early intervention programs, manifest changes in development into the middle preschool years.

The earliest study of contemporary importance concerning children at environmental risk was the classic work of Skeels (1966). A group of children in an institutional facility were moved to an orphanage where they received individualized attention from older residents, in contrast to the considerable deprivation experienced by the children who remained in the institution. As time passed, children who remained in the original setting showed an average decrease in measured intelligence, whereas children in the new setting showed significant increases in measured intelligence, apparently as a result of the greater attention they received.

Research on the influence of early education received great impetus when prominent scholars such as Bloom (1964) and Hunt (1961) emphasized the sensitive nature of children's earliest years. More recently, Shore (1997) summarized the mounting evidence regarding the influence of early experience on brain development. Federal funding of programs to serve preschool children from low-income families provided researchers with an opportunity to explore the application of their theories through various approaches to early intervention. In the mid–1970s, a group of individuals who had directed these model programs gathered to review the progress of the children they had served. The Consortium for Longitudinal Studies (1978) issued several reports based on its review (Lazar & Darlington, 1982). Longitudinal results also were reported independently for the Perry Preschool Project in Michigan (Schweinhart & Weikart, 1980) and the DARCEE Project in Tennessee (Gray, Ramsey, & Klaus, 1982). The Consortium for Longitudinal Studies and Perry Preschool reports described the following outcomes for children who had received early intervention compared to children who had not:

1. The number of special education placements and children who were retained in grade was significantly smaller for the early intervention groups when they entered school.
2. These children attained higher achievement test scores and were more committed to school.
3. Members of this group were less likely to show delinquent behavior outside of school or to get into legal trouble.

These are the more conservative outcomes of early intervention, representing the human aspect of the benefits. That is, children are more productive and perform better within and outside of school when they receive early intervention. Another aspect of the benefits is equally meaningful: Significant financial gains are realized as a result of serving preschoolers with disabilities from the youngest age possible. Studies on the cost-effectiveness of early intervention generally are in agreement that schools quickly recover the costs of early intervention through savings in the lesser amount of special services required and in less retention in grade. The cumulative cost of serving a child through age 18 decreases in proportion to how early intervention begins (Wood, 1981). Savings to society continue outside of school and even after the child leaves school altogether. Children who need services and who receive early intervention are less likely than those who do not to use public funds for maintenance in prison, for welfare payments, or for unemployment compensation. They are more likely to obtain gainful employment after leaving school and to pay taxes (Weber, Foster, & Weikart, 1978), and are more likely to complete high school and avoid trouble with the law (Oden, Schweinhart, & Weikart, 2000).

Palmer (1983), one of the Consortium for Longitudinal Studies members, urged caution in interpreting and generalizing the results. Gray (1983), another member, responding to comments that the outcome of her own project did not match the enthusiastic results of some other projects, placed intervention into perspective by noting that the families with whom her project worked had multiple and severe problems, including extreme poverty. She also noted that, compared with the amount of time a project child spent in impoverished surroundings, "the total input from our program occupied about two-thirds of one percent of the waking hours of the participants from birth to 18 years" (p. 128).

Several contemporary longitudinal studies provide additional insight into the influences of early intervention. For example, in a review of results of three long-term studies of children from low-income and undereducated families, Ramey and Ramey (1994) concluded the following:

> Maternal intelligence is a key factor in children's intellectual development, especially when these children are not provided with intensive early intervention. Fortunately, children whose mothers have low IQs respond positively to intensive, high-quality early intervention, which leads to a dramatic reduction in their rates of mental retardation during the intervention program. (p. 1066)

Another study followed a large cohort of infants living in poverty (Bradley, Whiteside, Mundfrom, & Casey, 1994). The Infant Health and Development Program found that, at 3 years of age, certain home factors and participation in the early intervention program differentiated those children who showed early signs of coping with environmental demands ("resiliency") from those who did not. The latter group was identified as having a poorer developmental prognosis. A study of specific types of early intervention with a low-birth-weight subgroup of this cohort found that the treatment group had significantly higher IQ scores than the children who did not receive early intervention services (Brooks–Gunn, McCarton, Casey, & McCormick, 1994).

A summary review of the evidence supports the benefits of early intervention on both personal and financial levels. More systematic research on children with biological impairments is needed, but the available evidence suggests a justification for early intervention. Of course, one must weigh anticipated outcomes against the intensity and duration of the intervention, and the intervention approach must be clearly delineated (Currie, 2000; Ramey & Ramey, 1998).

Take a moment to review the empirical evidence supporting early intervention. What additional research is needed for you to be forceful in your justification for early childhood special education programs?

Ethical Considerations

Individuals with special needs are likely to be dependent on others throughout their lives. Their dependence can be extremely burdensome financially and in terms of the quantity of resources. The cost of maintaining one person who is disabled in a state institution, for example, can exceed $50,000 per year. Within the community, adults with disabilities often require special housing, transportation, health services, sheltered employment or work training, food and clothing subsidies, and other support. The constant dependence of the individual on others and the inability to break away from the dependency promotes what Sameroff (1979) has called "learned incompetence." Continued dependence also contributes to negative attitudes on the part of the public toward people with disabilities. When so much public money is spent on expensive services for a small percentage of the population, a society under economic stress often looks for a scapegoat. The problem is compounded when resources are channeled to individuals with disabilities when it is too late to do more than support a subsistence level of living. Certainly, the evidence shows only limited success for intervention with older school-aged children and adults with disabilities.

Ethics is a system of moral principles that govern conduct.

The ethical arguments for early intervention, then, encompass three issues: (1) preventing the child from learning incompetence by promoting greater independence, (2) removing the continued burden to society by reducing the child's long-term needs for intensive and expensive resources, and (3) changing the public's attitudes toward individuals who are disabled by demonstrating the success of early intervention programs in decreasing their dependence on public support.

Ethical considerations in support of early childhood special education should be as important as empirical evidence. The forces that motivated passage of the Americans with Disabilities Act and those that refocused the attention of Americans on the future of our youth appear to be maintaining momentum to support educational opportunities for young children with special needs. But this trend could change quickly because Congress and the states reconsider funding and priorities on a regular basis. Early interventionists play a critical and challenging role in this advocacy process as well as provide competent delivery of high-quality services. They are in a position that demands both the persuasive discourse and oratory of a journalist and the controlled militarism of one who has seen battles on the front lines. The challenge is keen, but the outcomes are tangible and offer a significant contribution to individuals and to society.

> Congress reauthorizes special education laws every few years. Advocates must be knowledgeable and current to offer a rationale for supporting early childhood special education.

The Early Interventionist

Teacher Roles

The professional who works with young children with special needs and their families is called by many titles and wears many hats: those of teacher, social worker, psychologist, counselor, and public relations person. This is not always by design, but often out of necessity. The early interventionist may, after all, work in a public school classroom, in a center-based program operated by a nonschool agency, in a clinical setting, in a consulting capacity, or in the home, and he or she works with a population with which few people have much experience. Consequently, this professional becomes the resource for the parent, for education colleagues, and for community agency personnel.

> The early interventionist as teacher should be able to verbalize the basis for the early intervention strategies being used.

The teacher has several primary tasks. Ultimate responsibility for program planning and implementation belongs to the teacher, who may base the intervention approach on a central theoretical scheme or on a more generalized eclectic scheme. (See Chapter 5 for a discussion of program models.) In either case, the teacher should be able to justify the particular program used with any child.

Program implementation for a young child often demands identification of the many factors that influence development and learning. Recognition of the importance of the home environment and family members in this process frequently draws early intervention programs toward a homebound model, but, as we shall see, there are many ways to make an impact on a young child.

The role of early interventionist encompasses great diversity and requires certain personal qualities: quick thinking, flexibility, diplomacy, scholarship, and an inner drive for accomplishment. The daily schedule of a professional in a school system reflects the uniqueness of the job, as described in the following vignette.

Vignette 1.1

AN EARLY INTERVENTIONIST'S DAILY SCHEDULE

The first thing I do when I arrive in the morning is to go over the daily schedule with my "parapro" (paraprofessional), Ken. He's the best; I couldn't do without him! We have two groups of six parents and their children who come into school three times each week. One group comes Monday, Wednesday, and Friday; the other group Tuesday, Thursday, and Friday. Fridays get a little hairy, but it does the parents and kids so much good to get together with each other.

So my "parapro" and I start the day reviewing what we will do with the morning group. They are here from 9 until 11:30 and get our total attention during that time. From 11:30 to 12, we talk over what occurred, jot down notes, and transfer any data we collected to the kids' folders. It helps for us to keep an ongoing record of the kids' progress just so we can feel we're making a difference. And the parents appreciate it, too.

We usually brown-bag lunch at one of the local agencies in the area or go out for lunch with a few of the welfare caseworkers, public health nurses, school psychologists, or whoever is available. It helps us to know what's going on in other agencies and it sure helps for them to know us. A lot of our kids use other community resources, and it's nice to be able to pick up the phone and say, "Hi, Nick. Enjoyed lunch yesterday. By the way, I think Ms. Jones is having some problems again with Toni's braces. I'd appreciate it if you'd give her a call today." It works! And our colleagues around town do the same with us. Martha called me yesterday because she knew Ken had a visit scheduled with one of our mutual families. Martha wanted Ken to remind the family about their appointment at the orthopedic clinic next week. Happy to do it! It's also a lot more efficient than professionals tripping over each other trying to get to the family. Some of our families are followed by five or more agencies. Can you imagine all those visitors coming and going in your home!

Well, Ken and I each have two home visits scheduled for the afternoon. One of my visits today is to screen a new child for the program. The others are to continue working through our curriculum with the children and families.

I head back to school today after the visits for a staffing on another new child. Sometimes the special education director runs the staffing, but I'll be running this one. I was a little scared the first few times I ran staffings. I've settled in now and just try to get the parent and the other people there to share their thoughts on what the child needs. Everyone's concern for the child and desire to do the best thing usually come through loud and clear. And I think that some of my colleagues who hadn't thought much about serving preschoolers with disabilities are becoming strong advocates for the program!

Today's a little longer day than usual. I speak to a church group this evening. They have several kids in their neighborhood who have dropped out of school or have graduated but don't have jobs. I think I'd like to use some of them on a volunteer basis in our class. Maybe after they're trained, they'll be able to get a good job at a local child care center. The programs need good people, and we could sure use a few extra sets of trained hands around our kids.

No question about it, it's a challenging job. But we love it. Ken and I enjoy working with the children, of course, but the opportunities to work with parents and other community people make us feel that we're doing the most efficient job of addressing the total needs of the kids and helping to change community attitudes, too.

The early interventionist who works with the infant and toddler program of the community public health agency also brings personal perspectives, as described in the following vignette.

Vignette 1.2

PERSPECTIVE ON THE INFANT AND TODDLER PROGRAM

Sometimes my first visit with the child and parent is in the hospital right after the child is born. When an obvious disability is identified, the physician or hospital social worker calls us to begin the process of parent education and preparation for what is likely to be ahead. Having a young child of my own has made me a lot more sensitive to how I approach the parents. I recognize their many months of building happy expectations for a healthy baby, their desire but sometimes reluctance to accept and love the child, and the complications resulting from the impact that early medical interventions (neonatal intensive care units, technological devices, and limited physical contact, for example) may have on the parent–child relationship. And we talk about these issues. We talk about how I can help the family when the baby gets home and start talking about other family and community support resources that are available.

Teacher Competencies

It is relatively easy to see that an untrained person will not do well in the tasks just described. The complex roles that early interventionists take on require careful training and ongoing clarification of professional responsibilities (Buysse & Wesley, 1993). Certain minimum entry-level skills and knowledge are necessary to do an adequate job. Experience as well as further knowledge and skill allows the teacher to meet the challenges of the position with confidence and competence.

The complexity of the teacher's role may be thought of as a matrix with at least four dimensions:

1. The age of the child may range from newborn to 5 years or older.
2. The setting may be a hospital, the home, a clinic, a special preschool classroom, a parent–child group, or an inclusive setting with children with and without disabilities together.
3. The individuals involved in the intervention may be the child, the parents and other family members, community agency personnel, health professionals, and others representing a variety of cultures and backgrounds.
4. The task may be assessment, intervention, counseling and education, evaluation, report writing, case management, or coordination of a staffing.

Even without complete agreement among professionals about the order of importance of skills and knowledge (Hanson & Lovett, 1992), several competencies stand out logically for the early interventionist, as one teacher tells us in the following vignette.

Vignette 1.3

COMPETENCIES NEEDED BY THE EARLY INTERVENTIONIST

I couldn't believe all I was called upon to do and all I felt that I needed to do. It helps to enjoy the work and to be really committed to it. I believe it was Weikart (1981) who found that one's commitment to whatever approach is used is more closely related to the child's outcome than any one particular approach over another. Of course, the interventionist should know child development backward and forward and be ready to be amazed when a child does something unexpected!

I think I know what I'm doing. Each time I interact professionally with a child or parent or colleague I know what I want to accomplish and I have a plan to accomplish it. I also keep some alternate plans in my "back pocket." Flexibility helps!

I find it important to speak several languages, also. A language for parents and volunteers that is free of the professional jargon. Jargon can lose them really quickly. And there are the languages of the other professionals. I've learned a lot about occupational therapy, speech therapy, physical therapy, medications, and all types of physical and health problems that my kids have. I've had to if I am to keep my credibility with my colleagues. They've learned my language, too. I like the continuous learning aspect of the job anyway. It does a lot to prevent burnout.

Screening and assessing kids came pretty easy to me because I had done a lot in my university training program. I learned about a few more testing instruments pretty quickly, which let me concentrate on the child and parent instead of the test manual during a testing session. The school psychologist hasn't had much experience testing really young kids, so we work together most of the time. Testing young kids is tough even when you know what you're doing. I want to be sure we do everything possible to get an accurate assessment, so it's good that we work together.

What blew me away the most in my job was a late-night call I got from one of my parents. We had become close—it happens when you go into people's homes regularly and share their emotional highs and lows. Her child had been in the hospital with respiratory complications. The child had just died and I was the first person that the mom had thought to call. I wasn't prepared for that moment and was pretty disappointed that I couldn't do more. But maybe the fact that I was there to listen was enough for the parent at the time. I at least know now how, ideally, to deal with a situation like that—what to say, what to do. I've done some reading and talking to people about it.

It's a difficult balance to maintain when you work with parents of kids with disabilities. You want to remain objective but you need to give them support and get them actively involved in supporting their kids. I've got lots more learning to do but I'm sure working on it.

I get a lot of satisfaction out of seeing how far the classroom part of the program has progressed. It's taken a bunch of work to make the parents feel comfortable with me and with each other, and I think they could run the program themselves now (with a little guidance every once in a while). The routine we established for the sessions has helped. We try hard to model for the parents and to give them good feedback when they interact with their kids. Our parents also are becoming better able to identify the resources that they and their children need in the community. They seem more confident calling the health department or physician or counseling center, for example. I hope that we've helped to build their skills to mobilize community resources. Just as we're trying to teach the children to be more independent in making choices and decisions, we're trying to make parents less dependent upon us. That's not easy and sometimes I feel so tempted to make the call for the parent or handle a child's temper tantrum or bring toys into the home or do for the parents what they are ready to do for themselves. It's taken some time for me to know how fast to move with different families, and I still make mistakes. But I feel pretty comfortable now discussing my fallibility with the parents and they understand!

The early interventionist must have a broad knowledge base and diverse skills. For a good foundation, teachers must know where to seek needed information and skill-building experiences. Above all, they must recognize their own limitations. Teachers should use, to the maximum extent possible, public and university libraries, teacher centers, community resource people, and the Internet.

Over the course of the past several years, communities have made efforts to offer programs to young children with disabilities in the same settings as their peers without disabilities. This movement toward capitalizing on inclusive settings has demanded an examination of the practices used by programs that serve young children.

The National Association for the Education of Young Children (NAEYC) published a position paper in 1991 that was revised in 1997 titled *Developmentally*

Appropriate Practice in Early Childhood Programs Serving Children from Birth to Age 8 (Bredekamp, 1997). This document of general philosophy and program guidelines for early childhood educators led to the publication of a similar document for early interventionists by the **Division for Early Childhood (DEC)** of the Council for Exceptional Children. *DEC Recommended Practices in Early Intervention/Early Childhood Special Education* (Sandall, McLean, & Smith, 2000) provides the early interventionist with excellent guidelines against which to evaluate one's philosophy, knowledge, and skills. There are many similarities between the developmentally appropriate practices (DAPs) presented by NAEYC and DEC. However, the philosophical differences, characterized by a developmental approach in early childhood education (ECE) versus a remedial–prescriptive approach in early childhood special education (ECSE), have spurred considerable debate in the literature (Fox, Hanline, Vail, & Galant, 1994; Odom & McEvoy, 1990). The differences, however, do not appear to be an impediment for either discipline to work together for the good of each child and family (Kilgo et al., 1999). Furthermore, the changing faces of both ECE and ECSE within the community setting encourage a drawing together of the content of both documents:

> Analyses of the components of DAP reveal that practices valued by ECSE are not incompatible with what has been stated as important in educating typically developing children. In the areas of curriculum, adult-child interaction, and developmental evaluation, the practices that are important to ECSE fit within the breadth of what is considered developmentally appropriate. Furthermore, there appears to be a trend in ECSE, with a growing empirical base, to move towards interventions that reflect the practices articulated by NAEYC and away from a narrow, remedial approach to early intervention. (Fox et al., 1994, p. 253)

The unity of ECE and ECSE is reflected in the collaborative position paper by DEC, the Association of Teacher Educators, and NAEYC (1994) titled *Personnel Standards for Early Education and Early Intervention: Guidelines for Licensure in Early Childhood Special Education* (reaffirmed in 2000). This document offers a framework for the preparation of professionals to serve a unique population and a standardization of minimum competencies. The competent early interventionist is one who

- is knowledgeable about child development and disabilities
- follows a theoretical intervention model and can justify the approach
- supports and responds to children and parents but promotes their independence
- adapts quickly to new and demanding situations
- administers and interprets preschool test instruments
- interacts productively with colleagues, children, and parents
- evaluates program success routinely and systematically
- uses available resources to better understand and meet the needs of children and their families
- functions well in a variety of settings
- adapts to the cultural differences of families
- encourages and accepts input related to development and modification from families and other sources

Young Children with Special Needs and Their Families

Who Are Young Children with Special Needs?

IDEA defines children with disabilities as those children with mental retardation, hearing impairments including deafness, speech or language impairments, visual impairments including blindness, serious emotional disturbance, orthopedic impairments, autism, traumatic brain injury, other health impairments, specific learning disabilities, deaf-blindness, or multiple disabilities, and who because of those impairments need special education and related services (34 C.F.R. Ch. 111, Section 300.7 (a) (1), p. 13). Any child from birth through 21 years of age who meets the specific criteria for any of these categories may be eligible for services. For infants and toddlers, states also may choose to serve, under Part C of IDEA, children who are at biological or environmental risk for one of the specified disabilities. For children from 3 years of age, under Part B of IDEA, states may serve children who are experiencing "developmental delays" as defined by the state using objective measures of physical, cognitive, social-emotional, and adaptive development. The 1997 Amendments to IDEA extended the use of the "developmental delay" category to age 9.

There is a sound rationale for serving young children in at-risk and developmentally delayed categories. The range of variations in development is considerable,

For children with disabilities, legislation and research have provided support for early intervention services.

even in a group of children of the same chronological age, gender, and ethnic group (Wolff, 1981). In some children, the variation is so extreme that identification of a problem is relatively easy. In such cases, a child may clearly fit into a category described by IDEA. However, Behr and Gallagher (1981) propose that a more flexible definition is needed for young children who might have special needs not so much as a result of the extent of the developmental variation as of the type of variation. This would include those children who, prior to their third birthday, have a "high probability of manifesting, in later childhood, a sensory motor deficit and/or mental handicap which may be the result of a birth defect, disease process, trauma, or environmental conditions present during the prenatal and/or postnatal periods" (p. 114).

The use of the "developmental delay" category allows services to be provided to children who do not yet meet the criteria for traditional categories. Services to these children might lessen or eliminate the need for services later in childhood.

The advantage of a more flexible definition for young children with special needs, in particular, is that more serious impairments can be prevented by serving a child early. Children from poor environments are overrepresented in special education classes in the public schools relative to their number in the general population. Successful efforts have been reported with many different high-risk populations to prevent minor developmental delays from becoming serious impairments (Brooks-Gunn et al., 1994; Campbell & Ramey, 1994; Meyer-Probst, Teichmann, Hayes, & Rauh, 1991). By offering incentives to serve young children prior to the appearance of a clearly identifiable disability, the government thus may provide a vehicle for preventing more serious impairments as children grow up.

In our discussions in this text, we approach children's needs from a developmental perspective. A framework of typical development underlies descriptions of how children vary from the typical pattern and what programmatic modifications are helpful to support learning. We also have included information on how specific types of disabilities influence development in each skill area. Table 1.4 presents the number of young children by disability area who are receiving special education under IDEA. A brief description of these disability areas follows.

TABLE 1.4   Number of 3- to 5-Year-Old Children Served Under IDEA, Part B by Disability During the 2000–2001 School Year

Disability Category	Number of Children
Autism	15,590
Deafness/blindness	208
Traumatic brain injury	891
Developmental delay	149,535
Specific learning disability	20,022
Speech/language impairment	330,838
Multiple disability	12,662
Hearing impairment	8,259
Orthopedic impairment	10,685
Other health impairment	13,355

Source: From the U.S. Department of Education, Office of Special Education Programs, Data Analysis System (DANS).

Mental Retardation (Intellectual Disability).   The definition of **mental retardation** used most often was developed by the American Association on Mental Retardation (AAMR): Mental retardation refers to substantial limitations in present functioning. It is characterized by significantly subaverage intellectual functioning, existing concurrently with limitations in two or more adaptive skill areas (American Association on Mental Retardation, 2002).

Intellectual functioning has traditionally been assessed by performance on intelligence tests. Figure 1.2 shows the theoretical distribution of scores on a standardized intelligence test. Although not part of the current definition, it has become commonplace to provide labels for different levels of retardation. A score between 1 and 2 standard deviations below the mean (70–85) characterizes a child with borderline intellectual functioning. Children who score greater than 2 standard deviations below the mean of 100, an intelligence quotient of less than approximately 70, would fall in the category typically classified as mental retardation. The levels of retardation are as follows:

Mild or educable mental retardation	55–69 IQ*
Moderate or trainable retardation	40–54 IQ
Severe mental retardation	25–39 IQ
Profound mental retardation	Below 25 IQ

*IQ = (mental age/chronological age) × 100.

The AAMR modified the definition of *mental retardation* to abolish levels based on cognitive dysfunction, as described previously, to differentiate cases of mental retardation based on "needed levels of support" (MacMillan, Sipperstein, &

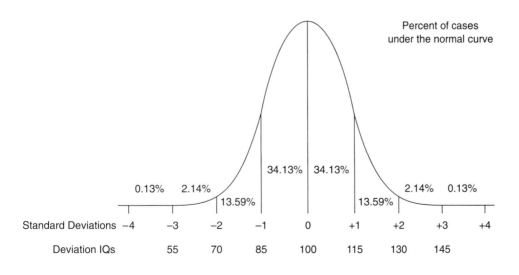

FIGURE 1.2   The theoretical distribution of IQ scrores

Gresham, 1996). In fact, the term **intellectual disability** has been proposed to replace **mental retardation.** It appears, however, that categorization based on the original definition persists and that the newer definition has been largely ignored.

Adaptive behavior describes a child's ability to deal with worldly demands. This may encompass components of communication skills, self-help skills, social skills, and psychomotor skills. Demands vary from setting to setting. A child, therefore, may show deficits in adaptive behavior and be considered mentally retarded in some settings but not in others. What constitutes mental retardation, however, is both subaverage intellectual functioning *and* deficits in adaptive behavior.

The characteristics of a child who is mentally retarded depend predominantly on the child's mental age, which is derived from an intelligence test. The more severely mentally retarded a child is, the greater the disparity between mental age and chronological age. Children of the same chronological age, then, may display very different characteristics. Mental age, more than chronological age, reflects a child's current level of ability and determines educational needs. It should be noted that few standardized intelligence tests are available and statistically sound for preschool children, particularly for infants and toddlers. Consequently, other strategies and instrumentation may be employed to measure the intellectual capabilities of these children.

An individual must show deficits in both intellectual functioning and adaptive behavior to be considered mentally retarded or intellectually disabled.

Hearing Impairments. Hearing losses are characterized by degree and type. Hearing is measured in units of intensity (i.e., loudness) and frequency (i.e., pitch). A child with normal hearing can hear sounds as soft as 0 to 25 decibels (dB) within a frequency range of approximately 40 to 4,000 hertz (Hz). Most conversational speech has an intensity of about 55 dB and a frequency range of 500 to 2,000 Hz. A child with a hearing loss of greater than 40 dB will probably miss a considerable amount of spoken information; a profound loss of greater than 90 dB will severely disable a child.

A hearing loss may be conductive or sensorineural. Conductive losses are caused by interference with the sequence of sound vibrations reaching the auditory nerve. Sensorineural losses are caused by defects in the inner ear or in the auditory nerve, which transmits electrical impulses to the brain for interpretation.

Hearing impairments may result from infection during the prenatal or postnatal period, from an accident, or from exposure to certain prescription drugs. The severity of the impairment depends on the degree of loss and the age of onset. A mild loss may allow a child to benefit completely from an auditory environment. A more severe loss may require alternative communication systems and modifications to the environment. In addition, a hearing loss that occurs prior to a child's learning language requires greater environmental modifications than a loss that occurs after mastery of language. Deafness is defined in IDEA as a hearing impairment that is so severe that a child is impaired in processing linguistic information through hearing, with or without amplification, and that the child's educational performance is thus adversely affected. Further discussion of hearing impairments is provided in Chapter 10.

Infection, accidents, and drugs may contribute to hearing loss.

Speech and Language Disorders. Because of differences in the rates of development of young children, it is difficult to clearly define what is and what is not a disorder. Certainly, some structural and functional aspects stand out as being atypical. For example, a child with a cleft palate who uses no words at 4 years of age or whose language is limited to repetition of what others say clearly can be categorized as having disordered speech and language. But the absence of certain speech sounds at times may reflect a disorder and at other times not. Great care must be taken in identifying a child as fitting this category, particularly when cultural diversity and environment play such critical roles in forming children's speech and language patterns.

Impairments of speech and language frequently accompany other disabilities and, in fact, may be the first suggestion of problems. Children with hearing impairments, cerebral palsy, emotional disturbances, or mental retardation all may exhibit atypical speech and language.

The ability of a child to communicate functionally is a requirement for independent living. A child who is unable to express needs and wants or to interact verbally and appropriately with other children and adults is at a serious disadvantage. Consequently, speech and language disorders must receive careful attention as soon as problems are identified.

Language must be viewed in the context of the child's environment and culture.

Visual Impairments. A child is considered to be blind if visual acuity is poorer than 20/200 in the better eye after correction or if the field of vision is limited to an angle of less than 20 degrees. A child with partial sight has an acuity of less than 20/70 but greater than 20/200. An acuity of 20/200 indicates that a child can see at 20 feet what a person with normal vision can see at 200 feet.

In education, children often are categorized in terms of their potential as either print or braille readers. Preschool children with visual impairments whose vision is too poor for them to benefit from even large-print materials should begin a program that sensitizes them to tactile learning materials. This provides an introduction to subsequent learning of pre-braille and braille reading skills.

Most vision problems in young children are attributable to prenatal factors. Infections, such as rubella, and certain hereditary factors may manifest themselves in blindness at birth or create a likelihood that a child will require special education services.

Serious Emotional Disturbance. The causes of severe emotional disturbance in young children are not well understood. Some experts attribute such problems to environmental factors and others to neurological or chemical factors. Strategies used to remediate emotional disturbance usually reflect the theoretical orientation of the program staff. Some programs may adjust the child's diet, others may restructure the child's physical environment, and still others may plan the child's interactions with other objects and people. It is most likely, however, that emotional disturbance encompasses many different types of problems, some biologically based and others environmentally based. Certainly, the variety of behaviors that characterize a child with emotional disturbance may be quite diverse: anxiety, withdrawal, aggression, impulsiveness, extreme fear, and so on. Diagnosis is based on the frequency, duration, and intensity of these behaviors. However, the conceptualization of diagnosing such a young child with a psychiatric disorder is not universally accepted.

Emotional disturbance probably encompasses many types of problems that are defined by their frequency, intensity, and duration.

Serious emotional disturbance is defined in IDEA as a condition exhibiting one or more of the following characteristics over a long period and to a degree that adversely affects a child's educational performance:

- An inability to learn that cannot be explained by intellectual, sensory, or health factors
- An inability to build or maintain satisfactory interpersonal relationships with peers and teachers
- Inappropriate types of behavior or feelings under normal circumstances
- A general pervasive mood of unhappiness or depression
- A tendency to develop physical symptoms or a physical focus associated with personal or school problems

Orthopedic Impairments.   The category of orthopedic impairments is so broad that it is difficult to identify many general characteristics. Any condition that interferes with the health or normal functioning of bones, joints, or muscles qualifies as an orthopedic impairment. Defects such as spina bifida, club feet, or cerebral palsy may be present at birth; other problems, such as amputations, may occur later in childhood.

Causes of orthopedic impairments are as diverse as the problems themselves. Some are a result of hereditary factors and some are a result of the influence of infection or toxic substances on the mother, particularly during the first trimester of pregnancy. Other impairments may be traced to birth injuries or to diseases or accidents after birth.

Many children with orthopedic impairments require no special education services. Adaptive equipment for some children may help them function independently in a typical setting. Special education staff may help children adjust to their impairment and adapt to the demands of their environment.

> Some children with orthopedic impairments require only adaptive equipment and training to adjust to environmental demands.

Other Health Impairments.   Based on the definition in IDEA, children in this category have limited strength, vitality, or alertness as a result of chronic or acute health problems related to a heart condition, tuberculosis, rheumatic fever, nephritis, asthma, sickle cell anemia, hemophilia, epilepsy, lead poisoning, leukemia, diabetes, or other conditions that adversely affect a child's educational performance.

Autistic Spectrum Disorder.   As defined by the law, **autism** is a developmental disability that significantly affects verbal and nonverbal communication and social interaction, is generally evident before age 3, and adversely affects a child's educational performance. Other characteristics often associated with autism are engagement in repetitive activities and stereotyped movements, resistance to environmental change or change in daily routines, and unusual responses to sensory experiences.

Traumatic Brain Injury (TBI).   TBI is an acquired injury to the brain caused by an external physical force, resulting in total or partial functioning disability or psychosocial impairment, or both, that adversely affects a child's educational performance. Although this definition appears to be fairly simple in its presentation, a plethora of issues surround this disability category (e.g., type of brain injury, severity of brain injury, and age at time of injury). In fact, this special education classification may be especially challenging for the early interventionist, particularly in regard to understanding the nature of recovery from a traumatic brain injury as well as specialized rehabilitation and intervention techniques.

Developmental Delay.   Most preschool children are served under this category. IDEA permits this label to be used with children from birth through 9 years of age. The Division for Early Childhood (2000) issued a position paper supporting the use of this category and defined developmental delay as

> a condition which represents a significant delay in the process of development. It does not refer to a condition in which a child is slightly or momentarily lagging in development. The presence of developmental delay is an indication that the process of development is significantly affected and that without special intervention, it is likely that educational performance at school age will be affected. (p. 1)

Supporters of this category believe that the early childhood years are too early to use traditional labels due to the plasticity of development. That is, there is a greater chance of making errors in diagnosis because children's development is molded by changes in the environment and by maturity, and guided by genetic factors, as well. Furthermore, some children show global problems during their early years, although they might not meet the criteria for traditional disability categories. These children would go unserved without a mechanism to make them eligible for appropriate services at a young age. The potential exists for those problems to become more serious and complex as time goes on without appropriate services.

During the 2000–2001 school year, more than 149,000 3- to 5-year-old children were served under the developmental delay category. IDEA mandates that states develop guidelines to determine eligibility of children. Children may be eligible for services under the developmental delay category if they satisfy two conditions: if they currently have a disabling or established risk condition or if they are considered to have a condition that, through informed clinical opinion, is deemed to place them at risk for a disabling condition in the future. States must develop a list of established risk conditions (e.g., Down syndrome and blindness) and set up a process to make children with other problems eligible using **informed clinical opinion.** Through this process, experts use all available information (intake reports, progress notes, test results, medical discharge summaries, etc.) to determine if a child's condition is likely to result in a disability at school entrance were the child not to receive early intervention services. The child's status is reviewed on a regular basis and a determination is made as to whether the child is eligible for services under one of the traditional categories and whether it is in the child's best interests to be served in that category.

The Family and the Community

It is difficult for even the experienced professional to have an accurate understanding of the dynamics of families with young children who are disabled. Prospective parents who have waited so many months for the birth of a baby may suddenly find that the child does not even approximate their idealized expectations. The amount of stress imposed on the family may depend upon how radically parental expectations are violated (Dyson, 1993; Powers, 1993). The degree of family stress is related to the specifics of the child's disability, with the greatest stress occurring in families with children who are most severely disabled (Wallander & Noojin, 1995). An outgrowth of dealing with the multiple needs of such children is isolation from normal community activities and interactions (Ehrmann, Aeschleman, & Svanum, 1995).

Consider for a moment the parents for whom every feeding session is a struggle because the child thrusts the food out with the tongue as soon as the parent spoons it in, or the parents who must still change diapers on their 4 1/2-year-old child, or the parents who must keep constant vigilance over their 3-year-old, who sleeps only 2 hours per night and is on the move the remainder of the time! One teacher's experiences with families coping with children with disabilities are described in the following vignette.

> The level of stress in a family with a child with a disability may range from mild to very severe. The impact is on all members of the family, including parents, siblings, and extended family members.

Vignette 1.4

COPING WITH DISABILITIES

I don't ever spend time anymore feeling sorry for myself. One of the first families I worked with cured me of that, and it's been reinforced by family after family. Myrna had twin boys. Both were deaf and had cleft palates and hip problems. John also had a cleft lip and a congenital cataract. Myrna was in an auto accident recently and has had medical problems of her own. She's spent most of her time since I've known her running from doctor to doctor and clinic to clinic for John and James. I bet she's had more experience with community agency people than anyone in the state. And she's shared with me a lot of her frustrations about the "hurry up and wait" games and not getting understandable answers from professionals. Yep, she's been through a lot, and I hope her struggles will make things easier for those who follow.

Myrna's husband left soon after the kids were born so she has been pretty much on her own. The kids are 5 years old now, and she's still shuttling them to the speech and hearing clinic regularly for hearing aid checks and to the medical center for monitoring of their cleft palate surgery, making sure they get to school, and trying to keep the house in order. I've never seen happier kids or a mom who could cope the way Myrna has. Sometimes when I'm driving in my car, I just think about her and wonder how she's handled it. I go crazy if my checkbook doesn't balance! Myrna's really given me an education. I hope I've helped her.

Another family that sticks out in my mind has taught me a lot, also. Vicky and Larry's daughter is 2 years old now and has Down syndrome. Her pediatrician recommended immediately after birth that Annie be institutionalized "for her own good and the good of the other children." Imagine that! It's been a tough few years for the family but somehow they manage to come through crisis after crisis a bit stronger and more reflective. Annie has had heart and respiratory problems, and Vicky spends most of her nights keeping watch while Larry gets some rest. He works the first shift at a local plant and rushes home after work to help feed Annie and the other kids, run errands, and handle chores. I don't think Vicky and Larry have been out alone together since Annie was born. They're still scared to leave her with a babysitter, and they have no relatives in the area. I've watched her for a few hours on a couple of nights so that the rest of the family could go out and eat casually at a restaurant. But those moments have been few for them. Mostly, it's feed, change diapers, run to doctors, come to school, and start the cycle again. Vicky and Larry have recently relaxed enough to talk with some of the other parents. I believe it's helped. Hopefully, they'll begin swapping childsitting chores and give each other support.

Sometimes I feel very limited. At other times I know I'm very limited. It's clear to me that I don't know about a child until I know about the child's family. And often the only way to help the child is to help the family. This takes getting to know and understand, as much as possible, the family and home environment. Fortunately, there have been some good folks working in the community who have been more than willing to get me through some rough moments and to help me get families through even more trying times. I remember people telling me about how I should stay away from Cathy Sue at the health department or Jimmy at the welfare office because they're so tough to work with. But these very colleagues—and I choose the word carefully—are my best friends now and some of the strongest advocates for my kids and families.

It's taken me a long time to be comfortable visiting homes routinely, but there's no other way to do my job well. At first, I also thought I was wasting my time stopping by different community agencies to say hello. But it's all helped; it really has. Parents need to know that I'm not interested in their child just as a clinical entity—because it's my job—but that I care about them, the whole family and the child together. Agency people also need to know that I take my job seriously. It makes them feel that their jobs are as important as they really are! I think I've made a difference.

IDEA mandates parent-related activities. Parents must approve individualized testing of their child, must be invited to and may attend the program staffing, must approve the child's special education program and placement, and must have the right to question and challenge decisions that are made for the child. In addition, the needs of the family are a central point of the IFSP:

> The evidence indicates that the family is the most effective and economical system for fostering and sustaining the development of the child. . . . Without family involvement any effects of intervention, at least in the cognitive sphere, appear to erode rapidly once the program ends. In contrast, the involvement of the parents as partners in the enterprise provides an on-going system which reinforces the effects of the program while it is in operation, and helps to sustain them. (Bronfenbrenner, 1974, p. 55)

Summary

The proliferation of early childhood special education programs represents a significant sociological and educational event. The long-term impact of early intervention has been demonstrated in terms of human and financial resources. Furthermore, early intervention offers opportunities to prevent or reduce deficits in children and stress in their families. However, the effectiveness of early intervention efforts depends to a great extent on the competence of the early interventionist. The diversity of children, families, and communities poses both problems and challenges. The ability of the teacher to apply a broad base of knowledge, to communicate well with families and other professionals, to use available resources effectively, and to monitor progress maximizes the ultimate benefits of programs for children.

The first years of children's lives are the most important for establishing a foundation for later learning. Young children with special needs require careful attention by trained individuals to ensure a path of development that, as closely as possible, parallels that of children without disabilities. This is achieved by providing for the child's physical and biological needs and by providing an environment rich in opportunities to learn. Although legal and ethical precedents have spawned an increase in the number of programs available, only the commitment of knowledgeable and skilled professionals can ensure that a high level of quality accompanies the increase in services.

Review Questions and Discussion Points

1. Describe the involvement of government in the education of young children with special needs.
2. You are asked to make a presentation to a legislative committee that is considering funding for early childhood special education programs. Make a case for funding based on empirical research in the area.
3. What qualities and characteristics contribute to being a successful early interventionist?
4. Discuss the similarities and differences between an IEP and an IFSP.
5. What are the differences between mandates for services to infants, toddlers, and preschoolers and for children over 5 years old?
6. How has the use of the "developmental delay" category affected the eligibility process?
7. This text was going to press just prior to the most recent reauthorization of IDEA. Compare and contrast it with the previous version. How has it changed?

Recommended Resources

Web Sites

Division for Early Childhood (DEC)
http://www.dec-sped.org

Individuals with Disabilities Education Act (IDEA)
http://www.ideapractices.org/law/index.php

National Early Childhood Technical Assistance Center (NECTAC, formerly NECTAS)
http://www.ectac.org

U.S. Department of Education, Office of Special Education Programs
http://www.ed.gov/offices/OSERS/OSEP/index.html

Publications and Other Media

*DEC Recommended Practices in Early Intervention/Early Childhood Special Education—*available at
http://www.dec-sped.org

*DEC Recommended Practices in Program Assessment: Improving Practices for Young Children with Special Needs and Their Families—*available at
http://www.dec-sped.org

*DEC Recommended Practices Video: Selected Strategies for Teaching Young Children with Special Needs—*available at
http://www.dec-sped.org

*Journal of Early Intervention—*subscribe at
http://www.dec-sped.org

*Young Exceptional Children—*subscribe at
http://www.dec-sped.org

*The Young Exceptional Children Monograph Series: Natural Environments and Inclusion—*available at
http://www.sopriswest.com

*ZERO TO THREE—*subscribe at
http://www.zerotothree.org

References

American Association on Mental Retardation. (2002). *Mental retardation: Definition, classification, and systems of supports* (10th ed.). Washington, DC: Author.

Badger, E. (1981). Effects of a parent education program on teenage mothers and their offspring. In K. Scott, T. Field, & E. Robertson (Eds.), *Teenage parents and their offspring.* New York: Grune & Stratton.

Battelle Institute of Columbus, Ohio. (1976). *A summary of the evaluation of the Disabled Children's Early Education Program.* Columbus: Author.

Behr, S., & Gallagher, J. J. (1981). Alternative administrative strategies for young disabled children: A policy analysis. *Journal of the Division for Early Childhood, 2,* 113–122.

Blair, C., Ramey, C. T., & Hardin, J. M. (1995). Early intervention for low birth weight, premature infants: Participation and intellectual development. *American Journal on Mental Retardation, 99,* 542–554.

Bloom, B. (1964). *Stability and change in human characteristics.* New York: Wiley.

Boyce, G. C., Smith, T. B., Immel, N., & Casto, G. (1993). Early intervention with medically fragile infants: Investigating the age-at-start question. *Early Education and Development, 4,* 290–305.

Bradley, R. H., Whiteside, L., Mundfrom, D. J., & Casey, P. H. (1994). *Journal of Clinical Psychology, 23,* 425–434.

Bredekamp, S. (1997). *Developmentally appropriate practice in early childhood programs serving children from birth to age 8.* Washington, DC: National Association for the Education of Young Children.

Bronfenbrenner, U. (1974). *A report on longitudinal evaluations of preschool programs.* Vol. 2: *Is early intervention effective?* DHEW Publication No. (OHD) 76-30025. Washington, DC: U.S. Department of Health, Education, and Welfare.

Brooks-Gunn, J., & Duncan, G. J. (1997). The effects of poverty on children. *The Future of Children, 7,* 55–71.

Brooks-Gunn, J., McCarton, C. M., Casey, P. H., & McCormick, M. C. (1994). Early interventions in low birth weight premature infants: Results through age 5 years from the Infant Health and Development Program. *Journal of the American Medical Association, 272,* 1257–1262.

Buysse, V., & Wesley, P. W. (1993). The identity crisis in early childhood special education: A call for professional role clarification. *Topics in Early Childhood Special Education, 13,* 418–429.

Campbell, F. A., & Ramey, C. T. (1994). Effects of early intervention on intellectual and academic achievement: A follow-up study of children from low-income families. *Child Development, 65,* 684–698.

Consortium for Longitudinal Studies. (1978). *Lasting effects after preschool.* (Final report of HEW Grant 90c-1311.) Denver, CO: Education Commission of the States.

Currie, J. (2000). *Early childhood intervention program: What do we know?* Washington, DC: The Brookings Institution.

Danaher, J. (Ed.). (2002). *Part C updates*. Chapel Hill, NC: NECTAS and Office of Special Education Programs.

Denenberg, V. H. (1981). Hemispheric laterality in animals and the effects of early experience. *Behavioral and Brain Sciences, 4,* 1–49.

Denenberg, V. H., Zeidner, L., Rosen, G. D., Hofman, M., Garbanati, J. A., Sherman, G. F., & Yutzey, D. A. (1981). Stimulation in infancy facilitates interhemispheric communication in the rabbit. *Brain Research, 227,* 165–169.

Devaney, B. L., Ellwood, M. R., & Love, J. M. (1997). Programs that mitigate the effects of poverty on children. *The Future of Children, 7,* 88–112.

Division for Early Childhood, Association of Teacher Educators, & National Association for the Education of Young Children. (1994). *Personnel standards for early education and early intervention: Guidelines for licensure in early childhood special education.* Reston, VA: Authors.

Division for Early Childhood. (2000). *DEC position statement on developmental delay as an eligibility category.* Retrieved from http://www.dec-sped.org

Dyson, L. L. (1993). Response to the presence of a child with disabilities: Parental stress and family functioning over time. *American Journal on Mental Retardation, 98,* 207–218.

Ehrmann, L. C., Aeschleman, S. R., & Svanum, S. (1995). Parental reports of community activity patterns: A comparison between young children with disabilities and their nondisabled peers. *Research in Developmental Disabilities, 16,* 331–343.

Erikson, E. H. (1963). *Childhood and society.* New York: Norton.

Fewell, R. R., & Oelwein, P. L. (1991). Effective early intervention: Results from the Model Preschool Program for children with Down syndrome and other developmental delays. *Topics in Early Childhood Special Education, 11,* 56–68.

Fox, L., Hanline, M. F., Vail, C. O., & Galant, K. R. (1994). Developmentally appropriate practice: Applications for young children with disabilities. *Journal of Early Intervention, 18,* 243–254.

Freud, A. (1965). *Normality and pathology in childhood: Assessments of development.* New York: International Universities Press.

Gallagher, J. J. (1991). Longitudinal interventions: Virtues and limitations. *American Behavioral Scientist, 34,* 431–439.

Galler, J. R., Ramsey, F., Solimano, G., & Lowell, W. E. (1983a). The influence of early malnutrition on subsequent behavioral development, II: Classroom behavior. *Journal of the American Academy of Child & Adolescent Psychiatry, 22,* 16–22.

Galler, J. R., Ramsey, F., Solimano, G., Lowell, W. E, & Mason, E. (1983b). The influence of early malnutrition on subsequent behavioral development, I: Degree of impairment in intellectual performance. *Journal of the American Academy of Child & Adolescent Psychiatry, 22,* 8–15.

Ginsburg, K. R., Alexander, P. M., Hunt, J., Sullivan, M., Zhao, H., & Cnaan, A. (2002). Enhancing their likelihood for a positive future: The perspective of inner-city youth. *Pediatrics, 109,* 1136–1143.

Gray, S. W. (1983). Controversies or concurrences: A reply to Palmer. *Developmental Review, 3,* 125–129.

Gray, S. W., Ramsey, B. K., & Klaus, R. A. (1982). *From 3 to 20: The Early Training Project.* Baltimore: University Park Press.

Haddad, P. M., & Garralda, M. E. (1992). Hyperkinetic syndrome and disruptive early experiences. *British Journal of Psychiatry, 191,* 700–703.

Hanson, M. J., & Lovett, D. (1992). Personnel preparation for early interventionists: A cross-disciplinary survey. *Journal of Early Intervention, 16,* 123–135.

Harlow, H. F. (1974). Syndromes resulting from maternal deprivation. In J. H. Cullen (Ed.), *Experimental behavior: A basis for the study of mental disturbance.* New York: Wiley.

Hauser-Cram, Warfield, M. E., Shonkoff, J. P., & Kraus, M. W. (2001). Children with disabilities: A longitudinal study of child development and parent well-being. *Monographs of the Society for Research in Child Development, 66.*

Hunt, J. McV. (1961). *Intelligence and experience.* New York: Ronald Press.

Keogh, B., Garnier, H. E., Bernheimer, L. P., & Gallimore, R. (2000). Models of child-family interactions for children with developmental delays: Child-driven or transactional. *American Journal on Mental Retardation, 105,* 32–46.

Kilgo, J. L., Johnson, L., LaMontagne, M., Stayton, V., Cook, M., & Cooper, C. (1999). Importance of practices: A national study of general and special early childhood educators. *Journal of Early Intervention, 22*(4), 294–305.

Kirk, S. A., & Gallagher, J. J. (1983). *Educating exceptional children* (4th ed.). Boston: Houghton Mifflin.

Lazar, I., & Darlington, R. (1982). Lasting effect of early education. *Monographs of the Society for Research in Child Development, 47* (Serial No. 495).

Leibowitz, G. (1991). Organic and biophysical theories of behavior. *Journal of Development and Physical Disabilities, 3*, 210–243.

Littlejohn & Associates, Inc. (1982). *An analysis of the impact of the Disabled Children's Early Education Program.* Washington, DC: Author.

Lizardi, H., Klein, D. N., Ouimette, P. C., & Riso, L. P. (1995). Reports of the childhood home environment in early onset dysthymia and episodic major depression. *Journal of Abnormal Psychology, 104*, 132–139.

MacMillan, D. L., Sipperstein, G. N., & Gresham, F. M. (1996). A challenge to the viability of mild mental retardation as a diagnostic category. *Exceptional Children, 62*, 356–371.

Meyer-Probst, B., Teichmann, H. H., Hayes, A., & Rauh, H. (1991). Follow-up of a cohort of risk children from birth into adolescence: The Rostock Longitudinal Study. *International Journal of Disability, Development and Education, 38*, 225–246.

Morgane, P. J., Austin, L. R., Borzino, J. D., & Tonkiss, J. (1993). Prenatal malnutrition and development of the brain. *Current Directions in Psychological Science, 17*, 91–128.

Oden, S., Schweinhart, L. J., & Weikart, D. P. (2000). *Into adulthood: A study of the effects of Head Start.* Ypsilanti, MI: High/Scope Press.

Odom, S. L., & McEvoy, M. A. (1990). Mainstreaming at the preschool level: Potential barriers and tasks for the field. *Topics in Early Childhood Special Education, 10*, 48–61.

Odom, S. L., Peck, C. A., Hanson, M., Beckman, P. J., Kaiser, A. P., Lieber, J., et al. (2000). *Inclusion at the preschool level: An ecological systems analysis.* Olympia, WA: Office of State Superintendent of Public Instruction (Special Education, P.O. Box 47200, Olympia, WA 98504).

Palmer, F. (1983). The continuing controversy over the effects of early childhood intervention: A perspective and review of Gray, Ramsey, and Klaus's From 3 to 20: The Early Training Project. *Developmental Review, 3*, 115–124.

Piaget, J., & Inhelder, B. (1969). *The psychology of the child.* New York: Basic Books.

Powers, L. E. (1993). Disability and grief: From tragedy to challenge. In G. H. S. Singer & L. E. Powers (Eds.), *Family, disability, and empowerment: Active coping strategies for family interventions.* Baltimore: Brookes.

Ramey, C. T., & Bryant, D. M. (1982). Evidence involving prevention of developmental retardation during infancy. *Journal of the Division for Early Childhood, 5*, 73–78.

Ramey, C. T., & Ramey, L. R. (1994). Which children benefit the most from early intervention? *Pediatrics, 94*(2), 1064–1066.

Ramey, C. T., & Ramey, S. L. (1998). Early intervention and early experience. *American Psychologist, 53*(2), 109–120.

Read, S. (1982). Malnutrition and behavior. *Applied Research in Mental Retardation, 3*, 279–291.

Ricciuti, H. N. (1993). Nutrition and development. *Current Directions in Psychological Science, 2*, 43–46.

Rosenzweig, M. R., Bennett, E. L., Diamond, M. C., Wu, Su-Yu, Slagle, R. W., & Saffron, E. (1969). Influence of environmental complexity and visual stimulation on development of occipital cortex in rats. *Brain Research, 14*, 427–445.

Sameroff, A. J. (1979). The etiology of cognitive competence: A systems perspective. In R. B. Kearsley & I. E. Sigel (Eds.), *Infants at risk: Assessment of cognitive functioning.* Hillsdale, NJ: Erlbaum.

Sandall, S., McLean, M., & Smith, B. (2000). DEC recommended practices in early intervention/early childhood special education. Reston, VA: Division for Early Childhood.

Schweinhart, L. J., & Weikart, D. P. (1980). *Young children grow up: The effects of the Perry Preschool Program on youths through age 15.* Ypsilanti, MI: High/Scope Educational Research Foundation.

Shonkoff, J. P., Hauser, C. P., Krauss, M. W., & Upshur, C. C. (1992). Development of infants with disabilities and their families: Implications for theory and service delivery. *Monographs of the Society for Research in Child Development* (Serial No. 230).

Shore, R. (1997). *Rethinking the brain: New insights into early development.* New York: Families and Work Institute.

Skeels, H. M. (1966). Adult status of children with contrasting early life experiences. *Monographs of the Society for Research in Child Development* (Serial No. 105).

U.S. Department of Education. (2001). *Twenty-third annual report to Congress on the implementation of the Individuals with Disabilities Education Act.* Washington, DC: Author.

Wallander, J. L., & Noojin, A. B. (1995). Mothers' reports of stressful experiences related to having a child with a physical disability. *Children's Health Care, 24*, 245–256.

Weber, C. U., Foster, P. W., & Weikart, D. P. (1978). *An economic analysis of the Ypsilanti Perry Preschool Project*. Ypsilanti, MI: High/Scope Educational Research Foundation.

Weikart, D. P. (1981). Effects of different curricula in early childhood intervention. *Educational Evaluation and Policy Analysis, 3*, 25–35.

Winick, M., Meyer, K. K., & Harris, R. (1975). Malnutrition and environmental enrichment by early adoption. *Science, 190*, 1173–1175.

Wolff, P. H. (1981). Normal variation in human maturation. In K. J. Connolly & H. F. R. Prechtl (Eds.), *Maturation and development: Biological and psychological perspectives* (Clinics in Developmental Medicine No. 77/78). Spastics International Medical Publications. Philadelphia: Lippincott.

Wood, M. M. (1981). Costs of intervention programs. In C. Garland, N. W. Stone, J. Swanson, & G. Woodruff (Eds.), *Early intervention for children with special needs and their families*. Monmouth, OR: WESTAR.

Yatkin, U. S., McLaren, D. S., Kanawati, A. A., & Sabbach, S. (1971). Undernutrition and mental development: A one-year follow up. In D. S. McLaren & N. J. Daghir (Eds.), *Proceedings of the 6th Symposium on Nutrition and Health in the Near East*. Beirut, Lebanon: American University.

2

Developmental Processes and Factors Affecting Development

Stephen R. Hooper and Carrie L. Mills

Denise and Nathaniel

*N*athaniel is Denise's third child. Denise is 21 years old and has struggled with a cocaine addiction for the past 4 years. She has been drug-free for the past year, although she clearly was using a variety of substances during her pregnancy with Nathaniel. As a single parent, she works hard to keep her part-time job and care for her three children. Although she receives some financial support from the WIC Program, she does not receive any child support. Her family is considered to be of low socioeconomic status and can afford only a one-bedroom apartment in an extremely old and poorly maintained building. Her first two children demonstrated some delays in their early development and are currently exhibiting some challenging behavioral difficulties in the classroom.

Denise did not seek medical services during her pregnancy with Nathaniel, in large part because of her struggles with cocaine, but she is now becoming increasingly concerned about his lack of developmental progress—even when compared to her other two children. At 23 months of age he is not able to stand without assistance, or walk, and is just beginning to use one-word utterances. Apprehensive about his slow progress, she made an appointment at the local child development clinic. Denise is frustrated with her lack of resources, feels alone in the process, and is overwhelmed by thoughts of what lies ahead for her and her family.

A sound knowledge of typical growth and development is essential for anyone interested in children, particularly for those who work with children in educational and developmental settings. For the student aspiring to work with young children with special needs, as well as for professionals already engaged in clinical practice serving such children, an understanding of typical growth and development provides a foundation from which many of the needs of children can be met. Not only does such knowledge contribute to an understanding of how children typically develop, but it also provides a basic yardstick for recognizing children with all kinds of exceptionalities and differences, and appropriately addressing their needs. Further, this knowledge base facilitates an understanding of the plethora of factors that can impinge on a child's developmental progress, some of which are illustrated in the vignette at the beginning of the chapter. An understanding of typical child development, including deviations and differences, along with an awareness of factors that affect development will guide the efforts of early interventionists to address the needs of young children with special needs.

This chapter provides an overview of the basic processes and principles of development. In addition to discussing definitional issues and specific stages of child development through the preschool years, selected risk factors that can impede development are highlighted.

Definitional Issues and Processes

Several questions arise in any attempt to define *development:* "Is there a time frame for the development of a specific behavior or repertoire of behaviors?" "How much change is needed in a behavior before it is recognized as development?" "Are there componential aspects to development?" How one conceptualizes human behavior and its development is a determining factor in how it is defined.

Definition

Development fundamentally involves systematic, cumulative change.

Unlike growth, through which new skills are acquired, development involves refining, improving, and expanding existing skills.

At its most fundamental level, development involves change. This change must be cumulative and systematic; however, random change is not considered to be developmental in nature. Whereas the concept of *growth* refers to the addition of new components or skills through the appearance of new cells, **development** refers to the refinement, improvement, and expansion of existing skills through the refinement of cells already present (Schuster, 1992). More specifically, three basic criteria must be met before change can be considered to be development:

1. The change must be orderly—not random fluctuations of behavior.
2. The change must result in a consistent modification in behavior.
3. The change must contribute to a higher level of functioning in the individual.

When a specific change in behavior satisfies these three criteria, development has occurred.

Development may be either qualitative or quantitative. For example, increases in height, weight, creativity, activity level, and vocabulary are quantitative changes;

that is, they are directly measurable. Progression toward maturity and the integration of complex physiological and psychological processes are qualitative changes; in other words, it is more difficult to gain an exact measure of these changes, but the changes are still noticeable. We see both types of change when children's shoes no longer fit, when they run faster and jump higher, when their increased proficiency in language helps them control their surroundings and their behaviors in a more accomplished manner, and when old toys and games lose their fascination in favor of new friendships and increased social contacts.

With these definitional components in mind, it also becomes important to distinguish between development and maturation. The concept of maturation is similar to that of development in that skills and functions are refined and improved over time. The concepts differ, however, in that **maturation** refers to the unfolding of personal characteristics and behavioral phenomena through the processes of growth and development. The concept of maturation reflects the final stages of differentiation of cells, tissues, and organs in accordance with a genetic blueprint wherein full or optimal development of a specific skill can be achieved (Schuster, 1992).

> Through the processes of growth and development an individual's characteristics and behavior unfold or mature.

Individual Differences

Another factor to consider in relation to development is the concept of individual differences. Children develop at different rates, and this in turn creates variations among individuals (i.e., individual differences). Again, these differences can be either qualitative or quantitative. For children in any preschool classroom setting, the differences in temperament, personality, intelligence, achievement, and physical factors such as height and weight, are noteworthy and reflect a wide range of normal variation. Some children grow rapidly and others grow more slowly. There also are racial and gender developmental variations. During the fetal stage, for example, females mature faster than males do. For example, at birth, the skeletal development of females is about 4 weeks ahead of that of males, and African American children show more rapid skeletal maturation than White children do (Lowrey, 1986; Russell et al., 2001; Tanner, 1989).

It is important to understand that the concept of individual differences is the basis upon which one child is compared to another. Also, the existence of these differences constitutes the fundamental premise underlying the development of standardized educational and psychological tests. An understanding of individual differences provides the foundation for recognizing normal variations as well as extreme differences among children, and thus for identifying those who may have special needs. In general, understanding of the various developmental levels is enhanced by familiarity with the concept of individual differences.

> Recognizing individual differences among children is the basis for determining special needs and for many testing procedures.

Principles of Development

Although children develop at different rates, and therefore the notion of interindividual differences exists, a single child can show more rapid change in some developmental areas than in others; thus, intraindividual differences also exist. Regardless of the perspective, there are certain principles of development that apply to all children. These include the following:

> Most principles of development apply to all children.

Normal variation is the rule in the development of a young child.

Children develop at varying rates, just as an individual child develops at varying rates in different areas.

- Development progresses in a step-by-step fashion. It is orderly, sequential, and proceeds from the simple to the complex. Each achieved behavior forms the foundation for more advanced behaviors.
- Rates of development vary among children as well as among developmental areas in a single child.
- Development is characterized by increasing specificity of function, or differentiation, as well as integration of these specific functions into a larger response pattern. A good example of this principle is the infant startle reflex. When an infant is startled, his entire body tenses and his arms move out to the side. With age, this reflex becomes integrated into more specific behavioral patterns such that a startled preschooler will tense only the shoulder and neck muscles.
- Neurological development contributes significantly to the acquisition of physical skills in young children. Physical development proceeds in cephalocaudal and proximodistal directions. **Cephalocaudal development** describes the progression of body control from the head to the lower parts of the body. For example, an infant will achieve head, upper trunk, and arm control before lower trunk and leg control. **Proximodistal development** describes progress from the central portions of the body (i.e., the spinal cord) to the distal or peripheral parts. In this developmental progression, gross motor skills and competencies precede fine motor skills. This developmental progression continues throughout early childhood, with

upper trunk control being achieved first, then arm control, and finally finger control. According to this principle, each change in the child's development should result in an increasingly refined level of skill development.

- Development of any structure follows a sequential pattern; however, there appear to be specific times during development in which a developing structure is most sensitive to external conditions. These **sensitive periods, or critical periods,** are the times during which a specific condition or stimulus is necessary for the normal development of a specific structure. Conversely, these periods also represent times when a structure may be most vulnerable to disruption (Rice & Barone, 2000). The concept of critical periods has created much debate in theoretical circles, particularly with respect to parent–infant bonding (Anisfeld et al., 1983) and language development (Lenneberg, 1967).

- All development is interrelated. Although it is convenient for the student or child practitioner to discuss development in terms of discrete developmental areas, such as motor skills, development in other areas such as social-emotional or communication functions does not cease, nor is it necessarily separate from other areas. The student or child practitioner must recognize how different areas of development are interrelated to understand how a particular child develops.

- Development is influenced by heredity and environment. Although there is much discussion by experts in the field about which is more important, there is no doubt that they both play a role in a child's development. A child's genetic inheritance (i.e., heredity) provides the basic foundation for many physical and personality attributes, but the influences of social, cultural, and familial variables (i.e., environment) also contribute to development.

> During sensitive, or critical, periods, a child must receive specific stimuli in specific conditions to develop normally.

> Both heredity and environment influence a child's development.

Processes of Development

An understanding of development requires resolution of a fundamental question: Do we develop primarily because we learn from our surroundings (environment) or because we are predisposed to grow in certain ways (heredity)? An explanation of each position provides an interesting framework for examining contemporary theories of child development.

> Heredity describes the inborn attributes of an organism.

Heredity. **Heredity** is the totality of characteristics transmitted from the parents to the offspring. The view that behavior and development are primarily directed by heredity, or nature, was initially set forth by **Jean Jacques Rousseau** in the 18th century. Rousseau was a French philosopher who believed that a child's growth and development were ultimately determined by nature, and that the child's surroundings had little influence on development. According to this viewpoint, nature provides the primary guidance for healthy growth and development. This philosophy has been advocated by Gesell (Gesell & Ilg, 1943), Jensen (1980), and others.

> Rousseau believed that a child's growth and development were determined by nature.

> John Locke believed that the environment was primarily responsible for growth and development.

Environment. The position that environment is primarily responsible for how a child develops can be traced to the work of 17th-century British philosopher **John Locke.**

Locke resurrected many of the teachings of Aristotle in describing the mind of an infant as a **tabula rasa**, or "blank slate." Locke believed that all of an individual's experiences contribute to filling the blank slate. The child was perceived as a passive receiver of information and thus easily shaped by environmental influences.

Watson (1924) and many other theorists (e.g., Skinner, 1961) have been strong advocates for the environmentalist position. Watson was a prominent force in American psychology and adhered almost exclusively to the nurture philosophy of the nature–nurture controversy. The basic tenets of his thinking are revealed in one of his earlier works (Watson, 1924):

> Give me a dozen healthy infants, well-formed, and my own specified world to bring them up in, and I'll guarantee to take any one at random and train him to become any type of specialist I might select—doctor, lawyer, merchant, chief, and yes, even beggar man and thief, regardless of his talents, penchants, tendencies, abilities, vocations, race of his ancestors. (p. 104)

Watson represented an extreme environmentalist position that downplayed biological influences on development and truly emphasized Locke's *tabula rasa* philosophy.

Interaction of Heredity and Environment.   As a resolution to these seemingly opposing positions, common sense dictates that neither heredity nor environment alone explains a child's typical growth and development. Heredity does not dominate development, nor are environmental influences solely responsible for one's personality, talents, or physical abilities. It seems that an interaction between these two positions most likely accounts for the multiple facets or elements of development. Although the interaction between heredity and environment is well accepted from a contemporary viewpoint, the exact degree of interaction remains a mystery; however, current scientific discoveries in the area of *genomics* (the study of genes and their expression) should provide clearer guidance with respect to the degree or magnitude of this interaction in the next several decades. The task for observers of child behavior and development should be to focus on describing the specific aspects of each philosophical position that may be affecting the development of any particular child. See Box 2.1 for a discussion of the Human Genome Project.

Periods of Development

This section explores the development of a child from conception through the early childhood years, including the prenatal period, the neonatal period, infancy, toddlerhood, and the preschool period. To complement the other chapters in this text, the emphasis here is placed on the prenatal and neonatal periods, although later developmental periods also will be described briefly. We begin with a brief review of some of the key biological foundations of development starting at the very beginning—the time of conception.

Growth and development begin at the time of conception.

Conception

Conception occurs when a sperm fertilizes an **ovum**, or egg. This union can take place only within approximately a 10- to 24-hour period after ovulation. The period

BOX 2.1	The Human Genome Project

In 1986 scientists embarked on a daunting mission of great significance—to map the human genome. Primarily under the direction of the National Institutes of Health and the Department of Energy, the primary purpose of the Human Genome Project is to identify the genetic code or DNA. Although each chromosome is made up of approximately 50,000 to 100,000 genes, scientists announced in February 2001 that they had mapped a rough draft of the human genome. One major discovery from this rough draft was that humans have no more genes than a common weed or worm (i.e., about 30,000–40,000). In April 2003, the human genome was completed— approximately two years ahead of schedule!

The medical, societal, and ethical implications of such an accomplishment are tremendous; however, several challenges remain. For instance, several diseases can be related to the same gene and, conversely, several genes can be related to one disease. In addition, some diseases are linked to the interaction of many genes, whereas other diseases need specific environmental conditions or "triggers" in order to be expressed. Despite these ongoing challenges, the potential contribution of such an undertaking likely will lead to revolutionary advances in health care. Not only do our genes contribute to our physical appearance, cognitions, and behaviors but they also contribute to what diseases we may develop or to which we may be susceptible (e.g., cancer, diabetes, heart disease). Although several concerns have been raised about potential ethical and legal ramifications, scientists believe that once the molecular structure is understood, they will be able to design drugs to treat the disease or even the genes involved in the disease process through gene therapy.

of ovulation, which corresponds to the release of an egg from an ovary, occurs in 28- or 29-day cycles in sexually mature females. In general, a high likelihood of conception occurs about 5 to 6 days before ovulation (Wilcox, Weinberg, & Baird, 1995). It is at this time of fertilization, or conception, that growth and development begin.

Cell Division, Chromosomes, and Genes.   After union of the sperm and egg, the fertilized egg begins to divide. Levitan (1988) estimates that approximately 44 geometric divisions of a single cell are required to transform it into a physiologically independent infant. In approximately 9 months, the single-celled fertilized ovum is transformed into a system of over 15 trillion cells. Each cell has a similar genetic composition, yet differs with respect to their specific function (Levitan). Cell division occurs by two processes, each serving a different function in development of the embryo. The first process is that of **mitosis**, in which a cell divides in half, thereby forming two new cells. It is through continuous cell division that a single cell evolves into a complex individual. Mitosis continues in body cells for one's entire life span; it contributes to growth as well as to replacement of dead and damaged tissue.

The second process of cell division is **meiosis**, which prepares a new cell for reproduction of the entire organism. Meiosis is a cell division that involves two highly specialized sex cells called **gametes**. These gametes are the ovum and the sperm, which are different from other cells in their chromosomal structure. When regular cells are formed, they contain 46 chromosomes arranged in 23 pairs. However, when the sex cells are formed, the chromosome pairs split so that the resulting sex cell has

In 9 months, the single-celled fertilized ovum transforms from a single cell into a system of over 15 trillion cells!

only 23 unpaired chromosomes. The gametes have a shorter life span than regular cells because they are missing a complete set of 46 chromosomes. They gain a full set of chromosomes, and consequently increase their life expectancy, only when the sperm fertilizes the egg (Vogel, 1986).

Chromosomes are hairlike particles of protein located in the nucleus of every cell. Each chromosome contains thousands of **genes** distributed in a balanced way among the pairs of chromosomes. Each gene carries coded information that combines to create unique human beings. It is precisely these informationally loaded particles that have been used in exploring revolutionary treatments involving gene replacement therapy for such genetic disorders as cystic fibrosis (see Box 2.1).

Genes may be either **dominant,** and always express their trait, or **recessive,** and express their trait only when paired with another recessive gene carrying the same coded information. For example, two tall parents, both carrying recessive genes for shortness in height, may have a short child if the recessive gene of each parent combines to form their child's gene for determining height. In this case, the child will not be as tall as the parents. This is an example of the genetic genotype. However, if one or both genes for tallness are transmitted, then the dominant gene will prevail and the child will be tall like the parents. This is an example of the genetic phenotype. In addition to the process of cell division, chromosomes and genes contribute to the hereditary construction of the individual. These processes and structures provide the blueprint for the unfolding of development.

Although specific types of genetic risk factors and inheritance mechanisms will be discussed later in this chapter, it is important to note that alterations in the chromosomes can contribute to a variety of birth defects as well as to spontaneous termination of the pregnancy. In fact, approximately 25% to 40% of conceptions are spontaneously terminated even before a woman knows that she is pregnant! Another 15% to 20% are spontaneously terminated after the woman knows about the pregnancy. Over half of these spontaneous abortions have been deemed secondary to genetic or chromosomal abnormalities, and they typically occur within the first trimester of pregnancy (Fogel, 2001; O'Rahilly & Muller, 1992). This stands in stark contrast to the 0.6% frequency of **chromosomal abnormalities** in live-born infants and the 4% to 12% rate in stillborn infants.

Prenatal Development

Prenatal refers to the time from conception to birth. The prenatal period may be divided into three stages. The first stage is called the **germinal stage** and lasts for about 2 weeks. The **embryonic stage** is next and lasts from about 2 to 8 weeks. The third stage, the **fetal stage**, follows and continues until birth. Although the variation of ovulation among women, as well as within the same woman, creates minor difficulties in accurately dating the pregnancy, this sequence of prenatal development holds true for all children. According to Deiner (1997), a general guideline to estimate the due date is to count back 3 months from the first day of the last menstrual cycle and then add 7 days, resulting in approximately 266 days postconception.

Sidebar notes:

Dominant genes will always express their trait, whereas recessive genes will express their trait only when paired with an identically coded recessive gene.

The hereditary construction of the individual provides the blueprint for the unfolding of development.

Chromosomal abnormalities can result in birth defects as well as spontaneous termination of the pregnancy.

To estimate a baby's due date, count back 3 months from the first day of the last menstrual cycle and then add 7 days.

Germinal Stage. The cell created by the union of the sperm and the egg is the zygote. Within 36 hours of fertilization mitosis begins, and this single cell rapidly divides. During the beginnings of mitosis the zygote slowly moves down the fallopian tube toward the uterus. This process takes about 3 to 4 days. Once its destination is reached, the zygote has transformed into a liquid-filled structure called a **blastocyst**, which floats in the uterus for about 24 to 48 hours. Mitosis continues and some of the cells of the blastocyst begin to clump on one side of the uterus to form the **embryonic disk.** This is the group of cells from which the baby will develop.

　　As the embryonic disk thickens, it begins to divide into three layers: the ectoderm, the endoderm, and the mesoderm. The **ectoderm** is the upper layer of cells in the embryonic disk and ultimately will become the epidermis, nails, hair, teeth, sensory organs, and central nervous system. The lower layer of cells, the **endoderm**, will eventually become the child's digestive system, respiratory system, and various other internal organs. The **mesoderm** is the last of the three layers to develop. It will evolve into the dermis, muscles and connective tissue, the skull, and parts of the circulatory and reproductive systems. The remaining parts of the blastocyst will create the prenatal structures required for intrauterine life. These include the **placenta**, which will nourish and protect the developing infant; the **umbilical cord**, which will connect the placenta to the developing child; and the **amniotic sac**, which will house the baby for the entire prenatal period. The outer layer of the **blastocyst**, called the **trophoblast**, eventually will produce microscopic, hairlike structures called **villi**. These villi adhere to the uterine lining until the blastocyst is totally implanted. Once uterine implantation is complete, the germinal stage is over, and the embryonic period begins.

> The baby ultimately develops from a group of cells called the embryonic disk. The embryonic disk provides the basis for the development of structures for prenatal life as well as for the development of all of the structures in postnatal life.

Embryonic Stage. This stage of development has been divided into 23 separate stages termed **Carnegie Stages**. It is beyond the scope of this chapter to review each of these stages in detail (for a review, see O'Rahilly & Muller, 1992); the main point to note is that during the embryonic stage, the embryo, as it is now called, experiences rapid growth. The amniotic sac, placenta, and umbilical cord are fully developed, and mitosis has progressed to the point that the **embryo** resembles a miniature human being. During this period, the developing embryo is extremely sensitive to toxic and infectious agents. Nearly all major birth defects, such as malformed limbs, cleft palate, blindness, and deafness, occur during this period or slightly after, but typically within the first 3 months of pregnancy (O'Rahilly & Muller, 1992). In fact, as noted earlier, many embryos spontaneously abort when their defects are markedly severe. Prenatal surgery is now possible to correct certain abnormalities (see Box 2.2).

　　By the end of this period, at about 8 weeks, the embryo has a beating heart, the beginnings of a skeleton, and a rapidly growing brain. This tiny developing human is now only about 2.5 to 3.8 cm (1−1½ in.) long and weighs about 0.9 gm (1/30 oz), but it clearly has begun to show distinct human characteristics (Moore & Persaud, 1993). For example, the head and brain are now visible, with the head accounting for approximately one half the length of the fetus, and a thin pink skin covers the body.

> Many major birth defects occur during the embryonic stage of development.

> By about 8 weeks of age, or about 2 months into a pregnancy, the embryo is about 2.5 to 3.8 cm (1 to 1/2 in.) long and about 0.9 gm (1/30 oz) in weight.

Fetal Stage. The fetal stage begins with the development of the first bone cell, which is produced from the cartilage of the developing skeleton at about 8 to 9

BOX 2.2   Prenatal Surgeries

Typical prenatal care activities may include obtaining a family and medical history, screening for hereditary conditions, conducting a variety of medical procedures such as blood work and urinalysis, discussing nutritional and physical needs, and perhaps performing genetic counseling. In addition to these important prenatal care activities, pioneering work in the field of fetal surgery is now being conducted. These delicate surgeries may involve inserting 2 shunt into the brain of the fetus to allow excess fluid to escape (thus minimizing brain damage), correction of urinary tract abnormalities, placement of the bowels back into the body, and fixing of abdominal hernias. Many of these procedures are still in their experimental stages and surrounded by many ethical concerns; however, the possibilities for contributing to positive growth and development are quite promising.

During the last 7 months of pregnancy, called the fetal stage, the baby experiences the most extensive rate of growth.

After 3 months, the baby measures 8 cm (3 in.) in length and is humanlike.

Life outside of the uterus is possible beginning around the fifth month of prenatal life.

weeks. The embryo now becomes a **fetus**. This final stage of the prenatal period lasts until birth, and it is during this time that the organism experiences the most extensive rate of growth in its lifetime. The length of the fetus increases until normal body proportions are achieved, and all internal systems and organs continue to increase their efficiency. At the end of the third month, the fetus is approximately 8 cm (3 in.) long and begins to show human characteristics. Its musculature is developing, and some spontaneous movements may be noted by the mother. Eyelids, teeth, fingernails, toenails, and external genitalia begin to form, and the gender is easily distinguished. During the fourth month the fetus grows another 2.5 to 5 cm (1 to 2 in.) in length and begins to develop hair, called **lanugo**, on its body. The eyelids begin to blink, the mouth begins to open, and the hands are capable of grasping. The fifth month is characterized by the mother typically feeling the fetus move for the first time. Eyebrows and hair appear, and the skin begins to take on the human shape. The length of the fetus is now roughly 25 cm (10 in.). At the end of the second trimester, the fetus has eyes that can open, taste buds on the tongue, and a functional respiratory system; it also is capable of making crying sounds. The fetus now weighs approximately 680 gm (1 lb 8 oz), and life outside of the uterus is possible.

The final trimester is a period of further growth and development of the fetus. This is manifested in greater structural differentiation and definition. At this point the fetus is viable; that is, its respiratory system and central nervous system are developed to a point at which it could survive independently outside of the uterine environment without undue difficulty. This growth continues until the point of delivery, or birth, typically somewhere between weeks 37 to 41 of the pregnancy. Figure 2.1 presents a month-by-month summary of the growth and development during the prenatal period.

The Birth Process

As delivery time nears, the mother's calcium level drops. This decrease is particularly marked in the pelvic area so that the mother's pelvis can be extended as widely as possible to accommodate the fetus. Simultaneously, muscles around the uterus and cervix also become larger and more flexible to accommodate the fetus during birth. In preparation for birth, the fetus rotates in the womb so that it will be born head

First Month *(1 to 4 weeks after conception)*
Conception, rapid growth
Fertilized egg embeds in uterine wall
Differentiation of individual from
    accessory structures
Three germ layers differentiated
Rudimentary body parts formed
Cardiovascular system functioning
Yolk sac begins to diminish

Fourth Month *(13 to 16 weeks)*
Much spontaneous movement
Moro reflex present
Rapid skeletal development
Meconium present
Uterine development in female infant
Downy hair (lanugo) appears on body
Weight: 120 gm (4 oz)

Second Month *(5 to 8 weeks)*
Formation of head and facial features
Very rapid cell differentiation and growth
Beginning of all major external and
    internal structures
External genitalia present, but gender
    not discernible
Heart functionally complete
Some movement by limbs
Yolk sac incorporated into the embryo
Weight: 1 gm

Fifth Month *(17 to 20 weeks)*
Begins to exchange new cells for old,
    especially in skin
"Quickening"—fetal movement felt by mother
Vernix caseosa appears
Eyebrows and head hair appear
Skeleton begins to harden
Strong grasp reflex present
Permanent teeth buds appear
Heart sounds can be heard with a stethoscope
Weight: 360 gm (12 oz)

Third Month *(9 to 12 weeks)*
Eyelids fused, nail beds formed
Teeth and bones begin to appear
Kidneys begin to function
Some respiratory-like movements exhibited
Begins to swallow amniotic fluid
Grasp, sucking, and withdrawal
    reflexes present
Moves easily (not felt by mother)
Gender distinguishable
Weight: 30 gm (1 oz)

Sixth Month *(21 to 24 weeks)*
"Miniature baby"
Extrauterine life first possible
    (but very unlikely)
Mother may note jarring but rhythmic move-
    ments of infant indicative of hiccups
Body becomes straight
Fingernails appear
Skin has a red, wrinkled appearance
Alternates periods of sleep and activity
May respond to external sounds
May try to find comfortable position
Weight: 720 gm (1½ lb)

FIGURE 2.1   A month-by-month summary of development in the prenatal period

Source: Adapted from Schuster, C. S.(1992). In C.S. Schuster & S.S. Ashburn (Eds.), *The Process of Human Development: A Holistic Life-Span Approach* (3rd ed., pp. 68, 70). Philadelphia: J.B. Lippincott Company. Adapted by permission.

first. This rotation is triggered by hormonal action in the mother and is the first indication of the onset of labor. If fetal rotation does not occur, the baby will be born feet first. This awkward type of delivery is called a **breech delivery** and occurs in about 3% to 4% of births (Kauppila, 1975), with increased frequency noted in preterm deliveries (i.e., 14% at 29 to 32 weeks gestation) (Haughey, 1985). A breech delivery can cause anoxia (lack of oxygen), intracranial hemorrhage (bleeding), and transient lowering of the fetal heart rate, particularly in the premature infant (Schifrin, 1982). Although a breech delivery typically is not of major consequence to outcome,

The fetus rotates in the uterus so that it will be born head first; if this rotation does not occur, a breech delivery will result.

Seventh Month *(25 to 28 weeks)*
Respiratory system and central nervous
    system sufficiently developed that
    many babies may survive with
    excellent and intensive care
Eyelids reopen
Assumes head-down position in uterus
Respiratory-like movement
Weight: 1,200 gm (2½ lb)

Ninth Month *(33 to 36 weeks)*
Continues fat deposits
Body begins to round out
Increased iron storage by liver
Increased development of lungs
May become more or less active because of
    space tightness
Excellent chance of survival if born
Lanugo begins to disappear from body
Head hair lengthens
Weight: 2,000 gm (6 lb)

Eighth Month *(29 to 32 weeks)*
Begins to store fat and minerals
Testes descend into scrotal sac in male
Mother may note irregular, jerky,
    cryinglike movements
Lanugo begins to disappear from face
Skin begins to lose reddish color
Can be conditioned to environmental sounds
Exhibits good reflex development
Good chance of survival if born
Weight: 2,000 gm (4 lb)

Tenth Month *(37 to 40 weeks)*
Lanugo and vernix caseosa both begin
    to disappear
High absorption of maternal hormones
Skin becomes smooth, plump
Firming of skull and bones
Continued storage of fat and minerals
Ready for birth
Weight: 3,200 to 3,400 gm (7 to 7½ lb)

FIGURE 2.1   *Continued*

some association has been made to abnormalities in the child, with central nervous system anomalies being noted most frequently (Mazor, Hagay, Leiberman, Biale, & Insler, 1985). In addition, nearly half of all cases of hydrocephalus, myelomeningocele, Prader-Willi syndrome, and trisomy are associated with breech presentation (Westgren & Ingemarsson, 1988).

Other factors that can affect the baby include pressure in the birth canal, the use of forceps during delivery, and the sedation of the mother. This latter factor can be critical because the baby's immature liver and excretory systems experience difficulties eliminating maternal medications and anesthesia from the body. This may contribute to sedation and, consequently, to a baby who initially may be less responsive to environmental stimulation—including its parents (Morgan, 1994; Murray, Dolby, Nation, & Thomas, 1981).

When there is a possibility of an abnormal vaginal delivery, a **cesarean section** (c-section) can be performed. In this procedure, the mother's abdomen and uterus are surgically opened, and the baby and placenta are removed. This procedure eliminates many of the risks associated with an abnormal delivery for the mother as well as for the child. One factor that can indicate the need for a c-section is **postmaturity.** Postmaturity refers to a baby being postterm, or after the 41st week. About 10% of babies are born after the 41st week of gestation (Coustan, 1995). Although most babies show no permanent signs of being postmature, largely because of routine and careful prenatal monitoring, some postmature babies do not obtain sufficient nutri-

A c-section can eliminate many of the risks of an abnormal delivery for the mother and baby.

ents and oxygen from the placenta to meet the demands of labor (Korones, 1986), and thus brain injury or death can occur.

Neonatal Period

The **neonatal period** is the transitional time from intrauterine to independent existence. Defined as approximately the first 4 weeks after delivery, the neonatal period is possibly the most tenuous in a human's lifetime. Of the nearly 4 million babies who are born alive annually in the United States, approximately 1% die within the first 24 hours, 1% die within the first week, and 1% die within the first year. Behrman and Kliegman (1983) note that an infant experiences a greater risk of death during the first 7 days of life than at any other time during the next 65 years. The largest number of deaths occurring during the first year of life are attributed to sudden infant death syndrome (SIDS). See Box 2.3 for further discussion.

The average newborn enters the world weighing between 2,500 and 4,300 gm (5 lb 8 oz) and (9 lb 8 oz), with the overall average being about 3,200 to 3,400 gm (7 lb to 7 lb 8 oz). About 90% of newborns are approximately 46 to 56 cm (18 to 22 in.) in length, with the average being about 51 cm (20 in.) (O'Rahilly & Muller, 1992). The baby's size is associated with a variety of factors including parental size, race, gender, maternal nutrition, and overall maternal health. Male newborns tend to be slightly longer and heavier than their female counterparts, and the first child in the birth order generally weighs less than any of the siblings who follow (Lowrey, 1986). The skin of newborns is often pale and thin. The skin also may be covered with **lanugo**, a light, fuzzy body hair, or **vernix caseosa**, an oily fluid that protects the baby from infection. Both of these substances disappear shortly after birth.

> The neonatal period—the first 4 weeks after birth—is considered a high-risk stage in human life.

> The average full-term baby weighs about 3,400 gm (7 lb 8 oz) and is about 51 cm (20 in.) long.

BOX 2.3   Sudden Infant Death Syndrome

Each year approximately 4,000 deaths of infants from 2 to 4 months of age are attributed to "crib death"—a problem best known as sudden infant death syndrome (SIDS). This accounts for the largest number of deaths occurring during the first year of life in developed countries with a rate of about 1–2.5 deaths per 1,000 live births. Researchers and medical professionals are still in the process of trying to understand the causes of this condition, particularly given that the majority of cases occur in apparently health infants. Although there are some indications that this condition is related to delayed development of physiological arousal and cardiorespiratory control, the actual mechanisms behind this problem remain unknown. What we do know is that premature infants have a five times greater risk for SIDS than full-term infants, that SIDS is seen more frequently in boys than girls, and that there also is higher risk for infants born to mothers who smoke, are not married, and/or come from impoverished backgrounds. In addition, many of the parents of babies succumbing to SIDS reported mild cold symptoms prior to the event. As might be expected, parents are devastated at the unexpected loss of their infant, and often experience intense guilt and grief. Prevention measures, such as keeping infants on their back as much as possible, avoiding overheating, and avoiding soft, loose bedding, all have contributed to reducing the occurrence of SIDS (American Academy of Pediatrics, 2000).

The skeletal system of the neonate is not totally developed, and consequently many of the bones are soft and pliable. For example, the **fontanelles**, or soft spots in the head, are the gaps between the bones in the skull that permit the skull bones to overlap during the birth process and allow for additional brain growth. The posterior fontanelle gradually closes up through the third month of life, whereas the anterior fontanelle is closed by 18 months of age.

The respiratory system of the newborn must adapt to a gaseous environment. Although the newborn consumes about twice the amount of oxygen as an adult does (Hubbell & Webster, 1986), respiration tends to be rapid, shallow, irregular, and unsynchronized, with the abdomen doing more work than the chest. The neonate may make peculiar wheezing and coughing sounds because the entire respiratory system is underdeveloped and inexperienced with the demands of the extrauterine environment. The digestive and circulatory systems also must make the transition to independent functioning. The visual system is incomplete because of underdevelopment of the retina and optic nerve; however, the newborn's eyes can follow a moving light as well as a moving target. In general, neonates can see best at a distance of about 19 cm ($7\frac{1}{2}$ in.). There also seems to be a preference for visually following human faces more than any other type of object (Johnson, Dziurawiee, Ellis, & Morton, 1991) and they seem to prefer faces judged by adults to be more attractive, regardless of age, gender, or race (Slater et al., 1998). Interestingly, these features may not be as true for newborns with emergent neurodevelopmental disorders (e.g., autism).

The neonate also maintains physiological reactivity to sound intensity, as indicated by increased heart rate and motor activity, as well as an orienting reflex in which the baby turns in the direction of the sound stimulus. The other senses of olfaction, taste, and tactile sensitivity also are intact (Maurer & Maurer, 1988). For example, the neonate is capable of distinguishing among sweet, sour, and bitter tastes, as well as distinguishing the odor of its mother's breast milk (MacFarland, 1975). Motor skills of the neonate are mainly characterized by primitive reflexes and random gross motor activity. Reflexes are automatic inborn behaviors of which the newborn has many. Further discussion of reflexes and motor development is provided in Chapters 7 and 8; Box 2.4 discusses neonatal intensive care facilities for infants with special developmental needs.

Newborns can see best at a distance of about 19 cm ($7\frac{1}{2}$ in.), and they seem to prefer attractive human faces.

Infant Period

Infancy describes the growth and development of the child from about the fourth week through the second year of life. The infant experiences rapid physical growth during this time. The birth weight doubles by the fifth month and triples by the end of the first year, and the infant gains about 2,300 to 2,700 gm (5 to 6 lb) per year for the next several years (Lowrey, 1986). The infant grows approximately 25 cm (10 in.) by the end of the first year, an average of 13 cm (5 in.) by the end of the second year, and 7 cm (3 in.) the following year (Deiner, 1997). In addition to weight and length, **head circumference** is an important physical feature to measure at regular intervals. Changes in head circumference are important because they denote brain growth. During the first year of life, head circumference increases from 33 or 36 cm (13 or 14 in.) at birth to about 43 or 46 cm (17 or 18 in.), with most of this growth occurring during the early months of development. The circumferences of the chest

The infancy period—from 4 weeks of age to 2 years—is a time of rapid physical growth.

Changes in head circumference indicate brain growth.

BOX 2.4	The Neonatal Intensive Care Unit (NICU)

Premature, low-birth-weight, and medically involved infants may need to spend time in a closely monitored environment where they can receive complex medical care and attention. The newborn or neonatal intensive care unit (NICU) is a specialized facility that can meet the needs of medically fragile infants and their parents. Length of stay in the NICU is determined by a number of factors including severity of the illness or condition and the rate of progress during care. Although the infant mortality rate has decreased 90% from 1915 to 1997 to about 7.2 per 1,000 live births (Centers for Disease Control and Prevention [CDC], 1999), the United States continues to have one of the highest rates of infant mortality among industrialized nations. Whereas the mortality rates have decreased with advances in medical technology, reducing the morbidity rates (i.e., negative outcomes) increasingly has become the focus of caregivers in the NICU environment.

A strong movement in NICUs within the United States and abroad is to integrate developmental care into the NICU environment. A training model and protocol developed by Heidelise Als around 1986, titled the Neonatal Intervention and Developmental Care Assessment Program, is a forerunner to the family-centered developmental care movement. This model suggests that the environment should be modified to simulate the in utero setting, yet stimulate and encourage development of the newborn on its schedule. Modifications in lighting, handling of the infant, and feeding practices are examples of variables that may need to be changed to suit the infant's specific developmental needs (Als, 1997).

and abdomen are about the same in the neonate, but during infancy the chest circumference becomes larger than that of the abdomen. Deciduous, or primary, teeth appear at about 6 to 8 months and continue to erupt until all 20 are in place by toddlerhood. The skeletal structure of the infant hardens, and the musculature increases in weight and density. Typically, African American children show more rapid skeletal growth than White children do, and the bones of females generally grow faster than those of males (Lowrey, 1986; Tanner, 1989).

> African American and female children typically grow faster than do White children and males.

Another manifestation of infancy is the apparent disappearance or, more accurately, the integration of many of the primitive reflexes into the baby's developing nervous system. This occurs as the cerebral cortex matures and begins to exert control over the lower central nervous system. This control is accomplished, in part, by a process called **myelinization**. Myelin is a soft, white, fatty substance that coats and protects many nerve cells. It allows for rapid transmission of neural messages from the brain to other parts of the body. Myelinization begins in utero at about the fourth gestational month, with some neural pathways (e.g., the brain stem) being fully myelinated by the 30th gestational week (Amand, Phil, & Hickey, 1987); however, myelinization is not complete at birth (Willis & Widerstrom, 1986). Although it will not be complete until adulthood, by 6 months many of the cortical fibers have been sheathed with myelin, thus facilitating greater cortical control and enabling the infant to achieve various developmental milestones such as sitting up, grasping, and walking, and various cognitive and adaptive skills necessary for maturation (Tanner, 1989).

> Myelinization is the process by which myelin, a soft, white, fatty substance, coats and protects nerve cells.

Infants begin learning about themselves and their environments as early as the first day of life.

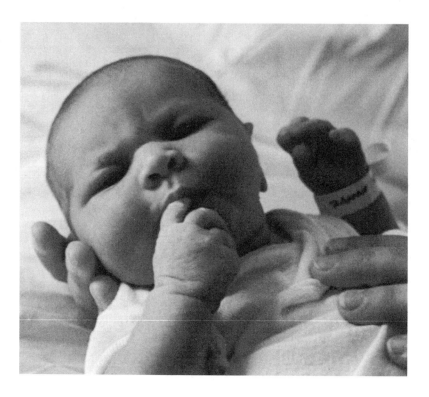

Toddler Period

The **toddler period** generally encompasses development during the second and third years of life. Strang (1969) has labeled this period "the first adolescence." It is a transitional time between infancy and early childhood, just as adolescence links childhood to adulthood. The toddler period is characterized by a slowing of physical development, although the toddler maintains a growth rate faster than any subsequent period except adolescence. At age 2 the average toddler is 81 to 89 cm (32 to 35 in.) tall and weighs approximately 11 to 14 kg (25 to 30 lb). The child now is capable of maintaining an upright physical posture, and development in all areas becomes more refined. Brain growth reaches about four-fifths of its ultimate adult weight by age 2, and by age 3 it is closer to its mature size than any other body part (Black & Puckett, 1996; Lowrey, 1986).

> Toddlerhood—the second and third years of life—is a transitional period of continued growth and development.

Bones continue to calcify and harden, with the composition of wrists and ankles changing from cartilage to bone. Nonetheless, the toddler still has a larger proportion of cartilage than hard bone, making possible skeletal damage resulting from disease or poor diet. A toddler normally has a full set of baby teeth by age 2. Muscle and fat tissues develop slowly during this period, with fatty tissue growth actually decreasing up to about age 30 months when it again begins to increase. Motor development improves, and well-balanced walking, jumping, and climbing without adult assistance are common. Fine muscle control is evident in the child's finger coordination in learning to handle pencils, crayons, and paintbrushes.

> By age 3, the brain is closer to its mature size than any other body part.

Play during the toddler period is increasingly exploratory and self-directed.

Memory and language skills also show significant gains during this period. The child learns the names of people, objects, and places and can recall them for later use. In the language domain, the child moves from word combinations at age 2 to sentences at age 3. Words and actions become more coordinated near the end of the toddler period. Social-emotional development moves from adult-assisted activities to more independent social-emotional activities, with play being exploratory and egocentric in nature. Self-help and adaptive behaviors also emerge during toddlerhood, with the major one being toilet training. In general, the toddler begins to use thought, language, movement, and emotions in a coordinated fashion and is learning to gain verbal control over actions (Tinsley & Waters, 1982).

> The toddler begins to coordinate thinking and language skills, as well as motor and emotional skills.

Preschool Period

As will be seen from the chapters in Part III of this text, the **preschooler** continues to experience refinement in growth patterns, particularly in physical structures and motor skills. Self-help skills, such as dressing, toileting, and language usage, become a regular part of day-to-day behaviors. Gender differences are minimal, although boys usually are heavier and have more muscle tissue than girls do. The head reaches about 90% of its adult size and the brain about 75% of its adult weight by the end of the preschool years (Lowrey, 1986; Tanner, 1989).

The preschool child is willing to try new games, tricks, and stunts, and self-confidence in this realm is growing. Preschoolers are excited about their surroundings

> The preschooler integrates self-help skills, such as dressing, toileting, and language usage, into daily behavior.

By the end of the preschool years, the head grows to 90% of its adult size and the brain to 75% of its adult weight.

and are curious enough to ask "Why?" questions. Speech and language skills have become more grammatically correct in their manifestations, and the child uses language in a functional manner. Social-emotional development is characterized by increased child-to-child and child-to-adult interactions as fears, fantasies, and a sense of self-respect emerge. Much of the preschooler's developmental activity forms the foundation for the social and learning challenges to be encountered when formal schooling begins around age 6 (Black & Puckett, 1996).

Factors Affecting Development

Nearly all of the preschooler's developmental activity forms the foundation for future learning and social challenges.

Although the unfolding of the developmental process is a fairly remarkable set of events, there are many factors that can influence the viability of the developing embryo and the subsequent condition of the young child. Some of these factors, such as maternal age and parity, exist prior to conception; some, such as maternal nutrition, substance use during pregnancy, and maternal illness, exist at or following conception, but prior to birth; some, such as prematurity and low birth weight, appear at the time of birth; and others, such as failure to thrive and child abuse or neglect, exist after birth. Many of these factors are interrelated, such as when poor maternal nutrition during the prenatal period contributes to low birth weight; however, these factors will be considered separately for the purposes of discussion. Further, it is important to note that this section is not meant to be an exhaustive listing of factors that can disrupt development; it is intended merely to illustrate the many possible factors that can disrupt the developmental process.

Maternal Age and Parity

Risks to the unborn child increase with advancing maternal age.

Maternal age and parity (i.e., number of pregnancies) provide clues relating to the course of development of the fetus. Women between the ages of 20 and 30 are in the prime of their childbearing years. Although today more women are waiting until their mid-30s or early 40s to have children (Martin et al., 2002), emergent research suggests that female fertility begins to decline in the early to mid-30s (Auyeuna, Klein, Ratts, Odem, & Williams, 2001). Further, although the risks during pregnancy at a later age are still relatively small, they do increase with advancing age (Dildy et al., 1996). For instance, the risk of Down syndrome increases with age, with rates being approximately 1 in 10,000 for 20-year-old mothers; about 3 in 1,000 for 35-year-old mothers; and 1 in 100 for 40-year-old mothers (Eisenberg, Murkoff, & Hathaway, 1991). In addition, mothers over 25 years of age are at a significantly increased risk of having babies with congenital malformations, such as clubfoot, not associated with chromosomal abnormalities (Hollier, Leveno, Kelly, McIntire, & Cunningham, 2000). Mothers who are 35 or older also may be at increased risk for high blood pressure, diabetes, cardiovascular disease, preterm labor, and postpartum hemorrhage. In some older mothers, a decrease in muscle tone and joint flexibility may contribute to more difficult labor, but this may not be a problem for women who have maintained good physical condition prior to and during pregnancy.

In general, women over the age of 35 and teenagers are more likely to have high-risk pregnancies. Reasons for the increased risk may include limited prenatal care and poor nutrition, as well as a number of negative social and emotional consequences. In addition, for teenagers, recent evidence also points to lower IQ as a key contributor to early childbearing (Shearer et al., 2002). This combination of factors may increase the teenage mother's chances of premature labor and delivery of a low-birth-weight child. Both teenage and older mothers have a greater likelihood of developing toxemia (Batshaw & Perret, 1992). Children of adolescent mothers also are at greater risk for a number of physical, emotional, and cognitive problems (Coley & Chase-Lansdale, 1998), although it is important to note that the rate of births to teenagers has been steadily dropping over the past decade (Martin et al., 2002).

> Teenagers and women over age 35 are more likely to face risks during pregnancy.

Regardless of the mother's age, the first birth carries an added risk because all of the maternal systems involved in pregnancy and delivery have yet to be tested. Subsequent births less than 2 years apart and after the third child also carry additional risks (Apgar & Beck, 1972; Holley, Rosenbaum, & Churchill, 1969), although many of these risks have been linked to poor prenatal care (Blondel, Kaminsky, & Breart, 1980).

> The first birth carries added risks to the child and mother.

Paternal Factors

Until recently, it was believed that a father's responsibility in the reproductive process was solely to fertilize the egg and that the male had no involvement in how the child developed in utero; however, this may not be an accurate reflection of the paternal role. It was discovered during the last century that the father's sperm decides the gender of the baby, and in the last few decades it has been suggested that an older father's sperm might contribute to birth defects such as Down syndrome (Abroms & Bennett, 1981). Just as in the case of the eggs of the older mother, it has been argued that the undeveloped sperm of the older father have had longer exposure to environmental hazards or teratogens and, consequently, might contain altered or damaged genes or chromosomes (Eisenberg et al., 1991). This finding has recently been challenged (Luetjens, Rolf, Gassner, Werny, & Nieschlag, 2002), but ongoing research is still needed to provide greater clarification, particularly as it may apply to *genetic counseling* (Hook, 1987). In addition, it has been postulated that a father's sperm may be a vehicle for transporting drugs, such as cocaine, to the egg during fertilization (Yazigi, Odem, & Polakoski, 1991). Therefore, many obstetricians are now considering paternal age and related factors (e.g., substance abuse) as risk factors to development in addition to the age of the mother.

Maternal Nutrition

More than 30 years ago, the Food and Nutrition Board published a landmark report titled *Maternal Nutrition During the Course of Pregnancy* (National Research Council, Committee on Maternal Nutrition/Food and Nutrition Board, 1970), which examined the relationship between nutrition and the course and outcome of pregnancy. This report made recommendations for weight gain and nutritional intake during pregnancy. It also suggested that women should be concerned about their nutritional habits from puberty through the childbearing years because these habits can help prepare them for childbirth. Adequate maternal nutrition is important to the health of the expectant mother as well as to that of her unborn child. Poor maternal nutrition will affect the child by not sufficiently meeting the nutritional requirements of the developing fetus and by weakening the mother and, consequently, the intrauterine environment (Herbert, Dodds, & Cefalo, 1993).

During pregnancy, many substances are exchanged between mother and baby as their blood passes through the placenta. Thus, dietary intake by the mother influences the developing fetus. Both quality and quantity of nutrient intake required by a woman increase during pregnancy. Qualitative deficiencies relate to the imbalance of proteins, vitamins, and minerals in the mother's diet. Quantitative deficiencies are simply those in which the mother lacks sufficient caloric intake. A review of data on nutrient intakes during pregnancy indicates that, on average, women probably meet their recommended daily allowance (RDA) for protein, thiamin, riboflavin, niacin, and vitamins A, B12, and C. Expectant mothers are less likely to meet requirements for folacin, iron, calcium, zinc, magnesium, and vitamins B6, D, and E. This does not necessarily mean that a woman's diet is deficient, however, as many of the RDA requirements are somewhat generous. Although a sensible, balanced diet, consisting of approximately 2,700 calories, is considered the optimal way for an expectant mother to pass nutrients to her baby, vitamin and mineral supplementation is common.

For example, for women who are on restricted diets, are carrying more than one fetus, are very young, use drugs, or have poor prepregnancy nutritional or physical status, selective supplementation may be warranted. For women who regularly follow suggested dietary guidelines, iron and folacin appear to be the primary nutrients for which requirements cannot be met reasonably by diet alone. The RDA for iron during pregnancy is more than twice as high as the average daily intake. Further, a deficiency in folate in the expectant mother's diet has been associated with **neural tube defects** (i.e., problems with the closing of the primary tubular structure that develops into the brain and spinal cord; Smithells et al., 1983), orofacial clefts (Shaw, Lammer, Wasserman, & O'Malley, 1995), and low birth weight (Scholl, Hediger, Schall, Khoo, & Fischer, 1996). In fact, the United States Public Health Service now recommends that all females of childbearing age consume 0.4 mg of folic acid every day during the periconceptual period; that is, one month before conception through the third month of pregnancy (CDC, 1995). In addition, the Department of Health and Human Services and the Food and Drug Administration (FDA) announced that many foods in the United States will be fortified with folic acid to prevent birth defects (Food and Drug Administration [FDA], 1996).

Several other dietary components are essential in the diet of a pregnant woman, and may have an impact on brain growth and subsequent cognitive development. For example, recent work has targeted choline as a key nutrient in this regard. Choline is one of the building blocks of cell membranes that aid functions such as the neurotransmissions that control memory. Following a dose of choline to a pregnant rat during the third trimester, her pups could negotiate a maze nearly 40% better than pups of mothers who were not given choline (Zeisel, 2000). Although the generalization of these findings to humans awaits confirmation, these findings generally suggest that the dietary needs of women of childbearing age should be monitored because preconception nutrition deficits may affect the developing fetus in positive as well as negative ways (House, 2000; King, 2000).

Poor prenatal care and insufficient food intake both are associated with poor pregnancy outcomes. Between the 1960s and 1980s it became common for doctors to recommend a **gestational weight gain** averaging 11 kg (24 lb) or more rather than the 9 kg (20 lb) or less recommended prior to the 1960s. Contemporary best practices suggest a range of weight gain for pregnant women based upon prepregnancy weight-for-height. This change in recommended weight gain for expectant mothers has been accompanied by an increase in mean birth weight of their infants and a reduction in low birth weight (Institute of Medicine, National Academy of Sciences, 1990a; Susser, 1991). A large body of evidence indicates that gestational weight gain during pregnancy, particularly during the second and third trimesters, is an important determinant of fetal growth. For example, inadequate nutritional intake during the last trimester can permanently reduce the number of brain cells by as much as 40%, and improved nutritional intake after such a period of malnourishment ultimately will not increase the number of brain cells (Winick, 1971). Poor fetal nutrition also has been associated with increased risk for problems in adulthood, such as coronary heart disease, stroke, and diabetes (Barker & Clark, 1997; Godfrey & Barker, 2000; Petry & Hales, 2000).

> Weight gain during gestation is important in determining fetal growth.

> Poor fetal nutrition has been associated with problems at developmental stages across the life span.

In general, low weight gain during pregnancy is associated with intrauterine growth retardation, which in turn can have adverse consequences for subsequent growth and possible neurobehavioral problems. It also increases the risk of infant mortality. Women with total individual weight gains of less than 10 kg (22 lb) were two to three times more likely to have growth-retarded full-term babies (Luke, Dickinson, & Petrie, 1981). Conversely, excessive weight gain in pregnancy can be associated with high birth weight and, secondarily, prolonged labor, shoulder dystocia (i.e., a disconnecting of the upper arm from the shoulder during the birth process in which muscles and nerve fibers can be damaged or destroyed), cesarean delivery, birth trauma, and asphyxia (Institute of Medicine, 1990).

The **Special Supplemental Food Program for Women, Infants and Children (WIC)**, which is administered by the U.S. Department of Agriculture, has had an increasing impact on the provision of food to low-income pregnant women since 1974 (Rush, 1988). In addition to food or food vouchers, WIC provides education, counseling, and referrals for women who meet state criteria for nutritional risk during pregnancy and the early childhood years of their babies. This program has had a positive impact on the health of pregnant mothers from lower socioeconomic strata and their babies: about a 25% reduction in low-birthweight infants and a 44% reduction in very-low-birth-weight infants (U.S. General Accounting Office, 1992).

> The WIC program has had a positive impact on the health of pregnant mothers from lower socioeconomic strata and their babies.

Exposure to Toxins During Pregnancy

Exposure to various toxins during child development has the potential for significant deleterious effects. A conceptual framework to organize neurotoxins, or teratogens, and their developmental consequences has been presented by Trask and Kososky

(2000). A **teratogen** is anything that is external to the fetus that causes later structural or functional disabilities. Teratogens typically fall under two main categories, exposure to environmental toxins, such as lead and mercury (see Stein, Schettler, Wallinga, & Valenti, 2002, for review), and exposure to drugs, such as alcohol and tobacco. Research indicates that the earlier the exposure, particularly during the prenatal period, the greater the potential for negative developmental outcomes as a result of the exposure. In addition to the direct effects of teratogens on the child, indirect effects of the teratogens may compromise other maternal systems (Williams & Carta, 1997). For instance, smoking or alcohol consumption may inhibit the availability of critical nutrients in the bloodstream, and further hinder the development of the fetus. Research that attempts to quantify the impact of teratogens on children, both short-term and long-term effects, are often hindered by the frequency with which potential negative influences, such as poverty and poor nutrition, tend to co-occur (Abel & Hannigan, 1995).

Substance Use During Pregnancy

Substance use during pregnancy is an area of serious concern, with contemporary estimates suggesting a prevalence of about 11% (Chasnoff, 1991). This figure could be even higher given that many expectant mothers do not report their use of illegal substances. This issue was brought to the fore during the early 1960s when a number of babies were born with no limbs and with other malformations because their mothers had taken thalidomide, a German-made tranquilizer to control vomiting during pregnancy. About 20% of the pregnant women who took thalidomide gave birth to babies with birth defects. This incident dramatically underscored the risks involved in taking any drug during pregnancy. Although detrimental effects have been suggested for a variety of drugs, such as heroin, marijuana, and lysergic acid diethylamide (LSD), it is difficult to document the individual impact of these specific substances because many users of illegal drugs experiment with a variety of substances, not to mention variants of the same drug. In addition to the negative effects of direct exposure to substances prenatally, infants and children are also affected by the parental illnesses related to substance use and are at risk for future substance abuse themselves (Richter & Richter, 2001). Many women who use illicit drugs often place their babies at additional risk resulting from poor nutrition and lack of adequate prenatal care.

In general, the specific effects of a drug on a developing fetus are determined by at least two key factors: the dosage level and the stage of pregnancy during which the drug is taken. In fact, drugs with addictive properties, such as heroin, can cross the placenta barrier and cause the baby to be born addicted to that particular substance. Unfortunately, the infant then must go through withdrawal symptoms similar to those of adult addicts to get the drug out of its system. For the sake of the unborn child, the use of any drug for recreational purposes during the prenatal period should be avoided. This precaution should be extended to include both over-the-counter and prescription drugs, and all medications should be used only when they are recommended *and* monitored by the expectant mother's physician (see Shehata & Nelson-Piercy, 2001).

Alcohol.   Alcohol is the drug most frequently used by women in the United States, with alcohol abuse present in 1% to 2% of all pregnant women in the United States. Estimates suggest that approximately 40,000 infants born each year are affected by prenatal alcohol exposure (National Council on Alcoholism and Drug Dependence, 1990). As such, alcohol use during pregnancy is cited as one of the leading causes of preventable birth defects and developmental disabilities in the United States (Weber, Floyd, Riley, & Snider, 2002). A number of detrimental short- and long-term effects have been associated with prenatal alcohol use. Some of the most consistent manifestations of significant alcohol exposure are intrauterine growth deficiency, low birth weight, cardiac defects, microcephaly (i.e., small head and brain), shortened fetal length, and subsequent cognitive delays (Abel, 1989). The cognitive delays have been documented across nearly every area of functioning including motor, sensory, attention, language, visual-spatial abilities, learning and memory, problem solving, and overall intelligence (Streissguth & Kanter, 1997). Further, abnormalities in specific brain structures (e.g., corpus callosum, basal ganglia, cerebellum) also have begun to be documented (Mattson & Riley, 1998).

> Limiting alcohol use during pregnancy is one of the leading ways to prevent birth defects and developmental disabilities.

A distinct cluster of characteristics, which have been linked to comprise a disorder termed **fetal alcohol syndrome** (FAS), has been identified in children of alcoholic mothers. These characteristics include (a) pre- and postnatal growth retardation; (b) abnormalities of major organ systems such as the heart and liver; (c) central nervous system abnormalities including microcephaly, mental retardation, or specific neurodevelopmental delays; and (d) distinctive facial characteristics (e.g., short palpebral fissures, a thin upper lip, a flattened and elongated philtrum, minor ear anomalies, and micrognathia; Shubert & Savage, 1994). These latter features are illustrated in Figure 2.2. It should be noted that many of the facial features may not be present if the mother did not consume alcohol during the time that these facial characteristics were forming (i.e., about the 20th day of pregnancy) and, when present, they may be seen most clearly between the ages of 2 and 10.

The estimated prevalence of FAS in the United States is approximately 0.5 to 2 cases per 1,000 births (May & Gossage, 2001). The incidence of FAS is approximately 1 to 3 per 1,000 live births (Gardner, 1997), and it is estimated that thousands more children may exhibit **fetal alcohol effects** (FAE); that is, they have some, but not the full range of FAS characteristics. The Institute of Medicine (1990b) termed brain dysfunction in the presence of significant prenatal exposure to alcohol but no physical deformities "**alcohol-related neurodevelopmental disorder**"; this may occur with at least 10 times the prevalence of FAS. Mattson, Schoenfeld, and Riley (2001) and others noted that children with FAE may show a variety of maladaptive behaviors, learning disabilities, speech and language problems, hyperactivity, and attention-deficit hyperactivity disorder.

Along with fragile X syndrome in males, FAS is one of the leading known causes of mental retardation in the United States (Deiner, 1997). Current research also indicates that there may be a dose-response relationship to development; in other words, detrimental effects on development seem to increase with the amount and frequency of alcohol consumption (Day & Richardson, 1991; Sood et al., 2001). Binge drinking appears to be more harmful than more continuous drinking patterns even if less

> One of the leading known causes of mental retardation in the United States is fetal alcohol syndrome.

FIGURE 2.2 Distinctive facial characteristics of FAS

Source: Reprinted with permission from the King County Medical Society, Seattle, WA.

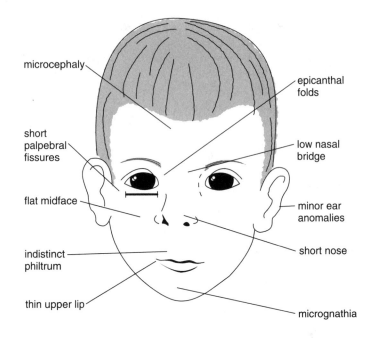

There are no safe levels of alcohol consumption during pregnancy.

alcohol is consumed during the period of binge drinking (Maier & West, 2001). In general, there may be no safe level of alcohol consumption during pregnancy (National Clearinghouse for Alcohol and Drug Information, 1995), although it appears that moderate-to-high levels of alcohol consumption early in pregnancy cause the most severe problems. A woman is thought to be at increased risk of delivering a baby with FAS when her daily alcohol intake exceeds 80 gm ($2\frac{1}{2}$ oz) of alcohol per day (10 gm = one glass of wine or half a pint of beer). In fact, fetal growth may be compromised by as little as 40 gm ($1\frac{1}{2}$ oz) of alcohol per day (Shubert & Savage, 1994). It is thought that one of the primary mechanisms of damage occurs when high blood concentrations of alcohol hinder the transfer of amino acids and other necessary nutrients from the mother to the fetus, thus contributing to fetal hypoxia, subsequent decreased brain weight, and perhaps brain abnormalities. The rate at which alcohol is metabolized also may contribute to these anomalies (Autti-Ramo & Granstrom, 1991). Recent evidence indicates that exposure to alcohol in utero may even contribute to a preference for alcohol later in life (Molina, Chotro, & Dominguez, 1995).

Tobacco.   One million babies are estimated to be at increased risk for low birth weight because their mothers smoke cigarettes (Floyd, Zahniser, Gunter, & Kendrick, 1991). In fact, smoking is one of the most preventable causes of low-birth-weight babies and is implicated in 20% to 30% of all the cases of low birth weight in the United States (Chomitz, Cheung, & Lieberman, 1995; Ogunyemi, Hullett, Leeper, & Risk, 1998). Unfortunately, reports of the rate of pregnant women in the United States who continue to smoke throughout pregnancy range from 13% to 30% (Hoyert, Freedman, Strobino, & Guyer, 2001; Slotkin, 1998). The potential impact of this problem has led to the identification of **fetal tobacco syndrome** (FTS), (Nieburg, Marks,

Smoking accounts for 20% to 30% of all low-birth-weight babies.

McLaren, & Remington, 1985). This syndrome is characterized by mothers who (1) smoke five or more cigarettes per day, (2) have no maternal history of hypertension in pregnancy, (3) have babies with fetal growth retardation at term, and (4) manifest no other causes for their baby's intrauterine growth retardation. A likely mechanism for FTS involves the vasoconstrictive properties of nicotine. Nicotine actually binds to fetal hemoglobin and, consequently, reduces oxygen availability to the fetus (Longo, 1976). This effect has also been found in cases where the mother is exposed to passive or secondhand smoke (Dollberg et al., 2000).

Passive or secondhand smoke also may impact negatively on the developing fetus.

There have been additional risks associated with smoking during pregnancy including spontaneous abortion, premature delivery, and stillbirth later in pregnancy (Kleinman & Madans, 1985). More recent concern also has focused on the effects of passive exposure to smoking, and correlations have been made to delays in intellectual, academic, and social-emotional development (Rush & Callahan, 1989). Prenatal exposure to nicotine is associated with general physiological dysregulation and higher risk for psychiatric problems (Ernst, Moolchan, & Robinson, 2001) including early onset conduct disorder and adolescent-onset drug dependence (Weissman, Warner, Wickramarante, & Kandel, 1999), an increased risk of cleft lip and cleft palates (Kallen, 1997), and a significant negative impact on the behavior of preschoolers (Day, Richardson, Goldschmidt, & Cornelius, 2000). Infants whose mothers were exposed to passive smoking also have been found to be at increased risk for illnesses such as pneumonia, bronchitis, laryngitis, otitis media (i.e., chronic ear infections; Floyd et al., 1991), and lung-related problems at birth (Milner, Marsh, Ingraham, Fox, & Susiva, 1999).

As is suspected with alcohol, a strong dose-response relationship seems to exist for smoking; that is, the more a woman smokes during pregnancy, the greater the likelihood that her baby will have low birth weight (Cnattingius, 1997). In fact, Cnattingius reported that the incidence of low birth weight is significantly higher for infants born to women who smoke than for those born to women who do not. More specifically, the rate of having infants with low birth weight is high for women who smoke less than 10 cigarettes per day versus those who don't smoke, but it is even higher for women who smoke more than 10 cigarettes per day. Further, Cnattingius reported that age is a significant mediating factor affecting these rates. For example, the risk of a baby being small for gestational age is about twofold for teenage mothers who smoke compared to teenage mothers who do not smoke, but the rate more than doubles to about 4.5 times for women over 40 years of age who smoke during pregnancy. In addition, women who stopped smoking within the first trimester reduced the risk for stillbirth and infant mortality to levels comparable to the rates for children of nonsmoking mothers, suggesting that whether or not a mother stops smoking by the 16th week of gestation may be critical (Wisborg, Kesmodel, Henriksen, Olsen, & Secher, 2001). Despite these findings, only about 25% of women who smoke stop smoking during pregnancy, and it may be even more difficult to encourage older smokers to quit than younger ones. Nonetheless, smoking remains one of the most preventable risk factors and quitting smoking, even as late as the seventh or eighth month of gestation, may have a positive influence on an infant's birth weight (Rush & Cassano, 1983).

A strong dose-response relationship seems to exist for smoking.

Other Substances.   Since the mid-1980s a number of studies have examined the impact of prenatal cocaine exposure on infant development. Early reports suggested that cocaine use during pregnancy was associated with a host of adverse effects spanning a continuum of severity from significant physical and neurological impairments to very subtle neurobehavioral differences. More recent studies, however, have been less conclusive, in part because of complex methodological issues (Zuckerman & Frank, 1994). The direct impact of cocaine is difficult to document because of its many variants, the concern that women using cocaine are likely to be using other drugs concomitantly (including tobacco), and the problem that there often are coexisting environmental factors of poverty and malnutrition, which can lead to less than optimal pregnancy outcomes. Children exposed to high-frequency cocaine use prenatally had poorer neurobehavioral outcomes (Schuler & Nair, 1999), significant cognitive deficits, were twice as likely to have a developmental delay (Singer et al., 2002), and were at increased risk for motor dysfunction (Swanson, Streissguth, Sampson, & Olsen, 1999). In contrast, other investigators have suggested that the effects of prenatal cocaine exposure are similar to the effects of other teratogens (Frank, Augustyn, Knight, Pell, & Zuckerman, 2001). In fact, one study did not reveal significantly lower IQ scores in a sample of prenatally exposed preschoolers tested at age 4 (Hurt et al., 1997). Nonetheless, studies have linked cocaine exposure to smaller babies, either as a result of early delivery or intrauterine growth retardation, or both (Datta-Bhutada, Johnson, & Rosen, 1998; Frank, Bresnahan, & Zuckerman, 1993; Richardson, Hamel, Goldschmidt, & Day, 1999; Robins & Mills, 1993).

Heroin use by expectant mothers also has received recent attention. The use of heroin during pregnancy is associated with decreased birth weight and length (Little et al., 1990), along with other perinatal and postnatal complications. Heroin quickly crosses the placenta, so if the mother is addicted, the infant is too. This addiction results in neonatal withdrawal symptoms affecting both the central and autonomic nervous systems (Strauss & Reynolds, 1983). Symptoms frequently include tremulousness and hyperirritability, a high-pitched cry, and possible neurologic regulation difficulties manifested by sleeping and eating disturbances. Methadone maintenance often is recommended for heroin-addicted women in conjunction with adequate prenatal care. This treatment has been shown to reduce the incidence of medical complications resulting from prematurity (Kaltenbach & Finnegan, 1987; Kandall, Doberczak, Jantunen, & Stein, 1999). Although the use of methadone during pregnancy also may have some early effects on the baby, long-term developmental problems are not suspected, or at least have not been documented.

Although minimal research has been conducted on the effects of prenatal exposure to marijuana, recent cross-sectional and longitudinal studies have reported deficits in specific areas of cognitive function, such as attention (Fried & Smith, 2001). Likewise, the effect of inhalant abuse during pregnancy is limited, yet appears to indicate several negative fetal outcomes (Jones & Balster, 1998).

Because heroin quickly passes through the placenta, the infant becomes addicted, too.

Maternal Illness

Some diseases minimally affect the expectant mother but can devastate her unborn child. Diseases and infections have the greatest influence during the first trimester, when the major body systems are being formed. The effects of rubella on the mother, for example, may be mild or even go unnoticed; however, the unborn child may

Some diseases that severely affect a fetus have minimal impact on the mother-to-be.

experience heart malformation or disease, microcephaly, retardation, vision and hearing deficits, or death. There is now a vaccine for rubella that can be administered to prepubescent females to prevent this from becoming a factor during pregnancy. Other maternal illnesses contracted during the prenatal period, such as venereal diseases, toxoplasmosis, toxemia, pica, chicken pox, mumps, measles, scarlet fever, tuberculosis, and urinary tract infections, also may cause children to have various intellectual, motor, physical, or sensory differences or deficits.

Diabetes.   With incidence rates between 1.5% to 11.3%, diabetes in expectant mothers can have negative effects on their infants (Magee, Walden, Benedetti, & Knopp, 1993). In pregnancy, there are two main forms of diabetes: **gestational diabetes mellitus (GDM)** and **pregestational diabetes mellitus (PGDM)**. GDM generally is limited to pregnancy and is not considered to be a maternal disease; it usually is resolved about 6 weeks after the birth of the baby (Ezra & Schenker, 1996). GDM occurs in about 2% to 6% of pregnancies (Sullivan, Henderson, & Davis, 1998). In contrast, PGDM is a maternal disease that can begin to exert an impact on the pregnancy at the point of conception, particularly if the mother-to-be has not achieved adequate glycemic control (Kitzmiller et al., 1991). This impact may be seen in the form of major and minor abnormalities in the fetus, with the incidence of major abnormalities falling between 5% and 13% (Gotto & Goldman, 1994; Omori et al., 1994). Although these abnormalities can involve nearly all of the body systems (Cousins, 1983), in particular there is a 2-to-19 times higher risk of central nervous system disruption (Reece & Hobbins, 1986) and a 4-to-7 times higher risk of cardiac anomalies (Ferencz, Rubin, McCarter, & Clark, 1990). The most frequent central nervous system malformation is anencephaly (no brain development), followed by spina bifida (Reece & Hobbins, 1986).

More generally, infants born to diabetic mothers tend to be larger, heavier, and born somewhat earlier than infants of nondiabetic mothers; they also tend to be more prone to critical levels of hypoglycemia (low blood sugar) after birth (Ezra & Schenker, 1996). Women with poorly controlled PGDM also experience a higher rate of spontaneous abortion (Katz & Kuller, 1994), intrauterine growth retardation (Van Assche, Holemans, & Aerts, 2001), and complications during delivery (Scholl, Sowers, Chen, & Lenders, 2001).

> Babies of diabetic mothers typically are larger, heavier, and born earlier than babies of nondiabetic mothers.

The offspring of diabetic mothers, whether diabetes is preexisting or limited to the gestational period, are at increased risk for a number of undesirable developmental outcomes, such as difficulties with attention span and motor function (Ornoy, Ratzon, Greenbaum, Wolf, & Dulitzky, 2001), obesity (Silverman, Rizzo, Cho, & Metzger, 1998), and a greater number of hospitalizations (Aberg & Westbom, 2001). One of the most significant fetal complications of GDM or PGDM is **macrosomia** (i.e., "large body," or an absolute birth weight greater than 4,000–4,500 gm [9–10 lb]), which occurs 10 times more frequently in infants with diabetic mothers than in infants with nondiabetic mothers. Macrosomia can lead to birth trauma, such as brachial plexus palsy, and asphyxia in labor secondary to difficulties in extracting the baby from the mother. Approximately 25% to 30% of fetuses born to diabetic mothers have macrosomia (Carrapato & Marcelino, 2001).

A number of etiological factors have been described as contributing to the formation of congenital abnormalities in babies of women with diabetes. These include metabolic abnormalities, such as hyperglycemia (high blood sugar levels), hypo-glycemia (low blood sugar levels), and hyperinsulinemia (high insulin levels); hyperketonaemia (high ketone [a sugar-based metabolic agent typically found in the blood and urine] concentrations), and general genetic susceptibility. Although a description of these etiological factors is beyond the scope of this chapter, the main point to note is that one of the key factors necessary for fetal development is glu-cose. For the fetus, glucose is completely derived from the blood circulation of the mother via diffusion through the placenta. Therefore, the condition of the mother's metabolic system is a critical determinant in fetal growth. Circulating glucose levels that are too high or too low force the fetus to adjust to these conditions because it is completely dependent upon these circulating levels, and this condition sets the stage for the potential of the abnormalities just described (Aerts, Pijnenborg, Verhaeghe, Holemans, & Van Assche, 1996).

Maternal Infections

Maternal infections can have significant deleterious effects on the developing fetus. An acronym to delineate various maternal infections that can cause similar malfor-mations is **STORCH**. This acronym stands for syphilis, toxoplasmosis, other infec-tions, rubella, cytomegalovirus, and herpes simplex virus. In addition, there are other maternal infections that can disrupt the developing fetus.

Acquired Immunodeficiency Syndrome.   One of the most serious conditions that infants can acquire from their mothers is acquired immunodeficiency syndrome (AIDS). AIDS in young children primarily is the result of congenital or perinatal maternal transmission of the human immunodeficiency virus (HIV) to the fetus or newborn infant. Transmission of this AIDS-causing virus affects about 20% to 30% of infants born to HIV-infected mothers (Crocker, 1999; Grant, 1995), with some esti-mates as high as 65% (Deiner, 1997). This transmission also can occur across the pla-centa or in utero, during delivery, or via breast milk (Deiner, 1997; Miotti et al., 1999). Not only can development in cognitive, physical, and social domains become slowed or arrested (Chase et al., 2000; Macmillan et al., 2001), but actual deterioration of previously achieved skills and milestones also can occur (Crocker, 1999).

> Infants affected with HIV can experience slowed, arrested, or even reversed development in cognitive, physi-cal, and social domains.

In addition, the mortality rate is high for these infants, with a median survival rate of approximately 38 months once the child exhibits symptoms of the virus. Although most infected infants may appear to be healthy at birth, symptoms report-edly can occur as early as 8 months of age (Scott et al., 1989). Initially, the incuba-tion period in young children appeared to be much shorter than in adults (Rubinstein, 1986), estimating that approximately one-third of the infected children die during infancy, another third before kindergarten, and another third before 20 years of age (Grubman, Gross, Lerner-Weiss, & Hernandez, 1995). More recent reports (Lindegren, Steinberg, & Byers, 2000) conclude that about 15% to 20% of chil-dren with HIV rapidly deteriorate and die within the first 4 years after infection, whereas the majority show disease progression at a rate similar to adults.

HIV affects the body's immune system, leaving the individual vulnerable to var-ious illnesses. The leading cause of death in HIV-positive children is opportunistic infections secondary to this compromised immune system (Hammill & Murtagh, 1993). Even those children who are fortunate enough to remain uninfected by the virus face a life filled with uncertainty because of their mother's infection and higher rates of anxious and depressive symptoms (Esposito et al., 1999).

Currently, more than 1 million children are infected worldwide and, unless prenatal care and other preventative measures are adopted, another million will be infected in the next 3 years (Wilfert & McKinney, 1998). Antiviral drug therapy, such as AZT, can reduce the prenatal transmission of AIDS by 67% to 75%, but it also may place the unborn baby at risk for a variety of birth defects (Chadwick & Yogev, 1995; Connor et al., 1994).

HIV affects the body's immune system, leaving the individual vulnerable to various illnesses.

Maternal Emotional State

Although it is clear that children of mothers with depression are at greater risk for developing depression or other forms of psychopathology than children of non-depressed mothers (Beardslee, Versage, & Gladstone, 1998), little is understood about the pathways that influence the child's developmental trajectory and increase the likelihood of transmission from parent to child (Cummings, Davies, & Campbell, 2000). A combination of genetic and environmental factors, particulary interactions between the parent and child, may contribute to depressive disorders in children as recent findings highlight the significance of prenatal influences. Specifically, preliminary findings suggest that adverse prenatal conditions, such as the exposure of the fetus to abnormal neuroendocrine functions, increased cortisol levels, or constricted blood flow to the fetus, may increase a child's vulnerability to future psychopathology (Goodman & Gotlib, 1999). Therefore, although the emotional state of the mother may not directly affect her developing child, the hormonal releases that accompany her emotions, particularly those associated with stress and anxiety, affect the baby both before and after birth (Glover, 1999). These hormonal releases have been associated with the neuroanatomical and biochemical organization of the brain of the fetus as early as 8 weeks following conception. Exposure of the mother to life stress appears to result in physiological changes, which in turn affects the future behavior and stress reactivity of her offspring (Fifer, Monk, & Grose-Fifer, 2001). In fact, even the physical health of the infant has been suggested as being compromised by maternal stress. For example, peptic ulcers related to maternal stress have been found in newborns (Herrenkohl, 1988).

According to preliminary research, adverse prenatal conditions may make a child more susceptible to abnormal behavior or mental health problems.

Stress creates changes in the nervous system that contribute to reduced blood flow to the uterus and, consequently, reduced flow of nutrients and oxygen to the fetus. One of the hormones triggered by increased stress is cortisol. Cortisol is a recognized teratogen to body organs, especially the organs of the reproductive system (Schuster, 1992). Herrenkohl (1988) has noted that the "prenatal stress syndrome" may contribute to the feminization and demasculinization of male offspring, and it may contribute to reproduction dysfunction in females. More generally, women who are highly anxious or who experience prolonged stress have complicated deliveries, spend about 5 more hours in labor, and have more spontaneous abortions and premature births than their less stressed counterparts. The presence of malformations in babies of mothers with critical stress during the first trimester is higher than in babies of mothers with lower levels of stress (Stott, 1971). DaCosta, Dritsa, Larouche, and Brender (2000) also found that mothers reporting less satisfaction with their social supports experienced greater stress during pregnancy, had more difficult deliveries, and delivered children of lower birth weight. For low-income women, the relationship between social support and positive pregnancy outcomes is particularly strong (Hoffman & Hatch, 1996). Examination of other maternal lifestyle variables has the potential to provide new insights about the effects of maternal emotional states on the fetus (Nathanielsz, 1995).

Blood Incompatibility

Early in pregnancy all women are tested to determine blood type (A, B, AB, or O) and Rh factor (positive or negative). If a woman's blood type is Rh positive (which is true of approximately 85% of women), or if both she and the baby's father are Rh negative, there is no cause for concern. If the mother is Rh negative and the father is Rh positive, however, the baby could inherit the father's positive blood type, which could cause a problem during pregnancy or at the time of delivery if the condition is not treated. When the baby's blood enters the Rh-negative mother's circulatory system during pregnancy, the mother's body produces antibodies to destroy the "foreign substance" in a natural protective immune response. The antibodies are intended to attack the baby's blood cells in the mother's circulatory system, but they can cross the placenta and destroy the fetus' Rh-positive blood cells. These antibodies may not be a problem during a first pregnancy, but they can lead to serious hemolytic or Rh disease in subsequent newborns. When there is a high level of antibodies produced by the mother, many of the fetus' red blood cells are destroyed, eventually leading to severe anemia or possible fetal death. If this condition is left untreated, live births can be complicated by severe jaundice, which can lead to mental retardation, hearing loss, or cerebral palsy.

Injections of gamma globulin, or RhoGam, can prevent hemolytic disease in the newborn.

Fortunately, hemolytic disease of the newborn can be prevented most of the time by injections of gamma globulin, or RhoGam. RhoGam acts to prevent the mother's immune system from reacting to the fetus's red blood cells and producing antibodies. At 28 weeks an expectant Rh-negative mother who shows no antibodies in her blood receives an injection of **RhoGam**, and another dose is administered within 72 hours following delivery, miscarriage, abortion, amniocentesis, or bleeding during pregnancy if the baby is Rh positive. If it is determined that the Rh-negative mother has begun producing antibodies during pregnancy and that her blood is incompatible with the fetus' blood, maternal antibody levels are carefully monitored. When the incompatibility is severe, which is rare, a fetal transfusion of Rh-negative blood may be necessary. In most cases, however, a transfusion is not necessary or can be done at the time of delivery.

In nearly 3% to 4% of newborns, defects are detected prenatally, at birth, or within the first few years of life.

Genetic Abnormalities

Although most babies are born healthy and develop normally, approximately 3% to 4% have defects that are detected prenatally, at birth, or within the first few years of life (National Society of Genetic Counselors, 1989). Some birth defects are inherited, some are a result of environmental influences, and others are attributable to the interaction of heredity and environment. Families with a history of genetic abnormalities may wish to consider genetic counseling, testing, or both as part of their family-planning process. It may be important for an expectant couple to be aware of any increased genetic risk so they can consider the possibility of prenatal screening. Parents of a child with developmental difficulties may decide, along with their pediatrician, to have a **karyotype** (i.e., chromosomal analysis) performed or to have other, more sophisticated genetic testing conducted to diagnose current problems.

Abnormalities caused by hereditary factors are of three types: autosomal inheritance, X-linked inheritance, and defective chromosomes. Table 2.1 shows examples of problems resulting from the three types of genetic abnormalities, their causes, their characteristics, and what is known about the developmental course of individuals with the abnormality.

Autosomal inheritance is a natural process by which traits are transmitted from parents to their children. Two autosomal patterns of inheritance include the autosomal recessive pattern and the autosomal dominant pattern, of which the chances of inheritance are equal for males and females. For an **autosomal recessive disorder** to occur, both parents must be carriers of a defective recessive gene and transmit this gene to their child; the risk of occurrence is 25% for each conception, as shown in Figure 2.3. Carriers are not usually clinically symptomatic.

One example of the autosomal type of inheritance pattern is the disorder phenylketonuria (PKU). PKU is an inherited inborn error of metabolism for which infants are routinely screened at birth. It is a condition whereby the body is unable to process adequately the food it consumes, particularly with respect to a component

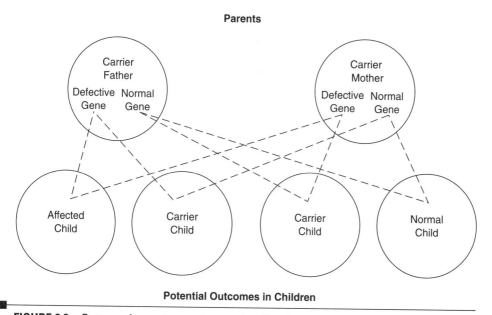

Parents

Carrier Father
Defective Normal
Gene Gene

Carrier Mother
Defective Normal
Gene Gene

Affected Child

Carrier Child

Carrier Child

Normal Child

Potential Outcomes in Children

FIGURE 2.3 Pattern of an autosomal recessive disorder

TABLE 2.1   Examples of Genetic Abnormalities

Abnormality	Cause/Early Detection	Characteristics	Developmental Course
AUTOSOMAL INHERITANCE Cystic fibrosis	Recessive gene/prenatal testing	Glands controlling production of mucus, sweat, tears, and saliva function incorrectly and make breathing difficult. Coughing, recurring pneumonia, large appetite, small size, and enlarged fingertips are symptoms.	Increased risk of severe respiratory infection; possible future candidate for gene therapy.
Phenylketonuria (PKU)	Recessive gene located on chromosome #12/ possible prenatal DNA analysis and routine newborn screening	Inborn error of metabolism; newborn lacks ability to process phenylalanine found in products like milk. If left untreated, can cause mental retardation.	Dietary restriction of phenylalanine beginning in infancy minimizes any effects.
Sickle-cell anemia	Recessive gene/prenatal screening and blood test after birth	Shortage of red blood cells causes pain, damage to vital organs, possible death in childhood or early adulthood.	Chronic illness; often treated medically but there is no cure.
Tay-Sachs disease	Recessive gene/prenatal screening	Progressive nervous system disease that allows a toxic product to accumulate in the brain as a result of enzyme deficiency. Leads to brain damage and death.	Normal development until 6 months of age. Neurological deterioration includes seizures, blindness, mental retardation, and death by age 5.
Achondroplasia	Dominant gene/prenatal testing	Disproportionately short stature, relatively large head, short limbs, trident hand, normal intelligence.	Possible delay in developmental milestone attainment; occasional deafness.
Marfan's syndrome	Dominant gene/no prenatal testing at this time; usually diagnosed by physical exam	Tall, thin with hypermobile joints; long, thin spiderlike fingers; spinal curvature, dislocated eye lens.	Prone to lung collapse with high incidence of heart and blood vessel defects; associated with ADHD and learning disabilities.
Neurofibromatosis	Dominant gene; linked to chromosome #17/no prenatal tests; diagnosis based on physical exam	Multiple "cafe-au-lait" spots on body; small nerve tumors on body and skin; some affected persons may have large heads, scoliosis, or variety of bone defects.	No known treatment. Wide variability in expression; may be associated with mild mental retardation or learning disabilities.

TABLE 2.1 *Continued*

Abnormality	Cause/Early Detection	Characteristics	Developmental Course
X-LINKED INHERITANCE			
Color blindness	X-linked recessive gene	Red-green color blindness.	No known cure.
Hemophilia	X-linked recessive gene	Blood lacks important clotting factor.	Blood-clotting factor is needed to stop bleeding. Frequent hospitalizations and chronic problems. No known cure.
Duchenne muscular dystrophy	X-linked recessive gene/prenatal testing	Normal development until 6 to 9 years of age; then muscular weakness appears and progresses.	Progressive disease affecting all muscles including heart and diaphragm; usually results in death during young adulthood.
Fragile X syndrome	X-linked fragile site/chromosomal testing available pre- and postnatally	The most common hereditary form of mental retardation in males, with associated physical features of prominent jaw, large ears and testes.	Children may have associated behavioral problems, hyperactivity, and some autisticlike features.
DEFECTIVE CHROMOSOMES			
Cri du chat syndrome	Deletion on top portion of #5 chromosome	Microcephaly, widely spaced eyes, small chins, and high-pitched cry ("cat cry"); severe retardation.	No known cure.
Down syndrome	Extra chromosome of 21st pair/prenatal testing	Cognitive deficits, hypotonia, facial characteristics, short stature, congenital heart disease.	Developmental progress appears to slow.
Klinefelter's syndrome	Extra X chromosome (45XXY)/prenatal testing	Male child with inadequate testosterone production resulting in abnormal sexual development. Usually tall, slender, with breast development and small genitalia. Close to normal intelligence.	Psychological and psychiatric abnormalities; small percentage has mental retardation, language delays. Medical treatment involves administration of male hormones.
Turner's syndrome	Missing X chromosome (XO or 45X)/prenatal testing	Only disorder associated with survival despite loss of chromosome. All are female, very short, and have webbed necks, widely spaced nipples, and nonfunctional ovaries. Usually of normal intelligence, with visual perceptual difficulties.	Majority of girls have learning disabilities; medical treatment with hormones.
XYY syndrome	Extra Y chromosome/prenatal testing	Usually tall with normal sexual development but low intelligence. Aggressive behavior; severe acne.	Associated with behavioral problems and learning disabilities. No known cure.

FIGURE 2.4 Pattern of an
autosomal dominant disorder

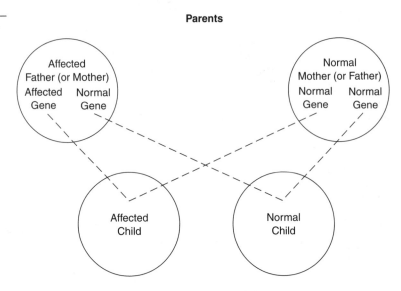

Potential Outcomes in Children

of protein called phenylalanine, and this incomplete metabolic process creates a toxin that can be damaging to neurological development. The fetus is unaffected by this metabolic defect prior to birth because excess materials pass freely from child to mother via the placenta (Ensher & Clark, 1994). Following birth, however, and without treatment, the body accumulates excess phenylalanine within tissues, which causes central nervous system damage including mental retardation by 1 year of age. Early identification of PKU can lead to restriction of the intake of phenylalanine (i.e., to reduce the amount of toxin in the body) in the diet within the first few weeks of life. Although this special diet may need to continue indefinitely, it has been proven to be effective in preventing adverse outcomes (Poustie & Rutherford, 2000).

Autosomal dominant disorders are different from autosomal recessive disorders in that the individual has the disease when he has a single abnormal gene, and thus the risk of transmission is increased to 50%. Autosomal dominant disorders usually involve structural abnormalities (Batshaw & Perret, 1992). This type of inheritance pattern can be seen in Figure 2.4. An example of the autosomal dominant pattern is neurofibromatosis. Neurofibromatosis is one of the most common genetic disorders, with an incidence rate of approximately 1 per 3,000 births. One of the common signs of this disorder is the presence of large tan spots, or "cafe-au-lait" spots, on the skin. These spots often are present at birth, and they may increase in size, number, and pigmentation with age. Small benign tumors under the skin may appear at any age, and other tumors may be present in and damage major neurological systems; tumors in the auditory nerve, for example, result in hearing impairment or deafness. The degree of involvement in any single case can vary widely, ranging from relatively few problems to significant learning and developmental problems. Currently, there is no prenatal test that can detect neurofibromatosis; the diagnosis is made by physical exam.

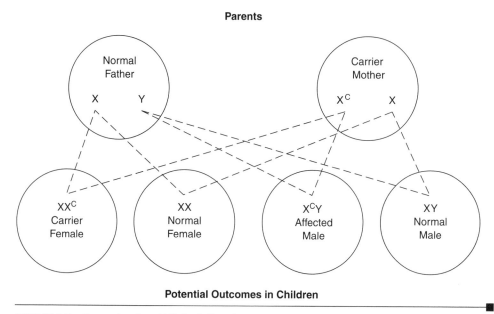

FIGURE 2.5 Example of an X-linked disorder inheritance pattern

The second form of genetic inheritance of abnormalities is referred to as sex-linked, or **X-linked**, because it involves genes located on the X, or female, chromosome. With this type of disorder females typically are carriers and males are affected—largely because males have only one X chromosome. One variant of an X-linked inheritance pattern can be seen in Figure 2.5. An example of an X-linked inheritance pattern is fragile X syndrome. As noted in Table 2.1, fragile X syndrome is the leading cause of inherited developmental delay in males (Hagerman, 1999). The prevalence of fragile X syndrome in males is about 1 per 4,000 compared to about 1 per 8,000 for females. As its name implies, this abnormality relates to a mutation at the bottom of the X chromosome. This mutation can result in a variety of physical (e.g., elongated face, large ears, increased head circumference), behavioral (e.g., attention deficits, self-injury), emotional (e.g., social anxiety), and learning problems ranging from subtle deficits in mildly affected children to severe levels of mental retardation (Bailey et al., in press; Cohen, 1995; Hagerman, 1996). Both males and females are affected by this disorder, although females tend to have less impairment (Hagerman, 1999).

The third type of genetically inherited abnormalities are caused by **chromosomal malformations** in which chromosomes are added to or deleted from the normal 23 pairs or they are damaged. Any of these disruptions can result in birth defects or death. The incidence of chromosomal aberrations is about 0.4%. Autosomal chromosomal abnormalities usually lead to mental retardation and are characterized by distinct physical characteristics (Batshaw & Perret, 1992).

Down syndrome is an example of this type of genetic abnormality, with an incidence rate of about 1 in 700 to 800 live births. As noted earlier, this rate tends to increase for expectant mothers over the age of 35 (Chan, McCaul, Keane, & Haan,

1998). The diagnosis of Down syndrome is typically suggested by clinical observations of physical characteristics and then confirmed by obtaining a karyotype (Cohen, 1999); however, prenatal testing also can determine its presence. Selected physical features include a variety of minor anomalies (e.g., flat nasal bridge and flat profile), although most individuals manifest only some of these features (Cohen, 1999). More severe involvement of musculoskeletal, hematological, neurological, endocrine, and cardiac systems also are common (McBrien, Mattheis, & Van Dyke, 1996). Although children diagnosed with Down syndrome tend to show pervasive developmental delays, they also manifest steady rates of positive development with appropriate educational and family interventions.

Prematurity and Low Birth Weight

Historically, the risk factors of prematurity and low birth weight have been used interchangeably. Certainly, these factors are intimately related in that prematurity tends to be a cause of low birth weight; however, it is important to note that infants

Children with Down syndrome and other genetic disorders can show positive development and growth when provided with a nurturing environment and early intervention.

born prematurely do not always have low birth weight and, conversely, infants with low birth weight are not always born prematurely. In fact, about 33% of babies with a birth weight of less than 2,500 gm (5 lb 8 oz) are actually small for their gestational age, perhaps secondary to **placental insufficiency**. Placental insufficiency reduces the flow of oxygen and nourishment to the fetus (Behrman, 1992).

A baby is defined as **premature** if the period of gestation is less than 37 full weeks (Korones, 1986). In the United States about 11% to 12% of newborns are classified as premature (March of Dimes Birth Defects Foundation, 1997), and this rate appears to be slowly rising (Martin et al., 2002). It is important to note, however, that the births of twins, triplets, and babies with diabetic mothers inflate this figure somewhat because prematurity is an expected outcome in these cases (Lin, Verp, & Sabbagha, 1993).

A premature baby is one that is born before 37 weeks of gestation.

Although most babies born after 37 weeks usually experience few problems and have good survival rates, babies born before this time can experience a myriad of problems and risks, including heightened mortality. Currently, most infants who are born at about 6 months' gestation survive, whereas of those born at 23 weeks, about 15% survive, and of those born at 22 weeks and below, very few survive (Allen, Donohue, & Dusman, 1993). There are several factors, such as inadequate prenatal care (Krueger & Scholl, 2000) and short interpregnancy intervals (Basso, Olsen, Knudsen, & Christensen, 1998), that contribute to premature births.

Many preterm infants manifest spasmodic and weak reflex movements and crying, show periods of apnea (i.e., not breathing), have problems maintaining body temperature, and may require respiratory assistance until the lungs mature. Lanugo and vernix may still cover the body of the preterm infant. Cerebral hemorrhaging, or bleeding in the brain, also is common in these infants. Improved medical technology has increased the survival rate of premature babies; however, as we shall see with the low-birth-weight babies, this higher survival rate has increased the vulnerability of surviving premature infants to a host of developmental abnormalities.

Fetal birth weight may be one of the most important predictors of fetal outcome.

Many professionals consider fetal birth weight to be one of the most important indices in the prediction of fetal outcome (Pollack & Divon, 1992). In general, a baby is deemed to be small at birth because it was born too soon (i.e., it is premature), because it grew too slowly in utero (i.e., it is small for its gestational age), or because of a combination of these two factors. More specifically, an infant is viewed as having low birth weight if it weighs less than 2,500 gm (5 lb 8 oz). It has been estimated that, at present, about 8% of all infants are born with low birth weight, with about 62% of these births culminating in neonatal deaths (Hoyert et al., 2001). The birth rate of very-low-birth-weight infants, or those weighing less than 1,500 gm (3 lb 5 oz) is approximately 1% to 2% (Guyer et al., 1998).

Survival rates for infants born with low birth weight have improved dramatically over the past decade, with infants weighing over 1,000 gm (2 lb 3 oz) having a survival rate of over 90%, and infants weighing 751 to 1,000 gm (about 1 lb 10 oz to 2 lb 3 oz) having a survival rate approaching 86% (Lemons et al., 2001). Infants with birth weights of 501 to 750 gm (1 lb 2 oz to 1 lb 10 oz) have about a 59% chance of survival at present (Finer, Horbar, & Carpenter, 1999). Infants weighing less than 500 gm (1 lb 2 oz) at birth rarely survive; however, rates of approximately 11% to

15% have been reported (Gould, Benitz, & Liu, 2000), and this likely will continue to increase with ongoing improvements in neonatal technology and prenatal care (e.g., prenatal surgery).

As a general rule of thumb, the farther the infant is from the 2,500-gm criterion, the greater the problems it experiences. The closer the infant is to the 2,500-gm birth-weight criterion, the better the prognosis. Although most low-birth-weight children function within the normal range across a variety of domains when compared to normal-birth-weight children, these children tend to show higher rates of mental retardation, cerebral palsy, blindness and deafness, psychomotor problems, school failure, subnormal growth, and related health problems (Hack, Klein, & Taylor, 1995). In fact, cognitive factors, such as intelligence level (IQ), show a direct relationship to birth weight; that is, as birth weight declines, so does IQ (Breslau et al., 1994). Further, school-aged children who had birth weights of less than 2,500 gm are nearly 50% more likely than their normal-birth-weight counterparts to be receiving some form of special education (Lewit, Baker, Corman, & Shiono, 1995). In contrast, in one of the few studies that has tracked premature very-low-birth-weight infants into adulthood, Hack et al. (2002) found that, despite the presence of learning disabilities and physical problems, many of these individuals were likely to complete high school and to engage in less risky behaviors (i.e., they were not prone to use alcohol and drugs, experience problems with the law, or become teenage parents).

Other complications of prematurity and low birth weight also have been shown to have an impact on later development. For example, children born prematurely, with very low birth weight (less than 1,500 gm [3 lb 5 oz]), or both, are at risk for chronic lung disease because of their lack of lung maturity. In fact, chronic lung disease, specifically bronchopulmonary dysplasia, is the most common chronic illness among very-low-birth-weight infants who survive the neonatal period, and occurs with an estimated prevalence of between 17% to 54% (Marshall et al., 1999). Outcome studies of infants born with chronic lung disease indicate that this condition is associated with an increased risk for developmental abnormalities over and above the problems attributed to very low birth weight (Farel, Hooper, Teplin, Henry, & Kraybill, 1998; O'Shea et al., 1996). In fact, the longer infants require mechanical oxygenation, the greater the likelihood of cognitive delay (Stephens, Richardson, & Lewin, 1997) with learning difficulties being documented into late childhood and early adolescence (Vohr et al., 1991). The use of artificial surfactant, a medication designed to facilitate the transfer of gases in the lungs until natural surfactant can form, has become part of the routine treatment for infants with immature lungs, and its use has increased the survival rate of infants with respiratory distress syndrome (RDS; Fujiwara, 1996); however, available research suggests that it has not lowered the risk for chronic lung disease nor its associated morbidity (Ferrara et al., 1994; Schwartz, Luby, Scanlon, & Kellogg, 1994). Antenatal steroids have also been found to be effective in reducing the incidence and severity of RDS and related disorders (Hagedorn, Gardner, & Abman, 2002).

Another problem resulting from prematurity and low birth weight involves the flow of oxygen to the fetus. **Anoxia** results from a lack of oxygen during the birth process, whereas **hypoxia** results from a reduced flow of oxygen. These conditions can occur during prolonged labor, when excessive pressure can rupture a blood

The farther a newborn is from the 2,500 gm birth weight, the greater are the chances for problems to arise.

Nearly 50% of school-aged children receiving some form of special education had birth weights less than 2,500 gm.

vessel in the brain (intraventricular hemorrhage), or during the birth process when the umbilical cord can become tangled or restricted. In each case, oxygen flow to the baby is disrupted and brain damage can result. In fact, chronic hypoxia has been found to be the cause of at least 60% of postnatal fetal deaths (Manning, Morrison, Lange, & Harman, 1982). In many instances, hypoxia and anoxia cause damage in the motor areas of the brain, and a variety of motor disorders can occur. These disorders, as a group, are called cerebral palsy, and the astute reader will note the various descriptions of children with these problems scattered through the development section of this text. Although most babies who experience anoxia or hypoxia do not suffer mental retardation or central nervous system involvement, the risk is higher for these babies than for their problem-free counterparts (Ensher & Clark, 1994; Mecham, 1996).

> At least 60% of all postnatal fetal deaths are the result of chronic hypoxia.

Failure to Thrive

Failure to thrive (FTT) is a chronic, potentially life-threatening disorder of infancy and early childhood. It strikes as many as 3% to 5% of all infants under 1 year of age (Mitchell, Gorrell, & Greenberg, 1980) and accounts for 3% of all pediatric hospitalizations (Dacey & Travers, 2002). The criteria used to diagnose FTT have been described as a "quagmire of factors" (Drotar, 1983), but generally the term refers to infants and young children whose weight is persistently below the third percentile for age on appropriate standardized growth charts (Dacey & Travers, 2002).

> Three percent of all pediatric hospitalizations are due to FTT.

In the past, some researchers (e.g., Homer & Ludwig, 1981) suggested three etiological categories for FTT: organic, nonorganic, and a combination of these. Most cases are of the combined type, however, and the organic-versus-nonorganic distinction is not used by most pediatricians practicing today (Alexander, 1992). Regardless of etiology, the common trait for all infants with FTT is the inadequate intake, retention, or use of calories. In addition to medical malnutrition, many of these children show poor physical growth; delayed motor, language, and cognitive skills; and emotional listlessness (Homer & Ludwig, 1981).

Although adequately controlled studies in FTT are rare, it appears that the prognosis is more favorable for the child's physical growth than for cognitive growth (Berwick, 1980). Sturm and Drotar (1989) noted in their longitudinal study of 59 infants with FTT that about 67% of their group achieved normal growth parameters at age 3 years of age; however, intellectual functioning for the group tended to fall within the borderline range. With respect to treatment, the earlier and more vigorous the intervention is, particularly when the parents are involved and multiple etiological factors are considered, the better the chances of recovery from FTT (Spinner & Siegel, 1987).

Child Abuse and Neglect

In addition to the medically based factors that can influence development, child abuse and neglect can exert a significant influence on the developing child. In 2001, approximately 3 million suspected child abuse and neglect cases were reported in the United States, with about 1 million of these cases (33%) being confirmed (U.S. Department of

Health and Human Services, Administration on Children, Youth and Families, 2003). Around 26% of abuse and neglect victims were children aged 3 or younger (U.S. Department of Health and Human Services, 2003). Abuse can come in several forms: physical, sexual, and psychological. All represent a significant and profound assault on a developing child. Child abuse occurs across racial, ethnic, and socioeconomic groups, and it may be difficult to recognize. Researchers have identified a variety of factors that may increase the risk of child maltreatment. These include parent, child, and family characteristics as well as features of the community or culture (Belsky, 1993; Cicchetti & Toth, 1998). In addition to the risk of abuse, the actual occurrence of abuse or neglect in the child may be a function of a combination of these characteristics, such as abuse of the parent as a child (Yehuda, Halligan, & Grossman, 2001).

Physical abuse and neglect may be the easiest forms to detect; other forms may be manifested by a child's internalizing (e.g., withdrawal, depression, anxiety) or by inappropriate externalizing behaviors (e.g., conduct problems, sexual acting out). Neglect refers to the failure of the caregivers to meet the child's emotional, physical, or medical needs, and can be difficult to substantiate.

Because the circumstances under which abuse occurs vary dramatically from case to case, and because data are often based on retrospective, or speculative, information from hesitant reporters (e.g., a single parent who could be in and out of jail), it is difficult to determine a direct causal relationship between detrimental developmental outcomes and various forms of abuse. Nonetheless, child abuse and neglect have been associated with negative short-term and long-term effects on children's physical development and mental health. Emergent data have begun to document structural abnormalities in the brains of these children with associated cognitive dysfunction (Beers & DeBellis, 2001; DeBellis, 2001).

> Child abuse and neglect have been associated with many negative short-term and long-term effects—including abnormal brain development.

For example, physical abuse in infancy can result in scarring or other deformities, as well as in problems such as mental retardation, seizures, cerebral palsy, or blindness following head trauma (e.g., shaken baby syndrome). Neglect of young children puts them at increased risk for poisoning, burns, cuts, and similar types of injuries (Rosenberg & Krugman, 1991). Abuse and neglect during infancy also have been associated with difficulties in the regulation of emotions, poor attachment, language delays, and problems with peers (Cicchetti & Rogosch, 1994). Early stress can influence neurotransmitter systems and brain structures thereby altering the development of the child, yet more research on the interaction of genes, the environment, and the development of future mental disorders is necessary (Heim & Nemeroff, 2001; Kaufman, Plotsky, Nemeroff, & Charney, 2000).

Maltreatment in childhood may lead to behavioral or psychiatric problems that manifest themselves in childhood or adulthood. Conditions such as posttraumatic stress disorder, depression, anxiety, personality disorders, self-injurious behaviors, substance abuse, eating disorders, interpersonal difficulties, and other forms of psychopathology also have been linked to child abuse (Briere & Elliot, 1994; Rosenberg & Krugman, 1991). In addition, abused children often demonstrate poor academic performance and have more difficulties at school (Kinard, 1999). Indeed, young children with special needs may be at increased risk for abuse and neglect because of the very nature of their needs and disabilities (Alexander & Sherbondy, 1996; Ammerman, Hersen, Van Hasselt, Lubetsky, & Sieck, 1994).

Summary

The development of an individual from conception through childhood is a complex unfolding that is influenced by the processes of heredity and environment. Numerous theories have been proposed to explain how these processes interact; however, no single theory appears to provide a satisfactory explanation for all the intricate events that comprise development. Certainly, children inherit many characteristics from their parents. The environment also shapes the way children behave, how and what they learn, and their rate of development. Selected aspects of the environment may impact neurological growth and development as well.

Stages of development are characterized by major milestones. The division and differentiation of the fertilized egg cell are the most important events during the early gestational period. Later in gestation, major organ systems are refined so that the fetus is prepared for entry into the world. During the gestational period, the developing mother's experiences also are key contributors to this process. For example, food and beverage intake, exposure to toxic substances and disease, and other activities of the mother (e.g., smoking) have an impact on intrauterine life—some positive and some negative. Once born, the child's interactions with the environment and the quality of parental care appear to be critical influences on the child's development. Furthermore, observations of developing children over time reinforce the concept that areas of development are interrelated. For example, as you will see in the following chapters of this text, language development and cognitive skills parallel each other in many ways, and in turn both of these are further influenced by a child's physical health, social-emotional development, family dynamics, school, and cultural expectations. No single theory integrates all of the factors of child development. Consequently, a holistic perspective of the child more readily lends itself to understanding the multitude of factors that are involved in development.

In reading the following chapters, it is important to consider how each area of development affects the others. With an understanding of the complexity of these phenomena, the early interventionist will be prepared to identify and address the many needs that young children with disabling conditions can manifest.

Review Questions and Discussion Points

1. Describe the differences among growth, development, and maturation. What three basic criteria must be met before change can be considered to be development?

2. Describe three events or changes that typically occur in each of the five developmental stages explored in this chapter.

3. Discuss potential factors that could affect each of the five periods of development. Be sure to note which factors are positive and which ones are negative.

4. How can nutrition impact on a developing fetus? With respect to having a baby, why is it worthwhile for a woman to think about such things as nutrition and physical health prior to pregnancy?

5. What questions would be important to gather from a woman who is planning to become pregnant? What questions would be important to know from a man who is planning to be a father?

Recommended Resources

Web Sites

America's Children—Key National Indicators of Children's Well-Being: 2002
http://www.childstats.gov/americaschildren/

March of Dimes Birth Defects Foundation
http://www.modimes.org

National Clearinghouse on Child Abuse and Neglect Information
http://www.calib.com/nccanch/stats/index.cfm

Parenting Resources for the 21st Century
http://www.parentingresources.ncjrs.org

Women, Infants and Children Program, U.S. Department of Agriculture
http://www.fns.usda.gov/wic/

Books

Fogel, A. (2001). *Infancy: Infant, family, and society* (4th ed.). Australia: Wadsworth Group.

Miller-Perrin, C. L., & Perrin, R. D. (1999). *Child maltreatment: An introduction.* Thousand Oaks, CA: Sage.

National Research Council and Institute of Medicine. (2000). *From neurons to neighborhoods: The science of early childhood development.* Washington, DC: National Academy Press.

References

Abel, E. L. (1989). *Fetal alcohol syndrome: Fetal alcohol effects.* New York: Plenum Press.

Abel, E. L., & Hannigan, J. H. (1995). Maternal risk factors in fetal alcohol syndrome: Provocative and permissive influences. *Neurotoxicology and Teratology, 17,* 445–462.

Aberg, A., & Westbom, L. (2001). Association between maternal pre-existing or gestational diabetes and health problems in children. *Acta Paediatrica, 90*(7), 746–750.

Abroms, K. I., & Bennett, J. W. (1981). Age dispersion of parents of Down and non-Down syndrome children. *American Journal of Mental Deficiency, 86,* 204–207.

Aerts, L., Pijnenborg, R., Verhaeghe, J., Holemans, K., & Van Assche, F. A. (1996). Fetal growth and development. In A. Dornhorst & D. R. Hadden (Eds.), *Diabetes and pregnancy: An international approach to diagnosis and management* (pp. 77–97). New York: Wiley.

Alexander, R. C. (1992). Failure to thrive. *APSAC Advisor, 5,* 1–13.

Alexander, R. C., & Sherbondy, A. L. (1996). Child abuse and developmental disabilities. In M. L. Wolraich (Ed.), *Disorders of development and learning: A practical guide to assessment and management* (2nd ed., pp. 164–184). Boston: Mosby.

Allen, M. C., Donohue, P. K., & Dusman, E. E. (1993). The limit of viability–neonatal outcome of infants born at 22 to 25 weeks' gestation. *New England Journal of Medicine, 329,* 1597–1601.

Als, H. (1997). Earliest intervention for preterm infants in the Newborn Intensive Care Unit. In M. J. Guralnick (Ed.), *The effectiveness of early intervention* (pp. 47–76). Baltimore: Brookes.

American Academy of Pediatrics. (2000). Changing concepts of Sudden Infant Death Syndrome: Implications for infant sleeping environment and sleep position. *Pediatrics, 105,* 650–656.

Amand, K. J. S., Phil, D., & Hickey, P. R. (1987). Pain and its effects in the human neonate and fetus. *New England Journal of Medicine, 317,* 1321–1329.

Ammerman, R. T., Hersen, M., Van Hasselt, V. B., Lubetsky, M. J., & Sieck, W. (1994). Maltreatment in psychiatrically hospitalized children and adolescents with developmental disabilities: Prevalence and correlates. *Journal of the American Academy of Child & Adolescent Psychiatry, 33,* 567–576.

Anisfeld, E., Curry, M. A., Hales, D. J., Kennell, J. H., Klaus, M. H., Lipper, E., et al. (1983). Maternal-infant bonding: A joint rebuttal. *Pediatrics, 72,* 569–572.

Apgar, V., & Beck, J. (1972). *Is my baby all right? A guide to birth defects.* New York: Trident Press.

Autti-Ramo, I., & Granstrom, M. (1991). The psychomotor development during the first year of life of infants exposed to intrauterine alcohol of various duration: Fetal alcohol exposure and development. *Neuropediatrics, 22,* 59–64.

Auyeuna, A., Klein, M. E., Ratts, V. S., Odem, R. R., & Williams, D. B. (2001). Fertility treatment in the forty and older woman. *Journal of Assisted Reproduction and Genetics, 18,* 638–643.

Bailey, D. B., Roberts, J., Hooper, S. R., Hatton, D., Mirrett, P., Roberts, J. E., et al. (in press). Research on fragile X syndrome and autism: Implications for the study of genes, environments, and developmental language disorders. In S. Rice & S. Warren (Eds.), *Developmental language disorders: From phenotypes to etiologies.* Mahwah, NJ: Lawrence Erlbaum Publishing.

Barker, D. J., & Clark, P. M. (1997). Fetal undernutrition and disease in later life. *Review of Reproduction, 2*(2), 105–112.

Basso, O., Olsen, J., Knudsen, J. B., & Christensen, K. (1998). Low birth weight and preterm birth after short interpregnancy intervals. *American Journal of Obstetrics and Gynecology, 178*(2), 259–263.

Batshaw, M. L., & Perret, Y. M. (1992). *Children with disabilities.* Baltimore: Brookes.

Beardslee, W. R., Versage, E. M., & Gladstone, T. R. G. (1998). Children of affectively ill parents: A review of the past 10 years. *Journal of the American Academy of Child & Adolescent Psychiatry, 37*(11), 1134–1141.

Behrman, R. E. (1992). *Nelson textbook of pediatrics* (14th ed.). Philadelphia: W. B. Saunders.

Behrman, R. E., & Kliegman, J. M. (1983). Jaundice and hyperbilirubinemia in the newborn. In R. E. Behrman, V. C. Vaughan, & W. E. Nelson (Eds.), *Nelson textbook of pediatrics* (12th ed., pp. 378–381). Philadelphia: W. B. Saunders.

Belsky, J. (1993). Etiology of child maltreatment: A developmental-ecological analysis. *Psychological Bulletin, 114,* 413–434.

Berwick, D. (1980). Nonorganic failure to thrive. *Pediatric Review, 1,* 265.

Black, J. K., & Puckett, M. B. (1996). *The young child: Development from prebirth through age eight.* Upper Saddle River, NJ: Merrill/Prentice Hall.

Blondel, B., Kaminsky, M., & Breart, G. (1980). Antenatal care and maternal demographic and social characteristics: Evolution in France between 1972 and 1976. *Journal of Epidemiology and Community Health, 34,* 157–163.

Breslau, N., DelDotto, J. E., Brown, G. G., Kumar, S., Ezhuthachan, S., Hufnagle, K. G., et al. (1994). A gradient relationship between low birth weight and IQ at age 6 years. *Archives of Pediatric and Adolescent Medicine, 148,* 377–383.

Briere, J. N., & Elliott, D. M. (1994). Immediate and long-term impacts of child sexual abuse. *The Future of Children: Sexual Abuse of Children, 4,* 54–69.

Carrapato, M. R., & Marcelino, F. (2001). The infant of the diabetic mother: The critical developmental windows. *Early Pregnancy, 5*(1), 57–58.

Centers for Disease Control and Prevention. (1995, March). Prevention program for reducing risk for neural tube defects: South Carolina, 1992–1994. *Morbidity & Mortality Weekly Report, 44*(8), 141–142.

Chadwick, E. G., & Yogev, R. (1995). Pediatric AIDS. *Pediatric Clinics of North America, 42*(4), 969–992.

Chan, A., McCaul, K. A., Keane, R. J., & Haan, E. A. A. (1998). Effect of parity, gravidity, previous miscarriage, and age on risk of Down's syndrome: Population based study. *British Medical Journal, 317*(7163), 923–924.

Chase, C., Ware, J., Hittelman, J., Blasini, I., Smith, R., Llorente, A., et al. (2000). Early cognitive and motor development of infants born to women infected with human immunodeficiency virus. Women and Infants Transmission Study Group. *Pediatrics, 106*(2), E25.

Chasnoff, I. (1991). Drugs, alcohol, pregnancy, and the neonate—pay now or pay later. *Journal of the American Medical Association, 266,* 1567–1568.

Chomitz, V. R., Cheung, L. W., & Lieberman, E. (1995). The role of lifestyle in preventing low birth weight. *The Future of Children: Low Birth Weight, 5,* 121–138.

Cicchetti, D., & Rogosch, F. A. (1994). The toll of child maltreatment on the developing child. *Child and Adolescent Psychiatric Clinics of North America, 3,* 759–772.

Cicchetti, D., & Toth, S. L. (1998). Perspectives on research and practice in developmental psychology. In I. E. Sigel & K. A. Renninger (Eds.), *Handbook of child psychology.* Vol. 4: *Child psychology in practice* (5th ed., pp. 479–582). New York: Wiley.

Cnattingius, S. (1997). Maternal age modifies the effect of maternal smoking on intrauterine growth retardation but not on late fetal death and placental abruption. *American Journal of Epidemiology, 145,* 319–323.

Cohen, I. L. (1995). A theoretical analysis of the role of hyperarousal in the learning and behavior of fragile-X males. *Mental Retardation and Developmental Disabilities Research Reviews, 1,* 286–291.

Cohen, W. I. (1999). Down syndrome: Care of the child and family. In M. D. Levine, W. B. Carey, & A. C. Crocker (Eds.), *Developmental-behavioral pediatrics* (3rd ed., pp. 240–248). Philadelphia: W. B. Saunders.

Coley, R. L., & Chase-Lansdale, P. L. (1998). Adolescent pregnancy and parenthood: Recent evidence and future directions. *American Psychologist, 53,* 152–166.

Conner, E. M., Sperling, R. S., Gelber, R., Kiselev, P., Scott, C., O'Sullivan, M. J., et al. (1994). Reduction of maternal-infant transmission of human immunodeficiency virus type 1 with zidovudine treatment. *New England Journal of Medicine, 331,* 1173.

Cousins, L. (1983). Congenital anomalies among infants of diabetic mothers: Etiology, prevention, prenatal diagnosis. *American Journal of Obstetrics and Gynecology, 147,* 333.

Coustan, D. R. (1995). Obstetric complications. In D. R. Coustan (Ed.), *Human reproduction: Growth and development* (pp. 431–455). Boston: Little Brown.

Crocker, A. C. (1999). Human immunodeficiency virus infection in children. In M. D. Levine, W. B. Carey, & A. C. Crocker (Eds.), *Developmental-behavioral pediatrics* (3rd ed., pp. 289–293). Philadelphia: W. B. Saunders.

Cummings, E. M., Davies, P. T., & Campbell, S. B. (2000). *Developmental psychopathology and family process: Theory, research and clinical implications.* New York: Guilford Press.

DaCosta, D., Dritsa, M., Larouche, L., & Brender, W. (2000). Psychosocial predictors of labor/delivery complications and infant birth weight: A prospective study. *Journal of Psychosomatic Obstetrics and Gynaecology, 21*(3), 137–148.

Dacey, J. S., & Travers, J. F. (2002). *Human development across the lifespan* (5th ed.). Boston: McGraw-Hill.

Datta-Bhutada, S., Johnson, H. L., & Rosen, T. S. (1998). Intrauterine cocaine and crack exposure: Neonatal outcome. *Journal of Perinatology, 18*(3), 183–188.

Day, N. L., & Richardson, G. A. (1991). Prenatal alcohol exposure: A continuum of effects. *Seminars in Perinatology, 15,* 271–279.

Day, N. L., Richardson, G. A., Goldschmidt, L., & Cornelius, M. D. (2000). Effects of prenatal tobacco exposure on preschoolers' behavior. *Journal of Developmental and Behavioral Pediatrics, 21*(3), 180–188.

DeBellis, M. D. (2001). Developmental traumatology: The psychobiological development of maltreated children and its implications for research, treatment, and policy. *Developmental Psychopathology, 13,* 539–564.

Deiner, P. L. (1997). *Infants and toddlers: Development and program planning.* Fort Worth, TX: Harcourt Brace.

Dildy, G. A., Jackson, G. M., Fowers, G. K., Oshiro, B. T., Varner, M. W., & Clark, S. L. (1996). Very advanced maternal age: Pregnancy after age 45. *American Journal of Obstetrics and Gynecology, 173*(3), 668–674.

Dollberg, S., Fainaru, O., Mimouni, F. B., Shenhav, M., Lessing, J. B., & Kupferminc, M. (2000). Effect of passive smoking in pregnancy on neonatal nucleated red blood cells. *Pediatrics, 106*(3), E34.

Drotar, D. (1983, August). *Outcome in failure to thrive: Implications for prevention.* Kennedy Center Lecture Series at Peabody College of Vanderbilt University, Nashville, TN.

Eisenberg, A., Murkoff, H. E., & Hathaway, S. E. (1991). *What to expect when you're expecting.* New York: Workman.

Ensher, G. L., & Clark, D. A. (1994). *Newborns at risk: Medical care and psychoeducational intervention* (2nd ed.). Gaithersburg, MD: Aspen.

Ernst, M., Moolchan, E. T., & Robinson, M. L. (2001). Behavioral and neural consequences of prenatal exposure to nicotine. *Journal of the American Academy of Child & Adolescent Psychiatry, 40*(6), 630–641.

Esposito, S., Musetti, L., Musetti, M. C., Tornaghi, R., Corbella, S., Massironi, E., et al. (1999). Behavioral and psychological disorders in uninfected children aged 6 to 11 years born to human immunodeficiency virus-seropositive mothers. *Journal of Developmental and Behavioral Pediatrics, 20*(6), 411–417.

Ezra, Y., & Schenker, J. G. (1996). The diabetic fetus. In F. A. Chervenak, & A. Kurjak (Eds.), *The fetus as a patient.* New York: Wiley.

Farel, A., Hooper, S. R., Teplin, S., Henry, M., & Kraybill, E. (1998). Very low birth weight infants at 7 years: An assessment of the health and neurodevelopmental risk conveyed by chronic lung disease. *Journal of Learning Disabilities, 31*(2), 118–126.

Ferencz, C., Rubin, J. S., McCarter, R. J., & Clark, E. B. (1990). Maternal diabetes and cardiovascular malformations: Predominance of double outlet right ventricle and truncus arteriosus. *Teratology, 41*, 319.

Ferrara, T. B., Hoekstra, R. E., Couser, R. J., Gaziano, E. P., Calvin, S. E., Payne, N. R., et al. (1994). Survival and follow-up of infants born at 23 to 26 weeks of gestational age: Effects of surfactant therapy. *Journal of Pediatrics, 124*, 119.

Fifer, W. P., Monk, C. E., & Grose-Fifer, J. (2001). Prenatal development and risk. In G. Bremner & A. Fogel, *Blackwell handbook of infant development* (pp. 503–542). Oxford, England: Blackwell.

Finer, N. N., Horbar, J. D., & Carpenter, J. H. (1999). Cardiopulmonary resuscitation in the very low birth weight infant: The Vermont Oxford Network experience. *Pediatrics, 104*, 428–434.

Floyd, R. L., Zahniser, C., Gunter, E. P., & Kendrick, J. S. (1991). Smoking during pregnancy: Prevalence, effects, and intervention strategies. *Birth, 18*, 48–53.

Fogel, A. (2001). *Infancy: Infant, family, and society* (4th ed.). Australia: Wadsworth Group.

Food and Drug Administration (1996, February 29). *Folic acid to fortify U.S. food products to prevent birth defects.* Press release.

Frank, D. A., Augustyn, M., Knight, W. G., Pell, T., & Zuckerman, B. (2001). Growth, development, and behavior in early childhood following prenatal cocaine exposure: A systematic review. *Journal of the American Medical Association, 285*(12), 1613–1625.

Frank, D. A., Bresnahan, K., & Zuckerman, B. (1993). Maternal cocaine use: Impact on child health and development. *Advances in Pediatrics, 40*, 65–99.

Fried, P. A., & Smith, A. M. (2001). A literature review of the consequences of prenatal marihuana exposure: An emerging theme of a deficiency in aspects of executive function. *Neurotoxicology and Teratology, 23*(1), 1–11.

Fujiwara, T. (1996). Surfactant therapy for neonatal respiratory distress syndrome. In F. A. Chervenak & A. Kurjak (Eds.), *The fetus as a patient.* New York: Parthenon.

Gardner, J. (1997). Fetal alcohol syndrome—Recognition and intervention. *American Journal of Maternal and Child Nursing, 22*, 318–322.

Gesell, A., & Ilg, S. (1943). *The infant and child: The culture of today.* New York: Harper Brothers.

Glover, V. (1999). Maternal stress or anxiety during pregnancy and the development of the baby. *Practicing Midwife, 2*(5), 20–22.

Godfrey, K. M., & Barker, D. J. (2000). Fetal nutrition and adult disease. *American Journal of Clinical Nutrition, 71*(Suppl. 5), 1344S–1345S.

Goodman, S. H., & Gotlib, I. H. (1999). Risk for psychopathology in the children of depressed mothers: A developmental model for understanding mechanisms of transmission. *Psychological Review, 106*(3), 458–490.

Gotto, M. P., & Goldman, A. S. (1994). Diabetic embryopathy. *Current Opinions in Pediatrics, 6*, 486.

Gould, J. B., Benitz, W. E., & Liu, H. (2000). Mortality and time to death in very low birth weight infants: California, 1987 and 1993. *Pediatrics, 105*, E37.

Grant, J. P. (1995). *The state of the world's children.* New York: Oxford University Press (in cooperation with UNICEF).

Grubman, S., Gross, E., Lerner-Weiss, N., & Hernandez, M. (1995). Older children and adolescents living with perinatally acquired human immunodeficiency virus infection. *Pediatrics, 95*, 657–663.

Guyer, B. MacDorman, M. F., Martin, J. A., Peters, K. D., & Strobino, D. M. (1998). Annual summary of vital statistics—1997. *Pediatrics, 102*, 1333.

Hack, M., Flannery, D. J., Schluchter, M., Cartar, L., Borawski, E., & Klein, N. (2002). Outcomes in young adulthood for very-low-birth-weight infants. *New England Journal of Medicine, 346*, 149–157.

Hack, M., Klein, N. K., & Taylor, H. G. (1995). Long-term developmental outcomes of low birth weight infants. *The Future of Children, 5*, 176–196.

Hagedorn, M. E., Gardner, S. L., & Abman, S. H. (2002). Respiratory diseases. In G. B. Merenstein & S. L. Gardner, *Handbook of neonatal intensive care* (5th ed., pp. 485–575). St. Louis, MO: Mosby.

Hagerman, R. J. (1996). Fragile-X syndrome. In M. L. Wolraich (Ed.), *Disorders of development and learning. A practical guide to assessment and management* (2nd ed.). Boston: Mosby.

Hagerman, R. J. (1999). Chromosomal disorders. In M. D. Levine, W. B. Carey, & A. C. Crocker (Eds.), *Developmental-behavioral pediatrics* (3rd ed., pp. 230–239). Philadelphia: W. B. Saunders.

Hammill, H. A., & Murtagh, C. (1993). AIDS during pregnancy. In R. A. Knuppel & J. E. Drukker (Eds.), *High-risk pregnancy. A team approach.* Philadelphia: W. B. Saunders.

Haughey, M. J. (1985). Fetal position during pregnancy. *American Journal of Obstetrics and Gynecology, 153*, 885–886.

Heim, C., & Nemeroff, C. B. (2001). The role of child-hood trauma in the neurobiology of mood and anxiety disorders: Preclinical and clinical studies. *Biological Psychiatry, 49*, 1023–1039.

Herbert, W. N. P., Dodds, J. M., & Cefalo, R. C. (1993). Nutrition in pregnancy. In R. A. Knuppel & J. E. Drukker (Eds.), *High-risk pregnancy; A team approach* (2nd ed.). Philadelphia: W. B. Saunders.

Herrenkohl, L. R. (1988). The impact of prenatal stress on the developing fetus and child. In R. L. Cohen (Ed.), *Psychiatric consultation in childbirth settings: Parent- and child-oriented approaches.* New York: Plenum Medical Books.

Hoffman, S., & Hatch, M. C. (1996). Stress, social support, and pregnancy outcome: A reassessment based on research. *Paediatric and Perinatal Epidemiology, 10*, 380–405.

Holley, W. L., Rosenbaum, A. L., & Churchill, J. A. (1969). Effects of rapid succession of pregnancy. In *Perinatal factors affecting human development.* Pan-American Health Organization, Pan-American Sanitary Bureau, Regional Office of World Health Organization.

Hollier, L. M., Leveno, K. J., Kelly, M. A., McIntire, D. D., & Cunningham, F. G. (2000). Maternal age and malformations in singleton births. *Obstetrics and Gynecology, 96*(5), 701–706.

Homer, C., & Ludwig, S. (1981). Categorization of etiology of failure to thrive. *American Journal of the Disabled Child, 735*, 848.

Hook, E. B. (1987). Issues in analysis of data on paternal age and 47, +21: Implications for genetic counseling for Down syndrome. *Human Genetics, 77*, 303–306.

House, S. (2000). Stages in reproduction particularly vulnerable to xenobiotic hazards and nutritional deficits. *Nutrition and Health, 14*(3), 147–193.

Hoyert, D. L., Freedman, M. A., Strobino, D. M., & Guyer, B. (2001). Annual summary of vital statistics: 2000. *Pediatrics, 108*(6), 1241–1255.

Hubbell, K. M., & Webster, H. F. (1986). Respiratory management of the neonate. In N. S. Streeter (Ed.), *High-risk neonatal care.* Rockville, MD: Aspen.

Hurt, H., Malmud, E., Betancourt, L., Braitman, L. E., Brodsky, N. L., & Giannetta, J. (1997). Children with in utero cocaine exposure do not differ from control subjects on intelligence testing. *Archives of Pediatric and Adolescent Medicine, 151*(21), 1237–1241.

Institute of Medicine, National Academy of Sciences. (1990a). *Nutrition during pregnancy.* Washington, DC: National Academy Press.

Institute of Medicine. (1990b). Broadening the base of treatment of alcohol problems. Washington, D.C.: National Academy Press.

Jensen, A. R. (1980). *Bias in mental testing.* New York: Free Press.

Johnson, M. H., Dziurawiee, S., Ellis, H., & Morton, J. (1991). Newborns' preferential tracking of the face-like stimuli and its subsequent decline. *Cognition, 40*, 1–19.

Jones, H. E., & Balster, R. J. (1998). Inhalant abuse in pregnancy. *Obstetrical and Gynecological Clinics in North America, 25*(1), 153–167.

Kallen, K. (1997). Maternal smoking and orofacial clefts. *Cleft Palate and Craniofacial Journal, 34*(1), 11–16.

Kaltenbach, K., & Finnegan, L. P. (1987). Perinatal and developmental outcome of infants exposed to methadone in utero. *Neurotoxicology and Teratology, 9*, 311–313.

Kandall, S. R., Doberczak, T. M., Jantunen, M., & Stein, J. (1999). The methadone-maintained pregnancy. *Clinical Perinatology, 26*(1), 173–183.

Katz, V. L., & Kuller, J. A. (1994). Recurrent miscarriage. *American Journal of Perinatology, 11*, 386.

Kaufman, J., Plotsky, P. M., Nemeroff, C. B., & Charney, D. S. (2000). Effects of early adverse experiences on brain structure and function: Clinical implications. *Biological Psychiatry, 48*, 778–790.

Kauppila, O. (1975). The perinatal mortality in breech deliveries and observations on affecting factors: A retrospective study of 2227 cases. *Acta Obstetrica et Gynecologica Scandinavica, 39*(Suppl.), 1–79.

Kinard, E. M. (1999). Psychosocial resources and academic performance in abused children. *Children and Youth Services Review, 21*(5), 351–376.

King, J. C. (2000). Physiology of pregnancy and nutrient metabolism. *American Journal of Clinical Nutrition, 71*(Suppl. 5), 1218S–1225S.

Kitzmiller, J. L., Gavin, L. A., Gin, G. D., Jovanovic-Peterson, L., Main, E. K., & Zigrang, W. D. (1991). Preconception care of diabetes: Glycemic control prevents congenital anomalies. *Journal of the American Medical Association, 265*, 731.

Kleinman, J., & Madans, J. H. (1985). The effects of maternal smoking, physical stature, and educational attainment on the incidence of low birth weight. *American Journal of Epidemiology, 121*, 832–855.

Korones, S. B. (1986). *High-risk newborn infants: The basis for intensive nursing care* (4th ed.). St. Louis, MO: Mosby.

Krueger, P. M., & Scholl, T. O. (2000). Adequacy of prenatal care and pregnancy outcome. *Journal of American Osteopathy Association, 100*(8), 485–492.

Lemons, J. A., Bauer, C. R., Oh, W., Korones, S. B., Papik, L., Stoll, B. J., et al. (2001). Very low birth weight outcomes of the National Institute of Child Health and Human Development neonatal research network, January 1995 through December 1996. NICHD Neonatal Research Network. *Pediatrics, 107,* E1.

Lenneberg, E. H. (1967). *Biological foundations of language.* New York: Wiley.

Levitan, M. (1988). *Textbook of human genetics* (3rd ed.). New York: Oxford University Press.

Lewit, E. M., Baker, L. S., Corman, H., & Shiono, P. H. (1995). The direct cost of low birth weight. *The Future of Children, 5,* 35–56.

Lin, C. L., Verp, M. S., & Sabbagha, R. E. (1993). *The high-risk fetus: Pathophysiology, diagnosis, and management.* New York: Springer-Verlag.

Lindegren, M. L., Steinberg, S., & Byers, R. H. (2000). HIV/AIDS in infants, children, and adolescents: Epidemiology of HIV/AIDS in children. *Pediatric Clinics of North America, 47*(1), 1–19.

Little, B. B., Snell, L. M., Klein, B. R., Gilstrap, L. C., Knoll, K. A., & Breckenridge, J. D. (1990). Maternal and fetal effects of heroin addiction during pregnancy. *Journal of Reproductive Medicine, 35,* 159–162.

Longo, L. D. (1976). Carbon monoxide: Effects on oxygenation of the fetus in utero. *Science, 194,* 523–525.

Lowrey, G. H. (1986). *Growth and development of children* (8th ed.). Chicago: Year Book Medical.

Luetjens, C. M., Rolf, C., Gassner, P., Werny, J. E., & Nieschlag, E. (2002). Sperm aneuploidy rates in younger and older men. *Human Reproduction, 17,* 1826–1832.

Luke, B., Dickinson, C., & Petrie, R. H. (1981). Intrauterine growth: Correlation of maternal nutritional status and rate of gestational weight gain. *European Journal of Obstetrics, Gynecology, and Reproductive Biology, 12,* 113–121.

MacFarland, A. (1975). Olfaction in the development of social preferences in the human neonate. *Ciba Foundation Symposium, 33.* New York: Elsevier.

Macmillan, C., Magder, L. S., Brouwers, P., Chase, C., Hittelman, J., Lasky, T., et al. (2001). Head growth and neurodevelopment of infants born to HIV-1-infected drug-using women. *Neurology, 57*(8), 1402–1411.

Magee, M. S., Walden, C. E., Benedetti, T. J., & Knopp, R. H. (1993). Influence of diagnostic criteria on the incidence of gestational diabetes and perinatal morbidity. *Journal of the American Medical Association, 269,* 609.

Maier, S. E., & West, J. R. (2001). Drinking patterns and alcohol-related birth defects. *Alcohol Research and Health, 25*(3), 168–174.

Manning, F. A., Morrison, I., Lange, I. R., & Harman, C. (1982). Antepartum determination of fetal health: Composite biophysical profile scoring. *Clinics in Perinatology, 9,* 285–296.

March of Dimes Birth Defects Foundation. (1997). *The March of Dimes StatBook: Statistics for monitoring maternal and infant health.* White Plains, NY: Author.

Marshall, D. D., Kotelchuck, M., Young, T. E., Bose, C. L., Kruyer, L., & O'Shea, T. M. (1999). Risk factors for chronic lung disease in the surfactant era: A North Carolina population-based study of very low birth weight infants. *Pediatrics, 104,* 1345–1350.

Martin, J. A., Hamilton, B. E., Ventura, S. J., Menocker, F., Park, M. M., & Sutton, P. D. (2002). Births: Final data for 2001. *National Vital Statistics Report, 51,* 1–102.

Mattson, S. N., & Riley, E. P. (1998). A review of the neurobehavioral deficits in children with fetal alcohol syndrome or prenatal exposure to alcohol. *Alcoholism: Clinical and Experimental Research, 22,* 279–294.

Mattson, S. N., Schoenfeld, A. M., & Riley, E. P. (2001). Teratogenic effects of alcohol on brain and behavior. *Alcohol Research and Health, 25*(3), 185–191.

Maurer, D., & Maurer, C. (1988). *The world of the newborn.* New York: Basic Books.

May, P. A., & Gossage, J. P. (2001). Estimating the prevalence of fetal alcohol syndrome. A summary. *Alcohol Research and Health, 25*(3), 159–167.

Mazor, M., Hagay, Z. J., Leiberman, J., Biale, Y., & Insler, V. (1985). Fetal abnormalities associated with breech delivery. *Journal of Reproductive Medicine, 30,* 884–886.

McBrien, D. M., Mattheis, P. J., & Van Dyke, D. C. (1996). Down syndrome. In M. L. Wolraich (Ed.), *Disorders of development and learning: A practical guide to assessment and management* (2nd ed., pp. 316–345). Boston: Mosby.

Mecham, M. J. (1996). *Cerebral palsy.* Austin, TX: PRO-ED.

Milner, A. D., Marsh, M. J., Ingraham, D. M., Fox, G. F., & Susiva, C. (1999). Effects of smoking in pregnancy on neonatal lung function [Fetal neonatal edition]. *Archives of Disease in Childhood, 80*(1), F8–14.

Miotti, P. G., Taha, T. E., Kumwenda, N. I., Broadhead, R., Mtimavalye, L. A., Va der Hoeven, L., et al. (1999). HIV transmission through breastfeeding: A study in Malawi. *Journal of the American Medical Association, 282*(8), 744–749.

Mitchell, W., Gorrell, R., & Greenberg, R. (1980). Failure to thrive: A study in a primary care setting. *Pediatrics, 65,* 971.

Molina, J., Chotro, M., & Dominguez, H. (1995). Fetal alcohol learning resulting from contamination of the prenatal environment. In J. P. LeCanuet, W. Fifer, N. Krasnegor, & W. Smotherman (Eds.), *Fetal development: A psychobiological perspective* (pp. 419–438). Hillsdale, NJ: Erlbaum.

Moore, K. L., & Persaud, T. V. N. (1993). *The developing human: Clinically oriented embryology.* Philadelphia: W. B. Saunders.

Morgan, B. (1994). Maternal anesthesia and analgesia in labor. In D. K. James, P. J. Steer, C. P. Weiner, & B. Gonik (Eds.), *High-risk pregnancy: Management options* (pp. 1101–1118). London: W. B. Saunders.

Murray, A. D., Dolby, R. M., Nation, R. L., & Thomas, D. B. (1981). Effects of epidural anesthesia on newborns and their mothers. *Child Development, 52,* 71.

Nathanielsz, P. W. (1995). The role of basic science in preventing low birth weight. *The Future of Children, 5,* 57–70.

National Clearinghouse for Alcohol and Drug Information. (1995). *Making the link: Alcohol, tobacco and other drugs & pregnancy and parenthood.* Washington, DC: Author.

National Council on Alcoholism and Drug Dependence. (1990). *NCADD fact sheet: Alcohol-related birth defects.* New York: Author.

National Research Council, Committee on Maternal Nutrition/Food and Nutrition Board. (1970). *Maternal nutrition during the course of pregnancy: A summary report.* Washington, DC: U.S. Government Printing Office.

National Society of Genetic Counselors. (1989, November). *Prenatal genetic counseling fact sheet.* Wallingford, PA: Author.

Nieburg, O., Marks, J. S., McLaren, N. M., & Remington, P. L. (1985). The fetal tobacco syndrome. *Journal of the American Medical Association, 253,* 2998–2999.

Ogunyemi, D., Hullett, S., Leeper, J., & Risk, A. (1998). Prepregnancy body mass index, weight gain during pregnancy, and perinatal outcome in a rural black population. *Journal of Maternal and Fetal Medicine, 7*(4), 190–193.

Omori, Y., Minei, S., Testuo, T., Nemoto, K., Shimizu, M., & Sanaka, M. (1994). Current status of pregnancy in diabetic women. A comparison of pregnancy in IDDM and NIDDM mothers. *Diabetes Research and Clinical Practice, 24* (Suppl.), 273.

O'Rahilly, R., & Muller, F. (1992). *Human embryology and teratology.* New York: Wiley-Liss.

Ornoy, A., Ratzon, N., Greenbaum, C., Wolf, A., & Dulitzky, M. (2001). School-age children born to diabetic mothers and to mothers with gestational diabetes exhibit a high rate of inattention and fine and gross motor impairment. *Journal of Pediatric Endocrinology and Metabolism, 14* (Suppl. 1), 681–689.

O'Shea, T. M., Goldstein, D. J., deRegnier, R., Sheaffer, C. I., Roberts, D. D., & Dillard, R. G. (1996). Outcome at 4 to 5 years of age in children recovered from neonatal chronic lung disease. *Developmental Medicine and Child Neurology, 38,* 830–839.

Petry, C. J., & Hales, C. N. (2000). Long-term effects on offspring of intrauterine exposure to deficits in nutrition. *Human Reproduction Update, 6*(6), 578–586.

Pollack, R. N., & Divon, M. Y. (1992). Intrauterine growth retardation: Definition, classification, and etiology. *Clinical Obstetrics and Gynecology, 35,* 99–113.

Poustie, V. J., & Rutherford, P. (2000). Dietary interventions for phenlyketonuria. *The Cochrane Library* (Issue 1). Oxford: Update Software.

Reece, E. A., & Hobbins, J. C. (1986). Diabetic embryopathy: Pathogenesis, prenatal diagnosis, and prevention. *Obstetrics and Gynecology Surveillance, 41,* 325.

Rice, D., & Barone, S. (2000). Critical periods of vulnerability for the developing nervous system: Evidence from human and animal models. *Environmental Health Perspectives, 108*(Suppl. 3), 511–533.

Richardson, G. A., Hamel, S. C., Goldschmidt, L., & Day, N. L. (1999). Growth of infants prenatally exposed to cocaine/crack: Comparison of a prenatal care and no prenatal care sample. *Pediatrics, 104*(2), E18.

Richter, L., & Richter, D. M. (2001). Exposure to parental tobacco and alcohol use: Effects on children's health and development. *American Journal of Orthopsychiatry, 71*(2), 182–203.

Robins, L. N., & Mills, J. L. (Eds.) (1993). Effects of in-utero exposure to street drugs. *Journal of Public Health, 83* (Suppl.), 8–32.

Rosenberg, D. A., & Krugman, R. D. (1991). Epidemiology and outcome of child abuse. *Annual Review of Medicine, 42*, 217–224.

Rubinstein, A. (1986). Pediatric AIDS. *Current Problems in Pediatrics, 16*, 361–409.

Rush, D. (1988). Evaluation of the Special Supplemental Food Program for Women, Infants, and Children. *American Journal of Clinical Nutrition Supplement, 48*, 512–519.

Rush, D., & Callahan, K. R. (1989). Exposure to passive cigarette smoking and child development. *Annals of New York Academy of Sciences, 562*, 74–100.

Rush, D., & Cassano, P. (1983). Relationship of cigarette smoking and social class to birth weight and perinatal mortality among all births in Britain, April 1970. *Journal of Epidemiology and Community Health, 37*, 249–255.

Russell, D. L., Keil, M. F., Bonat, S. H., Uwaifo, G. L., Nicholson, J. C., McDuffie, J. R., et al. (2001). The relation between skeletal maturation and adiposity in African American and Caucasian children. *Journal of Pediatrics, 139*, 844–848.

Schifrin, B. S. (1982). The fetal monitoring polemic. *Clinics in Perinatology, 9*, 399–408.

Scholl, T. O., Hediger, M. L., Schall, J. I., Khoo, C., & Fischer, R. L. (1996). Dietary and serum folate: Their influence on the outcome of pregnancy. *American Journal of Clinical Nutrition, 63*, 520–525.

Scholl, T. O., Sowers, M., Chen, X., & Lenders, C. (2001). Maternal glucose concentration influences fetal growth, gestation, and pregnancy complications. *American Journal of Epidemiology, 154*(6), 514–520.

Schuler, M. E., & Nair, P. (1999). Brief report: Frequency of maternal cocaine use during pregnancy and infant neurobehavioral outcome. *Journal of Pediatric Psychology, 24*(6), 511–514.

Schuster, C. S. (1992). Antenatal development. In C. S. Schuster & S. S. Ashburn (Eds.), *The process of human development: A holistic life-span approach* (3rd ed.). Philadelphia: J. B. Lippincott.

Schwartz, R. M., Luby, A. M., Scanlon, J. W., & Kellogg, R. J. (1994). Effects of surfactant on morbidity, mortality, and resource use in newborn infants weighing 500 to 1,500 g. *New England Journal of Medicine, 330*, 1476–1489.

Scott, G. B., Hutto, C., Makuch, R. W., Mastrucci, M. T., O'Connor, T., Mitchell, C. D., et al. (1989). Survival in children with perinatally acquired human immunodeficiency virus type I infection. *New England Journal of Medicine, 321*, 1791–1796.

Shaw, G. M., Lammer, E. J., Wasserman, C. R., & O'Malley, C. D. (1995). Risks of orofacial clefts in children born to women using multivitamins containing folic acid periconceptionally. *Lancet, 346*, 393–396.

Shearer, D. L., Mulvihill, B. A., Klerman, L. V., Wallander, J. L., Houinga, M. E., & Redden, D. T. (2002). Association of early birth and low cognitive ability. *Perspectives on Sexual and Reproductive Health, 34*, 236–243.

Shehata, H. A., & Nelson-Piercy, C. (2001). Drugs in pregnancy. Drugs to avoid. *Best Practices in Research in Clinical Obstetrical Gynecology, 15*(6), 971–986.

Shubert, P. J., & Savage, B. (1994). Smoking, alcohol, and drug abuse. In D. K. James, P. J. Steer, C. P. Weiner, & B. Gonik (Eds.), *High-risk pregnancy: Management options*. Philadelphia: W. B. Saunders.

Silverman, B. L, Rizzo, T. A., Cho, N. H., & Metzger, B. E. (1998). Long-term effect of the intrauterine environment. The Northwestern University Diabetes in Pregnancy Center. *Diabetes Care, 21*(Suppl. 2), B142–149.

Singer, L. T., Arendt, R., Minnes, S., Farkas, K., Salvator, A., Kirchner, H. L., et al. (2002). Cognitive and motor outcomes of cocaine-exposed infants. *Journal of the American Medical Association, 287*(15), 1952–1960.

Skinner, B. F. (1961). *Cumulative record* (enlarged ed.). New York: Appleton-Century-Crofts.

Slater, A., von der Schulenbur, C., Brown, E., Badenoch, M., Butterworth, G., Parsons, S., et al. (1998). Newborn infants prefer attractive faces. *Infant Behavior and Development, 21*(2), 345–354.

Slotkin, T. A. (1998). Fetal nicotine or cocaine exposure: Which one is worse? *Journal of Pharmacological and Experimental Therapies, 285*(3), 931–945.

Smithells, R. W., Nevin, N. C., Seller, M. J., Sheppard, S., Harris, R., Read, A. P., et al. (1983). Further experience of vitamin supplementation for prevention of neural tube defect recurrences. *Lancet, 1,* 1027–1031.

Sood, B., Delaney-Black, V., Covington, C., Nordstrom-Klee, B., Ager, J., Templin, T., et al. (2001). Prenatal alcohol exposure and childhood behavior at age 6 and 7 years: I. Dose-response effect. *Pediatrics, 108*(2), E34.

Spinner, M. R., & Siegel, L. (1987). Nonorganic failure to thrive. *Journal of Preventative Psychiatry, 3,* 279–287.

Stein, J., Schettler, T., Wallinga, D., & Valenti, M. (2002). In harm's way: Toxic threats to child development. *Developmental and Behavioral Pediatrics, 23*(1S), S13–S22.

Stephens, R. P., Richardson, A. C., & Lewin, J. S. (1997). Outcome of extremely low birth weight infants (500–999 grams) over a 12-year period. *Pediatrics, 99,* 619–622.

Stott, D. H. (1971). The child's hazards in utero. In J. G. Howells (Ed.), *Modern perspectives in international child psychiatry.* New York: Brunner/Mazel.

Strang, R. (1969). *An introduction to child study.* New York: Macmillan.

Strauss, M. E., & Reynolds, K. S. (1983). Psychological characteristics and development of narcotic-addicted infants. *Drug and Alcohol Dependence, 12,* 381–393.

Streissguth, A., & Kanter, J. (Eds.) (1997). *The challenge of fetal alcohol syndrome: Overcoming secondary disabilities.* Seattle: University of Washington Press.

Sturm, L., & Drotar, D. (1989). Prediction of weight-for-height following intervention in three-year-old children with early histories of nonorganic failure to thrive. *Child Abuse and Neglect, 13,* 19.

Sullivan, B. A., Henderson, S. T., & Davis, J. M. (1998). Gestational diabetes. *Journal of American Pharmacological Association, 38*(3), 372–373.

Susser, M. (1991). Maternal weight gain, infant birth weight, and diet: Causal sequences. *American Journal of Clinical Nutrition, 53,* 1384–1396.

Swanson, M. W., Streissguth, A. P., Sampson, P. D., & Olsen, H. C. (1999). Prenatal cocaine and neuromotor outcome at four months: Effect of duration of exposure. *Journal of Developmental and Behavioral Pediatrics, 20*(5), 325–334.

Tanner, J. M. (1989). *Fetus into man: Physical growth from conception to maturity* (Rev. ed.). Cambridge, MA: Harvard University Press.

Tinsley, V. S., & Waters, H. S. (1982). The development of verbal control over motor behavior: A replication and extension of Luria's findings. *Child Development, 53,* 746–753.

Trask, C. L., & Kosofsky, B. E. (2000). Developmental considerations of neurotoxic exposure. *Neurology Clinics, 18*(3), 541–562.

U.S. Department of Health and Human Services, Administration on Children, Youth and Families. (2003). *Child maltreatment 2001.* Washington, DC: U.S. Government Printing Office.

U.S. General Accounting Office. (1992). *Early intervention: Federal investments like WIC can produce savings.* Washington, DC: Author.

Van Assche, F. A., Holemans, K., & Aerts, L. (2001). Long-term consequences for offspring of diabetes during pregnancy. *British Medical Bulletin, 60,* 173–182.

Vogel, F. (1986). *Human genetics: Problems and approaches* (2nd ed.). New York: Springer-Verlag.

Vohr, B. R., Garcia-Coll, C. T., Labato, D., Ynis, K. A., O'Dea, C., & Oh, W. (1991). Neurodevelopmental and medical status of low-birthweight survivors of bronchopulmonary dysplasia at 10–12 years of age. *Developmental Medicine and Child Neurology, 33,* 690–697.

Watson, J. (1924). *Behaviorism.* New York: Norton.

Weber, M. K., Floyd, R. L., Riley, E. P., & Snider, D. E. (2002). National task force on fetal alcohol syndrome and fetal alcohol effect: Defining the national agenda for fetal alcohol syndrome and other prenatal alcohol-related effects. *Morbidity and Mortality Weekly Report, 51*(RR-14), 9–12.

Weissman, M. M., Warner, V., Wickramarante, P. J., & Kandel, D. B. (1999). Maternal smoking during pregnancy and psychopathology in offspring followed to adulthood. *Journal of the American Academy of Child & Adolescent Psychiatry, 38*(7), 892–899.

Westgren, L. M., & Ingemarsson, I. (1988). Breech delivery and mental handicap. *Baillieres Clinical Obstetrics & Gynecology, 2,* 187–194.

Wilcox, A. J., Weinberg, C. R., & Baird, D. D. (1995). Timing of sexual intercourse in relation to ovulation: Effects on the probability of conception, survival of the pregnancy, and sex of the baby. *New England Journal of Medicine, 333*(7), 1517–1521.

Wilfert, C. M., & McKinney, R. E. (1998). When children harbor HIV. *Scientific American, 279*, 94–95.

Williams, R. C., & Carta, J. J. (1997). Behavioral outcomes of young children with prenatal exposure to alcohol: Review and analysis of experimental literature. *Infants and Young Children, 8*, 16.

Willis, W. G., & Widerstrom, A. H. (1986). Structure and function in prenatal and postnatal neuropsychological development: A dynamic interaction. In G. W. Hynd, & J. Obrzut (Eds.), *Child neuropsychology* (Vol. 1). New York: Academic Press.

Winick, M. (1971). Cellular growth during early malnutrition. *Pediatrics, 47*, 969.

Wisborg, K., Kesmodel, U., Henriksen, T. B., Olsen, S. F., & Secher, N. J. (2001). Exposure to tobacco smoke in utero and the risk of stillbirth and death in the first year of life. *American Journal of Epidemiology, 154*(4), 322–327.

Yazigi, R. A., Odem, R. R., & Polakoski, K. L. (1991). Demonstration of specific binding of cocaine to human spermatozoa. *Journal of the American Medical Association, 266*, 1956–1959.

Yehuda, R., Halligan, S. L., & Grossman, R. (2001). Childhood trauma and risk for PTSD: Relationship to intergenerational effects of trauma, parental PTSD, and cortisol excretion. *Development and Psychopathology, 13*, 733–753.

Zeisel, S. H. (2000). Choline: Needed for normal development of memory. *Journal of the American College of Nutrition, 19*(Suppl. 5), 528S–531S.

Zuckerman, B., & Frank, D. A. (1994). Prenatal cocaine exposure: Nine years later. *Journal of Pediatrics, 124*, 731–733.

3

Partnerships with Families

Zolinda Stoneman and Mary E. Rugg

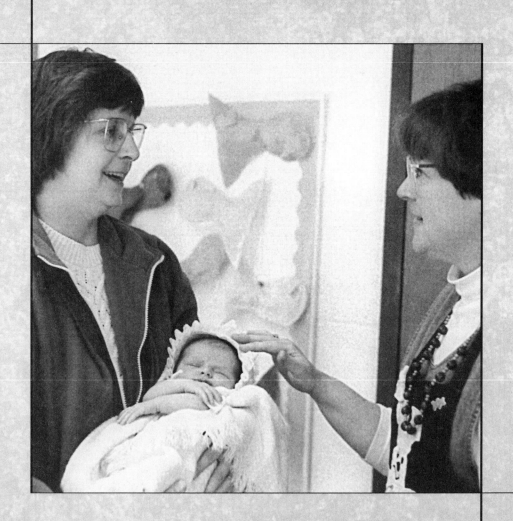

Chapter Outline

Tonya and Her Family

Tonya and her mother, Sheila, live in a mobile home in a rural area. Tonya, who is almost 3 years old, has two older sisters and a younger brother. Sheila works at a pancake restaurant from noon until eight in the evening, 5 days a week. While she is at work, her mother takes care of Tonya and her younger brother. The two older girls are in school during the day and are dropped off at their grandmother's house after school. Sheila picks up all of the children when she gets off work. On her days off, she is very busy doing laundry, grocery shopping, and taking care of the children. Tonya is quite delayed in her development. She does not yet walk. She makes sounds, but has no real words. She has large, bright eyes and a wonderful smile.

Tonya has received early intervention services since she was 14 months old. Parent to Parent connected Sheila with another single parent with a child with a substantial delay. When Sheila gets tired or discouraged, the two mothers talk on the phone and Sheila usually feels better. An early interventionist comes to Sheila's home on Saturday afternoons, one of Sheila's days off. She has helped Sheila think of ways that the limited time she has with Tonya can be the most fun for both of them, while, at the same time, teaching Tonya new skills. Sheila has learned to play sound games with Tonya when she bathes her and to help Tonya with her fine motor skills at snack time. The interventionist helped Sheila find ways to incorporate all of her children into activities with Tonya, so that the siblings would develop a close relationship with her. This was very important to Sheila. The interventionist also visits Tonya at her grandmother's home. She has arranged for Tonya to attend a local day-care center in the fall. The early interventionist will work with Sheila, the day-care provider, and with a physical therapist and speech-language therapist to create a developmentally stimulating inclusive preschool program for Tonya.

Families are the first, and most important teachers of young children. The family is responsible for the care of the child with a disability before interventionists, teachers, or therapists become involved with the child, and the family will remain the dominant force in the child's life long after these service providers have moved on to work with other children and families. Early intervention service providers are part of the child's life for a few years; families have a lifelong commitment to the child (see the Vignette on Sheila and Tonya). This thought was captured by Bruder (2000) when she wrote, "We must always remember that the children we serve belong to their families, and we are privileged to be in their lives for a short time" (p. 110).

For many years, educators and other professionals emphasized parent involvement in infant and preschool programs. Parents were encouraged to attend educational and support-oriented meetings, to assist the teacher in the preschool classroom, to implement intervention programs at home, and to provide information about the child and family to professional staff. It was believed that by involving parents, the best interests of young children would be served. These approaches to parent involvement retained professional control of services and programmatic decisions. Rather than being decision makers, the traditional role of parents has been one of "information providers" and of interventionists, reinforcing aspects of the service program at home (Morsink, Thomas, & Correa, 1991). In recent years, there has been a dramatic change in the role of families in programs for young children with disabilities. An emphasis on parent involvement has given way to a **family-centered approach**, in which families have the power to direct the services that they, and their children, receive.

Changes in the role of families were the direct result of federal legislation. When P.L. 99–457 was enacted into law in 1986, the role of families in the development and implementation of programs for young children with disabilities was radically enhanced. Subsequent reauthorizations of this Act (e.g., P.L. 105–17 and Amendments to the Individuals with Disabilities Act [IDEA], 1997) have further codified into law the central role of families in their children's early intervention programs. The family is formally recognized as the most important constant in each child's life, and the family environment as the richest context for social, emotional, cognitive, and physical development. The role of the service delivery system and service providers is seen to be that of supporting the family.

For children from birth through age 2, served by Part C of IDEA, the individualized family service plan (IFSP) expands the intervention focus to include families, as well as their children. Families are required to be invited to be a part of the team that develops the IFSP, to be asked for input concerning priorities and concerns, to have the family's needs addressed in the IFSP if the family so chooses, to assist in identifying the natural environments in which interventions will be delivered, to review the IFSP every 6 months, to decline or accept early intervention services offered to the family and child, and to be informed in writing before any change is made to the child's placement or services.

Part B of IDEA, which focuses on services to preschool children (aged 3 through 5) with disabilities, also stresses the important roles to be played by families. Parents of preschool children are given a significant role in the design and evaluation of services provided to their children, making them partners with the schools in developing individualized education plans (IEPs). Parents are to be included as members of teams making decisions about eligibility and placement of the child, as

Parents should be encouraged to take a leadership role on the intervention team.

well as members of the team developing the IEP. Parents must agree to and sign the IEP. Due process and mediation procedures are in place if families disagree with the IEP or with the child's placement. Both Part C and Part B of IDEA place strong emphasis on families and on family involvement in the early intervention process.

For a family-centered approach to early intervention to become a reality, early intervention professionals must embrace family-centered values, appreciate family diversity, understand family systems, be sensitive to parent emotions and beliefs, support learning in the natural environments experienced by families, and have the skills to work in partnership with families. This chapter is organized around these themes.

Family-Centered Values

Implementing family-centered approaches to intervention requires a dramatic shift in the way that many professionals think about families. To be successful, the interventionist must hold a set of attitudes, or values, that place the needs and desires of the family at the center of the intervention process. This value system is counter to the child-centered approach historically endorsed by early intervention professionals, regardless of disciplinary background. Family-centered approaches require that professionals relinquish the "expert" role, instead creating a partnership with families in which both the professional and the family members bring knowledge and expertise into the collaborative relationship.

Five primary values underlie family-centered early intervention:

1. Family strengths are identified and emphasized;
2. Families are actively included in planning and decision making;
3. Services and supports are developed for the whole family, not just for the child;

In the family-centered approach to intervention, the family members and the interventionist create a partnership.

4. Family priorities guide intervention goals and services; and
5. The preference of the family concerning their level of participation in the program is respected.

These program characteristics are directly related to a set of values and beliefs that form the foundation for family-centered interventions.

Family Strengths Are Identified and Emphasized

Family-centered early interventionists actively seek to identify and build upon the assets and strengths of the families whom they serve. They focus their attention on learning about positive aspects of the family, reflecting back to the family the strengths of the family unit, as well as the strengths and assets of the child with a disability. All families have strengths. All children, regardless of the severity of their disabilities, have strengths. Focusing on strengths does not mean that the interventionist denies or ignores the struggles and problems of the family. Rather, these challenges are understood and addressed in the context of the strengths possessed by the family to meet and overcome those challenges. Whereas the traditional intervention approach has often focused on identifying and remediating deficits, the family-centered approach reverses this focus.

Just as it is true that all families have strengths, it is also true that there are no perfect families. Consider, for a moment, your family of origin. Think about the feelings that would have been aroused in you, and in your family, if an interventionist had entered your home and talked with you about the things that were wrong about how your family was living. Too much fighting in front of the children? Meals consisting of too many fatty foods? Television playing too loudly for too many hours? Children staying up too late at night? Then think about the effect of the same interventionist noting positive aspects of your family. For example, the interventionist might note that there are many books and magazines present in the home. Grandparents are available to care for the children, as needed. The parents clearly love their children. These positive communications set the tone for collaboration and partnership. Every person, and every family, wants the acknowledgment that he or she is valued and has a positive contribution to make.

For some families, strengths are easy to identify; for other families, strengths are less obvious. To see the strengths of some families, professionals must shift the focus from the attention-grabbing problems and risk factors. With a family-centered focus, it is possible to discover strengths and assets in the most challenging family situations. Werner and Smith (1982, 1992), in their classic studies of resilient families and resilient children, identified numerous strengths that helped families rear competent children in the face of adversity, including the following:

1. one or more caring adults(s) in the child's life
2. adults who encourage trust, independence, and initiative
3. clear and consistent rules and structure in the home
4. parenting characterized by warmth and high expectations

> The family-centered approach focuses on the positive aspects in even difficult family situations.

5. harmony and lack of conflict between parents and caregivers
6. parents and caregivers with positive mental and emotional health
7. families that are stable over time
8. kin and neighbors available for emotional support
9. shared family values
10. a sense of family oneness
11. strong, positive sibling relationships

These and other strengths, when identified and nurtured, form a foundation for successful interventions with families.

Families Are Actively Included in Planning and Decision Making

In family-centered programs, families hold the power to make key decisions about their children. Professionals believe that families are capable of making wise and responsible decisions about their children and about the family as a whole. Parents are encouraged to take a leadership role on the intervention team (McBride, Brotherson, Joanning, Whiddon, & Demmitt, 1993), rather than acting as passive participants. Family decisions are respected, even when they conflict with the recommendations of professionals. Families are provided with the information and resources that they need to make informed decisions. Information is provided in a manner that is culturally relevant and is understandable and usable by the family.

To make decisions, families need choices. Too often, the service options available to families are very limited (Hanson et al., 2000). Consider the example of a family of a 2-year-old child served in a Part C program. This family wants their child to be in an inclusive preschool program as the child ages and moves into the Part B early childhood special education system. However, the Part B program in their community administers only segregated programs. Under the old service model, the family would be told that an inclusive preschool was not an option; to continue to receive services after the child turned 3 years old, the family would need to accept a placement in one of the segregated programs operated by the system. A family-centered service delivery model rejects this outcome, calling upon interventionists from both the Part C and Part B programs to be creative problem solvers and to work together with the family to develop an inclusive placement for the child.

Services and Supports Are Developed for the Whole Family

Forest and Pearpoint (1992) wrote that "families who . . . do not have support systems for all their members cannot adequately build support around their children" (p. 77). Supporting the whole family, including the mother, father, siblings, and extended family members, recognizes that family members are interdependent and that the development of the child with a disability is enhanced when the family is strong and all members' needs are respected. It is unrealistic to expect that early interventionists will solve all of the family's problems or meet the needs of every family member. Early

Development of the child is enhanced when the family is strong and all members' needs are respected.

interventionists are not omnipotent. It is realistic, however, for early interventionists to serve as facilitators, connecting families to other resources and assisting the family in developing creative solutions to problems and needs. This includes helping families to use the resources of their natural support systems (e.g., friends, relatives, clergy) to assist the family in achieving its goals. It also can include helping the family to expand these informal social resources, linking the family to others in the community who can provide support and assistance.

Family Priorities Guide Intervention Goals and Services

In family-centered early intervention programs, services reflect the choices and preferences of families and are tailored to their needs. McWilliam, Tocci, and Harbin (1998) cite a service provider who asks families, "When you're at home with your child and you're going through your day, what is the most difficult time of your day? What do we need to do . . . to make that a more pleasant time?" (p. 212). Questions such as these allow the interventionist to understand the family's perception of areas in which they need assistance. Every child and every family is unique. Goals on the IFSP or IEP are developed in partnership with the family. The interventionist understands that two families with the same identified needs may prioritize those needs differently and may desire very different approaches to meet those needs (Covert, 1995). Families have the opportunity to be actively involved in all aspects of their child's program, including assessment, writing the program plan, selecting appropriate services and service providers, implementing the intervention, and evaluating the outcomes of the intervention. The interventionist works with parents to generate intervention options and lets the family decide which options best fit their resources and desires (McWilliam & Winton, 1990).

> Every child and every family has unique needs.

The Preferred Level of Family Participation Is Respected

Some families prefer to be actively involved in all aspects of their child's program; others want professionals to plan and implement the intervention with little family involvement. In family-centered intervention programs, all families are given the option of controlling their child's program. Not all families want this level of responsibility, however. The extent to which they choose to engage in intervention activities may vary greatly between families, and they may change over time. For example, some parents may decline a particular service in order to have time for the family to participate in much-needed recreation or leisure or engage in other nondisability-related activities. The importance of such activities for the resilience and well-being of all family members is recognized, and their choices are validated.

Family members have the right to minimal participation in their child's program, if that is their choice, without being viewed as "bad" or "uninterested" parents. Interventionists are respectful of family routines and commitments, scheduling evening meetings, weekend home visits, and so on to accommodate the family's schedule (McBride et al., 1993). Families are never pressured into any choice of services, or denied those services at a later date if their needs change. Interventionists understand that families from different cultures may have differing views concerning the roles of family members and the manner in which family members interact with service providers. These cultural mores are respected.

Family Diversity

Respect for family diversity is critical to the provision of sensitive and effective early intervention services. Early interventionists are called upon to serve families representing a wide variety of situations, backgrounds, and philosophies. The following sections address changing family demographics, serving families from different cultures, and the interconnections of families, poverty, and early intervention.

Changing Family Demographics

Historically, the provision of human services has been based on the traditional definition of a family as a married couple with children living in the same household. Families in today's society are represented by many different types and structures. The 2000 U.S. Census revealed that 10 million children under age 18 live in single-mother households, whereas 2 million children live with single fathers (U.S. Census Bureau, 2001). Many other children live in blended families with stepparents, in foster or adoptive families, with grandparents or other relatives, with gay and lesbian couples, in families built around nonmarital relationships and parenting partnerships, and in multigenerational households. Service providers in early intervention must be prepared to recognize and honor each family's unique definition of membership. Such recognition will entail taking time to get to know each family, withholding judgments that criticize any nontraditional family form, and fashioning services that allow for the participation of all family members.

Serving Families from Different Cultures

Lynch and Hanson (1998) refer to the United States as having a "kaleidoscope of cultures" with a "changing pattern of color, customs, and language" (p. 492). According to the 2000 U.S. Census, America is becoming increasingly diverse. Approximately 75% of the population, 211,460,626 people, described themselves as White. African Americans comprise 12.3% of the population (34,658,190 people). More than 35.3 million people, 13% of the population, described themselves as Hispanic or Latino/Latina. Slightly over 3.5% of the population are of Asian origin (10,242,998 people); approximately 1% of the population are American Indian (2,475,956 people). Almost 1.5% or 6.8 million people, responded that they were of two or more races. If current population trends continue, no racial or ethnic group will be a majority in the U.S. population by midcentury. The increase in the proportion of the population that is non-White is especially dramatic for the age group of most interest to early interventionists, namely, infants and young children (U.S. Census Bureau, 2001).

Cultural
competence is
being aware of a
culture's beliefs,
attitudes, and
characteristics.

It is critical that early interventionists have the competence to support families from diverse cultural backgrounds, including families who are recent immigrants and speak a language other than English. It is not necessary for an interventionist to know everything about a particular culture in order to provide sensitive and appropriate services (Lynch & Hanson, 1998). **Cultural competence** is a set of personal beliefs and attitudes that shape behavior. Service providers who are open and eager to learn, respectful of differences, and willing to conduct thoughtful self-examinations and make personal change are most capable of developing cultural competence (Lynch & Hanson, 1998). These traits allow interventionists to identify and use cultural resources, strengthen their relationships with families, and provide the most effective services. A focus on the development of these personal characteristics, rather than on the acquisition of detailed knowledge of a culture, will also discourage service providers from stereotyping families based on their membership in a cultural group. Each family is unique, and any one family may be as different from a family in their own cultural group as they are from a family from another cultural group (Wayman, Lynch, & Hanson, 1990).

Several strategies enable early interventionists to work sensitively and effectively with families from diverse cultural backgrounds, including the following:

- Learn to view cultural diversity as an asset—something to celebrate, rather than as a problem to be overcome.
- Focus on the uniqueness and individuality of each family and of each child.
- Be aware of your own cultural beliefs and customs, including the beliefs that you hold about what constitutes a "strong" or an "ideal" family.
- Encourage families to share their stories, their hopes, and their histories. Try to understand what they want for their children and the cultural meanings they have concerning disability.
- Be sensitive to the ways that social interactions may differ across cultures. This may include personal space (how close to stand to someone), use of eye contact, gender roles, comfort in talking about oneself, comfort with silence, and use of touch.
- Learn to be comfortable around people who look or think differently than you do. Learn to make others feel comfortable. Show acceptance.
- Fight against the tendency to stereotype families, even if the stereotypes are positive.
- Be sensitive to the strong impact that current, as well as historic, discrimination has on families.
- Learn about what it means to immigrate to the United States. Think about the challenges of living in a country where you do not speak the dominant language. Learn to work with a language interpreter.

Families, Poverty, and Early Intervention

Although the United States is an affluent country, many families live in poverty. Young children are more likely to be poor than any other age group. Contrary to many stereotypes, the majority of poor young children live in working households; only 11% of poor children under age 3 live in families that rely primarily on public assistance. Almost one in five children under age 3, or 2.1 million young children, live in poverty. Young children living with single mothers are five times as likely to be poor as those living with married parents; 45% of young children living in mother-headed families are poor, whereas only 9% of young children living with married parents experience poverty (Song & Lu, 2002).

Poor children are more likely than affluent children to have disabilities. This is true for many reasons, including maternal and child malnutrition, inadequate pre-natal care for the mother, exposure to environmental toxins, poor access to health care, trauma related to unsafe environments, maternal drug and alcohol abuse, com-promised parenting, and lack of developmental opportunities. Poverty, by itself, does not cause disabilities in children, but the consequences of poverty place young, poor children at heightened risk for disabilities (Thompson, 1992). For many early interventionists, the majority of families they serve are living in poverty. Yet, most interventionists come from middle-class backgrounds and have limited understand-ing of what it means to live in persistent poverty.

> Poverty places young children at a higher risk for disabilities.

Homelessness is a poverty-related issue of importance to early interventionists. It is estimated that each week, more than 200,000 U.S. children experience home-lessness; 42% of these children are under 5 years of age (Burt et al., 1999). Young children whose families are poor, and subsequently homeless, are at high risk of developmental delays and emotional and behavioral disabilities. Developing early intervention strategies for families who are homeless (Kelly, Buehlman, & Caldwell, 2000) can support these families during trying times and can prevent or reduce developmental difficulties in their children.

Families of minority young children have significantly higher rates of poverty than do White families (Fujiura & Yamaki, 1997; Walker, Asbury, Maholmes, & Rackley, 1991). Hispanic young children living in two-parent families are three times as likely (24%) to experience poverty as African American children (8%), and almost five times more likely to be poor as White children (5%). Over half of all African American chil-dren aged 3 and under living in single-mother families are poor; nearly half of young Hispanic children living with single-parent mothers are poor (Song & Lu, 2002). These high poverty rates lead to increased rates of disability among minority children (Fujiura & Yamaki, 1997). Leung and Wright (1993) argued that people with disabilities who are also members of minority groups face "double discrimination and a double disadvan-tage" (p. 1). It is important for early interventionists to understand the complex rela-tionships among disability prevalence, poverty, and minority status and to be able to differentiate the effects of poverty from those of cultural or ethnic differences among families. Without an understanding of the overwhelming effects of poverty on children and families, it is impossible to provide early intervention services that are effective and that make sense for the family.

The Family as a System

In addition to adopting a family-centered values base and understanding family diversity, it is important that early interventionists appreciate the systemic nature of the family. A family is more than a collection of individual members. **Family systems**

theory (Broderick & Smith, 1979; von Bertalanffy, 1968) recognizes that there are complex interconnections among family members. In the family system, many roles and rules guide individual and family functioning. Within the larger system of the family are subsystems made up of smaller groups of family members. For instance, there may be a husband and wife subsystem, a parent and child subsystem, a grandparent and parent subsystem, and a sibling subsystem all within the same family. The members of these subsystems have strong influences on each other.

Each family subsystem influences other subsystems and the family as a whole. Thus, change or intervention in one part of the family can positively or negatively affect the entire family system (Minuchin, 1974). "Each family member influences the family as a whole. To separate one from another is like trying to put together a puzzle without all the pieces" (Beach Center on Families and Disability, 1997). A change in the relationship between the parent and one child, for example, might also affect the parents' marriage and the relationships between siblings. Similarly, when events impact one member of a family, all family members are changed in some way. When, for example, a mother is fired from her job, every member of the family is affected.

This conceptualization of the family as a system is important when intervention programs for young children are being planned. Interventions designed to help children learn, for example, can have unintentional negative effects if those interventions create stress or conflict in the family.

Expecting that parents perform painful physical exercises, certain demanding behavior modification strategies, or intensive educational strategies may have short-term benefits for the child. In the long term, however, the developmental progress of this child may be compromised by the stress and conflict created in the child's family by these additional demands.

Service providers who wish to deliver the most appropriate and helpful services to families of children with disabilities must spend time talking with all possible family members in an informal, open, and respectful manner before suggesting interventions. Fialka (2001) suggests asking the family a series of questions when discussing possible in-home programs or interventions: "How will this disrupt or change your life?" "How will this complicate your daily living?" "What do I need to understand from your side as the parent?" (p. 26). In general, families will be more open to suggestions, interventions, and changes that closely fit their already established values and behaviors. The following sections of this chapter will discuss the family roles often filled by parents, spouses, siblings, the child with a disability, and members of the extended family.

Parental Roles

Children with disabilities can place heavy time demands and role restrictions on families, including feeding, bathing, and dressing; these added role responsibilities fall disproportionately on mothers (Beckman, 1991; Krauss, 1993; Willoughby & Glidden, 1995). It important to note, however, that in some families, the father is the primary caretaker of the child. Other families are headed by single-parent fathers. Parents of

---

Family systems theory posits that family members are interconnected and that events that occur to one family member affect the whole family.

Family members interact as a whole, like the pieces in a puzzle.

Some interventions may create stress or conflict in the family.

The most well received suggestions and interventions are those that fit the family's values and behaviors.

Siblings can be a positive factor in young children with special needs.

children with disabilities are often expected to be educators, speech therapists, physical therapists, medical technicians, advocates, and service planners, and to assume numerous other roles not usually assumed by family members. Parents are asked to perform these other duties, sometimes to the exclusion of the primary role of all parents—that of nurturer.

Parents of children with disabilities are often expected to take on roles not usually performed by family members.

One of the most important roles of early interventionists is to support positive, developmentally enhancing relationships between parents and their young children with disabilities. Mahoney, Boyce, Fewell, Spiker, and Wheeden (1998) analyzed multiple early intervention outcome studies and found that the strongest predictor of positive developmental outcomes for children was the degree to which the intervention enhanced parents' responsiveness toward their children.

The strongest predictor of positive developmental outcomes was an increase in parents' responsiveness toward their children.

Responsive parent–child interactions can be disrupted by many factors, including parent stress or fatigue, hard-to-interpret cues or lack of responsiveness from the child with a disability, absence of positive parenting models, or lack of parenting information or skill. Parent responsiveness includes behaviors such as turn-taking, responding to the child's utterances, using the child's interests or focus of attention to guide the interaction, sensitivity to the child's cues, warmth, and minimal use of directives or commands. Intervention based on enhancing these parenting behaviors is often termed **relationship-focused early intervention** (Kelly & Barnard, 1999; Mahoney et al., 1998). Early interventionists often use the term *parents* when, in practice, they

Relationship-
focused early
intervention refers
to intervention
that seeks to
enhance the
relationship
between parents
and their children.

usually mean *mothers* (Pearl, 1993; Turbiville & Marquis, 2001). It is not uncommon for early interventionists to never meet the child's father, even if he is living in the home and actively involved in the care of his child. Turbiville and Marquis suggest that early interventionists are often not well prepared to work with mothers, and are even less prepared to work with fathers. It is vital that fathers be supported in their efforts to participate in their child's intervention programs, consistent with their preferred roles or levels of involvement. This may mean scheduling meetings when fathers can attend or communicating directly with fathers over the phone rather than immediately asking to speak with the mother. It also may mean planning activities that can be shared by both mothers and fathers.

Marital Roles

Parents are partners with each other as well as with their children. The relationship between parents is an important predictor of overall family functioning. Marital satisfaction and harmony have been associated with more positive parental attitudes, less strict beliefs about child discipline, more sensitive father–child interaction, and fewer feelings of parental annoyance with the child (Stoneman & Brody, 1993). Marital security and satisfaction have been identified as key variables in successful coping in families with children with disabilities (Nihira, Mink, & Meyers, 1981). Positive family functioning also has been related to decreased stress and increased well-being. Among parents of young children with disabilities, higher family resources, cohesion, and adaptability have been associated with lower stress (Boyce, Behl, Mortensen, & Akers, 1991; Shonkoff, Hauser-Cram, Krauss, & Upshur, 1992).

Some marriages
become stronger
from parenting
a child with a
disability.

Some marriages experience additional stressors related to parenting a child with a disability. It is important to recognize, however, that many marriages are not adversely affected by disability, and many become even stronger (Lambie & Daniels-Mohring, 1993). The importance of the marital relationship must be recognized, and service providers should support the maintenance of healthy marital partnerships through the provision of services, such as respite care, which allow the couple to spend time away from caretaking or disability-related duties. Similarly, for single parents, it is important to recognize the parent's need for time away from child-related responsibilities and to support the parent in maintaining a healthy network of social relationships.

Sibling Roles

Brothers and sisters serve as teachers, caretakers, friends, and playmates to each other. The relationships between the siblings in families of children with disabilities are similar to all sibling relationships. Few differences have been found in the levels of play, social activities, or conflict. In fact, siblings have been found to be good at choosing play materials and activities that allow for extended social interaction with their brothers and sisters with mental retardation (Stoneman, 1998, 2001). It is important for families, and for interventionists, to recognize the needs of siblings and avoid an exclusive focus on the child with the disability or disability-related issues and activities. Children without disabilities need the freedom and the support from their families to pursue their own interests and activities. Siblings benefit when parents are open and supportive in talking with them about their brother or sister with a disability. Interventionists should consider the impact of goals and strategies on siblings while planning services, and recognize the importance of family involvement in nondisability-related activities, including leisure time.

Brothers and sisters of children with disabilities have developmental needs of their own that can be addressed by early intervention. During home visits, it is helpful for the interventionist to include siblings in ongoing activities, listening to the siblings' communications, and providing play materials for siblings as well as for the child with a disability. By actively including siblings in the visit, interventionists can help siblings understand that they are an important part of the family, worthy of the interventionist's time and attention. Resources such as the **Sibling Need and Involvement Profile** (SNIP; Fish, McCaffrey, Bush, & Piskur, 1995) and **Sibshops** (Meyer & Vadasy, 1994) are tools that can be used to explore siblings' levels of awareness, feelings, and desired roles and responsibilities. Both resources include helpful reading lists for parents, siblings, and service providers. Sibshops, which are sibling support groups offered across the country, can help children share their experiences, as well as realize that there are many other children in similar family situations (Meyer & Vadasy).

Although there is still much to learn about the brothers and sisters of children with disabilities, we do know that, given appropriate support and opportunities, sibling relationships in these families are characterized by many of the same strengths and challenges found in all other families. Brothers and sisters of children with disabilities can benefit from the expanded opportunities for role enactment and personal growth when the family system responds positively to the child with the disability. Early interventionists can help make that happen.

> Instead of focusing solely on the child with the disability, families and interventionists must recognize the needs of siblings as well.

> With the right support and opportunities, sibling relationships in families with children with disabilities mimic those found in all other families.

The Role of the Child with a Disability

Parents, siblings, grandparents, and other family members develop relationships with the child with a disability based on their understanding of who the child is and what his or her unique qualities are. The formation of a holistic view of a child, along with clear and accurate information about the disability, reduce the possibility that the child could be labeled as the "vulnerable," "needy," or "special" one in the family, and have areas of strength and potential go unrecognized. Interventionists can promote this holistic perspective by frequently engaging in conversations with family members regarding characteristics of the child that are not directly related to the disability, including child strengths, interests, and personality traits. An interventionist who cannot see beyond the child's disability cannot support a family in taking a more holistic view. Because of the daily opportunity that families have to get to know their child with a disability in multiple contexts, it is often the members of the family who naturally develop a comprehensive, holistic view of the child. Ironically, it can be the family's task to help the interventionist to see beyond the disability and appreciate the complexity of the "whole child." Finally, as with all children, children with disabilities frequently shape their own roles in their families by their interests, personalities, and talents. The unique characteristics of each child must be recognized and celebrated.

The Role of the Extended Family

Increased family mobility and an emphasis on independence rather than inter-dependence have functioned to limit extended family networks as sources of support (Santelli, Turnbull, Lerner, & Marquis, 1993). Many families, however, do continue to strongly rely on extended family members to provide emotional and practical help with child rearing. In some families, including those with young single parents or parents with multiple life stresses, grandparents may be the primary caregivers for the child with a disability. With this in mind, it is important that interventionists ask specific questions regarding the involvement of extended family members, and their attitudes and behaviors toward the child. Grandparents, aunts, uncles, and other relatives often have emotional and informational needs related to the child's disability that could be met through involvement in early intervention. Additionally, they frequently have unique perspectives on the child and can be sources of additional information for the interventionist, as well as sources of family support. All people identified as members of the family should be offered the opportunity to participate in support groups, educational activities, or IFSPs and IEPs, when such involvement is desired by the parents.

Parent Emotions, Beliefs, and Parent-to-Parent Support

The birth or diagnosis of a child with a disability is usually an unexpected life event. Family members may react in a variety of ways. Possible parental responses include denial, blame, fear, guilt, grief, withdrawal, rejection, and acceptance (Berger, 1987). Grief or mourning have often been addressed as a common response to learning that a child has a disability, due in part to cultural norms that maintain health and able-bodiness as necessary for happiness and acceptance (Powers, 1993). Grief is sometimes viewed as the result of a family's attempt to cope with the loss of the "perfect" child they anticipated during pregnancy (Patterson, 1988). It should be noted, however, that these theories about grief or chronic sorrow have been challenged by some as the result of negative and pessimistic attitudes regarding the effects of disability on the lives of children and families. Indeed, not all family members report feelings of loss, grief, or sorrow.

Family members vary in their initial response to diagnosis or birth of a child with a disability, and responses can change over time. There is no singular "correct" or permanent reaction. Services and levels of involvement that are necessary at one stage of coping or decision making may be experienced as unnecessary, intrusive, or disrespectful at another stage. For example, some parents may be highly active and involved in planning and decision-making immediately following the initial diagnosis of a disability, and later wish to alter their roles to allow them more time to focus on other aspects of their child's life. Other parents may want more time to make decisions or define their roles, gradually increasing their levels of involvement. Milestones such as self-feeding, walking, talking, and toilet training that provide a sense of accomplishment and satisfaction for family members may be delayed or never occur, renewing feelings of sadness or grief. Service providers must be careful to monitor such changes and adjust their roles accordingly. It is clear that not all families are alike, and that it is inappropriate to make assumptions about what families (or individual members of a family) are feeling or experiencing, without talking with them and listening to their communications.

Parents often form their expectations for their children based on "facts" given to them by doctors, interventionists, educators, and various other professionals. This is particularly true during infancy and early childhood. It is frequently the case, however, that unambiguous answers regarding the implications of the disability for the child's health or development are not available. These situations can be particularly difficult for families. In the past, many service providers have presented worst-case scenarios as fact in order to prepare families for what might lay ahead. Although intended to save the family pain or disappointment later, this practice can limit child outcomes and jeopardize the formation of healthy attachments in the family. Service providers must be straightforward regarding the limitations of available knowledge, and provide parents and other family members the opportunity to talk about the challenges associated with living with such uncertainty.

> For many parents of children with disabilities, other parents in similar situations are their primary source of support.

Parents of children with disabilities face all of the typical demands associated with parenting, as well as the additional challenges posed by parenting a child with a disability. The first choice of support for many parents of young children with disabilities is other parents in similar situations (Fox, Vaughn, Wyatte, & Dunlap, 2002). **Parent-to-Parent programs** began in the early 1970s to meet this need, and quickly expanded across the nation. The success of these programs is based on the personalized support to new members offered by well-trained "veteran" parents who have children with similar disabilities or who share similar life experiences (Santelli et al., 1993; Santelli, Turnbull, Marquis, & Lerner, 1995; Singer et al., 1999). The shared information and emotional support received by the family reduces isolation and supports active involvement and decision-making related to disability issues.

Natural Environments as Sources of Everyday Learning Opportunities

The role of families in the delivery of early intervention was changed dramatically by the 1997 reauthorization of IDEA. As mentioned in Chapter 1, Part C of the Individuals with Disabilities Education Act (IDEA) Amendments of 1997 states that,

> To the maximum extent appropriate, early intervention services must be provided in natural environments, including the home and community settings in which

> children without disabilities participate. . . . Services can only be provided in a set-
> ting other than a natural environment when early intervention cannot be achieved
> satisfactorily in a natural environment. [IDEA, 1997, Sec. 303.12(b)(1)(2)]

As a result of the implementation of the natural environment provision of Part C of IDEA, programs and services for infants and toddlers have shifted from a clinic-based model to a model in which services are delivered in **natural environments,** those settings where children without disabilities spend their time (e.g., the home, community programs, child care programs, and a number of other settings in which the child and family live, learn, and play).

Families may no longer spend time taking their child to different therapy settings. Rather, the intervention comes to the child. Because most young children spend large amounts of time with their families, the family becomes a primary setting for early intervention. Using a family-guided, activity-based approach, family members are seen as the constant in their child's life and work in partnership with members of the early intervention team, often guiding the team of professionals from various disciplines to work together, sharing roles and responsibilities. Team members, along with the family, collaborate to develop IFSP outcomes that can be integrated throughout the day in naturally occurring play, routines, and activities using the child's interests, favorite toys and materials. Family members and care providers implement intervention within the context of changing diapers, reading books, folding laundry, or riding in the car. Service providers serve as "coaches" to family members, helping them gain confidence and competence to meet the needs of their child with a disability.

Addressing early intervention outcomes in the natural environment requires more than a change in location. It requires providers to consider the routines, materials, activities, and people common to the child and family in order to determine the best opportunities for teaching and learning. Family routines are the activities of daily living (e.g., eating, grocery shopping, bath time, etc.) that relate to family interests and priorities. For infants and toddlers, naturally occurring events include child-initiated actions and play (e.g., climbing into cupboards to play with the pots and pans, activating the mobile on the crib), daily routines (e.g., diapering, traveling to child care, washing up), and planned activities (e.g., taking a trip to the store; Bricker & Cripe, 1992).

Play-based approaches provide opportunities for infants and toddlers to use child-initiated action routines to develop and practice skills with their family members in a positive, natural, mutually satisfying context (Cook, Tessier, & Klein, 1996). Children learn about water while playing in the bathtub, washing hands in the sink, getting a drink, splashing in a puddle, or swimming in a pool. In addition to understanding what water is, children are learning self-help skills like drinking from a cup, hand and face washing, or motor skills like walking and jumping. Early intervention providers listen to families and support them in identifying priorities and concerns, family and child preferences, comfortable routines, and when and how to embed training within routines. Families share information about the day-to-day settings and activities that are of interest to the child and family and are potential sources of learning.

Different places are sources of multiple kinds of natural learning environments, and any one learning environment is the source of multiple kinds of learning opportunities. For example, a kitchen table is a place that affords a child such activities as listening to others talk, "asking" for a drink, learning to eat with a spoon, playing with toys, "drawing" with crayons, and so forth (Dunst, Bruder, Trivette, Raab, & McLean, 2001). Many of these opportunities occur as part of daily living, child and family routines, family rituals, and family and community celebrations and traditions (Goncu, 1999). What is especially appealing about using natural environments for promoting and enhancing learning is that these sources of children's learning opportunities are literally everywhere in a child's family and community (Dunst et al., 2001).

When early intervention and early childhood practitioners use natural learning environments as sources of children's learning opportunities, a meaningful difference can be made in the lives of children and their families. Dunst, Bruder, Trivette, Raab, and McLean (1998) report that in order to do so, practitioners must "think outside of the box" and take the time to listen to families' descriptions of their home and community lives and to understand the value and importance of child participation in naturally occurring learning environments. Although the natural environments provisions of IDEA are focused on Part C, intended for children birth through age 2, there is no magical change in the way that families function when the child turns 3 that makes these interventions any less appropriate or effective. Working collaboratively with families to embed intervention activities in the ongoing daily activities of the child and family is important throughout the preschool years. These strategies are as relevant to interventionists working with children with disabilities aged 3 through 5 as they are to interventionists working under Part C.

It is important for the interventionist to work collaboratively with families throughout the preschool years.

Skills for Effective Work in Partnership with Families

The Division for Early Childhood of the Council for Exceptional Children has identified four recommended family-based practices that form the foundation for high-quality services to young children with disabilities and their families (Trivette & Dunst, 2000). The first of these, *Families and professionals share responsibility and work collaboratively*, focuses on the partnership between interventionists and families (see Box 3.1). This partnership includes developing and working toward family-identified goals and outcomes, providing information to families, and respecting the cultural and ethnic heritage of the family. The second recommendation, *Practices strengthen family functioning*, highlights practices such as family choice and decision making, building supports and resources, and working to avoid interventions that disrupt family life. The third recommendation, *Practices are individualized and flexible*, focuses on practices attuned to the priorities of different family members and builds on family values and cultural mores. The final recommendation, *Practices are strengths- and assets-based*, stresses building on the competence of families and children.

| BOX 3.1 | DEC Recommended Practices: Family-Based Practices |

Families and professionals share responsibility and work collaboratively.

F1. Family members and professionals jointly develop appropriate family-identified outcomes.

F2. Family members and professionals work together and share information routinely and collaboratively to achieve family-identified outcomes.

F3. Professionals fully and appropriately provide relevant information so parents can make informed choices and decisions.

F4. Professionals use helping styles that promote shared family/professional responsibility in achieving family-identified outcomes.

F5. Family/professionals' relationship building is accomplished in ways that are responsive to cultural, language, and other family characteristics.

Practices strengthen family functioning.

F6. Practices, supports, and resources provide families with participatory experiences and opportunities promoting choice and decision making.

F7. Practices, supports, and resources support family participation in obtaining desired resources and supports to strengthen parenting competence and confidence.

F8. Intrafamily, informal, community, and formal supports and resources (e.g., respite care) are used to achieve desired outcomes.

F9. Supports and resources provide families with information, competency-enhancing experiences, and participatory opportunities to strengthen family functioning and promote parenting knowledge and skills.

F10. Supports and resources are mobilized in ways that are supportive and do not disrupt family and community life.

Practices are individualized and flexible.

F11. Resources and supports are provided in ways that are flexible, individualized, and tailored to the child's and family's preferences and styles, and promote well-being.

F12. Resources and supports match each family member's identified priorities and preferences (e.g., mother's, father's may be different).

F13. Practices, supports, and resources are responsive to the cultural, ethnic, racial, language, and socioeconomic characteristics and preferences of families and their communities.

F14. Practices, supports, and resources incorporate family beliefs and values into decisions, intervention plans, and resources and support mobilization.

Practices are strengths- and assets-based.

F15. Family and child strengths and assets are used as a basis for engaging families in participatory experiences supporting parenting competence and confidence.

F16. Practices, supports, and resources build on existing parenting competence and confidence.

F17. Practices, supports, and resources promote the family's and professional's acquisition of new knowledge and skills to strengthen competence and confidence.

Source: From "Recommended Practices in Family-Based Practices," by C. M. Trivette and C. J. Dunst, in *DEC Recommended Practices in Early Intervention/Early Childhood Special Education* (pp. 45–46), by S. Sandall, M. E. McLean, and B. J. Smith, 2000, Denver, CO: The Division for Early Childhood of the Council for Exceptional Children. Used with permission.

To implement these recommended practices, interventionists need skills that build on the family-centered values discussed earlier and include demonstrating respect, being realistic, using good listening and communication skills, helping the family to build natural support networks, being sensitive, forming partnerships and collaborations, and being flexible.

Demonstrating Respect

Respect for the family is the hallmark of all positive and effective intervention efforts. It is created and sustained by a fundamental belief in the importance of families and trust in the ability of families to make the most appropriate choices for the lives of their children. Early interventionists demonstrate respect when they ask families what they see as priority areas for intervention before offering an opinion. They offer their own opinions in a way that allows parents to comfortably disagree (McWilliam & Winton, 1990). Service providers who respect families honor their decisions, lifestyles, values, beliefs, and efforts to care for their children, even when this entails supporting choices the service provider would not have made. Interventionists must not only *feel* respect toward the families they serve, but they also must actively *demonstrate* that respect in their interactions with family members and in the way they talk about the family to others.

> Demonstrating respect is the hallmark of all effective intervention efforts.

> Interventionists must actively demonstrate respect in their interactions with family members and when discussing the family with others.

Being Realistic

It is easy for interventionists to forget that parents have other roles and responsibilities in addition to parenting a child with a disability. The day-to-day demands of rearing children and managing careers, finances, and households, as well as meeting other family responsibilities, can sometimes be overwhelming. Even more is demanded of parents of children with disabilities than is demanded of parents of typically developing children, and it is demanded for a longer period. Parents of children with disabilities are often expected to be "super parents," who attend meetings, work in their children's classrooms, advocate for their children's rights and needs, implement home-based intervention programs, collect daily data, attend workshops, support other parents, plan and implement IFSPs, IEPs, and home-based therapy programs, and transport their child to see doctors, therapists, educators, and other service providers.

Most families welcome the opportunity to participate in planning meetings, obtain multiple services for their child, and implement home-based intervention plans. For some families, however, these extra parenting tasks become overwhelming. When families are overburdened with intervention plans they cannot possibly implement, or when such plans have negative impacts on other areas of family functioning, members often feel guilty and discouraged and may avoid contact with the service provider they feel they have failed. Families that decline or fail to complete services may be labeled inappropriately by interventionists as "resistant" or thought to care less for their child. It is important to consider the many aspects of a family's day-to-day life when suggesting services or levels of involvement. Being realistic

The intervention-
ist must work
with the family to
design strategies
that are realistic
and can be easily
implemented by
the family.

Service providers
must be open and
sincere when
communicating
with families and
in trying to under-
stand their needs
and concerns.

means working together with the family to design intervention strategies that make sense and can be easily implemented in the everyday life of the family.

Using Good Listening and Communication Skills

Listening skills are critical for successful work with families. To be effective, service providers must want to hear what family members have to say and be truly interested in understanding each family's unique needs and concerns. While family members are talking, the provider should concentrate fully on what they are saying. This means paying careful attention to *what is being communicated and being sensitive to both verbal and nonverbal cues.* It is often helpful for the provider to repeat what she hears family members saying so that they have the opportunity to correct or clarify the provider's interpretation. Whenever possible, service providers should make notes after, rather than during, conversations, and review any notes with the family. Ample time should be allowed for talks to occur. Silences in conversation should not be filled because important information is often revealed after a period of silence. The provider should ask herself, "Do I really listen to families? Do I accept and respect what family members tell me, or am I actively trying to influence their beliefs or ideas?"

Service providers should be keenly sensitive to how their negative attitudes or disagreements with a family may be communicated, either directly or in more subtle ways. Such thoughts can undermine family confidence and responsibility, causing members to feel inadequate or defensive and seriously limiting the extent to which services will be used effectively. Helping professionals who always keep the overall goal of family empowerment in mind and who derive personal rewards from seeing families become more competent and self-sustaining are most likely to provide the most appropriate and effective services (Dunst & Trivette, 1994).

The provision of services to families of children with disabilities often necessitates the involvement of numerous service providers, many of whom have access to confidential and intimate information about the families. Boundary conflicts can arise between families and the service delivery system when service providers fail to recognize the roles and rights of all family members, or when professionals intrude too far into the lives of families. For example, in professional attempts to conduct family assessments, the parents of children with disabilities are sometimes asked very personal questions about their marital satisfaction and functioning, financial status, and family relationships. Such assessments can be experienced by the family as intrusive and unhelpful unless approached with sensitivity and a clear statement of purpose (Slentz & Bricker, 1992). Asking questions about family coping and marital adjustment is often unnecessary and can send a message that the interventionist believes that because the child has a disability, the parents must have problems as well (Slentz & Bricker, 1992). On the other hand, some families want to share this personal information with the interventionist. Sensitive communication and good listening skills allow the interventionist to understand the family's feelings and to be responsive to their desired level of disclosure.

Helping the Family Build Natural Support Networks

Families and their children live within neighborhoods and communities. They have many social connections, including religious organizations, work, clubs and civic organizations, and recreational settings. Bronfenbrenner (1979) developed an ecological model of human development that has had a major impact on public policy and on services for children with disabilities and their families. The **ecological model** stresses the important developmental influences exerted by the settings in which children and families live, and by the larger contexts in which those settings are embedded. It is possible for families, with the support of early interventionists, to use people and organizations in the family's ecology to provide important social and pragmatic support. In the disability field, organizing people already present in the family's environment to help the family achieve their goals is referred to as **natural support**. Members of a natural support network are not paid. They provide help and assistance from a sense of community and from a caring relationship they have developed with the family (Nisbet, 1992).

> Bronfenbrenner's theory claims that children's development is influenced by the settings in which children and families live.

It is important that early interventionists encourage the family's use of natural support networks when available, such as friends, neighbors, community or church resources, or extended family relationships. Involvement with these sources of support can enhance a sense of connection and community, normalize the need for support as something common to all families, and decrease reliance on paid service provision (Dunst & Trivette, 1994). Some families naturally develop these support networks with little assistance from the interventionist. For other families, who may be more isolated from their communities, the skill of the interventionist will be called upon to invite community members into the life of the family to provide emotional support (such as that described earlier from Parent-to-Parent programs) and pragmatic support (such as transportation or babysitting).

> Natural support is support provided by unpaid people who are present in the family's extended family, neighborhood, and community.

Being Sensitive

Being sensitive to families includes carefully listening and then responding in a way that is consistent with the cues and messages that families are sending. Interventionists must communicate a sincere sense of caring, warmth, and encouragement. Support is much easier to accept when it is offered by someone who is perceived to have a positive attitude and to be genuinely interested in helping (Dunst & Trivette, 1994). The interventionist must listen to herself talk to the family, making sure that her words communicate a strengths-based approach that is positive toward the family and toward the child, and focuses on assets rather than on deficits or problems.

> Families are more likely to accept support offered by someone who is genuinely interested in helping.

Fox et al. (2002) interviewed parents of young children with disabilities receiving services related to problem behaviors, and found that the professionals described as being the most helpful to the families were those who provided support and encouragement. Encouragement can be communicated by helping the family identify and successfully solve small problems or achieve short-term goals before moving on to tackle more difficult or long-range issues. Such successes bolster the self-esteem and confidence of family members and increase their investment in the intervention process (Dunst & Trivette, 1994).

It is important that providers envision what life is like for the families (Bruder, 2000). They might consider a scenario such as this: You missed an IEP or IFSP meeting because your car wouldn't start. Earlier in the day, your babysitter canceled and you have no option but to take your three young children to the meeting. Now you have no transportation. You are tired, one of your children is crying, and you really don't understand what this meeting is about and feel rather intimidated by the group of professionals who will probably attend. Wouldn't you be tempted to just stay home?

Thinking about life from the point of view of the family often helps interventionists to identify support needs and to put a positive frame on the behavior of the family. Sensitivity is based on understanding, and understanding is based on a vision of the world as experienced by the family.

To gain full perspective, an interventionist should spend time caring for a child with a disability and the child's family.

It is often a powerful experience for interventionists to spend a day (and a night) caring for the child with a disability and his or her siblings or to accompany the family throughout a typical day that might include a trip to the doctor or to the Social Security office. After this type of personal experience, the provider's point of view may never be the same. Looking at family life from the outside is a very different view than that obtained when walking beside the family, experiencing what their life is really like.

Reaching Out—Forming Partnerships and Collaborations

Early intervention is not a one-person or single-agency endeavor. In addition to forming partnerships with families, interventionists must develop collaborations with other community agencies and resources. Early intervention services often are delivered by teams whose members are employed by different agencies or departments. Team members must be able to work together with mutual respect to implement family-centered early intervention.

Knowledge of available community resources and the skills to interact with other professionals are two major requirements needed by interventionists.

Developing community partnerships is especially critical for families with complex living situations. Some families served by early interventionists are characterized by disorganization, multiple stressors, and severely limited resources (Baumeister, Kupstas, & Klindworth, 1992). These families may reside in substandard housing in neighborhoods where the crime rate is high and hope for the future is low. An interventionist may suspect, or may know, that a family is engaging in child abuse or neglect; such knowledge requires appropriate reporting and subsequent renegotiation of relationships with family members. Other families may be impacted by substance abuse problems, high levels of family conflict, homelessness, serious mental health problems in a parent, entanglement with the legal system, or extreme poverty. Thompson (1992) commented that "Tackling problems associated with poverty is not a challenge for the faint of heart" (p. 9). Complex family issues such as those described above are not challenges to be handled alone. Interventionists must be familiar with the resources available in their communities and have the skills necessary to interact with other professionals and agency personnel to obtain the supports and services that are needed for the children and families that they serve.

Being Flexible—Doing Whatever It Takes

The *Statement in Support of Families and Their Children*, published by the Center on Human Policy (1987), stated that family services should be "flexible, individualized, and designed to meet the diverse needs of families." This policy introduced the principle of "whatever it takes," representing the idea that interventionists working with families must be creative and adaptable, not limiting their actions or services to those prescribed by the service system. Implementing family-centered early intervention requires a willingness to create positive visions for the future with families and to listen to and share their dreams. The next step is to do whatever it takes to join in partnership with families to work toward achieving their goals for themselves, and for their young children with disabilities.

> Implementing family-centered early intervention requires a willingness to create positive visions for the future with families and to listen to and share their dreams.

Summary

This chapter has provided an overview of key issues for the early interventionist to consider when working with young children with special needs. In one sense, it is natural for service providers to care deeply about the families and children they serve and to have their own values and beliefs about what is best for them. As mentioned in several sections of this chapter, however, there will be times when family choices, goals, practices, or values will be different from those of the professional. This is not undesirable and, in fact, should be expected when a family is actively involved in early intervention services. Further, how the early interventionist responds to these situations will contribute significantly to the strength of the family-centered services (e.g., are the wishes of the family being honored?).

Across the nation, states are struggling to turn the promise of family-centered intervention into reality for families and young children. We have made much progress, but there is still much work to be done. Progress toward this goal will be enhanced when a new generation of early intervention professionals are trained who embrace family-centered values, appreciate family diversity, understand family systems, are sensitive to parent emotions and beliefs, support learning in the natural environments experienced by families, and have the skills to work in partnership with families.

Review Questions and Discussion Points

1. Why do you think it is so important for families to be in decision-making roles concerning the early intervention services received by their children with disabilities?
2. How would you go about helping parents become more responsive to their child with a disability using relationship-based early intervention? How could you implement this intervention while still maintaining a family-centered, partnership perspective?
3. How does your own cultural background influence how you interact with families? Have you had an experience where cultural differences caused you to judge a family negatively because of a

culturally based practice that was new to you? What did you do when this happened? Was your response successful in helping you to understand the family's point of view?

4. Can you think of other skills, not mentioned in this chapter, that are important for early interventionists who are implementing family-centered early intervention? What are those skills?

5. Have you had a particularly successful experience in working collaboratively with a family to address a problem or to reach a goal? What about the interaction caused it to be so successful?

Recommended Resources

Family and Disability Web Sites

Beach Center on Disability
http://www.beachcenter.org

Center on Disability and Community Inclusion; Family Support, Self-Determination, & Disability Training Curriculum
http://www.uvm.edu/_cdci/programs/familysupport

Family Support America
http://www.familysupportamerica.org

Family Village
http://www.familyvillage.wisc.edu

The Fathers Network
http://www.fathersnetwork.org

MUMS National Parent-to-Parent Network
http://www.netnet.net/mums

Parents Helping Parents
http://www.php.com

Sibling Support Project
http://www.thearc.org/siblingsupport

Books and Other Resources

Covert, S. B. (1995). *Whatever it takes! Excellence in family support: When families experience a disability.* St. Augustine, FL: Training Resource Network.

Family Support America. (1996). *Guidelines for family support practice.* Chicago: Author.

Jeppson, E. S., & Thomas, J. (1999). *Essential allies—Families as advisors.* Bethesda, MD: Institute for Family-Centered Care.

McWilliam, P. J., & Winton, P. (1990). *Brass tacks: A self-rating of family-centered practices in early intervention.* Chapel Hill: University of North Carolina, Frank Porter Graham Child Development Center.

Meyer, D. J., & Vadasy, P. F. (1994). *Sibshops: Workshops for siblings of children with special needs.* Baltimore: Brookes.

Pooley, L. E. (Ed.). *Learning to be partners: An introductory training program for family support staff.* Pittsburgh, PA: University of Pittsburgh, Family Resource Coalition of America.

Yuan, S. (2001). *Family support, self-determination and disability—Teacher's manual.* Burlington, VT: Center on Disability and Community Inclusion.

References

Baumeister, A. A., Kupstas, F., & Klindworth, L. M. (1992). The new morbidity. In T. Thompson & S. C. Hupp (Eds.), *Saving children at risk: Poverty and disabilities* (pp. 143–177). Newbury Park, CA: Sage.

Beach Center on Families and Disability. (1997). Family-centered service delivery. *Families and Disability Newsletter, 8*(2), 1–3.

Beckman, P. (1991). Comparison of mothers' and fathers' perceptions of the effect of young children with and without disabilities. *American Journal on Mental Retardation, 95,* 585–595.

Berger, E. H. (1987). *Parents as partners in education: The school and home working together* (2nd ed.). Upper Saddle River, NJ: Merrill/Prentice Hall.

Boyce, G. C., Behl, D., Mortensen, L., & Akers, J. (1991). Child characteristics, family demographics and family processes: Their effects on the stress experienced by families of children with disabilities. *Counseling Psychology Quarterly, 4,* 273–288.

Bricker, D., & Cripe, J. W. (1992). *An activity-based approach to early intervention.* Baltimore: Brookes.

Broderick, C., & Smith, J. (1979). The general systems approach to the family. In W. R. Burr, R. Hill, F. I. Nye, & I. L. Reiss (Eds.), *Contemporary theories about the family* (Vol. 2, pp. 112–129). New York: Free Press.

Bronfenbrenner, U. (1979). *The ecology of human development: Experiments by nature and design.* Cambridge, MA: Harvard University Press.

Bruder, M. B. (2000). Family-centered early intervention: Clarifying our values for the new millennium. *Topics in Early Childhood Special Education, 20,* 105–115.

Burt, M. R., Aron, L. Y., Douglas, T., Valente, J., Lee, E., Iwen, B. (1999). *Homelessness: Programs and the people they serve.* Washington, DC: Interagency Council on the Homeless.

Center on Human Policy. (1987). *Statement in support of families and their children.* Syracuse, New York: Author.

Cook, R. E., Tessier, A., & Klein, M. D. (1996). *Adapting early childhood curricula for children in inclusive settings* (4th ed.) Upper Saddle River, NJ: Merrill/Prentice Hall.

Covert, S. B. (1995). *Whatever it takes! Excellence in family support: When families experience a disability.* St. Augustine, FL: Training Resource Network.

Dunst, C. J., & Trivette, C. M. (1994). What is effective helping? In C. J. Dunst, C. M. Trivette, & A. G. Deal (Eds.), *Supporting and strengthening families.* Vol. 1: *Methods, strategies and practices* (pp. 162–170). Cambridge, MA: Brookline Books.

Dunst, C. J., Bruder, M. B., Trivette, C. M., Raab, M., & McLean, M. (1998, May). Increasing children's learning opportunities through families and communities. *Early Childhood Research Institute: Year 2 Progress Report.* Asheville, NC: Orleans Hawks Puckett Institute.

Dunst, C. J., Bruder, M. B., Trivette, C. M., Raab, M., & McLean, M. (2001). Natural learning opportunities for infants, toddlers, and preschoolers. *Young Exceptional Children, 4,* 18–25.

Fialka, J. (2001). The dance of partnership: Why do my feet hurt? *Young Exceptional Children, 4,* 21–27.

Fish, T., McCaffrey, D., Bush, K., & Piskur, S. (1995). *SNIP: Sibling Need and Involvement Profile.* Columbus: Ohio State University, Nisonger Center.

Forest, M., & Pearpoint, J. (1992). Families, friends, and circles. In J. Nisbet (Ed.), *Natural supports in school, at work, and in the community for people with severe disabilities* (pp. 65–86). Baltimore: Brookes.

Fox, L., Vaughn, B. J., Wyatte, M. L., & Dunlap, G. (2002). "We can't expect other people to understand": Family perspectives on problem behavior, *Exceptional Children, 68,* 437–450.

Fujiura, G. T., & Yamaki, K. (1997). Analysis of ethnic variations in developmental disability prevalence and household economic status. *Mental Retardation, 35,* 286–294.

Goncu, A. (Ed.). (1999). *Children's engagement in the world: Sociocultural perspectives.* Cambridge, England: Cambridge University Press.

Hanson, M. J., Beckman, P. J., Horn, E., Marquart, J., Sandall, S. R., Greig, D., et al. (2000). Entering preschool: Family and professional experiences in this transition process. *Journal of Early Intervention, 23,* 279–293.

IDEA (1997). IDEA final regulations—34 CFR Part 303, Early Intervention Program for Infants and Toddlers with disabilities.

Kelly, J. F., & Barnard, K. E. (1999). Parent education within a relationship-focused model. *Topics in Early Childhood Special Education, 19,* 151–157.

Kelly, J. F., Buehlman, K., & Caldwell, K. (2000). Training personnel to promote quality parent-child interaction in families who are homeless. *Topics in Early Childhood Special Education, 20,* 174–185.

Krauss, M. W. (1993). Child-related and parenting stress: Similarities and differences between mothers and fathers of children with disabilities. *American Journal on Mental Retardation, 97,* 393–404.

Lambie, R., & Daniels-Mohring, D. (1993). *Family systems within educational contexts.* Denver, CO: Love.

Leung, P., & Wright, T. J. (1993). Introduction: Minorities with disabilities. In T. J. Wright & P. Leung (Eds.). *Meeting the unique needs of minorities with disabilities: A report to the president and the Congress* (pp. 11–17). Washington, DC.: National Council on Disability.

Lynch, E. W., & Hanson, M. J. (1998). Steps in the right direction. In E. W. Lynch & M. J. Hanson, *Developing cross-cultural competence: A guide for working with children and their families* (pp. 491–512). Baltimore: Brookes.

Mahoney, G., Boyce, G., Fewell, R., Spiker, D., & Wheeden, C. A. (1998). The relationship of parent-child interaction to the effectiveness of early intervention services for at-risk children and children with disabilities. *Topics in Early Childhood Special Education, 18,* 5–17.

McBride, S. L., Brotherson, M. J., Joanning, H., Whiddon, D., & Demmitt, S. (1993). Implementation of family-centered services: Perceptions of families and professionals. *Journal of Early Intervention, 17,* 414–430.

McWilliam, P. J., Tocci, L., & Harbin, G. L. (1998). Family-centered services: Service providers' discourse and behavior. *Topics in Early Childhood Special Education, 18,* 206–221.

McWilliam, P. J., & Winton, P. (1990). *Brass tacks: A self-rating of family-centered practices in early intervention.* Chapel Hill: University of North Carolina, Frank Porter Graham Child Development Center.

Meyer, D. J., & Vadasy, P. F. (1994). *Sibshops: Workshops for siblings of children with special needs.* Baltimore: Brookes.

Minuchin, S. (1974). *Families and family therapy.* Cambridge, MA: Harvard University Press.

Morsink, C. V., Thomas, C. C., & Correa, V. I. (1991). *Interactive teaming: Consultation and collaboration in special programs.* New York: Macmillan.

Nihira, K., Mink, I. T., & Meyers, C. E. (1981). Relationship between home environment and school adjustment of TMR children. *American Journal of Mental Deficiency, 86,* 8–15.

Nisbet, J. (1992). Introduction. In J. Nisbet (Ed.), *Natural supports in school, at work, and in the community for people with severe disabilities* (pp. 1–10). Baltimore: Brookes.

Patterson, J. M. (1988). Chronic illness in children and the impact on families. In C. S. Chilman, E. W. Nunnally, & F. M. Cox (Eds.), *Chronic illness and disability* (pp. 69–107). Beverly Hills, CA: Sage.

Pearl, L. (1993). Providing family-centered early intervention. In W. Brown, S. K. Thurman, & L. Pearl (Eds.), *Family centered early intervention with infants and toddlers: Innovative cross-disciplinary approaches* (pp. 81–101). Baltimore: Brookes.

Powers, L. E. (1993). Disability and grief: From tragedy to challenge. In G. H. S. Singer & L. E. Powers (Eds.), *Families, disability, and empowerment:*

Active coping strategies for family interventions (pp. 119–150). Baltimore: Brookes.

Santelli, B., Turnbull, A., Lerner, E., & Marquis, J. (1993). Parent to Parent programs: A unique form of mutual support for families of persons with disabilities. In G. H. S. Singer & L. E. Powers (Eds.), *Families, disability, and empowerment: Active coping strategies for family interventions* (pp. 27–58). Baltimore: Brookes.

Santelli, B., Turnbull, A., Marquis, J., & Lerner, E. (1995). Parent to Parent programs: A unique form of mutual support. *Infants and Young Children, 8,* 53–62.

Shonkoff, J. P., Hauser-Cram, P., Krauss, M. W., & Upshur, C. (1992). Development of infants with disabilities and their families: Implications for theory and service delivery. *Monographs of the Society for Research in Child Development, 57*(6; Serial No. 230).

Singer, G. H. S., Marquis, J., Powers, L. K., Blanchard, L., Divenere, N., Santelli, B., et al. (1999). A multisite evaluation of Parent to Parent programs for parents of children with disabilities. *Journal of Early Intervention, 22,* 217–229.

Slentz, K. L., & Bricker, D. (1992). Family-guided assessment for IFSP development: Jumping off the family assessment bandwagon. *Journal of Early Intervention, 16,* 11–19.

Song, Y., & Lu, H. (2002). *Early childhood poverty: A statistical profile.* New York: Columbia University, National Center for Childhood Poverty.

Stoneman, Z. (1998). Research on children with mental retardation and their siblings: Contributions of developmental theory and etiology. In J. A. Burack, R. M. Hodapp, & E. Zigler (Eds.), *Handbook of mental retardation and development* (pp. 669–692) Cambridge, England: Cambridge University Press.

Stoneman, Z. (2001). Supporting positive sibling relationships during childhood. *Mental Retardation and Developmental Disabilities Research Reviews, 7,* 134–142.

Stoneman, Z., & Brody, G. H. (1993). Sibling relations in the family context. In Z. Stoneman & P. W. Berman (Eds.), *The effects of mental retardation, disability, and illness on sibling relationships* (pp. 3–30). Baltimore: Brookes.

Thompson, T. (1992). For the sake of our children: Poverty and disabilities. In T. Thompson & S. C. Hupp (Eds.), *Saving children at risk: Poverty and disabilities* (pp. 3–10). Newbury Park, CA: Sage.

Trivette, C. M., & Dunst, C. J. (2000). Recommended practices in family-based practices. In S. Sandall, M. E. McLean, & B. J. Smith, *DEC recommended practices in early intervention/early childhood special education* (pp. 39–46). Denver, CO: Division for Early Childhood of the Council for Exceptional Children.

Turbiville, V. P., & Marquis, J. G. (2001). Father participation in early education programs. *Topics in Early Childhood Special Education, 21,* 223–231.

U.S. Census Bureau. (2001). America's families and living arrangements. Washington, DC: U.S. Department of Commerce.

von Bertalanffy, L. V. (1968). *General systems theory.* New York: George Brazilles.

Walker, S., Asbury, C., Maholmes, V., & Rackley, R. (1991). Prevalence, distribution and impact of disability among ethnic minorities. In S. Walker, F. Z. Belgrave, R. W. Nicholls, & K. A. Turner (Eds.), *Future frontiers in the employment of minority persons with disabilities* (pp. 10–24). Washington, DC: President's Committee on Employment of People with Disabilities.

Wayman, K. L., Lynch, E. W., & Hanson, M. J. (1990). Home-based early childhood services: Cultural sensitivity in a family systems approach. *Topics in Early Childhood Special Education, 10*(4), 56–75.

Werner, E. E., & Smith, R. S. (1982). *Vulnerable but invincible—A longitudinal study of resilient children and youth.* New York: McGraw-Hill.

Werner, E. E., & Smith, R. S. (1992). *Overcoming the odds—High risk children from birth to adulthood.* Ithaca, NY: Cornell University Press.

Willoughby, J. C., & Glidden, L. M. (1995). Fathers helping out: Shared child care and marital satisfaction of parents of children with disabilities. *American Journal on Mental Retardation, 99,* 399–406.

PART II

Principles of Assessment and Intervention

CHAPTER 4

Assessment of Young Children: Standards, Stages, and Approaches

CHAPTER 5

Intervention

CHAPTER 6

Technology for Assessment and Intervention

4

Assessment of Young Children: Standards, Stages, and Approaches

Rebecca Edmondson Pretzel and Jennifer Hiemenz

Chapter Outline

- Current Standards for the Assessment Process
- Stages of Assessment
- Team Approaches and Typologies
- Considerations for the Assessment of Young Children

Joey

*M*rs. Nelson glanced over at Joey, her 34-month-old son, as they drove to the Developmental Center for his reevaluation for transition to the preschool program at the local elementary school. She couldn't help but think how different it felt going to this evaluation as opposed to his initial one when he was just 18 months old. She had been so nervous and scared, and really had no idea of what to expect. Mrs. Nelson remembered her early concerns that Joey was slower to sit, walk, and talk than her other two boys had been. She had talked to Joey's pediatrician about her concerns when Joey was 9 months old, and he had suggested that she wait until he was about a year and a half to see if he would catch up. When he still was not walking or using single words by that age, the pediatrician referred Joey to the Developmental Center for a comprehensive interdisciplinary evaluation. Mrs. Nelson had been exhausted after providing the team members with the information they needed, but she had realized how well she really knew her child and the important role she played in the assessment process. That evaluation, although quite difficult for both Mrs. Nelson and Joey, not only confirmed her concerns that he had delays in some areas but also helped her access numerous intervention services for him. Through the recommended center-based preschool program, Joey had been able to receive speech, occupational, and related educational services. His teacher monitored his developmental progress by assessing his skills every 4 to 6 months, and everyone was delighted with the gains he made. Even though Joey was still behind other children his age, Mrs. Nelson was comforted by the knowledge that he continued to make progress and enjoyed his classroom activities. As she arrived at the center, Mrs. Nelson felt a small twinge of nervousness because she knew she would once again hear about Joey's needs; but she also knew that the team would see Joey's strengths and appreciate the progress he had made.

Assessment is an ongoing, goal-oriented, problem-solving process.

Assessment is "a process designed to deepen understanding of a child's competencies and resources, and of the caregiving and learning environments most likely to help a child make fullest use of his or her developmental potential. Assessment should be an ongoing, collaborative process of systematic observation and analysis. This process involves formulating questions, gathering information, sharing observations, and making interpretations in order to form new questions" (Greenspan & Meisels, 1996, p. 11). More specific to the field of early childhood education, assessment is a process that uses various measures and techniques. It is a variable process that depends on the questions being asked, the type of challenges encountered by the child and family, and myriad social, developmental, and contextual factors. Thurlow and Ysseldyke (1979) defined *assessment* from an educational perspective as "a data-gathering process for the purpose of decision making." In this sense, assessment applies to all decision-making processes from the earliest concern about development through the ongoing determination points about a child's progress and program.

This chapter provides an overview of the complex process of early childhood assessment. In addition to current standards that regulate assessment in early childhood, this chapter discusses the different stages of the assessment process, including screening and specific components to be considered in a comprehensive evaluation, a variety of assessment approaches, and commonly used assessment techniques and measures. The importance of assessment-intervention linkages is also stressed, particularly in relation to current standards of practice. The chapter concludes with specific considerations for the assessment of young children with special needs. Although it is beyond the scope of this chapter to provide a comprehensive review of early childhood assessment measures (many of these measures will be described in subsequent chapters), it focuses on the standards for assessment and the specific approaches that can be employed. An understanding of these aspects of assessment and of child development across the various domains described in this text is far more useful to the early interventionist than is being able to identify the latest tests.

The early interventionist must understand the various assessment standards and approaches that are available.

Current Standards for the Assessment Process

Many legal mandates have been initiated over the past several decades that have contributed to the evolution of the assessment process for young children with special needs. Specifically, the Education for All Handicapped Children Act amendments (P.L. 99-457, 1986), later renamed the Individuals with Disabilities Education Act (IDEA, P.L. 102-119, 1998), and the previously reauthorized version of IDEA (P.L. 105-17, 1997–1998), have provided critical guidelines for the identification, assessment, and treatment of young children with special needs. In addition to these legal initiatives, several professional organizations have asserted a number of standards for assessment and treatment in the early childhood domain. Organizations such as the American Speech-Language-Hearing Association (ASHA; 1990), the National Association for the Education of Young Children (NAEYC; 1990; currently being revised), the National Association of School Psychologists (1999), and the Division for Early Childhood of the Council for Exceptional Children (1993, 2002) have offered specific statements pertaining to the assessment and treatment practices for young children with special needs. For example, NAEYC (2002) provided the following on assessment practices: "Information gained from assessments . . . should be used to improve practices and services and should not be used to rank, sort, or penalize young children."

In addition, the Division for Early Childhood (Neisworth & Bagnato, 2000) has recommended specific practices for assessment under five broad principles:

1. Professionals and families collaborate in planning and implementing assessment.
2. Assessment is individualized and appropriate for the child and family.
3. Assessment provides useful information for intervention.
4. Professionals share information in respectful and useful ways.
5. Professionals meet legal and procedural requirements *and* meet recommended practice guidelines.

Neisworth and Bagnato (1996) have distilled these position statements, in conjunction with their perspective of ongoing assessment models and practices, to reflect four major assessment standards: treatment utility, social validity, convergent assessment, and consensual validity. Although these standards seem quite reasonable, it is likely that they have not yet been fully implemented across all early childhood assessment settings to date.

Treatment Utility

One of the major considerations in the assessment process should be the **treatment utility;** that is, the usefulness of the measure or approach to guide intervention and educational planning (Bagnato, Neisworth, & Munson, 1997). Many of the traditional types of assessment strategies that have been applied to preschool as well as school-aged children have yielded little information useful for program planning and specific treatment strategies. Although traditional tools, such as formal cognitive measures, might be a component of a child's evaluation in terms of making a diagnosis or establishing eligibility, they should be augmented routinely with other measures that are more sensitive to treatment utility.

> Treatment utility refers to the usefulness of the scale and its findings for intervention planning.

Social Validity

The second standard, **social validity,** refers to the perceived value, acceptability, and appropriateness of the assessment. Several key questions should be asked in relation to this standard, such as "Is the assessment viewed as valuable for the specific situational factors presented by a child and his family?" and "Are the assessment methods acceptable to the participants?" Many of the items found on typical early childhood assessment measures require a child to perform tasks that represent isolated skills, but the tasks themselves have little validity with respect to that child's daily functioning. For example, whether or not a child can complete a pegboard may be an important normative finding (i.e., Can the child perform this task at the same level as other children of the same age?), but it may or may not relate to why the child is having trouble with buttoning, zipping, and other functional activities in his daily life. Social validity considerations may also increase the probability that the family and other professionals will become more involved in the assessment, treatment, and monitoring processes.

> Social validity refers to the value and appropriateness of an assessment method.

> Does the assessment task relate to activities within the child's daily routine?

Convergent Assessment

In tandem with the legal mandate that treatment planning not be based on a single assessment procedure, **convergent assessment** is critical to synthesize information collected from multiple sources and situations using a variety of methods. The exact methods by which this information is gathered are less critical than the key concern that the assessment process involve multiple sources (McLean & Odom, 1993), such as parents, teachers, and other professionals. The subsequent pooling of information offers a more comprehensive and valid picture of the child's strengths and needs across settings. As a result, it provides for a firmer foundation upon which to make diagnostic and programmatic decisions, and it establishes multiple mechanisms for monitoring development. This latter advantage is important in that it necessarily requires involvement on the part of the family and others; convergence assessment values and encourages their participation throughout this process.

Consensual Validity

The final standard, **consensual validity,** reflects the need to reach assessment decisions via consensus by the team members. This generally is much easier said than done. Although the general intent of multidisciplinary teams is to serve the best interests of the child and family, sometimes this intent can become clouded by problems in the team's group dynamics. Problems can occur, such as one professional not being able to communicate clearly to another professional because of discipline-specific jargon (i.e., no common language), no common assessment tools (i.e., their "measuring sticks" are different), a lack of clear leadership, an overpowering of one discipline over another, and little collaboration. Each of these can interfere with the mission of the team—to collaboratively determine the child's developmental and educational needs and link them to an appropriate plan of intervention. Although a number of assessment models have been proposed to address issues of consensual validity, such as the System to Plan Early Childhood Services (SPECS; Bagnato & Neisworth, 1990), the universal application of these models has not yet been achieved.

Stages of Assessment

As noted in the vignette at the beginning of this chapter, assessment is an ongoing and continuous process. In early childhood intervention, there are four major assessment stages that occur prior to and throughout the delivery of services. These stages include (1) early identification, (2) comprehensive evaluation, (3) program planning and implementation, and (4) program evaluation. Figure 4.1 illustrates these stages in a decision-point format.

Stage 1: Early Identification

A primary goal in early childhood intervention is to identify children who may be eligible for services as soon as possible. Identification in early childhood can occur at any point from conception through the first years of formal schooling and typically

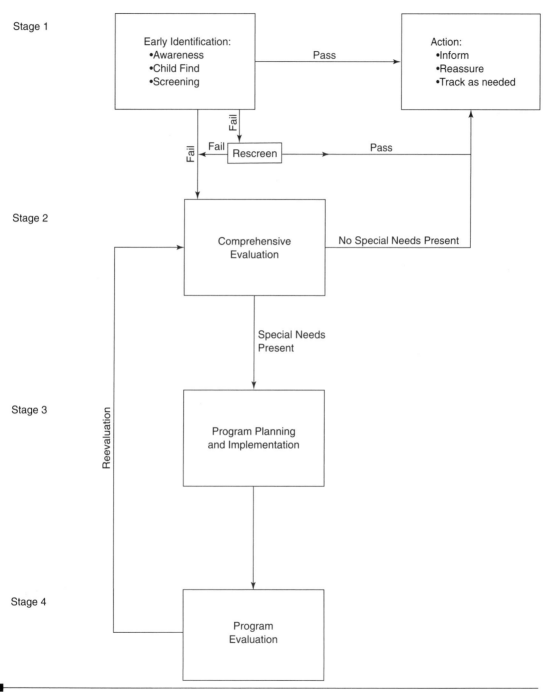

FIGURE 4.1 Stages of the assessment process

involves any procedure that leads to the identification of a child with special needs. Early identification is mandated by the Individuals with Disabilities Education Act and is usually under the jurisdiction of the lead agency, often the public schools. This process includes two major activities: Child Find and Screening.

Child Find. Federal legislation mandates that early intervention programs conduct comprehensive and coordinated activities in order to identify children as early as possible (Harbin, McWilliam, & Gallagher, 2000). **Child Find** is a community-wide effort involving many agencies that have contact with infants and young children. In this regard one key Child Find function is to increase public awareness in an effort to identify children who potentially may be eligible for intervention services.

Public Awareness. Awareness is one of the initial components of early identification and refers to the various methods (e.g., television, radio, pamphlets, newspaper releases) used to alert the public and professional communities about typical and atypical early childhood development. This involves organized efforts to inform and influence the public, especially community leaders and families, about programs for young children who have or are at risk for disabilities. Its purpose is to find children in need of special services and make families and the community at large aware of the referral procedures to access these programs. Awareness efforts not only promote support for intervention programs but also encourage close observation of the quality of these services.

Screening. The second major activity of early intervention is screening. In addition to increasing public awareness, Child Find activities are designed to locate infants, toddlers, and preschool children who will participate in a formal **screening** process to determine their need for a more comprehensive evaluation. As Lichtenstein and Ireton (1991) have noted, "The term screening technically refers to the process of selecting out for further study those high-risk individuals whose apparent problems might require special attention or intervention" (p. 487). Screening efforts typically employ brief, relatively inexpensive measures that can be quickly and easily administered by a variety of professionals and paraprofessionals.

Federal legislation has encouraged the implementation of large-scale, early identification screening, or **mass screening**, wherein a program attempts to screen every child in a specified population. Although this type of effort can be expensive, the cost should be viewed within a preventive framework, considering the probable reduction of long-term special education costs if earlier intervention services are received. Widespread screening increases the chances that young children with special needs will not be overlooked; furthermore, there tends to be little or no stigma associated with such screening practices because nearly everyone in the specified population participates (Lichtenstein & Ireton, 1991). Some programs may elect to engage in **selective screening** rather than mass screening. This approach to screening may target specific high-risk groups of children, such as children with a variety of chronic illnesses or children from poverty-stricken areas, or it might be used at specific developmental points in time, such as just prior to kindergarten entry.

Regardless of the type of screening approach, the basic premise of early childhood services is that early identification and intervention strive to lessen the impact of developmental disabilities on children.

Child Find refers to the systematic methods used to locate young children who may qualify for early childhood services.

Screening is a process through which individuals are selected for a more thorough evaluation.

The cost of widespread screening activities should be viewed within a preventive framework, with consideration given to the probable reduction of long-term special education costs if children and families are identified during early childhood.

Critical qualities of screening measures. Given that the focus of screening is to determine which children need further assessment, a key question is whether the decision to refer or not to refer a child for a comprehensive evaluation was accurate. There are several important concepts to consider in this regard: hit rates, sensitivity, specificity, false positives, and false negatives. Overall **hit rates** are important to screening in that they provide an index of the overall accuracy of the screening measure or measures.

As shown in Figure 4.2, there are four basic outcomes from a screening decision: two accurate and two inaccurate outcomes. When a screening decision suggests that a child may be at risk for a medical or developmental problem and the child indeed needs special services, then an accurate referral has been made. This is referred to as **sensitivity.** Ideally, a good screening device or program should capture at least 80% of children with problems (Glascoe, 1996). Conversely, when a screening decision indicates that a child is at low risk for having a medical or developmental problem and the child does not have the target problem, then an accurate nonreferral has been made. This is referred to as **specificity.** Glascoe (1996) suggests that this rate should be at least 90% to minimize overreferrals. Accurate decisions are represented in cells 1 and 4 of Figure 4.2.

Sometimes, a screening decision leads to a referral when in fact the child may not have the medical or developmental problem of concern. This leads to what is called a **false positive** and contributes to overreferrals, as shown in cell 2 of Figure 4.2. Additionally, screening decisions can suggest that a specific problem does not exist, but the child actually manifests the target problem. This type of decision-making error is shown in cell 3 of Figure 4.2 and is referred to as a **false negative.** False negatives can result in underreferral of children for specific problems which, in turn, may contribute to ongoing difficulties for those children and their families. The frequency of false negatives provides a strong rationale for conducting ongoing developmental monitoring, even when a child may not appear to have a problem.

> Hit rates reflect the degree of accuracy of screening measures.

> Sensitivity refers to accurate identification of a child who needs special services.

> Specificity refers to accurate identification of a child who does not need special services.

> A false positive occurs when screening suggests special services that are not needed.

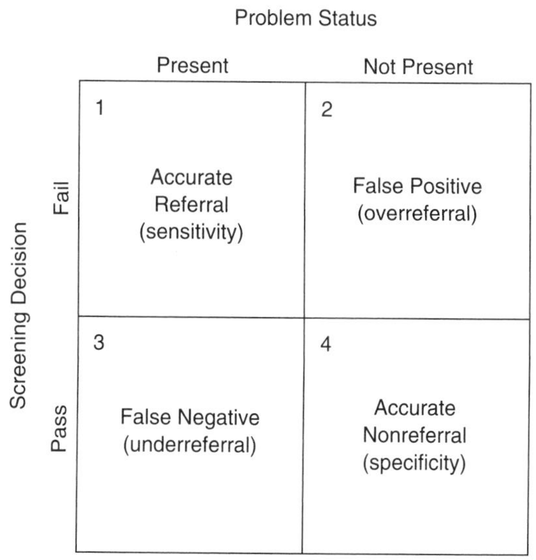

FIGURE 4.2   Types of screening decision outcomes

Obviously, the implementation of effective screening is a huge responsibility for a community and an integral part of the early intervention process. When choosing screening tools, it is critical that measures not only have adequate sensitivity and specificity but also have appropriate reliability and validity. These two dimensions are discussed later in this chapter. It is also critical for screening, or developmental monitoring, to take place on a recurrent or periodic basis and include input from a variety of professionals.

Formal Screening Procedures.   As part of the early identification process, and intimately related to Child Find, young children with special needs can be identified through formal screening procedures.

Prenatal and Neonatal Screening.   The initial identification of a disability often is made by a physician, such as the pediatrician, neonatologist, or the obstetrician, who may become aware of a disability as early as the first few weeks of pregnancy through prenatal diagnostic techniques (e.g., ultrasound). In some cases, early identification also has allowed for surgical correction of problems prior to delivery of the infant (Bruner et al., 1999; Manning, Jennings, & Madsen, 2000; Vanderwall & Harrison, 1996). Some of the more common prenatal screening or diagnostic procedures are presented in Table 4.1. Prenatal diagnosis is now a routine part of obstetric care, especially in the case of high-risk pregnancies.

An obstetrician is often able to recognize factors that can indicate a potential disability at the birth of an infant. These conditions include **anoxia** (lack of oxygen), possibly caused by a twisted umbilical cord; a prolonged, stressful labor during which the infant may aspirate **meconium** (fetal waste products) into the lungs; and prematurity or very low birth weight (Taylor, Klein, & Hack, 2000; Taylor, Klein, Minich, & Hack, 2001).

Other predictors of an abnormality may be observed during a routine examination of an infant immediately following birth. This process generally involves blood and urine tests for metabolic disorders such as phenylketonuria (PKU), and the **Apgar rating** (Apgar, 1953), which evaluates heart rate, breathing effort, muscle tone, reflex irritability, and skin tone. More detailed behavioral examinations of a newborn may be accomplished using such tests as the Brazelton Neonatal Behavioral Assessment Scale (NBAS; Brazelton, 1984), and other neurological examinations (Chervenak & Kurjak, 1996; Mindes, Ireton, & Mardell-Czudnowski, 1996). Scales such as the Brazelton NBAS allow a pediatrician or another appropriately trained professional to identify possible abnormalities in the central nervous system and in the sensory abilities of a newborn. According to Bergen and Wright (1994), the NBAS is a more sensitive predictor of later developmental outcomes than is the Apgar score. Further, it offers the opportunity for parents to observe and discuss their infants rather than to be directly taught about general infant behavior (Cardone & Gilkerson, 1989).

Early Childhood Screening.   Developmental screening has traditionally been viewed as the role of the physician; however, given the involvement of a variety of agencies in early childhood intervention and service delivery, numerous health care

TABLE 4.1   Common Prenatal Screening Procedures

Screening Procedure	Procedures/Utility
Urine Screen	A special stick is inserted in a urine sample at each prenatal visit to identify gestational diabetes. Low levels of sugar may indicate hypoglycemia, whereas high levels may indicate hyperglycemia. These conditions may affect the developing fetus.
Blood Pressure	Blood pressure is measured with a cuff and stethoscope at each prenatal visit. Abnormal pressure readings may suggest complications such as preeclampsia (maternal hypertension with high levels of protein in the urine and body swelling).
Hemoglobin Screen	Blood is drawn from an arm or finger prick at about 4 months gestation, and on a regular basis if necessary. The blood is examined for iron levels, with low levels indicating the presence of anemia.
Amniocentesis	A hollow needle is inserted through the abdominal wall into the uterus to withdraw a small amount of amniotic fluid. This procedure usually is done in conjunction with an ultrasound to avoid injuring the fetus, umbilical cord, or placenta. It is conducted at about 13 to 18 weeks gestation, and typically is performed for high-risk pregnancies (e.g., advanced maternal age and known family history of chromosomal abnormalities). Amniocentesis can provide relatively reliable information about open neural tube defects and genetic defects such as Down syndrome. It also reveals the gender of the fetus.
Alpha-Fetoprotein Test	Blood from a finger prick is used to screen for neural tube defects between 14 and 18 weeks gestation. A high AFP level is a possible indicator of neural tube defects (e.g., spina bifida and anencephaly), whereas a low level may suggest an increased risk of Down syndrome or other chromosomal problems. Abnormal levels indicate the need for additional AFP testing, a sonogram, and amniocentesis.
Chorionic Villi Sampling	A needle is inserted into the vagina or abdomen, and then into the uterine wall to the edge of the placenta. Chorionic villi (the fetal components of the developing placenta) are withdrawn and examined. This procedure is generally done between 9 and 12 weeks gestation. It can reveal chromosomal and genetic abnormalities (e.g., Down syndrome), Tay-Sachs disease and other inborn errors of metabolism, types of cystic fibrosis, and thalessemia (e.g., sickle cell anemia). Testing for other specific disorders and diseases can be done if the family history warrants it.
Ultrasound (Sonography)	Using sonography to generate a live outline of the fetus in utero, this procedure can reveal orthopedic impairment, problems with major organs, and other physical abnormalities. An ultrasound typically is performed between weeks 14 and 20 of the pregnancy.

providers (nurse practitioners, pediatric and public health nurses, dentists) and other professionals now participate in Child Find and associated screening efforts.

Most young children receive medical care from a pediatrician or other primary care provider through well-child visits. This system allows the health care provider the opportunity to observe a child's development frequently and over an extended period. A pediatrician may suspect possible disabilities if there is a record of stressful birth events, a history of pediatric illnesses, or a family history of developmental problems. Later, if a child does not achieve major developmental milestones (e.g., walking and talking) at expected times, then the pediatrician or health care provider might determine the need for further examination. Primary health care providers often are the main source of guidance when parents believe that their child is experiencing a problem or delay. Although it has been estimated that approximately 60% of pediatricians use some type of screening test or procedure to detect developmental abnormalities, most use them inconsistently or continue to depend upon clinical judgment (Dobos, Dworkin, & Bernstein, 1994; Glascoe, 1996; Scott, Lingaraju, Kilgo, Kregel, & Lazzari, 1993). In fact, the American Academy of Pediatrics (1986) suggested over 15 years ago that pediatricians should employ standardized screening procedures to detect developmental problems, and that these procedures should be employed at each of the 12 well-child visits planned between birth and 5 years of age.

There are formal screening instruments that can be used by health care providers as well as other professionals who are involved in screening. Two instruments that can be used with infants and toddlers are the Bayley Infant Neurodevelopmental Screener (Aylward, 1995) and the Denver–II (Frankenburg et al., 1990), which assess a child's gross motor, language, fine motor-adaptive, and personal-social skills in comparison with other children of the same age.

Child-care providers and early interventionists also play an important role in the early identification of children with special needs; they have the unique advantage of regular, often daily, observation of a child. Whereas other professionals are primarily concerned with a specific facet of a child's development, an early interventionist observes all aspects of a child's development, thus providing a more holistic view. Other professionals, such as social workers, may assist in the screening process by providing insight into the family strengths as well as familial and ecological risk factors.

Other popular screening measures that may be used by various professionals include the Ages and Stages Questionnaires (ASQ): A Parent-Completed, Child-Monitoring System, Second Edition (Squires, Potter, & Bricker, 1999); the Battelle Developmental Screening Test (Newborg, Stock, Wnek, Guidubaldi, & Svinicki, 1988); the Developmental Indicators for the Assessment of Learning–Third Edition (Mardell-Czudnowski & Goldenberg, 1998); the Early Learning Accomplishment Profile (Chapel Hill Training Outreach Project, 1995); and FirstSTEP (Miller, 1993).

Professional involvement is certainly valuable in the early identification of children with disabilities, but even more critical is the role of parents. In fact, as discussed in chapters 2 and 3, legislation has mandated that the family be involved as active participants throughout the early intervention process. As the primary observers of their child, parents have firsthand knowledge of their child's total development. If a problem is suspected, the parents may be the first to see evidence of it and subsequently seek advice from one or more professionals. Most parents are in a position to confirm, or at least discuss, the clinical suspicions of any professionals who may have expressed concerns.

> Child-care providers and early interventionists often have daily contact with young children, thus allowing them to observe a child's functional abilities in a natural environment.

> The involvement of the family in the early identification process is critical.

Stage 2: Comprehensive Evaluation

Once a child moves into stage 2, the purpose of the assessment changes from early identification of possible needs and concerns to determining whether or not a significant problem exists. Obviously, the primary purpose of a comprehensive evaluation can vary; it can include documentation of a delay, diagnosis of a disability, or the establishment of eligibility for intervention or education services. In addition, this stage should help to clarify the nature and extent of any problems that might be present, and should be clearly linked to stage 3, program planning and implementation.

Federal legislation mandates that the assessment of infants and young children with special needs be conducted with a team approach (specific approaches are discussed later in this chapter). An underlying premise of a team evaluation is that it should be comprehensive, covering the important domains of development, thus providing critical information for decision making. Most professionals would agree that several developmental domains should be assessed in a comprehensive evaluation due to the interrelated and integrated skills across these domains. The primary areas that are usually included are the cognitive, motor, communication, social/play, and self-care/adaptive domains. Many early intervention programs require information about a child's functioning in each of these domains in order to document eligibility for special education services and to plan a child's individualized education plan (IEP) or individualized family service plan (IFSP). Medical and family information also is critical at this stage, and should be complementary to information gained from the developmental domains.

Developmental Domains.   Five key developmental domains are typically considered in a comprehensive evaluation: cognitive, motor, communication, social/play, and self-care/adaptive skills.

Cognitive skills are those related to mental and intellectual development (see Chapter 9). In early childhood, these skills include concepts such as object permanence, imitation, means-end or causality, and spatial relationships. As a child reaches preschool age, the assessment of cognitive development includes more preacademic skills, such as literacy and early quantitative abilities.

Motor skills are related to the use of muscles, joints, and limbs. As discussed in Chapters 7 and 8, the assessment of motor skills typically is divided into two areas: gross motor and fine motor. Gross motor skills require the use of large muscles and movements such as walking, running, throwing, and jumping. Fine motor skills refer to the use of small muscles and more refined movements such as cutting, writing, grasping, and buttoning.

Communication skills are those that allow a child to give and receive information (see Chapter 10). Two types of communication skills that are frequently assessed are receptive and expressive language. Receptive language refers to a child's ability to understand and comprehend information being presented. Expressive language is a child's ability to communicate thoughts, feelings, or ideas. A child's speech production and ability to produce sounds and words may also be assessed. Communication includes not only the use of words but also gestures, pictures, facial expressions, and augmentative devices.

Social and play skills refer to a child's ability to interact with peers and adults, specific behaviors in social situations, and use of toys. The level of a child's play (i.e., manipulative, symbolic, pretend, constructive) can provide important developmental information. Frequently, an informal play assessment is conducted in order to understand a child's cognitive, motor, and communication skills as expressed

In early childhood, it is important to understand and appreciate that a child's development is both integrated and interactive, and takes place within a family and community context.

Observation of a child in his natural setting can facilitate the assessment process by allowing the child to function in his natural environment.

through the medium of play. As noted in Chapter 11, these skills are critical to children's social and emotional development.

Self-care or adaptive skills are related to a child's ability to function independently in meeting daily needs such as toileting, feeding, and dressing. Understanding a young child's needs for help or assistance during such daily care-taking activities can provide invaluable information for making decisions about placement and the need for individualized assistance and support. While many of the skills are described in the ensuing chapters, particular attention to this domain can be seen in chapter 8.

Medical Issues.   Because of the complex nature of many early childhood disabilities and conditions, it is imperative that medical issues receive consideration in the evaluation process. In addition to whatever information can be provided from the prenatal history of a child (e.g., findings derived from prenatal tests), a physical examination can help determine the nature of a child's disability. A thorough physical exam also can provide diagnostic (e.g., Fragile X syndrome, neurofibromatosis, or epilepsy) and selected prognostic information. Understanding a child's medical condition also can provide information about the need for specialized attention and assistance within the day-care or preschool setting. Medical factors can significantly impact a child's development and acquisition of new skills. For example, children with infectious diseases, metabolic disorders, and chronic illnesses require ongoing medical monitoring and perhaps medication or frequent hospitalizations. These factors also may dictate the setting in which services are provided.

Family Issues. The Individuals with Disabilities Education Act requires assessment practices to include an examination of the family's strengths and needs in addition to the child's. By establishing a collaborative partnership with families, professionals can gain a better understanding of a child's strengths, needs, and overall resources. Most parents know their child better than anyone else and can provide details about the child's past and current development. In addition, interviewing a child's parents or having them complete questionnaires can provide pertinent information about their parenting skills and attitudes, their discipline techniques, and their understanding of their child's developmental strengths and challenges. Having the family involved in the assessment process also elicits their input and cooperation in relation to ongoing developmental surveillance and monitoring.

Stage 3: Program Planning and Implementation

The comprehensive evaluation serves as a prerequisite and foundation for stage 3, program planning and implementation. It provides the information needed to discuss placement for a child and to develop relevant goals for an IEP or IFSP. This information is then translated into a plan of action for the preschool teacher, related services personnel, early interventionist, and family. Although more detailed information about intervention is provided in other chapters, it is important to note here that assessment does not stop once intervention begins. The teacher or early interventionist should continue to provide ongoing formal and informal assessment of a child's progress in target developmental domains and behaviors, as specified in the IEP or IFSP; assessment information pertaining to other aspects of growth, general development, and developmental readiness also should be obtained. From an assessment perspective, criterion-referenced types of measures can be useful for tracking progress frequently and in a developmentally sensitive fashion.

Stage 4: Program Evaluation

This stage involves assessment procedures that measure the progress of the child and the effectiveness of the intervention plan or program. The overall goal of this stage is to reassess the current developmental levels of a child, to monitor progress related to developmental goals established by the team and family members for the IEP or IFSP, and to determine the need for adjustments and modifications in the child's intervention program. In some instances, a child's developmental gains may have progressed to a point at which they are within age-appropriate levels, and no further services may be needed at that time.

Team Approaches and Typologies

There are a number of approaches and techniques that can be employed in the assessment process; indeed, an assessment team may elect to use a combination of these techniques, depending on the nature of the presenting problem (Neisworth & Bagnato, 1996).

Team Models

IDEA and accepted standards of best practice mandate that assessment strategies involve multiple disciplines as well as the family. Given the many different problems that children with developmental disabilities can have, and despite the financial costs inherent in bringing a (large) group of professionals together, a team approach clearly is the preferred method of gathering assessment data. The team can include, but not be limited to, a psychologist, social worker, early interventionist, audiologist, nurse, speech and language pathologist, nutritionist, occupational therapist, physical therapist, pediatrician, and parents. How this team operates, however, can be quite varied. At present, there are at least three versions of the team process: multidisciplinary, interdisciplinary, and transdisciplinary.

Multidisciplinary Team.   On the **multidisciplinary team,** whose origins are based on the medical model, the number of team members may be set or members may be selected to address the problems presented by the referral source (e.g., one referral problem may demand the presence of a physical therapist whereas another may not). Regardless of the team makeup, each professional on the team has a clearly defined role with specific areas of responsibility. Assessment takes place independently, and each discipline provides feedback to the parents or referral source, perhaps on different days; however, these professionals do not necessarily discuss their findings with the other team members. Clearly, this type of assessment process can result in conflicting results, perhaps with families or early interventionists receiving contradictory findings. Even when a selected professional is deemed responsible for presenting the results from all of the different disciplines involved, concerns may arise related to the comfort of that professional with all of the information being provided, and biases can emerge (Fewell, 1983). For example, such a situation could arise when an early childhood professional is trying to interpret the results of a geneticist or an occupational therapist.

> The multidisciplinary team consists of professionals from various disciplines who conduct independent assessments.

Interdisciplinary Team.   A variant of the multidisciplinary team is the **interdisciplinary team.** The number and type of professionals involved in multidisciplinary and interdisciplinary assessment may be very similar and disciplines may continue to do individual evaluations; the major differences lie in the interdisciplinary team's ongoing communication and the sharing of results by team members to develop a more integrated plan. Although the inclusion of ongoing communication may improve the information being provided to families and referral sources, there remain concerns that one professional may take charge and dominate a team meeting. Also, despite the fact that professionals may have the opportunities to talk to one another about their findings, this does not ensure that they will understand one another or reach consensus on the findings and recommendations.

> On the interdisciplinary team, although members are from different disciplines, they collaborate and communicate for a more integrated process.

Transdisciplinary Team.   A third variant of the team models is the **transdisciplinary team.** Using this model, team members meet regularly, share assessment and intervention responsibilities, and always include families as part of the team. An assessment approach often associated with this type of team is **arena assessment**. With this data-gathering approach, a team of professionals observes the child in some type of interaction with another professional or facilitator. One way for this process to unfold is for a single professional, such as a speech and language pathologist, to begin assessment and to have the other professionals observe and assist in various ways (e.g., "coaching" and taking notes). The basic premise is that many of the items of the various testing procedures will overlap or similar behaviors will be elicited. For example, a speech and language pathologist might be interested in whether a child can follow verbal directions necessary to perform a motor task, whereas an occupational therapist may be most concerned with the fine motor capabilities of the child. When the transdisciplinary team approach is used, professionals do not have to readminister the same type of item, which should save time, minimize the effects of practice, and preserve the child's stamina for other tasks. Linder (1993) described a six-component, transdisciplinary play-based assessment model that embodies this approach.

> Transdisciplinary team members commit to teaching, learning, and working across disciplinary boundaries to plan and provide integrated services (Garland, McGonigel, Frank, & Buck, 1989).

Transdisciplinary assessment can provide an enormous amount of practical information to clinicians, early interventionists, and parents across all of the key developmental domains of interest. One minor drawback to using a transdisciplinary assessment model, however, is that there are few assessment tools available that can be used well by a transdisciplinary team and that meet the reliability and validity standards of some of the more traditional single-discipline measures. On the other hand, when using "single-discipline" instruments in a transdisciplinary model, standardized procedures are difficult to maintain because the same task may have different specific directions in each of the different measures. For example, the Bayley Scales of Infant Development–Second Edition (Bayley, 1993), the Mullen Scales of Early Learning (Mullen, 1995), the Differential Ability Scales (Elliott, 1990), and the Denver–II (Frankenburg et al., 1990) all have a block-stacking task, but the blocks themselves, the directions to the child, and the scoring are all different. However, because the goal of this task in the transdisciplinary assessment is to determine whether or not the child can stack blocks, this problem may be relevant only to the scoring of the specific measures used. Obviously, observation of the child's ability and how it relates to daily tasks may be much more relevant to goal setting and program planning.

Assessment Typologies

To gain a comprehensive view of a young child, particularly one with delays or documented disabilities, it is especially important to choose a multidimensional assessment approach that employs multiple and often alternative measures, gathers information from multiple sources, examines several developmental and behavioral domains, and fulfills various purposes.

Although the intent of this section is not to review specific tests and procedures in any detail, it should be noted that over 15 years ago Neisworth and Bagnato (1988) provided an organizational typology of such procedures to help the early childhood professional make appropriate choices for the assessment process, and this still holds today. This typology of measures includes (1) norm-referenced, (2) curriculum-based, (3) adaptive-to-disability, (4) process, (5) judgment-based, (6) ecological, (7) interactive, and (8) systematic observation. Similarly, Benner (1992) has provided an organization of various approaches and techniques across strands, including formal/informal, normative/criterion-referenced, standardized/adaptive-to-disability, direct/indirect, naturalistic/clinical, and product/process. Use of these two typologies can provide a framework to organize and discuss specific assessment techniques. As tasks are described in subsequent chapters, these typologies should help you determine what kind of measure is being described.

Formal/Informal Assessment. This focuses on the type of information collected in the assessment process. In a formal assessment, the primary strategy for data collection involves the use of standardized tests, which are selected by the examiner(s) with a specific purpose in mind (e.g., screening, comprehensive evaluation, or program evaluation). A specific assessment plan then is set into action.

At the other end of the continuum are more informal assessment strategies. Rather than using standardized assessment strategies, the professional or team often uses nonstandardized assessment procedures. For example, a group of professionals may work together to observe the frequency of a specific behavior, and there is a clear structure of systematic data-collection strategies for these observations (see Box 4.1). An informal data-gathering strategy may indicate the need for and set into motion more formal data collection.

Normative/Criterion-Referenced Assessment. In normative data collection, one of the most frequently used strategies in early childhood assessment, the primary emphasis is on how one child compares with another child of the same chronological age. Although this type of data collection produces quantitative information about the overall level of functioning (e.g., developmental quotients and IQs), this information tends to have minimal influence on the selection of specific intervention initiatives. Further, although many normative-based tests have excellent psychometric properties (e.g., reliability), care should be taken when applying them to children with specific disabilities. Indeed, such an approach to assessment may contribute to underestimating a child's abilities if areas of disability are those that primarily are tapped.

Normative assessment compares a child's performance with that of age-level peers.

BOX 4.1	Systematic Data Collection

An important, but often difficult task is for teams to reach consensus during decision-making stages of service delivery.

One way to address team-based concerns, which affect all of the variants of the team approach, is to systematize the data-collection process. For example, the System to Plan Early Childhood Services (SPECS; Bagnato & Neisworth, 1990) comprises materials and procedures that assist the early intervention team in reaching consensus in the assessment process. Parents and professionals independently rate a child on 19 developmental and functional dimensions. From these ratings, the dimensions of concern or disagreement are identified, and the discrepant ratings are then discussed until a consensus is reached for a rating on each dimension. Once this occurs, the child's assessment profile can be detailed and appropriate programming options can be pursued.

Probably the most widely used normative-based instrument in early childhood assessment is the Bayley Scales of Infant Development–Second Edition (Bayley, 1993). The Bayley is designed for children aged 1 month to 42 months and provides a mental and a motor index. These two indices cover such items as imitation, visual-perceptual skills, language, eye-hand coordination, memory, and object permanence. In addition, the Bayley provides a behavioral rating scale whereby an examiner can rate a child's social and emotional characteristics.

By contrast, criterion-referenced assessment focuses on what specific skills an infant, toddler, or preschooler can demonstrate. In contrast to their norm-referenced counterparts, these types of data-gathering strategies may contribute significant information to a child's IEP or IFSP. Further, they can be quite informal—even created by a preschool teacher or early interventionist—and consequently can be used frequently for ongoing program planning and evaluation. Tying this data-gathering strategy directly into a developmentally sequenced curriculum (curriculum-based assessment) and task analysis also can be useful for developmental programming.

Curriculum-based assessment is one of the most representative assessment strategies of the criterion-referenced approach. This type of assessment allows the early childhood professional to assess a child's current skills and to monitor progress according to specific program objectives. Curriculum-based assessment even allows a teacher to delineate skills in the curriculum that a child has not yet mastered and to plan accordingly. A weakness of curriculum-based assessment is that the skills assessed are based upon a specific curriculum and may not generalize to another program.

Within the broad domain of criterion-referenced assessment, the Learning Accomplishment Profile–Revised (LAP-R) (Sanford & Zelman, 1981) is one instrument that is often used with preschool children with special needs. The LAP–R is designed to assess the skills of children aged birth to 72 months across the domains of cognition, language, fine and gross motor skills, self-help skills, and personal-social skills. Bufkin and Bryde (1996) also have tied this tool to specific programmatic goals and play activities. Similar instruments include the Early Screening Inventory (Meisels & Wiske, 1987), which assesses the visual-motor/adaptive domains, the language and cognitive domains, and gross motor/body awareness; and the Carolina Curriculum for Infants and Toddlers with Special Needs (Johnson-Martin, Jens, Attermeier, & Hacker, 1991).

Standardized/Adaptive-to-Disability Assessment. This category relates to the standardized nature of the data-gathering process. If an early childhood professional or team employs a standardized assessment, then a fixed set of procedures must be followed during data collection. In fact, some tests, such as many of the intellectual testing measures (e.g., Wechsler Preschool and Primary Scale of Intelligence–Third Edition Wechsler, 2002; Kaufman Assessment Battery for Children, currently being revised, Kaufman & Kaufman, 1983), provide specific wording of directions and prompts for the examiners to follow. Standardized procedures also typically include some kind of starting and stopping points from which it is assumed that a child will accurately perform (**basal level**) or fail (**ceiling level**) all items below and above

Criterion-referenced assessment can help identify specific tasks a child can and cannot do rather than compare him to his peers.

Curriculum-based assessment identifies skills, tasks, and behaviors that are important within a particular curriculum.

these points, respectively. Basal and ceiling levels are designed to reduce testing time (i.e., permits administration of only the necessary or developmentally appropriate items), and to allow for some variability at the easy (basal) and more challenging (ceiling) ends of the performance continuum. Although this approach may appear to be quite rigid, especially when considering the wide range of responses and behaviors that any infant or young child may exhibit, many standardized assessment strategies are norm-referenced; thus it is essential that the standardized procedures be followed to ensure that the data can be interpreted in a valid fashion. As Benner (1992) accurately notes, however, using these data-gathering strategies with some children with specific disabilities may yield invalid results (e.g., administering fine motor coordination or fine motor speed tasks to a child with cerebral palsy).

In this regard, adaptive-to-disability data-gathering strategies afford professionals and early childhood teams greater flexibility in attempting to gain a profile of a child's abilities. For example, Benner (1992) has proposed modifying the properties of the objects and materials used in an assessment. Such modifications might include making materials larger and brighter, adding visual contrast, reducing the number of possible response choices available, and using multidimensional scoring methods that are scaled on a continuum as opposed to having the child respond in a right-versus-wrong fashion. Relatedly, Neisworth and Bagnato (1988) suggest three types of adaptive approaches: (1) the examiner simply modifies the items and procedures as necessary, (2) systematic guidelines are provided for altering the test materials, and (3) the measure is designed for a specific disability. Bagnato and colleagues (1997) also discuss a dynamic modification in which a child might first be tested, then taught the task, and subsequently be retested to gain an estimate of learning rate. Additionally, Sattler (2001) provides a number of suggestions for testing limits of standardized procedures, particularly for older preschoolers (e.g., eliminating time limits and asking probing questions).

Direct/Indirect Assessment. According to Benner (1992), the direct/indirect continuum involves how examiners or early intervention teams collect information about a child. Using the direct strategy, a professional works with the child face-to-face. Benner notes that this strategy is in operation even when a videotape is used to observe and code a child's behaviors. Direct data gathering is likely the most frequently used strategy, and it should be part of every early childhood assessment.

The indirect data-gathering strategy involves the collection of information about a child via other assessment techniques. For example, interviewing parents and other caregivers (e.g., preschool teachers) would serve to provide some index of how a child is functioning in various settings. Rating scales also can be used for indirect data gathering. When indirect data-gathering strategies are combined with direct data-gathering strategies, the assessment process is a richer source of information for the early intervention team. Further, although indirect data-gathering strategies continue to focus on the child, they also can allow the gathering of related information critical to that child's development, such as information about family resources and parental discipline techniques. The Child Development Inventories (Ireton, 1992) fit this mold. These inventories are a multidimensional parent rating system comprising three separate instruments wherein parents answer yes–no items about their child's developmental status. In addition to gaining an appraisal of developmental status, parents are asked to describe their child's behavior and emotional functioning.

Naturalistic/Clinical Observations.   Observational data are critical components of all assessment processes. In fact, many of the tests and procedures available for early childhood assessment are little more than structured methods for collecting data on a youngster. With this basic understanding in mind, Benner (1992) describes a continuum of data-gathering strategies that employs observational techniques.

On one end of the continuum is natural observation. Naturalistic observational strategies require that information be collected in a child's natural environment under routine circumstances. Such strategies can involve observation of the child's overall behavior within the setting, or they can focus on more specific types of behaviors (e.g., temper tantrums, social skills during group activities, or fine motor skills during an art activity). Unless there is a good rationale for limiting the observations to specific behaviors—and in many cases this is a preferable type of behavioral observation (e.g., when it is necessary to focus on specific developmental problems)—care should be taken to include other aspects of the setting or caregiver to minimize bias in the interpretation of the observations. Benner (1992) notes that naturalistic observations can be one of the most ecologically valid data-gathering strategies for a child's day-to-day functioning. In fact, many of these assessment strategies are intimately linked to play scales, such as the Play Assessment Scale (Fewell, 1991) and the Symbolic Play Scale (Westby, 1991), and provide observational guidelines for interpreting developmental status (Fewell, 1993; Linder, 1993).

> Federal legislation suggests that natural environments are settings that are natural or normal for the child's same-age peers without disabilities.

Interactive and ecological types of assessment as described by Neisworth and Bagnato (1988) probably fall on this end of the continuum. In interactive types of measures, the reciprocity between and compatibility of child and caregiver(s) is examined. Dimensions of interactions that often are explored include the reading of and response to partner cues, the altering and managing of behaviors, and the ability to initiate and maintain interactions. For example, the Brazelton Neonatal Behavioral Assessment Scale (Brazelton, 1984) examines neonatal interactive and organizational behaviors by measuring elements such as states of arousal, habituation, state regulation, and orientation.

Similarly, ecological assessment techniques examine factors within a child's life that may contribute to developmental status, thus providing a more comprehensive profile of strengths and needs. A child's ecological context includes the family, home, and classroom characteristics such as room layout, materials, available opportunities for stimulation, peer interaction, social responsibility, discipline, and social support. Two ecological assessment tools that can be employed to examine a child's environments are the Home Observation for Measurement of the Environment–Third Edition (HOME; Caldwell & Bradley, 2001) and the Early Childhood Environment Rating Scale–Revised Edition (ECERS, Harms, Clifford, & Cryer, 1998). More specific measures relating to parenting stress (Parenting Stress Index; Abidin, 1986), parental behaviors (Parent Behavior Checklist; Fox, 1993), and other psychosocial areas also are available (Glascoe, 1996).

On the other end of the continuum is clinical observation. This type of observation occurs when a child is being evaluated in a clinical setting, such as when a pediatrician performs an examination or a child is receiving a comprehensive evaluation at a child development center. Although skilled evaluators can extract reliable and valid behaviors from young children, these same children also can become more constricted in their behavioral presentations during a clinic visit. Consequently, the use of different types of observations provides a more accurate picture of a child's overall functional capabilities.

For example, a formal evaluative process may need to include systematic observation of a specific behavior. Such observation should be objective, quantifiable, and collected over time. Observation may occur in the child's natural setting or in a simulated or staged situation. Systematic observation does not include interpretation of behaviors or judgments but, rather, objective, structured measures of overt behaviors (e.g., the number of times a child hits another child or the amount of time the child is off task during an assignment). For formal assessment of a behavior, dimensions that may be included are its frequency, duration, and intensity. Typically, data sheets or coding systems are developed that allow an examiner to observe and record behaviors of concern.

Product-/Process-Oriented Assessment. Similar to the normative/criterion-referenced dichotomy, the product-/process-oriented continuum relates to the type of information that should be gathered in the assessment process. A product-oriented data-gathering strategy generally involves administering to a child a battery of tests and procedures with the goals of describing how a child compares to same age peers and establishing initial developmental or instructional levels for programming. Measures such as the Bayley Scales of Infant Development (Bayley, 1993) and common preschool measures of intelligence (e.g., Wechsler Preschool and Primary Scale of Intelligence–Third Edition; Wechsler, 2002) fall under this category. Similarly, performance-based, or authentic assessment (Meyer, 1992; Wiggins, 1989), and portfolio data-gathering strategies for collecting samples of a child's work over time (Arter & Spanel, 1991; Meisels, 1993) also are included on the product-oriented side of the continuum. Product-oriented data-gathering strategies are important in that they likely will occur in the child's natural setting.

Process-oriented data-gathering strategies involve *how* a child interacts with the examiner and the environment; they even examine how a child passes *and* fails selected tasks and items. Piagetian types of measures, such as the Uzgiris-Hunt Scales (Uzgiris & Hunt, 1975), and dynamic assessment procedures, such as those advocated by Feuerstein (1979), Vygotsky (1978), and Lidz (1987), are data-gathering strategies that are process-oriented. With these types of assessment, children typically are exposed to a task and their performance is observed. If children experience difficulties in performing a selected task, they can be taught the task through mediated learning experiences (Tzuriel & Klein, 1987), and then the item is readministered. This **test-teach-test** type of format can occur as many times as is deemed necessary by the evaluator.

For many young children with significant disabilities (e.g., visual impairment or severe motor impairment), traditional assessment strategies are not appropriate. Consequently, alternative approaches are needed to tap into these children's developmental needs and less obvious competencies. Process assessment attempts to discover a child's unique capabilities, such as in memory and recall, attention, and information processing through indirect and inferential means. Although this is not

Portfolio assessment provides documentation of a child's work over time and can include artwork, journal writing, audiotapes, photos, and so on.

an ideal method of assessment, it is one alternative when other assessment approaches are not feasible.

Considerations for the Assessment of Young Children

Several factors must be considered when assessing a young child with special needs. These include the selection of assessment approaches and tools that link assessment and intervention, situational constraints including child and environmental variables, and the involvement of the family.

Selection of Assessment Measures and Methods

Assessment should be a process driven by questions pertinent to a child's development and specific developmental needs. Furthermore, the *purpose* of the assessment must be clearly established before selecting measures and methods (Bagnato et al., 1997). This process notwithstanding, the selection of assessment methods should be guided by basic canons of science (e.g., reliability and validity), cultural sensitivity, and good old common sense. In fact, many of these standards are described in the *Standards for Educational and Psychological Testing,* a joint effort by the American Educational Research Association, the American Psychological Association, and the National Council on Measurement in Education (AERA, APA, & NCME, 1999).

> The first step in the assessment process is to define a purpose or question to be answered.

The requirements include the following:

- Tests must not contain racial and/or cultural bias.
- Tests must be valid for their intended purpose and should be administered only by appropriately trained professionals.
- The procedures used should be able to address a variety of educational and developmental needs.
- A single assessment procedure must not be the sole contributor to a child's treatment plan.
- A multidisciplinary team or designated group of professionals must participate in the assessment process, and this group must include a teacher with specialized knowledge in that area of disability.
- A child must be tested in all educational and developmental areas related to the suspected disability.

Reliability and validity are critical scientific concepts that must be understood when selecting a specific assessment tool for any part of the assessment process (e.g., screening, diagnostic, or program evaluation). Does the test measure what it is supposed to measure in a dependable fashion? Obtaining dependable information from any young child is a challenge, and it is for examiners to choose tests that have adequate reliability. The test should have adequate **content validity** (Does the test reflect the content it is purportedly measuring?); **concurrent validity** (Does the test correlate with other accepted criteria of performance in each skill area?); **predictive validity** (To what extent do the obtained scores correlate with some criterion

> Reliability refers to consistency.

for successful performance in the future?); **construct validity** (Does the test address the theoretical constructs upon which the test is based?); and **discriminant validity** (Do subtests measure separate and distinct skills?). Although a detailed discussion of these psychometric issues is beyond the scope of this chapter, the early childhood professional should examine test manuals for such information prior to employing any test for screening, diagnostic, or program evaluation purposes.

> Validity refers to how well the test measures what it is supposed to measure.

In addition to the basic psychometric aspects of the assessment tools, it is critical that they be nonbiased and nondiscriminatory. These issues have been addressed in court cases (*Diana v. State Board of Education,* 1973; *Larry P. v. Riles,* 1979), and subsequently in our federal laws; however, it is the responsibility of early childhood professionals to be highly sensitive to these issues. Nondiscriminatory assessment refers to the multicultural nature of society and means that any assessment must be equally fair to all children. It is important to note that the nature of any assessment is discriminatory; its overarching purpose is to distinguish between those who need services and those who do not, but it *unfairly* discriminates if it does not allow for cultural differences. Allowing for cultural differences should include administering tests in a child's native language or other modes of communication and providing experiences that are familiar to the child. Closely related to nondiscriminatory assessment is the concept of **nonbiased assessment**. Duffey, Salvia, Tucker, and Ysseldyke (1981) define a biased assessment as having "constant errors in decisions, predictions, and inferences about members of particular groups" (p. 427). An example of an early childhood professional making a biased assessment is making premature judgments about the child being tested, especially when the child is tested in an unnatural setting.

> The assessment process should always be viewed as the first step in a potential intervention process (Meisels & Fenichel, 1996).

It is important for the early childhood professional to possess plain old common sense! Although it may seem obvious, it is critical that the tests selected actually assist in answering the referral questions. Will the tests provide and/or assist in the assessment-treatment linkages detailed by Neisworth and Bagnato (1996)? If so, how? Further, is the content appropriate for the child? Is the professional administering the test appropriately trained to administer and interpret it? Again, although they are basic, the application of these common-sense considerations lessens the misuse and abuse of assessment tools.

Situational Considerations

Traditional early childhood assessment has been described as . . . "the science of the strange behavior of children with strange adults in strange situations for the briefest period of time" (Bronfenbrenner, 1979). Situational constraints clearly contribute to the "strangeness" of the assessment process as described by Bronfenbrenner. Situational constraints can involve any number of concerns that may arise in the assessment process. One of the most common constraints encountered is when a child simply refuses to perform on request. The child might be frightened, fatigued, slow to warm up to the testing session, or, in the case of an infant, sleeping! Other children may present extreme behavioral difficulties that do not facilitate the assessment process. In assessing young children with special needs, it is of vital importance to take any functional impairments into account when observing behaviors, including possible vision or hearing impairments, motor impairments, or language impairments or differences. Testing materials should be appropriate to the child in terms of language, size, and ability. It is best to use a seating system in which the child is adequately and comfortably supported, and from which the child can interact with the testing materials appropriately. When a typical response modality cannot be used, it may be possible to gather the same information by using another communication system. For example, the child may use an augmentative communication device or a system of pictures, gestures, or eyeblinks to indicate a response. In all of these situations, it is important for the early childhood professional to be familiar with the many different types of data-gathering methods to take advantage of these situational constraints.

When establishing rapport with the child and family at the outset of the evaluation process, it is important to establish a solid play and work partnership with the child. When working with small children in particular it is vital to ask, "What's in it for the child?" Some children are extremely motivated by verbal praise and the undivided attention of adults; they are extremely easy to assess and eager to please. Others will require much more tangible reinforcement—such as stickers, snacks, or toys—in exchange for their efforts. Parents and other familiar caregivers should be partners in eliciting the child's best efforts, confirming if the child's performance is typical of his abilities, and suggesting how a task might be presented differently in order to gain greater effort.

At some times, it will not be possible to get a child to complete formal testing tasks for one reason or another. For example, when an examiner or team is trying to gain a formal assessment and a child is noncompliant, it might be useful to shift to more informal (e.g., observation), indirect (e.g., parent ratings or report), and process-oriented (e.g., play) types of data-gathering strategies. If an examiner has a strong background in child development, behavioral guidance, and management strategies, useful information can be gained from observation of the child's play or other naturalistic observations. If the examiner continues to make demands on the child to complete the formal assessment, on the other hand, opportunities to learn more about the daily, adaptive functioning of the child could be lost. It is also helpful to learn about the child's performance in the natural environment. This should include gaining knowledge about the child's day-care or preschool, child-care provider or the preschool teacher, therapists, and the homesetting.

Family and Parental Involvement

As discussed earlier, the importance of the family in the assessment process cannot be overemphasized. A critical facet of early childhood assessment is the collaborative, working partnership between the parents and professionals. This relationship goes beyond traditional "rapport" and includes respect, reciprocity, and flexibility (Meisels & Atkins-Burnett, 2000). Parents play a vital role in the gathering of information about the child, the family, and the home and community environments. As noted at the beginning of this chapter, family members need to view assessment and

It is logical to expect improved outcomes for children when parents and other care providers are actively involved in treatment planning and intervention.

intervention as consistent with their perceptions of and expectations for their child as well as with their current familial values and needs. Understanding a family's perspectives and concerns *prior to* initiating any assessment is critical in constructing the assessment process. This contributes to appropriate decisions about where the assessment will take place, what kind of data-gathering approaches are useful, and which specific tools (if any) may be used. The development of intervention plans in collaboration with the family can also increase the likelihood that the plans will be accepted, implemented, and successful.

Summary

This chapter provided an overview of the assessment process in early childhood. Several definitions of the term *assessment* were provided, and contemporary assessment standards were discussed. These included treatment utility, social validity, convergent assessment, and consensual validity, which should be applied to any assessment in early childhood to increase the accuracy and utility of the assessment information, and to provide for valid and functional intervention plans. The various stages of assessment were detailed with particular emphasis on early identification, including issues related to screening, and the major components of a comprehensive assessment. The ongoing process of assessment was highlighted, particularly in the intervention and program evaluation phases.

In addition to these aspects of assessment, a number of approaches to assessment were detailed in accordance with a set of strands, or typologies, as espoused by Benner (1992) and Neisworth and Bagnato (1988). The team approach to assessment in accordance with federal laws was highlighted, with a specific emphasis on transdisciplinary teams. Although the focus of this chapter was not on describing the many assessment tools available to the early childhood professional, selected tools were mentioned to illustrate the various strands of assessment. A discussion of some of the issues pertinent to the assessment process, such as test selection, situational constraints, and involvement of the family, also was provided. A good understanding of the assessment process together with a firm grounding in basic child development will allow the early interventionist to address the assessment of young children with special needs in a sensitive, thoughtful, and meaningful fashion.

Review Questions and Discussion Points

1. Describe current standards related to best practice in early childhood assessment.
2. What are three common assessment team models? Describe the similarities and differences among the three teams?
3. What are some of the advantages and disadvantages of formal, normative-based assessment tools?

4. In a difficult assessment situation in which a child refuses to comply with the testing process, what are some alternative ways to get the same information?
5. How can an evaluation-treatment team maximize the utility of the information gathered during assessment toward developing and evaluating treatment goals?

Recommended Resources

Bagnato, S. J., Neisworth, J. T., & Munson, S. M. (1997). *LINKing assessment and early intervention: An authentic curriculum-based approach.* Baltimore: Brookes.

Division for Early Childhood, Council for Exceptional Children. (2002). Assessment strategies. *Young Exceptional Children Monograph* (Series No. 4). Longmont, CO: Sopris West.

Sandall, S., McLean, M. E., & Smith, B. J. (Eds.). (2000). *DEC recommended practices in early intervention/early childhood special education.* Division for Early Childhood, Council for Exceptional Children. Longmont, CO: Sopris West.

Sattler, J. M. (2001). *Assessment of children: Cognitive applications* (4th ed.). La Mesa, CA: Sattler.

Sattler, J. M. (2002). *Assessment of children: Behavioral and clinical applications* (4th ed.). La Mesa, CA: Sattler.

References

Abidin, R. R. (1986). *Parenting Stress Index* (2nd ed.). Charlottesville, VA: Pediatric Psychology Press.

American Academy of Pediatrics. (1986). Committee on children with disabilities: Screening for developmental disabilities. *Pediatrics, 78,* 526–528.

American Educational Research Association, American Psychological Association, & National Council on Measurement in Education. (1985). *Standards for educational and psychological testing.* Washington, DC: Authors.

American Speech-Language-Hearing Association. (1990). *Guidelines for practices in early intervention.* Rockville, MD: Author.

Apgar, V. (1953). A proposal for a new method of evaluation of the newborn infant. *Current Research in Anesthesia and Analgesia, 32,* 260–267.

Arter, J. A., & Spanel, V. (1991). *Using portfolios of student work in instruction and assessment.* Portland, OR: Northwest Regional Educational Laboratory.

Aylward, G. P. (1995). *Bayley Infant Neurodevelopmental Screener.* San Antonio, TX: Psychological Corporation.

Bagnato, S. J., & Neisworth, J. T. (1990). *System to Plan Early Childhood Services.* Circle Pines, MN: American Guidance Services.

Bagnato, S. J., Neisworth, J. T., & Munson, S. M. (1997). *LINKing assessment and early intervention: An authentic curriculum-based approach.* Baltimore: Brookes.

Bayley, N. (1993). *Bayley Scales of Infant Development* (2nd ed.). San Antonio, TX: Psychological Corporation.

Benner, S. M. (1992). *Assessing young children with special needs: An ecological perspective.* New York: Longman.

Bergen, D., & Wright, M. (1994). Medical assessment perspectives. In D. Bergen (Ed.), *Assessment methods for infants and toddlers: Transdisciplinary team approaches* (pp. 40–56). New York: Teachers College Press.

Brazelton, T. B. (1984). *Neonatal assessment scale* (2nd ed.). *Clinics in Developmental Medicine,* No. 88. Philadelphia: Lippincott.

Bronfenbrenner, U. (1979). *The ecology of human development: Experiments by nature and design.* Cambridge, MA: Harvard University Press.

Bruner, J. P., Tulipan, N., Paschall, R. L., Boehm, F. H., Walsh, W. F., Silva, S. R., et al. (1999). Fetal surgery for myelomeningocele and the incidence of shunt-dependent hydrocephalus. *Journal of the American Medical Association, 282*(19), 1819–1825.

Bufkin, L. J., & Bryde, S. M. (1996). Young children at their best: Linking play to assessment and intervention. *Teaching Exceptional Children, 29,* 50–53.

Caldwell, B. M., & Bradley, R. H. (2001). *HOME Inventory.* Little Rock: University of Arkansas.

Cardone, I., & Gilkerson, L. (1989). Family administrated neonatal activities: An innovative component of family-centered care. *ZERO TO THREE, X*(1), 23–28.

Chapel Hill Training Outreach Project. (1995). *Early Learning Accomplishment Profile.* Chapel Hill, NC: Author.

Chervenak, F. A., & Kurjak, A. (Eds.) (1996). *The fetus as a patient.* New York: Parthenon.

Diana v. Board of Education, No. C-70-37 RFP, Consent Decree (N. D. Cal. 1973).

Division for Early Childhood, Council for Exceptional Children. (2002). Assessment strategies. *Young Exceptional Children Monograph* (Series No. 4). Longmont, CO: Sopris West.

Division for Early Childhood Task Force on Recommended Practices. (Eds.). (1993). *Recommended practices in early intervention.* Reston, VA: Council for Exceptional Children.

Dobos, A. E., Dworkin, P. H., & Bernstein, B. (1994). Pediatricians' approaches to developmental problems: Has the gap been narrowed? *Journal of Developmental and Behavioral Pediatrics, 15,* 34–39.

Duffey, J., Salvia, J., Tucker, J., & Ysseldyke, J. (1981). Nonbiased assessment: A need for operationalism. *Exceptional Children, 47,* 427–434.

Elliott, C. (1990). *Differential Ability Scales.* San Antonio, TX: Psychological Corporation.

Feuerstein, R. (1979). *The dynamic assessment of retarded performers: The learning potential assessment device, theory, instrument, and techniques.* Baltimore: University Park Press.

Fewell, R. (1983). Assessing handicapped infants. In S. G. Garwood & R. R. Fewell (Eds.), *Educating handicapped infants: Issues in development and intervention* (pp. 257–297). Rockville, MD: Aspen.

Fewell, R. (1991). *Play assessment scale.* Miami, FL: University of Miami.

Fewell, R. (1993). Observing play: An appropriate process for learning and assessment. *Infants and Young Children, 5,* 35–43.

Fox, R. A. (1993). *Parenting Behavior Checklist.* Brandon, VT: Clinical Psychology Press.

Frankenburg, W. K., Dodds, J., Archer, P., Bresnick, B., Maschka, P., Edelman, N., et al. (1990). *Denver–II.* Denver, CO: Denver Developmental Materials.

Garland, C. G., McGonigel, J. J., Frank, A., & Buck, D. (1989). *The transdisciplinary model of service delivery.* Lightfoot, VA: Child Development Resources.

Glascoe, F. P. (1996). Developmental screening. In M. L. Wolraich (Ed.), *Disorders of development and learning: A practical guide to assessment and management* (2nd ed., pp. 89–128). New York: Mosby.

Greenspan, S. I., & Meisels, S. J. (1996). Toward a new vision for the developmental assessment of infants and young children. In S. J. Meisels & E. Fenichel (Eds.), *New visions for the developmental assessment of infants and young children* (pp. 11–26). Washington, DC: ZERO TO THREE.

Harbin, G. L., McWilliam, R. A., & Gallagher, J. J. (2000). Services for young children with disabilities and their families. In J. P. Shonkoff & S. J. Meisels, (Eds.), *Handbook of early childhood intervention* (2nd ed.). New York: Cambridge University Press.

Harms, T., Clifford, R. M., & Cryer, D. (1998). *Early Childhood Environment Rating Scale.* New York: Teachers College Press.

Ireton, H. (1992). *Child Development Inventories.* Minneapolis, MN: Behavior Science Systems.

Johnson-Martin, N. M., Jens, K. G., Attermeier, S. M., & Hacker, B. J. (1991). *The Carolina curriculum for infants and toddlers with special needs* (2nd ed.). Baltimore: Brookes.

Kaufman, A., & Kaufman, N. (1983). *Kaufman Assessment Battery for Children.* Circle Pines, MN: American Guidance Service.

Larry P. v. Riles, 343 F. Supp. 1306, 502 F.2d 963 (N. D. Cal. 1979).

Lichtenstein, R., & Ireton, H. (1991). Preschool screening for developmental and educational problems. In B. Bracken (Ed.), *The psychoeducational assessment of preschool children* (2nd ed., pp. 486–513). Boston: Allyn & Bacon.

Lidz, C. (Ed.). (1987). *Dynamic assessment: An interactional approach to evaluating learning potential.* New York: Guilford Press.

Linder, T. (1993). *Transdisciplinary play-based assessment: A functional approach to working with young children* (Rev. ed.). Baltimore: Brookes.

Manning, S. M., Jennings, R., & Madsen, J. R. (2000). Pathophysiology, prevention, and potential treatment of neural tube defects. *Mental Retardation and Developmental Disabilities Research Reviews, 6,* 6–14.

Mardell-Czudnowski, C., & Goldenberg, D. S. (1998). *DIAL-3: Developmental Indicators for the Assessment of Learning– Third Edition.* Circle Pines, MN: American Guidance Service.

McLean, M., & Odom, S. (1993). Practices for young children with and without disabilities: A comparison of DEC and NAEYC identified practices. *Topics in Early Childhood Special Education, 13,* 274–292.

Meisels, S. J. (1993). Remaking classroom assessment with the work sampling system. *Young Children, 48,* 34–40.

Meisels, S. J., & Atkins-Burnett, S. (2000). The elements of early childhood assessment. In J. P. Shonkoff & S. J. Meisels (Eds.), *Handbook of early childhood intervention* (2nd ed.). New York: Cambridge University Press.

Meisels, S. J., & Fenichel, E. (1996). *New visions for the developmental assessment of infants and young children.* Washington, DC: ZERO TO THREE, National Center for Infants, Toddlers, and Families.

Meisels, S. J., & Wiske, M. S. (1987). *Early Screening Inventory.* New York: Teachers College Press.

Meyer, C. A. (1992). What's the difference between authentic and performance assessment? *Educational Leadership, 49,* 39–40.

Miller, L. J. (1993). *FirstSTEP Screening Test for Evaluating Preschoolers.* San Antonio, TX: Psychological Corporation.

Mindes, G., Ireton, H., & Mardell-Czudnowski, C. (1996). *Assessing young children.* Albany, NY: Delmar.

Mullen, E. (1995). *Mullen Scales of Early Learning, AGS Edition.* Circle Pines, MN: American Guidance Service.

National Association for the Education of Young Children. (1990). Position statement on school readiness. *Young Children, 46,* 21–23.

National Association for the Education of Young Children, National Association of Early Childhood Specialists in State Departments of Education. (2002). *Early learning standards: Creating the conditions for success* [joint position statement]. Retrieved December 13, 2002, from http://www.naeyc.org

National Association of School Psychologists. (1999). Position statement on early childhood assessment. Retrieved December 12, 2002, from http://www.nasponline.org

Neisworth, J. T., & Bagnato, S. J. (1988). Assessment in early childhood special education: A typology of dependent measures. In S. L. Odom & M. Karnes (Eds.), *Early intervention for infants and children with handicaps: An empirical base.* Baltimore: Brookes.

Neisworth, J. T., & Bagnato, S. J. (1996). Assessment for early intervention: Emerging themes and practices. In S. L. Odom & M. E. McLean (Eds.), *Early intervention/early childhood special education: Recommended practices.* Austin, TX: PRO-ED.

Neisworth, J. T., & Bagnato, S. J. (2000). Recommended practices in assessment. In S. Sandall, M. E. McLean, & B. J. Smith (Eds.), *DEC recommended practices in early intervention/early childhood special education* (pp. 17–28). Division for Early Childhood, Council for Exceptional Children. Longmont, CO: Sopris West.

Newborg, J., Stock, J. R., Wnek, L., Guidubaldi, J., & Svinicki, J. (1988). *Battelle Developmental Inventory.* Allen, TX: Developmental Learning Materials.

Sanford, A. R., & Zelman, J. G. (1981). *Learning Accomplishment Profile–Revised.* Winston-Salem, NC: Kaplan School Supply.

Sattler, J. M. (2001). *Assessment of children: Cognitive applications* (4th ed.). La Mesa, CA: Sattler.

Scott, F. G., Lingaraju, S., Kilgo, J., Kregel, J., & Lazzari, A. (1993). A survey of pediatricians on early identification and early intervention services. *Journal of Early Intervention, 17,* 129–138.

Squires, J., Potter, L., & Bricker, D. (1999). *Ages & Stages Questionnaires (ASQ): A Parent-Completed, Child-Monitoring System, Second Edition.* Baltimore: Brookes.

Taylor, H. G., Klein, N., & Hack, M. (2000). School-age consequences of birth weight less than 750 g: A review and update. *Developmental Neuropsychology, 17*(3), 289–321.

Taylor, H. G., Klein, N., Minich, N. M., & Hack, M. (2001). Long-term family outcomes for children with very low birth weights. *Archives of Pediatric and Adolescent Medicine, 155*(2), 155–161.

Thurlow, M., & Ysseldyke, J. (1979). Current assessment and decision-making practices in model LD programs. *Learning Disability Quarterly, 2,* 15–24.

Tzuriel, D., & Klein, P. S. (1987). Assessing the young child: Children's analogical thinking modifiability. In C. S. Lidz (Ed.), *Dynamic assessment: An interactional approach to evaluating learning potential.* New York: Guilford Press.

Uzgiris, I. C., & Hunt, J. M. (Eds.). (1975). *Assessment in infancy: Ordinal scales of psychological development.* Urbana: University of Illinois Press.

Vanderwall, K. J., & Harrison, M. R. (1996). Fetal surgery. In F. A. Chervenak & A. Kurjak (Eds.), *The fetus as patient.* New York: Parthenon.

Vygotsky, L. S. (1978). *Mind in society: The development of higher psychological processes.* Cambridge, MA: Harvard University Press.

Wechsler, D. (2002). *Wechsler Preschool and Primary Scale of Intelligence* (3rd ed.). San Antonio, TX: Psychological Corporation.

Westby, C. (1991). A scale for assessing children's pretend play. In C. Schaefer, K. Gitlin, & A. Sandgrund (Eds.), *Play assessment and diagnosis.* New York: Wiley.

Wiggins, G. (1989). A true test: Toward more authentic and equitable assessment. *Phi Delta Kappan, 70,* 703–713.

5

Intervention

Tina M. Smith and Tashawna Duncan

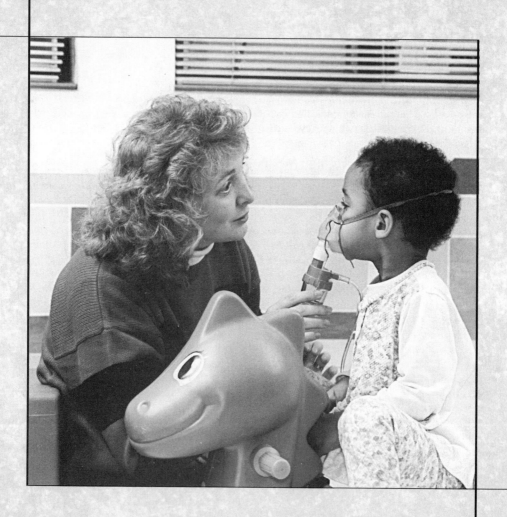

Jessica

*F*our-year-old Jessica receives early intervention services for developmental delay at Happy Acre Child Care Center. Jessica is the youngest of four children. Her pediatrician referred her for an evaluation at age 3 after her parents expressed concerns that she wasn't talking as well as her siblings had at the same age. Jessica's grandparents immigrated to the United States from Puerto Rico and her family speaks mostly Spanish at home. Currently, under Part B of IDEA, Jessica receives services from an early interventionist and a speech-language therapist.

Jessica attends Happy Acres, a regular child-care center, along with her older sibling. Her speech-language therapist, Ms. Watkins, visits Happy Acres once a week for 45 minutes. During that time, Ms. Watkins pulls Jessica and a few other children into a small group and works with them on language enrichment activities. The activities are designed based on Jessica's needs and she is the focus of them. The other children seem unaware of this and enjoy playing "Miss W's games." Because Ms. Watkins rarely sees Jessica's parents at school, she tries to send weekly notes to them describing Jessica's progress. Jessica's parents sometimes write back, but Ms. Watkins has difficulty understanding their English; she often finds herself wishing she spoke Spanish!

Jessica also received special education services at Happy Acres, but Jessica is oblivious to the services! Mr. Banks, an early interventionist, meets weekly with Jessica's regular child-care teacher, Ms. Taylor. They talk about Jessica's progress and any concerns Ms. Taylor has, and Mr. Banks helps Ms. Taylor modify the curriculum so that Jessica can participate in a meaningful way. Mr. Banks also is available as a consultant to Ms. Taylor any time concerns arise. Mr. Taylor tries to schedule his weekly visits to overlap with times when Jessica's parents pick her up or drop her off. He speaks some Spanish and has had some success establishing a collaborative relationship with Jessica's parents. He's offered to work with them on any concerns they have at home, but they always say that they don't have any concerns.

The concept of intervention represents the heart and soul of our work with children. In its broadest sense, intervention includes nearly every interaction that professionals have with children and families. The purpose of this chapter is to discuss intervention as it specifically relates to young children. We begin by offering a general definition of the term *intervention* to put the recent practice of early intervention into a historical context. Next, our discussion turns to more pragmatic aspects specific to early intervention and proceeds through planning, implementing, and evaluating intervention with young children.

Defining Intervention

Perhaps the most helpful way to begin a discussion of intervention is to define the basic concept. For the professional, a functional definition of the term *intervention* serves three purposes. First, it differentiates intervention from related but different clinical and educational endeavors, such as assessment. Second, a definition provides the framework necessary for formulating individual and program goals. For any field of study to progress, there must be at least some agreement regarding the goals and objectives. In the words of Yogi Berra, "You have to be very careful when you don't know where you're going, or you might never get there." A functional definition of intervention gives the professional an idea of "how to get there." Finally, a definition provides insight into the assumptions underlying professional practice and research.

A number of educational and psychological theorists have attempted to define intervention. Rhodes and Tracey (1972) describe it as any directed action intended to remedy the ill-fit between a child and the environment. Suran and Rizzo (1979) suggest that intervention is any professional effort to facilitate a child's ongoing healthy development. Some researchers (Adelman & Taylor, 1994) emphasize both planned and unplanned outcomes in their definition of early intervention. More recently, Hanson and Lynch (1998) have defined intervention broadly as "a comprehensive cluster of services that incorporates goals in education, health care, and social service for young children who are disabled or at risk for developing disabilities and their families."

These definitions overlap to a considerable degree and any of them may serve as a starting point for understanding intervention. However, each is also insufficient in certain respects. For example, Rhodes and Tracey do not address the outcomes of intervention. Intervention can have a multitude of outcomes, some desirable and some undesirable. Although a strong research base helps suggest what the outcomes of a planned intervention will be, unexpected outcomes always occur as well. In this regard, Adelman and Taylor's (1994) emphasis on outcomes is preferable in that the possibility of unintended and even undesirable outcomes is acknowledged along with planned outcomes.

Definitions that consider only problems or disabilities, such as that of Hanson and Lynch, also have limitations. Intervention should not automatically imply the presence of significant problems. Although intervention is usually intended to remediate a problem or area of need, it also can be used to establish and maintain positive functioning. For example, prevention is a type of intervention intended to avoid problems. If we define intervention this broadly, then every person is in need of some form of intervention at some point in development. The essential question is deciding when to intervene, who will be involved in the intervention, and the extent and type of intervention.

Finally, a definition of intervention also should account for the environmental influence of social systems beyond the individual and immediate family, such as school and the local community. Intervention is implemented in environments, not just for individuals. Notably, a person's functioning and development always occur in a given context. For the purposes of this chapter, intervention is broadly defined to refer to outcomes (both positive and negative, intentional and unintentional), conditions eliciting intervention (both positive and negative), and a consideration of the multiple systems affecting and affected by intervention (the individual, family, school, and community). Therefore, we offer the following definition of intervention:

> Intervention is a directed, purposeful process. It is the intentional application of resources with the aim of developing, improving, or changing conditions within an individual, environment, or interactions between an individual and the environment. Intervention always results in both intended and unexpected outcomes, which may be either positive or negative in nature.

Family-Centered Intervention

An important assumption in early intervention for infants and toddlers is that the family is the unit of intervention for services. By taking into account family needs, intervention efforts for infants and toddlers are likely to include goals that go well beyond the educational objectives mandated by special education laws relating to older children. For example, in the case of a family with three children, one of whom has a medical condition that requires constant attention and access to a respirator, one challenge faced by the parents may be how to give the other children the time and attention that they need. For this family, one relevant intervention goal would be the provision of respite services for the child with special needs so that the parents can spend time with their other children. Such needs can and should be addressed by early intervention. Ideally, parents take an active role in the education and development of their children at all ages.

In the example from the vignette at the beginning of the chapter, Jessica first began receiving early intervention services shortly after her third birthday. Based on the multidisciplinary team evaluation, the team decided that Jessica would benefit from language enrichment. The professionals on the team believed that Jessica would benefit from participation in a **self-contained class** for preschoolers with disabilities that was housed in public school. Her parents wanted Jessica to remain in her current child-care placement; one sister currently attended there, and her two older brothers had gone there as well. The professionals pointed out that the teacher in the self-contained classroom was well trained and certified, and could provide intensive intervention. Jessica's parents trusted the teachers at Happy Acres, and valued Jessica being near her sister and in the care of a known and trusted teacher. As a result, the team agreed to provide consultative speech services to Happy Acres personnel. Box 5.1 points out the important roles that families play in the intervention process.

BOX 5.1	Role of Families in Early Intervention

With the inclusion of Part C in P.L. 99-457, Congress acknowledged that families are an integral aspect of a child's life and worthy of intervention services in their own right. Although this legislation and its subsequent reauthorizations make clear the mandate to involve families in their children's early intervention, the definition of family involvement itself remains elusive. Bailey (2001) identifies three themes related to families and early intervention. First, he points out the importance of individualizing the ways in which parents are involved, taking into account cultural diversity, family resources, and family preferences. The second important point is the expectation that families will take an active, decision-making role in the planning and implementation of their children's interventions. Finally and perhaps most important, Bailey describes families as "the ultimate decision makers and long-term care providers for their children" (p. 1); therefore, intervention must have as a goal facilitating families' competence and confidence for advocating for their children.

Multiculturalism and Early Intervention

Because the United States is ethnically mixed, a respect for the uniqueness of cultural beliefs, values, and practices—that encourages newcomers to the United States to retain their cultural identity, while simultaneously becoming part of the larger "American" culture—is critical in educational settings.

One aspect of family-centered intervention that is becoming increasingly important and relevant is providing services in a multicultural society. American society is a diverse, dynamic, and interactive landscape comprised of communities and individuals. In 1970, 12% of the population in the United States under 5 years of age was non-White. By 1984, 36% of all babies in the United States were born to non-White, non-Anglo parents (Research and Policy Committee of the Committee for Economic Development, 1987). By the 1990s, our nation's growing diversity became even more apparent. For example, the 1990 census recorded that over 380 different languages were actively spoken by American citizens (U.S. Bureau of the Census, 1990). Predictions made by the Children's Defense Fund (1989) were that by the year 2000 there would be "2.4 million more Hispanic children; 1.7 million more African-American children; 483,000 more children of other races, and 66,000 more white non-Hispanic children" than there were in 1985 (p. 116). The predictions for the year 2030 are even more dramatic, projecting a decline of 6.2 million in the population of White, non-Hispanic children. This prediction also means that nearly half of all school-aged children will be non-White. As the number of children of color in the general population increases, we can expect a concomitant increase in the number of non-White, non-Anglo children requiring early intervention services. However, with so few minorities entering social service professions, the likelihood is that the majority of professionals providing early intervention services will continue to be White.

Current and predicted cultural mismatches between service providers and families offer new challenges for education professionals. Potential conflicts rooted in culture are likely and unfortunate because both interventionists and families share the same goal of wanting to help children. These potential cultural misunderstandings arise because people are bathed in a culture from birth. Brown and Lenneberg

(1965) found that children may establish a cultural identity as early as 5 years of age. Because our primary culture is a deeply set part of our values, attitudes, and behavior, we may easily misinterpret a second culture. In any case, the impact of culture on early intervention is indisputable.

Although many teachers, health care professionals, and psychologists often refer to "cultural issues," little consensus exists regarding a definition of culture. There are several formalized definitions of the term **culture**, but Turnbull, Turnbull, Shank, and Leal (2002) point out that many different factors shape our views of culture. However, most professionals do not rely on textbook definitions. Instead, they operate under the assumption that everyone has an implicit understanding of what is meant by the term *culture;* yet these connotative definitions frequently lead to disagreement and misunderstanding among professionals and between service providers and families. Frisby (1992) found that the term *culture* means different things to different people:

Culture A refers to differences in clothing, lifestyle, values, and traditions associated with a people's level of technological attainment or geographic location. For example, some anthropologists refer to Western or modern culture when discussing societies of Europe or the Americas.

Culture B is equated with the humanistic achievement of racial or ethnic groups. For example, when school classrooms celebrate Black History Month, administrators and teachers encourage students to explore the fundamentals of "Black culture."

Culture C designates common attitudes, values, and beliefs that guide an individual's identification with a particular group. For example, many African American community leaders garner great support because they are able to articulate the "Black experience" in America.

Culture D refers to the immediate context of an individual. For example, many anthropologists and politicians espouse the ideas of a "culture of poverty" and a "culture of the schools."

Culture E is associated with superficial lifestyle choices. For example, in the late 1970s there was a "punk culture" whose members were easily identified by their music, clothing, and appearance. Teachers and linguists use this meaning of culture when they identify certain patterns of speech as "Black English."

Culture F equates culture with race. This connotative definition of culture is the most superficial and simplistic. Not surprisingly, this definition of culture is also the primary source of misunderstandings between families and professionals. After all, should it be assumed that a family is culturally different simply because it is racially different?

Ethnocentrism: Views that emphasize one's own cultural or ethnic beliefs, attitudes, and traditions without regard for others' backgrounds, often identifying themselves and their own beliefs as "normal."

One of the primary concerns for early interventionists should be how to provide an effective and responsible delivery of services that is also sensitive to the needs of families whose language, culture, and experiences are different from theirs. Antibias curriculum goals are discussed in Box 5.2.

BOX 5.2	Antibias Curriculum

In order for children to develop a healthy self-identity, an educational environment that not only accepts but also respects and affirms their culture of origin is crucial. Increasingly, preschools are examining and modifying curricula to eliminate bias for one culture or group over another. This is often referred to as an *antibias curriculum*. The goal within this framework is to ensure that all children feel affirmed and accepted by their educational environment, regardless of their race, ethnicity, religion, gender, socioeconomic status, or disability. It's important to examine and evaluate every aspect of the environment for bias. For example, are there pictures on the walls that show women and men in nontraditional gender roles (e.g., female fire fighters, male nurses), as well as people of color wearing cultural dress in different roles? Classroom customs are important as well and teachers should give careful consideration to the holidays that are observed by the class.

Ultimately more important than the relatively superficial considerations of classroom decoration and costume is the way in which teachers convey respect and acceptance of difference to children. For example, art activities in which children draw self-portraits are perfect opportunities to model appreciation of differences and help children explore their own uniqueness. Rather than referring to children as "Black" or "White," teachers can use more precise language, such as "Justin's skin is a light tan color, with lots of reddish freckles that match his wonderful red hair; Jose's skin is light brown, and he has beautiful dark brown hair and eyes."

Barriers to Effective Family Involvement

Despite the intent of the law and the best efforts of professionals, parents often are inadvertently left out of the early intervention planning process. Part of the difficulty of including parents stems from the way services were provided in the past. Historically, education professionals have focused intervention efforts on the child. With IDEA's mandates for family-centered intervention, however, came a fundamental shift in the way professionals view themselves and families. Bailey, Buysse, Edmondson, and Smith (1992) outline four basic assumptions underlying family-centered practice that radically shift intervention efforts away from the individual child and onto the entire family (p. 299):

1. Children and families are inextricably intertwined. Intentional or not, intervention with children almost invariably influences families; likewise, intervention with and support of families invariably influence children.
2. Interventions involving and supporting families are likely to be more powerful than those focusing exclusively on the child.
3. Family members should be able to choose their level of involvement in program planning, decision making, and service delivery.
4. Professionals should attend to family priorities for goals and services, even when those priorities differ substantially from professional priorities.

In addition to the paradigm shift from child-centered to family-centered intervention, three types of barriers to full family participation have been identified: family, system, and professional barriers (Bailey et al., 1992). Family barriers include lack of parental skill (e.g., parents who are themselves developmentally disabled), inadequate resources (e.g., lack of time for parents to attend meetings because of the demands of their child's care), and attitudinal problems (e.g., lack of confidence or assertiveness). When these types of barriers exist, it is the responsibility of the professional to help the family overcome them so that fuller and more meaningful participation is possible.

System barriers, perhaps the most frustrating for professionals, are obstacles resulting from the bureaucracy or agencies responsible for service provision. System barriers include such difficulties as lack of time and resources, entrenched bureaucracies that are slow to change policies, and inflexible administrative practices. For example, one difficulty frequently encountered when professionals attempt to accommodate families is an inability to schedule meetings after work or on weekends so that working parents can attend. Although system barriers must be addressed at the administrative level, it is important for parents and professionals at all levels to bring their concerns to the attention of policy makers.

Professional barriers result from a lack of knowledge or skills, or from attitudinal problems on the part of the interventionist. Knowledge barriers can arise when professionals are not prepared by their **preservice** programs or **in-service** training to work effectively with families, or when they lack experience. Professional attitudinal barriers may present an even greater challenge than lack of knowledge or skill, because they involve the fundamental assumptions professionals hold about the ability of families to make decisions about their children's needs. Sometimes, the social service professional approaches intervention with an ethnocentric attitude, using his own culture and experiences as a measure of what is normal, expected, and superior. As one professional reported, "We seem to have the attitude that we know what's best for the child" (Bailey et al., 1992, p. 304).

> Policy makers include anyone who makes decisions about the policies and procedures that govern intervention services (e.g., superintendents, elected officials, state and federal employees charged with overseeing programs and funding).

> Preservice education refers to the training individuals receive *prior to* being certified or employed as educational professionals.

> Inservice education describes on-the-job training and professional development opportunities provided for employees after they are certified and employed.

Program Planning

An underlying principle of IDEA is that all children, including young children with disabilities, deserve a meaningful educational experience. This principle was further reinforced in the 1997 and more current Amendments to IDEA. To ensure the quality and richness of this experience for a child with special needs, the educational program must be based on individualized goals and objectives. IDEA requires that these goals and objectives be written down and that an individualized service plan be created for each child with special needs. This plan is intended to be the blueprint for the child's intervention program. This section of the chapter describes the planning process and the products of this process: the **individualized family service plan (IFSP)** and the **individualized education plan (IEP)**.

Step 1: Assessment

The first step in planning an intervention program is to identify areas of strength and need. To a large extent, the success of this process and ultimately the intervention itself depends on the success of the first phase; that is, the child's assessment. In early intervention, assessment is always accomplished through a multidisciplinary team evaluation and an in-depth assessment of every aspect of the child's development.

Multidisciplinary teams consist of professionals from at least two different disciplines (e.g., speech-language therapists, occupational therapists, early interventionists, and psychologists).

The transdisciplinary team, like the multidisciplinary team, consists of individuals from at least two different disciplines, but these individuals collaborate more closely to the point of sharing assessment and intervention activities.

By law, professionals from at least two disciplines (e.g., psychology, special education, regular education, and physical therapy) must participate in the assessment.

Many assessment experts recommend a transdisciplinary team evaluation as the most thorough and effective means of identifying young children's strengths and needs. As was discussed in Chapter 4, in transdisciplinary assessment, a team of professionals from several disciplines reaches a consensus regarding the unique combination of methods and procedures necessary to assess a child. In practice, the collaborative, transdisciplinary approach reduces overlap of assessment and intervention services because the focus of the assessment is to collect information specifically for the purpose of writing the child's personalized service plan. For example, within the transdisciplinary model, professionals from different disciplines collaborate to obtain the information necessary to plan the child's services.

The transdisciplinary model differs from the more traditional multidisciplinary team assessment in that, within the multidisciplinary model, professionals from each discipline conduct their own assessment independently and without regard for the assessments of other professionals. Because there is naturally occurring overlap among test activities across developmental domains (e.g., language, cognition, and motor domains), there also is overlap in the assessments. For example, both a psychologist and a speech-language pathologist would be interested in a child's ability to respond to the question "What is a cow?" Whereas the speech-language pathologist may be assessing the child's ability to use language to express herself, the psychologist is likely to be interested in the maturity of the child's cognitive abilities. Rather than asking the child the question twice, as would occur in a multidisciplinary assessment, within the transdisciplinary model one of these professionals administers the items and the two then work together to interpret the child's responses.

Multicultural Considerations in Assessment.

Families from diverse cultures pose special challenges at this stage in the intervention process. Many of the tests and procedures commonly used to determine a child's developmental and cognitive abilities have been criticized by families, teachers, and psychologists as being biased against ethnic and minority groups. For example, opponents of IQ tests frequently invoke the argument that they measure only skills and abilities valued by the dominant, Western culture and, therefore, children from non-Western or nondominant cultures may be at a unique disadvantage. Test bias is a complex issue, in part simply because we cannot conceive of the number of behaviors and mental processes that we might actually be measuring. For example, in some cultures, children convey respect by acting subdued around adults, especially strangers. Thus, when they are tested, these children may hold back meaningful interaction with their examiners. In such instances, the professionals may never obtain a clear idea of these children's potential or areas of need. Other researchers have found that children who are aware that they are being tested perform better than children who are oblivious to the situational demands of formal testing. Obviously, some cultures—particularly the mainstream culture of the United States—have more experience than others in test situations. Simply stated, a child's cultural experiences may dramatically influence the testing session. Therefore, the intervention professional should ask some difficult but necessary questions. Have children been referred for early intervention because of an objectively determined real need, or because of a value judgment on the part of social service professionals? Are screening and assessment instruments appropriate to the child's language and cultural background? Are families included in the assessment procedure or are they excluded? Are opportunities provided for reassessment?

Although many service delivery systems still adhere to a one-size-fits-all assessment protocol, a number of researchers and practitioners advocate that assessment be customized to reflect the unique needs, concerns, and priorities of the child and family (Sattler, 1992). Customizing assessment communicates to the family that its cultural differences will be recognized and honored throughout the entire intervention process. In the example of Jessica, because her family speaks Spanish at home, it was important that the assessment team include someone fluent in Spanish, both for interviewing the parents as well as testing Jessica. The fact that Jessica was referred for language problems exacerbated the need for a native speaker.

Step 2: The Individualized Service Plan

What Are Individualized Service Plans?   Once a child's needs and the family's strengths, concerns, and priorities have been identified, the intervention plan is outlined in detail. The program plan for most children aged 3 and older is called an individualized education plan (IEP). For infants and toddlers, service goals are outlined in an individualized family service plan (IFSP). Although most children older than 3 years receive services based on an IEP, federal law does allow states to use IFSPs for preschoolers or to use IEPs for 2-year-olds who will undergo transitions into preschool programs within the year. IEPs and IFSPs are legal documents, required by IDEA, and the law is very specific regarding their contents. The specific elements of IEPs and IFSPs required by IDEA are outlined in Figures 5.1 and 5.2; the following paragraphs briefly compare and contrast the two types of program plans. (For a more thorough discussion of IEPs, IFSPs, and the legal requirements for program planning, refer to Chapter 1.)

Similarities Between IEPs and IFSPs.   As Figures 5.1 and 5.2 indicate, both IEPs and IFSPs are statements of specific goals and objectives for providing services to children. To this end, both types of plans require that the specific services the child will receive be identified along with criteria and procedures that will be used to evaluate the services. Both IEPs and IFSPs specify when the services will begin and how long they are expected to last. In addition, although the wording is somewhat different, both IEPs and IFSPs document the environments in which the services will be provided. Emphasis is placed on providing services in the **least restrictive environment (LRE)**. Placement in a classroom or clinic specifically for children with special needs occurs only when specialized, one-to-one services are deemed necessary to meet the child's educational needs. This is most clearly delineated in the 1997 Amendments to IDEA which require justification when a child does not receive services in a natural setting. Finally, both IEPs and IFSPs contain provisions for making transitions to the next phase of the child's life.

Least restrictive environment refers to the educational placement most like that of typically developing children at the same age as the child with special needs.

1. A statement of the child's current functioning in the following areas:
   a. physical development
   b. cognitive development
   c. language development
   d. psychosocial development
   e. self-help skills or adaptive behavior
2. A description of the family's resources, priorities, and concerns.
3. The outcomes expected to be achieved as a result of intervention for the child and family. This should include the criteria that will be used to determine success, time lines for attaining goals, and whether modifications or revisions of the services or outcomes are needed.
4. The specific services—including frequency, intensity, and methods—that will be used to deliver the early intervention services. Also, the specific date that services will begin and the anticipated length of services should be included.
5. A description of where the intervention will take place, including the "natural environments" (i.e., inclusive environments as opposed to specialized clinic or school settings).
6. The name of the service coordinator who is responsible for overseeing the implementation of the plan and coordinating the efforts of various agencies.
7. Anticipated dates when services will begin and end.
8. A statement of the necessary services for the child's successful transition from an early intervention program to a preschool program (from Title I and Title II).

FIGURE 5.1   Elements of an Individualized Family Service Plan

Source: Data from *Birth to Five: Early Childhood Special Education,* by F. G. Bowe, 1995, New York: Delmar.

1. A description of the current educational performance of the child.
2. Annual goals and short-term instructional objectives.
3. Which specific educational services will be provided to the child.
4. The extent to which the child will be able to participate in regular educational classrooms or activities.
5. When the services will begin, and how long they are expected to last.
6. Objective criteria, evaluation procedures, and schedules for determining whether objectives are being achieved.

FIGURE 5.2   Elements of an Individualized Education Plan for Young Children

Source: Data from *Birth to Five: Early Childhood Special Education,* by F. G. Bowe, 1995, New York: Delmar.

Differences Between IEPs and IFSPs.   Although there are many similarities between IEPs and IFSPs, there also are several important differences. Some differences seem minor but have important implications for the ways services are provided. For example, although both plans contain a statement of the child's current functioning, IEPs address only educational performance whereas IFSPs require a broader statement of the child's overall development. This means that IFSPs address the family's concerns, resources, and priorities, as well as five specific domains of child functioning: physical development, cognitive development, language development, psychosocial development, and self-help skills. Because IEPs place less emphasis on the family, only characteristics describing the individual child are included.

Another difference relates to the way program goals are specified. IEPs must include specific short-term objectives, whereas IFSPs can be more general, including the outcomes that are expected but not specific goals and objectives. In contrast to IEPs, IFSPs allow that early intervention services for infants younger than 3 years may begin before specific details of the program are completed. IFSPs also provide for evaluation of objectives every 6 months rather than annually, as is required for IEPs. These provisions acknowledge the rapid development of infants and the importance of immediate intervention.

Family Involvement in Program Planning. One important difference between IEPs and IFSPs is that professionals are required by law to address families' resources, strengths, and priorities when they are providing early intervention services (usually based on IFSPs) to children younger than 3 years. The implications of this difference for the way services are provided are substantial and reflect fundamental differences in the underlying philosophies of intervention. Although the law allows IEPs to include instruction for parents, such instruction is not mandated or even emphasized. However, because IFSPs focus on the family's resources, strengths, and priorities, the plan should specify goals that are designed to build on the family's strengths in order to maximize child functioning.

The omnipresence of the family in the early intervention process highlights the need for the professional to work effectively with family members. As a first step in establishing a family–professional partnership, Lynch and Hanson (1993) suggest that the intervention professional learn culture-specific information about the various groups living in the family's immediate community. With the help of a cultural mediator or community guide, the professional can learn and recognize the family's patterns, beliefs, and practices. Such information is important in discerning which aspects of the family's involvement in the child's intervention result from personal preferences, lack of information, or cultural differences. In fact, what mainstream America views as passive indifference may be considered active, valid participation in some families and cultures (Lynch & Hanson, 1993). However, even if a family is perceived to be totally uninvolved in the planning process, the interventionist should never discount or exclude the family from the decision-making process. To ensure optimal parental participation during program planning meetings, Lynch and Hanson identify several steps.

- Retain an inclusive definition of family, recognizing that in many families, extended family members, and unofficial family members (e.g., godparents) are heavily involved in the care of, and decision making about the child. It's often helpful for families to bring people important to them, including clergy, friends, and relatives, to meetings.
- Adapt the meeting such that its pace is consistent with the preference of the family members. For some families, this may mean holding several

preliminary meetings to get to know each member of the family and transdisciplinary team.

- Many families are likely to be intimidated by American bureaucracy. In these cases, the professional should meet with the family beforehand and be prepared to present the family's perspective to others on the transdisciplinary team. The professional also should anticipate and answer the questions that the family may not even know to ask.
- Goals, objectives, and outcomes should be consistent with the family's culture and should reflect the family's own perceived needs and priorities.
- Identify community resources, especially individuals and groups that may share the family's language, unique experiences, and culture, that can be of assistance to the family (Lynch & Hanson, 1993).

In Jessica's case, her parents live next door to her maternal grandparents. Because Jessica's grandparents are a very important part of the family's life, her parents invited them to the meeting. As a result of their attending, Jessica's grandmother, who had initially been opposed to the evaluation, gained better understanding of Jessica's strengths and needs. According to Jessica's mother, Jessica's grandmother is able to be much more supportive and is less likely to dismiss her own daughter's concerns.

It also is important to note that different families perceive early intervention differently and their attitudes have a direct impact on the level of family involvement. For some families, the very idea of intervention may be foreign or unacceptable. One of the major tacit assumptions of early intervention is that circumstances for the child and family will change for the better. Some families, especially those new to this country, may resist change and perceive intervention efforts as a threat to the integrity of the family unit. Even families who have been in the United States for generations may perceive an interventionist's well-intended efforts as meddling. If the family has members who are undocumented immigrants, they may even fear the service provider.

Frequently, a family's attitude toward intervention is directly related to its perceptions of disabling conditions and causation. Hanson, Lynch, and Wayman (1990) found that family perceptions of disabilities fall on a wide continuum, with some families emphasizing the role of fate and other families directly assigning responsibility to family members, essentially blaming themselves for their child's disability. For example, Vietnamese families may perceive a child's disability as a stroke of fate and they resist intervention as being futile (Green, 1982). Other cultures may view a disability as punishment for past sins and, in some Native American cultures, it is thought that the child makes a prenatal choice to be born disabled. By understanding and honoring such cultural differences, the professional may avoid misunderstandings and engender a positive partnership with the child's most important resource: the family.

Who Writes Individualized Service Plans?   Individualized service plans, both IFSPs and IEPs, are developed through a collaboration of a child's parents and at least two early intervention professionals. In addition to these individuals, team members may include other family members (e.g., grandparents or siblings) or individuals designated by the family, a parent advocate, service coordinator, evaluators, and interventionists. For IEPs, the 1997 Amendments to IDEA expanded the number of team members by requiring participation of the special education teacher, the regular education teacher, where appropriate, a person who can interpret the educational implications of evaluation results, and other individuals, at the discretion of the parent or agency, who have expertise relative to the child's needs. For example, a team that is writing a program plan for a child with cerebral palsy would probably include a physical therapist, whereas a physical therapist might not be needed for a child whose primary problem relates to speech and language. A wide range of disciplines provides services in early intervention and may be involved in writing IEPs and IFSPs. Team members can include but are not limited to professionals in the areas of audiology, education, medicine, nursing, nutrition, occupational therapy, physical therapy, psychology, social work, special education, and speech-language therapy.

When Are Individualized Service Plans Written?   An IEP or IFSP should be written within 45 days of a child being referred for services. Typically, the plan is written at a meeting of the child's parents and the professionals who will work with them. This first official meeting can be very important in that it represents the beginning of the child's involvement with the educational system and, as such, sets the tone for later interactions between parents and professionals. The goal of the meeting is for parents and professionals to agree to a plan of services for the next year (or 6 months, for children under 3 years). This agreement is formalized by all members of the planning team—most important, the parents—when they sign the written document.

How Are Individualized Service Plans Written?   Clearly, an individualized service plan is a very important document in that it determines the nature and level of services that a child will receive. All too often, however, busy professionals view IEPs and IFSPs as nothing more than paperwork to be gotten out of the way. When this attitude is taken, the writing of the service plan is not taken seriously, which results in a document with little utility and a program of services that has not been well thought out. Because the writing of the service plan has such important implications for effective intervention, strategies for writing practical goals and objectives are described next.

Linking Assessment and Intervention.   Goals and objectives of a service plan are framed from the information gathered from the assessment. Thus, the starting point for writing the service plan is the report from the (transdisciplinary) team evaluation. When thinking about appropriate goals, the team should not only consider the child's needs or areas of weakness but also endeavor to create a document that reflects the family's resources and concerns. As each goal is considered, intervention strategies are generated that build on the child's and family's strengths. Effective service plans contain information that enables the team to identify those strengths and resources that can be used to address deficits.

Writing Goals.   Goals are intended to describe in practical detail exactly what a child is expected to accomplish within the next 6 months (for IFSPs) or year (for IEPs). They represent observable, incremental steps to intended outcomes, including the maximal degree of participation in natural environments and in a typical curriculum. Although the process may seem straightforward, many professionals find that writing appropriate, helpful goals is among their most difficult tasks. In many respects, the goals of the IEP and IFSP are identical; the basic sequence for establishing and selecting goals is the same for both documents. The fundamental difference is that goals written for the IFSP include family as well as child-centered outcomes. By asking the following questions, professionals increase the likelihood that the goals they write for any service plan will be accomplished and will result in positive changes for the child and family.

1. *Were the parents involved in a meaningful way in formulating the goal statements?* To ensure optimal parental involvement in program implementation, the goals of the IEP and IFSP must reflect the priorities and concerns of the family. Parents are more likely to participate in early intervention in a meaningful way if the goals of intervention are meaningful to the family. Professionals must be careful not to project their own values and choices onto the family but to address only concerns that are identified by the family (Bailey, 1988). Moreover, goals must consider the unique strengths and limitations of each family member. Child rearing is a complex task and certain aspects of caring for a child with special needs may be particularly difficult for some families. For example, many low-socioeconomic-status families struggle with a host of day-to-day survival problems stemming from poverty. Such conditions may make some long-range goals of the individualized plan unattainable. If families are struggling to meet basic survival needs, they will be unable to plan for the future. Therefore, family problems, such as unemployment and lack of adequate clothing and food, need to be incorporated into individualized plans.

Before service plans can target families' needs, professionals and families must work together to identify and prioritize areas for intervention. This process, known in early intervention as **family assessment**, is crucial to the success of intervention. A number of instruments and techniques have been developed to facilitate the assessment of family needs and priorities. Ideally, professionals use several methods of obtaining information about families' needs and priorities, including interviews and questionnaires.

2. *Are the goals functional and age appropriate?* Goals and objectives always should be embedded in the functional activities within a child's social system and environment; that is, goals and objectives must be useful. After all, the purpose of early intervention is to enhance children's functioning within the context of their family and environment. Therefore, in relation to the goals of intervention, it is important to include only those activities that will lead to improved functioning in the environment. Obviously, this means considering a child's overall environment as well as the child's specific characteristics. Further, if a child's impairment limits participation in regular educational or social settings, then the intervention plan should be geared toward helping the child move into the most naturalistic environment possible. This means helping to ensure that children in self-contained settings are working toward moving into regular classrooms.

Functional goals also are designed to help make caring for a child easier for the family. For example, in the case of a young girl with fine motor impairments,

Self-contained settings are specialized settings specifically designed to provide educational or therapeutic services to children with special needs.

one functional goal might address her ability to help dress herself. On the other hand, a nonfunctional goal might involve working to improve the time it takes her to complete a pegboard. Even though the second goal may serve to increase her experiences in the fine motor domain, it will have at best a remote relationship to the greater goal of helping her learn to function independently.

3. *Are the goals realistic?* Goals must be attainable given the specific strengths of a child and the demands of the environment. Achievable goals serve to increase the autonomy of the child and family by improving the caregiver's sense of self-efficacy. If expectations go unrealized because they were unrealistic, family members may interpret this as evidence of their failure. Worse, if the family of a child with special needs consistently believes that no progress is being made, the family may become either isolated and discouraged about social services or overly dependent on them.

One way to avoid setting goals that are unrealistic is to establish long-term goals as well as short-term objectives. Long-term goals acknowledge family members' dreams for their child and can serve to keep intervention efforts in line with the family's priorities across several years. Short-term objectives, on the other hand, act to keep intervention efforts in the present and help keep families and professionals from becoming discouraged or overwhelmed by goals that may require years of effort before they are realized.

The process of breaking a goal into its component parts is called **task analysis**. Once the family and interventionists have identified a child's current level of functioning and their goals, the next step is task analysis. In this step, every skill necessary to accomplish the ultimate goal is identified. If necessary, these skills may be broken into subskills until the tasks seem manageable. To gain an appreciation for the process of task analysis, consider a simple activity that you do every day, such as brushing your teeth. Next, think about all the steps involved in this seemingly simple routine. First you must find and pick up the toothpaste, then unscrew the cap. Next, you may pick up your toothbrush and then squeeze the toothpaste with the other hand, and so on. Most of us can complete such tasks with a minimum of mental and physical effort, but for a child with fine motor impairment, each step may require intensive concentration and practice.

4. *Does the goal account for all levels of learning?* The process of learning a new skill can be conceptualized as progressing through five phases: acquisition, fluency, maintenance, generalization, and adaptation (Haring, Whilte, & Liberty, 1980, in Wolery, 1989). **Acquisition** is the most basic level of learning and means that a child can successfully complete the basic requirements of a skill. **Fluency** refers to the child's ability to complete the task smoothly and quickly. Maintenance and generalization are related in that **maintenance** refers to the child's performance of the skill in settings similar to the training situation, whereas **generalization** refers to the child's ability to perform the skill in settings different from the training situation. **Adaptation** represents the highest level of achievement because it reflects the child's ability to modify the skill to fit environmental demands or conditions. All too often, intervention goals stop at the level of acquisition in that once a child demonstrates accurate task completion, the goal is considered to have been attained. This, however, does not ensure that the child

will be able to use the new skill in other settings or that it will actually improve the child's day-to-day functioning.

Step 3: Implementation of Intervention

Once goals have been written, they must be implemented. Implementation of intervention involves translating goals and intended outcomes into a planned program of activities. Just as service plans are individualized blueprints for service delivery, the implementation process likewise is unique for each child. Two children may have an identical goal, but the implementation of services to achieve this goal will likely be quite different, depending on each child's unique circumstances and the philosophies and resources of the programs providing the services.

Identifying Resources.   The first step in implementation is to identify all the resources needed to accomplish the desired goals and outcomes detailed in the service plan. Resources can take many different forms but always are the tools of the trade for the interventionist. Although the law mandates that a child's needs—not the agency's resources—dictate the services provided, the manner in which a child's needs are addressed is likely to vary according to the resources available.

Family Resources.   The most significant resource for a child is the primary caregiver (Gutkin & Curtis, 1990). As such, the caregiver's resources and priorities must be taken into account as intervention is implemented. For example, if the primary caregiver does not have reliable transportation, intervention involving clinic-based therapy is doomed to failure unless the problem of getting the child to the clinic is addressed. Also, the caregiver's resources should be reassessed periodically as family circumstances change. Many unforeseen events can interfere with or enhance family members' abilities to support or participate in their child's intervention. Negative events (e.g., illness, sudden unemployment, or a car needing repair) may cause a sudden shift in the family's priorities and necessitate a change in the manner in which services are provided to a child. Likewise, positive events (e.g., extended family members moving nearby or a job promotion) may enable the family to assume additional responsibilities.

In identifying the family's resources, it also is important for the interventionist to understand the family's developmental stage and its impact on perceptions of the child's special needs (Turnbull & Turnbull, 1986). Life-cycle theorists point out that all families go through a series of developmental stages that influence family functioning and needs. Normal life events, such as the birth of a new child or a change in employment, affect in a profound way the family's psychological and material resources. Therefore, it is important for professionals to remain flexible and sensitive to the family's changing needs and resources as they implement intervention.

Professional Resources.   To avoid having services provided to a child in a piecemeal fashion or in isolation, the critical task of implementing professional recommendations and treatment must be coordinated by a single person, who is usually known as the service coordinator. The responsibility of the service coordinator is to work with a child's primary caregiver in the integration of intervention services. The importance of a service coordinator is particularly pronounced for children who have multiple needs or whose families are struggling with multiple stressors.

Because program implementation is the most active component of the intervention process, it is also the stage at which a family's cultural differences become most apparent. Any misunderstandings related to the professional–parent collaboration are likely to manifest themselves during implementation. One way to avoid these misunderstandings is through the involvement of community guides. Community guides are respected individuals who are familiar with a family's cultural norms, attitudes, traditions, and perceptions. They may or may not be members of the transdisciplinary team, depending on the wishes of the family. Community guides may be religious leaders, interpreters, elders, or business leaders. They provide the interventionist insight into community norms and expectations and ensure that resources within a family's community are identified and utilized in a meaningful way.

> Norms refer to the beliefs, shared by a cultural group, regarding appropriate behavior of its members.

Next, intervention professionals must be identified and their efforts coordinated with those of the primary caregiver. Depending on the needs of a child, these professional resource people may include psychologists, teachers, speech pathologists, physical and occupational therapists, audiologists, physicians, dietitians, or social workers. Within the community, professional resource people may be identified through local schools, day-care programs, Head Start, mental health organizations, governmental agencies, or private nonprofit groups. For the purposes of this discussion, four categories of professional resources are considered: medical, allied health, mental health, and educational resources.

Medical Professionals.   For many children with disabilities, particularly those with severe or multiple disabilities, their problems are associated with medical conditions and are usually identified at or not long after birth. In some cases, this identification is made prenatally through amniocentesis, or other medical techniques (see chapter 4 for a description). Families of such children find themselves immediately involved with medical professionals. If a child's condition is identified at birth, it is likely that the child's first physician will be a **neonatalogist**, a physician who specializes in the care and treatment of newborns.

For most children, however, the primary health care provider is a **pediatrician** or pediatric nurse practitioner. Depending on a child's particular health care needs, the child may be involved with many types of medical specialists. Some specialists commonly encountered by young children with disabilities include **pulmonologists** (respiratory system), **neurologists** (nervous system), **orthopedists** (skeletal and muscular systems), **cardiologists** (heart and circulatory system), and **endocrinologists** (endocrine system). For children with multiple medical needs, pediatricians often assume the role of medical service coordinators. For nonmedical interventionists such as teachers and psychologists, pediatricians can be an important resource and should be viewed as colleagues in the development of intervention plans for children.

Nurses also are an important professional resource for many children with disabilities. A number of medical conditions require around-the-clock care or frequent medical procedures. Because of financial considerations and families' needs to resume their normal lives, many children, particularly those born prematurely, are released from the hospital with ongoing needs for medical intervention. These children are likely to receive home-based nursing care. In many instances, the nurse becomes one of the primary care providers and, as such, a vital agent of intervention.

Allied Health Professionals.   Included in this category are specialized therapists, including **speech-language pathologists** (SLPs), **occupational therapists** (OTs), and **physical therapists** (PTs). As their name implies, SLPs are concerned with disorders related to communication and oral-motor problems. Many young children with disabilities have difficulties with receptive or expressive language that can be addressed by SLPs. In addition, SLPs work with children who have typical language abilities but have difficulty communicating because of unclear speech. There also are SLPs who specialize in the oral-motor structures involved in speech and eating and may be called upon for children with feeding difficulties or structural deformities (e.g., cleft palate) that interfere primarily with eating and speaking. Physical and occupational therapists are similar in that both are concerned with motor abilities. As a general rule, however, the two professionals can be distinguished by the fact that PTs are primarily concerned with large muscle groups, or gross motor activities, such as walking, sitting, and jumping, whereas OTs typically address small muscle groups, or fine motor activities, such as writing and tying shoes. OTs also are called upon to assist with daily living tasks and, along with specially trained SLPs, to address feeding problems.

Depending on the specialized needs of a child, the expertise of other allied health professionals also may be required. For example, a child with visual impairments may receive services from a vision specialist who will assess the degree and developmental impact of vision loss, provide early mobility training, and recommend specialized equipment (Thomas, Correa, & Morsink, 1995). Similarly, audiologists and specialists in educational programming for children who are deaf work with children with hearing impairments.

Mental Health Professionals.   Families of children with disabilities are likely to encounter a number of mental health professionals as a result of their involvement with early intervention and various forms of social services. **Psychologists** are likely to be involved in the initial assessment of a child and often are called upon to provide estimates of children's cognitive abilities. Beyond the assessment phase of intervention, psychologists may provide grief counseling services or therapy to address specific problems (e.g., child behavior problems).

Social workers are another type of mental health professional likely to work with families of children with special needs. Social workers' unique understanding of social services and agencies make them a natural choice as service coordinators. Even if social workers are not designated as service coordinators, they often play a vital role in helping a family gain access to social services. Additionally, social workers may provide counseling, parent training, and other mental health services, as their training, interests, and job responsibilities permit.

IEPs and IFSPs are developed through collaboration of a child's parents and early intervention professionals.

Education Professionals. Perhaps the most common professional resource in early intervention is the early childhood educator. Two distinct types of educators can be identified: **early childhood educators** (ECEs) and **early childhood special educators** (ECSEs). Whether a child is served primarily by an ECE or ECSE depends in large part on the setting in which services are provided. ECEs commonly work with typically developing preschoolers, usually in a classroom-based early childhood setting. ECSEs, on the other hand, specialize in working with infants and young children with disabilities.

In addition to the different settings in which they work, ECEs and ECSEs have historically relied on different educational philosophies and practices (Bredekamp, 1993; Burton et al., 1992; Wolery & Wilburs, 1994). ECEs have typically attended teacher training programs that have been grounded in constructivism, whereas ECSEs have typically attended training programs that have been based largely on behavioral theory (Smith & Bredekamp, 1998; see also Wolery, Werts, & Holcombe, 1994; Wolery & Wilburs, 1994). Historically, more often than not, early childhood education and early childhood special education have maintained separate programs and services. Thus, it was possible for ECEs and ECSEs to keep their educational philosophies and practices separate (Smith & Bredekamp, 1998). In recent years, however, more children with special needs are being included in early childhood classrooms (Sexton, 1998; Wolery et al., 1993; Wolery et al., 1994), resulting in educators being called upon to instruct all types of children. Therefore, despite the traditional split among education professionals, as more children with special needs are served in regular educational settings, the gap between ECEs and ECSEs is narrowing (e.g., see most recent reauthorization of IDEA).

Location of Intervention.   The place where a child with special needs receives services has become a topic of great interest in the past several years. For many years, children with special needs of all ages received educational and therapeutic services in relative isolation. For example, a young child with cerebral palsy might have received educational services in a "preschool class for handicapped children" and received PT services in the therapist's office, rarely if ever interacting with typically developing peers. However, in recent years, the trend toward serving children with special needs in regular settings has gained momentum. The continuum of setting options ranging from clinic- or school-based self-contained classrooms to fully normalized settings is described next.

Self-Contained Settings.   Self-contained classrooms are the traditional setting for special education services. Placement in such settings has been based on the assumption that a child's disability prevented her from benefiting from standard classrooms and necessitated intensive, one-to-one instruction (Odom & McEvoy, 1990). Reviews of the research suggest possible advantages of such classrooms for some students, particularly those with severe disabilities such as deafness or autism (Heward, 1996). Similarly, other therapies (e.g., occupational, physical, and speech-language therapy) have traditionally been conducted in isolation, often in hospital-based or clinic settings.

Within the context of self-contained placements, a technique known as **reverse mainstreaming** has been used to increase contact between children with disabilities and their typically developing peers. With this technique, children without disabilities are brought into the special education classroom or therapy session for varying amounts of time.

Normalized Settings.   Federal law requires that intervention be provided in the least restrictive environment (LRE) possible. For infants and toddlers, this often means that services are provided in the child's home. Home-based intervention consists of an interventionist (e.g., an ECSE, SLP, PT, or OT) visiting a child's home on a weekly or biweekly basis, depending on the child's needs and IFSP or IEP goals, and providing direct therapy to the child and consultation for the care providers. Depending on a family's needs and the age of a child, early intervention services also may be provided in the context of regular child-care settings, such as preschools or day-care centers. In such cases, an interventionist may be called upon to assume a number of roles. For example, an SLP may work with a group of children, only one of whom has a disability, in a day-care classroom. An SLP also may function as a consultant to the regular teachers or assistants. A number of advantages have been identified for this type of service delivery (McWilliam & Bailey, 1994); most notably, by including intervention in a child's regular routine, the child is more likely to use the skills in everyday life. An additional advantage is that the skills addressed are more likely to be functional in nature. However, as the most appropriate setting for providing intervention services is determined, a number of factors must be taken into account. Within the context of family-centered intervention services, the family's preferences must be accommodated to as great a degree as possible, and the decision regarding the setting for service delivery must be made on a case-by-case basis.

For selecting the intervention setting, Bailey and McWilliam (1990) identify two primary considerations: effectiveness and normalization. **Effectiveness** refers to the intersection between a child's characteristics and environmental demands; that is, given a child's individual characteristics, what is the most effective means of reaching the goals identified by the family? If, for example, the family's priority is for the child to develop social skills, the most effective intervention is likely to be in a regular classroom. If, on the other hand, the family identifies learning sign language as the priority, this may best be accomplished in a self-contained classroom for children with hearing impairments.

Normalization refers to interventions that have as their primary goal facilitating "normal" experiences for children with disabilities. This is accomplished both through the location of the intervention and the strategies of the intervention. As described earlier, the location of the intervention should be the least restrictive environment (LRE); ideally, LRE is the school, center, or program the child would attend if the child had no special needs. Intervention strategies and activities can facilitate normalization by emphasizing functionality. For example, if the goal of the intervention is to improve fine motor skills, age-appropriate activities such as puzzles, tying shoes, coloring, and so on are preferable to less normal activities such as finger exercises.

The Debate Surrounding Inclusion.   Few professionals, parents, or individuals with disabilities would dispute that the goal of early intervention and special education is to enable children with special needs to participate fully in all the settings and environments enjoyed by those without special needs. This principle also is reflected in federal law. Increasingly, parents and professionals in special education and related fields have come to expect full inclusion of all children, including children with significant special needs. Although a range of definitions exists, advocates for full inclusion have defined an **inclusive school** as "a place where everybody belongs, is accepted, supports, and is supported by his or her peers and other members of the school community in the course of having his or her educational needs met" (Stainback & Stainback, 1992, p. 3). Further, within such a school, all types of children learn together, without regard for the nature or severity of their disabilities. Stainback and Stainback argue that, because children with special needs receive services from special educators, regular educators have begun to view special education as a dumping ground for "undesirable" children or children with problems. The only way to correct this, they argue, is to abolish special education completely.

Although the ideal of providing support for and acceptance of individuals with disabilities in all settings is appealing, some professionals worry that a small group within the educational community has gone too far on this issue (Fuchs & Fuchs, 1994). By arguing for full inclusion of children with disabilities, the more extreme advocates of inclusion also are calling for the abolition of the range of special services for children with special needs. Other professionals fear that such a move is not only unrealistic but would also threaten the quality of the education that could be obtained by children with special needs.

Clearly, the issues are complex and philosophical, and the debate is likely to be waged for some time. Whether or not schools and the ways in which children with special needs are educated are radically reformed remains to be seen. In the meantime, the Council for Exceptional Children (CEC), the major organization devoted to the education of children with special needs, has issued a middle-of-the-road position statement. The CEC supports inclusion as a meaningful goal but advocates a continuum of services, ranging from full inclusion to specialized settings (Heward, 1996). At this point in the debate, young children and their families are probably best served by professionals who are able to put their own positions on the issue aside and assume a pragmatic approach when developing service plans. Consistent with a family-focused view of early intervention, the setting in which each child receives services should be an individual decision based on the goals and priorities identified by the family.

Developing a Strategy.   Once the resources have been identified and the setting selected, the next salient issue is how to use these resources to facilitate the child's optimal development within the framework of the service plan. An instructional, therapeutic strategy is required. Several researchers (Barnett & Carey, 1992; Bricker & Cripe, 1998; Dunst, Hamby, Trivette, Raab, & Bruder, 2000) suggest that a **naturalistic, activity-based approach** is the best strategy for program implementation. Naturalistic intervention incorporates environmental variables into service delivery, and training goals are embedded in daily routines. Naturalistic, activity-based intervention is preferred for several reasons. First, intervention is most likely to be successful if it is linked to the caregiver's current living situation. Bricker (1989) reminds us that "the family situation itself dictates where, when, how, and in what areas to begin intervention" (p. 165). Second, skills acquired in naturalistic settings are most likely to generalize to different environments. Generalization of skills is best served by "providing the least artificial, least cumbersome, and most natural positive consequences in programming intervention. Such programming most closely matches naturally occurring consequences" (Stokes & Osnes, 1989, p. 341). Third, naturalistic intervention strategies emphasize the competency and involvement of caregivers. Finally, a naturalistic, activity-based approach ensures that targeted goals and outcomes are likely to be functionally appropriate and valued by the child and family. For the well-trained educator, everyday family and community settings provide varied and rich opportunities for intervention within the very contexts that matter most to families (Dunst et al., 2000).

> An activity-based approach is a functional approach to instruction that capitalizes on the use of naturally occurring activities as "teachable" opportunities.

Within the structure of naturalistic intervention, short-term, measurable objectives can facilitate the acquisition of new skills. Hanson (1987) advocates task analysis in the teaching of such objectives. Again, in task analysis, a target behavior is first identified and then broken down into a series of smaller tasks required to achieve the target. For example, a target behavior for an infant might be to roll over from her back to her front. The series of behaviors leading to successful completion of the target behavior might be that (a) the infant extends her arm to one side and rolls her shoulders, (b) the infant shifts her leg to align with her shoulders, and (c) the infant completes the roll by turning over to her front. Whereas the primary focus is on the target behavior, task analysis methods also provide the child and family with insight into the process of learning. Moreover, the emphasis on measurable objectives facilitates program evaluation.

Bricker (1989) recommends a combination of home-based and center-based implementation strategies. Home-based strategies are frequently used with infants up to age 3 years. As described earlier in this chapter, professionals visit the home on a regular basis and help the caregiver implement the selected treatments and activities. The advantages of home-based strategies are obvious: Parental involvement is increased and the interventionist is afforded the opportunity to observe parent–child interaction. In addition, home visits become training sessions for the parent.

Center-based models, on the other hand, rely on structured classroom activities and are usually employed with children above age 3. Head Start is an example of an intervention program that uses a center-based strategy. Center-based programs may include only children with special needs (self-contained setting) or children both with and without disabilities (inclusive or mainstreamed setting). Although preschools vary in terms of their philosophies, they typically stress the acquisition of developmental, cognitive, social, and self-help skills necessary for success in elementary school (see Box 5.3 on school readiness).

Center-based models and strategies also afford a child a new setting for practicing skills acquired in the home. A child's ability to generalize skills across settings is crucial for successful transition to new, less restrictive environments. For the family, center-based models also provide the opportunity to interact with other parents as well as needed respite from the child.

Philosophical Approaches and Developmental Theories. One of the crucial ways in which early intervention programs differ from one another is reflected by differences in their philosophical orientations. Early intervention relies on a rich history of developmental theory. Although no one school or theory is right or wrong, different developmental theories support different models of intervention. In addition, different programs focus on different areas of development, based on their underlying theories.

To be effective, intervention should be based on an underlying developmental theory. Not only are programs guided by the theoretical perspectives on which they are based, but professionals working with children and families also are influenced by their own varying beliefs about the ways children develop and the best

---

BOX 5.3	**School Readiness**

Educators, policy makers, and researchers have identified the early childhood years as critically important to children's success in school. Head Start has long had as a goal providing quality educational opportunities to children at risk for school failure due to economic disadvantage. In an effort to reach more children, a number of states have begun initiatives designed to provide high-quality preschool experiences to all children. The goal of these projects was derived largely from the National Educational Goals Panel—that all children enter kindergarten cognitively, emotionally, socially, and motorically ready to learn. As additional public funds are spent on early education, the opportunities for children with special needs to receive intervention with their typically developing peers is likely to increase as well.

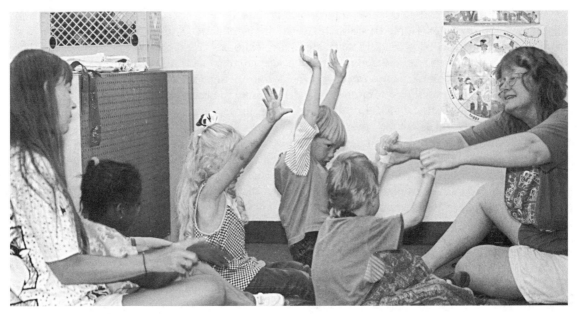

Whenever possible, children with special needs should participate fully in settings enjoyed by children without special needs.

ways to effect change, which are in turn influenced by their theoretical or philosophical perspectives. Given this central role of developmental theory in intervention, the following paragraphs briefly describe three of the most prevalent theoretical perspectives: those based on developmental, behavioral, and contextual models.

Developmental Models. Developmental models emphasize a child's biological makeup and maturation and are based largely on the theories of Piaget, Dewey, and Erikson. Intervention based on such models rests upon the assumption that development occurs along a natural course internal to a child. As the child encounters new and different experiences, she feels dissatisfied with her current means of solving problems and is motivated to accommodate new information and new ways of thinking.

Interventionists who adhere to developmental models believe that children are internally motivated to explore and master the world around them. For example, Piaget described young children as little scientists who explore the world around them through active manipulation (Bowe, 1995a). Further, this model maintains that the best and most efficient way for children to learn is through hands-on experiences and interactions with the material world. The role of the interventionist, then, is to provide experiences and create environments that support and facilitate a child's individual, self-directed growth. Jerome Bruner describes this process as "**discovery learning**," whereby children are their own teachers in an environment structured to encourage exploration (Bowe, 1995a).

Professionals who adhere to developmental models such as those based on Piaget's theories often refer to their philosophy as **developmentally appropriate practice (DAP)**. Developmental appropriateness was defined by the National Association for the Education of Young Children (Bredekamp & Copple, 1997) and refers both to age appropriateness (i.e., the predictable pattern and stages of development described by theorists such as Piaget and Erikson) and to an individual child's pattern of development (Black & Puckett, 1996). Montessori programs are often cited as examples of programs for young children that adhere to this definition of DAP. As the name suggests, Montessori programs are based on the work of Maria Montessori, an educator who worked in Rome in the early 20th century. Montessori methods include ungraded classrooms, instruction individualized to meet each child's unique educational needs, material that is ordered sequentially to reflect stages of development, and an absence of punishment (Richmond & Ayoub, 1993).

Behavioral Models.   These models are based on the structured principles of behavioral psychology. Unlike developmental models, behavioral models deemphasize the internal motivations of the individual. Instead, specific target behaviors are identified and taught using reinforcement, shaping, and modeling. In its simplest form, **behavioral theory** relies on the principles of reward and punishment: If a child is rewarded for a behavior, the child is likely to repeat the behavior, whereas punishing a child following a behavior decreases the chances that the behavior will be repeated. In contrast to programs guided by developmental theories, programs guided by behavioral theory typically rely more heavily on direct, one-on-one instruction.

An adaptation of behavioral theory is **social learning theory**, an approach emphasizing that children learn by observing and imitating. Within this framework, behavior is believed to be changed because of exposure to models. For example, in the case of a child who cannot play appropriately with other children because of her aggressive behavior, intervention based on social learning theory might include having the child watch other children play together without fighting.

Contextual Models.   Contextual models emphasize the role of the environment in shaping the development of a young child. Within such models, the roles of family and community, as well as the greater society, are considered. Urie Bronfenbrenner's (1986) **ecological model** is widely used as an intervention framework. Bronfenbrenner suggests that a child, family, community, and larger society can be viewed as concentric circles of influence that all affect the child's development. Similarly, Lev Vygotsky's **sociohistorical theory** has been used widely with students who have disabilities (Brown, Evans, Weed, & Owen, 1987). This model is sometimes called the functional model because it emphasizes the importance of social context in the acquisition of domestic, vocational, and communication skills that increase a child's self-sufficiency and independence in daily life. As one might expect, intervention based on this model seeks to facilitate the development of strong, supportive social networks for the family of the target child.

Within the contextual model, Sameroff and Chandler (1975) have developed a transactional approach that examines the intersection between characteristics of the individual and the environment. Because of its sensitivity to both dynamics, this approach provides a framework that is particularly relevant to early intervention. In the **transactional model**, Sameroff and Chandler suggest that development results from a cycle of ongoing, dynamic, and reciprocal interactions between a child and her environment, which includes parents and other caregivers. By introducing the notion of reciprocal interactions, the transactional model maintains that a child not only is influenced by her environment but also influences her environment. For example, consider a child who was born with health problems that have caused her to be irritable and to cry most of the time. Because the mother is unable to soothe the child, the mother begins to feel that she is a bad parent. Further, because of the negative feelings the mother experiences around her crying baby, she begins to avoid interacting with the child. Consequently, because the mother rarely talks to or interacts with the child, the child's language does not develop as rapidly as it otherwise would, and as a preschooler she is diagnosed with a language delay. Clearly, the child's language delay was not caused by either the mother's or the child's characteristics alone. Instead, the problem resulted from an interaction, or from the series of dynamic transactions, between the child's characteristics and the mother's feelings and behaviors.

Despite the apparent differences among the three broad kinds of models, all share a single, strong commonality. The thread running through all models of intervention and associated theories is that a child is an active, competent, and social organism. Therefore, although there certainly are biological components to a child's development, there also are interactions between the child and the environment that affect both the child's development and the larger social context. Accordingly, a child's developmental outcome is the result of biological constituents, the environment, and transactions between them.

Developmental theories guide our understanding of intervention with children and families by helping us to answer two fundamental questions: *Why* do children behave the way they do? *How* do children develop more mature behaviors? The following example of Jessica, a 4-year-old girl who is having trouble getting along with her peers, is presented to illustrate the differences among developmental, behavioral, and contextual theories.

Vignette 5.1

JESSICA

Jessica's parents are concerned because she has recently begun to hit other children in her preschool. Her parents asked three child development experts, each with a different theoretical orientation, to explain why Jessica hits other children and to offer solutions for helping her improve her peer relationships.

Jake is a developmental (cognitive) theorist, the first child development expert contacted by Jessica's parents. Jake believes that children's behavior is best understood in the context of their level of cognitive maturation. Therefore, in order to explain Jessica's behavior, Jake wanted to find out more about Jessica's development; that is, what does Jessica understand about the effects of her behaviors? After spending some time watching Jessica and talking with her, her parents, and her teacher, Jake decided that Jessica has been hitting other children because she does not understand that it hurts others when she hits them. Thus, Jake believes that cognitive immaturity, a deficit in the development of her understanding of the environment, explains Jessica's poor peer relationships. Jake believes that the best way to help Jessica learn more appropriate ways of interacting with her peers is to address this lack of understanding by first helping her learn to take the perspective of her peers. Jake recommended that Jessica's parents and teacher talk with Jessica about how her choices (hitting versus not hitting) affect others. Additionally, because Jake believes that children learn from their natural interactions with their environment, he also talked with Jessica's teacher about the classroom and ways to structure Jessica's environment so that she learns how to play appropriately.

Karen is a behavioral theorist. Unlike Jake, Karen does not believe that understanding Jessica's internal thought processes is very important for explaining or changing her behavior. Karen chose instead to focus only on the actual behavior (hitting others). She believes that Jessica hits other children because hitting them is rewarding for Jessica in some way. According to Karen, the key to understanding Jessica's behavior, then, is to discover what leads up to and

Particularly for children with behavior problems or other difficulties interacting with peers, a social skills-based preschool may be an appropriate form of intervention.

follows her hitting of others. To determine what is causing the hitting behavior, Karen decided to observe Jessica playing with her peers at school. After watching Jessica for several days and recording what leads up to and follows her hitting behavior, Karen decided that Jessica hits other children when they try to play with a toy she wants. Jessica is rewarded for hitting because, after she hits a child, the child leaves and Jessica can play with the toy of her choice. To help Jessica learn more appropriate play skills, Karen recommended that Jessica be rewarded with a sticker when she shares a toy without hitting other children and that she be sent to time-out when she hits others.

Sara is a contextual theorist, the third child development expert contacted by Jessica's parents. Sara believes that the environment shapes the way a child behaves. In order to understand why Jessica hits other children, Sara wanted to know about Jessica's environment and about the interactions between Jessica's characteristics and her environment. Sara wants to know not only about Jessica's classroom but also about Jessica's home life. Sara interviewed Jessica's parents and teacher and observed Jessica at home and at school. Sara decided that Jessica hits others because she hasn't learned social interaction skills from her environment. According to Sara, it is important for all of the people in Jessica's social network (e.g., parents, teachers, grandparents, and peers) to help Jessica learn more adaptive ways of dealing with conflict. Sara also emphasized that if Jessica's parents are anxious or overwhelmed by parenting responsibilities, Jessica may feel upset and act out at school. Therefore, Sara thinks that an important way for Jessica's parents to help Jessica is to seek some form of social support.

Types of Programs.   In addition to having different theoretical orientations, center-based early intervention programs focus on different areas of child development. Some programs develop their focus as a result of their theoretical orientations. For example, preschools based on developmental theories are likely to focus on children's play because of the belief that play is the most effective and developmentally appropriate way to encourage children's development. However, other programs focus on one area of development because they are specifically designed to serve children who demonstrate particular problems (e.g., language problems). Some of the most commonly encountered types of preschool programs, including play-based, academically oriented, language-based, and social skills-based programs, are described next.

Play-Based Programs.   No matter what their theoretical orientations are, most early interventionists believe in developmentally appropriate practice (Heward, 1996) and therefore agree that play is a vital component of every early childhood program. As the name implies, play-based early intervention programs recognize that children learn best through play. Preschools adhering to this philosophy typically are child-directed, meaning that children are encouraged to select their own activities. By creating a rich learning environment, teachers facilitate development through manipulation of materials and through children's interactions with each other and with adults. Most play-based classrooms are organized around centers (e.g., a house-keeping center, block center, and art center), and children are allowed to rotate among the activities at their own pace.

Academically Oriented Programs.   In contrast to play-based models, there also are traditional, academically oriented preschools. Academically oriented preschools strive to teach preacademic skills and prepare children for school. Rather than children being allowed to choose their own activities, as occurs in play-based preschools, children in academically oriented preschools spend most of their time engaged in teacher-directed activities. Often, these activities involve seatwork or circle time, in which the entire class gathers around the teacher for a lesson. Although some preschoolers may be able to cope with the demands of such a structured setting, most experts in child development agree that large-group activities and teacher-directed programming do not reflect developmentally appropriate practice and are not an efficient way to facilitate the cognitive, language, social, or motor development of young children.

Language-Based Programs.   One of the most important developmental tasks of the preschool years is learning language. Language deficits are among the developmental difficulties most frequently encountered by early intervention professionals. For this reason, many preschools are designed specifically to address language deficits. Language-based preschools employ a number of techniques to encourage the use of language and they often use environmental factors, such as the types of toys that are available, to encourage children to use language adaptively. For example, rather than having a large number of toys that encourage solitary play (e.g., puzzles), language-based preschools are likely to contain more social toys (e.g., dramatic play materials and games that require talking or turn taking). Teachers also may wish to set up language-based classrooms in such a way that children are encouraged to ask for help. For example, the most desirable toys may be kept on out-of-reach shelves so that children are motivated to ask for assistance.

Heward (1996) identifies two approaches for systematically promoting language development in the preschool: the **incidental teaching model** (Hart & Risley, 1975) and the **mand model** (Rogers-Warren & Warren, 1980). Within the incidental teaching model, the teacher uses naturally occurring opportunities to facilitate language use. Anytime a child wants something from the teacher, the teacher attempts to draw out the conversation. For example, if a child walks up to the teacher on the playground and points to the swings, rather than attempt to anticipate the child's desire to swing, the teacher might say, "Can you say *swing?*" If the child says the word, the teacher assists the child with the swing and gives praise. If the child does not say the word, the teacher still provides assistance without reprimand. In the incidental teaching model, it is very important that the child not perceive interactions with the teacher as punitive or unpleasant. This model assumes that language will be learned most effectively if children frequently initiate language opportunities with their teachers.

In the mand model, the interactions are typically initiated by the teacher. Within the context of regular activities, the teacher attempts to elicit a target response from a child, usually by asking a question. Using the example of the child who wants to swing, the teacher might say, "What do you want to do?" If the child does not respond, the teacher "demands" a response by saying something like, "Tell me." The teacher then attempts to elicit a more elaborate response by saying, for example, "Say, *Want to swing.*"

Social Skills-Based Programs.   A developmental task closely associated with language development is social skills development. For many children, preschool is their first opportunity to interact with peers. Particularly for children with behavior problems or other difficulties interacting with peers, a social skills-based preschool may be an appropriate type of intervention. Many such programs use model children—children who are competent social partners—to encourage appropriate play. As with language-based preschools, the environment can be manipulated to increase interaction opportunities. For example, limiting the number of toys available encourages children to play together and teachers can intervene to encourage appropriate sharing behavior. Therapeutic preschools—programs that incorporate psychological therapy along with educational goals—may be available for young children with severe emotional or behavioral problems.

Recommended Practices in Early Intervention.   To facilitate excellence in program implementation, it helps to have established standards of practice. Such recommended practices provide a benchmark for measuring the overall quality of any intervention program. Apart from the legal criteria mandated by Parts B and C of IDEA, there are no firmly established standards of practice for early intervention programs. However, several state educational agencies have proposed standards that are believed to be consistent with appropriate practice. Carta, Schwartz, Atwater, and McConnell (1991) and Johnson, Kaufman, and McGonigel (1989) suggest that best practices in early intervention include the following:

- a range of services that vary in intensity based on the needs of the children
- individualized teaching plans consisting of goals and objectives based on careful analyses of children's strengths and weaknesses and on skills required for future school and nonschool environments
- transdisciplinary assessment that is frequent enough to adequately monitor children's progress
- instructional approaches that are effective, efficient, functional, and normalized
- instructional approaches that actively engage children and their families
- activities that strengthen the abilities of families to "nurture their children's development and promote normalized community adaptation"
- program managers and workers who respect and acknowledge the diversity of patterns and structures within each family

Carta et al. and Johnson et al. also offer the following suggestions for best practices in early intervention:

- Families must be permitted to choose their level of involvement with the IFSP process. To help families with decision making, professionals must be clear and honest in their communications with them. Within the framework provided by parental involvement, professionals must respect families' rights to privacy and confidentiality.

- The program manager should strive to form a partnership and collaboration with a child's family. This relationship is fostered by adopting and adapting service delivery strategies that conform to the family's diversity and structure. Professionals also must be accessible and responsive to the family's questions and requests.
- Early intervention services should be flexible, accessible, and responsive to family-identified needs. To address these needs, the family and intervention team should compose goals and objectives that are functional and representative of the family's choices.
- Early intervention services should be provided according to the normalization principle; that is, families should have access to services that are provided in as normal a fashion and environment as possible and that promote the integration of the child and family within the community.
- Planning and service delivery should incorporate multiple agencies and disciplines. This approach acknowledges that no single agency or discipline can entirely meet the complex needs of children with special needs and their families.
- Family members should be present for all decision-making opportunities.

Step 4: Evaluation

Evaluation has become increasingly central to education, as recent federal and state legislation (e.g., the No Child Left Behind Act) emphasize educational accountability and mandate testing across grades in publically funded schools. Snyder and Sheehan (1993) define *evaluation* as "the process of systematically gathering, synthesizing, and interpreting reliable and valid information about programs for the purpose of aiding with decision making" (p. 269). Beyond political requirements for accountability, the bottom line for evaluation is the determination of the overall worth of a program (Bailey, 2001). In early intervention, program evaluation has two complementary purposes: to examine the effectiveness of a program and to determine the impact of a program on an individual child and family.

Evaluation is often synonymous with *accountability,* which can be loosely defined as the systematic activities through which professionals seek to demonstrate to their stakeholders that their actions have accomplished the desired outcomes. The "stakeholders" of early intervention include all parties with an investment in the early intervention program. The most obvious type of investment is financial. Like all state and federally funded programs, early intervention programs have a social and legal obligation to provide proof of their effectiveness. Because administrators, legislators, and other decision makers must determine which programs will receive funding, program evaluation provides vital information. In addition, by evaluating themselves and their programs, professionals help ensure that they will provide the best possible intervention to the families they serve.

Families who participate in early intervention also have investments of time and personal resources in the program and, as such, should be considered an audience for evaluation efforts (Simeonsson et al., in press). Program evaluation thus attempts to determine the impact of early intervention on individual children and their families. Accordingly, evaluation provides an index of program success related to three aspects of service implementation:

1. Efficiency of service delivery: Was intervention implemented as stated in the IEP or IFSP? Were services rendered in a timely and appropriate manner?
2. Overall child outcomes: What changes in the child's behavior occurred and can be demonstrated to be the result of intervention? What was the quality of these changes? Were any unexpected or undesired outcomes observed? To what extent were the desired outcomes of the IEP or IFSP achieved?
3. Overall family outcomes: Was the family satisfied with intervention? What are their attitudes regarding intervention? To what extent were the family's priorities addressed? (Bailey, 2001; Bricker & Gumerlock, 1988; Peterson, 1987; Snyder & Sheehan, 1993)

The Family's Role in Evaluation.   Part C of IDEA formalized the importance of the family in providing early intervention services. Several studies (e.g., Able-Boone, Sandall, Loughry, & Frederick, 1990) have confirmed that families want greater involvement in early intervention programs. Given the importance of the family in formulating objectives and implementing services, it is logical that families also should play a role in program evaluation. An obvious component of program evaluation that directly involves parents is consumer satisfaction. At a minimum, program evaluation should answer the question: "Are parents satisfied with the delivery of early intervention services?"

Frequently, professionals use specially designed questionnaires and rating scales to assess family satisfaction. One such rating scale used in program evaluation is the Family-Centered Program Rating Scale, or FamPRS (Murphy, Lee, Turnbull, & Turbiville, 1995), a rating scale designed to measure parents' perceptions of and attitudes toward service delivery. Sample items from the FamPRS ask parents to agree or disagree with evaluative statements such as the following:

1. Services can change quickly when my family's or child's needs change.
2. My family is included in all meetings about ourselves and our child.
3. Staff members do not rush my family to make changes until we are ready to.
4. Staff members ask my family's opinion and include us in the process of evaluating our child.

In general, parents who have greater involvement with the delivery of intervention services report greater satisfaction (Caro & Derevensky, 1991). In a study designed to isolate the source of parental satisfaction with early intervention programs, McWilliam et al. (1995) found that the individual case managers' behaviors were "often directly linked to families' positive impressions of early intervention services" (p. 53). Clearly, from the family's perspective, the individual interventionist is a principal source of their satisfaction. This finding should come as no surprise: The program manager is the primary channel through which the various intervention services flow. The program manager is the professional most visible to the family and represents the concerted efforts of everyone involved in the delivery of services. There is a need for further research to determine the specific personal and professional qualities of early interventionists that relate to parental satisfaction with services.

Not all research fully supports family involvement in early intervention. Innocenti, Hollinger, Escobar, and White (1995) evaluated the impact of parental involvement in the early intervention of 76 toddlers enrolled in a special classroom-based program. The researchers found that parental involvement had a relatively small initial effect on the toddlers' development and they concluded that parental involvement was not immediately cost effective. However, the authors also acknowledged that parental involvement may have a cumulative effect that is best evaluated over time. A parent may have the greatest impact not in the short term, but over the course of a child's lifetime. As Skeels (1966) noted more than 30 years ago, more longitudinal research is needed to assess the full impact of early intervention.

Planning the Evaluation.   To answer evaluation questions adequately, the interventionist must plan ahead. Because special education law requires that IEPs and IFSPs address evaluation at the program planning stage, evaluation should be a part of the intervention plan. By planning and implementing intervention with an eye toward evaluation, the interventionist can make the process much less time consuming and more systematic.

A first step in planning program evaluation is to determine the target audience for the evaluation. Who will use the information provided by the evaluation? Different target audiences require that different evaluative questions be answered. For example, if the information is to be used internally (i.e., by service coordinators working in a particular local agency), some questions that may be asked include "Are the children making suitable progress in meeting the objectives of the program plan?" and "Are families satisfied with the behaviors of the case manager?" However, if the information is to be used externally (e.g., by state education agencies), questions such as "What is the cost effectiveness of service delivery?" and "What percentage of children has been diagnosed with developmental disorders?" might be asked. The expectations and needs of the target audience determine the questions to be answered by the evaluation and thus frame its content.

The next step in planning an evaluation is to develop a design; that is, a systematic method for answering the questions posed for evaluation. This step in evaluation planning is crucial, yet it often is overlooked. One of the major problems in evaluating the effectiveness of early intervention programs occurs when researchers and agencies fail to employ a systematic methodology (Weatherford, 1986). A strong, systematic evaluation design not only provides insight into the overall quality of early intervention but also helps determine which specific components of an intervention program are most effective. The design should follow logically from the questions to be answered. Some questions, such as those relating to parental satisfaction, are best answered by simple rating scales and questionnaires. Other questions, such as those concerning a child's progress, may best be answered through a series of repeated skills tests. Still other questions, however, are too complex to be answered with a single methodology. For example, a case worker may want to know whether parental involvement is related to the ongoing severity of a child's impairment. This question is perhaps best answered with a combination of methods, including natural observations, structured and unstructured interviews, rating scales, and checklists. It may be necessary to further adapt the system of evaluation to the cultural characteristics of the family. For example, the professional may consider a combination of one-on-one interviews and short questionnaires in the family's native language. In all instances, the professional also should seek input from outside sources, especially community members, local advocacy groups, and other human services agencies regarding their perceptions of the program's effectiveness and sensitivity.

Conducting the Evaluation.   Once the professional has isolated the target audience, formulated evaluative questions, designed a methodology, and selected the necessary instruments, it is time to conduct the evaluation. This step consists of collecting and analyzing data relevant to the evaluation questions within the framework of the selected design. For the information collected during the evaluation to be useful, the professional must ensure that it is timely, reliable, and valid. Children develop rapidly; therefore, outdated information may simply not be relevant to the needs of the child. In addition, timely information cuts through bureaucratic red tape and facilitates decision making. To be considered reliable, information must be accurate and relatively free from error. For example, an interventionist may wish to evaluate a child's play behaviors. One method of gaining the necessary information is for the professional to ask the mother to report her child's play behaviors. Additionally, the interventionist may decide to observe the child playing with other children and the number of times the child displays positive play behavior in a specified time frame. To be considered valid, information must be relevant to the evaluation question and lead logically to recommendations for practice. The more information that is obtained, the more likely it is that the evaluation will be reliable and valid.

Reporting Results of the Evaluation.   The final step in program evaluation is reporting the results to the target audience. The results should be reported in a clear, succinct, and understandable manner. The report also should offer suggestions and recommendations based on the results of the data analysis. An evaluation is worthless if it does not lead to improvements in the quality of intervention. Hanson (1987) recommends providing decision makers with a brief executive summary as a means of calling attention to the significant findings of the evaluation. Naturally, the evaluation should be objective and not influenced by the biases of the interventionists who will be affected by the findings.

It is important to keep in mind that program evaluation is a process rather than a product. Ideally, evaluation should be conducted throughout the intervention program, not just at its conclusion. The purpose of such **formative evaluation**, occurring throughout program development and implementation, is to monitor the progress of the family and child, and to provide feedback to the family and interventionists on a regular basis. Formative evaluation is particularly important in refining the delivery of services during the initial stages of program implementation (Anastasiow, 1981). **Summative evaluation**, on the other hand, refers to the measurement of outcomes at the end of the program. Summative evaluation provides an estimate of the overall quality and success of the service delivery. Both formative and summative evaluations are required to accurately assess the effectiveness of an intervention program.

Summary

In this chapter, the process of intervention as it pertains to infants and young children has been discussed. At any given point in history, education and the provision of social services are governed to some extent by the prevailing philosophies and trends of the times. Naturally, notions about what constitutes best practice are constantly changing and predicting what tomorrow's priorities will be is a bit like fortune-telling. Nonetheless, a review of the literature suggests that a number of trends in practice may influence the provision of services in the next several years.

Now that early intervention is no longer a new field, as it was immediately following the passage of P.L. 99-457, a number of training programs have been developed that are devoted to the systematic training of early intervention professionals. Given the critical role of the individual interventionist in ensuring the success of intervention, the importance of maintaining high-quality professional training cannot be overstated. Reflecting the shift from child-centered to family-centered services, many of these programs are attempting to teach students the skills that are most valued by families.

If current trends continue, we can anticipate that inclusion will be an important force shaping the future of intervention with young children. As was indicated earlier in the chapter, inclusion refers to full incorporation of a child with special needs into normalized settings. If it is fully implemented (as it already has been in some states), inclusion will change not only the setting in which services are likely to be provided in the future but also the very nature of children's needs and the ways in which they are met. For example, very different skills are necessary for a child to function appropriately in a regular classroom from those that are necessary to function in a self-contained classroom with only a few other children who also have special needs. To meet these changing needs, intervention programs will need to be more flexible than ever before and

interventionists will be called upon to embrace a spirit of cross-discipline cooperation.

Some professionals are not content with the current continuum of services and argue for the abolition of all special education for children. Although most early intervention experts agree that inclusion is the goal for all children, the removal of service delivery options infringes on other ideals of early intervention, particularly the legal mandate and commitment of professionals to provide services consistent with family goals and priorities. As the inclusion debate rages on, early interventionists will be called upon to maintain a reasoned approach to the complex—and all too often political—issue of determining the most appropriate setting for service provision.

The spirit and letter of IDEA contain a mandate for service provision that crosses the boundaries of traditional professional disciplines. Increasingly, professionals have been collaborating in early intervention and this trend seems likely to continue. In particular, the collaboration between medical professionals and other professionals is likely to increase. Improvements in medicine have led not only to increased survival and improved developmental outcomes for medically fragile children but also to an increase in the number of technology-dependent young children. Given the complexities of such cases, improved collaboration between medical and nonmedical professionals can only contribute to more effective, less fragmented service delivery for children with special needs.

As the number of ethnic and language minorities increases, so will the need for cultural sensitivity in the provision of early intervention services. Recruiting interventionists from minority populations is likely to continue to be a pressing challenge for universities and agencies. In addition, interventionists will be called upon to develop an awareness of their own cultures and values while learning to accept and appreciate the cultures and values of others from diverse backgrounds.

The competition for the ever-shrinking public dollar has forced local and state intervention agencies to prove their effectiveness in concrete and definitive ways. As a result, outcome-based evaluation is becoming more important as agencies struggle to ensure continued funding. Because of the nature of intervention with children with special needs, such evaluation efforts are unlikely to reflect the impact of intervention in valid ways. Therefore, interventionists must approach evaluation proactively and begin to think creatively about efficient and accurate ways of demonstrating the effectiveness of their efforts. Given the current political climate, it seems likely that concerns about accountability will shape the way professionals provide services to children and families.

Despite ever-shifting national priorities and inconsistent funding, children with special needs and their families will continue to benefit from early intervention services.

Review Questions and Discussion Points

1. What are the theoretical and philosophical approaches that most commonly guide intervention with children? How would intervention planning differ depending on the approach taken?
2. What are the important components of individualized education plans (IEPs) and individualized family service plans (IFSPs)? How are they alike, and how are they different?
3. What factors or considerations should educators take into account when developing interventions for children with special needs?
4. The role of the family in intervention is critical. Describe ways in which professionals can involve families in meaningful ways.
5. Describe an evaluation plan for an intervention program. Who should be involved in the evaluation? How will the focus of the evaluation be determined?

Recommended Resources

Professional Associations for Intervention

The Center for Improvement of Early Reading Achievement (www.ciera.org) is a consortium of educators at 5 universities committed to sharing the latest research in effective practices in literacy education for young children.

The Division of Early Childhood of the Council for Exceptional Children (DEC) is a not-for-profit organization for professionals who work with young children with special needs and their families. Their website (www.dec-sped.org) includes position and policy statements, recommended practices, legislative updates, a calendar of training opportunities, lists of resources, and applications for membership.

The Head Start Bureau website (www.acf.hhs.gov) provides information for parents (e.g., how to enroll your child in Head Start), as well as professionals. Information on performance standards, publications, training opportunities, grant competitions, and related resources is provided online.

The National Association for the Education of Young Children (NAEYC) is a not-for-profit organization commited to promoting excellence in early childhood education. Their website (www.naeyc.org) contains information and updates on effective practices and public policies, guidelines for quality in early childhood education, an online store, and applications for membership.

The National Child Care Information Center (www.nccic.org) provides information and resources in hopes of ensuring that all children have access to high quality child care and education. Their website includes information for parents as well as tips for professionals working with young children. Links from the site allow the browser to find out more about other programs, grant opportunities, and publications.

The National Early Childhood Technical Assistance Center (NECTAC) is funded by the US Department of Education to provide information, resources, and techinical assistance to professionals working in early childhood (www.nectac.org).

The Parent Advocacy Center on Educational Rights (PACER) is an organization committed to providing information to parents and professionals in order to ensure that individuals with disabilities have access to appropriate opportunities, care, and education. The early childhood link from their website (www.pacer.org) includes research updates, training opportunities, and an online newsletter, *Early Childhood Connection.*

Zero to Three's website (www.zerotothree.org) contains information and resources for parents and professionals about very young children, child care and parenting, as well as briefs on breaking research and legislative updates.

References

Able-Boone, H., Sandall, S. R., Loughry, A., & Frederick, L. L. (1990). An informed, family-centered approach to Public Law 99-457: Parental views. *Topics in Early Childhood Special Education 10*(1), 100–111.

Adelman, H., & Taylor, L. (1994). *On understanding intervention in psychology and education.* Westport, CT: Praeger.

Anastasiow, N. J. (1981). *Socioemotional development.* San Francisco: Jossey-Bass.

Bailey, D. B. (1988). Considerations in developing family goals. In D. B. Bailey & R. J. Simeonsson, (Eds.), *Family assessment in early intervention* (pp. 229–249). Upper Saddle River, NJ: Merrill/Prentice Hall.

Bailey, D. B. (2001). Evaluating parent involvement and family support in early intervention and preschool programs. *Journal of Early Intervention, 24,* 1–14.

Bailey, D. B, Buysse, V., Edmondson, R., & Smith, T. M. (1992). Creating family-centered services in early intervention: Perceptions of professionals in four states. *Exceptional Children, 58*(4), 298–309.

Bailey, D. B., & McWilliam, R. A. (1990). Normalizing early intervention. *Topics in Early Childhood Special Education, 10*(2) 33–47.

Barnett, D., & Carey, K. T. (1992). *Designing interventions for preschool learning and behavior problems.* The Jossey-Bass Social and Behavioral Science Series and The Jossey-Bass Educational Series. San Francisco: Jossey-Bass.

Black, J. K., & Puckett, M. B. (1996). *The young child: Development from prebirth through age 8* (2nd ed.). Upper Saddle River, NJ: Merrill/Prentice Hall.

Bowe, F. G. (1995a). *Birth to five: Early childhood special education.* New York: Delmar.

Bowe, F. G. (1995b). Population estimates: Birth to 5: Children with disabilities. *Journal of Special Education 28*(4), 461–471.

Bredekamp, S. (1993). The relationship between early childhood education and early childhood special education: Healthy marriage or family feud? *Topics in Early Childhood Special Education, 13,* 258–273.

Bredekamp, S. & Copple, C. (1997). *Developmentally appropriate practice in early childhood* (Rev. ed.). Washington, DC: National Association for the Education of Young Children.

Bricker, D. (1989). *Early intervention for at-risk and handicapped infants, toddlers, and preschool children* (2nd ed.). Palo Alto, CA: VORT Corporation.

Bricker, D., & Cripe, J. J. (1998). *An activity-based approach to early intervention.* Baltimore: Brookes.

Bricker, D., & Gumerlock, S. (1988). Application of a three-level evaluation plan for monitoring child progress and program effects. *Journal of Special Education 22*(1), 66–81.

Bronfenbrenner, U. (1986). Ecology of the family as a context for human development: Research perspectives. *Developmental Psychologist, 22,* 723–742.

Brown, F., Evans, I. M., Weed, K. A., & Owen, V. (1987). Delineating functional competencies:

A component approach. *Journal of the Association for Persons with Severe Handicaps, 12*(2), 117–124.

Brown, R. W., & Lenneberg, E. (1965). Studies in linguistic relativity. In H. Proshansky & B. Seidenberg (Eds.), *Basic studies in social psychology* (pp. 244–252). New York: Holt, Rinehart and Winston.

Burton, C., Hains, A., Hanline, M., McLean, M., & McCormick, K. (1992). Early childhood intervention and education: The urgency of professional unification. *Topics in Early Childhood Special Education, 11*, 53–69.

Caro, P., & Derevensky, J. L. (1991). Family-focused intervention models: Implementation and research findings. *Topics in Early Childhood Special Education, 11*(3), 66–80.

Carta, J. J., Schwartz, I. S., Atwater, J. B., & McConnell, S. R. (1991). Developmentally appropriate practice: Appraising its usefulness for young children with disabilities. *Topics in Early Childhood Special Education, 11*(1), 1–20.

Children's Defense Fund. (1989). *A vision of America's future*. Washington, DC: Author.

Dunst, C. J., Hamby, D., Trivette, C. M., Raab, M., & Bruder, M. B. (2000). Everyday family and community life and children's naturally occurring opportunities. *Journal of Early Intervention, 23*, 151–164.

Frisby, C. L. (1992). Issues and problems in the influence of culture on the psychoeducational needs of African-American children. *School Psychology Review, 21*(4), 532–551.

Fuchs, D., & Fuchs, L. S. (1994). Inclusive schools movement and the radicalization of special education reform. *Exceptional Children, 60*, 294–309.

Green, J. W. (1982). *Cultural awareness in the human services*. Upper Saddle River, NJ: Prentice Hall.

Gutkin, T. B., & Curtis, J. (1990). School-based consultation: Theory, techniques, and research. In T. B. Gutkin & C. R. Reynolds (Eds.), *The handbook of school psychology* (pp. 577–611). New York: Wiley.

Hanson, M. (1987). *Teaching the infant with Down syndrome: A guide for parents and professionals*. Austin, TX: PRO-ED.

Hanson, M., & Lynch, E. W. (1998). *Early intervention: Implementing child and family services for infants and toddlers who are at risk or disabled* (3rd ed.). Austin, TX: PRO-ED.

Hanson, M. J., Lynch, E. W., & Wayman, K. (1990). Honoring the cultural diversity of families when gathering data. *Teaching of Exceptional Children in Special Education, 10*(1), 112–131.

Hart, B., & Risley, T. R. (1975). Incidental teaching of language in the preschool. *Journal of Applied Behavior Analysis, 8*, 411–420.

Heward, W. L. (1996). *Exceptional children* (5th ed.). Upper Saddle River, NJ: Merrill/Prentice Hall.

Innocenti, M. S., Hollinger, D. D., Escobar, C. M., & White, K. R. (1995). The cost-effectiveness of adding one type of parent involvement to an early intervention program. *Early Education and Development, 4*(4), 306–326.

Johnson, B. H., Kaufman, R. K., & McGonigel, M. J. (1989). *Guidelines and recommended practices for the individualized family service plan*. Bethesda, MD: Association for the Care of Children's Health.

Lynch, E. W., & Hanson, M. J. (1993). *Developing cross-cultural competence: A guide for working with young children and their families*. Baltimore: Brookes.

McWilliam, R. A., & Bailey, D. B. (1994). Predictors of service delivery models in center-based early intervention. *Exceptional Children, 61*(1), 56–71.

McWilliam, R. A., Lang, I., Vandiviere, P., Angell, R., Collins, L., & Underdown, G. (1995). Satisfaction and struggles: Family perceptions of early intervention. *Journal of Early Intervention, 19*(1), 43–60.

Murphy, D. L., Lee, I. M., Turnbull, A., & Turbiville, V. (1995). The Family-Centered Program Rating Scale: An instrument for program evaluation and change. *Journal of Early Intervention, 19*(6), 24–42.

No Child Left Behind Act of 2001, Pub. L. No. 107-110, 115 Stat. 1425 (2002).

Odom, S. L., & McEvoy, M. A. (1990). Mainstreaming at the preschool level: Potential barriers and risks for the field. *Topics in Early Childhood Special Education, 10*(2), 48–61.

Peterson, N. L. (1987). *Early intervention: An introduction to early childhood-special education*. Denver, CO: Love.

Research and Policy Committee of the Committee for Economic Development. (1987). *Children in need: Investment strategies for the educationally disadvantaged*. New York: Author.

Rhodes, W. C., & Tracey, M. C. (1972). *A study of child variance: Intervention, Vol. 2*. Ann Arbor: University of Michigan Press.

Richmond, J., & Ayoub, C. (1993). Evolution of early intervention philosophy. In D. M. Bryant &

M. A. Graham (Eds.), *Implementing early intervention: From research to effective practice.* New York: Guilford Press.

Rogers-Warren, A., & Warren, S. (1980). Mands for verbalization: Facilitating the generalization of newly trained language in children. *Behavior Modification, 4,* 220–245.

Sameroff, A., & Chandler, M. J. (1975). Reproductive risk and the continuum of caretaking casualty. In F. D. Horowith, M. Hetherington, S. Scarr-Salapetek, & G. Seigal (Eds.), *Review of child development research* (pp. 187–244). Chicago: University of Chicago Press.

Sattler, J. (1992). *Assessment in children* (3rd ed., Rev.). San Diego, CA: Author.

Sexton, D. (1998, December). *Measuring and comparing the developmentally appropriate beliefs of general and special education practitioners.* Paper presented at the 14th Annual DEC International Early Childhood Conference on Children with Special Needs, Chicago, IL.

Simeonsson, R. J., Huntington, G. S., McMillen, J. S., Dodds, A. H., Halperin, D., Zipper, I. N., et al. (in press). Services for young children and families: Evaluating intervention cycles. *Infants and young children.*

Skeels, H. M. (1966). Adult status of children with contrasting early life experiences: A follow-up study. *Monographs of the Society for Research in Child Development, 31*(3, Serial No. 105).

Smith, B. J. & Bredekamp, S. (1998). Foreword. In L. J. Johnson, M. L. Lamontagne, P. M. Elgas, & A. M. Bauer (Eds.) *Early childhood education: Blending theory, blending practice* (pp. xv–xx). Baltimore: Paul H. Brooks.

Snyder, S., & Sheehan, R. (1993). *Family-centered early intervention with infants and toddlers: Innovative cross-disciplinary approaches.* Baltimore: Brookes.

Stainback, S., & Stainback, W. (1992). *Curriculum considerations in inclusive classrooms: Facilitating learning for all students.* Baltimore: Brookes.

Stokes, T. F., & Osnes, P. G. (1989). An operant pursuit of generalization. *Behavior Therapy, 20*(3), 337–355.

Suran, B. G., & Rizzo, J. V. (1979). *Special children: An integrative approach.* Glenville, IL: Scott Foresman.

Thomas, C., Correa, V. I., & Morsink, C. V. (1995). *Interactive teaming: Consultation and collaboration in special programs* (2nd ed.). Upper Saddle River, NJ: Merrill/Prentice Hall.

Turnbull, A. P., Turnbull, H. R., Shank, M., & Leal, D. (2002). *Exceptional lives: Special education in today's schools* (3rd ed.). Upper Saddle River, NJ: Merrill/Prentice Hall.

Turnbull, S. K., & Turnbull, J. M. (1986). *Families, professionals, and exceptionality: A special partnership.* Upper Saddle River, NJ: Merrill/Prentice Hall.

U.S. Bureau of the Census. (1990). *Characteristics of the population: Vol. 1.* Washington, DC: U.S. Department of Commerce.

Weatherford, D. L. (1986). The challenge of evaluation: Early intervention programs for severely handicapped children and their families. In L. Brickman & D. L. Weatherford (Eds.), *Evaluation: Early intervention programs for severely handicapped children and their families* (pp. 1–17). Austin, TX: PRO-ED.

Wolery, M. (1989). Using assessment information to plan instructional programs. In D. Bailey & M. Wolery (Eds.), *Assessing infants and preschoolers with handicaps.* Upper Saddle River, NJ: Merrill/Prentice Hall.

Wolery, M., Holcombe-Ligon, A., Brookfield, J., Huffman, K., Schneider, C., Martin, C. G., Venn, M. L., Werts, M. G., & Fleming, L.A. (1993). The extent and nature of preschool mainstreaming: A survey of general early educators. *The Journal of Special Education, 27,* 222–234.

Wolery, M., Werts, M. G., & Holcombe, A. (1994). Current practices with young children who have disabilities: Issues in placement, assessment, and instruction. *Focus on Exceptional Children, 26,* 1–12

Wolery, M., & Wilburs, J. S. (1994). Introduction to the inclusion of young children with special needs in early childhood programs. In M. Wolery & J. S. Wilburs (Eds.) *Including children with special needs in early childhood programs* (pp. 1–22). Washington, D.C.: National Association for the Education of Young Children.

6

Technology for Assessment and Intervention

Kathryn Wolff Heller

Chapter Outline

- Types of Technology
- Assessment Considerations
- Augmentative Communication
- Computer Access
- Software for Early Learning
- Play and Technology

Maria

Maria is a 4-year-old girl who enjoys attending preschool. She has spastic quadriplegic cerebral palsy. She was born 4 weeks premature after a difficult delivery. She was not diagnosed with cerebral palsy until 5 months of age, when it became apparent that she was not achieving major developmental milestones and was showing signs of this motor disorder. Presently, Maria can not sit up, walk, talk, or manipulate small items, but she loves to play games and be around her friends. She uses an augmentative communication device to help her communicate with others in addition to using gestures and facial expressions. She uses adapted toys with switches during playtime. She is also learning to access a computer with a trackball and is being taught some early learning skills. For mobility, Maria uses a transitional motorized mobility device. Although she is unable to eat by mouth due to a severe gag reflex, she is getting sufficient nutrition through her gastrostomy tube feedings. After eating, she participates in brushing her teeth with an adapted toothbrush with the rest of her preschool class. Maria is making remarkable progress across several domains through the use of technology.

Technology has the potential for making a profound difference in the lives of infants and young children with disabilities, as shown in the story of Maria. Young children with developmental delays or physical, sensory, or cognitive impairments are often compromised in their ability to learn, interact, and access their environment. Technology can provide a means for these young children to more fully interact with their environment, gain access to learning opportunities, and become more independent (Judge & Lahm, 1998). The vast array of technological devices can assist these children to participate more fully in home, school, and community environments.

Technology can be used to assist young children with disabilities in a number of ways. For example, children with severe speech impairments may use communication devices to make their wants, needs, questions, and discoveries known to others. Adapted toys and computer games may provide an avenue for turn taking, interaction with peers, and independent play activities (Wershing & Symington, 1998). Wheelchairs and other mobility devices may allow children the opportunity to explore their environment. Alternate input devices will make the computer accessible to children with the most severe physical and visual impairments. Carefully designed software may promote learning and cognitive development in children with a wide range of disabilities. Adapted feeding devices, dressing aids, and other self-care equipment may permit children with physical disabilities to independently perform these activities.

It wasn't long ago that many types of technology were used only by older, elementary and middle school children or those who had achieved certain prerequisite skills. The current trend promotes technology use by much younger children. In fact, as the use of technology is increasing, the age of the user is decreasing. For example, infants as young as 3 months of age have interacted with computers, 18-month-olds have successfully used simple augmentative communication devices to communicate with others, and 18- to 24-month-olds have been able to operate powered mobility devices to move themselves to different locations (Behrmann, Jones, & Wilds, 1989; Butler, 1988; Cook & Hussey, 2002; Judge, 1998). Although young children may be able to use a specific technology, it is important that technology is not considered an end unto itself. Technology should be used as a tool for a means of accomplishing a targeted objective or task (Judge, 1998). For example, computers may be used as a tool to augment what is being taught in a preschool class, augmentative communication devices may be used to allow children with disabilities to communicate their needs, and switch adapted toys may be used to promote play. Careful assessment and matching of the technology to the young child is necessary for the technology to be successfully used to accomplish its specific purpose.

> Technology should not be used as an end unto itself, but as a tool to accomplish some task.

The National Association for the Education of Young Children (NAEYC) supports the use of technology and acknowledges that it can enhance children's cognitive and social abilities. Its position paper on technology stresses that technology is one of the many options that can be used to support children's learning. When technology is put in place, it should be integrated into the learning environment and used to enrich the curriculum. NAEYC also cautions that a professional judgment is required by the teacher to determine if the technology is age appropriate, individually appropriate, and culturally appropriate (National Association for the Education of Young Children, 1998).

This chapter provides information on the different uses of technology for young children with disabilities. First, five major types of technology will be discussed. This will be followed by a section on assessment considerations, specifically addressing assistive technology and instructional technology. Next, technology used for specific activities will be addressed: augmentative communication, computer access, software for early learning, and play. The important areas of mobility and self-care skills also could be included in a chapter on technology, but they will be covered in the chapters addressing gross (Chapter 7) and fine motor (Chapter 8) functioning. Due to the rapid changes that occur in the field of technology, each section addresses general concepts and principles that can be applied to young children with disabilities, regardless of the changes in the devices or software.

Types of Technology

Although many people initially think of computers or sophisticated devices when they hear the word *technology*, there are actually many different types of technology. There are typically five major types of technologies that are commonly used by young children with disabilities and their parents and teachers. These include medical technology, technology productivity tools, informational technology, assistive technology, and instructional technology.

Medical Technology

Advances in medical technology have made a profound impact in the lives of infants and young children. Children are surviving acute and chronic illnesses and medical conditions with the assistance of medical technology (Rapport & Lasseter, 1998). Children who are born very premature or with certain medical conditions would have been unable to survive a decade or so ago if it were not for advancements in medical technology. State-of-the-art neonatal intensive care units using the latest medical equipment, as well as technology-based surgical techniques and new medications, have increased the survival rate of many infants born prematurely or with various medical conditions. Some of these technologies may be needed for a short-term basis. Other technologies may be used for a lifetime, such as the use of a renal dialysis machine when no kidney donor is available or the use of an insulin pump to better control diabetes (Heller, Alberto, Forney, & Schwartzman, 1996). These and other devices have contributed to children's welfare.

As medical technological advances have been made, medical equipment has become smaller and more portable. This has allowed children with significant medical conditions to be included in schools and community. For example, ventilators used to be quite large, thus children who used them to breathe often stayed at home, in a hospital, or in a nursing care facility. Due to technological advances, ventilators are now so small that they can fit on the back of wheelchairs and accompany children as they go to home, school, and community environments (Jones, Clatterbuck, Marquis, Turnbull, & Moberly, 1996).

As medical advances are made, procedures and equipment that were rarely seen in schools are now commonly available in the school setting. It is not uncommon to see young children in nurseries, preschools, and schools receiving nutrition through tube feedings or eliminating wastes through colostomies. Other forms of medical technology also are being encountered in the schools, such as portable oxygen for children with respiratory problems, implanted insulin pump devices for children with diabetes, or vagal nerve stimulators for children with seizures (McBrien & Bonthius, 2000).

Advances in medical technology, as well as the trend to teach children with disabilities to be as independent as possible, have often resulted in children being taught to partially participate or independently perform their own health care procedure. For example, children as young as 5 years of age have learned to independently catheterize themselves to expel urine. Children as young as 2 and 3 years of age have learned to participate in a variety of health care procedures by washing their hands, getting into the proper position, holding equipment, or helping to clean equipment (Heller, Forney, Alberto, Schwartzman, & Goeckel, 2000). Having children partially or completely participate in their procedure and the proper care of their medical equipment increases independence and engagement. If the educational team decides to target teaching the child to assist in the performance of a procedure, teachers are needed to provide effective instructional strategies and the team will need to work together to plan appropriate instructional targets (Heller et al., 2000).

Medical technology has also increased an individual's capabilities. For example, body-powered or electric-powered artificial arms can allow a person to perform many routine daily activities (Heckathorne, 2002). Artificial legs can allow walking and running. Cochlear implants may be used with young children, typically over the age of 2, who have profound hearing losses to increase hearing ability (Russell, Coffin, & Kenna, 1999). Infants born with congenital cataracts eventually may have artificial lenses implanted in their eyes. These are only a few examples of the types of medical technologies that can enhance participation in daily life.

Teachers may help to determine the most appropriate instructional strategies to teach a child to perform a health care procedure.

Technology Productivity Tools

The second category of technology is known as technology productivity tools. This category includes tools that enable children and adults to work more effectively and efficiently (Blackhurst & Lahm, 2000). For young children, this often refers to the use of a computer to aid in learning and play. As computers have become more affordable and more widely used, their use has been increasing with younger and younger children. Computers are widely accepted as potential learning tools for preschool children (McBride & Austin, 2001).

Teachers of young children may use other types of technology productivity tools. Databases and spreadsheets may be used by teachers to keep information about their class. Videoconferencing is considered another form of productivity tool, allowing meetings and consultations with people over long distances. The use of word processing programs is another common technology productivity tool. Each of these tools must be carefully evaluated as to their functionality and ability to produce the desired outcome.

Informational Technology

Informational technology is often used by parents and teachers of young children with disabilities to find information. Informational technology includes all technological resources that serve as resources of information (Blackhurst & Lahm, 2000). This includes databases, such as the **Educational Resources Information Center (ERIC)** and **MedLine**. Databases provide a way to search much of the world's literature.

The Internet is the most frequently used informational technology. Teachers may use it to download lesson plans, information, and materials. Parents may use the Internet to learn about their child's disability, medical treatments, and educational materials. Information that may have been difficult to obtain years ago can often be easily accessed through the use of the Internet. However, sources of information must be carefully scrutinized for accuracy and reliability.

Assistive Technology

Assistive technology (AT) has provided a means for children with disabilities to participate in everyday activities. The Technology Assistance to the States Act (P.L. 100–407) defines assistive technology as "Any item, piece of equipment or product system whether acquired commercially off the shelf, modified, or customized that is used to increase, maintain, or improve functional capabilities of individuals with disabilities." This definition includes a wide range of technology from a pencil with a built-up handle to a powered wheelchair.

Assistive technology is often divided into low-technology (low-tech) tools and high-technology (high-tech) tools. **Low technology** (also referred to as *lite technology*) refers to devices that are inexpensive, simple to make, and can be easily obtainable. They are usually nonelectronic (or nonmotorized) devices. Examples of low-technology devices include a picture communication board, a built-up grip to be used with a pencil or crayon, a mouthstick for drawing, a bent spoon for eating, and a mitt-style washcloth. **High technology** usually refers to devices that are more complex, more difficult to create, and are typically more expensive. They often include electronic, electric, mechanical, or hydraulic components (Cook & Hussey, 2002). For example, electronic communication devices, powered wheelchairs, adapted access to computers, electric feeding devices, and switch-controlled computer games are considered high-tech devices. Further examples of low technology and high technology across various activities are provided in Table 6.1.

Some individuals make additional distinctions such as **middle technology** to mean something between high and low technology. The term **no technology** is also used to refer to adapted ways of performing an activity that do not involve using a tool or device, such as an adapted way of crawling up the stairs, using gestures to mean certain things, or requesting items by eye gazing (i.e., looking at them; King, 1999). The option of using no technology or an adapted means of performing an activity is usually evaluated first, before examining technology options. If assistive technology is needed, low-technology solutions are usually preferred over high-technology solutions, if the low-technology solutions result in optimum performance of the activity. A careful assessment is needed to select the best assistive technology for the child.

Assistive technology has the capability of providing experiences to young children with disabilities that may promote their development across cognitive, motor, perceptual, social, and communication domains (Cook & Hussey, 2002). AT provides

> Any item that improves the functional capability of a child with a disability is considered assistive technology.

TABLE 6.1 Examples of Low-Tech and High-Tech Assistive Technology

Activities	Low Technology	High Technology
Eating	Spoon with built-up handle	Mechanical feeder
	Scoop dish	Robotic arm
Play	Oversized building blocks	Computer game
	Card holder	Switch-controlled toy
Moving across room	Scooter board	Powered wheelchair
Requesting items	Communication board	Electronic device
Beginning reading	Book stand to hold book	Optical character recognition software
	Mouthstick to turn pages	Computer-read story
Drawing/writing	Pencil with built-up grip	Drawing program
	Dark-lined paper	Alternate keyboard
Counting	Counter	Early math software with alternate input

children with physical impairments the opportunity to manipulate objects; explore, interact, and learn about their environment through the use of mobility devices; play using adapted toys; use a computer through alternative access options (e.g., alternative keyboard); and participate in a wide range of activities. Children who do not have functional speech due to physical impairments, autism, or other developmental delays may use augmentative communication devices to request wants and needs, exchange ideas, clarify concepts, and engage in socialization. Young children with visual impairments may use **pre-cane devices**, devices that enlarge items or pictures, and software to make the computer more accessible. Children with hearing impairments may use devices that flash lights or vibrate to various sounds (e.g., telephone ringing). Children with mental retardation or developmental delays may use more direct methods to access a computer (e.g., a touch membrane mounted on the computer screen that allows them to directly touch the item on the screen to select it), or they may learn to use a switch to use software to promote **cause and effect** (i.e., understanding that a certain action, movement, or response results in a certain effect, such as pushing a switch causes a clown on the computer screen to move). Assistive technology has the potential to profoundly affect the capabilities of children, when developmentally appropriate technology is used and it is implemented in an effective manner.

Instructional Technology

Instructional technology refers to the use of technology to promote learning. It includes a wide range of technologies such as developmentally appropriate software delivered through **computer-assisted instruction** (also known as technology enabled instruction), multimedia and hypermedia software programs, Internet use, and virtual reality programs. Even video technology that is commonly used in preschool classrooms is considered a form of instructional technology (Higgins, 1993). Instructional technology has expanded over the years to include many forms of electronic media. Often the term **e-learning** is used to refer to the delivery of content by electronic media, which includes the Internet, satellite broadcasts, audio- and videotape, interactive TV, and CD-ROM (Meyen et al., 2002).

Many teachers of young children use computer-assisted instruction to teach a variety of skills. Computer-assisted instruction usually refers to direct, computer-to-child activity instruction that is tailored to the child's needs (Ray & Warden, 1995). Much of the computer-assisted instructional software teaches specific preacademic or academic skills. However, it has also been used with children with disabilities to promote skill development across a variety of areas. In one study by Lindstrand (2001), over 50% of the parents or children with disabilities found computer software to be important in the development of language, play, coordination, concentration, and overall development, as well as in learning colors and forms, new words and concepts, and specific (pre) academic skills. Several other studies have supported the effectiveness of computers with young children in increasing specific language skills (e.g., word knowledge and verbal fluency, Chute & Miksad, 1997); improving attention to visual analysis activities (Cardona, Martinez, & Hinojosa, 2000); increasing social interaction, play, and social-emotional growth (Hutinger & Clark, 2000; Speigel-McGill, Zippiroli, & Mistrett, 1989); and promoting specific skills (e.g., emergent literacy, cause and effect; Hutinger & Johanson, 2000; Mioduser, Tur-Kaspa, & Leitner, 2000).

> Carefully selected software can augment a teacher's instruction and promote learning and development.

Material may be presented using a multimedia or hypermedia format. **Multimedia** refers to the integration of different mediums of information, such as text, song, animation, audio, graphics, and video. Software for young children commonly uses multimedia. Traditional classroom presentations may be enhanced by using a multimedia format (by adding songs, videos, and pictures to a teaching lesson). Typically, multimedia presentations are sequentially presented in a linear fashion.

Unlike linear, paper-based learning products or traditional multimedia software, **hypermedia** software allows children to access the material in a flexible and interactive way, choosing the direction or order of the material. Basically, children get to choose how they will explore the material (Bitter & Pierson, 1999). Both multimedia and hypermedia have the advantage of providing multisensory experiences. They can be used to reinforce important concepts by providing multiple examples of the targeted material to be learned (Langone, Malone, & Kinsley, 1999).

The Internet can also be a form of instructional technology when used for instructional purposes. For example, a preschool class that is learning about different animals may use an Internet site to look at the pictures of the animals and engage in some developmentally appropriate activities on the site. Often Web sites present information using a multimedia format that further engages the children in learning the target material.

Virtual reality is one of the newest forms of instructional technology that allows children to simulate going places or performing actions in a safe environment. It has been defined as a computer-based technology that creates an interactive, multisensory artificial environment that gives the illusion of being real (Forcier, 1999). Often a helmet is used to create three-dimensional images, and the responses of the user create a feedback loop with the computer, making continual changes to what is being presented, based on the user's own movements.

The possibilities for virtual reality are limitless. Children who have never been to the beach before could experience being at the ocean as part of a lesson on geography. Children who are unable to walk could experience hiking in the mountains. The realism and motivational qualities of this type of instructional media have the potential of enhancing learning and understanding over a wide range of material.

Virtual reality has been used in special education. Children as young as 3 years old who have cerebral palsy have learned to operate a motorized wheelchair in a virtual reality environment, with the success being measured by their generalization to real-world environment (Ira, 1997). The use of virtual reality also has been explored in rehabilitation of physical disabilities, training activities for individuals with mental retardation and autism, social skills training for individuals with behavior disorders, and flexible thinking training for individuals with hearing impairments (Male, 2003; Roblyer & Cass, 1999).

Virtual reality programs have the ability to help promote understanding through the way they present various activities and actions. For example, virtual reality programs that allow the user not to just see events, but to experience them may aid in learning. For a child who uses a wheelchair, she may experience walking by moving her shoulders (e.g., when she moves her shoulders she sees legs move or the ground moves as if walking). Having the sensory component of movement may help aid understanding. Virtual reality also can offer modeling and shaping. For example, a child can superimpose his hand over a virtual reality hand and follow along and then fade the virtual reality hand (Fritz, 1991). It is predicted that this type of instructional technology will become commonplace in schools in the future (Best, Ollie, Weinroth, Dykes, & Heller, 1998).

Instructional technology has the capacity to promote learning and address specific learning challenges. Children with cognitive impairments, motor impairments, sensory impairments, or other developmental disabilities often have difficulties in discriminating the relevant details of a task or maintaining attention to them. Technology has the potential of helping children improve their attention on relevant stimuli due to the engaging nature of some programs and the ability to manipulate (on many of the software programs) the color, size, speech output, and visual output of what is being presented.

Perceptual problems and information processing issues may also be present in young children. Computer-based instructional programs providing visual and auditory information can increase attention and add to the child's perceptual understanding. The number and variety of stimuli can be increased and presented countless number of times to help children develop concepts, remember the information, and be able to use that information (Langone, 1998). In order to be successful, it is important that appropriate software is selected.

Instructional technology using virtual reality holds the capacity to provide a limitless array of experiences to children who may otherwise never have the opportunity

Assessment Considerations

Several individuals are often involved in determining the appropriate form of assistive and instructional technology for a particular child. Each individual, whether a parent, teacher, related service staff, technology expert, or other, brings a unique perspective to the assessment process. However, there are some general considerations that need to be taken into account, regardless of the type of technology. An overview of these factors will be presented across assistive technology and instructional technology.

Assistive Technology Assessment Considerations

Regardless of the type or complexity of an assistive technology device, a careful assessment is needed to match the child with the appropriate assistive technology to accomplish a specific activity. Assessment is often based on the **HAAT model** (Cook & Hussey, 2002), which stresses the interrelationship of human (H), activity (A), and assistive technology (AT). In this model, human performance is related to the specific task that involves technology in a given activity within a certain context. For the AT device to be successful, the specific activity, human factors, and the characteristics of the assistive technology need to be carefully assessed within the context they are to occur. Figure 6.1 depicts an adapted version of the HAAT model, stressing how performance is influenced by the three major areas.

> Assessment of AT must take into account the activity, child, assistive technology, and context of use.

Activity.   The first area to examine is the activity and the specific objective being targeted. For young children this can be any number of things, such as using a cup during lunchtime, requesting to play a game, turning on a favorite battery-operated toy, or moving the trackball to explore a computer program. How the child engages in the activity is closely examined to determine if adaptations are needed or if the current adaptations (or current AT devices) need to be changed. Based upon these observations, it may be determined that assistive technology or other assistive technology devices are needed.

Human Factors.   The second part of the assessment process involves examining the human factors that interface with technology. One human factor is a child's abilities. Assistive technology must closely match the child's current abilities in order to optimize performance. For example, if a child is unable to physically use a standard

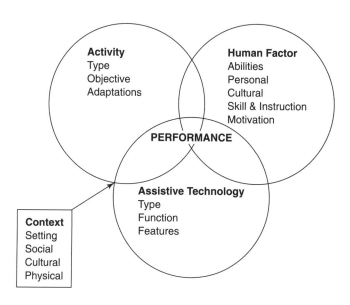

FIGURE 6.1   The activity, human factors, and assistive technology interact together to affect performance within a variety of contexts.

mouse, then this type of technology will fail. A different type of mouse or alternate input may be needed. If the child is not positioned properly to access the assistive technology device, then it may fail as well. Another human factor deals with personal preferences and cultural factors. These may strongly influence the success of a device. For example, if the child thinks that a head stick is unattractive and won't use it, then this technology will fail.

Other human factors that are important have to do with the child's skill and the instructional approach used with the child. Performing a specific activity using an AT device can fail if the child has not attained an appropriate skill level to use the technology, or received appropriate instruction in the activity and use of the device. Matching the best instructional methodology to the child's learning characteristics will be important to improve the child's skill level and reach optimal performance.

Another human factor to consider is motivation. The impact of motivation on AT is depicted by Baker's (1986) **basic ergonomic equation** that is elaborated by King (1999). In this equation, the human factor side of technology refers to the child's motivation to perform the activity, and the amount of physical effort, cognitive effort, linguistic effort, and time that is involved with using the device. If a particular assistive technology requires more physical effort, cognitive effort, linguistic effort, or time than the amount of motivation the child has to engage in the activity, then the AT will typically fail. The equation is depicted like this:

$$\frac{\text{Motivation of AT user to pursue and complete a task}}{\text{Physical effort} + \text{Cognitive effort} + \text{Linguistic effort} + \text{Time load}} = \text{Successful or unsuccessful AT use}$$

According to this equation, the use of the AT device may fail if a child with a severe motor impairment, for example, must expend a great deal of effort and time to use the technology and this effort is greater than the amount of motivation the child has to perform the task. In this example, a child with cerebral palsy who has difficulty activating a particular switch in an accurate or timely manner may begin to lose interest and require a different switch or means of activating a device to accomplish the task. In another example, if the AT is very complicated for the child with a developmental disability to use, the amount of cognitive effort (e.g., multiple steps are needed) and linguistic effort (e.g., uses complex symbols) may override the amount of motivation the child has to pursue the task. In this situation, a different form of assistive technology may be needed to accomplish the same task.

Types of Assistive Technology.   The third area to consider is the type of assistive technology itself. As discussed under activity, the selection of an AT device is based on the need to have assistive technology in order to perform some specific activity or objective. The human side of the equation will determine if assistive technology will be effective. There must be a close examination of the type and function of AT and its various features to be sure there is a good match for the child and activity.

Context.   The activity, human factors, and assistive technology must all be evaluated in regard to the specific contexts in which they are occurring. Contexts that must be considered are: (a) setting (e.g., home, school, community); (b) social contexts (e.g., family, familiar or unfamiliar adults, familiar or unfamiliar peers, alone); (c) cultural environment (e.g., within own cultural context or different cultural context); and (d) physical context (e.g., lighting, noise level, temperature; Cook & Hussey, 2002). For example, an augmentative communication device may work well in the school setting with familiar adults and peers, but work poorly in the community with unfamiliar people with poor lighting and lots of distractions.

Other Factors.   Another major consideration regarding assessment and implementation of an assistive technology is the need for families of young children with disabilities to be involved in the assessment and intervention process (Judge, 2002; Parette, Brotherson, & Huer, 2000). Teachers and other professionals need to build partnerships with parents that will empower them to make decisions regarding the assistive technology. In order to accomplish this, parents need information and hands-on experience with the devices to promote a level of comfort and knowledge. Involvement of families in assessment and selection of AT is particularly important because there is a greater likelihood that they will use the device and share ownership of the intervention plan when they play an active role in the assessment process. As the child grows older, he or she will often play an integral role in the decision-making process. Continued support and resources will be important for all concerned for proper use and maintenance of the AT device.

Instructional Technology Assessment

A careful evaluation is needed to determine if a young child with disabilities will benefit from computer-assisted instruction, multimedia or hypermedia software, Internet sites, or virtual reality programs. The appropriateness of a specific instructional technology will depend upon the child, the instructional technology, and the instructional objective. Because computer software is one of the most common forms of instructional technology used with young children, the remainder of this section will discuss software assessment.

> Software must be carefully evaluated to be sure it is developmentally appropriate, appropriate for the specific child, and appropriate for the concepts being targeted.

It is important to have a clear concept of the intended use of the software and the type of features that are important to a particular child. As seen in Table 6.2, there are several categories that should be examined: content area, developmental level, learning level, instructional method, input features, presentation features, presentation options, and feedback to answers (Bitter & Pierson, 1999; Lewis, 1993; Ray & Warden, 1995).

Content and Developmental Level.   There are a wide variety of content areas that young children may be taught. Some of these include cause and effect, language development, readiness level skills, and beginning literacy skills. Being sure that the software exactly matches the learning objective for the child and provides support to the material being taught by the teacher or parent are important for success. The program must also be at the appropriate developmental level. A program for kindergarten children may be inappropriate for preschool children. When a mismatch occurs, frustration can result in an inability to learn or attend to the material.

TABLE 6.2 Evaluating
Software

Categories	Example Subcategories
Content area	Numeral recognition, counting, letter-sound correspondence
Developmental level	Infant/toddler, preschool, kindergarten level
Learning level	Acquisition
	Proficiency
	Maintenance
	Generalization
	Application
Instructional method	Discovery/Exploratory learning
	Tutorial
	Drill and practice
	Educational games
	Simulation
	Problem solving
Input features	Consistency of requested input
	Appropriate motor and speed demands
	Accuracy demands (e.g., can backspace or erase input)
	Interfaces with alternate input (e.g., switch and scanning)
Presentation features	Presented logically, accurately, with adequate repetition
	Academic demands (e.g., reading, spelling level)
	Free of stereotypes or bias
	Degree of interactivity
	Consistent presentation format and ease of use
	Presence of graphics, audio, video, animation
	Visual and/or auditory prompts and features
Presentation options	Control presentation pace, difficulty level, lesson content
	Alternate presentation (e.g., high contrast, enlarge, scanning)
	Student-, teacher-, or program-driven starting point
Feedback to answers	Type of feedback to correct answers (reinforces)
	Type of feedback to incorrect answers (consistency)
	Provides another opportunity when incorrect
	Provides assistance when incorrect
	Teacher-controlled responses to wrong answers
	Provides reports of items missed

Learning Level.   Software should be evaluated to determine if it is targeting the desired learning level. As indicated in Chapter 4, learning levels are based on the stages of learning: acquisition, proficiency (or fluency), maintenance, generalization, and application (or adaptation; Mercer & Mercer; 1998). When children are first learning a skill, such as the names of the alphabet or learning to match shapes, they are at the acquisition stage of learning. Once they have achieved a high accuracy rate, they move into the proficiency stage in which accuracy and speed are emphasized. In this stage, the skill becomes more automatic. After mastering the skill at the proficiency stage, children then move to the maintenance stage which emphasizes knowing the skill over time. In the generalization stage, children are able to perform the skill in a different time, setting, or with different people or materials. It is important in this stage that the child demonstrates that he or she can perform the skill in a variety of actual situations, and not solely in the context of how it was initially presented. In the last learning stage, the application or adaptation stage, the learner applies the skill in new situations or applications.

Although factual information and comprehension of the material are emphasized at all learning levels, the application stage usually requires problem solving and may incorporate higher level thinking skills such as analysis, synthesis, and evaluation. Many software programs that are currently available promote these higher level thinking skills, including those for children with cognitive deficiencies who were thought to be unable to succeed at this level (Taber-Brown, 2000).

Instructional Method.   The instructional method used in the software program should correspond to the child's learning level. Children at the acquisition stage should use discovery or tutorial software. In **discovery software**, a child can explore concepts; in **tutorial software**, instruction is provided on a concept (or skill). As children move into the proficiency stage, **drill and practice software** may be used to promote quick and accurate responding. Once the child has demonstrated proficiency, the child may periodically be exposed to drill and practice software to help retain the information, or the child may be periodically exposed to the material in a game format. If the child has not retained the information, it may be retaught using tutorial software. In the generalization stage, other software programs targeting the same content may be used (as well as other material not on the computer) to be sure the child can perform the skill with different materials and settings. In the last stage, the application stage, **problem-solving software** or **simulation software** may be used (Blackhurst & Lahm, 2000). Problem-solving software presents problems based on concepts learned outside of the program, whereas simulation software presents real-life scenarios (Ray & Warden, 1995).

Input Features.   Software programs should be examined regarding the input demands placed on the child and the available input features. Input should be consistent in the type of response needed to maneuver through the program in order to avoid confusion. Also, the speed of the child's response and the motor demands of the program should match the child's ability. Another input consideration is the accuracy demands of the child's input. Some programs are more flexible, allowing the child to change a response before evaluating it. Because some children will need alternate input in the form of a different keyboard or a switch access with scanning features, it will need to be determined if the software will support these alternate access modalities.

Presentation Features.   The next area to examine is the presentation of the software. The presentation of the software should be logical, accurate, and provide enough practice and repetition of the material before going on to the next concept or level. Software that provides only a few samples, skips to more complex material too quickly, or does not provide enough practice of the material may need to be avoided. The demands of using the software, such as needing to know how to read, should be closely examined to see if it is appropriate for the child. It is also important to be sure the software eliminates stereotyping of any group and eliminates exposure to violence because young children are very impressionable (NAEYC, 1998).

Another presentation feature that varies in software programs is the amount of interactivity provided. The least interactive program provides minimal choices and has a predetermined path in terms of the order in which the child goes through the program. A software program with a middle level of interactivity provides multiple choices with a divergent path over which the child has some control. Usually graphics and text (if present) are fixed and cannot be controlled. The most interactive software tend to be hypermedia programs that give the child a wide variety of choices, with total control over the path, responses, text, sounds, graphics, and content (Hutinger & Johanson, 2000). The adult should carefully select the most appropriate level of interactivity given the child's ability and the intended purpose for using the software. In all cases, the presentation style should provide a consistent format that promotes easy maneuverability throughout the program.

Another presentation feature deals with the display of graphics, audio, video, animation, and prompting provided by the software program. The software should also match the child's learning style, including the child's sensory modality preferences (e.g., visual, auditory, kinesthetic; Schunk, 2000; Taber-Brown, 2000). Some children may learn best with visual presentations, whereas others perform better when most of the presentation is auditory. The software should support the type of sensory modality that is most conducive to learning for each child. In addition, the quality of the graphics, sound, and animation is important to determine whether they are adequate, as well as the types of prompts given to assist the child. Some software will not be appropriate for children who become easily distracted by extraneous visual or auditory input, or who have a visual impairment and have difficulty using a program that has a lot of visual clutter (extraneous graphics).

Presentation Options.   Many software programs come with options to alter the presentation of the program. One type of presentation option is the ability to control the difficulty level, presentation pace, and content being presented. For example, some children with motor impairments may need a longer time to respond than an allotted 10 seconds. Some programs will allow the presentation pace to be adjusted to allow time for the child to respond. Only certain programs will provide the flexibility to change the content by adding or deleting material.

The presentation format itself also may be adjustable. Some programs will come with a variety of scanning options to allow children to access the program using a switch. This is particularly useful for some children with severe physical impairments whose primary means of accessing a computer is using a switch that they activate when the desired response is visually highlighted (visual scanning) or spoken aloud (auditory scanning). Some programs will come with a high-contrast option that will alter the foreground or background colors to provide more contrast for children with visual impairments. Other format changes such as font size, symbol size, or low graphics option may also be available to assist children who have visual impairments.

Another presentation option is modifying the starting point. Many programs will keep track of where the child stopped the lesson so he can start where he left off the next time he uses the program. Some programs will allow the user or teacher to select the starting point, regardless of where the child ended.

Feedback to Answers.   One of the most critical areas to evaluate is how the software program provides feedback to the child. When the child provides a correct response, potentially reinforcing feedback should occur (e.g., dancing animal, positive comments, a gold star). Care should be taken that feedback to incorrect responses is not embarrassing (e.g., makes a negative sound for all to hear, makes negative comments) or results in frustration. Feedback to incorrect answers should be helpful and consistently made. Some programs will provide another opportunity when incorrect, whereas others will provide immediate assistance. Programs in which the teacher can manipulate how the feedback is provided (e.g., help screens, review content) will allow more individualized assistance to meet the child's needs. It also is important to evaluate if the program keeps track of the missed items. This will help the teacher to examine the areas in which the child is having difficulty and provide intervention.

Augmentative Communication

Children use augmentative communication when they are unable to speak, have unintelligible speech, or have speech that is not functional. Difficulty speaking may result from such conditions as severe motor disorders (e.g., cerebral palsy), autism, rare syndromes (e.g., Rett syndrome), and multiple disabilities (Hetzroni, Rubin, & Kondol, 2002; Ko, McConachie, & Jolleff, 1998; Miranda, 2001). Augmentative communication can provide a way for children with disabilities to ask for desired items, comment on interesting events, exchange information, form social bonds, and interact with others. Providing a means to communicate may even decrease aggressive behavior in preschool children (Frea, Arnold, Vittimberga, & Koegel, 2001). Being able to communicate with others promotes learning, socialization, and development and can even be viewed as the essence of human life (Glennen, 1997).

Augmentative communication (also referred to as augmentative and alternative communication or AAC) is the combination of all methods of communication available to a person including any speech, vocalization, gestures, communication behaviors, as well as specific communication methods and devices (Doster & Politano, 1996: Heller & Bigge, 2001). In many instances, children will use a combination of augmentative communication approaches such as gestures, vocalizations, and a communication device. The main objective is to promote effective communication with others, using the forms of communication that are most appropriate for the child and the situation.

Some children will use augmentative communication as a primary form of communication to replace speech, whereas others will use it to augment speech. In some cases, children may need to use augmentative communication to permanently augment speech (or replace speech); other times it may be used temporarily until speech improves. With young children, concern is often raised regarding the impact of using augmentative communication when speech is developing. It has been found that augmentative communication does not in any way inhibit speech production and, in some cases, may promote speech (Romski & Sevcik, 1993).

> Augmentative communication use does not interfere with the development of speech.

There are several different forms of communication devices that may be used by young children. Some are as simple as pictures displayed on a piece of cardboard or in a book format (i.e., low-tech, nonelectronic). Other communication devices are more sophisticated. Voice-output electronic communication devices may display only a few messages at one time, but have multiple levels or links to other vocabulary stored in the device. Electronic communication devices have the advantage of offering a variety of output modes. Devices with speech output can motivate children to use the AAC device by stimulating speech, allow children to gain another's attention to initiate communication, and promote self-correction of a message by being able to hear the message (Goosens & Kraat, 1985). Some children will have both a simple, low-tech, nonelectronic device as well as an electronic one. A simple low-tech device may be used in certain environments (e.g., sandbox, bathtub) and also serve as a backup should the electronic device need repair. As technological advances have been made, electronic communication devices are more commonly seen with young children due to their features and capabilities.

There are two main categories of electronic communication devices: dedicated devices and nondedicated devices. **Dedicated devices** are those that are designed with the sole or primary purpose of being a communication device. Dedicated communication devices may range from simple electronic devices that provide a few messages (e.g., BIGmack Communication Aid by AbleNet and Cheap Talk 4-Direct by Enabling Devices, Toys for Special Children) to complex programmable devices with hundreds of stored words, phrases, and sentences (e.g., DynaMyte by DynaVox Systems) to those in between (e.g., Macaw by Zygo Industries, AlphaTalker II by Prentke Romich Company). Augmentative communication devices come in a variety of shapes and sizes, from those that can be placed on a belt (Hip Talk by Enabling Devices, Toys for Special Children) to those that are rectangular in shape and can be easily carried or mounted on a wheelchair.

Nondedicated devices refer to computer-based augmentative communication systems that have software programs converting the laptop computer into a communication device. A nondedicated system allows children to have the flexibility of computer programs in addition to the communication device (Lipner, 1997). One example of a software program that can serve as a communication device as well as an educational tool is Speaking Dynamically Pro (Mayer-Johnson, Inc.).

The AlphaTalker is a dedicated communication device.

Means of Access, Storage, and Output

Electronic augmentative communication devices often come with a variety of access (or input) and output options. The most common means of accessing a device is **direct selection**, which refers to directly indicating, through touch or some other mechanism, the desired symbol. Whenever possible, direct selection is used with young children because it is faster and cognitively easier to learn than other access options (Judge, 1998).

The most preferred method of access of a communication device for very young children is direct selection through the use of touch. However, some young children have severe physical impairments that preclude them from directly touching the communication symbol with their fingers. Some children will be able to select the symbol using a pointing aid (e.g., mouthstick, headpointer) or a different body part (e.g., toe, eye gaze). Sometimes children with severe physical impairments can point using their finger, but it can be very fatiguing. When this occurs, they may switch to a less fatiguing system such as looking at the desired response. (This is also referred to as using eye gaze or eye pointing). A simple eye-gaze system often consists of a clear rectangular piece of plexiglass (usually with the middle cut out for the teacher to look through) and objects, pictures, or items attached with Velcro® around the opening. When asked a question, a child will look at the answer. This can be used to assess mastery of material (e.g., "Which number is the number 2?") or to communicate a snack selection (e.g., "Do you want a cookie, cracker, or potato chip?").

When a child with a physical disability cannot effectively access a communication device using direct access, **scanning** may be used. Some communication devices that have scanning highlight each symbol with a light, whereas other devices speak each choice. There are several different scanning patterns that may be used (e.g., row-column, group-item scanning), but the most commonly used by young children is linear scanning in which one symbol at a time is highlighted. To control the scanning process, the device may be set to automatically scan, or the child may push a switch each time to advance to the next selection. When the desired symbol is highlighted by a light (with visual scanning) or spoken (with auditory scanning), a switch is activated to make the selection. Although scanning is an option for children who are unable to use direct selection, children younger than 4 years of age may have difficulty using a scanning method because it is more difficult to learn and requires a longer period of attention than most direct selection methods (Glennen, 1992).

Different communication devices display the desired vocabulary in different ways. Very young children typically need all of the choices in sight. However, as the child has increasing vocabulary needs, more symbols are needed and a display cannot necessarily display all of the choices at one time. Some devices will come with different levels (or pages). These levels consist of additional symbols that may be accessed by touching a specific area on the device. For example, one child's device may display 36 symbols at one time and have 10 levels (pages) of 36 symbols each. This may be set up so that there are different pages for different activities (e.g., one for snack, one for circle time). Some devices have dynamic displays in which one symbol will link the child to other symbols. For example, if the child pushes the toy symbol, this may link the child to different types of toys from which to choose. In

> Touch is the most preferred method of access of a communication device.

order for this type of system to work, it is important that the child is able to categorize and understand where the desired symbol is located.

Electronic augmentative communication devices may come with visual or auditory output. Visual output usually consists of the printed message that may be temporarily displayed using liquid crystal displays (LCDs), or it may be permanently displayed using a printed hard copy. Auditory output voices the message using either digitized speech or synthesized speech. **Digitized speech** is recorded using a human voice, whereas **synthesized speech** is computer generated (Tanchak & Sawyer, 1995). In some augmentative communication devices, there are several computer-generated voices to choose from. Whenever possible, a child's voice of the same gender is usually selected.

Symbol and Vocabulary Selection

There are a wide variety of symbols that young children may use in augmentative communication systems. Symbols can include objects, partial objects, photographs, line drawings, pictures, icons, letters, words, or other representational items. Symbol selection will depend upon several factors, one of which is the cognitive skills of the child. For example, a young child may use an empty milk carton attached to her communication system to indicate "milk," whereas another child may have a picture of a milk carton programmed into her device to indicate the same thing. The more **iconic** a symbol (i.e., degree a symbol resembles what it represents), the easier it will be to learn (Heller & Bigge, 2001). Programs also are available to make pictures to use with various communication devices (e.g., Boardmaker by Mayer-Johnson; Overlay Maker by IntelliTools).

Careful consideration and assessment are needed to select the vocabulary that a child will need to successfully interact with others. Beginning vocabulary selection typically targets items that are reinforcing to the child. For instance, a child whose favorite activity is to play with blocks may have a block or picture of a block depicted on the communication device. If the child really enjoys drawing with crayons, a crayon or picture of a crayon may be on the device. It is important that the initial vocabulary is highly motivating to encourage the child to use the device to obtain the reinforcing item.

As the child's communication needs grow, families and teachers will need to examine the child's daily activities and make a list of the typical vocabulary that is used in that activity. For example, some of the vocabulary found in a snack activity include: "I want," "cookie," "milk," "more," "please," "thank you," "This is good," "Do you want one?" "no," "big one," and "small one". After a list is made, the vocabulary is then examined to determine which vocabulary is at the child's level and will be targeted at this time, and which will be targeted at a later time. For instance, one preschool child who is just beginning to communicate may have only the word "cookie" targeted whereas another child may target several of the messages.

It is also important to examine the type of messages that are being selected for the communication device. According to Cook and Hussey (2002) there are primarily eight different vocabulary categories. Some young children will be learning only a few of the categories, whereas others will have messages from all areas.

Category	Sample Message
Initiating an interaction	"Come talk to me."
Greeting	"Hi."
Responses	"I'm sleepy."
Requests	"I want a cookie."
Information exchange	"Can I go swing?"
Commenting	"That's yucky!"
Wrap-up farewell	"Bye-bye."
Conversational repair	"No. Not what I mean."

Augmentative Communication and Assessment

The child's ability to use an augmentative communication device should be carefully assessed to determine if changes should to be made to the access method, output method, type of symbol, vocabulary, instructional strategies, or other areas. Usually changes can be made using the same device, but sometimes a different augmentative communication device is needed. Changes are often necessary when the child is not making sufficient progress using the system or the child has outgrown the current system and needs a more sophisticated device that has more capabilities.

Careful assessment of the child's use of the augmentative communication device is important to determine not only device and instructional changes but also whether the device can be reliably used for assessment purposes. When a child is nonverbal, the tendency is to use the augmentative communication device to answer questions, whether these are over material being taught in school or items on some type of standardized test. However, if the child is still learning the device or is still trying to motorically access the device accurately, the augmentative communication device may not be the best option to use for assessment purposes. The child may have other responses that are more accurate to use. For example, some children will have a very accurate yes/no response or the child may use eye gaze when choices are given visually. Until the augmentative communication device can be used accurately, other means of response may need to be used when assessing the child. Systematic instruction of the device will need to continue until the device can be used accurately. Box 6.1 outlines some suggestions for teaching augmentative communication.

The child should use the most reliable means of responding for assessment. This is not necessarily the child's communication device.

Computer Access

Some children will have difficulty accessing a computer using a standard keyboard or mouse due to cognitive, physical, or sensory impairments. There are a variety of ways to make the computer accessible. Some of these options involve using a pointing aid (e.g., mouthstick, finger isolation glove), having a child with a motor impairment correctly positioned to promote optimal motor movement, or adjusting the position of the keyboard or monitor to a different height. Other options involve making changes to the computer such as using accessibility options, keyboard modifications, alternate keyboards, mouse alternatives, alternate input, processing aids, and alternate output.

BOX 6.1	Tips for Teaching Augmentative Communication

1. Be sure the augmentative communication device is placed where the child can use it (e.g., not in a closet) and that the child is positioned properly to promote optimal movement to access the device (e.g., sitting correctly in the wheelchair or adapted chair).
2. The vocabulary should be appropriate for the target activity.
3. The vocabulary should promote interaction between the child and other classmates.
4. If possible, the vocabulary should reflect several different functions or categories of communication (e.g., requesting, greeting, refusing, asking questions).
5. Provide opportunities for the child to use the augmentative communication device throughout the day.
6. Always use the augmentative communication device as a means to an end, not as a labeling activity. If the child touches milk, give him milk. Do not say "good talking" and move on to another symbol.
7. Give the child what she indicates, even if she doesn't like it. For example, if the child touches milk and prefers juice, give her milk and then provide another opportunity (with guidance, if needed) to select juice. The child must learn that what she touches is what she gets.
8. Arrange the environment to promote communication. For example, have a favorite toy out of reach to encourage the child to request it or give the child just a small amount of juice to request more.

Accessibility Functions and Keyboard Modifications

Some children with physical impairments may be able to use the standard keyboard with modifications. Most computers have accessibility options. (This is often found by opening "My Computer," selecting "Control Panel," and then clicking on "Accessibility Options.") There are several different accessibility options, such as filter keys that make the computer ignore brief or repeated keystrokes or slow down the repeat rate (so that the child gets "p" instead of "pppppppppp"). Another example of an accessibility option is Sticky Keys, which allows children to press one key at a time for a key combination like Ctrl + Shift or Ctrl + Alt. Some computers will come with alternate keyboard layouts, such as Dvorak, that can be used for one-handed typists instead of the standard QWERTY layout that is on most keyboards. (If an alternate keyboard layout is used, the keyboard must be relabeled or the keys can often be moved.)

Simple appliances may also be put over the keyboard to make it accessible. One example is a keyguard that is a plastic cover with holes for each key. This prevents children who drag their hand over the keyboard from accidentally pushing unwanted keys. Another simple modification is a moisture guard that fits over the keys to prevent spillage of liquids (or saliva) into the keyboard. Labels may also be placed over the keys to display lowercase letters or to provide high-contrast letters for children with visual impairments (e.g., bolded white letters with a black background). Certain keys may also be color coded to aid learning.

Alternate Keyboards and Alternate Input

Sometimes the keyboard is not the appropriate size or the keys are spaced too far apart or too close together. In these instances, alternate keyboards may be used. Some children will use smaller keyboards designed for young children that help accommodate children's small fingers (Little Fingers Keyboard by InfoGrip). Very small keyboards, such as WinMini (TASH, Inc.), are also available for use with children using mouthsticks or headsticks and for those with limited movement.

Some children may need larger keyboards or those arranged with a different configuration. For example, an IntelliKeys keyboard (by IntelliTools, Inc.) is larger and has the option of using several different overlays. Overlays may be of the alphabet in standard keyboard order or the alphabet arranged in alphabetical order. Mouse functions and overlays representing colors, shapes, and other concepts can be easily placed on the keyboard to allow the child to provide the answer by touching the overlay. Most of the software programs using the IntelliKeys keyboard provide both visual and auditory feedback (e.g., "Yes! That is the duck. Watch the duck swim on the water" as the duck is shown swimming). A variety of software programs for young children come with overlays to go with stories or activities that can be placed on the IntelliKeys keyboard. Overlays also can be made by parents and teachers for various activities using an overlay-maker software program. IntelliKeys keyboards also come with a place to plug in switches so children needing scanning programs that are controlled by switches have a means of access. Programs using IntelliKeys keyboards usually support scanning and switch access.

Some software programs may be controlled by using a mouse. However, some children may have difficulty with a standard mouse and may require one that is smaller in size or a different shape. Some children with physical disabilities will need alternatives to a mouse such as a trackball or a joystick.

Often very young children or children with developmental delays will have difficulty learning the association between the keyboard (or mouse) and what is being displayed on the screen. One option is to use a TouchWindow (Edmark, Riverdeep) or a touch monitor. A TouchWindow is a clear membrane that fits over the monitor screen and is used with a specially designed monitor that works by touch. Both of these devices allow the child to touch the item on the screen to select it. The computer interprets the touch as a selection, and the program responds accordingly. Programs also are available that provide on-screen keyboards that may be accessed with a TouchWindow (as well as a mouse, trackball, joystick, or by scanning).

Children with severe physical disabilities may use a switch connected to a computer to scan their selections (in the same manner that they may be connected to certain augmentative communication devices). Switches come in a variety of shapes and sizes and may be activated by almost any movement that different parts of the body can make. For example, a switch may be activated by pushing

> Whenever possible, direct selection options should be selected over slower, more difficult to learn scanning options.

IntelliKeys keyboards use overlays that can be adapted to meet an individual child's needs.

on it with a hand or foot, wrinkling an eyebrow, or breathing in and out of a tube (sip and puff switch). Various computer programs can be accessed by scanning and using a switch to make a selection. The child activates the switch when the desired item is highlighted by a light visually (visual scanning) or by voice output (auditory scanning).

Computer Output Options

There are a variety of output options that may be used to access a variety of computer programs. Screen magnification may be needed for children with visual impairments. This may be accomplished by using a large-screen monitor or specially designed software that offers magnification (e.g., ZoomText by Ai Squared). If the child is using print, most word processing programs will allow font and size changes, as well as foreground or background color options that may make the output more accessible. Some children will need higher contrast to discern what is on the computer screen and many software programs will provide high-contrast options.

Another output option that may help a variety of children with disabilities is voice output. Voice output can provide directions, inform the child of what is being

Switches, like these by AbleNet, allow children to access a computer or activate electrically controlled devices with simple muscle movements.

displayed on the computer monitor, and provide feedback regarding the selection the child made. Several educational software programs provide voice output in addition to what is visually displayed. There also are several software programs designed to read what is written on a computer screen (e.g., Write:OutLoud by Don Johnston Inc.; JAWS for Windows Screen Reading Software by Freedom Scientific, Inc.).

Printers are available to print out a child's work. Printers may also be used to print symbols, pictures, and words. Special printers, known as **braille embossers**, may be used to print braille or to construct pre-braille activities for young children.

Assessing Computer Access

A team of individuals will typically determine the appropriate computer access devices or modifications needed to make the computer accessible to a child with a disability. As the child grows and develops, computer access will need to be continually assessed. Changes may be needed due to changes in the child's motor, sensory, or cognitive abilities. Conditions that cause deteriorating motor or cognitive functioning may result in the need for different types of computer access. Conversely, as a child develops, more sophisticated computer technology may be used (e.g., voice recognition software or word prediction programs).

There are many computer programs that may be used as an adjunct to classroom teaching to reinforce concepts and to assess if children have mastered targeted skills. As with augmentative communication devices, it is important that children are not assessed on whether they know the material presented on the computer when there are unreliable access issues. Some children may have difficulty mastering the access technique and miss items due to motor or sensory problems, rather than not knowing the concepts being presented. To determine this, children can be presented with material that their teacher is confident they know and see how well they can access the computer to make their selection. If they are missing known items, then inaccurate responses are not due to learning issues, but may be attributed to motor or sensory access issues (e.g., not being able to reliably use the switch to make a selection with scanning software, or being unable to reach all of the keys on the alternate keyboard). Children will need to be assessed using reliable responses while they are still learning to use the computer. Also, the computer access technologies will need to be further evaluated to be sure that the correct technology has been selected.

Software for Early Learning

Software programs often are used with young children with disabilities to enhance classroom or home instruction. Software programs for young children often emphasize cause and effect, readiness and beginning level skills (e.g., matching, number recognition, beginning literacy), and language development. As mentioned earlier, a careful evaluation of the software program is needed to ascertain whether it matches the instructional objective in a manner that is effective for the particular child. Some examples are discussed in the following pages.

Cause-and-Effect Software

Cause-and-effect software is used to help children make the connection between performing an action (e.g., pressing a switch, touching a computer monitor, pressing a keyboard) and causing a visual or auditory response on the computer screen. Cause-and-effect software has been used successfully with children who have mental retardation. This type of software also has been used to teach cause and effect to very young children. Some infants younger than 1 year of age have been able to access a computer using a switch to play simple cause-and-effect games (Glickman, Deitz, Anson, & Stewart, 1996; Swinth, Anson, & Deitz, 1993).

Cause-and-effect software has been used to teach children with motor impairments how to use a switch to access a computer. How to use a switch may not be readily apparent, or the child may need repeated practice to be able to motorically activate it. This type of software has the advantage of giving immediate feedback when the switch is correctly activated. Cause-and-effect software also tends to be motivating, which encourages the child to make the physical effort to try.

There are many different software programs that target teaching cause-and-effect. Often they use colorful animated graphics and sound to provide positive feedback when the child has performed the correct action (e.g., pushing a switch). Depending upon the specific software program, the age range is infancy to adulthood. Examples of these programs are: Creature Antics (Laureate Learning Systems, Inc.), Creature Cartoons (Laureate Learning Systems, Inc.), Cause and Effect Carnival (Judy Lynn Software, Inc.), and Cause & Effect Sights & Sounds (Simtech Publications). These programs are designed to support alternate access devices (e.g., switches).

Language Development Software

Many computer software programs for young children focus on receptive and expressive language skills development. When speech output and graphics are combined, software programs can provide models of language use. Also, computer graphics and animation can enhance comprehension of the words being introduced. Concepts introduced in the classroom or at home can be reinforced and further explored using these software programs.

Many receptive language programs are designed to teach vocabulary, illustrate language concepts, and encourage language use through exploratory and discovery activities (Langone, 1998). For example, the word *dog* may be introduced by showing a dog barking and walking across the screen as the computer's speech synthesizer says "dog." When more expansive language is being targeted, the computer's speech synthesizer may say "the dog is barking" or "the dog is walking," depending upon what is occurring on the computer screen.

Software programs designed to expand expressive language abilities typically provide language models of the item or action on the screen. Some programs encourage the child to say the word or words or sing with them. More advanced expressive language programs provide activities that help children choose words and phrases to build sentences.

Software also has been used to promote expressive language by providing interesting events or actions for children and adults to discuss together. Exciting and motivating graphics, animation, music, and voice output can increase opportunities for expressive language use. For example, Katie's Farm (Lawrence Productions) provides information about farm animals, as well as the make-believe activities such as dressing the animals in human clothing. McGee at the Fun Fair (Lawrence Productions) provides graphics with Mom and Dad taking their child and a friend to a city park. The child using the software program can make choices as to where they go.

Many software programs target both receptive and expressive language skills. For example, First Words, First Words II, and First Verbs–Sterling Edition (Laureate Learning Systems, Inc.) teach early vocabulary using reinforcing graphics and voice output. These programs have the ability to use alternate input (e.g., adapted keyboards, switch with scanning) to make them accessible to a wide range of children with disabilities. Talking Nouns I and II (Laureate Learning Systems, Inc.) encourage language exploration using a multisensory approach to teach basic vocabulary. These software programs also support alternative input (e.g., adapted keyboard, switch with scanning, TouchWindow, and IntelliKeys).

Software for Readiness and Beginning Academic Skills

Many software programs target a variety of readiness and beginning level skills for young children with disabilities. In order for the programs to be effective with young children, they should emphasize interaction and discovery, provide information in a fun, interesting manner, teach children to make choices, and have easy maneuverability to allow independent work (Haugland & Shade, 1988; Murphy & Thuente, 1995; Okolo, 2000). Care should be taken not to introduce drill and practice software too early because it may be counterproductive and result in burnout, rather than increasing these skills (Langone, 1998). It also is important to carefully evaluate the software to be sure it is developmentally appropriate and does not have difficult text-based directions that may result in frustration.

Early learning software teaches a variety of skills. For instance, Early Learning I, II, and III or Suite (Marblesoft) teach skills from infant and toddler to elementary age. Some concepts include matching colors, learning shapes, counting numbers, matching letters, and doing basic addition and subtraction. These programs also provide alternate access. Stickybear's Early Learning Activities and Stickybear's Kindergarten Activities (Optimum Resource Inc.) provide activities pertaining to the alphabet, counting, grouping, shapes, as well as other skill areas. Children can learn through prompted directions or through discovery. In many of these early learning software programs basic cognitive processes, such as attention, perception, discrimination, and memory, also are addressed and reinforced.

There are numerous early learning software programs that emphasize beginning reading and writing skills. Earobics Step 1 (Cognitive Concepts, Inc.) targets phonological awareness, auditory processing, and introductory phonics skills. Simon Sounds It Out and Simon Spells It Out (Don Johnston Inc.) provide fun activities with letter sounds, combinations of letter sounds, and animated spelling exercises. Bailey's Book

A specially designed overlay on an alternate keyboard promotes early literacy skills by displaying the student's selection on the computer monitor and speaking what is selected.

House (Edmark, Riverdeep) provides activities in which children are exposed to letters, rhyming, storytelling, and experimenting with prepositions. They also can create greeting cards and make storybooks. Several programs also are available in which text is highlighted and read to the child, while providing choices and fun activities. For example, UKanDu Little Books: A Day at Play, On a Green Bus, Out and About, and Eensy and Friends (Don Johnston Inc.) target language arts, prereading, and reading through animated stories. All of these programs support the use of adapted keyboards and switch access, making them available to a wide range of children with disabilities.

Several software programs target early math skills. For example, Piggy in Numberland (Learning in Motion) provides fun sound effects and animation to improve number sense and counting skills. More advanced skills, such as addition, subtraction, and geometric shapes, also are addressed. Math Magic (MindPlay) uses arcade-type action with counting, addition, and subtraction. This software allows the child to count objects using the spacebar. Software programs also are available that teach coins (Coin Critters by Nordic Software, Inc.) and time (Clockworks by William K. Bradford Publishing Company).

Software Targeting Multiple Intelligence Areas

Although the concept of multiple forms of intelligence has been promoted over the past two decades (Gardner, 1982, 1993), research documenting their application to infants, toddlers, and preschoolers has been relatively nonexistent. Nonetheless, this concept has contributed to the growth of software addressing these various forms of intelligence. Whereas the evidenced-based utility of these programs has not been documented with young children, their use with this population is intriguing, particularly with respect to how such programs could facilitate the development of a young child with special needs.

Gardner (1982, 1993) theorized that there are several different types of intelligences, and most tasks require a combination of these. The way a child approaches learning, and the type of learning preferences the child has, is associated with the strengths and weaknesses of these various intelligences (Pracek, 1994; Taber-Brown, 2000). Gardner (1982, 1993) identified seven intelligences that can have an impact on learning: linguistic, spatial, logical-mathematical, bodily-kinesthetic, musical, interpersonal, and intrapersonal. Because it is important for young children to discover their own particular interests and abilities, they should be exposed to a variety of materials addressing these different intelligence areas. Children may also be given the opportunity to explore material using their more dominant intelligence(s), as well as to expand on less dominant ones (Hutinger & Johanson, 2000). Each of the different intelligences has been associated with certain software characteristics that are integrated into preschool software (Taber-Brown, 2000).

A child's dominant intelligence area or areas often correspond to a child's preferred learning style.

Linguistic intelligence refers to the capacity to use written or oral words in practical ways. Software programs targeting this type of intelligence contain speech, words, word games, and other literacy forms of expression (e.g., poetry, journal writing). Examples of software programs for young children that address linguistic intelligence are Bailey's Book House (Edmark, Riverdeep), Kid Works Deluxe (Knowledge Adventure), and Storybook Theatre (Sunburst Communications; Hutinger & Johanson, 2000; Taber-Brown, 2000).

Spatial intelligence refers to the ability to perceive the visual-spatial world accurately with sensitivity to color, line, shape, form, and space. Software programs addressing this area use point and drawing programs, reading software with visual cues or color coding, mazes, puzzles, maps, and diagrams. Some software programs that address spatial intelligence are Kid Pix Studio Deluxe (The Learning Company), Thinkin' Things Collection (Edmark, Riverdeep), and Kid Works Deluxe (Knowledge Adventure; Hutinger & Johanson, 2000; Taber-Brown, 2000). (Note that most software programs require the child to use more than one intelligence area; hence, Kid Works Deluxe is listed under two different areas.)

Logical-mathematical intelligence refers to the ability to use logic and numbers to perceive logical patterns and relationships. Software programs addressing this area include those that use problem solving, abstract patterns and relationships, puzzles, and activities using categorization. Some of these programs include Millie's Math House and Sammy's Science House (Edmark, Riverdeep) and Blocks in Motion (Don Johnston Inc.; Hutinger & Johanson, 2000; Taber-Brown, 2000).

Bodily-kinesthetic intelligence refers to the ability to learn through touch and manipulation, and the ability to use one's body or hands to produce things. Software programs addressing this area have such features as manipulatives that can be moved around the screen, animated graphics, and arcade-style games. The programs also allow for alternative input such as joystick, mouse, and TouchWindow. Programs addressing bodily-kinesthetic intelligence include Blocks in Motion (Don Johnston Inc.) and Stanley's Sticker Stories (Edmark, Riverdeep; Hutinger & Johanson, 2000; Taber-Brown, 2000).

Musical intelligence refers to the capacity to perceive and express musical ideas. Children with musical intelligence learn through rhythm and melody. Software programs addressing this level of intelligence use songs and sounds, use music as a reward for correct responses, and have associated activities that add music to their presentation. Programs include Monkeys Jumping on the Bed (SoftTouch, Inc.), Chicka Chicka Boom Boom (Knowledge Adventure), and Music Keys (Creative Communicating; Hutinger & Johanson, 2000; Taber-Brown, 2000).

Interpersonal intelligence pertains to learners who like to interact with others and be involved in social activities. Learning occurs best by relating and cooperating with others. Software targeting this area include programs that promote group participation or social issues. Several programs can be used as a group activity in which turn-taking and group discussion are promoted, such as Just Grandma and Me Deluxe (The Learning Company, Riverdeep) and Green Eggs and Ham (The Learning Company, Riverdeep; Hutinger & Johanson, 2000; Taber-Brown, 2000).

Intrapersonal intelligence pertains to those who like to be independent and who are self-motivated. These children typically learn best with self-paced instruction and individualized projects and games. Programs that are tutorials, self-paced, or encourage self-improvement usually appeal to this type of intelligence. Programs include Kid Pix Studio Deluxe (The Learning Company, Riverdeep) and Bailey's Book House and Millie's Math House (Edmark, Riverdeep; Hutinger & Johanson, 2000; Taber-Brown, 2000).

Play and Technology

Play is an important activity for children from which cognitive, social, communication, and motor skills can develop (Wershing & Symington, 1998). Piaget (1962), for example, emphasized the importance of object play in cognitive development. In some instances, the types of assistive technology children with disabilities use may be the same as children without disabilities. However, sometimes young children with disabilities may be unable to access typical toys or play activities and require various forms of assistive technology.

Adapted Toys

Toys can be easily adapted to promote enjoyment, social interaction, and development.

Some children with motor impairments will be unable to manipulate toys to play with them. In some cases, using larger toys that are easy to grip may prevent difficulties. However, some children have such severe motor problems that they are unable to pick up toys or move them to desired locations. One strategy is for the child to tell another person (possibly using augmentative communication) what they would like the toy to do. For example, when playing with dolls in a dollhouse, the child could indicate where to put the doll and what it is doing.

Children also may use battery-operated toys that have been adapted to operate with a switch. Any battery-operated toy can be adapted by placing a battery interrupt device between the batteries and connecting it to a switch (Bain, 1997a). The child can turn the device on and off by accessing the switch. For example, a child can make a battery-operated barking dog move and bark when pushing a switch. These adapted toys can be made inexpensively at home, purchased from companies, or borrowed from lending libraries targeting children with disabilities (e.g., Lekotec).

Infants as young as 3 months old have used toys to learn about the effect they can have on their environment (Male, 2003). Besides promoting play and learning, these switch-operated toys may stimulate movement when switches are positioned in certain ways. For example, a child may be motivated to extend her reach farther than before to activate a switch that makes a favorite toy dance. Motor milestones, such as rolling over, may be encouraged if the switch is positioned to activate a favorite toy upon rolling onto the switch.

Games, Recreational Devices, and Software Programs

Many games and sports for young children can be adapted to allow the child with a disability to play with other children. Board games may be adapted by using alternate spinners, larger game pieces, and simpler rules, among other adaptations. Sports can be modified by altering rules (e.g., allowing more swings at bat), modifying equipment (e.g., using balls that beep for children with visual impairments or a using a larger, lighter ball for children with physical impairments), or making the playing area accessible (e.g., having a ramp installed to allow the child to get onto the field). Many different types of adaptations and technology can be used to allow all children to participate.

Recreational devices, such as scooters and bicycles, also may be used to promote play. These devices can be modified to allow children with physical disabilities to use them (e.g., adding extra wheels or a seat that would secure the individual). Another option is to use an adapted device, such as an adapted bicycle, that is pedaled using the arms instead of the legs.

Software programs also can be used to promote play. Some of these will replicate various games and sports that are available in real life, and some will provide games or simulations of recreational devices. Many computer programs are set up to provide simple or complex games for the purpose of enjoyment, discovery, and play. Solitary play activities, such as using computer programs to color or draw, may be used as well as those that require multiple children to play. These software programs may provide additional learning in a game format, such as those targeting cause and effect, language, and early learning skills.

Providing Environments for Play

Some children may be unable to access activities in their environment, either because they are physically unable to access them or because the environment is inaccessible. One type of technology that can assist a child to access various electric devices is **environmental control units (ECUs)**. Environmental control units allow children with physical disabilities to turn on and off various items. For example, children can turn on a light to see a favorite storybook or turn on a tape player to sing along with the music. Young children can use ECUs during school activities, such as to activate an electric mixer during a fun cooking activity, or by turning on an electric toy or game (Bain, 1997b). Environmental control units work by having the item plugged into a control unit that is then plugged into the wall. The child has another control unit into which a switch is typically plugged. By activating the switch, the child's control unit sends out a signal to activate the item. This works similar to a remote control device.

Although all environments should be examined for accessibility, playgrounds need careful examination to determine if they are accessible and if they are conducive to children playing with each other. Playgrounds can be modified or created to allow children with disabilities to play and interact with typically developing children. The playground does not necessarily have to be high tech, but it should be **design tech**. This means that the playground is constructed with user-based design guidelines, accessible components, and accessible surfaces. For example, some of the playground surfaces may be repaved to allow a child who uses a wheelchair access to the various parts of the playground. A ramp may be available to allow a child to wheel onto a pretend ship on the playground. Often having play activities of different difficulty levels near each other allows children of different abilities to play and interact (Goltsman, 2002). Careful consideration and planning can result in accessible play activities and promote interaction among children.

Summary

There are several different types of technologies that may have an impact on the lives of young children, such as medical technology, technology productivity tools, information technology, assistive technology, and instructional technology. Assistive technology can provide children with a means to communicate using augmentative communication, use computers through modified or alternate computer access devices, move around the environment using a mobility device, engage in play using switch-controlled toys, and participate in performing self-care skills with the use of adapted devices. Instructional technology provides numerous learning opportunities, including software programs to promote learning and development. To make technology successful, it is important to carefully assess the specific technology device or material with respect to human factors and the context in which it will be used. The technology device or software should be developmentally appropriate and match the learners' needs. It also should be used as a tool to accomplish some task, not as an end in itself. When appropriate technology is used, it has the capability to make a significant difference in the lives of young children with disabilities.

Review Questions and Discussion Points

1. What are five types of technology and how can they have an impact on the life of a young child with a disability?
2. What modifications and alternate input devices may be used to access a computer?
3. What are the key areas to consider when evaluating whether a software program is appropriate for a young child?
4. What is augmentative communication and what type of vocabulary is often used with augmentative communication devices?
5. You are asked to provide an assessment and design an intervention plan for a 2-year-old who is totally nonverbal and has limited physical mobility. How would you proceed? What might you try?

Recommended Resources

Professional Associations

The Alliance for Technological Access is a national network of assistive technology resource centers, individuals, organizations, and vendors who promote the use of technology for individuals with disabilities. Information about this organization can be found online. (http://www.ataccess.org).

The Technology and Media Division (TAM) of the Council for Exceptional Children is a nonprofit organization advocating for individuals who work with or on behalf of children with special needs. This division addresses the need, availability, and effective use of technology and media for individuals with disabilities. (http://www.cec.sped.org).

Rehabilitation Engineering and Assistive Technology Society of North America (RESNA) is an interdisciplinary association of individuals (e.g., teachers, rehabilitation specialists) who have a common interest in technology and disability. The purpose of this association is to improve the potential of individuals with disabilities and help them achieve their goals through the use of technology. (http://www.resna.org).

Web Sites

Searchable Databases Specializing in Technology

AbleData
http://www.abledata.com

Closing the Gap
http://www.closingthegap.com

Sample Web Sites

Don Johnston Incorporated
http://www.donjohnston.com

Edmark
http://www.riverdeep.net/edmark

IntelliTools, Inc.
http://www.intellitools.com

Laureate Learning Systems, Inc.
http://www.laureatelearning.com

Lekotek
http://www.lekotek.org

Mayer-Johnson, Inc.
http://www.mayerjohnson.com

TASH, Inc.
http://www.tashinc.com

Trace Research and Development Center
http://trace.wisc.edu

Recommended Readings

Assistive Technology Journal

Journal of Special Education Technology

Judge, S. L., & Parette, H. P. (1998). *Assistive technology for young children with disabilities: A guide to family-centered services.* Cambridge, MA: Brookline Books.

National Association for the Education of Young Children. (1998). *Technology and young children—Ages 3 through 8.* Retrieved November 10, 2002, from http://www.naeyc.org/resources/position_statements/pstech98.htm

References

Bain, B. K. (1997a). Switches, control interfaces, and access methods. In B. K. Bain & D. Leger (Eds.), *Assistive technology: An interdisciplinary approach* (pp. 57–71). New York: Churchill Livingstone.

Bain, B. K. (1997b). *Environmental control systems.* In B. K. Bain & D. Leger (Eds.), *Assistive technology:*

An interdisciplinary approach (pp. 119–139). New York: Churchill Livingstone.

Baker, B. (1986). Using images to generate speech. *IEEE Biomedical Conference Proceedings,* Fort Worth, TX.

Behrmann, M. M., Jones, J. K., & Wilds, M. L. (1989). Technology intervention for very young children with disabilities. *Infants and Young Children, 1*(4) 66–77.

Best, G. A., Ollie, P. A., Weinroth, M. D., Dykes, M. K., & Heller, K. W. (1998). The education of students with physical and health disabilities: Past, present, and future. *Physical Disabilities: Education and Related Services, 16*, 55–76.

Bitter, G. C., & Pierson, M. E. (1999). *Using technology in the classroom.* Boston: Allyn & Bacon.

Blackhurst, A. E., & Lahm, E. A. (2000). Technology and exceptionality foundations. In J. D. Lindsey (Ed.), *Technology & exceptional individuals* (3rd ed., pp. 3–45). Austin, TX: PRO-ED.

Butler, C. (1988). High tech tots: Technology for mobility, manipulation, communication, and learning in early childhood, *Infants and Young Children, 1*, 66–73.

Cardona, M., Martinez, A. L., & Hinojosa, J. (2000). Effectiveness of using a computer to improve attention to visual analysis activities of five preschool children with disabilities. *Occupational Therapy International, 7*, 42–57.

Chute, R., & Miksad, J. (1997). Computer assisted instruction and cognitive development. *Child Study Journal, 27*, 237–254.

Cook, A. M., & Hussey, S. M. (2002). *Assistive technologies: Principles and practice* (2nd ed.). St. Louis: Mosby.

Doster, S., & Politano, P. (1996). Augmentative and alternative communication. In J. Hammel (Ed.), *AOTA Self-Paced Clinical Course: Technology and occupational therapy: A link to function.* Bethesda, MD: American Occupational Therapy Association.

Forcier, R. (1999). *The computer as an education tool: Productivity and problem solving* (2nd ed.). Upper Saddle River, NJ: Merrill/Prentice Hall.

Frea, W. D., Arnold, C. L., Vittimberga, G. L., & Koegel, R. L. (2001). A demonstration of the effects of augmentative communication on the extreme aggressive behavior of a child with autism within an integrated preschool setting. *Journal of Positive Behavior Interventions, 3*, 194–199.

Fritz, M. (1991). The word of virtual reality. *Training, 28*, 45–47.

Gardner, H. (1982). *Frames of mind: The theory of multiple intelligences.* New York: Basic Books.

Gardner, H. (1993). *Multiple intelligences: The theory in practice.* New York: Basic Books.

Glennen, S. (1992). Augmentative and alternative communication. In G. Church & S. Glennen (Eds.), *The handbook of assistive technology* (pp. 93–122). San Diego, CA: Singular.

Glennen, S. L. (1997). Introduction to augmentative and alternative communication. In S. L. Glennen & D. C. DeCoste (Eds.), *Handbook of augmentative and alternative communication* (pp. 3–20). San Diego, CA: Singular.

Glickman, L., Deitz, J., Anson, D., & Stewart, K. (1996). The effect of switch control site on computer skills of infant and toddlers. *American Journal of Occupational Therapy, 50*, 545–553.

Goltsman, S. M. (2002). Recreation and play environments. In D. A. Olson & F. DeRuyter (Eds.), *Clinician's guide to assistive technology* (pp. 451–469). St. Louis: Mosby.

Goosens, C., & Kraat, A. (1985). Technology as a tool for conversation and language learning for the physically handicapped. *Topics in Language Disorders, 6*, 56–70.

Haugland, S. W., & Shade, D. D. (1988). Developmentally appropriate software for young children. *Young Children, 43*(4), 37–43.

Heckathorne, C. W. (2002). Upper-limb prosthetics. In D. A. Olson & F. DeRuyter (Eds.), *Clinician's guide to assistive technology* (pp. 265–280). St. Louis: Mosby.

Heller, K. W., Alberto, P., Forney. P., & Schwartzman, M. (1996). *Understanding physical, sensory, and health impairments: Characteristics and educational implications.* Pacific Grove, CA: Brooks/Cole.

Heller, K. W., & Bigge, J. (2001). Augmentative communication. In J. Bigge, S. Best, & K. W. Heller (Eds.), *Teaching individuals with physical and multiple disabilities* (4th ed., pp. 229–277). Upper Saddle River, NJ: Merrill/Prentice Hall.

Heller, K. W., Forney, P. E., Alberto, P. A., Schwartzman, M. N., & Goeckel, T. (2000). *Meeting physical and health needs of children with disabilities: Teaching student participation and management.* Belmont, CA: Wadsworth.

Hetzroni, O., Rubin, C., & Kondol, O. (2002). The use of assistive technology for symbol identification by children with Rett syndrome. *Journal of Intellectual & Developmental Disability, 27*, 57–71.

Higgins, N. (1993). Preschool teacher uses of video technologies. *Journal of Educational Television, 19*, 153–167.

Hutinger, P., & Clark, L. (2000). TEChPLACEs: An Internet community for young children, their teachers, and their families. *Teaching Exceptional Children, 32*(4), 56–63.

Hutinger, P. L., & Johanson, J. (2000). Implementing and maintaining an effective early childhood comprehensive technology system. *Topics in Early Childhood Special Education, 20,* 159–173.

Ira, V. (1997). Virtual reality and mobility skills. *Exceptional Parent, 27,* 50.

Jones, D. E., Clatterbuck, C. C., Marquis, I. G., Turnbull H. R., III, & Moberly, R. L. (1996). Educational placements for children who are ventilator assisted. *Exceptional Children, 63,* 47–57.

Judge, S. (2002). Family-centered assistive technology assessment and intervention practices for early intervention. *Infants and Young Children, 15,* 60–68.

Judge, S. L. (1998). Providing access to assistive technology for young children and families. In S. L. Judge & H. P. Parette (Eds.), *Assistive technology for young children with disabilities: A guide to family-centered services* (pp. 1–15). Cambridge, MA: Brookline Books.

Judge, S. L., & Lahm, E. A. (1998). Assistive technology applications for play, mobility, communication, and learning for young children with disabilities. In S. L. Judge & H. P. Parette (Eds.), *Assistive technology for young children with disabilities: A guide to family-centered services* (pp. 16–44). Cambridge, MA: Brookline Books.

King, T. W. (1999). *Assistive technology: Essential human factors.* Boston: Allyn & Bacon.

Ko, M. L., McConachie, H., & Jolleff, N. (1998). Outcome of recommendations for augmentative communication in children. *Child: Care, Health, and Development, 24,* 195–205.

Langone, J. (1998). Technology. In W. Umansky & S. R. Hooper (Eds.), *Young children with special needs* (3rd ed., pp. 309–339). Upper Saddle River, NJ: Merrill/Prentice Hall.

Langone, J., Malone, D. M., & Kinsley, T. (1999). Technology solutions for young children with developmental concerns. *Infants and Young Children, 11,* 65–78.

Lewis, R. B. (1993). *Special education technology: Classroom applications.* Pacific Grove: CA: Brooks/Cole.

Lindstrand, P. (2001). Parents of children with disabilities evaluate the importance of the computer in child development. *Journal of Special Education Technology, 16,* 43–52.

Lipner, H. S. (1997). Augmentative and alternative communication. In B. K. Bain & D. Leger (Eds.), *Assistive technology: An interdisciplinary approach* (pp. 99–118). New York: Churchill Livingstone.

Male, M. (2003). *Technology for inclusion: Meeting the special needs of all students.* Boston: Allyn & Bacon.

McBride, K. M., & Austin, A. M. (2001). Computer affect of preschool children and perceived affect of their parents, teachers, and peers. *Journal of Genetic Psychology, 14,* 497–506.

McBrien, D. M., & Bonthius, D. J. (2000). Seizures in infants and young children. *Infants and Young Children, 12,* 21–31.

Mercer, C. D., & Mercer, A. R. (1998). *Teaching students with learning problems* (5th ed.). Upper Saddle River, NJ: Merrill/Prentice Hall.

Meyen, E. L., Aust, R., Gauch, J. M., Hinton, H. S., Isaacson, R. E., Smith, S. J., et al. (2002). e-Learning: A programmatic research construct for the future. *Journal of Special Education Technology, 17,* 37–46.

Mioduser, D., Tur-Kaspa, H., & Leitner, I. (2000). The learning value of computer-based instruction of early reading skills. *Journal of Computer Assisted Learning, 16,* 54–63.

Miranda, P. (2001). Autism, augmentative communication, and assistive technology: What do we really know? *Focus on Autism & Other Developmental Disabilities, 16,* 141–152.

Murphy, V., & Thuente, K. (1995). Using technology in early learning classrooms. *Learning and Leading with Technology, 22*(8), 8–10.

National Association for the Education of Young Children. (1998). *Technology and young children—Ages 3 through 8.* Retrieved November 10, 2002, from http://www.naeyc.org/resources/position_statements/pstech98.htm

Okolo, C. (2000). Technology for individuals with mild disabilities. In J. D. Lindsey (Ed.), *Technology & exceptional individuals* (3rd ed., pp. 243–301). Austin, TX: PRO-ED.

Parette, H. P., Brotherson, M. J., & Huer, M. B. (2000). Giving families a voice in augmentative and alternative communication decision making. *Education and Training in Mental Retardation and Developmental Disabilities, 35,* 177–190.

Piaget, J. (1962). *Play, dreams and imitation in childhood.* New York: Norton.

Pracek, E. (1994). *Gardner's multiple intelligences and types of software.* Miami, FL: Florida Diagnostic and Learning Resources System. Unpublished document.

Rapport, M. J., & Lasseter, D. J. (1998). Providing support services to students who are ventilator dependent. *Physical Disabilities: Education and Related Services, 16,* 77–94.

Ray, J., & Warden, M. K. (1995). *Technology, computers and the special needs learner.* Albany, NY: Delmar.

Roblyer, M., & Cass, M. (1999). Still more potential than performance: Virtual reality research in special education. *Learning and Leading with Technology, 26,* 50–53.

Romski, M. A., & Sevcik, R. A. (1993). Language learning through augmented means: The process and its products. In A. P. Kaiser, & D. B. Gray (Eds.), *Enhancing children's communication: Research foundations for intervention* (pp. 85–104). Baltimore: Brookes.

Russell, K. E., Coffin, C., & Kenna, M. (1999). Cochlear implants and the deaf child: A nursing perspective. *Pediatric Nursing, 25,* 396–401.

Schunk, D. (2000). *Learning theories: An educational perspective.* Upper Saddle River, NJ: Merrill/Prentice Hall.

Speigel-McGill, P., Zippiroli, S. M., & Mistrett, S. G. (1989). Microcomputers as social facilitators in integrating preschools. *Journal of Early Intervention, 13,* 249–260.

Swinth, Y., Anson, D., & Deitz, J. (1993). Single-switch computer access for infants and toddlers. *American Journal of Occupational Therapy, 47,* 1031–1038.

Taber-Brown, F. M. (2000). Software evaluation and development. In J. D. Lindsey (Ed.), *Technology & exceptional individuals* (3rd ed., pp. 133–160). Austin, TX: PRO-ED.

Tanchak, T. L., & Sawyer, C. (1995). Augmentative communication. In K. F. Flippo, K. J. Inge, & J. M. Barcus (Eds.), *Assistive technology: A resource for school, work, and community* (pp. 57–85). Baltimore: Brooks.

Wershing, A., & Symington, L. (1998). Learning and growing with assistive technology. In S. L. Judge & H. P. Parette (Eds.), *Assistive technology for young children with disabilities: A guide to family-centered services* (pp. 45–75). Cambridge, MA: Brookline Books.

PART III

Developmental Domains

7

Gross Motor Development

Carole W. Dennis and Kathleen A. Schlough

Emily

*E*mily *was diagnosed with cerebral palsy (spastic quadriplegia type) when she was 8 months old. She and her twin brother were born 7 weeks premature by emergency cesarean section. Emily had a prolapsed umbilical cord and, following her birth, she was transferred from the local hospital to the neonatal intensive care unit (NICU) in a nearby city. Emily weighed 4 lb 3 oz and her brother weighed 3 lb 14 oz. Her twin has no apparent side effects from the premature birth and his development has been typical. Emily also has a sister who is 2 years older.*

Shortly after her diagnosis of cerebral palsy, Emily was referred for early intervention services. She received an arena assessment, which included an occupational therapist, speech therapist, physical therapist, and developmental psychologist to evaluate her needs. Emily presented with very high muscle tone (spasticity), especially in her calf, hamstring, adductor (muscles that bring the legs together), and her hip flexor muscles. This gave her the typical scissoring posture of the legs, often seen in children with spacticity, when attempting active large motor movement or when standing with support. OT, PT, speech, and special education were recommended in the home. Four different disciplines entering the home several times a week can easily be overwhelming to a family; therefore, specialists in physical therapy and special education were considered the "core" interventionists by the team and were recommended twice weekly. Occupational and speech therapists consulted with the team and the family on a less frequent basis. Because of Emily's special needs, the team and family decided that the physical therapist and the early childhood educator co-treat during the session to lessen the impact of frequent home visits. Because Emily's physical needs were the greatest concern, the physical therapist would often help move and position her during the therapeutic session while the early childhood educator engaged her in age-appropriate play and cognitive skills. The parents and siblings were present at all sessions and were encouraged to become part of the therapeutic activities.

At the age of 2, Emily attended a private preschool for children with special needs. She attended full time until she was 5 years old and then was enrolled in a typical classroom in her school district. Parental concerns included her difficulty in mobility, breath support during vocalization, and need for positioning equipment. Intervention in the gross motor area included learning to walk with a walker, propelling her wheelchair, positioning needs, and learning to move in and out of her wheelchair independently.

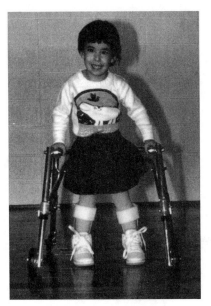

Emily using her rear walker (4 years old).

By the time she was 3 years old, Emily was using a rear walker to walk short distances with supervision. This walking ability was incorporated into her daily classroom routine. She also used a small wheelchair and was able to independently propel it around her preschool classroom, which increased her ability to explore her environment. Her sitting skills were good and no additional trunk support was needed for her wheelchair or adapted chair which she used in both the classroom and at home. Emily wore ankle-foot orthoses (AFOs) on both feet. They extended from just below her knee to her feet and helped keep her from standing on her toes. They also aided in giving her more stability. Emily also used a stander, especially in the classroom, so that she could stand at various activities like the water table with her peers. She used a specially designed floor sitter to give her stability in sitting during classroom circle time.

The classroom team, which included the OT, PT, SLP, classroom teacher, paraprofessionals, and adapted physical education teacher, met on a regular basis to discuss her progress. The team also met formally several times a year with the family and there was informal communication on a daily basis between the family and at least one member of the team. The entire team (including the family) generated discipline-free goals and objectives for Emily. That is, instead of separate goals for each discipline, the team decided on the most important areas that Emily needed to strengthen and then the objectives were tailored to meet those needs.

Gross motor development, the ability to control posture and movement using the large muscles of the body, represents a child's growing proficiency in producing movement that is appropriate to sensory stimuli and environmental demands. Its significance in the developing child is multifaceted. Through the development of motor skills, the child gains feelings of self-control, competence, and self-esteem. The ability to control one's own body in the immediate physical environment is primary to the development of feelings of mastery and motivation. Mobility is important for participation in educational, social, and community life. The International Classification of Functioning, Disability and Health (ICF) model proposed by the World Health Organization (WHO) defines **participation** as the way people live with their health conditions and how these conditions can be improved to achieve a productive, fulfilling life. The child's ability to effectively move and explore his environment is essential for the fulfillment of his life's roles (see the story of Emily at the beginning of the chapter).

In addition, gross motor skills support the development of abilities in the areas of fine-motor development, cognition, communication, adaptive skills, and social and emotional competence in the typically developing child. For example, a stable body position is necessary for children to control their arms and hands for object manipulation. Control of posture is important for respiratory support for speech. As children develop the ability to move about in the environment, they learn a great deal about perceptual properties of objects within that environment.

Motor skills also allow the expression of skills in other domains. Most assessments of cognition, language development, self-care skills, and socialization in the very young child require the demonstration of some type of motor behavior. For example, the behaviors an infant displays that indicate attachment to and separation from the primary caregiver are considered to be important milestones of social and emotional development. These behaviors all require some type of motor output (turning toward, gazing at, and smiling at the caregiver; moving away from the caregiver; and returning to the caregiver for comfort).

Those who work with young children who experience difficulties in gross motor control face several challenges. To help improve such children's motor development, it is important for the early interventionist to understand where delays exist and to hypothesize why they have occurred so that an appropriate intervention plan can be developed. Because motor deficits affect other aspects of development, it is not enough merely to attempt to improve motor skills; it is equally important to consider the impact of adaptation and compensation in relation to task mastery. The use of compensatory techniques for impaired function, adaptation of the environment, provision of specific adaptive equipment, and the modification of activities will have far-reaching implications for the overall development of the child.

Theories of Motor Development

The emergence of gross motor skills in the developing infant is an extraordinary process. Although most of us view a newborn as being helpless, a typical infant is born with all of the requirements necessary for movement. Infants appear to be born with an intrinsic motivation to move and, despite the lack of coordination typical of movement in early infancy, there appears to be some mechanism whereby infants can exert rudimentary control over their environment. In this section of the chapter, some of the theoretical models are discussed that explain motor development.

Reflex/Hierarchical Model

This model is a combination of two different models: the reflex model and the hierarchical model. The **reflex model,** advocated by Gesell and Amatruda (1947) and Sherrington (1947), attempts to explain the progression of motor development as the result of maturation of the central nervous system. According to this model, movement progresses from primitive, reflexive control to voluntary control of movement (Piper & Darrah, 1995). The **hierarchical model** proposed by Hughlings Jackson (Foerster, 1977) and Rudolf Magnus (Magnus, 1926) expands upon the reflex model by focusing on the role of the cerebral cortex, the highest level of central nervous system motor control, which also governs lower levels of the central nervous system (Mathiowetz & Haugen, 1994).

For many years, motor development was viewed in light of Sherrington's (1947) study of reflexes. He suggested that normal human movement was the result of the summation of preprogrammed reflexes (Piper & Darrah, 1995). Reflexes (often called **primitive reflexes**) are automatic, stereotypical movement patterns that are triggered

Primitive reflexes are involuntary, automatic, and stereotypical responses to specific sensory stimuli that are typically seen only in infancy.

Flexion refers to a decreased angle at a joint, or bending of the joint.

Obligatory primitive reflexes are automatic, stereotypic movements that always occur (without volitional control) in response to specific sensory stimuli.

The asymmetrical tonic neck reflex is a normal response in newborns to turning of the head, in which the arm and leg on the side of the body to which the head is turned extend while the limbs on the opposite side flex. Persistence beyond 3 months of age is considered atypical.

The Moro reflex is an infant response to a quick dropping of the head or a perception of falling, where the infant rapidly abducts and extends the arms, followed by an embracing motion.

by sensory stimuli such as touch, stretching of specific muscle groups, the position of the head in relation to the body, and the position of the head in relation to gravity. It is still believed that many of the infant's earliest movements are reflexive in nature and mediated by subcortical areas of the central nervous system. Primitive reflexes are thought to have a discrete function in development. For example, when an infant's cheek is touched, he turns his head toward the touch in a rooting response, which is necessary for suckling and, consequently, survival among mammals. Also, when an infant is lying on his back and a caregiver grasps his forearms and gently pulls upward, the infant responds by pulling his head and arms toward the center of his body (in a **flexion** response). These primitive reflexes should be integrated by the time the infant is 4 to 6 months of age; that is, the infant is no longer obliged to react to a stimulus with a stereotypical reflexive response. Volitional control becomes possible when conscious movement overrides the reflex. Although some vestiges of the primitive reflexes remain throughout life, they are no longer **obligatory** (the response to the stimuli is not always present) in the healthy individual after 4 to 6 months of age. Some typical primitive reflexes are the Moro, flexor withdrawal, palmar grasp, tonic labyrinthine, and asymmetrical tonic neck reflex (Figure 7.1). The **Moro reflex** is the body's response to a loss of head control when the infant is quickly tilted backward. If the infant loses head control, the response is to reach out his arms to the side, then back toward the chest, and finally cry. This reflex may serve to alert the caregiver that the infant is in danger. The **flexor withdrawal reflex** is elicited by a touch to the bottom of the foot; the infant responds by pulling his foot away. In the **palmar grasp reflex,** the infant responds by gripping the finger very tightly when a finger is placed in the palm of the infant's hand. The caregiver often interprets this reflexive response as a sign of strength in the infant. The **tonic labyrinthine reflex** is somewhat controversial in that its true expression is generally seen only in individuals with brain injury. However, in the young infant, there does seem to be a bias toward total body **extension** when the infant is supine (lying on his back) and a bias toward total body flexion when the infant is prone (lying on his stomach). The **asymmetrical tonic neck reflex** (ATNR) occurs when the infant turns his head to one side. The "face" side arm (and sometimes leg) extends and the "skull" side arm (and sometimes leg) flexes. This position is also referred to as the "fencer's position."

In children who have suffered specific brain injuries (as occurs in cerebral palsy, tumors of the central nervous system, or traumatic brain injury), the higher systems are unable to override early, primitive reflexes, and these children may not be able to move with volitional control. Theoretically, the higher centers of the central nervous system are unable to function as a result of an injury and lower level reflexes are released. In these children, primitive reflexes may not become integrated and subsequent movement may be obligatory and stereotypical. In children and adults who suffer brain injuries as a result of trauma or tumors, movement that was previously under volitional control may again be reflexively controlled following the injury. It is important for the educator to be aware of the obligatory nature of these reflexes because they may have a strong influence on the child's ability to move and learn.

As the infant matures, the primitive reflexes are replaced by **postural reactions** that help to keep the individual upright with respect to gravity and protect him in case of a fall. These reactions begin to develop during the sixth month of life (just

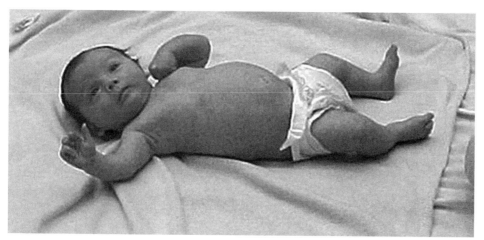

FIGURE 7.1 The asymmetrical tonic neck reflex (Noah, at corrected age 3½ weeks). Note the extension of the arm on the side of the body where his face is turned, and the flexion of the arm on the skull side of his head.

Source: Used by permission of Carole Dennis.

Extension refers to an increased angle at a joint, or the straightening of the joint.

The tonic labyrinthine reflex is a reflex where the position of the body in relationship to gravity influences muscle tone in early infancy. The prone position tends to facilitate flexion, and the supine position tends to facilitate extension of the head, trunk, and extremities.

Protective extension is an automatic reaction that occurs when people reach out to protect themselves from a fall.

Equilibrium reactions are balance/counterbalance responses characterized by muscle tension and movement in response to body movement.

as the primitive reflexes are becoming integrated and less obligatory) and continue throughout life. These reactions include protective extension, righting reactions, and equilibrium reactions. When people reach out to protect themselves during a fall, they are using a protective extension reaction. **Protective extension** may be forward, to the side, or backward and occurs automatically if there is a perception of an imminent fall. The legs may also be involved in the reaction by taking a step or extending toward the unstable direction. **Righting reactions** usually refer to the tendency for the head and trunk to align upright in relation to gravity. As a person starts to tip to one side, the body reacts by maintaining the head oriented to the vertical while the trunk curves to accommodate for this. If a person tips too far to one side, the opposite side arm and/or leg will reach out in an effort to counterbalance the movement. This is called an **equilibrium reaction** and may also involve rotation of the trunk. All three reactions may happen simultaneously or only one may predominate, depending on the need. Therapists will often try to discourage a primitive reflex in young children with head injury and try to encourage the use of equilibrium reactions.

Although most movement specialists today do not believe that the reflex model is sufficient to explain all aspects of motor control, early reflexes do appear to allow the infant to experience movement without conscious control, thus providing the possibility for use of the movement volitionally in the future. For example, when an infant turns his head to the left side, the ATNR is triggered, which promotes extension of his left arm out to the side of his body. If this movement results in contact with an environmental object, other sensory mechanisms are triggered. The body's **proprioceptive system** registers the position of the limb, the tactile system registers the feel of the object, and the visual system records the optical image of the hand touching the object. As this sequence of movement and feedback is repeated, the infant gradually begins to associate the movement pattern with the sensory rewards just noted and eventually learns to control this pattern volitionally with involvement of higher cortical centers of the central nervous system (Piper & Darrah, 1995). When the infant repeats a volitional movement pattern over and over again, myelination of the neural connections that imprint the movement pattern occurs, resulting in fast, automatic movement that requires no conscious thought for its execution. **Myelination** is the developmental process whereby nerve fibers are insulated with a fatty sheath (i.e., myelin), allowing rapid, efficient neural transmission.

In addition to the concept that purposeful, controlled, and voluntary movement evolves from primitive, reflexive movement, the reflex/hierarchical model embraces several other assumptions: that motor development progresses in a head-to-foot (cephalocaudal) direction, that movement control occurs in a proximal-to-distal sequence (from the center of the body toward the extremities), and that movement occurs in a predictable, sequential pattern among typically developing children (Piper & Darrah, 1995). Although these assumptions still guide much of current therapeutic practice, some important exceptions to the model have been demonstrated. The early domination of reflexive-based movement has been questioned by Touwen (1978), who argues that even neonates have variability of movement, and by Thoman (1987), who has demonstrated very early control of movement in premature neonates. Furthermore, the concept of proximal-to-distal control has been called into question by studies indicating that differential acquisition of motor skills may occur as a result of the type of movement valued in a specific cultural group (Super, 1976). In addition, Fetters, Fernandes, and Cermak (1988) have demonstrated through kinematic recordings that infants develop proximal and distal skills simultaneously when learning to reach for a block.

Dynamic Systems Model

The reflex and hierarchical models of motor development share a common basic assumption: Motor development occurs as a function of changes in the central nervous system, primarily from lower level control to higher level control. Whereas the systems model of motor development does not dispute the requirement of maturational change for motor development, it holds that maturation of the nervous system is insufficient to explain motor development (Thelen & Ulrich, 1990). Motor development, like many other areas of development, is part of an open system that is responsive to events occurring within other domains such as motivation, experience, and spatial orientation. In this model, the child is able to modify a motor plan while it is being enacted in response to specific task constraints and environmental events, rather than relying on a preprogrammed motor plan in its entirety (feed-forward) or relying on **feedback** produced by the movement (Mathiowetz & Haugen, 1994; Piper & Darrah, 1995). In a feedback mechanism, incoming sensory stimuli result in initiation or modification of movement. In a feed-forward mechanism, the child may initiate movement in response to sensory stimuli, but once the movement has begun, it is not modified. Feedback is used when the child is learning new skills that require careful monitoring, such as using a spoon to scoop up pudding. **Feed-forward**

The proprioceptive system is a sensory system that provides information through joint and muscle receptors about the body's position in space (i.e., "proprioception").

Feedback refers to the sensory stimulus that the body receives upon movement, which provides information about direction, force, timing, and accuracy resulting in a maintenance or correction of the movement.

Feed forward refers to a preprogrammed movement that, once initiated, continues to completion without modification based upon sensory feedback.

applies to movements that have been learned and practiced so the movements become more automatic. Scooping with a spoon may become a feed-forward movement in the older child. Both feedback and feed-forward are used to produce coordinated, goal-directed movement.

The dynamic systems model also takes into consideration the interaction of constraints of the environment, demands of the task, and self-organization of the body. With a change in any of the three conditions, the movement itself may change (Clark, 1995). For example, a toddler learning to walk may appear to lose his walking ability if the surface (environment) becomes very uneven. If the child wishes to move faster (changing demands of the task), the walking skill may not be sufficient and the child may change from a walk to a toddler's run or revert to a previously learned but faster skill such as crawling. As the child grows and changes body morphology (body shape and organization), his center of gravity slowly lowers which helps make him more stable, allowing for more demanding gross motor skills. Increases in muscle strength and force production, changes in height and weight, improved reactions, and a more efficient cardiorespiratory system also allow for the emergence of higher order skills.

Stages of Gross Motor Development

The progression of gross motor development in infants and young children is an amazing process. Infants must learn and process a multitude of information before they are able to walk. Learning to walk is one of the many important developmental events in the parent's and child's life. The gross motor skills acquired during the infant's development are necessary to eventually obtain the upright position. Walking and other early **developmental milestones** are presented in Table 7.1.

Developmental milestones are the average ages at which most typically developing children achieve targeted motor skills.

Birth to Six Months

Typical full-term infants are born in a position of physiological flexion which parallels the infant's posture in the cramped space occupied just prior to birth. The infant's head, legs, and arms tend to be drawn toward the center of the body. This early posture allows the infant to gather some basic information about his own body. The hands are in close proximity to the mouth allowing oral exploration, and allowing the infant to see the hands and other parts of the body. This may be contrasted with the position of prematurely born infants, whose extremities tend to hang away from the body. These infants require special positioning to allow bodily exploration and optimal motor development.

Extension.   The full-term infant's body at birth is in the flexor position. Therefore, the most likely option for movement is extension, in which the head and limbs move away from the body. Many primitive reflexes (including the Moro reflex and the asymmetrical tonic neck reflex) support the development of movement and strength in extension, thus preparing the infant for early functional behaviors. The infant uses extension to hold his head in an upright position when he is held and later to turn and lift his head

TABLE 7.1 Gross Motor Skills and Age of Acquisition in Infants

Position	Age of Acquisition*	Gross Motor Skill
Prone	less than 1 month	lifts head momentarily in prone, asymmetrically
	2½ months	bears weight on forearms (elbows ahead of shoulders)
	4½ months	bears weight on hands, arms extended
	6 months	rolls from prone to supine, without rotation
	7½ months	crawls on tummy
	8½ months	creeps on hands and knees, reciprocally
Supine	1 month	balances head in midline in supine
	2½ months	brings hands to midline in supine
	4½ months	brings feet to hands
	5½ months	rolls from supine to prone, without rotation
	6½ months	rolls from supine to prone, with rotation
Sitting	5 months	sits alone briefly
	6½ months	sits alone steadily
	8 months	moves from sitting to four-point (hands and knees)
Standing	8 months	pulls to stand at furniture
	8½ months	pulls to stand through half-kneel position
	10½ months	stands alone momentarily
Walking	9 months	cruises around furniture, without rotation
	11 months	walks independently, five steps
	11½ months	rises from supine to four-point to standing
	12 months	maintains squatting position

* Note: The age of acquisition reflects the age by which 50% of children attained this skill. Most skills were attained by 90% of the infants studied within 2 to 3 months after the mean age.

Source: Data from *Motor Assessment of the Developing Infant* by M. C. Piper & J. Darrah, 1995, Philadelphia: W. B. Saunders. Copyright 1995 by W. B. Saunders. Adapted by permission.

when placed on his tummy. This extensor control moves from the head in a downward direction, allowing the infant to shift his weight back toward the pelvis and to raise his upper trunk off the floor when placed in a tummy-lying position (prone). He can then move his arms underneath his body to support his weight on his elbows (see Figure 7.2).

As this extension continues to move downward, the infant is able to support his weight on his hands, with his arms extended, shifting his weight down to the pelvis. At about the same time in development, the infant becomes able to use this extension in the trunk to lift head, chest, arms, and legs off the floor in an airplane posture. By pushing with one arm and pulling with the other, the infant learns to pivot to attain toys that are out of reach.

Flexion. Flexion involves moving body parts toward the center of the body. The newborn is already in flexion, so not much more movement is possible in flexion until the infant attains some skills in extension. Once the infant can extend his head against gravity, he can begin to balance it in an upright position by using both flexion

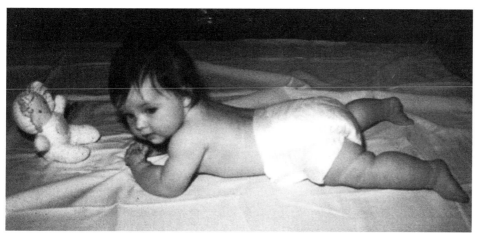

FIGURE 7.2 Lindsey, propped on elbows in the prone position (4½ months).
Source: Used by permission of Kathleen Schlough.

and extension. When the infant is able to reach away from his body while lying on his back (supine), the infant learns to bring his hands back toward the center of the body, allowing oral exploration, visual regard, and hand-to-hand play. This play in flexion and extension in the supine position prepares the infant for increased control in the prone position, thus allowing the infant to maintain stability when shifting weight to free one arm to reach for a toy. The infant develops this ability to shift weight first from an on-elbows position and later from an extended-arms position.

Similar control in flexion is achieved in the lower half of the body as the supine infant raises his legs against gravity to kick, lifts his feet to his hands, and finally lifts his feet to his mouth in play. This improvement in control and increase in muscle strength prepares the infant to move from the prone position into a position on his hands and knees.

Coactivation and Rotation. Typically developing infants achieve postural control along the continuum of control in extension, control in flexion, control of both flexion and extension together **(coactivation),** which is necessary for postural stability, and **rotation** (the turning of one body part in relation to another). This pattern of development repeats itself at each stage of the developmental sequence (Bly, 1983). For example, when a prone infant lifts his head to an angle of 20 degrees from the horizontal, extension is primarily used. However, when the infant balances his head at 90 degrees in a prone or upright position, he must exert control of both flexion and extension (coactivation) and, in order to turn his head to look at objects in the environment, the infant must use rotation, which incorporates differential control of flexion and extension. By about 6 months of age, the infant's body follows the head and he is able to roll from the stomach to the back. Shortly thereafter, rolling develops from the back to the stomach. Although early rolling is characterized by the body moving as a whole, it later becomes segmental, with rotation occurring at the head, neck, trunk, and pelvis.

Rotation is one of the four basic movements allowed by the skeleton; rotation is movement that occurs around the central axis of the body or a limb.

Another example of continuum of control that occurs later in the developmental sequence is when an infant is first placed in a sitting position and the trunk leans forward. The trunk is held upright primarily by extension of the muscles of the back. Through play in a supine position, including raising the head to look at the body, bringing the hands to midline, and bringing the feet toward the hands, the infant develops control of the muscles of the abdomen in flexion. In this way the infant is able to gradually use both extension and flexion for sitting in an upright, balanced position. In addition, the infant must develop control in rotation in order to turn the head and trunk to reach for toys in the environment.

During the first 6 months of life, an infant progresses from having a minimal repertoire of movement to an ability to roll, reach in all directions in prone, and maintain a propped sitting position. Primitive reflexes are very strong in the young infant but, by 4 to 6 months, most of these reflexes become integrated and start to fade as volitional control improves. The exhibition of strong primitive reflexes in an infant after 6 months of age (in premature infants, this age should be corrected for amount of prematurity) may signal a delay in gross motor development. There is, however, a range of typical development. The ages given in Tables 7.1 (p. 232) and 7.2 represent mean ages of acquisition of motor skills.

Depending on child-rearing practices, environmental issues and cultural backgrounds, the development of gross motor skills may vary within a range of what may be considered typical. For example, practices relating to the positioning of very young children for sleep has received a great deal of attention in recent years. Pediatricians have been guided by the National Institute of Child Health and Human Development (NICHD) and the the American Academy of Pediatrics to advise caregivers to place the infant in the supine position for sleeping ("back to sleep, stomach to play") to avoid the possibility of **sudden infant death syndrome** (SIDS; see Box 2.3 p. 51). Although this practice has significantly reduced the occurrence of SIDS, at least two studies have

Sudden infant death syndrome (SIDS) is the unexpected and sudden death of an infant during sleep, where no evidence of disease is found by physical examination or autopsy.

TABLE 7.2 Gross Motor Skills and Expected Ages of Acquisition in the Toddler and Preschooler

Age of Acquisition	Gross Motor Skill
15 months	creeps up steps
18–23 months	creeps down steps backwards
24–29 months	jumps off floor 2 inches using both feet
2–2½ years	climbs stairs and descends stairs with both feet on each step
2–2½ years	descends stairs with both feet on each step
2½–3 years	climbs stairs, alternating feet
3–3½ years	descends stairs, alternating feet
3–5 years	hops on one foot
4–5 years	gallops
5–6 years	skips, alternating feet
6–7 years	walks four steps on 4-inch balance beam

Sources: Bayley Scales of Infant Development: Second Edition. Copyright © 1993 by The Psychological Corporation. Adapted and reproduced by permission. All rights reserved. "Bayley Scales of Infant Development" is a registered trademark of The Psychological Corporation. Adapted from the *Peabody Developmental Motor Scales,* by M. R. Folio and R. R. Fewell. Copyright by Pro-Ed, Austin, TX. Adapted by permission.

found that infants whose parents report they sleep in the prone position attain early motor milestones significantly faster than nonprone sleepers (Davis, Moon, Sacks, & Otolini, 1998; Dewey, Fleming, Golding, & ALSPAC Study Team, 1998). This has raised the concern of many motor specialists because the prone position is felt to be very important in the development of strength and control in the arms, back, and neck muscles. It is often from this position that the infant learns to get into the creeping position and later to pull to stand. Many therapists strongly encourage parents to allow the infant time in prone during waking hours in order to develop the necessary skills. However, there is disagreement about the necessity of this. Developmental differences reported in the studies cited above may represent only a transient variation; by 18 months of age, Dewey and her colleagues found no significant differences in motor skill acquisition between prone and non-prone sleepers (1998).

Seven to Twelve Months

The period of time between the 6th and 12th month is marked by an increase in mobility in the baby. Many parents find they must "child proof" their homes as the curious infant begins to explore the environment. Although caregivers are usually excited and pleased with the infant's expanding abilities, they often realize these new abilities create safety issues. They may cover the electrical outlets, put up gates between rooms or staircases, tie up the blind cords, move the knick-knacks off the coffee table, lock cupboards, pad the corners of furniture, and generally make the home safer for the exploring child.

During the 7th and 8th months, a typical baby will begin learning to sit independently. There is sufficient strength in the back, hip, and leg muscles and increased strength in the abdominal muscles so the infant can maintain an upright sitting position without the need to prop with his arms. This frees up both hands for play and exploration which is advantageous to the child. To move out of the sitting position, the infant will often fall to the side or backward because, even though protective extension of the arms is now active when reaching forward, protective extension is just starting to emerge to the sides and backwards. So, if a child loses his balance to the side, he is likely to fall. The neck, back, and hip muscles are now very strong and, when the infant is in prone, he often will appear to "swim" by lifting up his arms, legs, and head. In the supine position, the infant expresses the strength of the abdominal and hip flexor muscles by lifting up his legs and bringing his feet to his mouth. From the prone position, the infant may start to push himself forward or backward with his stomach still on the surface. He may then push up into all-fours.

During the 9th and 10th months, the baby becomes even more mobile and begins creeping with his stomach off the surface. Many babies use this newly found crawling ability for many months, whereas other babies use it only as a transitional movement between sitting and pulling to stand. Often a baby at this age will assume a "bear walk" position with both hands and feet on the floor (rather than on the knees). The ability to attain a position on the hands and knees is necessary to develop control in flexion and extension of the whole body, so that the infant can move into a sitting position (the infant pushes back and slightly to the side with the arms), rock on his hands and knees, and crawl (move forward on hands and knees).

Crawling is the developmental stage in the prone position where the body is moved forward by pulling with the arms and pushing with the legs.

Creeping is the forward movement of an infant characterized by reciprocal arm and leg movements in the hands and knees position. In some texts and in everyday conversation, this movement may also be referred to as "crawling."

The infant gains additional control of flexion and extension when exploring on his hands and knees in preparation for the transition to standing. Most infants learn to move into a standing position using furniture at first, pulling upward with the arms while extending both legs. Later, the infant learns to bring one leg forward and push up, allowing the other leg to follow. This builds differentiated control in each leg in preparation for cruising or side stepping along furniture and, finally, walking. At this age, the infant loves to take steps with support and will often learn to push a piece of furniture (kitchen chair or highchair) around while taking steps to keep up with it.

During this time of increased mobility, but before the baby begins to walk independently, many well-meaning parents encourage the use of a babywalker. However, studies have shown that infants who use babywalkers achieve independent walking at a later age (Garrett, McElroy, & Staines, 2002; Siegel & Burton, 1999). Additionally, the use of babywalkers has been associated with serious injuries, such as skull fractures, contusions, lacerations, electrocutions, and burns. Many of these injuries have occurred even in the presence of adult supervision (Smith, Bowman, Luria, & Shields, 1997). Because infants this age usually enjoy the upright position, alternatives to babywalkers are standing devices that bounce, swivel, or sway but do not roll.

During the 11th and 12th months, many babies learn to stand independently. However, some typical babies take longer to learn to walk. If a child cannot stand independently or walk by the 15th month, this may be cause for concern as it may signal a delay in gross motor development. When an infant first attains a standing position, strong extension occurs throughout the body to remain upright. First, movements in standing are stiff, with the child swaying the body slightly from side to side ("toddle") to gain initial forward mobility. From a dynamic systems point of view, the child is using a stiff body posture (coactivation) in an effort to control his many **degrees of freedom**; that is, the child must learn to control all the muscles, joints, nerve pathways, and so on to accomplish the task. As he becomes more experienced with the task of standing, he can then "let go" of some of these degrees of freedom and the movement appears smoother and more coordinated and effortless.

Each time a child (or adult) learns a new motor task, he must first learn to control these many degrees of freedom in which, initially, the movement looks stiff and uncoordinated. With practice, the child learns to control these degrees of freedom. He shifts his body to one leg, allowing the other to advance forward reciprocally as he takes a step. Later, as rotation gradually develops, the child will walk with the counter rotation and arm swing that characterize mature walking. With full rotation, as one leg swings forward, the arm on the same side swings backward. During this period, protective extension has developed forward, to the sides, and backward so that the baby can protect himself better during a fall. Also, the development of righting reactions and equilibrium reactions allows for more complex movement patterns.

> Degrees of freedom refer to the possibilities for movement provided by the many muscles, bones, joints, and nerves that contribute to movement. These must be controlled when an individual learns to perform a motor task.

Twelve to Twenty-four Months

The continuing development of gross motor skills among toddlers is dependent upon the postural skills mastered earlier, as well as on the environmental experiences afforded to the child. As children develop increased strength, balance, endurance, and coordination, they are able to increase their motor patterns in relation to environmental demands. Continuing development of differentiated control of the body, that is, the ability to use one limb alone or use both flexion and extension in different joints of the same extremity, allows the child to gain higher level motor skills, such as squatting to the floor.

Postural reactions become more mature, so that movements become smoother and more controlled. Protective skills, such as reaching out with the arms or legs, are used only when falls are imminent. Righting and equilibrium reactions are now very strong and dependable. Independent stair climbing is first mastered by holding onto the railing and advancing the feet in a step-to-step progression by about 24 months. Later, at about 30 to 36 months, the child can use a reciprocal progression of the feet, without needing to hold the railing for balance and demonstrating a smooth, diagonal weight shift with trunk rotation. Acquisition of higher level motor skills has been demonstrated to parallel acquisition of early motor skills (Roberton & Halverson, 1984). When ball throwing is a new skill, for example, the arm moves while the trunk remains stable. As this skill improves, however, the trunk rotates in conjunction with arm and shoulder movements to add efficiency, speed, and force to the action.

Two to Five Years

Once children have mastered the basic movement skills, repetition allows smoother performance of specific motor patterns and combinations of these motor patterns. Preschool children enjoy practicing their skills, challenging themselves, and mastering the environment. Children begin to use these skills in simple social games, such as Duck, Duck, Goose and Tag, in which movements must conform to changing speed and position of the other children playing. Children master more difficult motor skills, such as climbing stairs, jumping, hopping, and running (Figure 7.3). Each of these skills has a predictable pattern of development as well. Table 7.2 provides a list of toddler and preschool gross motor skills and the age at which children typically attain them.

Beginning at about age 3, movement patterns are combined for mastery of galloping and, later, skipping. As movements are sequenced for learning more complex tasks, adequate **motor planning**, or **praxis**, is required. Praxis demands adequate sensory capabilities to provide feedback about the correctness of a given motor act and to allow adaptation to environmental demands during execution of the motor plan. Children with poor motor praxis often do not exhibit any motoric difficulty until age 3, when they begin playing simple games that require planning out a sequence of prescribed movements. The child may appear clumsy, confused, or uncooperative when, in fact, he cannot process and react to all the information required for the task.

During the preschool years, many gross motor skills are based on core abilities. The ability to stand on one foot while maintaining one's balance is needed to go up and down stairs without holding on, step over obstacles, hop, kick a ball, climb on playground equipment, ride a tricycle, and walk a balance beam. The ability to control total body extension and flexion is needed for age-appropriate skills in activities, such as going down a slide and swinging on a swing.

Motor planning refers to how a person plans and sequences a movement or skill.

Praxis is the ability to plan and execute a skilled movement (Goodgold-Edwards & Cermak, 1989).

FIGURE 7.3   Emilio (3 years 9 months) is just about to enter the 'flight' phase of running, when both feet are off the ground. Note the reciprocal pumping of his arms and the rotation through his trunk. Children generally master running between the ages of 2 and 4, gaining control over stopping and starting at age 5 or 6.

Source: Used by permission of Carole Dennis.

Factors Affecting Gross Motor Development

Variations in Early Motor Development

The sequence of development just described is fairly uniform and predictable for typically developing infants who are exposed to similar experiences; however, developmental variations may be noted when structural or environmental conditions are different. For example, infants who have experienced thoracic surgery may find play in the prone position uncomfortable and may have weak abdominal control. These children may not learn to move from a position on hands and knees to a sitting position or to develop the ability to creep when they are expected to; they may move about by scooting in a sitting position. Transitions to standing often do not develop in the typical manner and the child may learn to walk before he is able to move to and from the floor. Due to an imbalance in development of flexion and extension, good control in coactivation and rotation may not occur. These children may be quite fearful of movement.

The failure of a child to attain developmental milestones on time may be cause for concern for parents and professionals. Often, the observant parent or friend may notice that the child's movements don't look quite right, or that he may seem floppy or stiff. In addition to being aware of atypical posture, observers may note that transitions from one position to another are not possible or are accomplished in unusual ways. Figure 7.4 lists movement patterns that may signal motor delays and indicate the need for additional assessment of motor development.

Variations in musculoskeletal development, postural tone, and sensory processing, as well as variations in the child's physical and social environment, may alter development of motor skills. Children raised in situations in which social and environmental interactions are severely restricted may suffer from sensory deprivation. Adequate sensory stimulation is necessary for typical development to occur. Much of an infant's early experience is sensory in nature, resulting in the formation of neural connections in the brain; neurons that do not form connections with other neurons will die (Vander Zanden, 1997). The consequences of sensory deprivation have been observed recently in institutionalized children in Romania, where custodial care was provided but interaction with people and toys was severely limited. Sensory and motor deficits have been well documented in these children (Haradon, Bascom, Dragomir, & Scripcaru, 1994; Sweeney & Bascom, 1995).

Race, Ethnicity, and Culture

In various cultural groups, differences in motor development may occur due to genetic differences, environmental influences, and variations in child-rearing practices. McClain, Provost, and Crowe (2000) investigated the motor development of 2-year-old children of Native American background and found that more than a third of the sample scored at least one standard deviation below the mean. The authors suggested that some biological differences may have played a part in this disparity, but also noted that the children in general were very shy and probably did not give their best performance. The functional independence of young Chinese children was examined in another study. Chinese children performed significantly better than their U.S. counterparts in self-care and mobility skills (Wong, Wong, Chan, & Wong, 2002). The investigators attributed the differences to the early attendance of the Chinese children in preschool settings where self-care was promoted.

Two separate studies of Brazilian children compared to children from the United States and Great Britain showed that the Brazilian children were more advanced in the gross motor area by the age of 4 (Victoria, Victoria, & Barros, 1990), but that their mean motor scores were significantly lower during the 3rd, 4th, and 5th months of age (Santos, Gabbard, & Goncalves, 2001). The study concluded that the differences may have been due to variations in child-rearing practices and the influence of biological factors. A study of babies from Yucatan, Mexico, compared to infants from Denver, Colorado, concluded that, although the Mexican babies were more advanced in fine-motor development, they were delayed in gross motor development at the end of their first year (Solomons, 1982). Capute, Shapiro, Palmer, Ross, and Wachtel (1985) found that African American infants tended to attain motor milestones sooner than White infants; however, ethnic or cultural differences have not been adequately explained. These apparent differences in motor development for various groups of children must be considered in light of the environment, child-rearing practices, and cultural differences.

PRONE
- newborn assumes position of relative extension, rather than flexion of utero
- infant is unable to lift head off floor by 3 months
- infant maintains a uniform posture; no variety of position or movement in prone
- infant is unable to balance head in a midline position by 5 months
- arms remain pulled into flexion, close to infant's body by 4 months
- infant is unable to assume a position of support on both forearms by 5 months, or on hands by 7 months

SUPINE
- infant is unable to balance head at midline by 4 months
- infant remains in extended position, unable to lift legs from floor, past 6 months
- infant maintains a consistently asymmetrical posture

CREEPING
- infant is unable to crawl on tummy by 8 months
- infant is unable to creep, or utilizes one of the following patterns:
  - commando crawling: pulling self forward on elbows, legs extended
  - bunny creeping: arms and legs move together bilaterally, rather than reciprocally
  - creeps with exaggerated turning of head as arm on same side extends

SITTING
- sits with rounded head, neck, and back past 6 months
- infant is unable to sit independently for extended periods by 9 months
- infant is able to sit, but falls when he or she turns head or reaches for objects past 10 months
- infant is able to sit, but posture is characterized by one of the following:
  - narrow base of support (posterior pelvic tilt, trunk rounded, and head hyperextended)
  - wide base of support (legs spread wide, or habitual sitting in a W pattern)
- infant is unable to prevent falls by extending arms to front, side, and back by 12 months
- infant is unable to move into and out of sitting from other positions by 12 months or uses unusual movement patterns to change position

STANDING AND WALKING
- child is unable to stand independently by 14 months or walk independently by 15 months
- child bears weight on toes, rather than flat on feet
- child stands with significant knee hyperextension or swayback (lordosis) beyond 15 months

TODDLER AND PRESCHOOL SKILLS
- child has met most early milestones, but walking is stiff, unsteady, or met with many falls
- child has difficulty with activities requiring single-limb stability, such as climbing stairs, standing on one foot, and hopping
- child has mastered most basic skills, but has more difficulty than peers when learning new, sequenced motor tasks
- child appears clumsy when compared with typically developing peers

FIGURE 7.4 Movement Patterns That May Signal Postural and Gross Motor Development Delays
Source: Used with permission of Carole W. Dennis.

More studies need to be done describing the contributions of ethnic or cultural differences to motor development in diverse populations of young children before more definitive statements can be made; however, it remains important for these potential differences to be considered when working with young children with special needs and their families.

Prematurity

A premature infant is one born at 37 weeks of gestation or younger. Approximately 11% to 12% of all births in the United States occur before 37 weeks. Recent advances in medicine have greatly decreased the **morbidity** and mortality rates for premature infants; those born as young as 24 weeks' gestation can now survive. However, their gross motor development may diverge from the typical pattern. Infants born at term (37 to 42 weeks) are characteristically in physiological flexion, which means they are in a flexed posture secondary to prolonged positioning in the uterus. Children who are born prematurely will often exhibit **hypotonicity** (low muscle tone) and do not exhibit physiological flexion. They demonstrate a classic posture that consists of the head turned to the side and the arms and legs splayed. The arms may fall into a W pattern and the legs are "frogged" (Hunter, 2001). If this is not corrected with therapeutic positioning, infants may develop deformities that will affect their posture and movement throughout their lives. Typically, an occupational or physical therapist will calculate the infant's adjusted or corrected age by subtracting the amount of prematurity from the expected due date and use this "adjusted age" to determine true ages for acquisition of developmental milestones.

Disorders of Postural Tone

Variations in muscle tone are frequently seen in children who show delayed gross motor development. Muscle tone is the degree of tension that exists in a muscle when it is at rest. **Postural tone** (muscle tone response to demands of gravity and movement) may range on a continuum from lower than normal to greater than normal tone or it may fluctuate. Each of these conditions is discussed in more detail later in this chapter. For example, the condition of postural tone in children with traumatic brain injuries follows a more transitional and dynamic versus static process.

The involved extremities may be initially **flaccid** (completely lacking tone) with a gradual increase over time to hypertonicity. Although not all children with motor delay exhibit atypical tone, some generalizations can be made with respect to those who do. Children diagnosed with cerebral palsy may have any type, degree, or distribution of atypical tone depending on the site and extent of central nervous system dysfunction. Children with Down syndrome typically have varying degrees of hypotonia, or low muscle tone, throughout the body. Some children diagnosed with learning disabilities and mental retardation may have mild hypotonia, resulting in clumsiness.

Hypertonia.   **Hypertonia** refers to tight muscles or **spasticity**; postural tone thus is increased. Hypertonia is characteristic of the spastic and rigid subtypes of cerebral palsy, but the degree of tone can range from mild to severe involvement. Distribution of hypertonia in the body can vary from child to child. Patterns typically seen

Morbidity is the state of being diseased or sick.

Hypotonia refers to decreased tension and resistance to stretch in a muscle. Occupational and physical therapists may use these terms to describe the same condition: *decreased tone*, *low tone*, or *floppy*.

Flaccid describes a muscle or limb that is relaxed, having defective or absent muscle tone.

Hypertonia refers to increased tension and resistance to stretch in a muscle (i.e., "high tone" or "tight").

Spasticity means increased resistance to passive stretch of a muscle, or increased muscle tension or tone within the muscle.

Contracture is the loss of motion or fixation at a joint caused by atrophy and shortening of muscle fibers.

A child often must compensate for atypical muscle tone, posture, or movement by responding with a complementary movement (e.g., if a child sits with the trunk deviated to one side, he must center his balance by deviating his head in the opposite direction).

include increased tone in one extremity **(monoplegia),** increased tone primarily in the lower extremities with some mild involvement in the upper extremities **(diplegia),** increased tone in all extremities **(quadriplegia)** or increased tone or paralysis on one side of the body **(hemiplegia),** which results in asymmetrical posture and movement. Hypertonia reduces mobility and range of motion (joint flexibility), potentially leading to deformities such as **contractures,** scoliosis (curvature of the spine), or hip dislocation. Hypertonia often results in characteristic problems with posture and movement. When spasticity is present in the lower extremities, the legs tend be adducted (movement of the limbs toward the midline of the body) and internally rotated, with the ankles extended and the feet rotated inward. The hamstring muscles at the back of the upper leg are often tight and tend to rotate the pelvis backward (posterior pelvic tilt), resulting in compensatory rounding of the trunk (Figure 7.5) and extension of the head and neck in sitting. Gross motor deficits in children with increased tone are more fully covered in the discussion of cerebral palsy later in this chapter.

Clonus may be present along with spasticity. Clonus is a hyperactive stretch reflex consisting of repetitive, jerky movements occurring most commonly at the wrist or ankle when the muscles are put on stretch. Associated reactions (mirror movement in the opposite limb) may occur on one side of the body when there is excessive effort on the other side.

Hypotonia.   As stated earlier, hypotonia refers to low muscle tone that occurs symmetrically throughout the body. Low muscle tone is characteristic of

FIGURE 7.5   Poor sitting position in a toddler with spastic diplegic cerebral palsy. Note the posterior pelvic tilt, rounded back, and adducted legs with toe clawing, resulting in a narrow base of support and requiring the use of one arm to maintain balance.

Source: Used by permission of Jean Patz.

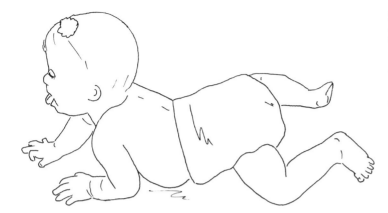

FIGURE 7.6   Low muscle tone in a year-old child with Down syndrome. Note the widely spread legs, poor trunk control, and immature weight-bearing on arms, which interfere with play and crawling.
Source: Used by permission of Jean Patz.

hypotonic cerebral palsy, prematurity in the first months (Hunter, 2001), myelomeningocele (a form of spina bifida; Hinderer, Hinderer, & Shurtleff, 2000), and many conditions associated with mental retardation including the following syndromes: Down syndrome, Cri du chat syndrome, fragile X syndrome, Prader-Willi syndrome, and early Rett syndrome (McEwen, 2000). Children with hypotonia have difficulty moving against gravity. Parents may describe the quality of such children's tone as "floppy," "double-jointed," or "like that of a rag-doll." Excessive range of motion (hypermobility) occurs at the joints. When a child with hypotonia is positioned in supine or prone, the lower extremities exhibit wide hip abduction and external rotation, frequently termed the frog-leg position (Figure 7.6). Children with low muscle tone tend to assume a characteristic posture when standing, with the legs hyperextended or locked at the knees, pelvis rotated forward (anterior pelvic tilt), lumbar spine in lordosis (swayed back), and thoracic spine in kyphosis (rounded back, Figure 7.7).

Sensory Registration and Processing Disorders

Sensory difficulties that influence motor skill development may include problems in the registration, discrimination, processing, and organization of sensory stimuli. Skillful execution of motor skills requires sensory input to plan what action needs to occur, as well as sensory feedback to plot the action that has occurred, and to help determine whether that action was successful. Children with cerebral palsy, particularly those with hemiplegia, may have difficulty accurately perceiving their own movement and be unable to identify that the involved extremity has been touched, or they may have difficulty describing the nature of the touch or identifying where on the body it occurred. These phenomena represent problems with registration and discrimination. Difficulties with the processing and organization of sensory stimuli may result in motor incoordination in children with pervasive developmental disorders (e.g., autism), in some children with learning disabilities and attention-deficit hyperactivity disorder (ADHD), and in children raised in situations lacking sufficient sensory stimulation.

FIGURE 7.7   Supported standing in a toddler with low muscle tone. Note how the child leans into the supporting surface, with locked knees, anterior pelvic tilt, lordosis of lumbar spine, and shoulder instability.
Source: Used by permission of Jean Patz.

Gross Motor Development in Young Children with Special Needs

In this section, common exceptionalities that result in atypical gross motor development are discussed. The anticipated developmental progression of motor skills in children with selected diagnoses is provided. It is important to recognize that the common exceptionalities presented here are subsumed under the educational classifications described in Chapter 1. For example, Down syndrome typically is included under the classification of mental retardation, whereas cerebral palsy may fit within one of several classifications (e.g., orthopedic impairment).

Cerebral Palsy

> Dyskinesia is an impairment of the ability to execute voluntary movements. When used with cerebral palsy, this term refers to tonal abnormalities that involve the whole body.

Cerebral palsy is a group of nonprogressive disorders of movement and posture caused by damage to an immature brain (Batshaw & Perret, 1992). These lesions can occur during the rapid growth of the brain in the prenatal or perinatal period or up to 3 years following birth (Bennett, 1984). The results of these defects often are motor, cognitive, and sensory deficits. The motor involvement may include poor balance, awkward movement, and decreased repertoire of movement. Depending on the specific location of lesions, the individual may display spasticity (hypertonia), hypotonia, **dyskinesia**, ataxia, or a combination of these types

(Molnar, 1985; Olney & Wright, 2000). Spasticity is the most frequently occurring movement disorder in cerebral palsy and is characterized by stiffness or tightness in the affected limbs. Dyskinesia includes **athetosis** (writhing movement patterns of the limbs), **dystonia** (changes in muscle tone), **choreiform** (rapid, jerky movement patterns), **ballismus** (uncoordinated flailing of the limbs and jerky movements), and **tremor** (fine shaking movement noted especially in the head and hands).

Another, less typical type of cerebral palsy is **ataxia** in which the individual maintains a wide base of support and has little trunk rotation. Because of atypical postural tone, children with cerebral palsy do not experience normal movement and develop compensatory patterns of movement and posture that may further impede their progress. They also may develop muscular and skeletal anomalies secondary to abnormal muscle pull and poor movement patterns.

Postural problems that accompany cerebral palsy were discussed earlier in this chapter. A child with spastic quadriplegia (the most severe type of cerebral palsy) generally experiences increased extensor tone in the lower extremities with flexor tone predominating in the upper extremities. The persistence of primitive reflexes results in the child being pulled into gravity and, therefore, having great difficulty moving against gravity in the prone and the supine positions. It is usually difficult for the child to raise his head and trunk off the floor when in prone. If rolling is mastered, it is characterized by limited rotation through the trunk with posturing of the arms in flexion and the legs in extension (Figure 7.8).

In floor sitting, the pelvis is pulled into a posterior tilt. Compensatory trunk flexion results in further compensatory neck and head hyperextension to maintain balance in sitting (as was shown in Figure 7.5). If the child is able to attain sitting, the legs are often internally rotated with the knees together and the feet out to either side of the body, creating a "W" with the legs. The child may favor this position because it provides improved stability and frees the arms for use. However, this position is discouraged for several reasons: It may promote dislocation of the hips, it limits trunk rotation in sitting, and it does not require the child to use the lower extremities to assist in maintaining posture, which is necessary for later walking. When the child with spastic quadriplegia crawls, he pulls his body forward with his

Athetosis is a neuromuscular condition characterized by slow, writhing, continuous, and involuntary movement of the extremities, as seen in some forms of cerebral palsy, specifically athetoid cerebral palsy.

Ataxia is a condition characterized by impaired ability to coordinate movement, frequently including a staggering gait and postural imbalance.

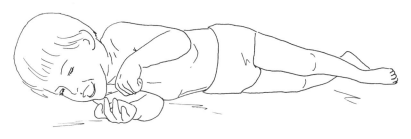

FIGURE 7.8 "Log" rolling in a 4-year-old child with spastic quadriplegic cerebral palsy. Note the extensor tone in the lower body, with flexor tone in the upper extremities.

Source: Used by permission of Jean Patz.

arms close to the body, whereas the legs usually remain extended and adducted. Some children move on the floor by lying in supine and pushing with the feet, while arching the body into extension.

Children with spastic diplegia typically creep in a "bunny hop" pattern, with arms and legs moving together in a bilateral, symmetrical pattern rather than reciprocally. When these children walk, the increased extensor tone in the lower extremities results in adduction and internal rotation, with the legs moving in a pattern often termed "scissoring." Often, the ankles are braced to prevent walking on the toes. The upper extremities, though only mildly involved, often pull into a high-guard position as a result of associated reactions, or overflow. **High guard** is a position that children may use in standing or walking when they are unstable. The child holds his arms up and away from the body with the elbows bent. A typical child learning to walk often uses this position to help maintain his balance; with maturation and improved balance, the arms move down to the side. Children with motor impairment may use the high-guard position for a similar reason, but for a much longer time.

> Many typically developing children use the W sitting position during floor play because it is very stable; however, unlike children with special needs, they are not limited to this position.

Children with hemiplegia have increased tone on one side of the body, resulting in asymmetrical posture and movement. These children typically master the early gross motor developmental milestones and are very mobile. High-level preschool skills are difficult for them, but children with hemiplegia often try to do all that their peers do. The involved ankle is often braced to maintain muscle length, to help break up the extensor tone in the leg, and to promote walking with the foot flat on the floor.

Children with athetosis have fluctuating muscle tone and variable motor capabilities. Some children with athetosis learn to walk independently, but many never advance beyond moving on the floor. Their posture is very unstable and movements are asymmetrical and uncontrolled because the fluctuating tone makes it difficult for them to control flexor and extensor muscles together for coactivation. It is difficult for a child with athetosis to maintain a midline position because of asymmetrical movement and persistence of the asymmetrical tonic neck reflex. This creates difficulty in any activity requiring the maintenance of a midline position such as eating, writing, reading, or any focused attention directly in front of the child.

Children with ataxic cerebral palsy are generally considered very clumsy with poor balance and coordination especially in more upright positions, such as standing. They tend to take sideways steps rather than follow a straight path when walking.

Traumatic Brain Injury and Brain Tumors

Traumatic brain injury (TBI) is the leading cause of death and disability in children in the United States. The most common causes of TBI in children are motor vehicle accidents, falls, and abuse. More than one million children in the United States receive TBIs each year and more than 30,000 of these children are significantly disabled as a result, as reported by the National Rehabilitation Information Center (1994). Depending on the severity and extent of the injury, the child may exhibit a variety of symptoms. Also, the age of the child when the injury occurred will have an impact on the progression of secondary impairments.

In general, the child may experience problems in three different areas: physical, cognitive, and behavioral-emotional. Physical impairments may include problems with muscle tone (spasticity or paralysis), poor balance, speech, vision, and hearing. Cognitive impairments may include short- or long-term memory loss, slowed thinking, and difficulty learning. Behavioral and emotional problems may include lability (i.e., extreme mood swings), agitation, poor emotional control, and depression. Agitation and angry outbursts, in particular, may decrease over time as some healing occurs.

Brain tumors are another type of central nervous system disorder. The incidence of brain tumors in the pediatric population is between 2.5 and 3.5 per 100,000 (Lannering, Marky, & Nordborg, 1990). Tumors can occur in a variety of locations in the brain. Clinical signs and symptoms depend on the location and type of tumor. Tumors of the central nervous system may occur in the **cerebellum** (causing ataxia, tremor, hypotonia, and poor balance), the **brainstem** (causing problems with gait, **torticollis,** quadriparesis, or hemiparesis), or the cerebral cortex (causing seizures and spasticity; Kerkering & Phillips, 2000).

Gross motor development will vary in infants and young children depending on the severity and extent of the injury or tumor and the age of the child during the onset. Because infants and young children are considered very "plastic" in their musculoskeletal development, care must be taken to avoid secondary problems associated with these systems such as contractures, decreased range of motion in the joints, and abnormal bone formations. Often, the infant or preschooler who has sustained a TBI also develops spasticity (and sometimes flaccidity, or limpness) of the muscles corresponding to the area of the brain that was injured. With both TBI and brain tumors, the clinical signs and symptoms are similar to that of cerebral palsy; consequently, the physical and occupational therapist may treat the child in a comparable manner.

Spina Bifida (Myelodysplasia)

Spina bifida is second only to Down Syndrome as the most common birth defect in the United States with a prevalence rate of 1 in every 1,000 live births. The National Institute of Neurological Disorders defines spina bifida as a type of neural tube defect that includes an incomplete closure of the fetus' spine during early fetal development. The severity of this defect can range from spina bifida occulta (incomplete closure of the vertebra of the spine with no nerve involvement) to complete avulsion of the spinal cord and meninges (spinal cord's protective covering) into a cyst called **myelomeningocele**. In the more severe form, the child may have hydrocephalus (excessive cerebral spinal fluid in the brain), be bowel and bladder incontinent, and have partial or full paralysis of the lower extremities (Botto, 1999). Folic acid taken by the mother before conception and during the early months of the pregnancy has been shown to prevent certain birth defects including spina bifida (Berry et al., 1999).

Some or all of the muscles of the lower extremities may be paralyzed, causing the growth of muscles and bones to be underdeveloped. Children with spina bifida may also have low muscle tone and some developmental delay. **Hydrocephalus,** an obstruction of cerebrospinal fluid causing increased intracranial pressure, is common in children with myelomeningocele. This pressure on the brain tissue may result in

---

The brainstem is a portion of the brain responsible for motor, sensory, and reflexive functions.

The cerebellum is the posterior portion of the brain that primarily coordinates voluntary muscular activity.

Torticollis is an abnormal condition where the head is inclined to one side resulting from a shortening of the muscles on that side of the neck.

Myelomeningocele is a form of spina bifida in which part of the spinal cord protrudes in a cyst, resulting in neurological, motor, and sensory deficits below the level of the cyst.

additional central nervous system problems. Children with hydrocephalus often have a shunt surgically implanted, which drains fluid from the brain into the abdominal cavity. Recent efforts in prenatal surgery, largely conducted to relieve the hydrocephalus, also have shown emergent positive impact on the gross motor development of children with spina bifida. A malformation on the back of the fetus may be observed with ultrasound and, under the correct circumstances, an early cesarean section may be performed. The lesion is then closed surgically to save some nerve function and hopefully decrease the severity of the paralysis (Luthy et al., 1991).

Therapeutic intervention in the gross motor area may include encouraging balance, coordination, range of motion, strengthening, and proper positioning (Figure 7.9). Therapeutic intervention for the affected lower extremities may include positioning, bracing, and range of motion exercises. Briefly standing in a weight-bearing position may be appropriate for the infant. Later, standing either in a special standing frame (a parapodium, which "walks" when the child sways from side to side) or with the assistance of crutches and lower extremity braces may commence when the child is developmentally ready for this position. Depending on the level of the spina bifida, bracing may range from the ankle to the calf using an **ankle/foot orthosis** (AFO), to the hips using a **hip-knee-ankle orthosis** (HKAFO), or to the lumbar area (low-back) or thoracic area (mid-back) using a **thoracic-hip-knee-ankle orthosis** (THKAFO). In some cases, a **reciprocating gait orthosis (RGO)** that extends from the foot to the pelvis, or a parapodium may be used as additional standing and mobility devices. A wheelchair or other rolling device may eventually be the most appropriate and efficient form of mobility for a very high thoracic lesion.

Ankle-foot orthosis (AFO) is a protective external device that can be applied to the ankle area to provide support and prevent deformities.

Generally, care must be taken to prevent deformity of the legs and a possible secondary problem of scoliosis. Lack of sensation in the legs may cause skin breakdown. Obesity is also a concern for this population because of the difficulty in being physically active. As the child ages and has had very little weight bearing in the standing position, he may develop osteoporosis. Stuberg (1992) suggests that a regular standing program would be beneficial to increase bone density in children with developmental disabilities including spina bifida. The professional should work closely with the physical and occupational therapist in understanding correct positioning to prevent deformity, osteoporosis, and the possibility of associated fractures. The educator should also be aware of signs of shunt dysfunction, which may include fever and malaise, extreme irritability, onset or increased seizures, and decreased activity levels (Shurtleff, Stuntz, & Hayden, 1986).

Degenerative Conditions (Neuromuscular Disorders)

Degenerative diseases are those that cause progressive weakness, muscle atrophy, and increasing disability. Unlike cerebral palsy, spina bifida, Down syndrome, and spinal cord injuries, which are considered static and do not progress, degenerative diseases including spinal muscular atrophy (SMA) and Duchenne's muscular dystrophy (DMD) pursue a steadily progressive deterioration.

Duchenne's Muscular Dystrophy.   DMD is one of the most common forms of muscular dystrophies. It is an X-linked disorder inherited through the mother that

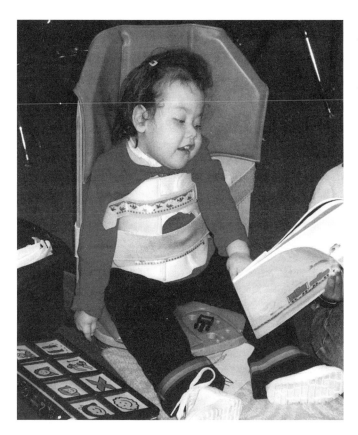

FIGURE 7.9 Positioning in a corner seat to allow floor play for a child with spina bifida (and associated Arnold Chiarri Malformation), wearing a thoracic brace for scoliosis.

Source: Used by permission of Jean Patz.

affects mostly males. It is a defect of the gene for the protein dystrophin, which is necessary to maintain healthy muscle fibers (Koenig et al., 1987). Incidence of DMD may vary from 13 to 33 per 100,000 live male births (Dubowitz, 1978).

DMD may be detected by the caregiver as early as 3 years or as late as 6 years of age when the child appears to lose motor skills he had previously achieved. The caregiver may note that the child cannot climb the stairs as easily, has more difficulty on the playground equipment, or that the child falls or tires easily. The caregiver may also notice a characteristic maneuver called "Gowers sign" in which the child gets up off the floor by first getting into the all-fours position, straightening the legs, and then using the arms to push on the thighs to stand. Often the calf muscle becomes larger (pseudo-hypertrophy) as muscle fibers are replaced by increased fibrous connective tissue.

Progressive weakness follows a typical course and, although intervention cannot prevent the eventual loss of muscle strength, it can help prevent secondary problems such as contractures, scoliosis, and decreased respiratory function. Most boys can walk unaided until the age of 6 to 7 years and by 9 to 10 years may require assisted ambulation including the use of AFOs, crutches, or a walker. By 12 years, many children require the use of a powered wheelchair for mobility (Brooke et al., 1983). A child with DMD should be allowed to self-limit his activities especially when he is very young. If a child shows signs of fatigue during the school day, he may be allowed an extra rest period and his school day may be reevaluated to optimize the times when the child has more energy. Evidence is conflicting regarding the amount and type of exercise in which a child with DMD should participate (Brooke et al., 1989; Florence & Hagberg, 1984); however, a stretching program is often prescribed to prevent contractures and enhance function.

Spinal Muscular Atrophy. Spinal muscular atrophy (SMA) may be one of three forms: childhood-onset Type I and Type II (Werdnig-Hoffmann disease), or juvenile-onset type III (Kugelberg-Welander disease) (Stuberg, 2000). They are all inherited autosomal recessive disorders and affect the anterior horn cell of the spinal cord, which is the area that sends impulses to the muscles. When there are no electrical impulses to the muscles, they eventually atrophy.

Children with the type I SMA are extremely flaccid and weak as early as 3 months of age. These children rarely live beyond 3 years of age and often die of complications secondary to respiratory problems. They are considered medically fragile and often require life support. Type II SMA also affects very young babies, but not as severely as the type I form. These children may survive up to early adulthood. They are also very weak and flaccid. One must be cautious when picking up a child with SMA under the arms, because the reflexive tightening of the muscles in the axillary area is very weak and the child may literally "slip" through the hands of the caregiver. Often these children do not learn to walk and use standing frames to provide stability in a standing position, preferably in a supine stander that supports the head. They may learn to use a motorized wheelchair as early as 18 to 24 months. Contractures, scoliosis, and **kyphosis** are concerns and careful positioning and range of motion exercises are often part of the gross motor intervention. Although the sensory nerves are not affected, many children complain of increased sensitivity to touch, passive range of motion and handling. The juvenile form (type III) of SMA is often not diagnosed until later childhood or adolescence (Stuberg, 2000).

Kyphosis is exaggeration of the normal thoracic curve of the spine.

| **Vignette 7.1** |

RAMON

Ramon is a bright, curious, and engaging 4-year-old who enjoys his school program and the company of his peers. His motor skills, however, are severely limited by spinal muscular atrophy, a progressive neuromuscular disorder. He no longer is capable of independent floor mobility and is not able to propel the manual wheelchair that was prescribed when he was 2 years old. Because of his weak neck and back muscles, he requires significant external support and a slightly reclined back to support his head and trunk in order to sit. When his forearms are supported on a smooth surface, he is able to slide his arms from point to point and use his hands quite well in play. However, he does not have sufficient strength to raise his arms off the table.

The preschool team that works in his classroom has carefully considered his capabilities, interests, and needs to design a program that includes him in all classroom activities. He has just received a power wheelchair, which he controls with a joystick. He travels between home and school on a school van with a power lift to accommodate his wheelchair. As in many preschool programs, the day begins with time for free play and toileting. He is capable of controlling bowel and bladder functions and is able to communicate his needs to use the toilet effectively. He uses a special potty chair that supports his trunk and head well and which has a detachable tray to support his arms. Before the structured school program begins each day, he often spends time resting in a side-lying position on a mat placed so that he can reach toys on the bottom shelf in the play area.

The children then gather for circle time where he is positioned in a floor corner seat, which places him at the same level as his classmates when they sit on the floor. This piece of adaptive equipment provides head and trunk control and a tray for arm support. He is able to participate fully in circle time, needing help only to pass materials to the next child in the circle. He uses this same chair later in the day to support him in free play. He enlists his peers to help him get the toys he wants and to play with him. A snack is served at semicircular tables. Ramon is transferred to a fully adjustable classroom chair that fits well under the table. Other than needing help setting up his snack and refilling items as needed, he feeds himself independently. His food is placed on a rimmed plate on top of a raised wooden stand made by the school custodian. His right arm rests on this stand and he is able to control his wrist and fingers well to feed himself finger foods or to scoop food and pivot the spoon to his mouth. His cup has a long plastic straw for liquids; he can slide the cup toward his mouth with his left hand.

When the children go outside to play or walk, Ramon uses his power chair to move through those parts of the play structure that are accessible to wheelchairs. He requires assistance to use most of the outdoor play equipment. When the children engage in water or sand play, Ramon uses a supine stander, which supports his feet, pelvis, trunk, and head in an upright position to play beside his friends. Ramon uses his adapted classroom chair to join his friend in computer games. He controls the computer using a WinMini, a small keyboard that allows him to operate mouse and keyboard functions with his fingers. This keyboard allows him to reach all necessary keys without needing to lift his arms to reposition his hands.

Although this equipment allows Ramon to engage in all classroom activities, it is clear that Ramon needs a well-coordinated team to ensure that his equipment is adjusted correctly and to move him from one piece of equipment to another, as necessary. His team strives to change his position every 30 minutes to ensure his comfort and to maintain skin integrity. A full-time classroom aide assigned to Ramon assists his special education instructor. An occupational and physical therapist each work in the classroom with the special education teacher during one full session a week, where they provide direct services to Ramon and consultation to the other team members. Biweekly meetings are held to carefully coordinate team activities. Ramon's mother and father are delighted with their son's program. Because of the progressive nature of Ramon's condition, they know that his muscles will continue to grow weaker. They anticipate that he may have only a few more years of life left; thus, it is tremendously important to them that Ramon be just "one of the kids" for as long as possible.

Spinal Cord Injury and Tumors of the Spinal Cord

Spinal cord injury (SCI) is any injury causing a complete or partial disruption of neural impulses from the spine to the affected muscles, skin, and other organs resulting in complete or partial paralysis. The leading cause for SCI at all ages is trauma from motor vehicle accidents, falls, and violence and abuse (Shakhazizian, Massagli, & Southard, 2000). Depending on the level of the injury, the individual may have paralysis of different areas of the body. Injury to the spinal cord at the cervical level (neck vertebra) may result in quadriplegia or paralysis from the neck down. Injury to the thoracic area (midback) and lumbar area (low back) may result in paraplegia or paralysis from the waist or low-back area continuing down through the legs and feet. There may be full paralysis or partial paralysis depending on the extent of the lesion. Similar clinical findings are found with spinal cord tumors in young children.

The young child with a spinal cord injury or spinal tumor requires special care. The toddler and preschooler may require special devices to learn to sit. A soft back brace may assist the child with sitting balance so that he can use his hands more easily and also to prevent scoliosis (especially if the lesion is high). Preschoolers can use **knee-ankle-foot orthoses** (KAFOs) or long leg braces to learn to walk and also require the use of a walker or crutches. This form of ambulation requires a great deal of energy and the child may eventually prefer to use a wheelchair. A manual wheelchair may be appropriate for a child with a lumbar or low thoracic cord injury in that he still has the strength of the arms and necessary sitting balance needed to propel the wheels. A powered wheelchair may be a better choice for a child with a higher thoracic or cervical cord injury. Many children (and adults) prefer to activate a powered chair with a joystick, but other forms of activation are available for the child with less active movement of the arms. With close supervision, a child as young as 18 to 24 months may be taught to use a wheelchair.

Pressure sores are a problem for children with any level of cord injury, because of the loss of sensation in the affected parts. Special wheelchair cushions are available to help alleviate this, but it is important for all caregivers to be aware that the child should be repositioned on a regular basis for pressure relief. Standing frames and other classroom positioning devices are also available for alternative positioning.

Down Syndrome

Down syndrome is a genetic disorder that results from a chromosomal abnormality causing a number of physical and cognitive anomalies (Blackman, 1997). Children with Down syndrome typically have low muscle tone, short stature, and mental retardation. A number of health problems may accompany this disorder such as congenital heart disease, visual deficits, and lowered resistance to infection. Instability between the first two cervical vertebrae, called **atlantoaxial subluxation,** occurs in a small percentage of children with Down syndrome. X-rays of the neck are often recommended to rule out this condition because, in rare instances, pressure on the head and neck may result in damage to the spinal cord (Blackman, 1977).

Although gross motor delays are typical in children with mental retardation, the degree of delay is greater in Down syndrome than in retardation due to other factors. Typically developing children begin to walk without support anywhere from 9 to 15 months; children with Down syndrome begin to walk from 13 to 48 months (Cunningham, 1982). In general, the age of acquisition of developmental milestones is late and the range of ages in which skills may be acquired is broad.

Lack of trunk rotation, variability, and poor balance characterize the quality of movement in children with Down syndrome. It is felt that these problems are caused by low muscle tone and limited coactivation around the joints (Lauteslager, 1995), resulting in poor stability at the shoulders and hips and leading to limited ability to shift weight. In infancy, resistance against gravity is minimal and range of motion is greater than in typically developing children. Children with Down syndrome tend to use atypical posture in static positions, such as sitting, in which the legs tend to be widely abducted providing a wide base and eliminating the need for weight shift. In sitting, children with Down syndrome tend to avoid rotating the trunk to retrieve objects; instead, they may lean far forward with a rigid trunk or scoot in the sitting position to move toward a desired object.

Atypical movement patterns are often observed when these children move from one position to another. Movement often occurs in straight planes, with limited trunk rotation. For example, whereas the typical child moves from sitting to a modified side-sitting position to the hands-and-knees position, a child with Down syndrome is more likely to vault straight forward over the legs into the hands-and-knees position (Lauteslager, 1995). In walking, children with Down syndrome are more likely to have their legs widely abducted and use lateral trunk movements to achieve weight shift for much longer periods than typically developing children do. Few children with Down syndrome develop the mature counterrotation and arm swing present in most typically developing 6-year-old children.

It may be hypothesized that although the movement patterns of young children with Down syndrome are efficient based upon their musculoskeletal features, the stereotypical movement patterns they display will result in further delays in the future. For example, when typically developing children move from sitting to hands and knees, they get practice with trunk rotation and have better developed equilibrium reactions, more strength, and more variability of movement to prepare them for higher level skills, such as walking. Children with Down syndrome often do not have the same range of experiences in sitting and do not gain the same degree of control before learning to walk; therefore, the walking pattern is more restricted. To allow the child to experience greater variability of movement, intervention is often focused on tone building and facilitation of coactivation, weight shift, and rotation in movement activities.

Disorders of Motor Coordination

For many years, researchers and experts in child development have used various terms to describe children who exhibit difficulty with motor coordination, including *minimal brain dysfunction, developmental apraxia* (or *dyspraxia*), *sensory integration disorders*, or *somatodyspraxia* (Cermak, Gubbay, & Larkin, 2002; David, 2002;

Developmental
coordination dis-
order (DCD) is
poor motor coordi-
nation that is not
related to primary
cognitive, sen-
sory, or neurologi-
cal impairment.

Missiuna & Polatajko, 1995; Reeves & Cermak, 2002). This problem with nomenclature has resulted in confusion that has hindered research and intervention in this area. Within the last 10 years the term **developmental coordination disorder** (DCD) has been used more frequently to describe motor deficits in children whose incoordination is not associated with primary cognitive, sensory, or known neurological impairment (American Psychiatric Association, 2000). These motor deficits include significant delays in achieving typical motor milestones (development is below cognitive levels), clumsiness in the execution of motor skills, difficulty with handwriting tasks, and poor performance in sports. The motor impairment must significantly impede functional self-care activities and academic achievement. It should be noted that DCD often coexists with learning disabilities and attention-deficit hyperactivity disorder (Dewey, 2002).

Experts remain divided about classifying children into subgroups of DCD. Dewey has suggested that it may be useful to describe children based on whether they have difficulty with motor planning or with motor execution (Dewey, 2002). Children with motor planning problems may be described as having "developmental dyspraxia," a term used widely by occupational therapists, neuropsychologists, and neurologists (Cermak et al., 2002). Developmental dyspraxia refers to clumsiness that is due to impairment in the ability to plan nonhabitual motor tasks. Problems with motor planning may be the result of difficulty integrating sensory information from the body or from difficulty with sequencing motor tasks. Children with developmental dyspraxia use excessive effort and energy to plan complex motor tasks such as buttoning, cutting with scissors, tying shoelaces, riding a bicycle, writing, skipping, hopping, and playing on playground equipment. A skilled observer often can recognize problems in the preschool years, but typically the disorder is not identified until the first, second, or third grade when demands on time, organization, and participation increase (Cermak, 1991; Levine, 1987). Early diagnosis can help prevent some of the difficulties and frustration that these children may encounter. Therapists may identify these children by analyzing clinical observations, pertinent historical information, and standardized testing.

Autism

Although the identifying features of autism and other pervasive developmental disorders are primarily related to qualitative deficits in communication and social interaction, atypical responses to sensory stimuli and stereotypical motor movements also are common diagnostic findings.

Gross and fine-motor development in young children with autism, although often the most successful area of development (Cox, 1993), are nonetheless often significantly delayed (Watson & Marcus, 1986). These children may appear to be physically agile and often do quite well in activities such as completing puzzles and block designs, but they may have difficulties in tasks requiring the planning and sequencing of movement (e.g., pedaling a tricycle, drawing, and folding paper). The ability of children with autism to gather accurate information about their own bodies through proprioception and the bodies of others through visual perception—both of which are required for imitation of motor movement—is in question. Young children with autism are notably poor at imitating the behavior of others, which some feel may account for the problems of socialization and communication inherent in children with autism (Meltzoff & Gopnik, 1993). Specific deficits related to motor development that have been noted in children with autism include decreased postural tone, toe walking, drooling, clumsiness, delayed onset of walking (Rapin, 1988), decreased balance, incoordination, and poor finger-to-thumb movements (Jones & Prior, 1985).

Specific Strategies for Gross Motor Assessment

There are several reasons for assessing the gross motor competence of young children. The identification of a discrepancy between age-expected performance and actual performance is the first step in determining whether intervention is necessary and is imperative if services are sought under early intervention and preschool legislation. However, the assessment should do more than merely identify disparity. It should provide the evaluation team with sufficient information to establish functional goals and objectives to facilitate motor development. In addition, it should allow one to hypothesize causes for identified motor delays, and it may provide information that will help to explain other areas of delay (see chapter 4).

The assessment of gross motor skills must include both a quantitative and a qualitative evaluation of motor performance. A very young child may be meeting developmental milestones, but a careful examination of the quality of posture and movement may provide information that will identify the probability of future delay. For example, a child with low muscle tone may roll and sit when expected, but his posture in sitting will be qualitatively different from that of a typically developing child. The experienced therapist may help parents and educators understand how the hypotonia may limit the ability to move in and out of sitting, to creep, to pull to stand, and to walk in a normal fashion. In addition, the therapist may be able to suggest therapeutic activities that will minimize potential future problems with motor skills. Assessment results should be interpreted in light of the child's cognitive, communicative, psychosocial, self-care, and fine motor skill development. Children who have difficulty performing motor tasks at a level with their peers may experience decreased self-esteem, may avoid physical activity, or may be fearful of situations that require gross motor control.

Gross motor assessment may occur as part of an interdisciplinary team-based assessment or may occur as a "specialty" evaluation. In the case of the interdisciplinary team, evaluation may be accomplished by a group of professionals, each assuming responsibility for specific areas of function. Depending on the child's perceived needs, the evaluation may occur in an arena format (i.e., many disciplines evaluate the child, usually during the same appointment), a core format (i.e., usually two key disciplines evaluate the child), or with separate appointments by one discipline in the home, school, or clinic. Many early intervention and preschool programs prefer that the examination be done in the child's home or another natural environment with the primary caregivers present. When children are assessed in unfamiliar environments, they may be constrained in their willingness to explore and move.

Professionals who perform team evaluations often use measures that allow assessment across many domains of function. Examples of these broad-based assessments that might be used to evaluate young children include the Bayley II (Bayley, 1993) and the Bayley Infant Neurodevelopmental Screener (Aylward, 1995), the Battelle Developmental Inventory (Newborg, Stock, Wneck, Guidubaldi, & Svinicki, in press), the Infant-Toddler Developmental Assessment (Provence, Erikson, Vater, & Palermi, 1995), the Early Intervention Developmental Profile (Rogers et al., 1981), and the Hawaii Early Learning Profile (HELP; Furuno et al., 1984). The HELP is designed for children from 0 to 3 years of age, and the HELP for Preschoolers Assessment Strands, Charts, and Checklists (VORT Corporation, 1995) were designed for children 3 to 6 years of age. These assessments provide information on a child's functioning in self-care, gross motor, fine-motor, cognitive, and social and emotional development. The Ages and Stages Questionnaire (Bricker & Squires, 1995), which is written in terms easily understood by caregivers, can be completed by parents.

An excellent measure for assessing self-care, mobility, and social function in context, which may not meet the needs of educational teams related to eligibility for services, is the Pediatric Evaluation of Disability Inventory (PEDI; Haley, Coster, Ludlow, Haltiwanger, & Andrellos, 1992). In some settings in which a transdisciplinary approach is used and **discipline-free goals** are developed—which are becoming more favored, particularly in the provision of early intervention services and for children with multiple disabilities—a team-based contextual evaluation may be preferred, such as the Transdisciplinary Play-Based Assessment (Linder, 1990; see Chapter 4 for a description). When concerns exist in the gross motor areas, the motor specialist on the team may conduct a more in-depth evaluation. Some assessments designed specifically to measure development of gross and fine-motor skills include the Peabody Developmental Motor Scales II for children from birth through 5 years (Folio & Fewell, 2000), the Toddler and Infant Motor Evaluation (Miller & Roid, 2002), and the Bruininks-Oseretsky Test of Motor Proficiency for children, which is useful only with children who are at least $4\frac{1}{2}$ years of age (Bruininks, 1978).

In addition to using assessments that measure gross motor performance, occupational and physical therapists may use standardized and criterion-referenced assessment tools and qualitative measures to assess components of motor skills and sensory processing. A clinical evaluation by the therapist will identify contributing factors that may have an impact on motor functioning, such as reflexive development, atypical postural tone, decreased or increased range of motion, atypical movement patterns and components, poor musculoskeletal integrity, inadequate positioning for function, and disorders in sensory registration, discrimination, and tolerance. There are a number of measures designed primarily to gather information about a child's ability to process sensory information; these provide supplemental information and do not take the place of an assessment of gross motor performance. The Infant/Toddler Sensory Profile (Dunn, 2002) and the Sensory Profile (Dunn, 1999), for children aged 3 and above, use a questionnaire format to provide information about a child's sensory performance. The DeGangi-Berk Test of Sensory Integration (DeGangi & Berk, 1983) is designed to measure postural control, bilateral motor integration, and reflex development in children from 3 to 5 years of age. The Sensory Integration and Praxis Test (Ayres, 1989) measures visual, tactile, and kinesthetic perception, as well as motor performance in children from 4 to 8 years of age.

Discipline-free goals are goals that focus on a child's needs within a given context, rather than upon skills within a specific service provider's domain.

The results of the gross motor assessment should be considered together with information about the child's function in other developmental areas, and family information and concerns to develop appropriate intervention plans that consider the whole child.

Selected Strategies for Intervention

Models and Frameworks for Meeting Gross Motor Needs

Meeting the needs of children with gross motor impairment can be accomplished in a number of different ways. Each model of service delivery has specific strengths that, depending upon the needs of the child, the skills of team members, and the nature of the organization providing services, may be considered most appropriate for the individual child. For children younger than 3 years, federal legislation mandates a family-centered approach, which recognizes that infants and toddlers are part of an integrated family system where each individual influences the behavior of all other individuals. The family makes decisions about intervention, with the early intervention team providing information and support in this process. Although this approach is not mandated for children older than 3, the family is still tremendously important. It behooves the team to include parents and support their wishes as much as is possible in assessment, intervention, and program planning. Parents who become empowered through their child's early intervention program tend to expect to be involved in making decisions about their child's educational experiences at age 3. Suggestions on motor interventions should support the role of the parent and be tailored to the parent's interests and capabilities.

The needs of the child and the family are considered in light of community and agency resources to determine a service program to meet the needs of the child. When a child has specific motor needs, the appropriate specialist from the team (e.g., the occupational or physical therapist) must determine how services should be provided. The **occupational therapist** views the child within his physical, social, and cultural environment, examining how the environment influences the child's performance in such areas as self-care, play, and schoolwork. The occupational therapist addresses issues related to feeding, dressing, positioning, handwriting, and psychosocial needs, and often is helpful in adapting tasks and the environment for optimal function. Occupational therapists must be certified by the American Occupational Therapy Association in order to practice; in addition, many states also require a professional license. An occupational therapist may be prepared at the basic bachelor's level or at the master's level, whereas a certified occupational therapy assistant holds a certificate or associate's degree.

The **physical therapist** is concerned with children's function related to posture and movement. Physical therapists address issues related to mobility and gross motor skill acquisition, and often provide adaptive equipment to support these functions. Physical therapists in practice today may have been prepared at the bachelor's or master's level, although in the future, a master's or a doctoral

An occupational therapist is a professional who helps individuals participate in those activities (or occupations) that are meaningful and purposeful for them, through remediation of individual skills, or modification of the task or environment.

The physical therapist is a professional who focuses on managing a patient's movement system, by evaluating and treating the musculoskeletal and neuromotor system.

degree will be required to enter the field. A physical therapy assistant holds an associate's degree. Physical therapists and assistants must be licensed by the state in which they practice.

It should be noted that under early intervention legislation, occupational and physical therapists may provide a "primary" service to the child and family. These therapists, in fact, may represent the only service a child receives if that service is all that is deemed necessary by the early intervention team. When working with pre-school and school-aged children, however, occupational and physical therapists are "related" service providers. These services are considered necessary in order for a particular child to benefit from the special education program. In this case, the therapist works with the special education teacher and other members of the team to meet the child's educational needs.

Special physical educators work with children who "cannot benefit from or safely participate in a regular physical education program" (Jansma & French, 1994, p. 3). This is a specialty area within physical education designed to serve children with special needs. Such teachers may be involved in adapting physical education activities for students or providing programs that foster development of fitness and gross motor skills or that help to correct specific problems related to posture and body movement. Several different approaches may be needed to assist a child with motor problems.

Intervention by the physical or occupational therapist may be provided through direct therapy, monitoring, consultation, or a combination of these models (Dunn & Campbell, 1990). However, decisions should be made based upon a careful analysis of the child, family, and school situation rather than upon staff availability or what has been done in the past (Palisano, Campbell, & Harris, 1995).

Direct Therapy.   Intervention that is individually designed and carried out by the therapist with one child or a group of children is referred to as direct therapy. This may occur within a natural environment, such as the child's home, the educational classroom, or the cafeteria, or it may occur in an isolated environment, such as a therapy room. Isolated therapy in a school setting should be provided only when the service the child requires is inappropriate in the natural environment.

Monitoring.   When the motor specialist designs a service plan to meet a child's needs, but another person (such as a classroom aide) is trained to carry out the activities, the specialist remains responsible for the implementation of the plan. This is accomplished through monitoring whereby the therapist maintains contact with the child and modifies the intervention as necessary.

Consultation.   In the consultation model, the motor specialist provides expertise to another person or program to address concerns identified by that person. In this model, the specialist no longer assumes responsibility for the intervention plan. For example, the occupational therapist may have expertise in developing handwriting programs for children with mild motor delays, but does not provide direct services to individual children.

Positioning the Child

Regardless of how treatment is conducted, postural control is central to the development of most sensorimotor skills and often represents the initial consideration in intervention. For very young children who have problems with postural tone, simple environmental modifications may promote successful interaction with the environment and may help prevent the development of atypical posture and movement. For example, placing rolled towels under the head and extremities of an infant with hypotonia in supine will facilitate bringing the head, hands, and legs toward midline. This will support the child's visual and tactile exploration of his own body in midline, which many consider to be the first position of learning. For the child with hypertonia, primitive reflexes often dominate the prone and supine positions, making volitional movement difficult. Placement in the side-lying position may eliminate the influence of tonic reflexes by minimizing the effects of gravity on postural tone, allowing the child to move with greater freedom and control.

> Postural control is critical to the evolution of most sensorimotor skills.

For children who need postural control at higher levels of functioning, adaptations to infant seats, strollers, highchairs, classroom tables and chairs, toilet seats, and even swings may greatly improve the child's functional success. Considerations for fostering posture and mobility through technology are discussed later in this chapter.

Postural and Gross Motor Control

When postural control is significantly impaired, the physical or occupational therapist may develop a treatment program keyed to the specific needs of the individual child. Treatment programs may include activities to promote more normal muscle tone, to maintain range of motion, and to improve the ability to use protective and equilibrium reactions in functional activities. Because different underlying mechanisms may cause postural deficits in children, the early interventionist should not implement a motor program without guidance from these professionals.

When a young child is not able to move about independently, professionals must do their best to provide the child with as much control as possible over his environment. For example, promoting and responding to communicative attempts by young children with significant motor impairment will allow them some ability to direct others to move them through the environment or to bring the environment to them. In addition, it is important to position these children on a level with peers to foster social interaction and to make the environment as accessible to them as possible.

> Positioning children at the level of their peers will foster social interactions and make their surroundings more accessible.

For children with mild motor impairments, such as those with developmental motor disorders, modifying activities to lessen motor demands may be particularly helpful. Children who have problems with motor coordination are often cognizant of their difficulties and see their performance in motor activities as inferior to those of their peers. They may avoid engaging in activities with other children because of fear of failure and, therefore, limit their own opportunities to improve motor skills performance. Children with motor incoordination may find relative success in activities that provide the opportunity for practice and that do not require constant interaction with changing environmental conditions. The special physical educator may be especially helpful to classroom teachers in finding ways to modify motor tasks for success.

For children with specific medical diagnoses, such as cerebral palsy, spina bifida, and juvenile rheumatoid arthritis, it is important to consult with the physical and occupational therapists before instituting a program. This is because there are often contraindications for movement that must be considered.

For children with mild-to-moderate motor impairment, the most important consideration in improving skills is a firm understanding of the present motor, sensory, and cognitive capabilities of the child. When the goal of an activity is motor performance, the activity should be structured so that it represents the *"just-right challenge,"* or the point at which the task is just difficult enough to entice the child to try to succeed, but not so difficult so as to result in poor performance or failure (Koomar & Bundy, 2002).

Assistive Technology for Gross Motor Intervention

As discussed in chapter 6, low- and high-technology supports for children can be of great help when designing curricula to support development of a child with motor impairment. Low-tech supports include simple seating modifications that may provide better posture and allow more optimal function. Figure 7.10 provides an illustration of simple postural modifications to typical preschool furniture, including a seat belt, a back insert to reduce seat depth, footrests, and a cut-out table.

FIGURE 7.10   Seating modifications to typical preschool chairs designed to enhance fine-motor function.

Source: Used by permission of Jean Patz.

When homemade adaptations are not practical, special adaptive equipment may be purchased commercially. There are many adaptive devices to support sitting on the market, including floor sitters, **corner seats** (see the photo on p. 249), and various special classroom chairs. Wheelchairs are typically used for postural support by children with severe motor impairments. In such cases, it is imperative that all members of the assistive technology team consider mobility needs, transfer capabilities, communication needs, and the support necessary for feeding and fine-motor activities. Family concerns must be foremost. Family members may benefit from a lightweight wheelchair that they can carry in their car and can get into their home. Depending on the services available and the problems that need to be addressed, the assistive technology team may include the developmental pediatrician, the physical and occupational therapists, the speech-language pathologist, the orthopedist, the rehabilitation technology supplier, the early interventionist, and the family.

The interventionist should be knowledgeable about how to handle children when placing them in and out of adapted positioning devices to reduce the influence of atypical tone or primitive reflexes, if these are present. The interventionist also should know about the application of seating accessories for wheelchairs such as anterior chest supports, lap trays, and headrests.

The more physically involved child may require a specialized stander if he cannot stand unaided. There are several different types of standers: supine, prone, box, or floor standers. The **supine stander** is usually for the most severely involved child who requires extensive positioning. The child lays supine and the stander is positioned horizontally while the child is strapped in. Then the stander is moved into a standing position. This is often used for children with SMA, severe cerebral palsy, high-level spina bifida, or a spinal cord injury. A **prone stander** allows the child to lean forward on the stander and usually is not positioned completely vertical. The child must use some neck and upper back muscles to keep his head and shoulders erect. Often children with less involved cerebral palsy or lower level spina bifida use this type of stander. A **box stander** is used less frequently because better positioning may be available with different types of standers. A **floor stander** usually has a wide base of support so the child does not tip, and bars and straps are available for correct alignment. The child needs to have good trunk and neck strength to use this device.

Other adaptive equipment includes walkers and braces. Different types of walkers are available, but generally the favored walker is a **backward (or reverse) walker** with the wheels and the bar in the back. This device allows the child to stand up straighter. Ankle-foot orthoses (AFOs) have been described earlier. Additionally, some children may require more or less lower leg control. The hip-knee-ankle-foot orthoses (HKAFO) may be used by a child with very high spina bifida, spinal cord injury, or advanced Duchenne's muscular dystrophy. Less support might be provided by lower cut AFOs or SMOs **(supramalleolar orthoses)** for children with mild cerebral palsy, Down syndrome, or sacral-level spina bifida.

Powered mobility devices represent high-tech options for children with significant motor impairment; children who are as young as 18 to 24 months may safely operate them. Powered mobility devices that resemble children's toys may be accepted more readily by parents and may promote peer play in children with significant motor impairment (Deitz, 1998). Carlson and Ramsey (2000) provide

A corner seat, or floor sitter, is a chair where the back is fashioned in a right angle, or corner, which provides postural support to young children so that they can sit on the floor with their peers.

The early interventionist must be knowledgeable of a child's adapted positioning needs and devices, and how to move the child from one position to another.

Rear walker is a device to support walking where the horizontal bar is positioned behind the person.

a concise review of the developmental benefits of power wheelchair provision to young children with disabilities. The use of power wheelchairs has been found to result in increased communication and peer interaction, increased interaction with objects in the environment, increased motivation for independent mobility, and decreased family perceptions of the child's helplessness. Scull (1996) discusses additional benefits of powered mobility for children as young as 2 years of age. The assistive technology team, the child, and the family determine the best method to access the power wheelchair, depending on the child's physical and cognitive readiness. Wheelchair controls can be activated by any part of the body: pushing a joystick with the hand or extremities, pressing switch controls mounted on a headrest with the head, moving a chin cup, blowing into a sip-and-puff control, or activating a tongue-touch control plate (newAbilities Systems Inc., 1994) placed on a child's palate.

Summary

This chapter has presented typical gross motor development in infants and young children, including the acquisition of postural and gross motor skills. Some of the situations and conditions that may result in atypical gross motor development were described, and guidelines to help the early interventionist determine when motor development is not following the expected path were provided. Some suggestions for intervention with children who have gross motor deficits were given, with indications of when the help of a motor specialist is needed.

Early interventionists are often the first to observe motor deficits, particularly in children with mild-to-moderate impairment, because they have the benefit of seeing the child with other children of the same age. When an early interventionist has concerns regarding the gross motor development of a child, careful observation of the child is required in order to clearly articulate the reason for concern. A discussion of these concerns with the intervention team will help the early interventionist determine when additional evaluation is necessary and who should perform the evaluation.

It is important for the early interventionist to gather as much information from the motor specialists on the team as possible so that they have a good understanding of the gross motor needs of the child. It is equally important for the early interventionist to inform the motor specialist (therapist or special physical educator) about the child's function in the home and classroom to aid the motor specialist in understanding the skills the child needs to be able to perform successfully. Only when there is the opportunity for open and ongoing communication among the family, early interventionist, and motor specialist can the benefits of gross motor intervention be optimized.

Review Questions and Discussion Points

1. What does the term *integrated* mean with respect to infant primitive reflexes?
2. Why does a child appear to "toddle" from side to side when he first learns to walk?
3. How does muscle tone influence posture and movement in young children? How is it different in young children with special needs?

4. Why is it important for a child to learn to stand on one foot? What are some gross motor skills that require this ability?

5. How could a young child with spastic cerebral palsy who uses a wheelchair or walker be included in activities such as a fieldtrip to the park?

Recommended Resources

American Occupational Therapy Association
4720 Montgomery Lane
PO Box 31220
Bethesda, MD 20824-1220
301-652-2682
http://www.aota.org

American Physical Therapy Association
  Pediatrics Section
1111 N. Fairfax St.
Alexandria, VA 22314-1488
800-999-2782, ext. 3254
http://www. PediatricAPTA. org

Brain Injury Association (formerly the National Head
  Injury Foundation)
105 N. Alfred St.
Alexandria, VA 22314
Telephone: 800-444-6443; Family Helpline: 703-236-6000
E-mail: FamilyHelpline@biausa.org
http://www.biausa.org

Early Childhood Technical Assistance Center
Campus Box 8040, UNC-CH
Chapel Hill, NC 27599-8040
919-962-2001
http://www.ectac.org

National Institute of Child Health and Human
  Development
Bldg. 31, Room 2A32, MSC 2425
31 Center Dr.
Bethesda, MD 20892-2425
800-370-2943
http://www.nichd.nih.gov

Therapy Skill Builders
Psychological Corporation
PO Box 839954
San Antonio, TX 78283-3954
http://www.tpcweb.com

References

American Psychiatric Association. (2000). *Diagnostic and statistical manual of mental disorders* (4th ed.). Washington, DC: Author.

Aylward, G. P. (1995). *Bayley Infant Neurodevelopmental Screener.* San Antonio, TX: Psychological Corporation

Ayres, A. J. (1989). *Sensory Integration and Praxis Tests.* Los Angeles: Western Psychological Services.

Batshaw, M., & Perret, Y. (1992). *Children with disabilities: A medical primer* (3rd ed.). Baltimore: Brookes.

Bayley, N. (1993). *Bayley Scales of Infant Development* (Rev. ed.). New York: Psychological Corporation.

Bennett F. C. (1984). Cerebral Palsy: The how and why of early diagnosis. *Consultant, 24,* 151–173.

Berry, R. J., Li, Z., Erickson, J. D., Li, S., Moore, C. A., Wang, H., et al. (1999). Prevention of neural tube defects with folic acid in China. *New England Journal of Medicine, 341,* 1485–1490.

Blackman, J. A. (1997). *Medical aspects of developmental disabilities in children birth to three* (3rd ed.). Gaithersburg, MD: Aspen.

Bly, L. (1983). *The components of normal movement during the first year of life.* Chicago: Neuro-Developmental Treatment Association, Inc.

Botto, L. D., Moore, C. A., Khoury, M. J., & Erickson, J. D. (1999). Neural tube defects. *New England Journal of Medicine, 341,* 1509–1510.

Bricker, D., & Squires, J. (1995). *Ages & Stages Questionnaires.* Baltimore: Brookes.

Brooke, M. H., Fenichel, G. M., Griggs, R. C., Mendell, J. R., Moxley, R., Miller, P., et al. (1983). Clinical investigations in Duchenne dystrophy. Part 2. Determination of the "power" of therapeutic trials based on the natural history. *Muscle & Nerve, 6,* 91–103.

Brooke, M. H., Fenichel, G. M., Griggs, R. C., Mendell, J. R., Moxley, R., Florence, J., et al. (1989). Duchenne muscular dystrophy: Patterns of clinical progression and effects of supportive therapy. *Neurology, 39,* 475–481.

Bruininks, R. (1978). *Bruininks-Oseretsky Test of Motor Proficiency.* Circle Pines, MN: American Guidance Service.

Capute, A. J., Shapiro, B. K., Palmer, F. B., Ross, A., & Wachtel, R. C. (1985). Normal gross motor development: The influences of race, sex and socioeconomic status. *Developmental Medicine and Child Neurology, 27,* 635–643.

Carlson, S. J., & Ramsey, C. (2000). Assistive technology. In S. K. Campbell, D. W. Vander Linden, R. J. Palisano (Eds.), *Physical therapy for children* (2nd ed., pp. 671–708). Philadelphia: W. B. Saunders.

Cermak, S. (1991). Somatodyspraxia. In A. Fisher, E. Murray, & A. Bundy (Eds.), *Sensory integration: Theory and practice.* (pp. 137–168). Philadelphia: Davis.

Cermak, S. A., Gubbay, S. S., & Larkin, D. (2002). What is developmental coordination disorder? In S. A. Cermak & D. Larkin (Eds.), *Developmental coordination disorder* (pp. 2–22). Albany, NY: Delmar.

Clark, J. E. (1995). On becoming skillful: Patterns and constraints. *Rehabiliation Quarterly, 66,* 173–183.

Cox, R. D. (1993). Normal childhood development from birth to five years. In E. Schopler, M. E. VanBourgondien, & M. M. Bristol (Eds.), *Preschool issues in autism* (pp. 39–57). New York: Plenum Press.

Cunningham, C. C. (1982). *Down syndrome: An introduction for parents.* London: Souvenir Press.

David, K. S. (2000). Developmental coordination disorders. In S. K. Campbell, D. W. Vander Linden, A. J. Palisano, (Eds.), *Physical therapy for children* (2nd ed., pp. 471–501). Philadelphia: Saunders.

Davis, R. E., Moon, R. Y., Sachs, I., & Otolini, M. C. (1998). Effects of sleep position on infant motor development. *Pediatrics, 102,* 1135–1140.

DeGangi, G. A., & Berk, R. A. (1983). The DeGangi-Berk Test of Sensory Integration. San Antonio, TX: Psychological Corporation.

Deitz, J. C. (1998). Pediatric augmented mobility. In D. B. Gray, L. A. Quatrano, & M. L. Lieberman (Eds.), *Designing and using assistive technology: The human perspective* (pp. 269–284). Baltimore: Brookes.

Dewey, D. (2002). Subtypes of deevelopmental coordination disorder. In S. Cermak & D. Larkin (Eds.), *Developmental coordination disorder* (pp. 40–53). Albany, NY: Delmar.

Dewey, C., Fleming, P., Golding, J., & ALSPAC Study Team. (1998). Does the supine sleeping position have any adverse effects on the child? II. Development in the first 18 months. *Pediatrics, 101* (1), p. e5. Retrieved from. http://www.pediatrics.org/cgi/content/full/101/1/e5.

Dubowitz, V. (1978). *Muscle disorders in childhood.* London: Saunders.

Dunn, W. (1999). *Sensory Profile: User's manual.* San Antonio, TX: Psychological Corporation.

Dunn, W. (2002). *The Infant/Toddler Sensory Profile manual.* San Antonio, TX: Psychological Corporation.

Dunn, W., & Campbell, P. H. (1990). Designing pediatric service provision. In W. Dunn (Ed.), *Pediatric occupational therapy* (pp. 139–160). Thorofare, NJ: Slack.

Fetters, L., Fernandes, B., & Cermak, S. (1988). The relationship of proximal and distal components in the development of reaching. *Physical Therapy, 68,* 839–845.

Florence, J. M., Hagberg, J. (1984). Effect of training on the exercise responses of neuromuscular disease patients. *Medicine and Science in Sports and Exercise, 16,* 460–465.

Foerster O. (1977). The motor cortex in man in the light of Hughlings Jackson's Doctrines. In O. D. Payton, S. Hirt, & R. Newman (Eds.), *Scientific basis for neurophysiologic approaches to therapeutic exercise* (pp. 13–18). Philadelphia: Davis.

Folio, M. R., & Fewell, R. R. (2000). *Peabody Developmental Motor Scales, Second Edition.* San Antonio, TX: Psychological Corporation.

Garrett, M., McElroy A. M., & Staines, A. (2002). Locomotor milestones and babywalkers: Cross sectional study. *British Medical Journal, 324,* 1494.

Gesell, A., & Amatruda, C. (1947). *Developmental diagnosis* (2nd ed.). New York: Harper & Row.

Goodgold-Edwards, W. A., & Cermak, S. A. (1989). Integrating motor control and motor learning concepts with neuropsychological perspectives on apraxia and developmental dyspraxia. *American Journal of Occupational Therapy, 44,* 431–439.

Haley S. M., Coster, W. J., Ludlow, L. H., Haltiwanger, J. T., & Andrellos P. J. (1992). *Pediatric Evaluation of Disability Inventory.* San Antonio, TX: Psychological Corporation.

Haradon, G., Bascom, B., Dragomir, C., & Scripcaru, V. (1994). Sensory functions of institutionalized Romanian infants. *Occupational Therapy International, 1,* 250–260.

Hinderer, K. A., Hinderer, S. R., & Shurtleff, D. B. (2000). Myelodysplasia. In S. K. Campbell, D. W. Vander Linden, & R. J. Palisano, (Eds.), *Physical therapy for children* (2nd ed, pp. 621–670). Philadelphia: Saunders.

Hunter, J. G. (2001). The neonatal intensive care unit. In J. Case-Smith, (Ed.), *Occupational therapy for children* (4th ed., pp. 636–707). St. Louis: Mosby.

Jansma, P., & French, R. (1994). *Special physical education.* Upper Saddle River, NJ: Merrill/Prentice Hall.

Jones, V., & Prior, M. R. (1985). Motor imitation abilities and neurological signs in autistic children. *Journal of Autism and Developmental Disorders, 15,* 37–46.

Kerkering, G. A., & Phillips, W. E. (2000). Brain injuries: Traumatic brain injuries, near-drowning, and brain tumors. In S. K. Campbell, D. W. Vander Linden, & R. J. Palisano, (Eds.), *Physical therapy for children* (2nd ed., pp. 597–620). Philadelphia: Saunders.

Koenig, N., Hoffman, E. P., Bertelson, C. J., Monaco, A. P., Feener, C., Kunkel, L. M. (1987). Complete cloning of the Duchenne muscular dystrophy (DMD) cDNA and preliminary genomic organization of the DMD gene in normal and afffected individuals. *Cell, 50,* 509–517.

Koomar, J. A., & Bundy, A. C. (2002). The art and science of creating direct intervention from theory. In A. Bundy, S. Lane, & E. Murray (Eds.), *Sensory integration: Theory and practice* (2nd ed., pp. 251–314). Philadelphia: Davis.

Lannering, B., Marky, I., & Nordborg, C. (1990). Brain tumors in childhood and adolescence in West Sweden, 1970–1984: Epidemilogy and survival. *Cancer, 66,* 604–609.

Lauteslager, P. E. M. (1995). Motor development in young children with Down syndrome. In A. Vermeer, & W. E. Davis (Eds.), *Physical and motor development in mental retardation* (pp. 74–98). New York: Karger.

Levine, M. D. (1987). *Developmental variation and learning disorders.* Cambridge, MA: Educators Publishing Service.

Linder, T. W. (1990). *Transdisciplinary play-based assessment: A functional approach to working with young children.* Baltimore: Brookes.

Luthy, D. A., Wardinsky, T., Shurtleff, D. B., Hollenbach, K. A., Hickok, D. E., Nyberg, D. A., et al. (1991). Cesarean section before the onset of labor and subsequent motor function in infants with myelomeningocele diagnosed antenatally. *New England Journal of Medicine, 324,* 662–666.

Magnus R. (1926). Some results of studies in the physiology of posture. *Lancet, 2,* 531–585.

Mathiowetz, V., & Haugen, J. B. (1994). Motor behavior research: Implications for therapeutic approaches to central nervous system dysfunction. *American Journal of Occupational Therapy, 48,* 733–745.

McClain, C., Provost, B., & Crowe, T. K. (2000). Motor development of two-year-old typically developing Native American children on the Bayley Scales of Infant Development II Motor Scale. *Pediatric Physical Therapy, 12,* 108–113.

McEwen, I. (2000). Children with cognitive impairments. In S. K. Campbell, D. W. Vander Linden, & R. J. Palisano, (Eds.), *Physical therapy for children* (2nd ed., pp. 502–532). Philadelphia: Saunders.

Meltzoff, A., & Gopnik, A. (1993). The role of imitation in understanding persons and developing a theory of mind. In S. Baron-Cohen, H. Tager-Flusberg, & D. J. Cohen (Eds.), *Understanding other minds: Perspectives from autism* (pp. 335–366). New York: Oxford University Press.

Miller, L. J., & Roid, G. H. (2002). *The T.I.M.E.® Toddler and Infant Motor Evaluation.* San Antonio, TX: Psychological Corporation.

Molnar, G. E. (1985). *Pediatric rehabilitation.* Baltimore: Williams and Wilkins.

National Rehabilitation Information Center. (1994). Traumatic brain injury: A NARIC resource guide for people with TBI and their families. Silver Springs, MD: Author.

newAbilities Systems, Inc. (1994). *newAbilities UCS1000™ with Tongue-Touch Keypad™* [brochure]. Palo Alto, CA: Author.

Newborg, J., Stock, J. R., Wneck, L., Guidubaldi, J., & Svinicki. (in press). *Battelle Developmental Inventory—Revised.* Chicago: Riverside.

Olney, S. J., & Wright, M. J. (2000). Cerebral palsy. In S. K. Campbell, D. W. Vander Linden, & R. J. Palisano, (Eds.), *Physical therapy for children* (2nd ed., pp. 533–570). Philadelphia: Saunders.

Palisano, R. J., Campbell, S. K., & Harris, S. R. (Eds.), (2000). Clinical decision making in pediatric physical therapy. In S. K. Campbell, D. W. Vander Linden, & R. J. Palisano, (Eds.), *Physical therapy for children* (2nd ed., pp. 198–224). Philadelphia: Saunders.

Piper, M. C., & Darrah, J. (1995). *Motor assessment of the developing infant.* Philadelphia: Saunders.

Provence, S., Erikson, J., Vater, S., & Palmeri, S. (1995). *Infant-Toddler Developmental Assessment.* Itasca, IL: Riverside.

Rapin, I. (1988). Disorders of higher cerebral function in preschool children. Part II: Autistic spectrum disorder. *American Journal of Diseases of Children, 142,* 1178–1182.

Reeves, G. D., & Cermak, S. A. (2002). Disorders of praxis. In A. Bundy, S. Lane, & E. Murray (Eds.), *Sensory integration: Theory and practice* (2nd ed., pp. 71–100). Philadelphia: Davis.

Roberton, M. A., & Halverson, L. D. (1984). *Developing children—Their changing movement. A guide for teachers.* Philadelphia: Lea & Febiger.

Rogers, S. J., Donavan, C. M., D'Eugenio, D. B., Brown, S. L., Lynch, E. W., Moersch, M. S., et al. (1981). *Early Intervention Developmental Profile.* Ann Arbor: University of Michigan Press.

Santos, D. C., Gabbard, C., & Goncalves, V. M. (2001). Motor development during the first year: A comparative study. *Journal of Genetic Psychology,* 162, 143–153.

Scull, S. A. (1996). Mobility and ambulation. In L. A. Kurtz, P. W. Dowrick, S. E. Levy, & M. L. Batshaw (Eds.), *Handbook of developmental disabilities* (pp. 269–326). Gaithersburg, MD: Aspen.

Shakhazizian, K. A., Massagli, T. L., & Southard, T. L. (2000). Spinal cord injury. In S. K. Campbell, D. W. Vander Linden, & R. J. Palisano (Eds.), *Physical therapy for children* (2nd ed., pp. 571–596). Philadelphia: Saunders.

Sherrington, C. S. (1906/1947). *The integrative action of the nervous system.* New Haven, CT: Yale University Press.

Shurtleff, D. B., Stuntz, J. T., & Hayden, P. (1986). Hydrocephalus. In D. B. Shurtleff (Ed.), *Myelodysplasias and exstrophies: Significance, prevention and treatment* (pp. 139–180). Orlando, FL: Grune & Stratton.

Siegel, A., & Burton R. (1999). Effects of babywalkers on early locomotor development in human infants. *Developmental Behavorial Pediatrics, 20,* 355–361.

Smith, G. A., Bowman, M. J., Luria, J. W., & Shields, B. J. (1997). Babywalker—Related injuries continue despite warning labels and public education. *Pediatrics, 100,* (2), p. 1 Retrieved from http://pediatrics.aapublications.org/cgi/content/full/100/2/e1.

Solomons, H. C. (1982). Standardization of the Denver Developmental Screening Test on infants from Yucatan, Mexico. *International Journal of Rehabilitation Research, 5,* 179–189.

Stuberg, W. A. (1992). Considerations related to weight-bearing program in children with developmental disabilities. *Physical Therapy, 72,* 35–40.

Stuberg, W. A. (2000). Muscular dystrophy and spinal muscular atrophy. In S. K. Campbell, D. W. Vander Linden, & R. J. Palisano (Eds.), *Physical therapy for children* (2nd ed., pp. 339–368). Philadelphia: Saunders.

Super, C. M. (1976). Environmental effects on motor development: The case of African precocity. *Developmental Medicine and Child Neurology, 18,* 561–567.

Sweeney, J. K., & Bascom, B. B. (1995). Motor development and self-stimulatory movement in institutionalized Romanian children. *Pediatric Physical Therapy, 7,* 124–132.

Thelen, E., & Ulrich, B. D. (1990). Dynamic processes in learning to walk. *Monographs of the Society for Research in Child Development, 56,* 36–46.

Thoman, E. (1987). Self-regulation of stimulation by prematures with a breathing blue bear. In J. J. Gallagher & C. T. Ramey (Eds.), *The malleability of children.* Baltimore: Brookes.

Touwen, B. C. L. (1978). Variability and stereotypy in normal and deviant development. In C. Apley (Ed.), *Care of the handicapped child* (pp. 99–110). Series title: *Clinics in Developmental Medicine,* No. 67. Philadelphia: Lippincott.

Vander Zanden, J. W. (1997). *Human development* (6th ed.). New York: McGraw-Hill.

Victoria, M. D., Victoria, C. G., & Barros, F. C. (1990). Cross-cultural differences in developmental rates: A comparison between British and Brazilian children. *Child Care, Health and Development, 16,* 151–164.

VORT Corporation. (1995). *HELP for preschoolers.* Palo Alto, CA: Author.

Watson, L. R., & Marcus, L. M. (1986). Diagnosis and assessment of preschool children. In E. Schopler & G. Mesibov (Eds.), *Social behavior in autism* (pp. 285–303). New York: Plenum Press.

Wong, V., Wong, S., Chan, K., & Wong, W. (2002). Functional Independence Measure (WeeFIM) for Chinese children: Hong Kong cohort. *Pediatrics, 109,* 317–319.

8

Fine Motor, Oral Motor, and Self-Care Development

Jean A. Patz and Carole W. Dennis

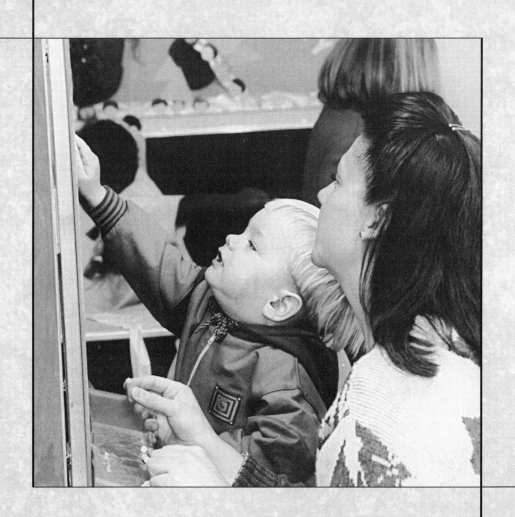

Chapter Outline

Lily

Lily, a 17-month-old fraternal twin, was delivered at 30 weeks with a birth weight of 2 lb 3 oz. The mother indicated that at 27 weeks gestation, Lily developed intrauterine growth retardation. At 1 year of age, it became apparent that Lily had delayed motor skills. Her twin sister had learned to crawl and speak, whereas Lily could only roll over and make basic vowel sounds. Lily was initially diagnosed with hypotonia (low muscle tone) of unknown cause. She currently has signs of hypertonia (high muscle tone) as well which interferes with her ability to manipulate toys and objects, chew or drink effectively from a cup, sit or move in her environment, and participate fully in age-appropriate self-care skills.

Despite her physical limitations, the parents report that Lily is a happy, bright, and healthy child. Lily started seeing a physical therapist (PT) when she was 7 months old, an occupational therapist (OT) when she was 10 months old, and an early intervention teacher when she was 14 months old. The OT addresses issues related to fine motor, oral-motor, and self-care skills. In the fine motor area, Lily needs assistance with reach, grasp, release, and manipulation of toys. No definite hand preference has developed yet. The parents want help with her eating because she thrusts her tongue during meals, making it difficult to eat food textures appropriate for her age level. She now eats soft foods such as bread, macaroni and cheese, and pasta, as well as mashed and pureed items. Also, Lily needs additional postural support during play, eating, and transportation due to her inability to sit independently. Lily will be referred to throughout this chapter to exemplify early intervention approaches and considerations that relate to fine motor, oral-motor, and self-care development.

This chapter examines development, assessment and intervention in the areas of fine motor, oral motor, and self-care skills. **Fine motor skills** reflect a child's ability to manipulate and control objects and tools through control of the upper extremities and small muscle movements of the hands. **Oral motor** refers to movement of the tongue, jaw, lips, and cheeks during sucking, swallowing, munching, chewing, spoon-feeding and drinking from a bottle or cup. **Self-care skills** refer to basic activities such as dressing, toileting, bathing, grooming, self-feeding, and communicating. They also can include functional mobility and more mature skills such as maintaining health, taking medication, and managing emergencies (Shepherd, 2001). Other terms used to address the same domain include *self-help*, *adaptive skills*, or *activities of daily living.*

Fine motor development provides the means by which children interact with and learn about the world around them. A child learns about the perceptual features of objects in the environment by holding objects, bringing them to the mouth, and manipulating them so that what is felt can be paired with what is seen. It is through the hands that a child can experiment with cognitive concepts such as object permanence, cause and effect, classification, and conservation. It is through the development of fine motor skills that the child learns how to connect with and have an effect upon his world. In fact, it is through the hands that a child can demonstrate what he has learned. Most measures of cognitive function rely on the child's ability to control objects with the hands. Clearly, fine motor skills are necessary for children to fully participate in activities that form much of the curriculum in early childhood learning environments. Even in second-grade classrooms, 50% of the time is devoted to fine motor tasks (McHale & Cermak, 1992).

Oral motor, fine motor, and self-care skills have several common attributes. Each requires the coordination of movement with sensory processes, which may include **tactile** sensation, proprioception, and vision. In addition, each is dependent to some degree upon gross motor and postural skills, which provide the scaffold upon which fine motor, oral motor, and self-care skills develop. As the child's developmental tasks in each area increase with age, the child's ability to control the head, trunk, and limbs becomes more crucial.

Tactile refers to the child's ability to perceive touch to the skin.

Theories of Fine Motor Development

Current views of the development of fine motor control reflect the theoretical models for motor development described in Chapter 7. The reflex/hierarchical model has influenced most descriptions of motor development in very young children. The earliest voluntary movements of newborns appear to be random and lacking in coordination. Postural and motor reflexes provide the very young infant with ways of interacting with the environment (Case-Smith, 2001). As noted in Chapter 7, primitive reflexes are stereotypic, predictable movement patterns that are triggered by specific sensory stimuli. Many of the primitive reflexes observed in very young children have a function in development of voluntary control of movement. Some examples follow: (1) When an infant's head is turned to one side, the arm on that side of the body will extend in the asymmetrical tonic neck reflex (ATNR). This reflex provides the first opportunity for eye-hand coordination in the very young child. (2) When touch is applied to the back of an infant's hand, the baby will open his fingers in an **avoidance response.** (3) When an object is placed in the palm of a month-old infant, the hand will close around the object in the grasp reflex.

This combination of reflexes provides the necessary components for voluntary grasp and release. These gross responses gradually become more differentiated as the infant matures. By 6 months of age, only the fingers that are in contact with an object will flex and the hand will begin to move in the direction of the tactile stimulus. At about this same time, infants can use information from both the tactile and visual systems to reach toward an object and open the hand to grasp an object, representing a transition from reflexive grasp to purposeful, voluntary grasp. This transition from reflexive to voluntary movement is representative of a shift in motor control from lower centers of the central nervous system to higher, cortical control. Practice in reach and grasp results in a smoother motor pattern through structural changes in the brain brought about by learning. Treatment approaches developed from the reflex/hierarchical model include **neurodevelopmental treatment (NDT)** and **sensory integration (SI);** these intervention approaches will be discussed later in this chapter.

Thelen, Corbetta, Kamm, and Spencer (1993) have suggested that, although movement appears to develop in a sequential way, the idea that different movement patterns are stored in the brain and called into use to address movement needs should be questioned. The authors believe that such a system of motor control would be inefficient to meet all motor demands. They suggest that motor behavior changes in response to the demands of the situation. Development and motor learning occur through a number of different systems.

For example, differences in body size and composition as well as object properties will yield different patterns for reach and grasp. The findings of this study support a dynamical systems view of fine motor development (Shumway-Cook & Woollacott, 2001), wherein motor control is a dynamic process that responds to properties and constraints of the body and the environment. There are few treatment approaches that have been developed around these newer theories of motor control and development; however, sensory integration therapy considers the motivation of the child and the meaningfulness of the task as important parameters of treatment (Reeves & Cermak, 2002).

Stages of Fine Motor Development

Fine motor skills are comprised of precise movements of the hands and fingers, supported by **stability** of the trunk and control of the shoulder girdle and arms. The skilled, preferred use of one hand **(hand preference),** the ability to use two hands

Avoidance response is a primitive hand reflex set off by touch to the back of the hand.

Neurodevelopmental treatment (NDT) therapeutic practices are used for children with neurological involvement to facilitate improved posture and movement for functional tasks. NDT uses touch and the forces of gravity to stimulate improved movement.

Sensory integration (SI) is the ability of the child to organize basic sensory information including tactile (touch), proprioceptive (perception of body and joint movement), vestibular (tone and posture), visual (sight), auditory (hearing), olfactory (smell), and gustatory (taste) in order to make an active response to environmental demands.

Stability is the ability to maintain a posture against gravity.

Sensory processing is the way a child receives (sensory registration), regulates (sensory modulation), and habituates to incoming sensory information.

together, and the ability to perform different tasks with each hand also are needed for children to carry out complex movements. In addition to motor control, fine motor skills require adequate cognition and **sensory processing** of tactile, proprioceptive, and visual information (Mulligan, 2002).

Fine motor control is defined as a child's ability to functionally reach, grasp, and release objects for purposeful manipulation of toys and tools. Development in each of these areas is supported by a child's increasing control in flexion, extension, coactivation, and rotation of the shoulder girdle, forearm, and hand. The foundational components of reach, grasp, and release mature within the first 2 years, allowing for development of higher level manipulative skills in the toddler and preschool-aged child.

Reach

Reaching is the movement of the arm toward an object. Components for the development of reach are mature by approximately 6 months in supine, 7 months in prone, and 12 months in sitting (Erhardt, 1994b). The development of reach patterns is outlined in Table 8.1.

When a newborn is placed on his stomach, arms are flexed and close to the body. Weight is centered mostly at the head and shoulders. As extension develops from head to toe, the infant learns to lift and turn the head. The infant then progresses from bearing weight on forearms to pushing up on extended arms, which helps to develop stability in the shoulder girdle for reach. The ability to free an arm for reaching occurs when the infant can stabilize the pelvis and shift weight toward one side, thus freeing an arm for reach.

Arm movements of the newborn in supine are random and disorganized and the ability to look at hands has not yet developed. At 2 months of age, when the

TABLE 8.1 Development of Reach

Age of Acquisition	Fine Motor Skills
2 months	arms activate upon sight of object
3 months	swipes at object
4 months	hands to midline
	bilateral reach
	contacts object in midline
5 months	underreaches for object
	reaches in prone on forearms
6 months	overreaches for object
	circular reach in sitting with one arm
7 months	reaches in prone on extended arms
8 months	direct reach in sitting with one arm
12 months	forearm supination with reach

Source: Adapted from *Developmental Hand Dysfunction* (2nd ed.): *Theory, Assessment, and Treatment* by R. Erhardt, 1994a, San Antonio, TX: Therapy Skill Builders. Copyright is held by author. Adapted by permission.

infant turns his head to one side, the arm on that same side extends while the opposite extremities flex as a result of the influence of the asymmetrical tonic neck reflex. This action provides the first visual connection between the eyes and the arm. Swiping with one hand occurs as the infant is able to look at interesting faces and objects. Reach progresses from this random swiping to purposeful reaching with both arms together. When the infant is supine, the surface of the floor or crib provides stability for the shoulder girdle. Two-handed reaching is replaced as the infant matures by the use of one arm in a direct approach toward an object. This movement demonstrates the ability to differentiate one arm from the other. Further refinement occurs when the infant is able to supinate the forearm while reaching (Erhardt, 1994). **Supination,** which is a critical component of controlled use of the thumb and fingers, is the ability to rotate the forearm so that the thumb moves in an upward direction and the object within the hand is clearly visible to the infant.

Grasp

Grasp is the attainment of an object with the hand. Grasp is usually described according to the placement of the object held within the hand; however, wrist stability and forearm rotation are important factors that affect grasp. Grasp on an object is reflexive during the first 2 to 3 months; an infant does not have voluntary control of grasp. A primitive squeeze grasp is the child's first attempt to grasp smaller objects against the palm (Halverson 1931); the thumb is not actively used with this grasp (Erhardt, 1994b). Over the next few months, grasp of small objects progresses from the middle of the palm **(palmar grasp)** to the radial or thumb side of the hand **(radial palmar grasp),** and finally to the thumb and digits **(radial digital grasp)** (Erhardt 1994b; Gesell & Amatruda, 1947). For tiny objects, such as a pellet, very young children will attempt to rake the object with the fingers and trap it against the palm. Next the child will grasp an object on the side of the index finger with the thumb **(scissors grasp)** (Gesell & Amatruda, 1947). A **fine pincer grasp** (Erhardt, 1994b) reflects the ability to pick up a small, pellet-sized object between the tips of the index finger and thumb forming an open web space, with the other fingers flexed and the wrist held in slight extension (Figure 8.1). A mature pincer grasp indicates that the child has developed the ability to use one side of the hand actively while the other side is quiet. The development of grasp patterns is outlined in Table 8.2.

The developmental sequence of pencil grasp progresses from an immature grasp to a **transitional grasp** to a mature pattern (Schneck & Henderson, 1990). Initially, a child uses an immature palmar grasp on a crayon. The shoulder is stable while the entire arm moves as a unit when scribbling (Erhardt, 1994b). Immature grasp on a tool includes holding the object in the palm of the hand with the fingers flexed around the shaft and with the forearm turned in **pronation** (Figure 8.2) or supination.

In a transitional grasp, movement is initiated from the hand and forearm. The **dynamic tripod grasp** (Figure 8.3), the most commonly used mature grasp, incorporates dynamic and precise alternating movements of the index finger, middle fin-

A transitional grasp refers to grasp patterns that evidence a "transition" from immature grasps to mature patterns.

Pronation is the movement of the forearm in a direction toward the body, resulting in the palm turning downward.

Pronated palmar grasp refers to the grasp of an object where the arm and forearm position the hand so the palm and thumb are facing downward.

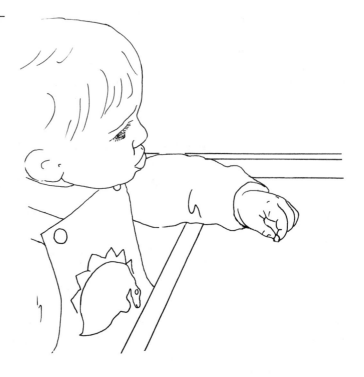

FIGURE 8.1   Pincer grasp in a 2-year-old child. Note the tip-to-tip prehension and open web space

Source: Used by permission of Jean Patz.

Supinated palmar grasp refers to the grasp of an object where the arm and forearm position the hand so the palm and thumb are facing upward.

ger, and thumb during writing, with the ring finger and little finger stabilized in flexion (Long, Conrad, Hall, & Furler, 1970; Rosenbloom & Horton, 1971). The wrist is stable, and the space between the thumb and index finger is rounded, forming an open web space. Young children tend to hold a pencil in the middle of the shaft, whereas mature finger placement is closer to the tip of the pencil.

Release

Release is the purposeful letting go of an object held within the hand. Voluntary release begins when the infant mouths toys, transferring objects from hand-to-mouth and back to hand. At this stage, the infant releases toys by stabilizing the object in the mouth and pulling it with the opposite hand or releasing it against a surface. Direct transfer from hand-to-hand occurs by approximately 7 months (Erhardt, 1994b). Active release occurs by 10 to 11 months, along with the development of object permanence as the child purposefully drops objects from the highchair, for example, with full arm, wrist, and finger extension (Case-Smith, 1995).

Erhardt (1994b) indicates that controlled release of a cube and pellet into a small opening develops by 12 months and 15 months, respectively. As control of release continues, the child is able to place objects into small containers, build towers (Figure 8.4), and release a ball. The development of voluntary release is outlined in Table 8.3.

TABLE 8.2 Development of Grasp

Age	Cube/Pencil/Utensil	Pellet
1 month	Hands mostly fisted Grasp reflex	
3 months	Hands mostly open-loosely closed in supine, fisted in prone Grasp reflex diminishes Brief grasp with ulnar digits— sustained if placed, no active reach	
4 months	Primitive squeeze grasp	
5 months	Palmar grasp	
6 months	Radial palmar grasp	Raking grasp
7 months		Inferior scissors grasp
8 months	Radial digital grasp Active palmar arches	Scissors grasp
9 months		Inferior pincer grasp
10 months		Pincer grasp
12 months	Palmar grasp on crayon	Fine pincer grasp
15 months	Pincer grasp with ulnar fingers stabilized	
2 1/2–3 years	Begin digital pronate on crayon	
3–4 years	Adult grasp on spoon begins	
4–5 years	Use transitional grips on pencil (cross thumb, 4 finger, lateral tripod); Static tripod grasp on pencil	
5–6 years	Dynamic tripod grasp on pencil	

Source: Adapted from *Developmental Hand Dysfunction: Theory, Assessment and Treatment* (2nd ed.), by R. Erhardt (1994a), San Antonio, TX: Therapy Skill Builders. Adapted by permission. Adapted from Descriptive analysis of the developmental progression of grip position for pencil and crayon control in nondysfunctional children by C. Schneck & A. Henderson, 1990, The *American Journal of Occupational Therapy, 44,* 893–900.

Fine Motor Development in Toddlers and Preschoolers

Manipulation

This section addresses how young children combine reach, grasp, and release to perform functional tasks, such as those involved in play, prewriting, and cutting with scissors. The focus is on tasks that often are problematic for young children with special needs, including the poor use of both hands to manipulate objects, the lack of development of a hand preference, and the inability to move an object within the hand.

Bilateral Development. Asymmetry is noted in an infant's arm movements during the first few months of life. Then, the infant begins to move his arms together at approximately 3 months of age when the hands are brought to the chest in midline.

FIGURE 8.2 Pronated palmar grasp on a crayon in a 2-year-old child. Note that the writing arm moves as a unit, while the left hand supports the paper.

Source: Used by permission of Jean Patz.

FIGURE 8.3 Tripod grasp on a marker with slight forearm supination, wrist extension, thumb and finger opposition, and an open web space.

Source: Used by permission of Jean Patz.

FIGURE 8.4 Controlled release enables the child to successfully build a tower.

Source: Used by permission of Jean Patz.

TABLE 8.3 Development of Voluntary Release

Age	Skill
0–2 months	No voluntary release; avoiding-response reflex
1 month	Immediate involuntary release of objects after brief retaining
3 months	Involuntary release of objects after sustained grasp
5 months	Beginning direct transfer of object from hand-to-hand
6 months	Indirect transfer from hand-to-mouth-to-hand
7 months	Successful hand-to-hand transfer; releases objects against a surface; object permanence
8 months	Clumsy release into large container
9 months	Controlled release into large container
10 months	Drops object from high chair
12 months	Precise release with cube; minimal finger extension
	Begins graded hand opening; begins to stack blocks
15 months	Precise release of pellet into small container
2–3 years	Smooth, graded release of objects

Source: Adapted from *Developmental Hand Dysfunction: Theory, Assessment and Treatment* (2nd ed.), by R. Erhardt 1994a. San Antonio, TX: Therapy Skill Builders. Copyright is held by author. Adapted by permission.

Bilateral activities include reaching with two hands at 4 to 5 months, transferring from hand to hand by 6 to 8 months, and clapping hands or banging objects together by the end of the first year. Between 12 and 18 months of age, the child uses one hand for manipulation and the other for stabilization (Exner, 2001) (e.g., holding a bucket while pouring sand with a shovel or stabilizing a bowl while scooping with

FIGURE 8.5 Complementary use of both hands as seen in stringing beads. The child uses in-hand manipulation (shift) while threading the bead

Source: Used by permission of Jean Patz.

a spoon). The ability to use opposing hand and arm movements for highly differentiated activities emerges at approximately 18 to 24 months and matures by 2 to 3 years of age (Connor, Williamson, & Siepp, 1978; Exner, 2001). Stringing beads (Figure 8.5) and cutting with scissors are examples of the complementary use of both hands. By 3 1/2 to 4 years of age, a child can hold scissors correctly and rotate the forearm to guide the scissors; the child is able to move the paper in coordination with cutting by 6 years of age (Lopez, 1986). Development of **bilateral hand skills** is the ability to use the hands together during functional tasks.

Hand Preference.   Development of hand preference allows the child success with precise control of one hand for skilled tasks. Right- or left-handedness is noticed around 18 months (Batshaw, 1997) and a clear hand preference becomes apparent during the preschool years (Gesell & Ames, 1947; Harris & Carlson, 1988; McManus et al., 1988; Tan, 1985). A history of a persistent and strong hand preference under 1 year of age may be indicative of a motor deficit.

In-Hand Manipulation.   Whereas grasp patterns capture children's abilities to statically hold objects and to use objects efficiently in many daily tasks, children must be able to move objects within the hand. For example, a child who is given several coins will pick them up with his fingertips and transfer them to a palm one at a time **(translation).** When stringing beads, a child needs to move the end of the string in

BOX 8.1	Fine Motor Empathy Exercises

- Pick up several coins, one at a time, and store them in your palm. This skill is finger-to-palm translation with stabilization. Now pretend you have increased postural tone. Pull your thumb in toward your palm and hold your wrist slightly bent and try the same task. Imagine a child with spastic cerebral palsy trying to pick up small objects in a timely manner
- Cut with a pair of scissors. Note the positions and mobility of your forearm during cutting,. Now pronate your forearm (thumb points down toward the floor as in a child with increased postural tone). Keep your forearm in that position while cutting. What do you experience?
- Grasp your pencil and write your name noting the position of your 4th and 5th fingers. Now write your name again with those same fingers extended instead of flexed. What happens to the quality of your writing? This exercise points out the need to stabilize the non-working side of the hand during coloring and writing.
- Grasp your pencil and write a sentence noting which direction the end of the pencil points. Typically it points back toward your shoulder. Now try writing the same sentence with the eraser end of the pencil pointing straight up toward the ceiling. Do you feel less control of the writing tool?

the fingers for more accurate placement **(shift)** (refer to Figure 8.5), and, when using a key, a child may need to rotate the key in a hand so that the correct end faces the keyhole **(rotation).** Exner (2001) proposes that these "in-hand manipulation skills" represent a higher level of fine motor skills than grasp alone. These skills begin to emerge between 12 and 15 months of age. A key time for development is from 2 to 4 years of age, with increasing speed, efficiency, and refinement of in-hand manipulation skills occurring through 12 years of age. See Box 8.1 to learn about fine motor empathy exercises.

Factors Affecting Fine Motor Development

When considering atypical fine motor development, it may be helpful to conceptualize three distinct areas of concern. The first is the ability to use the body as a stable base or a foundation for arm use. The second is the development of the basic components of reach, grasp, and release. The third is the combined use of these components for object manipulation in functional activities such as play and self-feeding.

Although problems may exist in postural control in addition to reach, grasp, and release, often fine motor difficulties are not identified until the child demonstrates problems integrating these skills for object manipulation. Parents may find that they have difficulty selecting toys for the child because the child is unable to play with age-appropriate items. They may note problems when the child is expected to use two hands together to manipulate toys or to use objects as tools.

Fine motor difficulties may result from atypical postural tone, persistent primitive reflexes, sensory processing deficits, poor motor planning, perceptual difficulties, and cognitive delay. Red flags suggestive of fine motor problems (Figure 8.6) can alert a teacher to potential difficulties in postural control, reach, grasp, release, and manipulation.

REACH
- inability to bring the hands to midline after 4 months of age
- motor inability or lack of interest in reaching for objects by 6 months of age
- tremors upon reach
- inaccurate or indirect reaching after 9 months of age

GRASP
- continual fisting of the hands with thumb in palm beyond 3 months of age; hands are typically open by three months
- lack of variety of grasp patterns to accommodate size and shape of objects
- lack of ability to isolate the index finger for pointing after 10 to 12 months of age
- persistence of a palmar grasp beyond 12 months of age
- lack of supination of the forearm
- lack of development of a pincer grasp by 15 months of age
- awkward grasp on the pencil during manuscript or cursive writing; thumb wrapped around pencil; presses too hard when writing
- refusal to use eating utensils during preschool years

RELEASE
- excessive dropping of objects
- inability to actively transfer (coordinate grasp and release) after 6–7 months
- unable to stack a few blocks after 15–18 months

MANIPULATION
- strong preferred use of one hand under 1 year of age (hand preference is generally not seen before 12 months of age)
- poor visual attention to toys
- inability or unwillingness to manipulate toys; cannot play with age-appropriate toys
- extreme difficulty learning how to manipulate scissors by age 3–4 years or later; inability to coordinate after much instruction (dependent on exposure)
- lack of a hand preference by first grade; continual switching of hands while eating or using a pencil
- frequent dropping of objects
- poor handwriting skills
- difficulty copying from the chalkboard

PARENTAL CONCERN
- difficulty choosing toys for the child

FIGURE 8.6   Red flags suggestive of fine motor problems

Source: Used by permission of Jean Patz.

Neuromotor dysfunction is a condition characterized by atypical muscle function, tone, or movement.

As noted earlier, a child with hypertonia may sit with a posterior pelvic tilt, resulting in a rounded trunk and limited ability to raise the arms (see the story of Lily in the opening vignette). Such a child may compensate by elevating his shoulder and leaning forward when reaching for objects, rather than extending the arm, as a result of decreased range of motion. In addition, shoulder retraction and elevation (pulling back and raising the shoulders) may limit his ability to bring the hands to midline. Tremors may be a red flag indicating the possibility of specific **neuromotor dysfunction** or generalized weakness.

Hypotonia in the trunk interferes with upright sitting, which limits the range available to reach forward. If trunk rotation has not developed as a result of poor proximal stability, reach across the midline will be affected. The child subsequently is forced to reach with the hand closest to the object. The child may have difficulty stabilizing his arm against gravity to reach for objects.

FIGURE 8.7 Child with spastic quadriplegic cerebral palsy with similar atypical positioning in both arms resulting from increased tone. Note elbow flexion, forearm pronation, wrist flexion, and ulnar deviation upon grasp with a built-up handled spoon and scoop dish.

Source: Used by permission of Jean Patz.

Wrist stability in slight extension is needed for mature grasping patterns; poor control of the trunk, shoulder, elbow, and forearm affects the ability to control the wrist and subsequently the hand for grasp. Wrist flexion with ulnar deviation resulting from increased muscle tone (Figure 8.7) interferes with fine motor control. Thumb adduction into the palm, a pattern seen in children with more involved neuromotor problems, prevents any oppositional use of the thumb. Persistent use of the entire hand in an immature palmar grasp indicates that the child cannot differentiate one side of the hand from the other. Inability to isolate the index finger to point (in a child who is cognitively ready for this skill) may be a red flag indicating poorly differentiated movements; the child may not have the motor ability to separate one finger from the others. The lack of development of rotational patterns, which is typical in children with fine motor delay, also interferes with a mature grasp. For example, the lack of forearm rotation in supination makes it difficult for the child to mechanically use mature grasps and to see and learn about the object grasped as the palm faces downward. Also, limited rotation in the proximal joints of the fingers, and particularly the thumb, interrupts the finger-to-thumb opposition needed to grasp small objects or a pencil.

A child with poor hand use may develop compensatory patterns during grasp that are not efficient or precise. For example, a child with hypotonia will have difficulty with finger stability in the fine pincer grasp as a result of increased mobility in the joints. In addition, a child with hypotonia or poor sensation in the hand may grip a pencil by wrapping the thumb tightly over the pencil shaft instead of opposing the tips of the thumb and index finger on the pencil. With this type of compensatory pencil grip, key clues include a closed web space, lack of distal finger movements during pencil use, and heavy markings with occasional tearing of the paper. Poor motor planning, or dyspraxia, may be suspected when a child with no apparent motor dysfunction has more difficulty than expected learning how to grasp tools such as scissors, pencils, or eating utensils after repeated instruction.

Persistence of a primitive grasp pattern, fisting of the hand, exaggerated wrist flexion, limited thumb extension, or lack of forearm supination may all interfere with controlled release. Fisting of the hand, typically seen in children with neuromotor dysfunction, prevents voluntary opening of the hand for release. The inability to bring the hands to the midline will inhibit direct hand-to-hand transfer of an object, the first stage of release. Poor proximal stability of the wrist and lack of forearm supination prevent control in midposition for precise release.

During the toddler and preschool years, a child may demonstrate continued resistance to using age-appropriate tools such as scissors, a pencil, or a spoon and instead prefer direct contact with his hands, or a child may prefer to play with the toys of younger children. A child who has difficulty manipulating objects within one hand will use compensatory patterns rather than in-hand manipulation skills. Common compensatory substitution patterns include assistance in object manipulation by supporting the object with the other hand, the chest, or a table surface. These children frequently drop objects.

Fine Motor Development in Young Children with Special Needs

In this section, sensorimotor characteristics related to selected diagnostic categories are discussed. The anticipated developmental progression of motor skills in children with these exceptionalities also is provided. It is important to recognize that the common concerns presented here are subsumed under the educational classifications described in Chapter 1. For example, Down syndrome typically is included under the classification of mental retardation, whereas cerebral palsy may fit within one of several classifications (e.g., orthopedic impairment).

Cerebral Palsy

Fine motor dysfunction in children with neurological problems such as cerebral palsy may be caused by tonal abnormalities, sensory deficits, and existence of primitive postural reflexes such as the asymmetrical tonic neck reflex (ATNR). For example, if the ATNR is present because of delayed integration, turning the head to the side dictates increased tone, thus creating extension in the extremities on the face side and increased flexion on the skull side. This persistent primitive reflex makes it difficult for the child to bring his hands together or maintain visual attention to the hand engaged in an activity that requires elbow flexion, such as bringing a cup to the mouth (Erhardt, 1994). Hypertonia restricts the range of motion available during reach. Hypotonia, on the other hand, may prevent lifting the arms up against gravity to meet in the midline or to reach.

A child who has variable or fluctuating postural tone, as in athetosis, demonstrates difficulty in grading movements for reach. The child will attempt to minimize **involuntary movements** by using compensatory stabilizing patterns such as elevating the shoulders to stabilize the head for eye-hand coordination during reach, locking the elbows in **hyperextension,** or adducting and internally rotating the arms.

Flexor spasticity in the arm interferes with grasp patterns (refer to Figures 8.7 and 8.8). The child often is unable to see what he has grasped and to use the thumb-to-fingertip opposition needed to prehend small objects or maintain grasp on a pencil.

> Involuntary movement refers to a movement produced without volition or voluntary control.

> Hyperextension describes excessive or unnatural movement in the direction of extension.

FIGURE 8.8 Atypical posturing in a preschool-aged child with left spastic hemiplegic cerebral palsy. The effort of work with the right hand further increases muscle tone in the left extremity, causing the left arm to pull toward the body with elbow flexion, deviation of the wrist, and fisting of the hand.

Source: Used by permission of Jean Patz.

A child with decreased or variable tone uses primitive grasp patterns such as the palmar grasp for stabilization.

Bilateral (two-handed) control needed during manipulation may be affected by the existence of tonal abnormalities. A child with spastic hemiplegia displays asymmetry in movement as a result of both motor and sensory involvement (Figure 8.8). As a child with spastic hemiplegia manipulates objects with the noninvolved hand, overflow or associated reactions may be noted in the involved extremity. Typically, the child disregards or neglects the involved upper extremity because of poor sensory awareness in that arm. Additionally, restricted active movement and posturing of the involved side behind the noninvolved side reinforces this neglect. Exaggerated movements may eventually develop in the noninvolved extremity because of overuse of compensatory patterns with that arm (Connor et al., 1978). A child with hemiplegia may not tolerate being touched on the involved arm and will resist any attempts to integrate that arm into fine motor activities.

Down Syndrome

Children with Down syndrome have small, slender bones with poor calcification, low-set thumbs, short fingers, and delayed development of the carpal bones causing initial instability in the hand (Benda, 1969). As in gross motor skills development, the child with Down syndrome is likely to use bilateral, symmetrical movements of

Hypermobility is defined as excessive mobility or range of motion in joints.

the upper extremities instead of differentiated movements, with minimal use of trunk rotation to support efficient reach. Low muscle tone results in **hypermobility** in the proximal finger and thumb joints which interferes with grasp. Grasp patterns may be immature, with continued use of palmar grasps instead of thumb and index finger opposition, poor differentiation of finger use and poor prepositioning of the hand for grasp. Cognitive limitations also affect fine motor skill development. Edwards and Lafreniere (1995) provide a good overview of assessment and intervention strategies to use with children who have Down syndrome.

Some researchers have suggested that children with Down syndrome may have deficits in receiving sensory information. Cole, Abbs, and Turner (1988) found that children with Down syndrome displayed an inability to adapt grip forces to characteristics of objects which was unrelated to hypotonia. In addition, the skin of children with Down syndrome may be thick and dry, possibly impairing sensation as age increases (Edwards & Lafreniere, 1995).

Disorders of Sensory Regulation

Children with disorders of sensory regulation may have heightened or diminished responsivity to sensory stimuli. Children who are hyperresponsive to stimuli may be very sensitive to lights, sound, touch, or movement and demonstrate overarousal and difficulty in focusing attention to the task at hand. In addition they may have significant difficulty interacting appropriately with peers and adults. They may find some stimuli noxious, and may avoid these stimuli as much as is possible. A child who has difficulty integrating tactile stimuli, for example, may avoid certain types of clothing, play things, and food, thus limiting experiences. They may find the touch of another person irritating, and may strike out when touched accidentally by a child, or avoid being hugged by their parents. Studies have found that moderate to severe regulatory difficulties in infancy are highly predictive of perceptual, language, sensory integrative, and behavioral and emotional problems at the preschool ages (DeGangi, Breinbauer, Roosevelt, Porges, & Greenspan, 2000; Gutman, McCreedy, & Heisler, 2002).

Vestibular functions relate to structures in the inner ear that are involved in posture and balance maintenance.

Early identification of children with disorders of sensory regulation is important so that parents and professionals can intervene to prevent the worsening of these problems. Information about such problems is usually gained from parent interviews and child observations. Questionnaires such as the Infant/Toddler Sensory Profile (Dunn, 2000), the Sensory Profile for children ages 3 and older (Dunn, 1999), and the Evaluation of Sensory Processing (Bundy, 2002; Parham & Ecker, 2002) along with clinical observations are measures that an occupational therapist may use to screen for possible problems with sensory regulation.

Autism

Children with autism and other pervasive developmental disorders frequently demonstrate difficulties responding appropriately to sensory stimuli. A number of anomalies involving registration, modulation, and response to sensory stimuli have been described in children with autism. Miller, Reisman, McIntosh, and Simon (2001) reported hyporeactive physiological responses to sensory information, yet severe hyperreactive behavioral responses to tactile, taste, smell, movement, visual, and auditory sensations in a small sample of children with autism. Volkmar, Cohen, and Paul (1986) reported that most parents described their young children with autism as being hyporeactive to sound and pain stimulation, yet hyperreactive to visual, tactile, and auditory stimuli. The apparent contradiction in responsivity to auditory stimuli may be explained by reports that children with autism may not respond to verbal commands and may have difficulty processing auditory information, but they may become very upset at the presence of specific environmental sounds or loud or unusual auditory stimuli (e.g., a vacuum cleaner, door bell). Other frequent sensory manifestations are a fascination with some visual stimuli (e.g., rotating fans and moving lights), an apparent insensitivity to pain, a tendency to lick or smell objects, and an aversion to specific foods (Rapin, 1988). Differences in tactile processing may be seen in avoidance or obsession with specific textures of objects or foods or the avoidance of touch to particular body parts.

Gross and fine motor development in young children with autism, although often the most successful area of development (Cox, 1993), is nonetheless often significantly delayed (Watson & Marcus, 1986). These children may appear to be physically agile and often do quite well in activities such as completing puzzles and block designs, but they may have difficulties in tasks requiring the planning and sequencing of movement (e.g., pedaling a tricycle, drawing, folding a paper). The ability of children with autism to gather accurate information about their own bodies through proprioception and through visual perception, both of which are required for imitation of motor movement, is questionable. Young children with autism are notably poor at imitating the behavior of others, which may be primary to the problems of socialization and communication inherent in children with autism (Meltzoff & Gopnik, 1993).

Specific deficits related to motor development that have been noted in children with autism include decreased postural tone, toe walking, drooling, clumsiness, delayed onset of walking (Rapin, 1988), decreased balance, incoordination, and poor finger-to-thumb movements (Jones & Prior, 1985). Stereotypic motor movements are commonly seen among children with autism. These behaviors may involve hand and arm flapping, finger flicking, rocking, and body spinning. There are two divergent schools of thought regarding the function of these behaviors. Lovaas, Newsom, and Hickman (1987) state that stereotypic movements represent the child's attempt to achieve a state of optimum arousal. King and Grandin (1990), on the other hand, speculate that these behaviors serve the function of calming an overaroused system. Although self-injurious behavior, which is not uncommon in children with autism, has been described as an attempt at communication or as a response to frustration (Van Bourgondien, 1993), it might also represent an inability to cope with intense sensory discomfort. Grandin (1995), in her description of sensory problems in individuals with autism, explains that severe sensory processing problems may result in great bodily discomfort. Deep pressure stimulation has been reported to be effective in dealing with overarousal in children and adults with autism (Grandin, 1995; Nelson, 1984).

For children with autism, severe sensory problems may create significant bodily discomfort.

Because of the sensory processing difficulties often present in children with autism, **sensory integrative therapy,** which is a method of improving registration, modulation, and adaptation to sensory input (Ayres, 1985), has been suggested as an intervention approach (Grandin, 1995; Mailloux & Roley, 2001; Siegel, 1996; Williamson & Anzalone, 1997). Efficacy studies have supported the use of SI intervention in children with autism (Case-Smith & Bryan, 1999; Ray, King, & Grandin, 1988). Case-Smith and Bryan found a decrease in nonengaged behavior and an increase in goal directed play in preschool children with autism who received SI intervention.

Indirect sensory integrative therapy for the child with a sensory processing disorder includes explaining behavior to parents and teachers, thus building better interaction, and modifying the environment to allow optimal function (Williamson & Anzalone, 1997). Direct approaches to intervention may include providing graded, specific sensory input to the child in a supportive environment. Stimuli may be designed to improve arousal and attention, or it may be designed to help calm the child. The goal is always for the child to respond appropriately to the sensory input by demonstrating improved emotional responses or to participate in goal-directed play or work experiences.

Vignette 8.1 describes an autism case study.

Vignette 8.1

JAKE

Jake is a 3 1/2-year-old child diagnosed with autism. He was referred to his county's early education program. Occupational therapy (OT), speech therapy, special education, and psychological services were involved in the evaluation process. Following the evaluation, he was found to be eligible for special education services with an educational disability of autism. The occupational therapist used the Hawaii Early Learning Profile (Furuno et al., 1997). Information was gathered from the family regarding his response to movement, sound, vision, and touch as well as oral sensory processing using the Sensory Profile (Dunn, 1999).

An individualized education plan (IEP) was developed with input from the family. It was recommended that Jake be placed in a full-day preschool program where he would receive OT services to increase the variety of his food intake, expand his play skills, and improve his response to sensory input. Jake's play primarily consists of dashing around a room with no "obvious" purpose, crashing against walls or onto the floor. He swings for lengthy periods and often has a temper tantrum when asked to stop. Jake will play with familiar puzzles, preferring letter and number puzzles, and he will stack and line up his toys. He constantly puts these toys in his mouth. When angry or frustrated, Jake will kick family members. He covers his ears when he hears a vacuum cleaner or a lawnmower. Jake does watch other children and family members at play, but prefers to observe rather than to interact with them. He can remove all his clothes, in addition to having strong preferences about the types of clothes he wears.

Jake prefers eating "beige" and crunchy foods such as cereals, french fries, bread, cookies, and crackers. Attempts at introducing other foods result in severe temper tantrums. He eats no fruits or vegetables and only occasionally will he eat chicken.

A sensorimotor program was developed by the occupational therapist to increase Jake's tolerance to light touch, decrease his need for strong proprioceptive input, decrease his strong need for movement, and increase the variety of his food intake. Modifications and techniques were introduced one at a time in order to evaluate the effectiveness of the various sensory interventions which consisted of tactile, proprioceptive, and vestibular activities. This program was explained to the parents and educational team and was integrated into the classroom routine. For example, suggestions included Jake sitting on a special movable cushion or therapy ball during circle and work time in order to better attend to his work and give him opportunities for movement. Also, an OT created a new feeding program that was carried out daily at snack and lunch.

Disorders of Sensory Discrimination

Some children may have difficulty perceiving or discriminating sensory stimuli accurately. As noted in Chapter 7, some children with developmental dyspraxia and developmental coordination disorder cannot effectively integrate sensory information provided by their own bodies and their environment. **Dyspraxia** is an impairment in the ability to plan nonhabitual motor tasks, which results in clumsiness; this is usually not a problem with motor execution but with motor planning (Reeves & Cermak, 2002). Children with developmental dyspraxia may have difficulty integrating sensory information from their own bodies with environmental information, and often they cannot adapt their motor behavior to changing environmental demands (Goodgold-Edwards & Cermak, 1989; Reeves & Cermak, 2002). These children have difficulty with complex fine motor tasks across developmental stages. A toddler might find it difficult to motor plan building a block tower, manipulating an unfamiliar toy, or using tools such as a crayon or spoon. During the preschool years, poor motor planning would be evident in such fine motor tasks as coloring, drawing, cutting with scissors, putting puzzles together, working with small manipulatives (such as beads and Legos®), and manipulating fasteners on clothing.

Unfortunately, many children with these difficulties are not referred to occupational therapy until they demonstrate problems keeping up with their peers in school, which can result in significant problems with self-esteem (Missiuna & Polatajko, 1995). However, the skilled professional can identify motor planning deficits at a much earlier age and plan interventions to allow the child to experience success and maintain feelings of self-adequacy.

Somatodyspraxia.   The term *somatodyspraxia* (Ayres, 1989) refers to a specific type of developmental dyspraxia caused by dysfunction in the ability to discriminate tactile information. Children with somatodyspraxia have impaired tactile and proprioceptive processing, which interferes with learning new motor tasks. Once the skill is learned, the child can accomplish the task, but generalization to other similar activities is difficult (Cermak, 1991).

The clinical picture of somatodyspraxia includes clumsiness, poor discrimination of tactile information, poor sequencing and timing of movements, difficulty learning self-care activities such as buttoning, problems in gross motor and fine motor activities including handwriting, and inadequate body schema (Cermak, 1991). These children have minimal oral motor problems related to feeding; oral problems are more commonly associated with oral dyspraxia. Poor motor planning may affect self-feeding skills, for example, by causing difficulty in using utensils. Reliance on finger feeding may therefore persist for an extended period to avoid frustration with utensils. Other characteristics may include sloppiness, poor attention span, and the inability to sit through an entire meal.

Early motor milestones such as crawling and walking are reported as age appropriate for children with somatodyspraxia, but they have difficulty with tasks such as manipulating fasteners and using scissors. A skilled observer often can recognize problems in the preschool years, but typically the disorder is not identified until the early school years, when demands on time, organization, and participation increase (Cermak, 1991; Levine, 1987). Early diagnosis can help prevent some of the difficulties and frustration that these children may encounter.

The diagnosis of somatodyspraxia is usually made by an occupational therapist after the analysis of results from clinical observations, pertinent historical information, and standardized testing using, for example, the DeGangi-Berk Test of Sensory Integration (Berk & DeGangi, 1983) for 3- to 5-year-olds or the Sensory Integration and Praxis Tests (SIPT; Ayres, 1989) for children 4 to 8 years of age. The SIPT is a standardized assessment tool measuring sensory integrative functions. Intervention for disorders of motor coordination is often based on the etiology of the disorder. For example, if the lack of coordination is believed to be due to problems with sensory integration, intervention may involve providing rich sensory experiences to provide the child with more information about the environment and the child's own body. Sensory integrative therapy would also structure the environment to maximize performance. An SI approach emphasizes the active processing of sensation by the child whereas sensory stimulation implies that the child is a "passive recipient of environmentally imposed stimuli" (Spitzer & Roley, 2001, p. 8).

Specific Strategies for Fine Motor Assessment

Keen observation of the child performing fine motor tasks within his own environment along with input from the parents provide useful information regarding the child's level of independence. The information gathered from medical and educational records, history from the caregivers, educators, and child, and direct observations in the child's environment is analyzed to give a functional picture of the child's level of mastery. The evaluator will want to ask the following questions: Are there developmentally appropriate toys and materials available in the child's environment? What structural barriers interfere with a child's mobility at home, school, or on the playground? What are the child's favorite toys? Do the parents have difficulty choosing toys for their child? Does the child dislike touching objects of different textures?

The cultural background of the family must be considered as well. The parents' concerns guide the evaluation when dealing with infants and toddlers. The occupational therapist interprets results of fine motor testing by critically analyzing how cognitive, motor, sensory, physical, psychosocial, behavioral, medical, and environmental issues affect performance. An evaluation is incomplete if the only areas considered are range of motion, strength, postural tone, and attention. The overall picture of the child's **occupational role** within the home, school, and community needs to be addressed.

Fine motor evaluation is often performed by an occupational therapist and includes clinical observations of the degree and distribution of postural tone, symmetry, range of motion, existence of primitive reflexes, righting and equilibrium reactions, and quality of movement. The level of mastery and independence in reach, grasp, release, manipulation, bilateral skills, and in-hand manipulation are evaluated during functional activities such as manipulating toys, scissors, or accessing a computer.

The Toddler and Infant Motor Evaluation (Miller & Roid, 1994) is a comprehensive standardized assessment to identify quality of movement and motor organization in infants and toddlers. Training in neurodevelopmental treatment (NDT) is recommended in order to adequately analyze test results. The Erhardt Developmental Prehension Assessment (EDPA)–Second Edition (Erhardt, 1994b) is a criterion-referenced test that addresses the presence of primitive reflexes and basic components of prehension, including reach, grasp, release, manipulation, and prewriting for children with developmental disabilities or neurological impairments. The Peabody Developmental Motor Scales II (Folio & Fewell, 2000) is a standardized, normed, and criterion-referenced test that evaluates both fine and gross motor abilities in children from birth through 5 years of age.

Broad-based developmental assessments such as the Hawaii Early Learning Profile (HELP) (Furuno et al., 1997), the HELP for Preschoolers (VORT Corporation, 1995), and the Learning Accomplishment Profile–Diagnostic Edition (LAP-D) (Nehring, Nehring, Bruni, & Randolph, 1992) include sections on fine motor development. The LAP-D divides the fine motor section into two subtests: manipulation and writing. These curriculum-based assessments cover the period from birth to 6 years of age (HELP) and 2 1/2 to 6 years (LAP-D).

Play is a primary occupation of a child and the early intervention professional will evaluate play skills through the use of play assessment tools such as the Test of Playfulness (Bundy, 1997), the Preschool Play Scale (Bledsoe & Shepherd, 1982; Knox, 1997), and the Transdisciplinary Play Based Assessment (Linder, 1993).

> Occupational role refers to the daily activities a child performs such as playing, dressing, bathing, or writing within the context of his environment.

Use of Technology in Fine Motor Assessment and Intervention

Technology provides opportunities for children who have significant motor impairment to have a degree of personal control over play activities that would otherwise be impossible. High-tech solutions generally involve the use of electronics—especially the use of computerized devices. Some examples of low-tech options for children with motor impairment might include using Dycem® to prevent a toy from sliding, a pencil grip to allow efficient grasp of a writing implement, or a battery interrupter in a toy to allow single switch use. The ability to activate a single switch with any reliable body movement can allow the child to turn on and off battery-operated toys and electrical devices (such as tape players or boom boxes) directly. With the addition of devices such as the Single Switch Latch and Timer for battery-operated toys or the PowerLink for electrical devices (both by AbleNet, Inc.), single switches can be used in several different modes. The direct mode keeps the toy on for as long as the switch is activated. The timed mode can be set to operate the toy for a predetermined amount of time. In the latched mode, one activation turns on the toy and a second will turn it off. There is a wide range of switches to meet specific motor and sensory needs. Switches vary in size and composition; they may be hard, soft, or cushioned. They may be activated by pressing, squeezing, or altering body position. They may vibrate, light up, or produce sound upon activation.

With the appropriate software and hardware, single switches also can be used to control computer games, interactive "books," and on-screen keyboards that the user can control by starting and stopping the cursor. These switches can be used simply for leisure activity or they may be used therapeutically to increase a child's motivation to reach or grasp with improved control, speed, and accuracy.

Whereas single switches can be used with many applications, they are quite slow when used with computers, especially when compared to direct-selection options. Some examples of direct-selection alternatives include the Touch Window™ by Edmark; the use of Morse Code for text-writing; the use of alternative mice like trackballs and HeadMouse; and keyboards such as IntelliKeys by IntelliTools or the WinMini by Tash Inc.

Computer-related technology includes the use of items such as a headstick; a touch screen; a switch with head array to access computer controls; expanded, enlarged key pads on keyboard or small keyboards; keyguards; keyboard emulators; screen enlargers; one- or three-finger typing; adjustable height table and chair; portable keyboards; and laptop computers (Struck, 1996).

Most states have lending libraries (often provided through United Cerebral Palsy or Easter Seals, or the local education agency) that provide free loans of assistive technology devices. Local special education departments or teachers and therapists with experience providing services to children with significant motor impairment should be able to supply information about these sources of equipment. Sources also can be found through a Web search (keyed to an assistive technology lending library in the city or state of interest). Whenever possible, it makes sense to test these devices before purchase, because mistakes can be costly.

Selected Strategies for Fine Motor Intervention

When considering intervention for the young child with fine motor or sensory needs, the most efficient approach is to first address that which will make the greatest difference in the functional performance of the child. Often, for example, better performance will result simply by improving the child's posture. Next, the objects used in performance of the task and the nature of the task itself need to be examined. The use of different objects or different placement of objects may result in better success. Perhaps the task can be done in a simpler way. When these options have been considered but problems still remain, the interventionist needs to systematically plan how to foster improved development of fine motor skills.

The child's sensory needs are as important to address as motor needs. Infants, toddlers, and preschoolers who have sensory processing disorders may need special accommodations at home or in the classroom. Often a child's perceived behavior problem is actually a response to inadequate sensory processing. The early interventionist, knowledgeable about sensory integration methods, can support a child with a sensory processing problem by providing alternative methods to address his sensory needs. The OT can assist the early interventionist by identifying a sensory processing problem and consulting about intervention.

Examples of accommodations might include the use of sensory preparatory activities prior to engaging in fine motor skills, addressing the child's level of arousal before expecting functional performance within the classroom, giving the child who is slow in processing sensory information extra time for completion of tasks, or allowing the use of movable equipment within the classroom for children who crave movement. Equipment within the classroom can be provided or adapted to allow the child to choose what can fulfill his sensory needs. For example, a child can sit on a movable, dynamic surface while doing table top activities to help with arousal. Push toys with added weight provide proprioceptive feedback which can be organizing for the child. Toys with various tactile properties can address tactile needs for those who are over- or underresponsive to touch. Once these children have their sensory needs met, they may have a better chance of interacting effectively within their environment.

Positioning the Child

It is important to consider specific ways to carry, move, or position children with atypical postural tone during their daily routines because this can influence fine motor functioning. Finnie (1997) addresses methods to position and carry children with cerebral palsy according to their atypical postural tone. For example, the parent or teacher can actively use her body as a positioning support for a young child who cannot sit independently due to poor postural tone and persistent primitive reflexes. Carrying the child in a manner to foster head and trunk control, with arms toward midline, and facing the child forward allows her to take in the environment. During floor sitting, the child's head, trunk, arms, and legs would be supported by the adult's body to enhance fine motor functioning.

An **adapted chair** (see Figure 8.9), including such items as a hard, solid back insert and solid seat insert, **seat belt,** lateral trunk and pelvic supports, anterior chest support, or **lap tray** may be indicated for an older child who cannot sit independently because of poor trunk control.

Working on sitting with stability and on hand skills simultaneously is counterproductive for a child with poor trunk control. Depending on the child's degree of involvement, appropriate positioning during fine motor tasks may include sidelying,

An adapted chair is a homemade or commercially available chair with added supports to provide optimal positioning for a child.

A seat belt is the simplest means of stabilizing the pelvis. The line of pull should be in a posterior, inferior direction (45 degrees) and inferior to the anterior-superior iliac spine (ASIS).

Lap tray refers to a wooden or clear plastic tray attached to a wheelchair that provides a working surface as well as some trunk support. Accessories can include padded top, easel, hand dowel, and activity bar.

FIGURE 8.9 Child with minimal head and trunk control positioned in an adapted chair to enhance fine motor and communication skills within the classroom

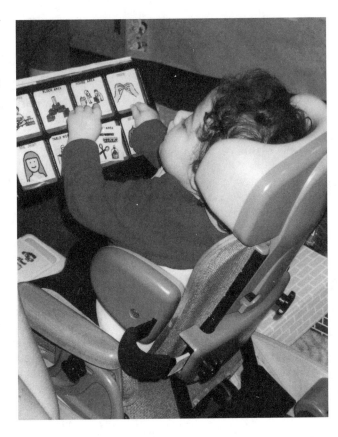

Chin jut refers to the atypical position of the head in which the chin juts forward due to atypical tone (if "high tone," the head is pulled into hyperextension; if "low tone," the head reacts to gravity and falls into hyperextension).

A chin tuck is the normal resting posture of the head in which the chin is in a neutral position and the neck is elongated.

prone or supine lying, sitting, or standing. For example, in the sidelying position, the child is therapeutically positioned on the left or right side using homemade or commercial devices to counteract the influence of atypical postural tone.

In the older child who is embarking on prewriting or writing skills, ideal positioning includes a chair height that allows the child to place his feet firmly on the floor and a desk height approximately 2 inches above the bent elbow at 90 degrees when the child is seated symmetrically and erect (Benbow, 1995). A child may lean into the table if the surface is too low; a table that is too high tends to turn the arms inward and thumbs downward, resulting in poor control and opposition of the thumb and index finger (Exner, 2001).

Positioning of Objects

How an object is presented to the child can make a difference in postural control. If a child demonstrates atypical head hyperextension with a **chin jut** when sitting (Figure 8.10), for example, the early interventionist can present objects closer to the child below chin level to promote active head flexion with a **chin tuck** (Figure 8.11). Lily typically would reach for toys with her arm turned inward (prona-

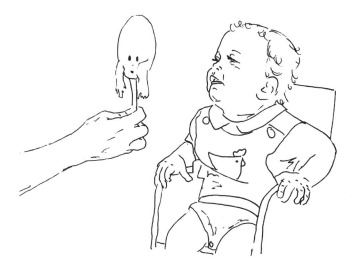

FIGURE 8.10 Inappropriate object presentation to toddler with spastic diplegic cerebral palsy, reinforcing chin jut, shoulder retraction, and head and neck hyperextension.
Source: Used by permission of Jean Patz.

FIGURE 8.11 Improved presentation of object below eye level, fostering appropriate head (chin tuck), trunk, and upper extremity control.
Source: Used by permission of Jean Patz.

tion), making it difficult to effectively reach and grasp a toy. Placing objects at the child's midline is important, particularly for children with central nervous system dysfunction, to minimize the influence of persistent primitive reflexes such as the asymmetrical tonic neck reflex. Optimal placement of the paper during writing tasks can be determined by having the child grasp her hands in the midline while resting on the desktop and pre-positioning the paper under the writing arm so it slants parallel to that arm (Benbow, 1990).

It is important to evaluate the **ergonomics** for computer use because many younger children are using computers for longer periods of time (National Center for Education Statistics, 2000). Musculoskeletal problems and eye strain can cause problems for a child who is inappropriately positioned while using the computer at home and in school. An OT can assist with positioning a child to facilitate use of the computer. Positioning at the computer to prevent injury in children includes: lower back and foot support with hips, knees and ankles at 90 degrees; eyes level with the monitor and directly in front of the child about an arms length away to prevent neck strain; arms close to the side with elbows at 90 degrees or greater; the keyboard placed for a neutral wrist position; and child sized keyboards and mouse (Healthy Computing for Kids, n.d.).

Fine Motor Materials

Larger toys may assist the child who has a poor grasp or weak grasp. Large lacing beads, easy-grip pegs, and **knobbed puzzles** are available commercially and from special-order catalogs. Lily was cognitively ready and interested in grasping and manipulating toys but she had difficulty maintaining grasp on toys due to her motor involvement. She is able to complete a puzzle by using puzzle pieces that have a knob with a 1-inch clearance for ease in grasp (Figure 8.12). A variety of beginner puzzles have single shapes with vegetables, fruits, animals, geometric figures, or flowers. Switch-activated toys are particularly useful for children with restricted arm use. Switches can be activated with any part of the body such as the head, arm, foot, or knee.

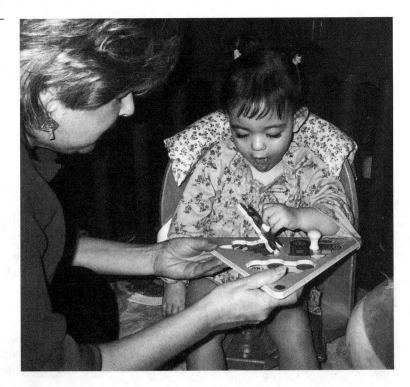

FIGURE 8.12 Lily uses a puzzle with knobs to assist in grasping. She is positioned in an adapted corner chair for added support in sitting so that her hands are free to manipulate toys.

Prewriting Adaptations

Adaptations may be needed to assist the child in holding a pencil in a more mature pattern. Splints can be individually fabricated by an occupational therapist to assist fine motor functioning at home and within the classroom (Figure 8.13).

Pencil grips come in a variety of shapes, sizes, and textures, such as pear-shaped grips, to guide placement of the index finger and thumb and prevent cramping, Super-Grips® for large 1/2-inch-diameter pencils, triangular pen grips, round rubber or soft foam grips, bulb-design built-up grips (Figure 8.14), and Stetro™ grips. Choice of the grip depends on the child's needs and comfort. The Handi-Writer™ (Figure 8.14) is a device that can assist with correct pencil angle and stabilization of the lateral fingers. The child holds a plastic charm attached to the Handi-Writer™ within the fourth and fifth fingers for stabilization. The loop encourages appropriate angle of the pencil resting within the web space and pointing back toward the shoulder. Adjustable-angle tabletops can assist the child in maintaining a more upright posture during prewriting or writing activities. Nonslip mats may be used to stabilize a child's writing paper or self-adhesive strips can be used to wrap around utensils or other tools for a better hold.

Prewriting Programs

There are a number of resources that can assist the interventionist in developing a prewriting program for preschool-aged children. For example, Klein's (1990a) illustrated book describes typical prewriting development, the necessary prerequisite

FIGURE 8.13 A preschool child seated in an adapted chair using a splint to hold the marker and a slant board to assist in maintaining an upright head position while coloring.

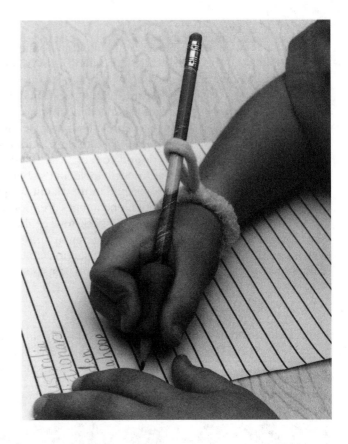

FIGURE 8.14   A child uses a large bulb shaped pencil grip for improved grasp, a Handi-Writer™ for correct angle of the pencil, and raised-line paper. The small side of the pencil grip is positioned toward the tip of the pencil and the letters R or L on the grip help the child position the thumb correctly.

skills, and suggestions for intervention. Witt and Klein (1990) have compiled activities that address kinesthetic and sensory awareness needed for the development of writing and school readiness, and Levine (1995) has developed a visual analysis of the normal components necessary for prewriting as well as scissor skills from birth to 6 years of age.

Scissors Skills

Equipment for Scissor Skills.   Appropriate scissors should be selected to address the child's needs (Klein, 1990b). For children who have not developed handedness, scissors for use with either the right or left hand are indicated to avoid frustration. Fiskar® scissors for preschoolers require the child to squeeze while cutting, but open automatically, helping a child who has difficulty with the opening action. A child with poor or weak grasp can easily squeeze loop scissors that consist of one large, flexible loop. Benbow (1995) has developed scissors designed especially for a child's hand that are only 3 1/2 inches in length with small loops to encourage isolated use of the index and thumb while cutting.

Care should be taken to select scissors that cut well; many standard scissors sold for children's use do not. **Four-loop training scissors** have an extra pair of loops placed adjacent to the child's loops; the interventionist places a hand over the child's for extra guidance. Another type of training scissors, **double-loop scissors,** have an extra pair of loops placed vertically to the child's loops. The interventionist holds the distal loops while the child holds the proximal loops. This procedure can be useful for a child who is tactually defensive to the interventionist's hand touching the child's or for one who finds touch uncomfortable (Klein, 1990b).

Pre-scissor Programs. An illustrated workbook for preschool and school-aged children that is designed to foster pre-scissor skills has been developed by Klein (1990b). Schneck and Battaglia (1992) suggest precutting activities to develop eye-hand coordination, hand strength, and fine motor dexterity in children who are not ready to use scissors. Activities include modeling clay for building strength and manipulating squeeze toys or squirt guns for opening and closing the hand, as well as bilateral activities such as snapping and unsnapping pop beads, sewing cards, or stringing beads. If the child has poor coordination because of tremors or jerkiness, the interventionist can provide external stabilization to the shoulder, arm, forearm, or wrist while cutting. This support can be gradually reduced. When the child begins cutting, Schneck and Battaglia suggest using long, narrow strips of paper, increasing the width as the child's skills develop, and grading the thickness of paper from thick paper to thin followed by nonpaper items.

In summary, the fine motor domain consists of the motor and sensory aspects of reach, grasp, release, manipulation, and bilateral control. It is important to examine how the child puts these components together to perform functional tasks within their daily routine. Environmental issues such as materials and toys available to the child, cultural values, or parental and school expectations play a major role in the child's development of these skills. Intervention addresses the child's needs, their participation in skills, and adaptations or adjustments to their environment.

Theories of Oral Motor Development

Although no theoretical approaches to oral motor development are found in the literature, it would appear that the theories used to describe gross and fine motor development apply to oral motor development as well. Certainly, some therapeutic approaches to swallowing and feeding disorders follow a neurodevelopmental framework, which is consistent with a reflex/hierarchical model of motor control. There are a number of primitive oral reflexes in the neonate that support feeding. For example, when the caregiver places a finger in the infant's mouth, the infant loosely closes the mouth around the finger and initiates sucking. This early **sucking reflex** allows the infant to attach to the nipple when nursing, a function that is later replaced by volitional control of sucking. When a finger is placed on an infant's gum, the infant will open and close the mouth repetitively on the finger, in a **biting reflex.** Biting and chewing are not useful for neonates, but may form a substrate for movement that will be used later in development because biting and chewing are necessary for ingesting solid foods. Wolf and Glass (1992) discuss how an infant's muscle tone, position, state, and physiologic control can alter oral motor control, which is consistent with a dynamic systems approach. Traditional therapeutic approaches to problems with oral motor control have followed a neurodevelopmental framework. In fact, the most common models of practice employed when children present with impaired oral motor control due to neuromotor dysfunction is neurodevelopmental treatment. Sensory integration may be used with children whose eating problems seem to be related to the inability to process sensory information.

Stages of Typical Oral Motor Development

Oral motor development incorporates coordinated movements of the jaw, tongue, lips, and cheeks during sucking, swallowing, munching, chewing, spoon-feeding, and cup drinking. In addition to the motor control necessary for eating, it is important to consider positioning of the child's head in relationship to the body and to gravity; positioning of the person feeding the child in relationship to the child; positioning of the bottle, cup, or spoon; and the selection of types and textures of food that are suitable for the developmental level of the child. As noted earlier in relation to the development of fine and gross motor skills, sensory processing skills also are necessary for feeding so that the child can respond appropriately to the texture, temperature, taste, and smell of food. The nature of oral motor skills required is quite different; for example, when a child eats a raw apple the response is different from when he eats pudding. Higher textured foods provide the sensory stimulus for the development of more mature oral motor skills. Developmental eating milestones from birth through 2 years of age are listed in Table 8.4.

Positioning During Meals

Typically, an infant enjoys being held in a semireclined position during feedings. By the age of 7 months, most infants can sit independently in a highchair with support provided by a seat belt or tray. Most children can sit in a small chair by 18 months of age (Morris & Klein, 2000). These positions parallel the development of oral structures as well as oral motor skills. Most infants can safely be fed in a reclined

TABLE 8.4 Stages of Typical Oral Motor Development

Age	Skills
Infancy	Infant is held by the caregiver during bottle or breastfeeding.
By 6 months	Infant may be introduced to new food textures (baby cereals, strained or pureed baby food, soft crackers that melt in the mouth), and utensils (cup and spoon) depending on cultural expectations and medical advice.
7–12 months	Child may be gradually introduced to higher textured foods (mashed or soft cooked table food) as chewing skills develop.
12–24 months	Child progresses from eating chopped table food to meats and uncooked vegetables within this time frame. Also develops skill in drinking from a straw and cup.

position because the relationship of the oral structures to one another makes it unlikely that **aspiration,** the passage of liquids or food into the lungs, will occur (Case-Smith & Humphrey, 1996).

As an infant approaches 12 months of age, however, the throat elongates and additional space is created between the base of the tongue and the epiglottis, which covers the trachea during swallowing. This growth change provides a greater opportunity for aspiration to occur when a child is in a reclined position because of the effect of gravity on foods. Thus, by this age, children should be in a more up-right position which facilitates the ability to handle solid foods safely, to chew, and to drink from a cup.

Aspiration is the passage of liquid or food during swallowing into the trachea and lungs.

Sucking

The **rooting reflex,** which the newborn exhibits from birth to 3 months of age, enables the child to locate the source of food. The infant's head turns toward the stimulus and he opens his mouth when touched around the oral area. Reflexive swallowing occurs with the **suck-swallow reflex,** which diminishes around 2 to 4 months of age (Connor et al., 1978). A healthy, full-term infant has the ability to initiate suckling, maintain a strong grasp on the nipple using an extension-retraction pattern of the tongue, and ingest the required amount of liquid efficiently within 20–30 minutes (Morris & Klein, 2000). Liquid loss may be apparent as a result of incomplete development of a lateral lip seal around the nipple and wide, yet rhythmical, jaw excursions. According to Morris and Klein, the mature sucking pattern emerges around 6 to 9 months of age. This action involves a cupped tongue around the nipple, up-and-down tongue movements creating negative intraoral pressure, smaller movements of the jaw and complete lip closure around the nipple.

Within about 20–30 minutes after birth a healthy, full-term infant will begin sucking effectively

Swallowing

Morris and Klein (2000) discuss the tongue, jaw, and lip movements during the oral phase of swallowing. Initially, tongue extension-retraction is used during swallowing and sucking; swallowing occurs after every second or third suck. Tongue movement changes at 6 to 8 months of age from slight protrusion to an up-and-down pattern and finally tongue-tip elevation around 2 years of age (Morris & Klein). The mouth is closed at the point of swallow. This is important to know because many children with oral motor dysfunction do not have mouth closure when swallowing and this can interfere with eating and swallowing. The pharyngeal phase of swallow begins when the bolus moves through the pharynx, triggering the **swallow reflex;** the final phase involves passage of liquid or food through the esophagus into the stomach (Logemann, 1998).

Protective mechanisms to prevent aspiration of liquid or food include elevation of the soft palate to close off the nasal cavities and the backward movement of the epiglottis to cover the airway. A sphincter at the top of the stomach prevents **reflux** (i.e., the back-up of food contents into the esophagus and into the pharynx).

Munching and Chewing

Munching occurs around 5 to 6 months of age as food is simply mashed against the palate with vertical tongue and jaw movements when the child manipulates a cracker (Morris & Klein, 2000). Food stays in the front of the mouth at this stage of development because lateral tongue and circular jaw movements have not developed. Tongue lateralization and circular or rotary jaw movements, which are needed to carry food to the side of the mouth and pulverize it for chewing, begin around 7 to 8 months, with mature chewing abilities developing by 2 years of age (Morris & Klein, 2000). Morris and Klein outline the developmental progression of the introduction of solids. Timelines for the introduction of solid foods vary according to pediatricians' recommendations and a family's culture, beliefs, and past experiences. Children are introduced to cereals and pureed or strained baby foods around 4 to 6 months of age. Ground or mashed table foods, referred to as "lumpy solids," are generally introduced at approximately 8 months, followed by coarsely chopped table food around 1 year of age. Most meats and some raw vegetables are appropriate for an 18-month-old.

Spoon-Feeding

Developmentally, the ability to quiet the tongue and jaw upon seeing the spoon approach occurs around 6 months of age (Morris & Klein, 2000). This resting posture of the tongue and jaw is important for preparing the mouth to receive food. Another important milestone during spoon-feeding is the child's ability to actively use the upper lip to clear food from the spoon and keep the bottom lip stable. This actively begins around 7 to 8 months of age (Morris & Klein, 2000).

Cup Drinking

A child with oral motor dysfunction is at risk for potential aspiration if swallowing occurs while his head is in hyperextension.

Cup drinking generally begins around 4 to 6 months of age as the mother holds a cup to the child's mouth for a taste. The child drinks with the head in a normal resting posture, slightly flexed. The infant initially uses a suck-swallow pattern. Because jaw stability has not yet developed, liquid loss occurs, necessitating use of a cloth or bib under the child's chin. The parent may offer cups with spouted lids to avoid spillage and the child will use more of a sucking pattern when drinking from this type of cup. Gradually, jaw stabilization develops, allowing closure of the lips on a regular cup rim. Jaw stability progresses from wide vertical jaw movements to biting on the cup rim at 15 to 18 months and the child achieves mature internal jaw stability at approximately 24 months (Morris & Klein, 2000). Movement of the tongue changes from the up-and-down pattern noted in sucking to a simple tongue protrusion pattern during the first year, followed by mature elevation of the tip of the tongue by 2 years (Morris & Klein, 2000). Initially, the child takes individual sips; however, continuous swallowing, or taking several sips in succession, indicates a more mature swallowing pattern. The child generally can drink successfully from a cup held by the feeder by 12 to 15 months of age and will do so with no liquid loss by 2 years of age. See Box 8.2 to learn about oral motor empathy exercises.

BOX 8.2	Oral Motor Empathy Exercises

- Take a drink and notice what your jaw does at the point of swallowing. Does your jaw totally close? How much?
- Now swallow with your mouth slightly open (similar to what children do who have oral motor dysfunction). What happens to your tongue during swallowing if the mouth is slightly open? Was it difficult to swallow this way? Did you cough?
- Hyperextend your head slightly by looking upward (similar to positioning seen in children with motor disabilities) and *carefully* swallow a small amount of water. How does it feel? How do you think a child with oral motor dysfunction would feel if someone fed her in this position?
- Take a drink and experience what happens to your breathing when you swallow. What impact might this have on a child with respiratory difficulties and oral motor dysfunction?
- Take a bite of a cracker. Chew it *without* moving your tongue to the side. Use straight up-and-down tongue movements. How does it feel? Can you taste the cracker? Does it take longer to chew the cracker? You are munching like a 5- to 6-month-old child.
- Take another bite of a cracker, chew normally, and pay close attention to your tongue movements. Does your tongue move to the side when chewing? Do you notice a side preference? You are experiencing mature tongue lateralization needed for effective chewing.
- Take a third bite and notice your jaw movements. Does your jaw move straight up and down, diagonally, or in a circular movement? Watch another person's jaw movements while chewing and note the movements needed to grind food.
- While using a spoon, notice if the upper or lower lip works more when removing food from the spoon. How much more? Note how efficiently the lip removes food from the spoon.
- Take a drink and describe movements of your tongue from the time the liquid enters your mouth to the time you swallow.

Factors Affecting Oral Motor Development

In the preceding section, the oral motor components of positioning, sucking, swallowing, chewing, spoon-feeding, and cup drinking were described. There are many issues which can interfere with eating including medical, structural, motor, sensory, behavioral, environmental, and/or neurological problems. Atypical oral motor development may occur when there are problems with postural tone. Sensitivity to texture and temperature also may result in resistance to eating or difficulties coping with different foods. For some children, prematurity, illness, **gastroesophageal reflux (GER),** or surgical intervention can result in an interruption of normal feeding procedures. For these children, the discomfort associated with alternative feeding methods such as **nasogastric** and **gastrostomy tube feedings** and lack of appropriate oral stimulation may result in complicated behavioral issues related to feeding. In addition, parents and interventionists should keep in mind that some medical conditions and medications may result in diminished appetite. Any of these problems can contribute to poor intake and low weight gain. The next section provides information that may be helpful in determining the need for further evaluation. Figure 8.15 summarizes this information.

Gastroesophageal reflux is the backward movement of liquid or food from the stomach up to the esophagus which may cause a child to spit up.

POSITIONING
- parent has difficulty holding or positioning the child in a chair during meals
- child is extremely fussy when held
- child has trouble sitting independently during meals as a result of poor postural control (independent sitting generally occurs by approximately 6–8 months)

SUCKING
- persistent difficulty initiating sucking when hungry and alert
- weak grasp or suction on the nipple when hungry and alert; poor intake
- consistently takes too long to complete a bottle when hungry and alert—more than 40–60 minutes
- frequent choking or gagging when drinking from bottle or breast
- tongue pushes nipple out of mouth involuntarily
- persistent, involuntary biting on the nipple
- parent feels the need to cut a hole in the bottle nipple to increase intake
- parent has difficulty finding a nipple that the child will consistently use

SWALLOWING
- coughing during or after eating and drinking
- history of aspiration pneumonia
- gurgly voice
- frequent vomiting
- persistent drooling beyond the teething phase of 6 to 18 months
- open mouth posture; excessive loss of liquid

CHEWING
- persistence on only baby food (strained, pureed, or mashed) beyond 12–15 months

(strained or pureed food is generally offered between 3 and 8 months; mashed by 8 months, followed by coarsely chopped regular food by 12–15 months)
- negative reaction to solid foods such as crying or spitting; "picky eater"
- lack of tongue lateralization; therefore, food stays in the front of the mouth after the first year; food loss
- persistent choking or gagging on solid food
- consistent asymmetry of the tongue, jaw, and lips during chewing, crying, or smiling

SPOON-FEEDING
- persistent, involuntary biting or clamping down on the spoon
- tongue involuntarily and forcefully pushes spoon out of the mouth on a consistent basis
- persistent choking or gagging when being spoon-fed
- inability to clear or wipe thickened food off the spoon with the upper lip after 9–12 months of age

CUP DRINKING
- excessive liquid loss beyond 1 year of age when drinking from a cup held by the caregiver
- coughing during or after drinking thin liquids from a cup
- difficulty transitioning from the bottle to a cup at a developmentally appropriate age
- inability to get enough liquid in by cup; history of dehydration
- report from the parent that cup drinking is stressful
- inability of a child over 1 year of age with at least 2 months of cup-drinking experience to take consecutive sips

FIGURE 8.15 Red flags suggestive of oral motor problems
Source: Used by permission of Jean Patz.

Positioning

Poor positioning due to atypical postural tone can have a considerable impact on all feeding functions. These problems may be reflected in an infant who is consistently difficult to hold, seems extremely fussy when held, or prefers being left alone. Caregivers may report that the child's body feels limp or stiff and that they do not have enough hands to support the child during eating. A child's need for additional support in sitting upright beyond the 8-to-12-month level is cause for concern because independent sitting generally develops by 6 to 8 months.

> A typical posture can place a child at risk for aspirating.

Poor postural alignment is not conducive to swallowing. Head hyperextension tends to place the oral structures in a position incompatible with normal swallowing. The atypical posture mechanically opens the airway, placing a child at risk for aspirating.

Sucking

Many factors can interfere with normal sucking including structural deformities; weakness resulting from poor health; poor oral motor control, resulting from central nervous system dysfunction; and behavioral issues stemming from inadequate sensory processing. Absent or weak oral reflexes can impede the sucking process. **Tongue thrust,** a forceful protrusion of the tongue, which is seen in some children with cerebral palsy and Down syndrome, interferes with sucking because the tongue is either bunched, as a result of increased tone, or flat, as a result of low tone (Morris & Klein, 2000). This makes it difficult for the tongue to wrap around the nipple to assist in channeling the liquid back into the mouth for swallowing. In short, the thrusting motion of the tongue may push the nipple out of the mouth and the presence of an atypical **tonic bite reflex** sets off a biting-versus-sucking response on the nipple. A tonic bite reflex, which is an atypical clamping of the jaw in response to stimulation on the gums or teeth (Morris & Klein, 2000), is an abnormality seen in children with more severe neuromotor dysfunction. Increased tone can create retraction of the upper lip, making it difficult to achieve lip closure around the nipple. An open mouth posture, resulting from hypertonia or hypotonia, prevents jaw and lip approximation around the nipple. All of these factors can increase feeding times and decrease liquid intake.

Swallowing

Children with neuromotor dysfunction are at risk at all stages of swallowing. Poor oral motor control, resulting from atypical tone, makes it difficult for a child to collect the bolus and time the swallow. Problems may also occur in the pharyngeal and esophageal phases of swallow. Coughing may be a sign of direct or indirect aspiration of food or liquid into the airway. Aspiration without coughing is termed **silent aspiration.** Frequent burping or vomiting may be an indication of reflux. Delayed or atypical oral motor control can contribute to an open mouth posture which fosters drooling. A persistently soaked bib, beyond the time when teething occurs, can indicate oral motor dysfunction.

Chewing

A child's inability or refusal to progress from pureed or strained baby food to more highly textured food beyond the 12-to-15-month level, after repeated introductions of solids, warrants further investigation. A child manipulates food between the molar surface when chewing; inefficient chewing would be suspected if food remained in the front of the mouth. Consistent choking when solids are given after the expected developmental range also is cause for concern. Poor oral motor control, such as that evidenced by tongue thrusting in children with cerebral palsy or Down syndrome (Figure 8.16), may appear to be purposeful spitting when in fact it is an involuntary tongue protrusion that expels food from the mouth. A child's difficulty carrying food back in the mouth to swallow combined with forward protrusion of the tongue can cause excessive food loss.

A child may not have the oral motor capabilities to maneuver food laterally between the molars for chewing and then back for swallowing. Persistent gagging may indicate a hyperactive gag reflex seen in some children with central nervous system dysfunction. Persistent negative responses to chunky or solid foods (e.g., crying, turning the head away, or spitting) may indicate a strong food preference. However, the resistance may be accounted for by a more serious condition, such as oral hypersensitivity, which occurs when a child is unable to tolerate the tactile qualities of the food, or oral motor dysfunction. Asymmetry in oral movements may be a symptom of motor dysfunction on one side of the body, as in spastic hemiplegia. Signs include an uneven smile, asymmetrical mouth posture when crying, and persistent pocketing of food on one side of the mouth. Another indicator of oral motor problems is the level of stress exhibited by the child and parent.

FIGURE 8.16 Tongue thrust in a child with Down syndrome

Source: Used by permission of Jean Patz.

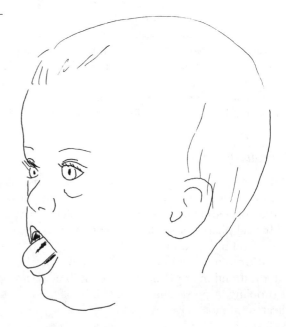

Spoon-Feeding

Consistently biting down on a spoon with clenched jaws may be a sign of a **tonic bite reflex,** which is a form of tactile hypersensitivity (Morris & Klein, 2000). A tonic bite reflex is a strong bite set off by touch to the gums or teeth that is difficult to release and this atypical reflex interferes with eating. A parent may unknowingly stimulate the tonic bite again by attempting to pull the spoon out of the child's clenched mouth. Lack of development of lip closure due to delayed maturation or neurological impairment can interfere with removing food from a spoon with the upper lip.

Cup Drinking

Morris and Klein (2000) discuss various factors that cause difficulties with cup drinking. These include oral motor delay, which can cause a primitive sucking pattern on the cup; atypical tone, which can result in poor oral motor control; and abnormalities in sensory processing, which can lead to oral hypersensitivity. Typically, a child loses liquid when he begins to drink from a cup. Excessive loss beyond the first year may indicate poor development of jaw stability, tongue control, or lip closure. A persistent cough while drinking may indicate aspiration of fluid into the lungs. Oral motor dysfunction, oral hypersensitivity, delayed development, or behavioral resistance might be suspected if the cup has been introduced in the typical developmental time frame, the child repeatedly refuses to drink from a cup, and the parent expresses concern. Further investigation is warranted by an occupational therapist or speech and language pathologist to evaluate what might be causing these problems.

> When drinking from a cup, excessive fluid loss beyond the first year may be suggestive of an oral-motor problem.

Oral Motor Development in Young Children with Special Needs

Cerebral Palsy

Children with cerebral palsy often exhibit a number of characteristics that may interfere with voluntary and involuntary motor control necessary for eating. These characteristics may include atypical postural and oral tone; atypical movement; persistent primitive postural reflexes (e.g., asymmetrical tonic neck reflex) and oral reflexes (e.g., gag, rooting, and sucking reflexes); sensory deficits (hyposensitivity or hypersensitivity); pharyngeal involvement (which can cause aspiration); or esophageal involvement leading to reflux.

> Jaw thrust is an atypical, forceful, downward thrusting of the lower jaw that interferes with mouth closure needed for food intake (Morris & Klein, 2000).

Hypertonia in the oral area can cause restriction in oral movements (e.g., difficulty opening the mouth) that interfere with eating. Oral asymmetry and atypical oral motor patterns can include tongue thrust, **jaw thrust,** tonic bite reflex, and lip retraction leading to lengthy feeding time and poor food intake. Mature oral movements such as isolated, lateral tongue movement needed in chewing may not develop.

Hypotonia in the oral area may cause sluggish oral movements. An open-mouth posture prevents a good lip seal on a cup, nipple, or spoon and results in drooling and food and liquid loss. The child with hypotonia may remain on lower textured foods well beyond the expected range of development. Tongue protrusion and tongue thrust interfere with food intake and channeling liquid and solids posteriorly for swallowing.

A child with variable or fluctuating tone, as with athetoid cerebral palsy, may exhibit involuntary, uncontrolled, extraneous oral movements. The child has difficulty sustaining movements such as maintaining lip closure on a nipple or cup rim. Stability of the head and trunk is lacking, making it difficult for the child to keep his body quiet and still for feeding. A greater degree of tongue thrust or jaw thrust occurs as a result of involuntary movements.

Down Syndrome

The child with Down syndrome has delays from mental retardation, hypotonia, and oral hyposensitivity. Inadequate postural control may result in head hyperextension, which can interfere with safety in swallowing. Infants may exhibit a poor suck resulting from the hypotonia or general weakness from other medical conditions such as associated heart abnormalities. An open-mouth posture and tongue thrusting lead to excessive drooling and poor oral intake. As the child matures, delayed chewing with a lack of progression to more highly textured food, as well as poor spoon-feeding and cup-drinking skills, may become more apparent.

Autism

The diet of children with autism may be limited to particular foods and food textures, as a result of atypical tactile, gustatory, or olfactory processing. Children with autism may have hypersensitivity to temperature, smell, touch, taste, sound, and movement (Kientz & Dunn, 1997) which can interfere with mealtime.

Sensory overload during feeding may produce tantrums, stereotypical behaviors, or a withdrawal of attention. Poor communication during mealtime might include non-responsiveness to the caregiver, limited turn-taking vocalizations, poor communication of needs, and lack of ability to engage the caregiver. Deficits in motor planning can make it difficult for these children to learn how to use utensils. **Pica,** the consumption of inedible substances, is common in autism and may be due to impaired taste perception in children with autism (Van Bourgondien, 1993).

Cleft Lip or Palate

Children with a cleft lip or palate may have difficulty with sucking due to poor oral pressure from an open cleft. Nasal regurgitation, air swallowing, choking, and vomiting may occur until surgical repairs of the cleft are completed.

Low Vision

Children with impaired vision may exhibit behavioral problems during meals as they may not feel in control (e.g., not seeing when a caregiver is approaching with a spoon). There may be resistance to new foods that cannot be seen. Self-feeding may be delayed due to difficulty locating utensils or food on their plate.

Myelomeningocele

Poor oral control in children with myelomeningocele may occur when an accompanying brain anomaly called **Arnold-Chiari malformation** is present. This deviation results from a herniation of the brainstem which can result in delayed swallowing and choking (Batshaw, 1997), and vomiting (Morris & Klein, 2000).

Congenital Acquired Immunity Deficiency Syndrome (AIDS)

Children with AIDS may exhibit recurrent, chronic diarrhea; failure to thrive; poor weight gain; progressive and dysfunctional oral motor control similar to neurological problems described under cerebral palsy; and oral thrush.

Learning Disability

Some children with learning disabilities exhibit minor oral motor problems during mealtimes, particularly oral dyspraxia. Poor motor planning may affect self-feeding skills because it will be difficult for the child to hold and coordinate use of utensils. Extended use of fingers occurs to avoid use of utensils. Parents may report sloppiness during mealtimes and poor attention.

Specific Strategies for Oral Motor Assessment

The early interventionist may be the first to suspect that children they are serving have an oral motor problem. In such cases, they would refer a child for evaluation. Oral motor problems are evaluated by occupational therapists or speech-language pathologists who have training in typical and atypical oral motor development. Videofluoroscopic swallow studies are done in radiology to rule out problems such as aspiration and gastroesophageal reflux. Other critical team members in the evaluation of swallowing disorders include a developmental pediatrician, gastroenterologist, neurologist, otolaryngologist, physical therapist, plastic surgeon, pulmonologist, and radiologist (Arvedson & Lefton-Greif, 1998).

> Oral motor problems are evaluated by professionals in occupational therapy and speech-language pathology.

Preassessment information is gathered from medical and nutritional records. An extensive interview is conducted with the primary caregivers about concerns related to their child's eating abilities. During the oral motor evaluation, the therapist observes the parent feeding the child, noting the method of feeding, communication between caregiver and child, positioning, and types of utensils, equipment, and food textures used. The therapist may then feed the child, evaluating typical and atypical sensory and motor aspects of sucking, swallowing, chewing, spoon-feeding, and cup drinking. Behavior during meals is noted. Various assessment tools are available for evaluating oral motor skills including the Clinical Feeding Evaluation of Infants (Wolf & Glass, 1992), Mealtime Assessment Guide and Developmental Prefeeding Checklist (Morris & Klein, 2000), the Pre-Speech Assessment Scale (Morris, 1982), and the Oral Motor/Feeding Rating Scale (Jelm, 1990). The therapist develops a treatment plan once the evaluation is completed, together with the child, parents, educational staff, and feeding team. The plan addresses quality of oral motor skills and needs within the child's eating environment.

Selected Strategies for Oral Motor Intervention

When providing intervention for a child with poor oral motor control that affects eating, the early intervention team includes the parents, physician, early interventionist, occupational therapist or speech-language pathologist, nutritionist, and nurse. The oral motor specialists will address positioning of the child, the caregiver, and equipment; functional eating tasks including sucking, swallowing, chewing, spoon-feeding, and cup drinking; diet texture modifications; and provision of adapted equipment when indicated. Consultation from appropriate professionals regarding possible food allergies and swallowing irregularities also may be necessary.

Positioning the Child

If the child must be held for feeding, he should be held in as upright a position as possible, with the head slightly flexed. The arms should be supported forward and the hips bent at approximately 90 degrees (Figure 8.17). The person feeding the child cradles the child's head in the crook of an elbow in order to actively move that arm to counteract tonic head hyperextension in a child with increased postural tone due to spastic cerebral palsy. The feeder may cross her leg to create a seat for the child, which bends the child's hips in flexion counteracting the atypical extension.

FIGURE 8.17   A grandfather holding his grandson for feeding, supporting the child's head with his arm while maintaining the child's arms forward and supporting the child's hips in flexion. The child has severe spastic quadriplegic cerebral palsy.
Source: Used by permission of Jean Patz.

Positioning of the Feeder

Positioning of the feeder is important as well. Generally, the feeder needs to sit directly in front of the child, not to the side (Figure 8.18), and at eye level to foster symmetry and to decrease the influence of atypical primitive reflexes. The plate of food is placed on the side of the feeder's dominant hand for efficiency when feeding. The person feeding the child should ensure her own comfort in a suitable chair.

Sucking

Medical issues must be ruled out prior to initiation of any program addressing sucking problems in infants. Intervention may address the type of equipment used to foster more efficient sucking from a bottle. Characteristics of nipples such as type, configuration, size, and ease of flow should be evaluated. Various choices of bottles are available. For example, angled-neck bottles, available commercially, allow the child to be fed in a more upright position, thus reducing air intake and decreasing head hyperextension. Special positioning may be indicated to enhance a neutral or slightly forward flexion of the head needed for sucking from the breast or bottle. Oral facilitation techniques such as jaw support (Figure 8.19) may be warranted to provide better oral stability during sucking.

FIGURE 8.18 Inappropriate spoon presentation from the side, which triggers the expression of the asymmetrical tonic neck reflex in a child with spastic quadriplegia cerebral palsy. The feeder should sit directly in front/of the child and at eye level to foster more normal tone and position for better success with eating.

Source: Used by permission of Jean Patz.

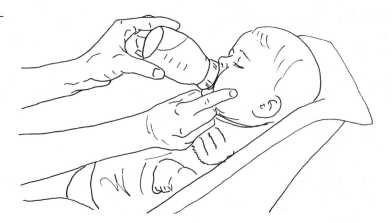

FIGURE 8.19 Jaw support provided to an infant with a weak suck. The lateral surface of the middle finger supports the jaw, while the index finger and thumb support the infant's cheeks.

Source: Used by permission of Jean Patz.

Swallowing

Intervention for swallowing dysfunction should be addressed by professionals skilled in oral motor evaluation and intervention. For a child who aspirates fluids, intervention can range from thickening the child's food or liquid texture to gastrostomy feeding. Whatever type of problem the child has, early interventionists should be familiar with modifications. Johnson and Scott (1993) have developed a resource guide addressing assessment and intervention for management of drooling.

Chewing

Children can easily choke on small pieces of food; therefore, caution is required when developmentally young children are given higher textured foods. Consultation with a professional trained in oral motor assessment and intervention is recommended. Chewing requires coordinated movements of the tongue, jaw, lips, and cheeks. Given the complexity of chewing, children with severe oral motor problems may not acquire this skill, thus necessitating adjustments to the type of food given. Intervention addresses factors which interfere with normal chewing, such as tongue thrust, tongue retraction, jaw thrust, tonic bite reflex, lip retraction, jaw instability, and oral hypersensitivity (Morris & Klein, 2000).

A change in food texture may foster chewing development. The child may move from low-textured foods, such as cereals and strained or ground foods that do not require chewing, to foods thickened with baby cereals, rice cereal, dehydrated fruit flakes, and lumpy, soft foods (Morris & Klein, 2000). Foods that melt in the mouth, such as graham crackers, are used when the child has progressed to the stage of beginning to orally manipulate small pieces. Foods that make noise when they are crunched, such as cereal bits, can be fun for the child; however, these foods can present a choking hazard depending on the size. Special handling techniques may be necessary to assist the child who has oral motor difficulties accept and manipulate more highly textured foods. Particularly for children who exhibit oral hypersensitivity, tolerating more highly textured foods will be a major challenge.

Textured foods may present a challenge for a child with oral-motor difficulties.

The therapist can assist in training the interventionist and parents in oral motor techniques. The feeder must be aware of the sensory and proprioceptive components of feeding and positioning. The feeder should be sensitive to the temperature of her own hand used when touching the child as well as to how much pressure she is exerting, for example, when applying oral control techniques. A cold hand may startle the child. A light touch can be noxious to a child who has overly sensitive responses to touch, whereas a firm touch might restrict necessary jaw movements. Therefore, moderation is recommended.

Diet Texture

The primary goal related to diet texture is that the child can experience and accept developmentally appropriate food textures. The primary goal for parents is that they can prepare appropriately textured foods to accommodate their child's oral motor capabilities. Adjusting food texture and liquid consistency for a child with special needs is the responsibility of an occupational therapist or speech pathologist who has performed a thorough oral motor and pharyngeal evaluation. The therapist often will consult with the pediatrician and nutritionist prior to making recommendations. The interventionist should know what texture has been recommended for the child.

Spoon-Feeding

A proper approach with the spoon can promote a more normal head position and easier swallowing. When spoon-feeding a child, the feeder should sit in front of the child at eye level to encourage midline positioning of the head and to discourage head hyperextension. When the feeder approaches with the spoon from below chin level, the child looks slightly down, creating a chin tuck. Also, it is important to bring the spoon close enough to the child so that he actively tucks the chin instead of jutting the chin forward to approach a spoon offered too far away. The feeder waits for the child to actively flex the head slightly (chin tuck) to clear food from the spoon. The spoon is inserted and removed in a horizontal fashion to encourage lip closure instead of wiping the spoon in an upward fashion, which negates the need for active lip closure on the spoon.

This method is also helpful for a child with cerebral palsy who has a tonic bite reflex because the approach avoids stimulating the gums or teeth upon spoon removal. The feeder should avoid pulling the spoon out of the child's mouth once the tonic bite reflex has been elicited because this will further strengthen the response. Instead, the feeder should wait for the child to relax. The therapist can show the feeder effective methods to help reduce overall postural tone to address this problem. A calm and quiet feeding environment is also helpful because these children over-respond to sensory stimulation. Coated spoons are recommended to protect the child's teeth and provide a soft biting surface. Many types of spoons are available from medical supply companies to meet the needs of children with feeding problems. These include coated spoons, shallow-bowled spoons, built-up-handled spoons, weighted spoons, adjustable-angle spoons, swivel spoons, and spoons with horizontal or vertical palm grips. A universal cuff may provide a means to hold different utensils; this is a strap wrapped around the palm of the hand with a pocket to hold utensils in place.

Cup Drinking

A cut-out cup is a therapeutically designed cup with a portion of the rim cut away to allow space for the nose when tipping the cup during drinking. It prevents head hyperextension during drinking.

Introduction of a cup into play situations prior to initiation of a cup drinking program is recommended so that the child will have seen and handled a cup. General principles can be applied to teaching cup-drinking skills. Positioning the cup appropriately ensures that the child does not have to wait too long to drink, which could set off tongue thrusting. The feeder tips the cup enough so that the liquid is close to the rim prior to bringing the cup to the mouth. **Cut-out cups** are often recommended to foster a more normal head position. Lily is given liquids from a cut-out cup because she has a tendency to hyperextend her head during drinking which would put her at risk for aspiration (Figure 8.20). The cut-out portion allows space for her nose when the cup is tipped up preventing head hyperextension.

Thickened liquids may be used initially to slow the flow for ease in swallowing. Age-appropriate foods, such as strained baby fruit, rice cereal, mashed bananas, and yogurt, can be mixed with the liquid. It is important for the caregiver to prepare the recommended thickness of liquid.

Handling techniques to provide jaw control can be used when recommended if the difficulty is an open-mouth posture, as noted in Lily's case. The feeder

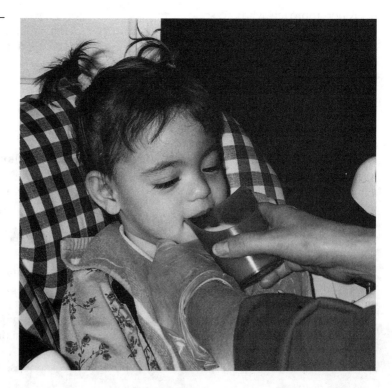

FIGURE 8.20 A cut-out cup is placed on Lily's lower lip while providing oral control

approaches the child slowly with the cup to avoid eliciting any primitive or atypical oral movements. The uncut side of the cup, opposite the cut-out portion, is placed on the midsection of the lower lip, not between the teeth. A small amount of liquid is poured slowly into the child's mouth to encourage one sip at a time when the child is first learning the skill; the amount is increased gradually to foster consecutive swallowing. If jaw control is recommended, the feeder maintains the jaw control until the child swallows the liquid. The child's reactions should be observed continuously to monitor what he can handle.

The goals for the parents are that they will (1) understand the oral motor strengths and needs of their child; (2) solve feeding problems that may arise outside of the intervention sessions; (3) know where to find resources regarding eating; (4) teach other family members how to skillfully feed the child; (5) use adapted equipment appropriately and in the most efficient manner; (6) prepare appropriate textured foods that are consistent with the child's oral motor capabilities; (7) integrate the oral motor intervention into the daily routine; and (8) identify safety issues in the feeding process. Vignette 8.2 illus trates oral motor development in a child with cerebral palsy.

Vignette 8.2

ANN

Ann was first seen at 11 months of age by a developmental pediatrician; she was diagnosed with spastic cerebral palsy, mental retardation, and failure to thrive during the initial evaluation. She was referred for early intervention services. The early interventionist, occupational therapist, physical therapist, speech-language therapist, and parents conducted an arena assessment to determine Ann's strengths and areas of difficulty.

The parents were concerned because it was difficult to feed, hold, and console their daughter. She had poor weight gain. The mother reported it took "forever" to complete a bottle—more than 45 minutes for each feeding. Ann's "tongue was in the way" when inserting the nipple which resulted in poor initiation of a suck. The parents tried several shapes, sizes, and textures of nipples and finally resorted to cutting a larger hole in the nipple. By report, Ann would periodically "stiffen up" when fed on her mother's lap and the parent's interpreted this behavior as rejection. The mother was the most successful in feeding her daughter; Ann did not tolerate being fed by other family members. Transition to solid foods was not smooth; Ann gagged and coughed on lumpy textured foods. The mother reported difficulty inserting a spoon because Ann would bite down on the spoon, have difficulty letting go, and lose about 50% of each spoonful. Periodically she would cough while swallowing.

Ann sat in a jumper seat that the parents padded with towels during spoon-feeding because she would fall to the side; Ann "stiffened" when bouncing in this seat and the increased tone interfered with eating.

It was difficult for Ann to grasp toys because her hands would fist during reach. She was unable to bring her hands to the midline and one arm was noticeably tighter than the other. This asymmetry was noted at less than 1 year of age.

Areas of concern in the self-care domain were dressing and bathing. As the mother diapered Ann, the child's legs would cross due to the hypertonicity, making it hard to open her legs. Her stiff arms were difficult to insert into a sleeve when dressing. She could not sit independently in a tub, so bathing was challenging.

The occupational therapist assisted in developing goals for feeding, fine motor, and self-care areas. Goals included proper positioning for seating and carrying; adaptive equipment for eating, bathing, and play; and oral motor handling techniques; neurodevelopmental treatment techniques to address postural issues that affected functional skills; and family education. The PT and OT taught the early interventionist about adapted positioning of Ann in a chair and on the parent's lap to decrease the influence of the atypical postural tone. The use of the bouncy seat during meals was discontinued because it set off primitive postural reflexes, increasing overall postural tone which adversely affected eating.

A coated spoon was recommended because Ann had a tonic bite reflex. The parents were discouraged from using metal or plastic utensils that might hurt or break off in her mouth as a result. A cut-out cup with thickened liquid was recommended to avoid hyperextension of the head while drinking. The bottle was discontinued gradually and cup drinking was introduced because bottle drinking encourages tongue thrust. The nutritionist was consulted during this transition to ensure adequate fluid and caloric intake.

Successful oral motor handling techniques were demonstrated to the parents. The parents were given resource materials along with explanations of the impact of cerebral palsy on a young child. The goal was to give the parents as much information as possible so they could independently understand why their child reacted negatively to touch, movement, and sound. In this way, it was hoped they would understand that her "pushing away" was actually spasticity and not a rejection of their parenting.

Adaptive positioning, such as playing in sidelying, allowed Ann better use of her hands in midline and counteracted the influence of her asymmetrical tonic neck reflex. The parents were shown how they could affect her tone by speaking softly and moving slowly.

An adapted bath seat with head cushion and reclining back was suggested to provide safety in the tub and to avoid back strain for the parents. A home program was specifically designed to address the family's daily routine. Written instructions with illustrations were given to the parents to share with other family members so they could participate in helping Ann become more functional in her environment.

After several therapy sessions and home visits, the parents stated that mealtimes were getting easier. Ann's irritability diminished and her eating improved as well. The father was able to feed her, giving the mother some much needed respite. The family was less stressed about mealtimes in general.

Adapted positioning devices or methods are designed or prescribed by a team to foster optimal positioning during functional activities.

Stages of Typical Self-Care Development

Stages in the development of self-care skills are outlined in Table 8.5.

Stages of Self-Feeding Development

Drinking From a Bottle.   Self-feeding with a bottle consists of the child inde-pendently holding and drinking from the bottle with two hands beginning at about 4 to 5 months of age. The child progresses to a one-handed grasp on the bottle. The majority of typically developing children will give up the bottle by 2 years accord-ing to Morris and Klein (2000).

Finger Feeding.   Finger feeding typically occurs at about 9–12 months of age (Coley, 1978; Haley, Coster, Ludlow, Haltiwanger, & Andrellos, 1992; Parks, 1995). Initially, the child picks up a large object, such as a cracker, using a **palmar grasp** then progresses to a smaller object, such as a Cheerio, when a **pincer grasp** (thumb and index finger) develops. This indicates that the child is able to isolate the index finger and thumb for grasping while the other fingers are closed for stability.

Use of a Spoon.   The child will initially use the spoon as a toy to bang on a surface. Appropriate use occurs when the child holds the spoon first with a palmar grasp, dipping the spoon into the food. The spoon turns upside down upon approach because the forearm is turned downward (pronated). Scooping sticky food inde-pendently and bringing it to the mouth with some spilling occurs between 18 to 24 months (Coley, 1978; Haley et al., 1992; Parks, 1995). As forearm supination develops by 2 years of age, spoon insertion without turning and minimal spilling generally occur (Haley et al., 1992). With the combination of a mature grasp, wrist rotation, and forearm supination, more successful spoon feeding occurs by 24 to 30 months of age (Parks, 1995).

> The functional use of a spoon, fork, and knife evolves from about 2 years to 8 years of age in most children.

Use of a Fork.   Stabbing with a fork requires some strength to push through the food. This skill develops at about 2 to 2 1/2 years, independence by 2 1/2 to 3 years (Parks, 1995), and a mature grasp on a fork by approximately 4 1/2 years (Coley, 1978).

Use of a Knife.   Spreading with a knife requires bilateral coordination. The child stabilizes the bread with one hand and spreads with the other. Rotation of the fore-arm and wrist are prerequisites needed to spread effectively. Spreading is accom-plished between 4 1/2 and 5 1/2 years, according to Parks (1995), 5 to 5 1/2 years according to Haley et al. (1992), and 6 to 7 years according to Coley (1978). The ability to cut through soft food, like a sandwich, develops around 5 to 5 1/2 years (Haley et al., 1992), to use a knife and fork by 5 1/2 to 6 1/2 years (Parks, 1995), and to cut meat by 7 to 8 years (Coley, 1978).

Drinking From a Cup.   Generally, a child is exposed to cup drinking around 6 months of age. A parent holds a cup to the child's lips, giving a sip with a bib under the chin for spillage. By approximately 12 months, the child is able to hold a cup and drink with some spilling. The child progresses to holding a small cup in one hand with minimal spillage by 2 years of age (Morris & Klein, 2000).

Straw Drinking.   Hunt, Lewis, Reisel, Waldrup, and Adam-Wooster (2000) found successful straw drinking in a majority of a small sample of children between 8 and 12 months of age. Morris and Klein (2000) attribute early development of this skill to earlier exposure to straw drinking, such as eating at fast-food restaurants.

Stages of Dressing Development

Dressing and undressing are not typically mastered until age 5 years.

Dressing and undressing are complex activities that are not typically mastered until age 5. Prerequisites for independent dressing are the ability to sit or stand without assistance, to use the hands in a coordinated fashion, to sequence complex tasks, and to organize clothing spatially. In most dressing tasks, children learn to undress before they can dress and undo fasteners before they can close them. The child begins assisting the caregiver with undressing when less than a year old by pulling the arm or leg from garments that are partially removed by the caregiver. At about 12 months of age, the child is able to hold out arms or feet for dressing (Finnie, 1997). Independent undressing begins at about 18 months of age, when the child can purposely pull off hat or socks. Between 2 and 3 years of age the child can usually remove all clothing that does not require the control of closures (buttons, snaps, etc.). The child can complete all dressing (including orienting clothing correctly), except for closures, between 3 and 4 years of age. Control of fasteners begins at about 2 years of age with opening large buttons and continues through 6 years of age, when tying is finally mastered (Shepherd, 2001). Stages of normal dressing are detailed in Table 8.5.

Stages of Toileting Development

The age at which a child becomes independent in toileting depends on cultural and environmental expectations, physical and emotional readiness of the child, and parental knowledge of and persistence with toilet learning practices (Shepherd, 2001). Stages of development are listed in Table 8.6. Beginning a successful toileting program is dependent on the readiness of the child. Readiness signs include the ability to indicate in some manner that he is wet, can stay dry for at least 1 to 2 hours at a time, can regulate bowel movements, desires being dry and wearing underpants, can follow simple commands, shows an interest in toileting, and understands toileting concepts such as wet and dry (Eisenberg, Murkoff, & Hathaway, 1994). There also is pressure on the child and family to accomplish bowel and bladder control for entry into school and community programs (Shepherd, 2001).

TABLE 8.5   Stages of Typical Self-Care Development

Age	Self-Feeding	Dressing	Toileting	Sleeping	Bathing and Grooming
Birth–3 months				Sleeps 16 to 17 hours per 24-hour day, 3 to 4 hours at a time	
6–12 months	Holds own bottle		Wears diapers	Sleeps 13 to 14 hours per day Takes several naps	
	Finger feeds Bangs or plays with spoon Holds spoon with poor control Takes sip from cup held by parent, shows an interest				
12–18 months	Uses spoon; spills	Cooperates— holds out arms and legs	Indicates when wet	Sleeps 12 to 13 hours per 24-hour day	Opens mouth to brush teeth
	Holds spoon with pronated grasp	Removes hat, socks, shoes, mittens		May take one or two naps per day (1 hour each)	
	Inserts spoon in dish, fills spoon poorly	Puts on hat	Has regular bowel movements by 1 year	May transition out of crib	
	Brings cup to mouth with two hands, spills Sucks from straw	Attempts to put on shoes Unsnaps in front			
18–24 months	Turns spoon before arriving at mouth	Removes coat, dress, pants	Indicates need	Sleeps 12 to 13 hours per 24-hour day	Attempts to wash body
	Scoops food, some spill Holds cup, some spill	Puts shoes on wrong feet Moves large zipper		May take one nap per day May sleep 11 hours at night	Attempts to blow nose
2–3 years	Feeds self; little spilling	Undresses with no help; removes pullover, dress	Expresses verbal anticipation	From 2 to 5 years of age, may sleep 11 to 13 hours per 24-hour day	Performs incomplete toothbrushing
	Holds spoon independently	Unbuttons	Uses control during the day, some accidents, needs reminders	May not need afternoon nap	Wipes nose when told
	Pours from small container	Buttons one large front button	Helps with clothes		Combs hair with supervision

Continued

TABLE 8.5   *Continued*

Age	Self-Feeding	Dressing	Toileting	Sleeping	Bathing and Grooming
	Holds cup in one hand, releases cup without spilling	Puts on shorts, front-opening shirt, and pants with help			
3–4 years	Begins adult grasp on utensils	Unties bow, unbuckles belt, unzips front zipper, unsnaps in back	Has bladder control at night		Washes hands and body well
	Pours from pitcher	Buttons large buttons	Attempts wiping		Wipes nose without being told
	Stabs with a fork; spreads with a knife	Puts on coat, dress, pullover shirt, boots, socks correctly	Manages clothing during toileting		
4–5 years	Eats independently, with minimal to no spilling	Dresses completely with supervision	Goes to the bathroom independently		Brushes teeth
	Cuts soft foods with a knife	Unzips back zipper	Maintains full independence		
	Chooses menu	Buttons shirt or coat	Has volitional control of bladder		
		Zips front zipper			
		Laces and is able to Velcro shoes, puts shoes on correct feet			
		Buckles belt			
		Knows front from back, right from wrong side; can turn inside out			
5–6 years		Ties shoes	Majority of children have day and night bladder control	Sleeps 9 to 11 hours per 24-hour day	Washes face well
			Wipes self well		
		Zips back zipper			
6–7 years	Prefers fork to spoon	Ties bow			Wipes and blows nose independently
	Does not use napkin	Snaps and buttons in back			

Sources: Adapted from Eisenberg, Murkoff, & Hathaway (1994); Haley, Coster, Ludlow, Haltiwanger, & Andrellos (1992); Henderson (1995); Hunt, Lewis, Reisel, Waldrup, & Adam-Wooster (2000); Morris, & Klein (2000); Shepherd, Procter, & Coley (1996).

Self-Care Development in Young Children with Special Needs

There are a variety of factors that can negatively impact on the self-care development of young children with special needs. When one or any combination of factors is present, there are a number of behaviors that can indicate a problem with self-care development. Figure 8.21 provides a list of some of these key behaviors. Specific functional areas of interest include self-feeding, dressing, and toileting,

Self-Feeding

Separating one side of the hand from the other to finger feed can be a difficult task for children with neuromotor dysfunction. For example, a child with spastic cerebral palsy may have a fisted hand due to increased postural tone in the flexors making it

Self feeding	Poor postural control that interferes with self feeding
	Lack of finger-feeding beyond 12 months of age
	Poor use of utensils (extended use of an immature grasp pattern, poor bilateral hand use)
	Refusal to use utensils by the appropriate developmental age
	Overly messy or sloppy eater
	Inability to sit still for a meal
	Extreme resistance to finger feeding certain textures of food
Dressing	Poor postural control that interferes with dressing
	Delayed dressing skills beyond expected age
	Poor fine motor skills (unable to button, zip, snap by the expected developmental age)
	Intolerance to certain clothing textures
	Parental report indicating that it took forever to teach dressing skills such as tying shoes
Bathing	Inability to independently sit in a bathing device after 8 months of age
	Parental concern about lifting child in and out of the bathtub
	Extreme resistance to washing hair
	Inability to maneuver in and out of the bathtub by the expected age
Toileting	Difficulty opening legs of a child when diapering
	Cannot sit independently on toilet when developmentally appropriate
	Lack of independence in managing clothing after the expected developmental age
	Delayed bowel and bladder control
Grooming	Poor fine motor skills to manage grooming tools such as comb, toothbrush, washcloth and soap
	"Hates" having hair cut
Sleep	Persistent tantrums at bedtime
	Frequent waking at night beyond infancy
	Absence of or excessive bedtime rituals
	Excessive demands of parent after child is in bed
	Persistent asymmetrical posturing of child in bed due to atypical postural tone; muscles do not relax during sleep

FIGURE 8.21   Red flags related to self care

difficult to open the hand, rotate the forearm in pronation and supination, or release the finger food once grasped.

Use of a spoon requires motor planning and dexterity. A child with a weak grasp due to atypical postural tone from cerebral palsy may have trouble holding and maintaining grasp on the spoon. For example, a child with athetoid cerebral palsy will have trouble maintaining grasp on a utensil and inserting it into the mouth due to involuntary movement. The child's body is in constant motion making the mouth a moving target. A child with a learning disability and dyspraxia may have difficulty motor planning use of a utensil and resort to using his fingers well beyond a socially acceptable age. Lack of a hand preference seen in some children with **sensory integrative dysfunction** can make it difficult to develop skilled tool use as the child switches from hand to hand. Limited cognitive abilities in a child with mental retardation may delay understanding the use of utensils.

> Sensory integrative dysfunction is an inability to organize and process sensory information in the absence of known neurological or sensory receptor abnormality.

Dressing

Atypical postural tone may interfere with positioning for dressing; the child may not tolerate or be able to be positioned to help in dressing. One side of the body may be tighter, as in hemiplegia, making it difficult for the child to independently dress with the involved side. Poor fine motor control may prevent manipulation of fasteners. Increased postural tone may make it difficult to insert a tonically extended foot into a shoe or a tightly fisted hand into a glove. Children with poor motor planning abilities may have difficulty figuring out how to tie shoes or distinguish the front from back or right from left. A child who has a sensory impairment may resist wearing certain types and textures of clothing.

Toileting

A child with spina bifida may have a flaccid bladder. Toilet learning may not be possible. The term toilet "learning" versus "training" emphasizes that any approach needs to be a child-centered learning experience (Eisenberg et al., 1994; Mack, 1978). Intervention can be beneficial if the lesion is above the lumbar region (Shepherd, 2001). **Spina bifida occulta,** a less severe form of spina bifida, also can cause delayed bladder control and a toileting program can be successful with this population (Maizels, Rosenbaum, & Keating, 1999).

Children with motor impairment may have problems due to atypical postural tone and limited movement. As was noted earlier, an infant with an abnormally tight musculature in the legs due to spastic cerebral palsy may be unable to open the legs for diapering. A child with neurological impairment may have unstable posture due to atypical tone which will make it difficult to independently sit on a toilet in a relaxed manner. The child may not feel safe due to the postural instability. Weakness or decreased range of motion in the arms can impede use of fasteners during toileting.

Inappropriate parental expectations also can lead to frustration with their child's accidents and resistance to toilet learning practices. The early interventionist can have a positive impact here by addressing parental frustration and by providing information to help adjust parental expectations.

Specific Strategies for Self-Care Assessment

Self-care assessment addresses a child's level of development and independence in self-feeding (finger feeding, use of utensils, use of bottle or cup); dressing (undressing, dressing, fasteners, and directionality); toileting (bowel and bladder control); bathing (washing hands, face, and body); grooming (brushing teeth, combing hair); and sleeping. Evaluation tools, such as the Hawaii Early Learning Profile (Furuno et al., 1997; Parks, 1995) provide a developmental framework for determining the child's ability in the self-care domain.

The early interventionist will collaborate with the OT when postural and sensory problems interfere with self-care tasks and there is a need for adaptive equipment. For example, how can a child with limited range of motion reach the soap in the bathroom to independently wash their hands? Can adapted equipment, such as a wheelchair, fit through the bathroom door and around the classroom? What adaptive equipment is needed to help the child be more independent in self-care skills? How do sensory components, such as tactile properties of clothes or food, noise level, lighting, and smells within the environment, affect self-care performance in a child with **sensory defensiveness**?

> Sensory defensiveness is the hypersensitivity to normal sensations (i.e., the child reacts defensively to sensory input rather than discriminately).

Assessment is performed within a cultural context that may be revealed through answers to the following questions: When are solid foods typically introduced into an infant's diet? What foods are restricted? What type of socialization is expected during meals? What level of independence is deemed appropriate at various ages? What type of clothing does the child wear that may be different from that expected by the evaluator? When and how is toilet learning addressed in the child's culture? What utensils are used at the meal; spoon and fork or chopsticks for example? Planning intervention to address manipulation of a spoon or fork is pointless if the child typically uses chopsticks. The evaluator observes the child within his own environment and integrates the family into the assessment process as much as possible.

Selected Assessment Tools That Evaluate Self-Care Skills

The Hawaii Early Learning Profile (HELP) is a curriculum-based, criterion-referenced, interdisciplinary assessment tool (Furuno et al., 1997). The HELP for infants and toddlers is family centered, covering birth to 3 years of age. HELP for Preschoolers (Parks, 1995) continues up to age 6. Content of the test includes cognition, language, gross motor, fine motor, social-emotional, and self-help. The self-help area addresses oral motor development, dressing, independent feeding, sleep patterns and behaviors, grooming and hygiene, toileting, and household independence/responsibility. Results are reported in developmental age levels.

The Battelle Developmental Inventory (BDI) covers activities of daily living including eating, dressing, toileting, and grooming and it addresses the birth to 8-year population (Newborg, Stock, Wnek, Guidubaldi, & Svinicki, in press).

The Pediatric Evaluation of Disability Inventory (PEDI), developed by Haley and colleagues (1992), is a structured interview-judgment-based standardized evaluation given to parents or clinicians familiar with the child. It measures three domains (self-care, mobility, and social function) in children with moderate to severe motor impairment between 6 months and 7 years. The PEDI also addresses the level of assistance and modifications needed. The self-care domain includes 73 items that include adaptability to food texture; use of utensils; use of drinking containers; toothbrushing; hair-brushing; nose care; hand, body, and face washing; maneuvering pullover garments, fasteners, pants, shoes and socks; toileting; and managing bowel and bladder.

The Functional Independence Measure for Children (WeeFIM) is appropriate for children with physical disabilities functioning within the age range of 6 months to 6 years (Hamilton & Granger, 1991). The self-care section includes feeding, dressing, and grooming.

Use of Technology in Self-Care Assessment and Intervention

An adapted toilet seat with accessories (e.g., tray, harness, back pad, footrest) provides extra trunk and head support during toileting.

As noted in chapters 6 and 7, adaptive equipment may be necessary when a child has a physical impairment. Equipment is prescribed with consideration for the child's chronological and developmental age as well as the environment in which the equipment will be used. Selected adaptive equipment such as adapted eating utensils or **adapted toilet seats** for the self-care domains are presented in Figures 8.22, 8.23, 8.24, and 8.25 on the following pages.

Use of Technology in Toileting

Some typically developing children independently learn toileting quickly whereas others, to the parents' distress, take much longer. Children with disabilities have added disadvantages that can make toilet learning all that more difficult. Some examples of adapted equipment used to enhance independence in toileting are listed in Figure 8.25. An **enuresis alarm** is one aspect of a multidimensional approach for children diagnosed with **nocturnal enuresis** (i.e., urinating during the night due to deep sleep patterns). Other methods may be indicated for children with special needs. A thorough evaluation is conducted to determine if wetting is due to issues such as deep sleep, small bladder size, neurological problems, overproduction of urine, stress in the family, or food sensitivities (Maizels et al., 1999). The alarm is used only when the child has been diagnosed with enuresis. It is not appropriate for a child with **incontinence.** Incontinence indicates that the child does not have a typically functioning urinary tract. The alarm sounds when the child wets during the night. The device includes a moisture sensor that is attached to the outer part of the child's underwear and an alarm that is attached near the shoulder on the child's pajamas. The comprehensive program generally shows success within a matter of months if used consistently (Maizels et al., 1999).

Bottles	Angled-neck bottles to decrease hyperextension of the head and air swallowing in children with atypical swallow
	Specially shaped bottles, grips, or adapted rings added to the bottles to allow for two-handed use
Spoons	Swivel spoons to accommodate lack of arm position and movement
	Weighted spoons for children with tremor, athetosis, or sensory disorders
	Right- or left-handed curved spoons
	Coated spoons to protect the teeth if the child has a tonic bite reflex or sensitivity to temperature
	Flexible utensils that can be adjusted to fit the child's changing needs
	Various sized and shaped spoons (narrow, wide, shallow, deep) to accommodate the child's needs and the feeder's comfort
Cups	Cut-out cups used to prevent head hyperextension and foster more normal swallowing
	Spouted cups to make transition to a regular cup easier. Spouted cups are discouraged if a child has a tongue thrust
	Easy-grip and two-handled cups for manageability
	Weighted cups for those needing sensory feedback and added stability
Dishes	Scoop dishes with a nonskid bottom and a higher, rounded edge to help the child scoop
	Plates with suction cups so they do not move while scooping
Straws	Straws of various widths, lengths, and thicknesses to provide added oral stability
Other	Handles on utensils to enhance grip
	Built-up handled utensils for children with poor or weak grasp
	Universal cuff, a device consisting of a cuff attached to an elastic strap wrapped around the hand that helps a child with minimal to no grasp
	Long-handled utensils for a child with limited reaching
	Sandwich holders for children who cannot maintain grasp on a sandwich
	Winsford Feeder for a child with severe arm involvement to self-feed by activating a spoon with a chin switch

FIGURE 8.22   Selected adaptive equipment for self-feeding

Available from: Sammons Preston (2003). Pediatrics Catalog: Special needs products for schools and clinics. Bolingbrook, IL: An Ability One Corporation.

Selected Strategies for Self-Care Intervention

Intervention approaches for development of self-care skills in children include (1) developmental; (2) remedial; (3) compensatory; and (4) educational approaches (Shepherd, 2001). These approaches can be used in isolation or combination. In the developmental approach, tasks are taught in a developmental sequence. A child's chronological and developmental age are used as guidelines for progression of skills. This approach is most useful for children with mild disabilities. The remedial approach focuses on direct intervention to address missing components that interfere with acquisition of self-care skills. The OT or PT will use **neurodevelopmental treatment techniques** (NDT), for example, to modify atypical postural tone or

Buttons	Velcro in place of buttons
	Button hook for limited bilateral control
	Larger buttons for ease in handling
	Cuff and collar button extender
Zippers	Zipper pull to accommodate a poor grasp
	Button hook with zipper pull
Laces	Elastic or coiled laces for poor dexterity
	Lace locks for one-handed child
	One-handed shoe-tying technique
Clothing	Pullover shirts to eliminate the need for fasteners
	Velcro or slip-on shoes
	Elastic waistbands on pants
Other	Lightweight reacher for dressing
	Pant clip for limited mobility or weakness
	Sock and stocking aid

FIGURE 8.23 Selected adaptive equipment and modifications for dressing

Available from: Sammons Preston (2003). Pediatrics Catalog: Special needs products for schools and clinics. Bolingbrook, IL: An Ability One Corporation. (1-800-323-5547)

- Reclining chair with adjustable seat and back angle with removable mesh fabric that comes in various sizes and includes a chest strap, hip strap, leg strap, and head support
- Wrap-around bath support that is height adjustable used for less involved children needing extra support for safety. It fits around the child's trunk so he can sit upright in the bathtub
- Optional shower stands
- Long-handled shower spray
- Tub-transfer seat

FIGURE 8.24 Selective adaptive equipment for bathing

Available from: Sammons Preston (2003). Pediatrics Catalog: Special needs products for schools and clinics. Bolingbrook, IL: An Ability One Corporation.

sensory integration (SI) to modify sensory integrative dysfunction for functional skill development. For example, Lily wanted to help with undressing, yet she was unable to accomplish this because she could not sit independently and her atypical postural tone prevented her hands from coming to the midline to reach and grasp effectively. The therapist consulted with the parents and early interventionist about special handling techniques to diminish the atypical tone and movement so that she could participate in undressing.

The **compensatory approach** includes the use of adaptive equipment to compensate for missing skills. In addition, Shepherd (2001) discusses how to grade

- Toilet seat reducer ring
- Toilet support-adjustable, wrap-around trunk or high-back toilet support that attaches to an existing toilet for a less involved child
- Adapted toilet seats with attachments suitable to the child's level of involvement
- Combined toilet and shower chair
- Toilet safety frame with adjustable arm support that attaches to the frame for support and push off
- Portable, pediatric commodes with chest strap
- Raised toilet seats
- Toilet safety locks for very young, mobile children (Miller, 1991)

FIGURE 8.25   *Selected adaptive equipment for toileting*

Available from: Sammons Preston (2003). Pediatrics Catalog: Special needs products for schools and clinics. Bolingbrook, IL: An Ability One Corporation.

activities through task analysis, personal assistance, partial participation, backward and forward chaining, and verbal, gestural, or physical prompts to modify a task.

The **educational approach** is a component of all the other intervention methods. The interventionist collaborates with the family, child, and educational staff to disseminate information in a manner that addresses the best learning style of each child. The interventionist uses open dialogue, modeling, and clear and concise written information that may include illustrations. Additional resources are suggested to the parents for further reading or specific assistance in an area of need.

Early intervention service providers target the family's concerns as a priority during evaluation and intervention. Goals are determined together with the parents. Team members analyze the barriers to independence. Cultural values and practices are considered as well. The program that is developed should be consistent with the daily family and school routines.

Summary

Early postural control and gross motor skills provide the child with the necessary tools to become independent from caregivers as well as caregivers themselves eventually. Development of a sense of "self," however, comes from an ability to do many things for oneself. Fine motor and self-care competence helps to build self-esteem in the young child.

Intervention in the areas of fine motor, oral motor, and self-care skills may be implemented by a number of specialists. The occupational thera-

pist may be the most knowledgeable member of the team regarding fine motor dysfunction. The occupational therapist or the speech-language pathologist may be best able to address assessment and program planning for oral motor skills. However, it is the early interventionist who most often introduces the child to fine motor and self-care tasks, working closely with the parents and other professionals. In order to have a successful program, good communication and mutual respect among all team members are imperative.

Review Questions and Discussion Points

1. Divide a paper into three columns. Label the columns *cerebral palsy, Down syndrome,* and *autism.* List characteristics of fine motor and oral motor development for children with each of these special needs.
2. Identify several indicators of fine motor problems in young children.
3. Identify several indicators of oral motor problems in young children.
4. Describe five strategies for enhancing the development of fine motor skills.
5. Describe five strategies for enhancing the development of oral motor skills.
6. Discuss ways that a teacher can adjust her classroom to address the needs of children who have sensory processing problems.

Recommended Resources

Recommended Reading

Autism

Janzen, J. (1999). *Autism: Facts and strategies for parents.* San Antonio, TX: Therapy Skill Builders.

Janzen, J. (2002). *Understanding the nature of autism: A practical guide* (2nd ed.). San Antonio, TX: Therapy Skill Builders.

Knight, J., & Decker, M. (1994). *Hands at work and play: Developing fine motor skills at school and home.* San Antonio, TX: Therapy Skill Builders.

Dressing

Klein, M. (1983). *Pre-dressing skills.* San Antonio, TX: Therapy Skill Builders.

Family

Batshaw, M. (Ed.). (2001). *When your child has a disability: The complete sourcebook of daily and medical care.* Baltimore: Brookes.

Cerebral Palsy

Finnie, N. (1997). *Handling the young child with cerebral palsy at home* (3rd ed.). Woburn, MA: Butterworth-Heinemann.

Geralis, E. (Ed.). (1991). *Children with cerebral palsy: A parents' guide.* Bethesda, MD: Woodbine House.

Safety

Miller, J. (1991). *The perfectly safe home.* New York: Simon & Schuster.

Sensory Integration Dysfunction

Arkwright, N. (1998). *An introduction to sensory integration.* San Antonio, TX: Therapy Skill Builders.

Ayres, A. (1979). *Sensory integration and the child.* Los Angeles: Western Psychological Services.

Inamura, K. (1998). *SI for early intervention: A team approach.* San Antonio, TX: Therapy Skill Builders.

Kranowitz, C. (1998). *The out-of-sync child: Recognizing and coping with sensory integration dysfunction.* New York: Berkley.

Roley, S. (2001). *Understanding the nature of sensory integration with diverse populations.* San Antonio, TX: Therapy Skill Builders.

Trott, M., Laurel, M., & Windeck, S. (1993). *SenseAbilities.* San Antonio, TX: Therapy Skill Builders.

Toileting

Maizels, M., Rosenbaum, D., & Keating, B. (1999). *Getting to dry: How to help your child overcome bedwetting.* Boston: The Harvard Common Press.

Mack, A. (1978). *Toilet learning: The picture book technique for children and parents.* Boston: Little, Brown.

Catalogs

Pediatric Catalogs for Adapted Equipment

Achievement Products for Children. (2003). *Catalog.* Canton, OH. (http://www.achievementproducts.org/index.html).

Mealtime Catalog (2003). A resource for oral-motor, feeding, and mealtime programs. Faber, VA: New Visions (http://www.new_vis5.com)

Sammons Preston Rolyan. (2003). *Pediatrics catalog.* Bolingbrook, IL: AbilityOne. (1-800-323-5547)

Southpaw Enterprises. (2003). *Southpaw products catalog.* Dayton, OH: Southpaw Enterprises. (1-800-228-1698; **therapy@southpawenterprises.com**)

Sportime Abilitations. (2003). *Catalog.* Atlanta, GA. (**http://www.abilitations.com.**)

Therapy Skill Builders. (2003). *Assessment and therapy resources catalog.* San Antonio, TX: Psychological Corporation/Harcourt Assessment.

Websites

Ergonomics and Computer Use
http://ergo.human.cornell.edu/cuweguideline.htm
http://www.kidstation.com/ergonomics/index.shtml
http://www.healthycomputing.com/kids/computers.html
http://www.askergoworks.com/cart_ergo_kids.asp

Technology

AbleNet
http://www.ablenetinc.com
1-800-322-0956

Don Johnston
http://www.donjohnston.com
1-800-999-4660

Enabling Devices
http://www.enablingdevices.com
1-800-832-8697

IntelliTools
http://www.intellitools.com
1-800-899-6687

Tash Inc.
http://www.tashinc.com
1-800-463-5685

References

Arvedson, J., & Lefton-Greif, M. (1998). *Pediatric videofluoroscopic swallow studies.* San Antonio, TX: Communication Skill Builders.

Ayres, A. J. (1985). *Sensory integration and the child.* Los Angeles: Western Psychological Services.

Ayres, A. J. (1989). *Sensory Integration and Praxis Tests.* Los Angeles: Western Psychological Services.

Batshaw, M. (1997). *Children with disabilities* (4th ed.). Baltimore: Brookes.

Benbow, M. (1990). *Loops and other groups: A kinesthetic writing system.* San Antonio, TX: Therapy Skill Builders.

Benbow, M. (1995). Principles and practices of teaching handwriting. In A. Henderson & C. Pehoski (Eds.), *Hand function in the child: Foundations for remediation* (pp. 255–281). St. Louis, MO: Mosby.

Benda, C. D. (1969). *Down syndrome: Mongolism and its management.* New York: Grune & Stratton.

Berk, R., & DeGangi, G. (1983). *DeGangi-Berk Test of Sensory Integration.* Los Angeles: Western Psychological Services.

Bledsoe, N., & Shepherd, J. (1982). A study of reliability and validity of a preschool play scale. *The American Journal of Occupational Therapy, 36,* 783–788.

Bundy, A. C. (1997). Play and playfulness: What to look for. In L. D. Parham & L. S. Fazio (Eds.), *Play in occupational therapy for children.* (pp. 52–66). Baltimore: Mosby.

Bundy, A. (2002). Assessing sensory integrative dysfunction. In A. Bundy, S. Lane, & E. Murray (Eds.), *Sensory integration: Theory and practice* (2nd ed., pp. 194–196). Philadelphia: F. A. Davis.

Case-Smith, J. (1995). Grasp, release, and bimanual skills in the first two years of life. In A. Henderson & C. Pehoski (Eds.), *Hand function in the child: Foundations for remediation* (pp. 113–135). St. Louis, MO: Mosby.

Case-Smith, J. (2001). Development of childhood occupations. In J. Case-Smith (Ed.), *Occupational therapy for children* (4th ed., pp. 71–94). St. Louis MO: Mosby.

Case-Smith, J., & Bryan, T. (1999). The effects of occupational therapy with sensory integration emphasis on preschool-age children with autism. *The American Journal of Occupational Therapy, 53,* 489–497.

Case-Smith, J., & Humphrey, R. (1996). Feeding and oral motor skills. In J. Case-Smith, A. S. Allen, & P. Nuse-Pratt (Eds.), *Occupational therapy for children* (3rd ed., pp. 430–460). St. Louis, MO: Mosby.

Cermak, S. (1991). Somatodyspraxia. In A. Fisher, E. Murray, & A. Bundy (Eds.), *Sensory integration: Theory and practice* (pp. 138–161). Philadelphia: F. A. Davis.

Cole, K., Abbs, J., & Turner, G. (1988). Deficits in the production of grip forces in Down syndrome. - *Developmental Medicine and Child Neurology, 30,* 752–758.

Coley, I. L. (1978). *Pediatric assessment of self-care activities.* St. Louis, MO: Mosby.

Connor, F., Williamson, G., & Siepp, J. (1978). *Program guide for infants and toddlers with neuromotor and other developmental disabilities.* New York: Teachers College Press.

Cox, R. D. (1993). Normal childhood development from birth to five years. In E. Schopler, M. E. VanBourgondien, & M. M. Bristol (Eds.), *Preschool issues in autism* (pp. 39–57). New York: Plenum Press.

DeGangi, G. A., Breinbauer, C., Roosevelt, J. D., Porges, S., & Greenspan, S. (2000). Prediction of childhood problems at three years in children experiencing disorders of regulation during infancy. *Infant Mental Health Journal, 21,* 156–176.

Dunn, W. (1999). *Sensory Profile.* San Antonio, TX: Psychological Corporation.

Dunn, W. (2000). *The Infant/Toddler Sensory Profile.* San Antonio, TX: Psychological Corporation.

Edwards, S., & Lafreniere, M. (1995). Hand function in the Down syndrome population. In A. Henderson & C. Pehoski (Eds.), *Hand function in the child: Foundations for remediation* (pp. 299–311). St. Louis, MO: Mosby.

Eisenberg, A., Murkoff, H., & Hathaway, S. (1994). *What to expect the toddler years.* New York: Workman.

Erhardt, R. (1994a). *Developmental hand dysfunction: Theory, assessment and treatment* (2nd ed.). San Antonio, TX: Therapy Skill Builders.

Erhardt, R. (1994b). Erhardt Developmental Prehension Assessment (EDPA), Revised. Tucson, AZ: Therapy Skill Builders.

Exner, C. (2001). Development of hand skills. In J. Case-Smith (Ed.), *Occupational therapy for children* (4th ed., pp. 289–328). St. Louis, MO: Mosby.

Finnie, N. (1997). *Handling the young child with cerebral palsy at home* (3rd ed.). Woburn, MA: Butterworth-Heinemann.

Folio, M. R., & Fewell, R. R. (2000). *Peabody Developmental Motor Scales* (2nd ed.). Chicago: Riverside.

Furuno, S., O'Reilly, K., Hosaka, C. M., Inatsuka, T. T., Allmann, T., & Zeisloft, B., (1997). *Hawaii Early Learning Profile.* Palo Alto, CA: VORT Corporation.

Gesell, A., & Amatruda, C. (1947). Developmental diagnosis. New York: Harper & Row.

Gesell, A., & Ames, L. E. (1947). The development of handedness. *The Journal of Genetic Psychology, 70,* 155–175.

Goodgold-Edwards, W., & Cermak, S. (1989). Integrating motor control and motor learning concepts with neuropyschological perspectives on apraxia and developmental dyspraxia *American Journal of Occupational Therapy, 44,* pp. 431–439.

Grandin, T. (1995). *Thinking in pictures.* New York: Doubleday.

Gutman, S. A., McCreedy, P., & Heisler, P. (2002). The psychosocial deficits of children with regulatory disorders. *OT Practice, 7,* CE4–CE8.

Haley, S. M., Coster, W. L., Ludlow, L. H., Haltiwanger, J. T., & Andrellos, P. J. (1992). *Pediatric Evaluation of Disability Inventory.* Boston: New England Medical Center Hospital Inc., and PEDI Research Group.

Hamilton, B., & Granger, C. (1991). *Functional Independence Measure for Children (WeeFIM).* Buffalo: Research Foundation of the State University of New York.

Harris, L. J., & Carlson, D. F. (1988). Pathological left-handedness: An analysis of theories and evidence. In D. L. Molfese & S. J. Segalowitz (Eds.), *Brain lateralization in children: Developmental implications.* (pp. 289–372). New York: Guilford Press.

Healthy Computing for Kids (n.d.) Ergonomics for kids: Computers. Retrieved June 6, 2003, from http://healthycomputing.com/kids/computers.html.

Henderson, A. (1995). Self-care and hand skill. In A. Henderson & C. Pehoski (Eds.), *Hand function in the child: Foundations for remediation* (pp. 164–183). St. Louis, MO: Mosby.

Hunt, L., Lewis, D., Reisel, S., Waldrup, L., & Adam-Wooster, D. (2000). Age norms for straw-drinking ability. *The Transdisciplinary Journal, 10,* 1–8.

Jelm, J. (1990). *Oral Motor/Feeding Rating Scale.* Tucson, AZ: Therapy Skill Builders.

Johnson, H., & Scott, A. (1993). *A practical approach to saliva control.* Tucson, AZ: Therapy Skill Builders.

Jones, V., & Prior, M. R. (1985). Motor imitation abilities and neurological signs in autistic children. *Journal of Autism and Developmental Disorders, 15,* 37–46.

Kientz, M., & Dunn, W. (1997). A comparison of the performance of children with and without autism on the Sensory Profile. *American Journal of Occupational Therapy, 51* (7), 530–537.

King, L. J., & Grandin, T. (1990). *Attention deficits in learning disorder and autism: A sensory integrative treatment approach*. Workshop presented at the Conference Proceedings of the Continuing Education Programs of America, Milwaukee, WI.

Klein, M. (1990a). *Pre-writing skills* (Rev. ed.). San Antonio, TX: Therapy Skill Builders.

Klein, M. (1990b). *Pre-scissor skills* (3rd ed.). San Antonio, TX: Therapy Skill Builders.

Knox, S. (1997). Development and current use of the Knox Preschool Play Scale. In L. D. Parham & L. S. Fazio (Eds.), *Play in occupational therapy* (pp. 35–51). St. Louis, MO: Mosby.

Levine, K. (1995). *Development of pre-writing and scissor skills: A visual analysis* [Videocassette]. San Antonio, TX: Therapy Skill Builders.

Levine, M. (1987). *Developmental variation and learning disorders*. Cambridge, MA: Educators Publishing Service.

Linder, T. W. (1993). *Transdisciplinary play-based assessment: A functional approach to working with young children*. Baltimore: Brookes.

Logemann, J. (1998). *Evaluation and treatment of swallowing disorders* (2nd ed.). San Diego, CA: College-Hill Press.

Long, C., Conrad, P., Hall, E., & Furler, S. (1970). Intrinsic-extrinsic muscle control of the hand in power and precision handling. *Journal of Bone and Joint Surgery, 52–A,* 853–867.

Lopez, M. (1986). *Developmental sequence of the skill of cutting with scissors in normal children 2 to 6 years old*. Unpublished master's thesis, Boston University.

Lovaas, O. I., Newsom, C., & Hickman, C. (1987). Self-stimulatory behavior and perceptual reinforcement. *Journal of Applied Behavior Analysis, 20,* 45–68.

Mack, A. (1978). *Toilet learning: The picture book technique for children and parents*. Boston: Little, Brown.

Mailloux, Z., & Roley, S. S. (2001). Sensory integration. In H. M. Miller-Kuhaneck (Ed.), *Autism: A comprehensive occupational therapy approach* (pp. 101–132). Bethesda, MD: American Occupational Therapy Association.

Maizels, M., Rosenbaum, D., & Keating, B. (1999). Getting to dry: How to help your child overcome bedwetting. Boston, MA: Harvard Common Press.

McHale, K., & Cermak, S.A. (1992). Fine motor activities in elementary school: Preliminary findings and provisional implications for children with fine motor problems. *American Journal of Occupational Therapy, 45* (8), 701–706.

McManus, I. C., Ski, G., Cole, D. R., Mellon, A. F., Wong, J., & Kloss, J. (1988). The development of handedness in children. *British Journal of Psychology, 6,* 257–273.

Meltzoff, A., & Gopnik, A. (1993). The role of imitation in understanding persons and developing a theory of mind. In S. Baron-Cohen, H. Tager-Flusberg, & D. J. Cohen (Eds.), *Understanding other minds: Perspectives from autism* (pp. 335–366). New York: Oxford University Press.

Miller, L. J., Reisman, J., McIntosh, D., & Simon, J. (2001). An ecological model of sensory modulation: Performance of children with Fragile X syndrome, autistic disorder, attention-deficit/hyperactivity disorder, and sensory modulation dysfunction. In S. Smith Roley, E. Blanche, & R. Schaaf (Eds.), *Understanding the nature of sensory integration with diverse populations* (pp. 57–79). San Antonio, TX: Therapy Skill Builders.

Miller, L. J., & Roid, G. H. (1994). *Toddler and Infant Motor Evaluation (TIME)*. San Antonio, TX: Psychological Corporation.

Missiuna, C., & Polatajko, H. (1995). Developmental dyspraxia by any other name: Are they all just clumsy children? *The American Journal of Occupational Therapy, 49,* 619–627.

Morris, S. (1982). *Pre-speech Assessment Scale: A rating scale for the measurement of pre-speech behavior from birth to 2 years*. New Jersey: J. A. Preston.

Morris, S., & Klein, M. (2000). *Pre-feeding skills: A comprehensive resource for mealtime development*. San Antonio, TX: Therapy Skill Builders.

Mulligan, S. (2002). Advances in sensory integration research. In A. Bundy, S. Lane, & E. Murray (Eds.), *Sensory integration theory and practice* (2nd ed., pp. 400–401). Philadelphia: F. A. Davis.

National Center for Education Statistics. (2000). *Internet access in public schools and classrooms: 1994–99*. Washington, DC: U.S. Department of Education, Office of Educational Research and Improvement.

Nehring, A., Nehring, E., Bruni, J., & Randolph, P. (1992). *Learning Accomplishment Profile-Diagnostic Standardized Assessment*. Lewisville, NC: Kaplan Press.

Nelson, D. L. (1984). *Children with autism*. Thorofare, NJ: Slack.

Newborg, J., Stock, J. R., Wnek, L., Guidubaldi, J., & Svinicki, A. (in press). *Battelle Developmental Inventory–Revised*. Chicago: Riverside.

Parham, D., & Ecker, C. (2002). Evaluation of sensory processing. In A. Bundy, S. Lane, and E. Murray (Eds.), *Sensory integration: Theory and practice* (2nd ed.), pp. 194–196). Philadelphia. PA: F. A. Davis.

Parks, S. (1995). *Inside HELP: Administration and reference manual for the Hawaii Early Learning Profile (HELP)*. Palo Alto, CA: VORT Corporation.

Rapin, I. (1988). Disorders of higher cerebral function in preschool children. Part II: Autistic spectrum disorder. *American Journal of Diseases of Children, 142*, 1178–1182.

Ray, T., King, L., & Grandin, T. (1988). The effectiveness of self-initiated vestibular stimulation in producing speech sounds in an autistic child. *Occupational Therapy Journal of Research, 8*, 186–190.

Reeves, G. D., & Cermak, S. A. (2002). Disorders of praxis. In A. Bundy, S. Lane, & E. Murray (Eds.), *Sensory integration: Theory and practice* (2nd ed., pp. 71–95). Philadelphia: F. A. Davis.

Rosenbloom, L., & Horton, M. (1971). The maturation of fine prehension in young children. *Developmental Medicine and Child Neurology, 13*, 3–8.

Schneck, C., & Battaglia, C. (1992). Developing scissor skills in young children. In J. Case-Smith & C. Pehoski (Eds.), *Development of hand skills in the child* (pp. 79–89). Rockville, MD: American Occupational Therapy Association.

Schneck, C., & Henderson, A. (1990). Descriptive analysis of the developmental progression of grip position for pencil and crayon control in nondysfunctional children. *The American Journal of Occupational Therapy, 44*, 890–893.

Shepherd, J. (2001). Self-care and adaptations for independent living. In J. Case-Smith (Ed.), *Occupational therapy for children* (4th ed., pp. 489–527). St. Louis, MO: Mosby.

Shepherd, J., Procter, S., & Coley, I. (1996). Self-care and adaptations for independent living. In J. Case-Smith, A. Allen, & P. Pratt (Eds.), *Occupational therapy for children* (pp. 461–501). St. Louis, MO: Mosby.

Shumway-Cook, A., & Woollacott, M. H. (2001). *Motor control*. Philadelphia: Lippincott Williams & Wilkins.

Siegel, B. (1996). *The world of the autistic child*. New York: Oxford University Press.

Spitzer, S., & Roley, S. (2001). Sensory integration revisited: A philosophy of practice. In S. Smith Roley, E. Blanche, & R. Schaaf (Eds.), *Understanding the nature of sensory integration with diverse populations* (pp. 3–27). Tucson, AZ: Therapy Skill Builders.

Struck, M. (1996). *Assistive technology in the schools. AOTA self-paced clinical course*. Rockville, MD: American Occupational Therapy Association.

Tan, L. E. (1985). Laterality and motor skills in four-year-olds. *Child Development, 56*, 119–124.

Thelen, E., Corbetta, D., Kamm, K., & Spencer, J. (1993). The transition to reaching: Mapping intention and intrinsic dynamics. *Child Development, 64*, 1058–1098.

Van Bourgondien, M. E. (1993). Behavior management in the preschool years. In E. Schopler, M. E. Van Bourgondien, and M. M. Bristol (Eds.), *Preschool issues in autism* (pp. 129–145). New York: Plenum Press.

Volkmar, F. R., Cohen, D. J., & Paul, R. (1986). Classification and diagnosis of childhood autism. *Journal of the American Academy of Child & Adolescent Psychiatry, 25*, 190–197.

VORT Corporation. (1995). *HELP for Preschoolers*. Palo Alto, CA: Author.

Watson, L. R., & Marcus, L. M. (1986). Diagnosis and assessment of preschool children. In E. Schopler & G. Mesibov (Eds.), *Social behavior in autism* (pp. 285–303). New York: Plenum Press.

Williamson, G. G., & Anzalone, M. (1997). Sensory integration: A key component of the evaluation and treatment of young children with severe difficulties in relating and communicating. *ZERO TO THREE, 17*, 29–36.

Witt, B., & Klein, M. (1990). *Prepare: An interdisciplinary approach to perceptual-motor readiness*. San Antonio, TX: Therapy Skill Builders.

Wolf, L. S., & Glass, R. P. (1992). *Feeding and swallowing disorders in infancy*. Tucson, AZ: Therapy Skill Builders.

We would like to thank the children, their families and teachers for sharing their wonderful stories; Betsy Cohen for her expertise related to the case studies; and Amy Fink for her helpful editing advice.

9
Cognitive Development

Warren Umansky

Chapter Outline

- The Range of Cognitive Skills
- Piaget's Theory of Cognitive Development
- Piaget's Stages of Development
- Other Theories of Development
- Relationships Between Developmental and Cognitive Processing Models
- Factors That Affect Cognitive Development
- Cognitive Development and the Child with Special Needs
- Facilitating Cognitive Development

Carrie

Carrie, a 4-year-old child with cerebral palsy, participates in an inclusive preschool class at a local synagogue. Her teacher has set up a classroom with a multisensory flavor. Children learn by doing and by experiencing the consequences of learning activities.

The painting center has cardboard boxes of different sizes that children have the opportunity to paint. The boxes then will become storage space for each child's belongings or mobiles that hang from the ceiling.

Carrie is having a grand time painting with blue and gold paint. In some places on the carton the colors have mixed, producing a vivid green color. "What color is that?" the teacher asks. "It's green," Carrie responds. "Where did you get green paint?" the teacher asks with a smile. Carrie looks at her containers of blue and yellow paint and her bright eyes reflect the thoughtful activity taking place behind them.

The casual observer of a 4-year-old child hard at play may be mystified by the intensity and variety of the child's behavior. Objects seem to take on life, simple problems evoke interesting attempts at solutions, and newly discovered skills are repeated and applied in different ways. The newborn presents quite another picture—that of a child whose day is spent mostly asleep, whose movements appear to be spontaneous and random, and whose communication repertoire consists only of crying and silence.

The transitions that occur in the typical child during the early years are as exciting to behold as a well-performed ballet is. The acquisition and refinement of skills are evidence that the higher levels of the brain are establishing control and that the child is developing into a cognitive being.

Cognition is difficult to define other than in terms of the many processes it comprises. The word describes mental activity and other behaviors that allow us to understand and participate in events around us. Fundamental to cognitive development is a person's ability to translate objects and events into a symbolic form that can be stored in the brain. The developing thinker is able to store increasingly complex and abstract information, and is able to manipulate the information in a variety of ways. The facility of a child to acquire, store, and manipulate information also is intimately related to development of language, social competence, and purposeful motor skills. For this reason, children who score low on intelligence tests that purport to measure levels of cognition frequently show delays in other areas of development as well.

This chapter examines the development of cognitive processes in young children and the impact that disabling conditions may have on cognition. By understanding how a child's overt behaviors reflect the unfolding of mental processes, one is better able to interpret a child's performance and thereby plan a developmentally appropriate program. The chapter concludes with suggestions and principles for providing experiences to children to facilitate cognitive development.

The Range of Cognitive Skills

Perception is the link between our senses and our experiences.

We receive information through five senses: vision, hearing, taste, smell, and touch. Relating that information to what we have accumulated from past experiences is called **perception.** Perception, then, is sensation with meaning. At yet a higher level of cognitive development, **logical thought** (the ability to use meaningful information to make decisions and solve problems) emerges. This marks the appearance of conceptual skills.

Even in a newborn, the foundations of cognition are apparent. At birth, a child reveals a varied repertoire of perceptual skills that expands rapidly during the early weeks and months of life. Soon after birth, infants fix briefly on visual stimuli (often the mother's eyes and face because of an attraction to forms with sharp contrasts) and even track moving objects over short distances. They turn away from strong odors, change their sucking patterns for fluids with different tastes, and become quiet in response to certain patterns of sound. Table 9.1 presents an array of perceptual skills present in most typical children during the early years of development.

One must be impressed by the capabilities of a young child, who progresses in about 9 months from the fusion of two cells to a complex and skilled organism. In 9 more months, the child is able to discriminate among information in the

Visual	Auditory	Tactile	Olfactory	Gustatory
Fixing	Localization	Discrimination	Localization	Discrimination

Tracking	Auditory memory	Form
		   Temperature
		   Texture
		   Pressure
			Discrimination	

Depth perception	Discrimination:
	   Sound
	   Speech			

Discrimination:
   Pattern
   Color
   Form
   Size				

Visual memory				
Figure ground				

TABLE 9.1 Normal Perceptual Skills

environment and remember a few meaningful experiences. He seems to recognize his caregivers, anticipate feeding, and show definite preferences for types and textures of food. During the third 9 months, the child remembers more experiences and begins attaching labels to people and things, permitting finer distinctions among similar stimuli and forming the basis for spoken language. For example, the 18-month-old child is unable to name colors, but he has internal labels for different colors that allow him to distinguish one color from another. The inner language represented by this labeling system is described by Vygotsky (1962). It is the means by which a child manipulates information in more and more complex ways. No longer controlled by the physical characteristics of things, a child suspects that the staunch-looking refrigerator carton might be empty and offer an excellent place to play. He indicates a grasp of temporal concepts by wanting something now rather than later. He anticipates the arrival of his mother from work when the sun begins to set. His spatial awareness and ability to pull together numerous bits of old and new information permit him to think through possible ways to get to the cookie jar on the refrigerator and to try only the solution he thinks is most likely to work. This is quite a change from the infant for whom time and space were dimensions too abstract to understand. A child who attaches the label "book" to all varieties of books, who knows that there are many kinds of four-legged animals, and who can sort blocks by color or shape or texture also demonstrates a grasp of classification concepts, reflecting another step on the ladder of cognitive skills.

As a child gets older, perceptual skills are refined and integrated into higher level thought processes. Random scribbling on paper, for example, develops into drawings that reflect a similarity to the model. Piaget and Inhelder (1969) have described children's unique efforts at this stage of emerging conceptual development:

The facility of the child to acquire, store, and manipulate information is intimately related to the development of language, social competence, and purposeful motor skills.

A face seen in profile will have a second eye because a man has two eyes, or a horseman, in addition to his visible leg, will have a leg which can be seen through the horse. Similarly, one will see potatoes in the ground, if that is where they are, or in a man's stomach (pp. 64–65).

A child's developing language is also indicative of the expanding range of cognitive skills. He must first sort out the meaningful sounds in his environment. He also must use sound differences to identify and store words for later recognition and speech production (Ferguson, 1978). Initial words tend to be names for people, very familiar objects, and function forms, such as *there, stop, gone,* and *more*. This vocabulary dominates a child's spoken language from approximately 12 to 18 months. When, in the second half of the second year, a child strings words together, it is a demonstration of his capacity to represent relationships between objects and events. There is support for the belief that a child at the stage of one-word utterances actually knows considerably more about sentence structure than he is able to demonstrate. He is prevented from exercising his knowledge by a limited short-term memory and oral-motor control.

> In many areas, young children appear capable of processing more complex information than they are able to demonstrate.

Length and complexity of a child's utterances increase within a speaking environment that provides a rich variety of language samples. A child's choice of words in speech then becomes a means to express the ways in which he thinks. Piaget based much of his theory of cognitive development on talks he had with children.

Piaget's Theory of Cognitive Development

Jean Piaget contributed the most comprehensive theory of how cognitive development progresses in children. He viewed development as an unfolding of ever more complex skills as children modify their mental structures to deal with new experiences.

Development is a continuous process that may vary in the rate at which it occurs in different children, but it always progresses in the same sequence. As with a house, for which the foundation first must be laid, then the outside structures, the wiring, the plumbing, and finally the interior walls, so cognitive development follows an orderly, unchanging progression. Substantial research on children with disabilities has documented the slower rate of development of children with disabilities compared with children who do not have disabilities; however, the same sequence of development as that which typically developing children have has been documented in children with visual impairments (Celeste, 2002; Fraiberg, 1975), mental retardation (Kahn, 1976; Silverstein, McLain, Brownless, & Hubbey, 1976; Weisz & Zigler, 1979), hearing impairments (Best & Roberts, 1976), and cerebral palsy (Tessier, 1969–1970).

> Development progresses in the same sequence for all children, but the rate may vary.

Piaget gave the name **schemata** to the cognitive structures responsible for maintaining a child's internal representations of objects and experiences. As a child engages in different experiences, receives novel sensory input, and is called upon to respond in new ways, new schemata are formed or old ones are modified. A child organizes his experiences, as he develops, into more complex mental structures. By coordinating schemata, for example, he is capable of generalizing behaviors to new situations. Reaching for an interesting-looking toy might be viewed as the coordination of the schemata of vision, reaching, and wanting a familiar object.

Piaget described two processes by which a child adapts to new or unique demands from the environment. In **assimilation,** a child interprets new experiences only in terms of schemata that he already has. If, for example, his schema for flying things includes only birds, he may inaccurately identify all flying things as birds. All four-legged animals may be "horses" if someone has once identified a specific four-legged animal for him as a horse. These overgeneralizations that children make are a reflection of how they perceive the world based on a limited store of experiences and information. A second process helps them bring their perspectives more in line with reality. Through **accommodation,** a child's schemata are modified with experience. By being shown a kite or a plane or by having the differences among a kite, a plane, and a bird described, the child expands his schema for flying things to include the new information. He also may begin to expand his store of information about birds to include different types of birds.

> Assimilation is a process by which the child interprets new information in terms of current schemata.

> In accommodation, the child modifies current schemata in light of information from new experiences.

Interactions with the environment almost always involve assimilation and accommodation. In the former, it appears that children change the world by fitting new experiences into their understanding. In the latter, the world changes children by altering their understanding to conform to reality. The continuous changing of cognitive structures, or schemata, occurs throughout life.

Young children identify characteristics of the world based upon physical attributes. That is, they cannot comprehend that a large box may be full or empty; they can perceive it based upon its surface qualities only. These percepts often provide erroneous information to a child. As he interacts more with his environment, he may

In the early stages of cognitive development, a child is drawn to the surface characteristics of objects. Later, objects become meaningful for what they do or represent.

be bound less and less to physical attributes. He may formulate concepts based upon how things are used and of what they are made, and he uses more discrete differences among objects and experiences to solve problems and make logical decisions.

Organization of Development

Through the principle of equilibrium, the child modifies his understanding of experiences in the world to achieve balance.

Qualitative changes mark the development of cognitive abilities in children. Piaget described the **principle of equilibrium** as one of the mechanisms that facilitates change as a child seeks balance in his interactions with the environment. With organization of and adaptation to new experiences through assimilation and accommodation, he achieves stability, or equilibrium.

Piaget presented the significant developmental accomplishments of children in terms of periods and stages. Again, he emphasized the sequence of changes more than the specific ages at which they occur. This explains why we frequently find children with disabilities experiencing a period of cognitive development associated with much younger children. Awareness of this developmental pattern provides valuable direction in program planning for the cognitively young child.

The first two periods of cognitive development—**sensorimotor** and **preoperational thought**—describe a child's progress through a mental age of about 7 or 8 years. The periods of **concrete operations** and **formal operations** describe mental processes of older children. Discussion of the latter two developmental periods is beyond the scope of this book; however, the interested reader is referred to some of the earlier works of Piaget (e.g., Piaget & Inhelder, 1969).

Piaget's Stages of Development

Sensorimotor Period

A child's earliest behaviors are reflexive in nature; the child gives the same motor response to the same types of stimuli with little understanding of what is happening. A loud noise or sudden movement elicits a startle. Stimulation of the area around the mouth elicits a rooting or suck-swallow response. During the sensorimotor period, mental operations go through a transition from being exclusively overt and motoric to being partially internalized. The child makes more effort at understanding the world. He begins to reflect on sensory information and selects a response from a number of alternatives. He can categorize many stimuli appropriately. Experiences provide the opportunity for the child to recognize the uniqueness of certain stimuli through accommodation. During this period, then, certain people and objects take on greater importance in the child's life.

A child also recognizes his ability to make things happen. He may throw his spoon on the floor and watch its descent intently. He may repeat this over and over, thrilled at his power over matter and at the responses he elicits from his parents.

One of the most significant changes during this period is the development of **object permanence,** the knowledge that an object continues to exist even though it is out of sight (Baillargeon, 1987; Schutte & Spencer, 2002). A keen observer notes that when a very young child drops a rattle out of his crib, he may cry briefly, but does not search for it. At about 12 months, however, he looks for it where he thinks it fell. A child's remembering the existence of an object after it is out of sight indicates that the child has internalized a symbolic representation of the object. The symbolic image is maintained by the child even in the absence of the sensory image. This mental operation is a most significant milestone in a child's development of cognition. The gradual unfolding of object permanence occurs sequentially during the sensorimotor period, as shown in Table 9.2.

> Object permanence requires that a child maintain a symbolic representation of the object in memory so that it continues to exist although out of sight.

Reflexive Stage. Cognitive development begins in a child as a group of invariant reflex behaviors. The cerebral cortex is still immature, permitting lower centers of the central nervous system to maintain dominance over sensorimotor performance. A child sucks, roots, grasps, and startles almost indiscriminately, and often in the absence of a stimulus. A child will suck, for example, even when a nipple is not present. Piaget observed that when a schema of particular importance is present, there is a tendency to exercise it. This process, called **functional assimilation**, allows

TABLE 9.2 Stages in Attainment of Object Permanence

Age	Behavior
0–4 months	Does not actively search for objects that have moved out of sight
4–8 months	Searches for partially concealed objects
	Anticipates the destination of a moving object that is lost from sight
8–12 months	Searches for objects seen being hidden
12–18 months	Searches for objects hidden in visible changes of location
18–24 months	Searches for objects in hidden displacements by recreating the sequence

a child to refine the behavior and to begin extending it to other situations. Thumb sucking, which has been observed even in utero, is one such extension of a schema. **Recognitive assimilation** also appears early, as the child begins to discriminate among objects to which a schema applies and those to which it does not. A child selects a nipple over other suckable objects when he is hungry, for example.

Infants enter the world prepared to receive and distinguish a variety of sensory information. Refinement of skills occurs quickly. A newborn's explorations and interactions with the environment reflect primitive behaviors, an immature nervous system, and schemata that assure the child's survival. These experiences provide the foundation for building more complex cognitive structures and prepare the child to become more directed in his actions.

Primary Circular Reactions.   This stage in a child's development of cognition is characterized by attempts to repeat an action that has been done reflexively or by chance. These actions are described as **primary** because they are limited to basic actions involving a child's own body, and as **circular** because they are repeated. An infant cannot yet initiate new actions. If, by chance, he brought his thumb to his mouth, he might try to repeat the event. By positioning his hand and head appropriately he may accomplish the task after a number of misses. Through accommodation a child modifies his schemata until he becomes more precise in repeating actions.

A child at this stage also begins to show anticipatory behavior. Whereas a newborn begins purposeful sucking when his lips are in contact with a nipple, a child now may begin to suck when he is placed in a position that he associates with feeding.

Several other important signs appear at this stage indicating a child's growing alertness to stimuli in his surroundings. At approximately 3 months of age, a typical child begins to look in the direction of a sound. He also responds differentially to various visual stimuli. Novel and complex objects or pictures are likely to draw a more lengthy and intent gaze than do things familiar to the child. Continued exploration of novel stimuli in the environment through gross coordination of the senses enables an infant to begin developing schemata for the structure of the environment (Parker, 1993). This then becomes the foundation for relating new information to former experiences and further modifying schemata. This process is the basis for cognitive functioning and is refined during the third stage of the sensorimotor period.

The child becomes interested in and begins interacting with objects in the secondary circular reactions stage.

Secondary Circular Reactions.   Many parents claim that the most enjoyable stage in infancy comes at about 4 to 8 months of age. By this time, a baby focuses his attention on objects rather than on his own body. He reaches and grasps, providing himself greater freedom in manipulating and exploring objects. His random movements may cause his hand or foot to strike the mobile above the crib, and he begins to refine these movements until he is able to keep the mobile going with purposeful swipes. A child also begins responding in the same way to objects that appear the same to him. This type of primitive classification system develops through recognitive assimilation. A child will swipe at another mobile or something that looks like a mobile until he discovers a more appropriate way to approach the new object. Observing this type of activity and the perception of sameness in his daughter, Lucienne, prompted Piaget's belief (1952) that actions are the precursors of thought processes.

Rattles are interesting toys for children at this age who are able to reach, grasp, and shake them, and who find the sound pleasing. The significance of specific objects and people signals the development of **object concept**, upon which Piaget put great emphasis. In the first stages of development of object concept, infants perceive an object only in terms of themselves; that is, something to suck, hold, or drop. During this later stage, however, objects begin to gain importance in relation to other objects. They become something with which to learn about spatial relationships and the stability of the universe (Piaget, 1954). Related to this is the concept of object permanence. During the early phase of **object permanence**, children show a fascination for hide-and-seek games. They can find partially hidden objects, and when a toy is moved under a blanket in a predictable trajectory, they may anticipate where it will reappear. The search for hidden objects is likely to be brief, however, perhaps as a function of infants' short memory span and attention (Bower, 1974). Nevertheless, as they develop, the images of objects and experiences beyond their immediate surroundings become more permanent residents of their schemata (Mareschal, Plunkett, & Harris, 1999).

A child's ability to sit independently at this stage and the appearance of teeth afford him a new perspective. Sights, sounds, smells, tastes, and tactile information are likely to increase in quantity and diversity, permitting the child to further refine his schemata for the environment. A child can make finer distinctions between the people and objects nearby. He can distinguish a familiar person or toy from others and can recognize them in different positions or when they are partially hidden from view.

Sitting in an upright position enhances a child's view of his world.

Coordination of Secondary Schemata.

This stage is marked by three important characteristics: **intention**, **imitation**, and **anticipation**. A child applies old schemata in new situations to attain a goal. For example, he uses a hitting action for the first time to move a barrier out of his path to get to a toy. He moves his parent's hand to a container that he cannot open himself. This intentional behavior is reflective of the child's beginning awareness of **causality**, the concept that people and things around him can cause change.

A child at this stage also begins to imitate on two planes: verbal and gestural. At earlier stages, the child tried to imitate sounds that he made and were repeated by someone else. Now, through approximations of his own sounds and then sounds he hears, the child begins to refine his verbal imitation skills. The first imitations to appear are the most closely related to sounds already in the child's repertoire. The same progression is seen in gestural skills. A child first attempts to repeat movements already in his repertoire and then modifies his movements to approximate those of someone else. One of the earliest gestural imitations seen in children is waving bye-bye, which is a modification of children's schemata for reaching, grasping, and releasing.

The child's emerging understanding of how the world works is reflected in behaviors that are intentional, imitative, and anticipatory.

Children of approximately 10 months of age show rather sophisticated anticipatory behavior. They may begin to cry when adults put on their coats, in anticipation of the adults' departure, or when food is placed before them that they do not like. It is not necessary at this stage for the parents to actually depart or for the child to taste the food in order for the child to cry; he can anticipate the outcome.

Also at this stage, the function of objects assumes greater importance to a child than does merely their appearance. The child is most interested in objects that can be manipulated in different ways, that make sounds, and that have visual fascination when they are explored. The child no longer perceives an object merely by its surface characteristics. He is able to hypothesize what things do by looking at them and, in play, uses the objects in purposeful ways (Frye & Zelazo, 1996).

Tertiary Circular Reactions.   Primary reactions involve the child's own body. Secondary reactions involve simple exploration with objects. In the stage of tertiary circular reactions, the child approaches objects with an attitude that can be characterized as curiosity. He will repeat the same behavior, then experiment with variations. A child in a high chair might drop his spoon on the tray in the same way several times. He might then begin to drop it from different heights, letting it fall straight or allowing it to spin. The child also begins to use a spoon and can drink from a cup at about this time. Spilling milk on the floor or tossing food across the kitchen is part of a child's exploration. The child may participate in this trial-and-error experimentation until he finds one strategy that is particularly satisfying or effective. In the same way, a child engages other objects in similar unsystematic explorations and continues to broaden his understanding of relationships in his universe.

Decentration is the process through which the child realizes that events occur in the world in which he is not involved and has no control.

There is good evidence that, in this stage, **decentration** evolves on the action level, wherein the child learns that events take place in the universe without his involvement or control. He is still limited in interpreting cause-effect relationships for actions but enjoys watching an activity in which he does not participate. When a child watches someone hide an object and then move it to another hiding place, he searches for the object where it has been moved. Formerly, he would have looked in its original position.

Because a typically developing child usually stands and walks during this stage, his ability to explore sights and sounds in the environment increases dramatically. He can classify objects by function or action in addition to shape. Nelson (1973a) found that children of 15–20 months initially classify objects by form or shape. After they have an opportunity to manipulate the objects, however, they classify them by action or function.

Invention of New Means Through Mental Combinations.   Near 2 years of age, a typical child no longer is tied to his actions, but can think through solutions to simple problems without the need for acting them out. The development of symbolic function marks the transition from the sensorimotor to the preoperational period.

The earliest symbols used by a child are probably internal images derived from his perceptual actions. That is, he retains the memory of an experience in some symbolic form. This allows for what Piaget called **deferred imitation.** A child can watch an action, store the image of the action in memory, and repeat it at a later time. A child's ability to imitate also improves because he is able to work through an action internally before acting it out.

A child's internal symbolic representations are also expressed in his understanding that pictures represent objects. He enjoys looking through a storybook and touching pictures of familiar objects. A child's language also may be a reflection of the experiences he considers most important. **Action terms** predominate in early language, as do names for objects that children associate with action (Nelson, 1973b).

At the end of this stage, a child perceives objects as permanent and independent. He understands that if an object is out of sight, it may be in one of several other places and he may seek it out in a more systematic way. He recognizes spatial relationships among objects, as when he places forms in a form board correctly or holds a chip in his hand to drop it through a slit in the top of a can.

During the first 2 years of life, then, a child has learned about the physical properties of his environment. Initially, all behavior is overt and related to the child's body. Gradually, the child becomes more interested in other objects and actions and is able to translate these into symbols that he internalizes. More complex manipulations of symbolic representations characterize the next period of cognitive development.

By the end of the sensorimotor period, the child has internalized images of objects and experiences, but makes many errors.

Preoperational Period

As a child enters this period in cognitive development, thought processes are still immature. A child often is misled by his perceptions of the environment. The broad changes that take place on the action level during the sensorimotor period are matched by similar changes on the level of representational thought during the preoperational period.

Piaget began formulating his theory relating to this period by talking with and observing many different children. He focused on children's egocentrism in relation to communication skills, morality, and reasoning. He later refined his method and gave children specific problems to solve. He then described their thought processes based upon their approaches to problem solving. He called their first attempts at constructing ideas or notions **preconcepts** to signify that children's conceptualization of the universe is still perceptually dominant.

Flavell (1963) described some of the marked changes that take place during the preoperational period. These are presented in the following paragraphs.

Egocentrism.   An egocentric child is unable to view things from another perspective. On the three-mountain problem used by Piaget (see Figure 9.1), a child is asked to indicate what a doll would see by looking at the scene from different sides of the

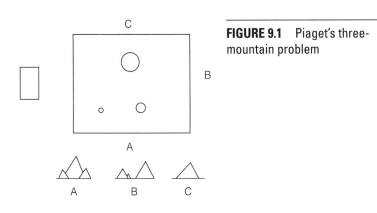

FIGURE 9.1   Piaget's three-mountain problem

table. Not being able to imagine that someone can have a different viewpoint, the child chooses his own point of view.

Children's language also reflects egocentricism. Piaget's daughter Jacqueline, for example, defined *daddy* as "a man who has lots of Jacquelines" (Piaget, 1951). McClinton and Meier (1978) have identified three forms of egocentric speech: **monologue**, **collective monologue**, and **repetition**. In the first, a child talks continuously while working or playing, apparently practicing the synthesis of action, language, and thought. Collective monologue takes place in a group situation. A child speaks with no apparent connection to what another child is saying. Although the social setting is different, the reasons for collective monologue appear to be the same as for simple monologue. Repetition is the third form of egocentric speech. A child repeats what another child has said but presents it as if it were a unique contribution.

A child in the preoperational period is unable to anticipate the strategies that another will use in game-playing or problem-solving situations, yet he assumes that others know what he is thinking. In relating a story, for example, he may present it disjointedly or leave out parts, yet believe that the listener understands as he does (Girbau, 2001).

> A child in the pre-operational period cannot yet view things from another's perspective or consider multiple attributes of an object at one time.

Centration. Successful problem solving requires that a child attend to many attributes of an object at one time. A preoperational child shows centration in thinking. He is unable to consider multiple attributes simultaneously, which causes errors in problem solving. If a child watches while a ball of clay is rolled into a snake, returned to its original form, and rolled again, he focuses on only one dimension when telling why the ball and snake are not equal. One child may say the ball is taller; another may say the snake is longer. Their inability to see the reciprocal changes in dimensions interferes with logical thinking and problem solving. The following problem provides another example of centration.

Given a group of red blocks and blue blocks that are all the same size and shape, a child has little difficulty putting together the blocks that are alike because they differ in only one attribute. However, if the child is given a group of red and blue blocks and red and blue disks, he will be confused. He tends to focus on one attribute at a time; therefore, he may group them all into two piles, or his attention may shift to another attribute during sorting and he may produce a conglomerate of piles.

Similarly, if a child is given seven blue and three white wooden beads, he will correctly name the color of the majority of the beads. But the child will be confused if he is asked whether there are more blue or wooden beads. Again, the child cannot focus on multiple attributes of the whole and its parts.

Irreversibility and Focus on Successive States. A preoperational child does not see that all logical operations are reversible. This is apparent in different types of problems. A child does not understand that if a ball of clay is rolled into a snake, it can just as easily be returned to its original form. Similarly, a child who is asked whether he has a brother may say "yes," but when he is asked whether his brother has a brother, he says "no."

This process also is associated with a child's focusing on successive stages of change rather than on the smooth transformation from one state to another. Piaget referred to a child's thought as being like a sequence of individual frames on a film. Flavell (1963) described a child's difficulty in arranging a series of pictures to reconstruct the movement of a stick falling from a vertical to a horizontal position to exemplify a child's view of changed states.

In conservation problems, the child must be able to recognize transformations from one state to another.

Conservation problems require that a child be able to focus on the transformation from state to state in relation to mass, length, number, volume, and area. Figure 9.2 presents some simple tests of conservation. Conservation of number is usually achieved by age 6. By age 7, a child attains conservation of mass and length; by age 9, weight; and volume after age 11.

Conservation of substance

a. The experimenter presents two identical clay balls. The child sees that they have equal amounts.

b. One of the balls is rolled out flat. The child is asked whether they still contain the same amount.

Conservation of length

a. Two sticks are lined up in front of the child. The child sees that they are the same.

b. One of the sticks is moved to the left. The child is asked whether they are still the same.

Conservation of number

a. Two rows of counters are placed in one-to-one correspondence. The child sees that they are equal.

b. One of the rows is elongated (or contracted). The child is asked whether each row still has the same number.

Conservation of area

a. The child and the experimenter each have identical sheets of cardboard. Wooden blocks are placed on these in identical positions. The child is asked whether each card has the same amount of empty space.

b. The experimenter moves the blocks around on the card. The child is asked the same question.

Conservation of liquids

a. Two glass jars are filled to the same level with water. The child sees that they are equal.

b. The liquid of one container is poured into a tall tube (or a flat dish). The child is asked whether each contains the same amount.

FIGURE 9.2   Simple tests of conservation

Transductive Reasoning.   Logical reasoning requires induction and deduction. In inductive reasoning, one generalizes from specific cases. In deductive reasoning, one applies general rules to specific cases. These processes require a child to recognize the stability of attributes despite changing circumstances and differences among attributes under the same circumstances. A preoperational child is not capable of deductive or inductive reasoning. Birds remain birds whether they are perched in a tree in the park or flying in the air. There are distinctive differences between the birds in the two cases. Yet the child who uses transductive reasoning assumes that the two birds he sees are one and the same. He sees relationships at a perceptual level without considering the possibility of higher order relationships.

Problem-solving and decision-making abilities signal the emergence of logical thought.

The Beginning of Concept Formation.   The emergence of logical thought in a child is manifested in problem-solving and decision-making abilities. He begins to put things and events into some type of order. Objects show similarities and differences in their physical attributes, in their functions, and in their relationships to other objects. The child begins to group what he sees into classes and subclasses. Lavatelli (1973) summarized the logical processes of classification, space and number, and seriation as they develop in a young child. These processes are presented in Table 9.3.

TABLE 9.3   Development of Simple Classification, Space and Number, and Seriation Concepts

Classification	Space and Numbers	Seriation
Simple sorting: Groups according to single perceptual attribute.	*One-to-one correspondence:* Establishes equality between two sets of objects that visually correspond.	*Orders objects* according to one property.
True classification: Abstracts common property in group of objects. Finds some property in other objects in group.	*One-to-one correspondence in absence of physical correspondence:* Recognizes equality in absence of spatial equivalence.	*Orders two inversely related series:* Arranges two series at once in inverse order.
Multiplicative classification: Classifies by more than one attribute at a time. Sees that object can belong to several classes at same time.	*Conservation of quantity:* Quantity does not vary even when it occupies a different space.	*Seriation and visual representation:* Draws a picture of objects he arranged in series. Then, draws in advance of ordering.
All-Some relation: Distinguishes classes based on property of all members and subclasses based on property of some members.	*Conservation of the whole:* The whole does not vary even when divided into parts.	*Seriation of geometric shapes:* Orders shapes based on area or number of sides.
Class-inclusion relation: Forms subclasses of objects and includes subclasses in larger class.	*Conservation of area:* Area is conserved even if appearance is changed.	
	Transformation of perspective: Pictures objects from different perspective when they are moved.	

Source: From *Piaget's Theory Applied to an Early Childhood Curriculum*, by C. S. Lavatelli, 1973, Nashua, NH: Delta Education, Inc. Copyright © 1973 by Delta Education, Inc. Reprinted by permission.

Other Theories of Development

Vygotsky's Theory

Whereas Piaget focused on the natural laws of intellectual development, Russian psychologist **Lev Vygotsky** (1978) concentrated on the role of language and culture, describing the roles of instruction, play, help, and learning. He explained cognitive development in terms of social systems comprised of productive interactions between the child and caregiver. Not unlike Piaget, he saw a responsive environment as the key to intellectual development.

Vygotsky used the term **zone of proximal development** to describe the distance between actual and potential development. **Actual development** is measured by watching a child's independent problem solving. **Potential development** is what the child does with help or guidance and it becomes actual development through the mechanism of **internalization**. This mechanism describes the developmental progression of a child from other-regulation, wherein another individual (an adult or more advanced child) guides the child's activities, to self-regulation, wherein the child initiates purposeful action with other available individuals who provide necessary support only. The successful negotiation of this shift toward greater independence and control requires **intersubjectivity**.

> Zone of proximal development describes the gap between what the child can currently do on his own and what he can do with help or guidance.

According to Rochat (2001), intersubjectivity occurs when both parties share an understanding of the purpose of a given task and each recognizes this of the other. For a productive interaction to occur between an adult and child, there must be a shared social reality such that both are working on the same problem. When shared understanding does not exist, some negotiation between the two parties must occur, requiring communicative interaction or semiotic mediation. Trevarthen (1988) suggests that there is a **primary intersubjectivity** present at birth between an infant and his caregiver. At 7 to 8 months of age, the infant enters a period of **secondary intersubjectivity**. At this point, the child and caregiver can share meanings at a higher cognitive level. Although Vygotsky stressed the language component of mediation, mechanisms such as joint eye gaze, following other's pointings, and catching other people's attention by using gestures and pointing also can be successful in the formulation of intersubjectivity (Rogoff, Malkin, & Gilbride, 1984). The adult can strive for a new level of intersubjectivity by representing objects and events in different ways, thereby stimulating cognitive development in the infant.

Vygotsky also proposed a sociocultural theory of disability in which compensation comes from cultural enlightenment and socialization. He offered a comprehensive and practical approach to educating children with special needs. The foundation of this **theory of disontogenesis**, or distorted development, is that children have two classes of defects. Organic impairments (primary defects) result from both endogenous and exogenous biological causes. Children also experience distortions of higher psychological functions (secondary defects) as a result of social factors. Vygotsky's view was that the development of a child with a disability is determined by the social implications of the organic impairment, but that social support systems can overcome the obstacles imposed by that impairment.

> Vygotsky emphasizes the importance of social support systems in bringing children with disabilities to higher levels of skill.

The main objective of special education and, especially, early intervention, is the application of the principles just described to the development of the child's higher psychological functions by capitalizing on the child's current abilities and by providing meaning to new experiences. Children with caregivers who offer verbal and nonverbal support and who seek a shared understanding with the child of the task to be accomplished, for example, appear to be more motivated to persist with other challenging tasks on their own (Hauser-Cram, 1996; Stremmel & Ru, 1993). The objective of early intervention, therefore, must be the identification of a child from the point of strength rather than disability (Gindis, 1995). Social support systems can help children with disabilities overcome obstacles as they evolve processes to adapt to environmental demands.

Behavioral Theories

Not everyone endorses the theory that cognition evolves through developmental changes in the organization of mental structures or that these changes are reflected in children's behavior in learning situations. There are numerous theories about how children learn, or how they ascend to adulthood with growing sophistication in their ability to relate to their environment. From the behaviorist perspective, cognitive development is the result of the method and amount of learning children gain from their surroundings. Although most theories of development emphasize predictable and measurable changes in behavior that are governed by interactions with the environment, the classical research behind the development of these theories took place in the laboratory. The results of these laboratory studies have been applied in natural settings to study particular processes related to learning and the development of cognitive skills.

Attention. A developing child is exposed to a large and diverse group of stimuli at any given time: the sound of a car in the street; the clothes dryer rumbling its tune in the next room; the radio playing; the brightly colored wallpaper; the toys, books, and magazines scattered around the room; the soup and roast cooking in the kitchen; and the family talking.

> Cognitive development requires that a child be able to attend to the critical details in his environment.

Very young children sustain attention for only brief periods. When they do attend, it is likely to be to the most intense stimuli in the environment—bright objects, loud noises, and strong smells. As children develop, they begin to concentrate on stimuli with the greatest functional value to the task at hand (Huang-Pollock, Carr, & Nigg, 2002). They are less apt to be distracted by irrelevant and incidental attributes, and more apt to focus on the relevant details of an object or situation. Kagan and Kogan (1970) postulate that neurological changes contribute to a child's improved attention over time. Attention theory is considered to be the critical factor for developmental transitions in perception, memory, thought, and problem solving. Children's ability to focus on the meaningful stimuli in their surroundings plays a significant role in the development of cognition (Colombo, 2001).

Perception. Children differ in how they interpret sensory information. They may perceive the same situation in different ways depending upon their dominant sensory mode and dimension preferences. A newborn may give the same response for many types of stimuli but, as he develops, fewer stimuli elicit the same response. In addition, at different ages an infant shows shifts in the sensory mode he prefers for receiving information. Infants are more tactually attuned to the environment. As they get older, their explorations of the environment shift toward a more visual orientation.

Predictable shifts also occur in a child's preference for characteristics of stimuli during a problem-solving task. For example, a dimension is a category that includes all the variations of an attribute. Whereas color comprises numerous qualities, it is considered a single dimension. Similarly, shape and size are other dimensions in the visual mode. The earliest preference for a stimulus dimension occurs at about age 2, when the child attempts to solve a choice problem by continually selecting the stimulus on the same side (left or right). Older children select stimuli based first on color or size, then based on shape at about 6 years of age.

A child also becomes better able to distinguish among stimuli as he develops. Gibson (1969), in her classic **differentiation theory**, proposes that, through a child's rich experiences with stimuli, he learns to differentiate attributes of objects and situations and then selects those that are relevant. In addition to becoming aware that different objects and events have different characteristics, he learns through experiences that some attributes are invariant. His toy car is the same whether it is in his hand or across the room, where it appears to be smaller. Similarly, it is the same toy car whether it is viewed from the front, the back, or the side.

Memory.   The distinction between perception and conception is often characterized by the quantity of information stored in the brain's data bank and the extent to which a child can take new information and make associations with past knowledge. A child becomes more of a conceptual thinker when the data bank is full of verbal labels for objects and events and there are clusters of related information or symbols to be drawn upon.

Children's retention of information for short and long periods follows different paths of development (Carver & Bauer, 2001). The capacity of short-term memory is small. If we tell a child what to order at a fast-food restaurant, he is likely to forget unless he uses the information quickly. Even then, if the phrase or word string is too long or has little meaning as a whole, he will probably forget it quickly. A 3-year-old child can repeat a string of three numbers presented to him orally. A 7-year-old can recall five numbers; to put this in perspective, most adults do not have a much greater capacity in **short-term memory** (seven numbers). Short-term memory also allows a child to look for an object that moves out of sight (i.e., object permanence) and facilitates manipulation of information in problem solving later in the preschool years (i.e., **active working memory**).

Long-term memory has a greater storage capacity and shows greater differences among ages. It is likely that increased memory capacity over time is a result of a richer abundance of material already in the brain's data bank to which new information can be related. The more meaningful new information is, the easier it is to memorize. Retention of new material also appears to be related to the inhibition of irrelevant information (Merrill & Taube, 1996) and to the speed of processing (Kail, 1993).

Conceptual thinking requires a rich bank of symbolic labels to be stored in memory.

Three strategies used to memorize new information appear to be related to children's use of verbal labels and their ability to group stimuli on the basis of more complex perceptual and conceptual attributes. First, memory through **rehearsal** increases with age (Flavell, 1970). When children were shown a series of pictures and asked to recall the order in which the examiner pointed to them, Flavell found that younger children who said the words for the pictures to themselves had much better recall. Flavell found the use of verbal mediation to increase with age. Also, when pictures were named for the children who did not use verbal rehearsal, their memory was greatly improved. In fact, very young children were able to point to many named pictures with the same proficiency as adults had! Apparently, the inability to produce the verbal mediators may be a hindrance in certain memory tasks. The acquisition of verbal labels appears to account for age changes in memory capacity. In preverbal children, active manipulation of stimuli may facilitate memory.

Imagery is a second strategy for committing new information to memory. It entails superimposing mental images of one or more stimuli upon each other so that the association of each with the other aids recall. For example, if a child is shown pictures of a dog, a wagon, a toothbrush, and a key, the child might formulate the image of a dog riding in a wagon with a toothbrush in one paw and a key in the other. Although imagery is more effective with concrete stimuli, abstractions may be incorporated into a mental image if they are paired with a concrete object, such as a large orange.

The third strategy reflects some of the more interesting data on developmental progressions. **Organization** of stimuli into meaningful clusters appears to contribute to their acquisition and recall; however, children organize information in different ways at different ages. Rossi and Wittrock (1971) presented a series of words that could be organized in different ways to children between 2 and 5 years of age. The 2-year-olds tended to cluster together words that rhymed; the 3-year-olds clustered words that had syntactic meaning (such as *eat—apple* and *men—work*); the 4-year-olds clustered words by functional similarity (such as *hand—leg* and *peach—apple*); and the 5-year-olds recalled the words most often in the order in which they had heard them. Clustering based on more and more complex factors is consistent with what we have already learned about cognitive processes.

Hypothesis Testing.   Children under 6 years of age do little systematic testing of hypotheses. Trying to guess the answer in a game of *I'm Thinking of Something*, a young child's questions are not likely to reflect strategy: "Is it a horse?" "Is it something to eat?" "Is it something I like?" As the child gets older, however, he uses a strategy that involves asking questions that gradually focus on the answer: "Does it move?" "Does it have wheels?" "Does someone drive it?" "Is it a car?"

Complex techniques of hypothesis testing may not be attained until adulthood. Even then, the problem-solving strategies used may be insufficient or ineffective in producing the correct answer.

Relationships Between Developmental and Cognitive Processing Models

It is important to keep in mind that the differences among the theories of cognitive development are not great. Piaget, representing a developmental approach, focused on the gradual organization of cognitive structures that permits a child to solve problems and perform logical operations. According to Piaget, cognition provides a means to adapt to environmental demands by assimilating new information and modifying cognitive structures—schemata—that are already present. Even a newborn has a basis for interacting with the environment in a motoric, reflexive way.

Proponents of behavioral models focus on the operations involved in receiving, storing, and recalling information. Although they do not disavow recognition of internal processes, behaviorists believe that "it is not profitable to speculate about these internal processes since they cannot be directly observed or controlled" (Maccoby & Zellner, 1970, p. 34). They believe that behavior is controlled by stimuli and that development progresses as behaviors are modified to the demands of stimuli.

Kamii and Ewing (1996) proposed that Piaget's theory explains all phenomena studied by other theorists, whereas other theories are unable to explain many phenomena described by Piaget. For example, in the situation involving blue and white wooden beads described in the earlier section on centration, Piaget's theory explains that 4-year-olds do not have the ability to consider a part of a class (i.e., only the blue beads) and the whole class (all wooden beads) at the same time. Once they think about a part, the whole no longer exists. By 8 years of age, however, children are able to separate the whole into parts and put them back together as an internal operation. Behavioral models do not explain the development of these types of logical operations.

Furthermore, developmental theorists assert that forcing development to occur by selectively reinforcing behaviors that are chronologically age-appropriate for a child is probably wasteful—if not harmful. Such is the case when children are expected to learn to read because they are 5 years old. If they do not yet have the cognitive structures to assimilate the new information, reading becomes a meaningless exercise for them. To memorize something without understanding it epitomizes teaching without learning. In addition, if a child is force-fed information that his cognitive perspective of the universe says is wrong, it may cause future conflicts in his perspective of reality.

Behaviorism may be viewed as a complement to certain aspects of developmental theory. When the cognitive structures for simple number concepts have developed, for example, repetition is the best way to learn counting and basic skills in arithmetic. Similar strategies from behavioral theory are effective for learning the alphabet and sight words.

Theories of development, although certainly distinct in description, are rarely applied in quite so secular a fashion by educators. Robinson and Robinson (1976)

> Cognition provides a means to adapt to environmental demands.

> Behaviorism can nicely complement selected aspects of developmental theory.

emphasize the use of a more eclectic approach in relation to children with mental retardation:

> It is probably wise . . . to employ a number of concepts in considering the process of psychological development. Just as it is meaningful to characterize a mentally retarded child from etiological, behavioral, social, and educational perspectives, one need not be impatient if several theoretical systems prove useful in understanding behavior. (p. 242)

Factors That Affect Cognitive Development

According to developmental theory, cognition unfolds gradually and in a consistent sequence as a function of maturation. Skills are modified and refined, however, as demanded by a child's needs to balance his interactions with the environment. We call this **equilibration**.

Many factors can interfere with the processes involved in the typical cognitive development of a child. Grossman (1977) classified them into nine groups: infection and intoxication, trauma or physical agents, metabolic or nutritional disorders, gross brain disease, unknown prenatal influences, chromosomal abnormalities, psychiatric disorders, gestational disorders, and environment. Some of these factors have a direct influence on the developing brain and may interfere with the transmission or processing of information. Others may impair a child's ability to receive or respond to information. Many of these factors were discussed in Chapter 2. This section addresses only environmental factors.

Cognition and the Environment

The continuum of reproductive casualty and the continuum of caretaking casualty explain the outcomes of children with disabilities.

In 1961, Pasamanick and Knobloch made the classic proposal that children are susceptible to a continuum of damage as a result of reproductive complications. The damage may range from minor and undetectable trauma to significant serious disabilities affecting one's mental, physical, and emotional capacities. The researchers called this a **continuum of reproductive casualty** and identified five disorders related to reproductive casualty: epilepsy, behavior disorders, cerebral palsy, mental retardation, and reading disabilities (Pasamanick & Knobloch, 1966). Several years later, Sameroff and Chandler (1975) presented their **continuum of caretaking casualty**. They emphasized that a poor caretaking environment may similarly yield a range of deviant developmental outcomes for children. In fact, the influence of the environment on a child and the transactional nature of a child's relationship with those in the environment (Sameroff, 1979) are generally considered to be more potent and expansive than biological factors are in determining how a child will develop. Reports of several longitudinal studies (Duncan & Brooks-Gunn, 1997; Duncan, Brooks-Gunn, & Klebanov, 1994; Jordan, 1980) that followed thousands of children revealed that the effects of perinatal stress on intellectual status was greater in children from low socioeconomic areas. It is not the socioeconomic status itself that contributes to the child's poorer performance, but associated factors—less education of the parent(s), a greater likelihood of a single parent and a less stable home, and fewer educational materials in the child's environment.

A substantive body of research now exists that documents the positive influences on cognitive development when the environment is made more stimulating for the child (Rutter, 1979, 1980). Children moved from poor institutional settings into adoptive homes showed significant IQ gains (Dennis, 1973). Results from the Milwaukee Project (Garber & Heber, 1977) indicate that disadvantaged African American children made IQ gains of as much as 20 points when an educational intervention program was provided. Other research shows similar consistency in pointing to a strong relationship between a supportive environment and measures of cognitive development (Baydar & Brooks-Gunn, 1991; Brooks-Gunn, Klebanov, & Liaw, 1995).

A child, however, is not a passive learner. A parent's approval and nurturing of the exploratory behavior of a child experimenting with his surroundings facilitate typical cognitive development in the child. A child's early social environment appears to be a better predictor of how development will progress than are biological factors at birth (Duncan & Brooks-Gunn, 1997). From the first visual and physical contact a child has with his parent(s), he asserts his influence on the parent(s). If the child shows extremes in temperament that conflict with the parent's personality, it creates a more adverse relationship between parent and child. A variety of other family and environmental characteristics also may cause stresses in the home. The traditional nature of parent-child relationships (i.e., the child and caregiver influencing and being influenced by the other) increases the likelihood that a single stress will lead to others (Rutter, 1979). Sameroff (1979, 1982; Sameroff & Fiese, 1990) has concluded that cognitive competence during the early years depends for much of its continuity not on the unfolding of innate capacities, but on environmental constraints.

> Cognitive competence depends on the unfolding of innate capacities *and* on environmental constraints.

Kearsley (1979) observed that some children may learn to be cognitively incompetent. He used the term **iatrogenic retardation** to describe children who have the potential for typical development—that is, who are structurally normal but "whose development [has] taken place in an environment characterized by prolonged parental anxiety and inappropriate caretaking practices" (p. 155). For the past several decades, professionals concerned with early intervention have directed their efforts toward refining procedures and materials for stimulating the development of these children and others who are likely to have disabilities later in life. These efforts have generated programs for applying numerous theoretical and conceptual models that explain how infants develop and learn. The presumption upon which many of the approaches were founded was that the quality of the caregiver (parent or teacher) and the quality of the environment contribute to facilitating development and learning. By improving the input the infant received, the thinking went, development would be maximized within the biological and genetic limits of the child. This thinking led to a plethora of curricula dedicated to this stimulus-based (or stimulation-oriented) approach.

Recently, there have been challenges to what had become the traditional approach to intervention with young children who are developmentally disabled. With the proposal of greater emphasis on **co-occurrences** in relation to young children's development—that is, the detection by children that two events occurring together or in close temporal proximity are associated—a new conceptual framework for intervention has evolved (Brinker & Lewis, 1982; Gasser & Colunga, 2002).

Piaget (1952) viewed the influence of co-occurrences on a child as having four aspects: They orient the child to aspects of the environment; they arouse the child and help to modulate his state; their detection provides satisfaction and confidence; and they exercise memory processes as the foundation for development of more complex mental structures. These influences are most easily viewed within the context of parent-child interactions and, particularly, maternal responsiveness to a child's actions and cues. Studies, for example, provide evidence that in infants through 2 years of age, maternal responsiveness is significantly related to a child's later development (Wakschlag & Hans, 1999) and significantly more related to development than is maternal stimulation (Jaskir & Lewis, 1981; Landry, Swank, Assel, Smith, & Vellet, 2001; Lewis & Coates, 1980). In addition, the quality of responsiveness is related to an infant's development. These studies defined *stimulation* as the quantity of time the mother spent smiling at, holding, and talking to the child and *responsiveness* as the frequency of time the mother performed these behaviors immediately following the infant's actions. Quality was related to the type of responsiveness. Proximal responsiveness (touching, holding, and rocking) was positively correlated to Bayley scores in the youngest children. This relationship lessened as the children got older and the relationship between distal responsiveness of the mother (talking to, looking at, and smiling at) and Bayley scores increased.

Although the relationship between a child's development and maternal responsiveness has not been shown to be causal in nature, a contingent environment facilitates important aspects of a child's cognitive development (Lewis & Rosenblum, 1974). Piaget's emphasis on a child's discovery of the environment during the sensorimotor period is founded on this concept. In the intact child, circular reactions provide the child with information about the nature of objects in the environment and his influence on them. In children with developmental problems, detection of these simple relationships and more complex relationships may be more fleeting and less available (Brooks-Gunn & Lewis, 1979; Detterman, 1979).

Thus, an unresponsive or stressful environment or one in which the expectations for a child are low may contribute to generalized retardation of cognitive development. An unknown but significant number of children with cognitive impairments probably fall into this category.

Cognitive Development and the Child with Special Needs

It is beneficial to consider, from time to time, the amazing ascent of a human being from the union of egg and sperm to a mature, cognitive being. With this perspective, we are better able to appreciate the plight of individuals with disabilities, who must function in a world that makes the same demands upon them as upon intact persons. Imagine a child who is congenitally blind trying to understand what an airplane is or what colors are. Consider how much worldly learning a child who is deaf misses or the social learning opportunities a child with physical disabilities never gets because he cannot participate in games and sports. Developmental theorists look upon the limitations in sensory experiences as restricting the growth and refinement of schemata. Cognitive learning advocates view the same limitations as restricting opportunities for appropriate behaviors to be reinforced, practiced, built upon, and generalized to other situations. From either perspective, a child with an impairment that limits his ability to receive, process, or respond to sensory information is likely to demonstrate delays or gaps in cognitive development.

Considerable research has investigated the effects of various disabilities on cognitive development. However, it contributes little to our understanding of children when they are described in broad categorical terms, such as "retarded" or "delayed." The following discussion therefore looks at the state of our knowledge regarding specific aspects of cognition in young children with disabilities.

Mental Retardation

As noted in Chapter 1, the term *mental retardation* implies cognitive deficits. Much evidence points to problems in memory and attention being responsible for the atypical performance of a child with an intellectual disability with that of his typical peers. In addition, differences in brain structure of children with disabilities might create these performance deficits (Raz et al., 1995).

Several theories have been proposed to explain memory deficits. Broadbent's (1958) **limited buffer theory** suggests that individuals with mental retardation have a smaller than normal capacity to store information, and that the addition of new information requires the purging of "old" information. The **"bottleneck" theory** was proposed by Tulving (1968). Slamecka (1968), in his elaboration of this theory, asserted that memory is impaired by the inability of a child to retrieve information, not by a limited storage capacity. This theory is supported by the superiority of our recognition memory skills over our recall skills. For example, consider a child who is shown a card with eight pictures on it and told to try to remember all the pictures, then the card is removed. The child will remember more pictures if he is given an opportunity to tell whether a certain picture was present or not (recognition memory) than if he must name the pictures he saw (recall memory). In comparisons of recognition memory of typical children and children with Down syndrome, the latter group still showed significant delays consistent with general developmental lag (Fantz, Fagan, & Miranda, 1975). McDade and Adler (1980) further extended the investigation of this problem by comparing visual and auditory memory skills in preschool-aged children with Down syndrome. Their findings revealed limitations in the storage and retrieval of auditory information and severe impairment in the storage of visual information. The differential memory for visual and auditory information was consistent with other findings for young children (Rohwer, 1970), although the subjects with Down syndrome and the control subjects of the same mental age performed significantly worse than did typical subjects of the same chronological age.

Ellis (1970) proposed that memory problems are caused by the absence of rehearsal strategies and an inability to store information. Zeaman (1973) concurred with the rehearsal strategy hypothesis, but argued that the problem is not with storage but with the acquisition of information.

As noted earlier, acquisition of information first requires attention to the relevant stimulus. Some children who are severely impaired may be unaware of their

Children with mental retardation might have a smaller memory capacity, difficulty acquiring and storing information, or a decreased ability to retrieve stored information.

surroundings and, consequently, be unable to benefit from the stimulation that appears spontaneously in the environment. Environments of children from low-income families, on the other hand, may be abundant in stimuli that are often ambiguous or excessive (Bernstein, 1960; Wachs, Uzgiris, & Hunt, 1971). The inability of a child to orient and attend to relevant stimuli, particularly if they are complex or demanding, has been implicated as a cause for the poor performance of children from low-income families on cognitive tasks (Finkelstein, Gallagher, & Farron, 1980) and of infants exposed to cocaine (Mayes, Bornstein, Chawarska, & Granger, 1995). It is likely, however, that early intervention can minimize the impact of these factors.

Similar deficits appear to be inherent in children with mental retardation. Sustained attention to a stimulus requires two components: orientation, or awareness of the stimulus, and comparison and relating of the stimulus to other sensory input or stored information (Laucht, Esser, & Schmidt, 1994; Lewis 1971). From a Piagetian perspective, a child orients to a stimulus through arousal of one or more of the senses. He then compares the input with schemata for similar sensory information. The inability of a child with mental retardation to retain or recall numerous or complex representations restricts the meaningful interpretation of new stimuli. Consequently, there is no motive for sustaining attention to that stimulus.

Visual Impairments

Piaget and Inhelder (1969) observed a hierarchy of deficits in the cognitive development of children who were blind from birth. Departures from typical development were most obvious during the third stage of the sensorimotor period, when children who were blind failed to reach for objects. Limitations in visual sensory experiences prevented these children from forming basic sensorimotor schemata. This affected their acquisition of higher level cognitive skills.

Obviously, children who are blind and partially sighted do not gain the same perceptions of the nature of their environment as do children with sight. Their inability to be lured by objects that promote sustained attention and require them to change their physical position or to judge positions in space delays the development of object concept. Reaching and attaining an object that makes sound may not occur until late in the second year. Only then does a child begin mobility that facilitates his construction of the environment (Adelson & Fraiberg, 1976). Furthermore, pretend play occurs infrequently in children who are blind before 18 months of age, whereas it is common for their sighted peers (Preisler, 1995). Langley (1980) noted the following:

> Limited in independent mobility until approximately 19 months, the blind child is not able to explore various rooms of the house, to touch objects of interest, and to have them labeled. Unless the blind child is taught systematic scanning and exploration strategies, the similarities between objects and the ability to make generalizations may not develop. The absence of visual opportunities to associate tactual properties with auditory input often leads to meaningless rote verbalization (p. 18).

Object concept appears 1 to 3 years later in children who are blind.

Fraiberg (1968) and Warren (1984) found that object concept appears from 1 to 3 years late in children who are blind. Consequently, the lack of knowledge of the permanence of objects in space and critical relationships hinders progress in these children's cognitive development. A child who is unable to use vision to integrate auditory and tactile cues learns much later than sighted children how to maintain contact with his environment. Even very limited vision significantly alters how a child perceives and interacts with the world (Preisler, 1991).

Still, there is evidence that children who are and who are not visually impaired show approximate equivalence in certain concepts (Brekke, Williams, & Tait, 1974; Friedman & Pasnak, 1973). Reynell (1978) indicated that parallel development is most likely to appear at about 3 or 4 years of age, when logical thought begins to replace visual perception as the major learning process. Certainly, the abilities of people such as Helen Keller and Stevie Wonder show that visual impairments from early in life need not limit development of abstract thought. Children who are impaired from birth may develop complex cognitive skills if they are taught to make maximal use of action learning (Piaget & Inhelder, 1969).

> Vision allows a child to be more mobile and to explore his environment, thus facilitating cognitive development.

Hearing Impairments

Children with hearing impairments are more often identified by their failure to exhibit appropriate language milestones than by difficulties in sensorimotor or pre-conceptual abilities. This suggests that cognitive development can progress normally in the absence of hearing.

Much of the alienation from the environment of a child with a hearing impairment results from the influence of the impairment on language reception and production. Unfortunately, many tests of intelligence rely on language. Children with hearing impairments, therefore, may be erroneously identified as retarded. The negative reinforcement a child receives based on the lower expectations people have for him as a "retarded" child may contribute to a poorer performance. Blank (1974) found that children with hearing impairments also have the greatest difficulties with tasks for which instructions cannot be easily conveyed with gestures. The widening gap between the performance of children who do and do not have hearing impairments that occurs as they get older may result, in part, from the increasing complexity of instructions required for tasks at older ages. Meadow (1975) suggested that the cumulative effect of decreased cognitive stimulation and poor interpersonal relations contributes to poorer demonstrated performance by children with hearing impairments. Nevertheless, Best and Roberts (1976) reported that children who are deaf are equal to children who are not in the development of gestural imitation. In fact, they may actually be superior in the rate at which they learn to imitate. Furthermore, young children with deafness develop eye-hand coordination and fine motor skills more quickly than most children do, perhaps because they rely upon gestures for much of their communication.

Can we develop thought processes without language? Piaget (1952) and Vygotsky (1962) believed that the two develop along parallel and independent courses. "At a certain point these lines meet, whereupon thought becomes verbal and speech rational" (Vygotsky, p. 44). Furth (1966) expounded on the belief that a child does not need a linguistic symbol system to think. Furth's research, based upon Piaget's works, indicates that children with hearing impairments follow a normal course through the early stages of cognitive development. Beyond that, Furth (1973)

If the environment is contingently responsive, then cognitive development can progress normally in a child with hearing impairment. .

concluded, development is more similar to that of children from impoverished environments. He found no differences between children who did and did not have hearing impairments on simple visual memory tasks involving concrete objects, but greater differences were found when the task involved digits (Furth, 1961). Children with hearing impairments have greater difficulty on tasks of a more abstract nature. They are able to perform most classification tasks on a par with other children, but they have greater difficulty on tasks requiring analogy and superordinate reasoning in which problem solving requires a combination of concepts.

This discussion demonstrates that doubts remain about how a hearing impairment affects cognitive development. In fact, poor research methodology has prevented a definitive answer. Jamieson (1994) applied Vygotsky's theoretical framework to the interactions between parents and their children who were deaf. She found that parents altered their mediational strategies to meet the child's evolving communicative needs. The degree to which the parent and child can jointly understand a task determines the extent of learning problems the child may have. We can conclude that, in the absence of a linguistic symbol system, children with hearing impairments have the potential to develop typically if their environment is contingently responsive, thereby enabling them to build an alternate system of symbolic representations.

Physical Impairments

A child's first years are ones in which he formulates a perception of the universe through action. A child who is unable to move freely is at a great disadvantage. He may miss the opportunity to see his arms and legs move about—at first, erratically, then in predictable, voluntary ways. He may be unable to manipulate objects or recognize his influence on the universe. He may not change position in order to view his surroundings from different perspectives.

Care should be taken not to assume the presence of cognitive deficiencies in a young child with motor and/or language problems.

Children with central nervous system damage, as in cerebral palsy and spina bifida, and children with chronic illnesses and orthopedic problems may perceive their universe in a different way from that of the typical child because of the limitations or uniqueness in how they interact with their surroundings. Preschool-aged children with physical disabilities display lower levels of persistence on problem-solving tasks than do their peers without disabilities (Jennings, Conners, & Stegman, 1988).

Several classic British studies (Douglas, 1964; Rutter, Tizard, & Whitmore, 1970) and an American study (Wrightstone, Justman, & Moskovitz, 1953) revealed that children who are chronically ill are significantly behind typical children in academic achievement. Long periods in the hospital, lack of motivation, and negative feedback from environmental interactions account for at least some of the cognitive deficits.

It also has been estimated that approximately 75% of children with cerebral palsy have cognitive deficits; half of children with hydrocephalus and spina bifida have IQs under 80 (Young, Nulsen, Martin, & Thomas, 1973). As with children who are chronically ill, however, the impairment alone probably does not account for the total deficit. Severe language problems combined with limited movement create an atmosphere whereby we perceive children as being disabled because of their inability to communicate or perform appropriately. The insufficiency of traditional test instruments to assess cognitive functioning in the absence of adequate language and movement has led to inaccurate and sometimes harmful judgments about children. Some efforts have been made toward forming more objective determinations about the cognitive functioning of children with severe physical impairments.

For example, Zelazo (1979; Zelazo, Hopkins, Jacobson, & Kagan, 1974) and Lewis (Brooks-Gunn & Lewis, 1979; Lewis & Baldini, 1979) used an attention paradigm to test children who were unable to respond to test items in traditional ways. **Habituation** is the term for the decrement in an individual's response to a repeatedly presented stimulus. When one is presented with a new or novel stimulus, attention to the stimulus and one's heart rate increase. After repeated presentations, attention wanes and heart rate decreases as one learns to anticipate the event. Monitoring attention and heart rate in children during repeated presentations of the same stimulus, followed by the introduction of a subtle variation and then a return to the original stimulus, enables the examiner to estimate a child's cognitive processing skills (Fagan, 1990). Cognitive level is a function of the speed with which a child habituates to the original stimulus, recognizes and dishabituates to the variation (evidenced by increased attention and heart rate), and recognizes the original stimulus when it is presented again by habituating more quickly (Zelazo, 1979).

> Habituation paradigms have been used to measure cognitive levels of young children and children with disabilities, but few normative standards have been established.

Additional research has helped to specify the influence of physical impairment on various perceptual and cognitive tasks. Visual perception problems appear in children who have spent little time in an upright position. These children have difficulties performing form-board tasks (Berko, 1966), discriminating among various shapes, and organizing their spatial environment (Shurtleff, 1966). Poor visual and auditory perceptual skills of children with cerebral palsy have been attributed to the absence of the motor skills that train the visual and auditory systems. Rolling elicits visual pursuit, fusion, and accommodation of the lens to focus on objects at various distances and from different perspectives. Poor muscle stability in the neck may inhibit visual fixation; poor stability in the shoulders and arms may cause poor reaching patterns. Similar types of deficits interfere with perceptual development (Rosenbaum, Barnett, & Brand, 1975) and later reading and writing skills (Shurtleff, 1966) of children with spina bifida.

Autism

Children with autism pose an interesting puzzle of perceptual and conceptual skill development. They have difficulty processing sensory input and, as a consequence, may show exaggerated responses or no response to stimuli. They may show no response even to intense auditory or visual stimuli, yet they may engage in rubbing textures, spinning objects, or scratching surfaces. Children with autism appear to show decreased visual fixation and attention, but they can receive information quite well through kinesthetic and tactile means. Ornitz and Rivto (1976) found children with autism to be skillful at tasks requiring fine motor manipulations. However, the fact that they treat very different objects and experiences in stereotyped ways (Rutter, 1978) probably limits the refinement of cognitive processes. The application of more sophisticated assessment instruments (e.g., the attention paradigm described earlier) to large numbers of children with autism and the examination of behavioral self-regulation, task persistence, and perseverative tendencies (Adrien et al., 1995) may shed more light on the development of cognition.

Facilitating Cognitive Development

Children are born to learn. From their first noisy expression of hearty crying, they are storing and using information to make simple decisions. It is only when new information is no longer available in a form the child can use that cognitive development slows. This may represent an attitude of neglect on the part of the caregiver, for the nature of all children is to take advantage of the learning opportunities in their environment. Infants explore tactual stimuli with their hands, feet, and mouths, and slow their movements to listen to new sounds. Children with visual impairments gravitate toward auditory stimuli and children with hearing impairments toward those visual and tactile cues in their environment that carry new information. Children with mental retardation attend to complex stimuli around them when the input is simplified and clarified. In all situations in which a child is in an environment where he is unable to participate independently, the abilities of the teacher and caregiver grow in importance.

Many early intervention programs are founded on the belief that, if children are busy, they are learning. Paper and crayons, puzzles, pegboards, and shape boxes are placed before a child to stimulate learning. The teacher returns periodically to see whether the child has finished the task. When the paper is full of crayon marks, the puzzle pieces are in place, a peg fills each hole, or the shapes rest securely in the container, the child is praised for having learned. Has the teacher missed valuable opportunities to facilitate learning? Unquestionably!

With all young children, but particularly with those who are disabled, learning cannot be left to chance. We know, by studying children who are disadvantaged, that undesirable consequences result from poor caregiving strategies and a disorganized environment (Brooks-Gunn et al., 1995; Sameroff, Seifer, Baldwin, & Baldwin, 1993). We also know the benefits of a sound home environment. The distinctions between high and low quality in a child's home life also can be made in an educational program. As goes the parent, so goes the quality of the child's home life. Similarly, as goes the teacher, so goes the quality of the child's educational program. Fancy facilities and elaborate equipment may enhance a good program, but they cannot create one. An orientation toward the *way* a child does something rather than *what* he does is the basic approach that provides a cognitively stimulating environment.

> The early interventionist must have a rock-solid understanding of (cognitive) development.

In light of the glut of educational materials on the market today—some of which are promoted particularly for young children with disabilities—it is easy to conclude that equipment and curricular materials are the most important factors in facilitating cognition. But such is not the case. Materials are not as important to the early interventionist as sound guidance and a rock-solid understanding of development.

Focusing on the Process

Although there are dozens of manuals on the market that contain teaching-learning activities for young children with special needs, they are of limited value to a limited audience. They may be helpful to educational technicians who lack the flexibility or the authority to tailor their approach to individual children's needs. They also may be useful for interventionists seeking ideas around which to develop their own activities. Restricting themselves to teaching by the numbers, however, may mean that their focus is on accomplishing an activity rather than on how children process information as the activity is presented. Fewell and Sandall (1983) have provided a review of curricula for young children with disabilities that emphasizes how children learn and develop rather than just what they learn.

Education is often more concerned with the product than with the process of learning. Is it any wonder, then, that children have difficulty applying concepts and skills in different appropriate situations? In the vignette at the beginning of the chapter, Carrie would have produced a very colorful carton that she might have used for storage or that might have been hung from the ceiling as a mobile. She then would have gone on to another activity. With the minimal intervention of the teacher in the learning process, however, it is more likely that Carrie will now experiment with mixing other colors of paint. She may mix them in different proportions and begin to experiment with controlling color shades and tones. She may even extend the concept to mixing fluids or different colors of sand, thereby learning other principles about the attributes of matter.

Skills of the Interventionist

Good interventionists and caregivers are notable for their consistent and nurturing approach with children. Beyond that, however, they exhibit specific skills that are particularly effective in facilitating cognitive development. These skills are useful with all children, but their application may differ when the child is disabled (Hawkins, 1979).

Use Materials and Activities That Catch and Sustain a Child's Interest.   As discussed earlier, attention is a prerequisite for learning. To attract a child's attention to a specific object or task, we must win the competition with many other stimuli in the environment that are also vying for the child's attention. The primary consideration is appropriate positioning of the child. Equipment should be modified or created to place the child in a position in which he is most free to move and most in contact with his surroundings. Stimuli can then be modified to maximize the child's awareness.

With very young children and children with severe disabilities, increasing the intensity of a stimulus may be sufficient to draw their attention. Loud sounds may improve auditory attention, bright colors and lights may attract visual attention, and varied textures may enhance attention for grasping and manipulation. With older children and children who are less severely disabled, novel variations of familiar activities are most likely to hold their interest. The hazard in using the same familiar tasks over and over is that, although children may retain the skill longer as a result of overlearning, responses reach only the very basic rote level of cognition. There are decreasing incentive and challenge to apply skills in new ways to accomplish the same task. When an activity is changed slightly during subsequent presentations, benefits may include accelerated cognitive development and better generalization of skills to varied situations. Play at a sand table becomes even more exciting and stimulating when new measuring devices and containers are substituted for the familiar ones. The listening center holds a child's interest when there are new sounds and pictures to match. A new puppet that requires finer manipulations than the old ones do may visit the dress-up area and stimulate many new skills and concepts.

Select Activities with Intrinsic Termination Points.   One interventionist prided herself on integrating prevocational skills into her preschool classroom. She had the children sand a block of wood for 10 minutes each day, after which they punched holes in soft leather for 5 minutes. The utter futility of the task would be obvious if one watched the children's attention meander the entire time. The teacher made two fatal errors. First, she provided a task totally out of context to what is meaningful to children. Had she shown the children a toy wagon or a set of blocks that would result from their efforts, the activity might have had some merit. Her second error was not building in a point of successful termination. Time, an extraneous element in the activity, is not an appropriate reason for ending a task. What logic is there for a child when, working through a task, the teacher says that time is up? Each task should be in the form of a problem or challenge for which the child must find a resolution. An activity should not be ended until there is resolution and the child is aware of it. With the sanding task, the teacher could have colored an area on the block with a marker. The children could then have sanded until the marker's color was no longer visible. With the hole punching, she could have outlined holes in geometric patterns, numbers, or letters, and the children could have stopped when the pattern was complete.

In teaching children to control their own behavior, it is desirable that they rely on the teacher as little as possible for continuous directions. Even though it is a good teaching strategy to provide guidance, feedback, and reinforcement to each child, it is equally important to offer developmentally appropriate activities that provide the child with feedback from his own performance and the knowledge of when he has solved the problem. This best occurs, of course, with activities of the self-testing variety. With these, a child knows whether he has performed the task correctly and, if not, he can try another approach immediately. During this phase and at the completion of the task, the teacher can investigate the cognitive processes leading to the child's solution. This is a difficult but necessary skill for interventionists to master.

Use Language as a Cognitive Tool.   A substantial body of literature supports the close link between language and thought. For a child to perceive relationships and attain development of concepts, he must have labels to represent objects, people, and feelings. The teacher must provide these word labels for the child until he is able to use them to synthesize thoughts and to solve problems. The interventionist who names new objects for a child, describes what that child or other children are doing, gives names to feelings, and discusses the relationships among things and events in the child's environment is contributing to language competence in the child and, therefore, to development of cognitive skills.

Ask the Child Questions That Provide Challenge and Satisfaction.   When a child has created a clay structure or paste-up and the teacher responds with "What's that?" it gives the child a clear message. What the child thought to be a realistic imitation of an object or person is not good enough to be identified as such by the teacher. A more reinforcing and thought-provoking response, whether the teacher recognizes the child's creation or not, is "I like what you made. Tell me about it." This approach gives the child a feeling of worth, while allowing the teacher to investigate the development of the child's skills.

The key ingredients in a good teacher's response to a child's task are acknowledgement of the child's efforts and extraction of the child's problem-solving strategy. Was it just luck that allowed a child with a visual impairment to place the round shape in the round slot and not the square or triangular slot, or did the child use a particular strategy to place it correctly? "Good, Joan. Why does that round shape go where you put it?" the teacher should ask.

> The master teacher acknowledges a child's efforts and extracts the child's problem-solving strategy.

With children who are nonverbal, the challenge to the teacher is greater. In these cases, the teacher may verbalize through the problem-solving process and demonstrate the strategies leading to a correct response. For example, "Good, this pile has pictures of things we eat and this pile has pictures of things we eat with." Or, "Let's do it again so that one pile has things we eat and another pile has things we eat with. I'll do the first ones; now you do the rest."

Questions should be nonjudgmental and purposeful—not "Why did you do it like that?" but rather "Why do you think those go together?" Put yourself in the place of a child. Given a task to perform, consider the logic involved and the variety of ways to perform the task. Then try to determine the child's approach to performing the task by asking questions that reveal the child's strategy.

Allow for Learning Through Discovery and for the Child to Choose Learning Tasks.   In European schools, one rarely finds materials stored away in cabinets or on high shelves. The Montessori approach, begun in Italy, advocates the availability and accessibility of materials to children in the classroom. Through exploration and teacher guidance, children learn what materials are on and off limits to them, how to use new materials, and how to select materials of interest to them.

Discovery is important in the development of cognitive skills. Through exploration, children assimilate information about the order of their surroundings. In many programs, teachers demonstrate how to use new and challenging pieces of equipment, such as graded cylinders or matrix puzzles. They give children an opportunity to work on the task with guidance and then place it in an accessible location so the children may use it at other times. This move toward nurturing independence can work very well with young children with disabilities. However, when interventionists tell children what to do or give them every task to perform, they deprive the children of the rich developmental opportunities that discovery and independent decision making provide.

Some children have difficulty selecting tasks. The following progression indicates how children at different developmental levels can be challenged to participate in activity selection.

1. Let's paint. (noncommunicative child)
2. Do you want to paint? (verbal or nonverbal response acceptable)

Children learn more quickly and retain information better when a multisensory approach is used—one combining two or more senses in the learning activity.

3. Do you want to paint or play at the sand table? (verbal, imitative response; the list of choices can be expanded)
4. Show me what you would like to do now. (nonverbal, open-ended response)
5. Tell me what you would like to do now. (verbal, open-ended response)

Children at any level of development can be included in the scheme of selecting and discovering through their own initiative. For this to occur, they must feel secure moving about in their environment (aided by consistency of objects' locations), and materials must be accessible to them. Finally, the interventionist can help children to discover how materials are used, where they are located, and what pleasures they hold. For example, children with visual impairments should be able to expect that their tactual materials are arranged on specific shelves, with the least difficult items on the lower shelves. Similar patterns may be established for children with other disabilities.

Identify and Use Each Child's Primary Input Mode.   All learners show a differential preference for receiving and processing information; some learn more effectively from auditory input, and others from tactile or visual input. Children with disabilities are not excluded from this learning characteristic, but if the preferential input mode is the locus of the impairment, learning may be considerably more difficult. The adaptability of young children makes it incumbent upon the interventionist to take advantage of input channels through which accurate information is likely to be received and to nurture and stimulate the secondary input channels that are the site of the impairment.

Young children and children with severe disabilities learn initially through movement. The kinesthetic stimulation of one's arms and legs moving in space, along with watching them move and hearing the sounds of objects they touch or strike, offers the initial learning experiences for a child. Physical movement remains an important mode of learning throughout life.

Education tends to become more and more auditory as a child progresses through formal schooling. Many children discover that they learn more from textbooks or field trips than they do from lectures. Children with disabilities show the same individual differences in how they learn. Consequently, interventionists must be flexible in their approaches. One child may learn a task quickly with a verbal explanation. Another child may require demonstration as well as verbal explanation or may have to be moved through the task, hand-over-hand. Interventionists should, therefore, give careful consideration to how children process different forms of input and use this information in their instructional strategies.

Structuring the Curriculum

The most important criterion for program success is a staff made up of people who know how to teach. Nevertheless, interventionists also must be able to organize the educational program so that it includes aspects that are most beneficial to children's intellectual growth. Using the structure of Lavatelli (1973) outlined earlier, a program should help children progress from a concrete to a symbolic level in classification, space and number, and seriation operations, from which all concepts are constructed. These may be used as the focus for activities in early intervention programs. The teacher also can organize materials based upon the same principles. Puzzles can be ordered by difficulty based not only on the number of pieces, but also on the spatial complexities of the position of pieces. Different groups of objects and pictures can be available for children to sort or classify. Some groups can contain objects that are very different and other groups can have objects or pictures with only subtle differences. Children can be given dolls to hold that are progressively bigger in size or can be asked to draw another one that is smaller, and then one that's even smaller. Containers at the water table can be color-coded to correspond with the daily color of the water to which food dye has been added. An infant can be given different-sized bottles from which to drink his milk.

If activities are considered in terms of the cognitive processes they require or nurture, program planning can yield more individualization and challenge for children. The works of Johnson-Martin, Jens, Attermeirer, and Hacker (1991); Lavatelli (1973); and Weikart, Rogers, Adcock, and McClelland (1971) provide more specific activities using this approach.

The structure and application of a curriculum are critical to a young child's cognitive development—but the most important element is good teaching!

Summary

For all children, the road to understanding and using complex concepts is quite similar. Children first learn about their worlds by their looks, smells, sounds, tastes, and feel. By seeing how different people and objects in their environments interact, children begin to formulate basic constructs of their worlds based on the simple relationships they perceive. As they add word labels to their experiences and observations, their understanding of the world increases significantly.

A disability may interrupt the cognitive process in four ways: It may interfere with a child's ability to attend to a stimulus, as in a neurological or sensory impairment; it may impede reception of potentially valuable stimuli, as in a visual or hearing impairment; it may disrupt the storage and processing of information, as in brain damage associated with mental retardation; and it may interfere with a child's ability to express his cognitive abilities, as in speech disorders and orthopedic impairments. A Piagetian framework was emphasized in this chapter because it helps us to interpret children's cognitive development even in light of these extreme differences. Furthermore, it provides the interventionist with a foundation from which to plan a program based on a child's current level of performance rather than on his chronological age.

The skills that have been described are caregiver skills and cannot be considered the province of the interventionist alone. Through home visits, parent participation in the classroom, and other broad strategies that include all of the caregivers, the child will be the beneficiary of an environment that has the potential to maximize intellectual development.

Review Questions and Discussion Points

1. Discuss Piaget's theory of development and its relationship to young children with special needs.
2. How does each type of disability potentially influence development of the young child?

3. Compare the three theories of development discussed in the chapter in relation to young children with special needs.
4. What factors contribute to development of cognitive skills in an early intervention program?

Recommended Resources

Web Sites

Cognitive Development in Young Children with Down Syndrome: Developmental Strengths, Developmental Weaknesses (Riverbend Down Syndrome Parent Support Group)

http://altonweb.com/cs/downsyndrome/index.html

Cognitive Development Theories
http://www.education.indiana.edu/~p540/webcourse/develop.html

Publications and Other Media

Bybee, R. W., & Sund, R. B. (1990). *Piaget for educators* (2nd ed.). Prospect Heights, IL: Waveland Press.

High/Scope Educational Research Foundation. *High/Scope Preschool Curriculum.* (600 North River Street, Ypsilanti, MI 48198.)

Johnson-Martin, N. M., Jens, K. G., Attermeier, S. M., & Hacker, B. J. (1991). *The Carolina curriculum for infants and toddlers with special needs* (2nd ed). Baltimore: Brookes.

Kamii, C., & Ewing, J. K. (1996). Basing teaching on Piaget's constructivism. *Childhood Education, 72,* 260–264.

Leong, D. J., & Bedrova, E. (1996). *Tools of the mind: A Vygotskian approach to early*

childhood education. Upper Saddle River, NJ: Merrill/Prentice Hall.

Singer, D. G., & Ravenson, T. (1996). *A Piaget primer: How a child thinks.* New York: Plume Books.

References

Adelson, E., & Fraiberg, S. (1976). Sensory deficit and motor development in infants blind from birth. In Z. S. Jastrzembska (Ed.), *The effects of blindness and other impairments on early development.* New York: American Foundation for the Blind.

Adrien, J. L., Matrineau, J., Barthelemy, C., Bruneau, N., Garreau, B., & Sauvage, D. (1995). Disorders of regulation of cognitive activity in autistic children. *Journal of Autism and Developmental Disorders, 24,* 249–263.

Baillargeon, R. (1987). Young infants' reasoning about the physical and spatial characteristics of a hidden object. *Cognitive Development, 3,* 179–200.

Baydar, N., & Brooks-Gunn, J. (1991). Effects of maternal employment and child-care arrangements on preschoolers' cognitive and behavioral outcomes: Evidence from the children of the National Longitudinal Study of Youth. *Developmental Psychology, 27,* 932–945.

Berko, M. J. (1966). Psychological and linguistic implications of brain damage in children. In M. Mecham, F. G. Berko, M. F. Berko, & J. Palmer (Eds.), *Communication training in childhood brain damage.* Springfield, IL: Charles C. Thomas.

Bernstein, B. (1960). Language and social class. *British Journal of Sociology, 2,* 271–276.

Best, B., & Roberts, G. (1976). Early cognitive development in hearing impaired children. *American Annals of the Deaf, 121,* 560–564.

Blank, M. (1974). Cognitive functions of language in the preschool years. *Developmental Psychology, 10,* 229–245.

Bower, T. G. R. (1974). *Development in infancy.* San Francisco: Freeman.

Brekke, B., Williams, J. E., & Tait, P. (1974). The acquisition of conservation of weight by visually impaired children. *Journal of Genetic Psychology, 125,* 89–97.

Brinker, R. P., & Lewis, M. (1982). Discovering the competent handicapped infant: A process approach to assessment and intervention. *Topics in Early Childhood Special Education, 2,* 1–16.

Broadbent, D. (1958). *Perception and communication.* London: Pergamon Press.

Brooks-Gunn, J., Klebanov, P. K., & Liaw, F. (1995). The learning, physical, and emotional environment of the home in the context of poverty: The Infant Health and Development Program. *Children and Youth Services Review, 19,* 251–276.

Brooks-Gunn, J., & Lewis, M. (1979, September). *Handicapped infants and their mothers at play.* Paper presented at the annual meeting of the American Psychological Association, New York.

Carver, L. J., & Bauer, P. J. (2001). Memory in infants: The emergence of long and short-term explicit memory in infancy. *Journal of Experimental Psychology (General), 130,* 726–747.

Celeste, M. (2002). A survey of motor dvelopment for infants and young children with visual impairments. *Journal of Visual Impairment & Blindness, 96,* 169–175.

Colombo, J. (2001). The development of visual attention in infancy. *Annual Review of Psychology, 52,* 337–367.

Dennis, W. (1973). *Children of the Creche.* New York: Appleton-Century-Crofts.

Detterman, D. K. (1979). Memory in the mentally retarded. In N. R. Ellis (Ed.), *Handbook of mental deficiency, psychological theory and research.* Hillsdale, NJ: Erlbaum.

Douglas, J. W. B. (1964). *The home and the school.* London: Mackgibbon & Kee.

Duncan, G. L., & Brooks-Gunn, J. (1997). *Consequences of growing up poor.* New York: Russell Sage Foundation.

Duncan, G. L., Brooks-Gunn, J., & Klebanov, P. K. (1994). Economic deprivation and early childhood development. *Child Development, 65,* 296–318.

Ellis, N. R. (1970). Memory processes in retardates and normal infants. *International Review of Research in Mental Retardation, 4,* 1–32.

Fagan, J. F. (1990). The paired-comparison paradigm and infant intelligence. *Annals of the New York Academy of Sciences, 608,* 337–364.

Fantz, R. L., Fagan, J. F., & Miranda, S. B. (1975). Early visual selectivity as a function of pattern variables, previous exposure, age from birth and conception, and expected cognitive deficit. In L. B. Cohen & P. Salapatek (Eds.), *Infant perception: From sensation to cognition.* Vol. 1: *Basic visual processes.* New York: Academic Press.

Ferguson, C. A. (1978). Learning to pronounce: The earliest stages of phonological development in the child. In F. D. Minifie & L. L. Lloyd (Eds.), *Communicative and cognitive abilities: Early behavioral assessment.* Baltimore: University Park Press.

Fewell, R. R., & Sandall, S. R. (1983). Curricula adaptations for young children: Visually impaired, hearing impaired, and physically impaired. *Topics in Early Childhood Special Education, 2,* 51–66.

Finkelstein, N. W., Gallagher, J. J., & Farron, D. C. (1980). Attentiveness and responsiveness to auditory stimuli of children at risk for mental retardation. *American Journal of Mental Deficiency, 85,* 135–144.

Flavell, J. H. (1963). *The developmental psychology of Jean Piaget.* Princeton, NJ: Van Nostrand.

Flavell, J. H. (1970). Developmental studies of mediated memory. In H. W. Reese & L. P. Lipsitt (Eds.), *Advances in child development and behavior,* Vol. 5. New York: Academic Press.

Fraiberg, S. (1968). Parallel and divergent patterns in blind and sighted infants. *Psychoanalytic Study of the Child, 23,* 264–300.

Fraiberg, S. (1975). The development of human attachments in infants blind from birth. *Merrill-Palmer Quarterly, 21,* 315–334.

Friedman, J., & Pasnak, S. (1973). Attainment of classification and seriation concepts by blind children. *Education of the Visually Handicapped, 5,* 55–62.

Frye, D., & Zelazo, P. D. (1996). Inference and action in early causal reasoning. *Developmental Psychology, 32,* 120–131.

Furth, H. G. (1961). Visual paired-associates task with deaf and hearing children. *Journal of Speech and Hearing Research, 4,* 172–177.

Furth, H. G. (1966). *Thinking without language: Psychological implications of deafness.* New York: Free Press.

Furth, H. G. (1973). *Deafness and learning: A psychosocial approach.* Belmont, CA: Wadsworth.

Garber, H., & Heber, F. R. (1977). The Milwaukee Project: Indications of the effectiveness of early intervention in preventing mental retardation. In P. Mittler (Ed.), *Research to practice in mental retardation,* Vol. 1: *Care and intervention.* Baltimore: University Park Press.

Gasser, M., & Colunga, E. (2002). Pattern learning in infants and neural networks. In P. Quinlan (Ed.), *Connectionist models of development.* Brighton, England: Psychology Press.

Gibson, E. J. (1969). *Principles of perceptual learning and development.* New York: Appleton-Century-Crofts.

Gindis, B. (1995). The social/cultural implication of disability: Vygotsky's paradigm for special education. *Educational Psychologist, 30,* 77–81.

Girbau, D. (2001). Children's referential communication failure. *Journal of Language and Social Psychology, 20,* 81–90.

Grossman, H. J. (Ed.). (1977). *Manual on terminology and classification in mental retardation.* Washington, DC: American Association on Mental Deficiency.

Hauser-Cram, P. (1996). Mastering motivation in toddlers with developmental disabilities. *Child Development, 67,* 236–248.

Hawkins, F. P. (1979). The eye of the beholder. In S. Meisels (Ed.), *Special education and development: Perspectives on young children with special needs.* Baltimore: University Park Press.

Huang-Pollock, C. L., Carr, T. H., & Nigg, J. T. (2002). Development of selective attention: Perceptual load influences early versus late attentional selection in children and adults. *Developmental Psychology, 38,* 363–375.

Jamieson, J. R. (1994). Teaching as transaction: Vygotskian perspectives on deafness and mother-child interaction. *Exceptional Children, 60,* 434–449.

Jaskir, J., & Lewis, M. (1981, April). *A factor analytic study of mother-infant interactions at 3, 12, and 24 months.* Paper presented at the annual meeting of the Eastern Psychological Association, New York.

Jennings, K. D., Conners, R. E., & Stegman, C. E. (1988). Does a physical handicap alter the development of mastering motivation during the preschool years? *Journal of the American Academy of Child and Adolescent Psychiatry, 27,* 312–317.

Johnson-Martin, N. M., Jens, K. G., Attermeier, S. M., & Hacker, B. J. (1991). *The Carolina curriculum for infants and toddlers with special needs* (2nd ed.). Baltimore: Brookes.

Jordan, T. E. (1980). *Development in the preschool years: Birth to age five.* New York: Academic Press.

Kagan, J., & Kogan, N. (1970). Individual variation in cognitive processes. In P. Mussen (Ed.), *Carmichael's manual of child psychology* (Vol. 1). New York: Wiley.

Kahn, J. (1976). Utility of the Uzgiris and Hunt scales of sensorimotor development with severely and profoundly retarded children. *American Journal on Mental Deficiency, 80,* 663–665.

Kail, R. (1993). The role of global mechanisms in developmental change in speed of processing. In M. L. Howe, & R. Pasnak (Eds.), *Emerging themes in cognitive development,* (Vol. 1: pp. 97–116). New York: Springer-Verlag.

Kamii, C., & Ewing, J. K. (1996). Basing teaching on Piaget's constructivism. *Childhood Education, 72,* 260–264.

Kearsley, R. B. (1979). Iatrogenic retardation: A syndrome of learned incompetence. In R. B. Kearsley & I. E. Sigel (Eds.), *Infants at risk: Assessment of cognitive functioning.* Hillsdale, NJ: Erlbaum.

Landry, S. H., Swank, P. R., Assel, M. A., Smith, K. E., & Vellet, S. (2001). Does early responsive parenting have a special importance for children's development or is consistency across early childhood necessary? *Developmental Psychology, 37,* 387–403.

Langley, M. B. (1980). *The teachable moment and the handicapped infant.* Reston, VA: ERIC Clearinghouse on Handicapped and Gifted Children.

Laucht, M., Esser, G., & Schmidt, M. H. (1994). Contrasting infant predictors of later cognitive functioning. *Journal of Child Psychology, Psychiatry, & Allied Disciplines, 35,* 649–662.

Lavatelli, C. S. (1973). *Piaget's theory applied to an early childhood curriculum.* Nashua, NH: Delta Education,

Lewis, M. (1971). Individual differences in the measurement of early cognitive growth. In T. Hellmuth (Ed.), *Exceptional infants: Studies in abnormality* (Vol. 2). New York: Bruner/Mazel.

Lewis, M., & Baldini, N. (1979). Attention processes and individual differences. In G. Hale & M. Lewis (Eds.), *Attention and cognitive development.* New York: Plenum Press.

Lewis, M., & Coates, D. L. (1980). Mother-infant interactions and cognitive development in 12-week-old infants. *Infant Behavior and Development, 3,* 95–105.

Lewis, M., & Rosenblum, L. (Eds.). (1974). *The effect of the infant on its caregiver.* New York: Wiley.

Maccoby, E. E., & Zellner, M. (1970). *Experiments in primary education: Aspects of Project Follow-Through.* New York: Harcourt Brace Jovanovich.

Mareschal, D., Plunkett, K., & Harris, P. (1999). A computational and neuropsychological account of object-oriented behaviors in infancy. *Developmental Science, 2,* 306–317.

Mayes, L. C., Bornstein, M. H., Chawarska, K., & Granger, R. H. (1995). Information processing and developmental assessments in 3-month-old infants exposed prenatally to cocaine. *Pediatrics, 95,* 539–545.

McClinton, B. S., & Meier, B. G. (1978). *Beginnings: Psychology of early childhood.* St. Louis: Mosby.

McDade, H. L., & Adler, S. (1980). Down syndrome and short-term memory impairment: A storage or retrieval deficit? *American Journal on Mental Deficiency, 84,* 561–567.

Meadow, K. P. (1975). The development of deaf children. In E. M. Hetherington (Ed.), *Review of child development research* (Vol. 5). Chicago: University of Chicago Press.

Merrill, E. C., & Taube, M. (1996). Negative priming and mental retardation: The processing of distractor information. *American Journal on Mental Retardation, 101,* 63–71.

Nelson, K. (1973a). Some evidence for the cognitive primacy of categorization and its functional basis. *Merrill-Palmer Quarterly, 19,* 21–39.

Nelson, K. (1973b). Structure and strategy in learning to talk. *Monographs of the Society for Research in Child Development, 38* (Serial No. 149).

Ornitz, E. M., & Rivto, E. R. (1976). Medical assessment. In E. R. Rivto (Ed.), *Autism: Diagnosis, current research and management.* New York: Spectrum.

Parker, S. T. (1993). Imitation and circular reactions as evolved mechanisms for cognitive construction. *Human Development, 36,* 309–323.

Pasamanick, B., & Knobloch, H. (1961). Epidemiologic studies on the complications of pregnancy and the birth process. In G. Caplan (Ed.), *Prevention of mental disorders in children.* New York: Basic Books.

Pasamanick, B., & Knobloch, H. (1966). Retrospective studies on the epidemiology of reproductive casualty: Old and new. *Merrill-Palmer Quarterly,* *12,* 7–26.

Piaget, J. (1951). *Play, dreams and imitation in childhood.* New York: Norton.

Piaget, J. (1952). *The origins of intelligence in children.* New York: International Universities Press.

Piaget, J. (1954). *The construction of reality in the child.* New York: Basic Books.

Piaget, J., & Inhelder, B. (1969). *The psychology of the child.* New York: Basic Books.

Preisler, G. M. (1991). Early patterns of interaction between blind infants and their sighted mothers. *Child: Care, Health, and Development, 17,* 65–90.

Preisler, G. M. (1995). The development of communication in blind and deaf infants—similarities and differences. *Child: Care, Health, and Development, 21,* 79–110.

Raz, N., Torres, I. I., Briggs, S. D., Spencer, W. D., Thornton, A. E., Loken, W. J., et al. (1995). Selective neuroanatomic abnormalities in Down's syndrome and their cognitive correlates: Evidence from MRI morphometry. *Neurology, 45,* 356–366.

Reynell, J. (1978). Developmental patterns of visually handicapped children. *Child: Care, Health, and Development, 4,* 291–303.

Robinson, N. M., & Robinson, H. B. (1976). *The mentally retarded child.* New York: McGraw-Hill.

Rochat, P. R. (2001). Social contingency detection and infant development. *Bulletin of the Menninger Clinic, 65,* 347–360.

Rogoff, B., Malkin, C., & Gilbride, K. (1984). Instruction with babies as guidance in development. In B. Rogoff & J. V. Wertsch (Eds.), *Children's learning in the "zone of proximal development".* San Francisco: Jossey-Bass.

Rohwer, W. (1970). Images and pictures in children's learning. *Psychological Bulletin, 73,* 393–403.

Rosenbaum, P., Barnett, R., & Brand, H. L. (1975). A developmental intervention program designed to overcome the effects of impaired movement in spina bifida infants. In K. S. Holt (Ed.), *Movement and child development.* Philadelphia: Lippincott.

Rossi, S., & Wittrock, M. C. (1971). Developmental shifts in verbal recall between mental ages two and five. *Child Development, 42,* 333–338.

Rutter, M. (1978). Language disorder and infantile autism. In M. Rutter & E. Schopler (Eds.), *Autism: A reappraisal of concepts and treatment.* New York: Plenum Press.

Rutter, M. (1979). Maternal deprivation 1972–1978: New findings, new concepts, new approaches. *Child Development, 50,* 283–305.

Rutter, M. (1980). The long-term effects of early experience. *Developmental Medicine and Child Neurology, 22,* 800–815.

Rutter, M., Tizard, J., & Whitmore, K. (1970). *Education, health, and behavior.* London: Longmans, Green.

Sameroff, A. J. (1979). The etiology of cognitive competence: A systems perspective. In R. B. Kearsley & I. E. Sigel (Eds.), *Infants at risk: Assessment of cognitive functioning.* Hillsdale, NJ: Erlbaum.

Sameroff, A. J. (1982). The environmental context of developmental disabilities. In D. D. Bricker (Ed.), *Intervention with at-risk and handicapped infants: From research to application.* Baltimore: University Park Press.

Sameroff, A. J., & Chandler, M. J. (1975). Reproductive risk and the continuum of caretaking casualty. In F. D. Horowitz (Ed.), *Review of child development research* (Vol. 4). Chicago: University of Chicago Press.

Sameroff, A. J., & Fiese, B. H. (1990). Transactional regulation and early intervention. In S. J. Meisels & J. P. Shonkoff (Eds.), *Handbook of early childhood intervention.* New York: Cambridge University Press.

Sameroff, A. J., Seifer, R., Baldwin, A., & Baldwin, C. (1993). Stability of intelligence from preschool to adolescence: The influence of social and family risk factors. *Child Development, 64,* 80–97.

Schutte, A. R., & Spencer, J. P. (2002). Generalizing the dynamic field theory of the A-and-B error beyond infancy: Three-year-olds' delay- and experience-dependent location memory biases. *Child Development, 73,* 377–404.

Shurtleff, D. T. (1966). Timing of learning in meningomyelocele patients. *Journal of the American Physical Therapy Association, 46,* 136–148.

Silverstein, A. B., McLain, R. E., Brownless, L., & Hubbey, M. (1976). Structure of ordinal scales of psychological development in infancy. *Educational and Psychological Measurement, 36,* 355–359.

Slamecka, N. (1968). An examination of trace storage in free recall. *Journal of Experimental Psychology, 76,* 504–513.

Stremmel, A. J., & Ru, V. R. (1993). Teaching in the zone of proximal development: Implications for responsive teaching practice. *Child and Youth Care Forum, 22,* 337–350.

Templin, M. (1950). *The development of reasoning in children with normal and defective hearing.* Minneapolis: University of Minnesota Press.

Tessier, F. (1969–1970). The development of young cerebral palsied children according to Piaget's sensorimotor theory. *Dissertation Abstracts International, 30A,* 4841.

Trevarthen, C. (1988). Infants trying to talk. In R. Söderbergh (Ed.), *Children's creative communication.* Lund, Sweden: Lund University Press.

Tulving, E. (1968). Theoretical issues in free recall. In T. Dixon & D. Horton (Eds.), *Verbal behavior and general behavior theory.* Upper Saddle River, NJ: Prentice Hall.

Vygotsky, L. S. (1962). *Thought and language.* Cambridge, MA: MIT Press.

Vygotsky, L. S. (1978). *Mind in society: The development of higher psychological process.* Cambridge, MA: Harvard University Press.

Wachs, T. D., Uzgiris, I. C., & Hunt, J. McV. (1971). Cognitive development in infants of different age levels and from different environmental backgrounds. *Merrill-Palmer Quarterly, 17,* 282–317.

Wakschlag, L. S., & Hans, S. L. (1999). Relation of maternal responsiveness during infancy to the development of behavior problems in middle childhood. *Developmental Psychology, 35,* 569–579.

Warren, D. H. (1984). *Blindness and early childhood development* (2nd ed.). New York: American Foundation for the Blind.

Weikart, D. P., Rogers, L., Adcock, C., & McClelland, D. (1971). *The cognitively oriented curriculum.* Washington, DC: National Association for the Education of Young Children.

Weisz, J. R., & Zigler, E. (1979). Cognitive development in retarded and nonretarded persons: Piagetian tests of the similar sequence hypotheses. *Psychological Bulletin, 86,* 831–851.

Wrightstone, J. W., Justman, J., & Moskovitz, S. (1953). *Studies of children with physical handicaps: The child with cardiac limitation.* New York: City Board of Education.

Young, H. F., Nulsen, F. E., Martin, H. W., & Thomas, P. (1973). The relationship of intelligence and the cerebral mantle in treated infantile hydrocephalus. *Pediatrics, 52,* 38–44.

Zeaman, D. (1973). One programmatic approach to retardation. In D. K. Routh (Ed.), *The experimental psychology of mental retardation.* Chicago: Aldine.

Zelazo, P. R. (1979). Reactivity to perceptual-cognitive events: Application for infant assessment. In R. B. Kearsley & I. E. Sigel (Eds.), *Infants at risk: Assessment of cognitive functioning.* Hillsdale, NJ: Erlbaum.

Zelazo, P. R., Hopkins, J. R., Jacobson, S. M., & Kagan, J. (1974). Psychological reactivity to discrepant events: Support for the curvilinear hypothesis. *Cognition, 2,* 385–393.

10

Communication

Susan R. Easterbrooks

Chapter Outline

Ian

*I*an is a 12-month-old boy whose hearing loss was identified while he was in the newborn nursery as a result of new laws regarding universal newborn hearing screening. Because there were some problems with the equipment, screening results were questioned. He was retested, yet the second set of equipment also malfunctioned. This led his parents to assume that all was well. Subsequent testing revealed that there was a severe loss in one ear and a moderately severe loss in the other. Additional testing revealed genetics to be the cause of the loss.

A professional in the field suggested cochlear implants, which are devices implanted in the inner ear, but because Ian had usable residual hearing, his parents opted not to go this route. Ian received hearing aids using advanced technology at 10 months of age. He has been attending a private auditory verbal program weekly, where his mother receives instruction in assisting him to learn to listen and use spoken language. A parent-infant advisor available through his state's parent-infant program also sees him twice monthly. Ian babbles consistently when wearing his hearing aids. He is able to match sounds to objects, such as "brrrmm, brrrmm" to an airplane. He is progressing very well.

The ability to understand and use language is a distinctly human trait. Language permits us to express our basic needs, provides a vehicle through which we learn about the world, and fosters social interactions. Children who are delayed in communication, for whatever reason, are at risk within a world that primarily conveys its demands and changes through language.

Listening to typically developing toddler language is a charming experience. The errors that infants and toddlers make during the language development process are a constant source of delight to adults. The preschool years are those during which language acquisition unfolds. By the time children enter school, they are using all the sentence types produced by adults (Owens, 1996). According to Chomsky (1957), the critical period for language acquisition is before the age of 5. Youngsters whose parents have recognized their special needs early in childhood are fortunate because intervention can be initiated before these precious years of learning have passed. This chapter reviews theories and stages of language development, factors that affect communication development, and intervention approaches.

Language: A Framework and Definitions

Communication

Communication is the exchange of information and ideas.

The term **communication** refers to an exchange of information and ideas. This broad definition requires that we view communication as occurring vocally, non-vocally, gesturally, pictorially, through sign language, through written language, or through any number of representational systems such as those used with communication boards.

Speech

Speech refers to the acoustic-articulatory code by which spoken languages are conveyed.

Speech refers to auditory-articulatory code by which we represent spoken languages. Speech includes phonation and articulation of the specific **phonemes** (the sounds of letters and letter combinations) of a language. Disorders of speech include but are not limited to articulation, dysfluency (stuttering), and voice disorders such as hoarseness or harshness. However, speech is not the only means by which we represent language.

Language

Language represents a culture-based code of arbitrary symbols used to communicate.

Language, as defined by Bloom and Lahey (1978), is a "code whereby ideas about the world are represented through a conventional system of arbitrary signals for communication" (p. 4). In spoken language, we represent this code through numerous conventional systems, including phonology, morphology, syntax, semantics, and pragmatics. Some children have difficulty mastering a first language because of problems with these systems. Others have difficulty because the language spoken at home differs from the language spoken at school or by the larger community. Others must learn signed or coded forms of English (e.g., Signing Exact English or

Cued Speech); still others must learn American Sign Language, which is a distinctly separate language from signed forms of English.

Form, Content, and Use

Language is a subject that has both perplexed and fascinated scholars. It has been studied from many perspectives. Bloom and Lahey (1978) proposed that communication could be organized into three aspects and that language competence was dependent upon interactions among these aspects. They saw language as being comprised of elements of **form, content,** and **use.** The form of language is comprised of phonology, morphology, and syntax; the content of language is often referred to as semantics; and the use of language includes functions and contexts, or pragmatics.

Table 10.1 identifies some of the basic components of the form, content, and use elements in the language of young children. For example, here is a conversation between a mother and her baby that demonstrates aspects of form, content, and use:

Mother:	Good morning, honey. Time to get up.
Baby:	(Reaching for mother) Up?
Mother:	That's my girl. Are you hungry? Are you ready for breakfast?
Baby:	Want eat.
Mother:	Good. I'm glad you're hungry, but let me change you first.
Baby:	(Crying) No! No! Want eat, want eat. Want eat!

Regarding form, this child is at the presyntactic stage, combining words into two-word utterances. The baby is not demonstrating any of the morphological elements such as word endings that convey tense and number, but we still get the message. Content is illustrated by the baby being able to understand and talk about concepts in her daily experience. She has certain semantic categories such as action (eat) and rejection (no change). Use is demonstrated by the child's mastering early pragmatic uses of her communication, such as mutuality and protesting.

Now recall Ian, our young friend who is deaf, in the opening vignette. In terms of form, he is communicating at the one-word, presyntactic level and is expressing declarative, imperative, and question forms through facial expression and voice intonation. Content-wise, he understands some vocabulary items in the categories of object and agent (see Table 10.1) because he will look for a toy or for his mother when someone asks, "Where's Mama?" He also uses the category of rejection, using grunts, whines, and gestures to let others know when he does not want something. Pragmatically, he uses his communication to seek attention, request, protest, and greet albeit vocally but not necessarily verbally.

Phonology

Chomsky and Halle (1968) studied the phonological components of language, which are the sound patterns of speech, or the articulatory-acoustic properties that allow us to represent our thoughts. **Phonology** is the study of speech sounds. Jakobson (1968) proposed that the phonemes of any language (i.e., the basic units of speech

Phonology refers to the study of sound units of speech.

TABLE 10.1 Elements of Form, Content, and Use in Young Children

Aspect	Linguistic Categories	Components	
Form	Morphology and Syntax	Declarative, imperative, and question sentence types	
		Simple sentences: one subject, one verb, simple verb tense	
		Simple transformations: passive voice, negation, conjunction, complements, *there* as sentence starter	
		Questions forms: *Wh-* questions, yes/no, *What . . . do*, tag questions, subject-auxiliary inversion questions	
		Complex sentences: dependent and independent clauses, relative clauses, complementation, verbs requiring special consideration, advanced verb tense	
Content	Semantics	Agent	Recurrence
		Entity	Disappearance
		Object/Patient	Denial
		Recipient	Rejection
		Action	Attribute
		transitive verb	Location/Position
		intransitive verb	Manner
		Process	Time
		Transitive verb	Frequency
		Intransitive verb	Duration
		Stative verb	Purpose
		Possessor	Intensifier
		Vocative	Inclusion
		Existence	Question forms
		Nonexistence	
Use	Pragmatics	Mutual	
		Repair of failed message	Closes conversation
		Ritualized gestures	Communicative intention
		Mutuality	Attention seeking
		Reciprocity	Requesting
		Synchronicity	Protesting
		Turn taking	Commenting
		Whispering	Greeting
		Hints	Answering
		Opens conversation	Teasing, taunting
		Sustains topic	Knowledge of context
		Changes topic	Knowledge of audience

Sources: Bloom & Lahey, 1978; Coggins & Carpenter, 1981; Owens, 1996.

TABLE 10.2 Latest Ages at Which Most Children Acquire Specific Phoneme Use

Age	Phonemes Typically Acquired	
3 years	*m* (mama)	*n* (nose)
	p (pat)	*t* (toy)
	k (kite)	*b* (baby)
	d (duck)	*h* (hot)
	w (water)	*g* (go)
4 years	*j* (yellow)	
5 years	ξ (jump)	
6 years	*r* (red)	*l* (little)
	tf (choo-choo)	*n* (ring)
7 years	θ (this)	δ (think)
	s (sun)	ʃ (shock)
	v (vase)	*z* (zipper)

Sources: Adler & King, 1994; Prather, Hedrick, & Kern, 1972; Templin, 1957.

sounds) can be classified in terms of their articulatory and acoustic properties, and that these features are universal. Table 10.2 indicates the ages by which most children acquire specific use of phonemes. Knowledge of the expected sequence of development is crucial in determining appropriate intervention goals. Babies develop the ability to use speech through distinct stages.

Morphology

Morphology is the study of the smallest meaningful units of language, such as *-ed*, *-s*, and *un-*. Berko (1958), in one of the original studies on morphology, devised a task for eliciting grammatical morphemes with nonsensical sentences and pictures. For example, in one task, a researcher showed a child a picture of an animal that looked like a bird, then a picture of two animals. The examiner said, "This is a wug. Here are two _____." The examiner then asked the child to supply the missing word, which is referred to as the **cloze** procedure. Other tasks based on the cloze procedure were used to study a number of grammatical morphemes and to chart their developmental sequence. Brown (1973) added to the basic understanding of morphology in young children and proposed the **mean length of utterance** (MLU), or the average number of morphemes in an utterance, as a way of quantifying language (deVilliers & deVilliers, 1978). The MLU is considered a good indicator of potential language problems because it correlates with many aspects of syntactic development (Brown, 1973; Sharf, 1972). It also is better than age as an indicator of language growth up to the 5-MLU level. (See Owens, 1996, for the rules of calculating MLU.)

Morphology is the study of grammatical units of words.

Syntax

Syntax is that aspect of language pertaining to the organizational rules of sentences. Syntax and morphology combine to form what is called grammar and include **phrase structure rules** (e.g., basic sentence patterns), **transformational operations** (e.g., passive voice and conjoining), and **morphological rules** (e.g., pluralization and noun-verb agreement).

Lenneberg (1967) postulated that individuals possess an **innate language acquisition device** (LAD). The LAD codes information two ways: first, as the deep structure of an utterance, which carries meaning; and second, as the surface structure of an utterance, which can take many forms. For example, although "Buddy hit Billy" is the deep structure, one might instead say "Billy was hit by Buddy" on the surface. Language becomes the process of moving from meaning (deep structure) to increasingly sophisticated forms of expression (surface structure). Once the individual has internalized the associated language rules, she is able to generate an infinite number of utterances.

Semantics

Even though syntax and morphology dominated the language scene in the 1960s and 1970s, a shift toward a semantic perspective took place in the 1970s (McLean & Snyder, 1977). **Semantics** is the study of meaning and content; that is, what one is talking about. Researchers call the object, event, or interaction to which we refer the **referent** (Bates, Camaioni, & Volterra, 1975; Bloom & Lahey, 1978; Clark & Clark, 1977; Ervin-Tripp, 1978; Lucas, 1980), and referents, or ideas to which a word refers, are related to one another in specific ways. Important adults in a child's life play a significant role in how children label things. During normal conversations, adults typically label objects, events, and relationships that form the child's **lexicon,** or vocabulary (Clark, 1974; Ervin-Tripp, 1978). A rich base of experiences with the world is essential to the language acquisition process. Without experiencing objects and events and how they relate, a child has nothing to which a marker or lexical item can be attached (see chapter 9). Semantic study is especially pertinent to the fields of preschool development and special education; thus, the early interventionist should become familiar with this subject.

Pragmatics

Pragmatics refer to the social contexts around which we learn and use language (Muma, 1998). Language develops in a social context, and the culture of the family as well as the broader culture has a significant impact on what a child learns. Early researchers (Bates, 1976; Dore, 1974, 1975; Halliday, 1975) identified taxonomies of pragmatic skills that identify the components of pragmatics. Once a child is involved in a social context where communication is fostered, pragmatic skills evolve into those rules that determine when and where to use language.

The **speech act** is considered to be the basic unit of pragmatics, just as the morpheme is the basic unit of morphology and syntax (Austin, 1962; Searle, 1969). Several theorists have suggested outlines for common speech acts. In addition, Halliday (1975) grouped the uses of language into three categories that emerge between 18 and 24 months of age: interpersonal (or pragmatic), intrapersonal (or mathetic), and ideational (problem solving). Between 2 and 3 years of age, children begin to use contingent queries to clarify the meaning of what someone has said (Gallagher, 1977), and they engage in rapid topic change (Shulman, 1985). The 3-year-old is very competent at **code switching** (Sachs & Devin, 1976), produces contingent queries to maintain conversations (Garvey, 1975), and is temporarily able to assume the perspective of another person through language (Selman, 1971).

Conducting a conversation, or engaging in **discourse,** although seemingly effortless, actually requires a complex set of practical skills. The first of these is **turn taking.** Before any kind of conversation takes place, the speakers must agree to certain characteristics of an interchange that result in orderliness. If these rules are violated, orderliness ceases, and the result is that they are unable to communicate with their conversational partner. Each set of communicative turns is referred to as an **adjacency pair.** Common, early adjacency pairs include opening, question-answer, greeting-greeting, offer-acceptance/rejection, assertion-acknowledgement, compliment-acceptance/rejection, request-grant, summon-answer, and closing-closing.

Discourse consists of any extended utterance beyond a single unit, including monologues and dialogues.

A set of communicative turns is called an adjacency pair.

Stages of Normal Language Acquisition

No matter what language you are referring to, a child's ability to use that language develops through a series of characteristic patterns (Brownlee, 1998; Tomasello, 1992). These forms emerge best when they are developed from a rich base of experiences. A child must experience the world for language to hold any meaning.

Prelinguistic and Babbling Stage

Long before they utter their first words, infants are able to refer to the world around them through their bodies (Bates et al., 1975). Infants express what they mean through perlocutionary and illocutionary acts (Bates, 1976). **Perlocutionary acts** are nonverbal means of communication such as gazing, crying, touching, smiling, laughing, grasping, and sucking. **Illocutionary acts** are vocal means of expression such as the use of vocalizations, intonation, and grunts and nonverbal acts including giving, pointing, and showing. According to Bates and Johnston (1977), the number of illocutionary acts an infant uses is a good prognostic indicator of later language ability. Studying an infant's perlocutionary and illocutionary skills may be helpful in determining any need for intervention.

Canonical babbling consists of reduplicated consonant-vowel combinations.

A baby goes through several stages of **canonical babbling,** referred to as precanonical, canonical, and postcanonical babbling (Oller, 1980; Stoel-Gammon,

1998). **Precanonical vocalizations** occur from birth to 6 months and include grunt-like vocalizations, squeals, quasiresonated vowels, raspberries, clicks, cries, and laughter that lack the form of true syllables. **Canonical vocalizations** emerge from 6 to 10 months when the child combines vowels (V) and consonants (C) into true syllables that sound very speechlike. **Postcanonical vocalizations** emerge from 10 to 18 months and include closed syllables (CVC) and open (CV) syllables. Babies also acquire greater articulatory control. Spencer (1993) found that the rate at which a child with a hearing loss produces canonical babblings is predictive of her spoken language production at 18 months, indicating that, at least in children with a hearing loss, canonical babbling may be a useful diagnostic indicator.

A later stage of prelinguistic development is the **jargon stage,** which overlaps babbling stages and may begin as early as 9 months. In this stage, children continue to develop strings of utterances that carry the stress and intonational patterns of adult speech (deBoysson-Bardies, Sagart, & Durand, 1984; Morgan, 1996). They appear to be talking but say no distinguishable words. Jargoning overlaps into the **one-word** and **combined-words stages,** and children often produce strings of inflected babbling with a real word included. Jargon usually disappears by 2 years of age (Trantham & Pedersen, 1976).

> Jargon is babbling that contains the intonation of adult speech.

One-Word Stage

Children utter recognizable words somewhere around their first birthday (Owens, 1996; Veneziano, Sinclair & Berthoud, 1990). A child who uses one-word utterances, or **holophrases,** is said to be in the holophrastic stage. During this phase a child uses one word to represent a whole phrase, and context is needed to understand what the child means. For example, the word *ball* might mean "I want the ball," "I have the ball," or "The dog is chasing the ball." As every parent knows who has experienced a child screaming "Ball! Ball! Ball!", context and intonation are not always enough to make meaning apparent.

> Holophrases are single words representing whole phrases.

Vocabulary during the one-word stage must be able to assist a child in causing change (Nelson, 1973). Words such as *bush* and *table* are not very common in early vocabularies because children's use of these words is not likely to bring about much change. However, the use of words such as *milk, blanket,* and *ball* are likely to result in some kind of action. Also in this stage, children engage in **overextensions.** When a child does not know the specific lexical item for a particular referent, she uses familiar words as substitutes, thus overextending the actual meaning of that particular marker (Clark, 1973). For example, the word *Mama* may refer to all females, especially female caregivers. Children often apply concepts of shape when referring to something for which they have no label (Clark & Clark, 1977). For example, the word *ball* may be applied to a toy, an orange, or the moon. Other concepts that form the basis for overextensions are movement, size, sound, texture, and taste. Shortly after children label objects, they begin to use spatial prepositions and adjectives. If a child experiences disruptions in perception of location in space, spatial terminology will be extremely problematic (Lucas, 1980).

> Overextensions refer to the application of a word (*ball*) to an object whose label is unknown (moon) based on a similar feature or trait of that object (roundness).

Once the child utters her first word, her vocabulary increases exponentially, reaching approximately 50 words by 16 to 18 months of age (Dromi, 1999; Fenson et al., 1994). At this time the child enters into a stage of rapid vocabulary development called **fast-mapping,** where she maps meaning to new words with very few examples of the word (Spencer & Lederberg, 1997).

At about 18 months of age, a child will have about 50 words in her expressive vocabulary.

Early Word Combinations

Before young children start to put words together, they combine a word with the pointing gesture (Iverson, Volterra, Pizzuto, & Capirci, 1994). Initially the pointing gesture is a repeat of the word, but just prior to two-word combinations, it represents a different function "apparently signaling a cognitive readiness for the expression of relations between symbolic elements" (Spencer & Lederberg, 1997, p. 222). Soon after children enter the period of accelerated vocabulary growth, multiword combinations emerge.

As young children learn to put words together, they leave out such extraneous language as verb tense but preserve the nouns and verbs. Children also leave out verb expansions and the determiner system (e.g., *a* and *the*) and say, for example, "Baby fall" or "Puppy jump." The auxiliary system develops during the period from 18 months to 3 years. Early word combinations generally are in the form of **semantic-syntactic pairs,** such as agent-action ("Kitty jump") or notice-object ("There shoe").

Multiword Combinations

Overlapping the stages from single words to adult grammar is a period during which children use **overgeneralizations** of the grammar they have just learned (Ervin-Tripp, 1964). For example, although children begin to use specific irregular verbs at a very young age, they often overgeneralize the use of the regular marker *-ed*, as in "runned" for *ran*, and "hided" for *hid*, and even add an *-ed* to some irregular forms, thereby producing "satted" for *sat* and "sawed" for *saw*. Children also overgeneralize plural forms, as in "foots," "mouses," and "mans."

Overgeneralizations are defined as the application of a regular grammatical feature (*-ed*) to a word requiring an irregular form (*runned*).

Simple Sentence Structure

Following the development of all semantic categories and the verb and auxiliary systems, children move into higher order transformations of basic sentence patterns. Children produce basic transitive sentences (e.g., "He cried"), intransitive sentences (e.g., "He ate the ice cream"), predicate nominative sentences using linking verbs (e.g., "He is a fireman"), predicate adjective sentences using linking verbs (e.g., "He is tired"), and sentences where linking verbs tie the subject to adverbial complements (e.g., "He is in the treehouse"). These basic forms and later transformations (e.g., questions, negation, passive voice, etc.) complete children's journeys toward the use of adult forms.

The rapid development of normal communication in such a brief period is truly remarkable. Never again does a child learn a skill of such magnitude in so little time. All the areas of language are closely intertwined such that a deficit in one area can lead to a deficit in another. Careful analysis of each component is essential in identifying deficits and planning appropriate remediation.

Theories of Communication Development

As in all avenues of study, various theories have developed to explain the phenomenon of communication development. Although each theory has had its heyday, in fact, children may benefit from various aspects of each as they approach the formidable task of learning to communicate. The four major theories of language acquisition are the behavioral theory, the innatist theory, the cognitive theory, and the social interaction theory.

Behavioral Theory

The behavioral theory, associated most notably with Skinner (1957), holds that language is a subset of learned behaviors and, as such, is learned through a process of reinforcement. Ogletree and Oren (2001) summarized the work of others (Alberto & Troutman, 1999; Skinner, 1957) into a set of language instructional principles, paraphrased below. These include:

- **Stimulus control**—the provision of certain antecedent behaviors that serve as a cue for other behaviors; for example, showing a picture as a stimulus to assist a child to learn pronouns.
- **Responses**—the child's behaviors after receiving a stimulus; for example, saying "cats" when shown a picture of more than one cat.
- **Consequences**—the direct results of a child's response to a stimulus; for example, receiving a toy to play with after correctly identifying the toy.
- **Positive reinforcement**—the functional relationship between two events that increases a behavior; for example, receiving praise every time a child makes a correct response.
- **Extinction**—the elimination of a behavior where reinforcement is no longer needed; for example, when a student no longer uses false starts to an utterance.
- **Negative reinforcement**—the functional relationship between two events that increases a behavior when a stimulus is removed; for example, modifying an intimidating situation so that a communication act can occur.
- **Punishment**—the functional relationship between two events that decreases a behavior; for example, placing a child in time-out after a tantrum.

Applied behavior analysis principles are commonly used with students with severe disabilities such as autism or severe retardation (Durand & Merges, 2001) and include such techniques as prompting, chaining, modeling, and cuing.

Innatist Theory

The innatist theory has been described under many labels—psycholinguistic theory, syntactic theory, and biological theory among them. Attributed to Chomsky (1957) and Lenneberg (1967), among others, the innatist theory holds that there is a biological basis for language acquisition, and that all humans are prewired to learn language because of the existence of a **language acquisition device**; it is just a matter of what aspect and at what rate language skills develop. Language is processed as a culturally determined set of rules, which is developmentally organized, and all infants pass through this developmental sequence in the same order, albeit at differing rates. The fact that all children go through the developmental sequence appropriate for the language of their cultures is cited as evidence of the existence of the language acquisition device. Although this theory fails to consider the importance of meaning and context in language development, it does provide great insight into how we process sentences.

Recently, there has been a resurgence of interest in the biological basis of language (Dale et al., 1998) as genetic research continues to bring us closer and closer to the understanding of the **human sentence processing mechanism** (HSPM) (Altman & Steedman, 1988; Crago & Gopnik, 1994; Frazier, 1993). Such a mechanism may be responsible for our ability to process sentences and may be genetically predetermined. Clarification of the existence of such a mechanism would have implications for therapy.

Cognitive Theory

Alternately known as psycholinguistic/semantic theory, case grammar theory, and information processing theory, cognitive theory argues that language development is based on meaning, or semantics, rather than on syntax. Bloom (1970) argued that there is a set of presyntactic, semantic relationships that precede true syntax. The order of their development reflects the order of development of cognitive structures (Bloom, 1973; Brown, 1973). For example, children develop the cognitive skill of object permanence before they talk about the appearance or disappearance of objects.

The semantic/cognitive theory has contributed significantly to our understanding of what young children talk about, when, and why. It explains language within the overall context of child development and forms the basis for models of intervention that stress active involvement of children with their environment.

Social Interaction Theory

The social interaction theory focuses on the social and personal purposes for which we use language. Social interaction theorists (Bruner, 1981; Dore, 1974; Halliday, 1975; Prutting, 1979) see language as culturally driven and based on the human need to communicate. Children learn to communicate within the context of their environment under the guidance of an important adult caregiver. The need to communicate springs from the need for human interaction. Social interaction theorists feel that the naturalistic environment is a key element in early intervention (Noonan & McCormick, 1993). Play-based intervention, multidisciplinary teaming, and parent involvement are all components of instruction in naturalistic environments.

Factors Influencing Communication Development

The process of acquiring language is extremely complex and requires an intact individual in an intact environment. Certain prerequisite systems are functioning in the typically developing youngster and, when they are delayed, defective, or absent, they have a significant impact on this acquisition process. An inefficient neurophysiological system, a damaged sensory system, limited intellectual potential, and high-risk medical and social environments significantly influence communication development. This section discusses the relationships of hearing, vision, intelligence, memory, and attention to language development.

Hearing

Even a minor or temporary hearing loss can disrupt language development in the first 3 years of life.

A hearing loss represents one of the most serious of all deterrents to spoken language development. We talk because we hear. Youngsters are surrounded by a world that is constantly being labeled, described, and defined by adults. Parents of a child with normal hearing unconsciously revise their language to meet the child's needs (Snow, 1972). They naturally babble and repeat intonational patterns in a fashion that will support a youngster's comprehension. When hearing is deficient, the natural interaction between adults and infant breaks down and the typical developmental sequence is disrupted. So much occurs linguistically in the first 3 years of life that even a minor or temporary hearing loss can be very disruptive.

When a child does not have normal hearing, she struggles to learn every sound, every concept, every word, and every structure of the spoken language. When young children experience mild fluctuating losses that result from colds and ear infections, the interference with language may never be overcome (Ling, 1972). Referring the child with chronic colds, allergies, and ear infections to an otologist may save that child needless problems in developing language as a preschooler and in learning core academic skills. For children who are learning language, a mild **conductive loss** (i.e., a loss caused by problems with the outer or middle ear) places them under great stress. Sarff (1981) reported that an unusually high percentage of students who were labeled as being learning disabled and who were reported to have normal hearing had past histories of medical problems with their ears as well as fluctuating hearing losses.

Universal newborn hearing screening and intervention (UNHSI) is the process of screening the hearing of all infants before they leave the hospital and instituting services for those who need them.

One innovation that holds potential for alleviating the impact of a hearing loss is **universal newborn hearing screening and intervention** (UNHSI). Every day, 33 babies (or 12,000 each year) are born in the United States with permanent hearing loss. With 3 of every 1,000 newborns having a hearing loss, it is the most frequently occurring birth defect (National Center for Hearing Assessment & Management, 2002). In 1993 the National Institutes of Health recommended the initiation of universal newborn hearing screening and intervention. Prior to that time, only about 30% to 50% of those children born with significant hearing loss were identified early, with the remaining children identified by 3 years of age. Screening technology, such as **Auditory Brain Response** (ABR) and **Transient Otoacoustic Emissions** (OAE), is rapid, reliable, sensitive, and easily administered (National Institutes of Health, 1993). However, universal newborn screening is not a replacement for vigilance during the developmental years because 20–30% of children acquire hearing loss during early childhood.

Although universal screening is essential, it must go hand-in-hand with early intervention. Yoshinaga-Itano and Apuzzo (1998) found that children with hearing loss, who began early intervention programs before the age of 6 months, showed significantly more progress in language acquisition than did their subjects who began early intervention programs after 6 months of age. New resources and new tools are becoming available more and more rapidly to assist states in implementing appropriate services to infants and toddlers who are deaf and hard of hearing. Yet without concerted efforts toward the development of appropriate services available to all parents, this potential may not be realized.

Vision

The role of vision in language learning is often discussed in terms of the higher linguistic functions of reading and writing. Visual disorders of perception, discrimination, memory, and the like have been associated with the inability to read and write; however, the impact of visual impairment becomes far more significant in reviewing the stages of language development in infants.

One of the first significant developments in language is **joint attending.** In joint attending, the caregiver and child view the same object, and the caregiver provides the label, thus helping to organize the child's world. Joint attending for a child with vision problems requires a more deliberate action; the caregiver must bring the object to the child's tactile and auditory awareness. At around 9 to 12 months of age, infants develop a gestural system by which they communicate to adults. The assumption is that the adult will see the child's gesture or gaze, follow the direction of the gaze or gesture, and see the object or event that the child intends to share. Infants who have never been able to see and who have no language skills are unaware that adults *can* see, so they do not engage in communicative gazing and gesturing in the same fashion as do children who are sighted. Thus, the language acquisition process for children who are blind is different from that of children who are sighted (Stremel & Wilson, 1998).

Even a slight deficiency in vision can impact language learning. Being able to see does not necessarily mean that children are able to look at or to make sense out of what they are viewing. Problems with depth perception, color blindness, uncorrected near- or farsightedness, nystagmus, and astigmatism interfere with how children perceive and interpret what they see. Whereas hearing is primarily used to detect temporal aspects and changes, vision is primarily used to detect spatial aspects and changes (Ling, 1972). The sense of touch is not as effective as the eye in dealing with spatial information. Spatial adjectives and prepositions present a challenge to a child with a vision impairment.

Intelligence

The role of intelligence in language has been explored for many years (Luria, 1961; Piaget, 1952; Vygotsky, 1962), yet the relationship is still not fully understood. Language and thought are not synonymous. A complex relationship between intelligence and language exists, and they may be bidirectional in their influence. Environmental factors, social pressures, inadequate sensory experiences, or perceptual problems may diminish the experiences of a youngster and cause poor test performance because all tests, whether they purport to measure intelligence, aptitude, or achievement, measure what a child has learned (Sattler, 2001). Difficulty in receiving information does not necessarily mean low intelligence. Further, children can develop near-normal ability in some areas of intelligence yet be quite deficient in others.

All other things being equal, language delays become more prevalent as mental age becomes more negatively disparate from chronological age (Dunn, 1973), and children with diminished capacity appear to make gains in language more slowly than those with normal capacity (Mervis & Bertrand, 1997). However, the variety of factors and their interrelationships are so numerous and complex that one cannot assume a one-to-one correspondence between intelligence and language.

Memory

Memory plays a significant role in the acquisition of language. A child must formulate and hold a visual image in memory so that the auditory symbol used to represent what they saw will have a point of reference. The process of **categorization** is extremely important to learning in general and to learning language in particular (Bruner, Goodnow, & Austin, 1956). Children need help seeing likenesses and differences in the world around them in order to organize their worlds. Efficient organization of experiences assists in the memory and retrieval processes.

Youngsters who are developing language rehearse that language both out loud and in their heads. Language **rehearsal** plays an important role in memory. Children with language problems often have difficulty with language rehearsal (Montgomery, 2000). Further, information that is taken in by a faulty sensory system or interpreted by a faulty perceptual system will be coded in the fashion in which it is experienced. Inaccurate, poorly rehearsed, or incomplete concepts and language are stored in that fashion, and when retrieved for use, they will be employed in inaccurate and incomplete ways.

Attention

Children at risk for attention disorders often have difficulty with language development (Warner-Rogers, Taylor, Taylor, & Sandberg, 2000). Attention is a neurobiological process, and attention deficits are real. They are not a result of poor parenting or lack of motivation or ignorance; however, they are difficult to diagnose in preschool children.

Attention implies the ability to focus actively on a stimulus. Sometimes we are required to focus by choice. In order for children to attend, they must consciously take in specific information while inhibiting a whole array of competing messages. Selection and inhibition require a judgment on the part of the child that a particular piece of information is worthy of attention. Children with problems in selective attention often have problems with language as well as with its impact on interpersonal relationships (Ratner & Harris, 1994). For children who have not matured neurologically in their ability to inhibit competing stimuli, or for those who have specific neurochemical dysfunctions, it is important that the interventionist assist in the selection and inhibition process by making information more readily accessible. Factors such as pitch, voice quality, loudness, spatial localization, and time of onset affect attending abilities. Further, the interventionist must assist in the judgment process by making what is to be learned meaningful and worthwhile to the child. To do this, the interventionist must have a good understanding of what is interesting to youngsters at different mental ages and of how to make linguistic information more auditorily and visually salient.

Separating vision, hearing, attention, memory, and intelligence for discussion purposes may be appropriate, but to think of them as individual blocks, stacked neatly one upon the other, is an inaccurate view of the learning process. These aspects are interdependent and, thus, mutually influential.

Communication Development in Young Children with Special Needs

When a child's sensory, cognitive, motor, or social-affective systems are compromised, language development may be impaired. This next section describes the impact of various disabilities on the development of communication in children.

Mental Retardation

Mental retardation appears to have an impact on language learning, with greater degrees of retardation accounting for greater problems with communication (Facon, Facon-Bollengier, & Grubar, 2002; Mar & Sall, 1999). Disorders of grammar and vocabulary influencing both receptive and expressive skills have been noted. In addition, speech delays are typically found in children with mental retardation. Yoder and Miller (1972) estimated that between 70% and 90% of all children with moderate and severe retardation make articulation errors. Dunn (1973) reported that children with IQs below 25 may never learn to speak.

Studies of the morphological characteristics of the language of children with mental retardation (Dever, 1972; Facon et al., 2002) show that children with mental retardation learn all the morphological components of language but do so at a slower rate. Kamhi and Johnston (1982) and Krivcher-Winestone (1980) looked at syntax skills and found that, like morphological skills, syntax skills are delayed but not different for children with mental retardation.

With the present emphasis on including children with disabilities in regular school classes, interest in pragmatic language skills has increased. Baum, Odom, and

Boatman (1975) found that language develops more quickly in children with mental retardation when it is intended for highly functional purposes. Abbeduto and Rosenberg (1980) found that the turn taking and illocutionary acts of older children with mental retardation are near normal, whereas Cunningham, Reuler, Blackwell, and Deck (1981) found the opposite in preschool children with mental retardation. Abbeduto and Rosenberg (1992) found that children with mental retardation have difficulty establishing a referent when they speak, are delayed in all aspects of speech act performance, and cannot repair communication. Pragmatic issues must receive specific program attention with preschool-aged children. Environmental approaches that stress the inclusion of a child's natural communication partners seem most effective in enhancing development (Owens, 1996).

Learning Disabilities

Learning disabilities are difficult to diagnose in preschool-aged children and are rarely identified as such; however, a look at the histories of older children who have learning disabilities indicate language problems in the preschool years. Learning disabilities are neurologically based, and children whose families have a history of learning disorders often have language learning problems (Lyytinen, Poikkeus, Laaks, Eklund, & Lyytinen, 2001). Although children with learning disabilities may have normal vision and hearing, their brains have difficulty interpreting what they hear or see. These processing deficits may result in problems with spatial orientation, sequencing, discrimination, and memory. Children with learning disabilities often experience word retrieval problems (Wiig & Semel, 1984). To carry on a conversation, one must be able to pull words from one's memory bank on demand. Inefficiency in this area interferes with communicative interaction essential to the language learning process and creates frustration in social situations.

Children with learning disabilities may have inefficient or immature neurophysiological systems (Arehole, 1995). To pay attention to what others say as well as to one's own thoughts, one's body must cooperate. The bodies of children who have learning disabilities do not cooperate with them, and they may exhibit poor listening skills, hyper- or hypoactivity, distractibility, perseveration, disinhibition, and other qualities, and these may evolve into later problems. Many children with learning disabilities need extra time to master the basics of oral language before they are ready to handle the kindergarten curriculum. Many will always have language-based problems, and these will contribute to later problems with reading, math, writing, and perhaps social-behavioral functioning. The semantic and pragmatic aspects of language in particular often are involved as well.

Behavior Disorders

There are numerous reasons why some children have behavior disorders. For example, when children have not matured neurologically to the point where they can inhibit their responses to stimuli, they may act out. Inability to inhibit a language response may result in a child's blurting out information at inappropriate times.

Many children have undetected hearing and vision problems that result in behavioral manifestations and concomitant language problems. Often, a youngster with learning disabilities who does not have the cognitive, motor, speech, or language abilities to interact with the world appears to have a behavior disorder because her responses to language and nonlanguage events are inappropriate. Children who have received no supervision or have had inappropriate role models may say and do unexpected things. These children need a highly structured, organized environment in which expectations are made clear and natural consequences to actions are meted out firmly but fairly. It also is essential to provide a structured language environment in which words make sense and are consistently applied to experiences.

Specific Speech Disorders

There are many forms of disordered speech. Each disability impacts speech development in its own way. However, three categories are recognized as common among children with speech disorders. These are disorders of fluency, articulation, and voice. Physical disabilities such as cleft palate and other anomalies may also be found.

Fluency. **Fluency** involves the forward flow of speech. A child whose speech is dysfluent (i.e., to a greater degree than is typical of preschoolers) used to be referred to as a stutterer. More males are dysfluent than females, and the onset of dysfluency usually occurs between the ages of 3 and 5. Dysfluency cannot be picked up by the imitation of speech patterns of another child. It is often hereditary and may be found in combination with other problems. It almost always influences a child's social and emotional status (Adler & King, 1994). Problems of fluency require real help to overcome, and the speech-language pathologist and parent must work as a team.

> Fluency is defined as the natural flow of the breath stream and vocalization during speech.

Articulation. Young children typically make **articulation** errors that adults find charming (e.g., *yap* for *lap*), but when baby talk is not outgrown, parents may become concerned. It is necessary to be clear about what articulation errors are typical and what is the result of a delay. Table 10.2 shows the average rate of acquisition of phonemes and provides a standard against which to judge articulation development. When articulation is severely delayed, professional assistance is needed.

> Articulation refers to the correct placement of the articulators (teeth, tongue, lips, jaw, etc.) during speech.

Voice Disorders. **Voice disorders** include problems with pitch, such as when the voice register is too high or too low, and with loudness, such as when a child is unable to monitor the loudness or softness of her voice. Voice quality features such as harshness, hoarseness, breathiness, hyper- or hyponasality, and problems of resonance may occur in young children with speech disorders. These require professional intervention.

> Voice disorders consist of problems with duration, intensity, pitch, and voice quality.

Cleft Palate and Other Craniofacial Anomalies. Cleft palate and other craniofacial anomalies are medical conditions that require specialized care. Often, surgery is involved and, for many newborns, even the act of sucking is affected. Children with cleft palates may be hesitant to speak, resulting in delayed production.

Those with severe impairments may have limited social contacts as a result of either increased illnesses or hospitalizations or fear of rejection by the child or parent. The teacher, parent, and medical professional must work together closely to develop and carry out a program to meet the child's comprehensive needs.

Specific Language Impairment

Specific language impairment results from problems with language comprehension and production unaccounted for by intellectual, social, emotional, or experiential factors.

Language impairments may occur secondary to hearing loss, mental retardation, autism, emotional conflict, learning disabilities, physical disabilities, and lack of English in the home environment. Still, when all these are ruled out, there remains a population of children whose language problems are of an unknown source. They are said to have **specific language impairment.** Fey and Leonard (1983) define specific language impairment (SLI) as "a pronounced deficit in the comprehension and/or expression of language in the relative absence of impairments in other areas of development" (p. 65). Children with SLI lag behind their peers in word acquisition and initial grammatical skills (Rice, Buhr, & Nemeth, 1990). There is evidence that young children with SLI have family histories of the same (Tallal et al., 2001), that SLI has an impact on later reading and academic success, and that SLI may continue into adulthood (Crago & Gopnik, 1994). When assessing a preschooler for the presence of SLI, it is helpful to determine if a family history exists. A distinguishing characteristic of the SLI population is that development among language components occurs differentially, with "moderate levels of difficulty with several linguistic domains, such as the lexicon, in conjunction with significant and long-lasting problems with grammatical morphology" (Watkins, 1997, p. 173). It is this discrepancy among the child's proficiency with various components of language that is the hallmark of SLI.

Hearing Loss

The majority of children who are deaf and have parents who can hear remain significantly delayed in communication throughout their lives, whether the comparison is to children and parents who can hear or children and parents who are deaf (Johnson, Liddell, & Erting, 1989; Spencer, 1993). Language development, whether spoken or signed, is dependent upon the opportunities a child has for uptake of the language (Lederberg & Spencer, 2001). Many children who are deaf and hard of hearing and have parents who can hear grow up linguistically impoverished. Spencer and Lederberg (1997) and Lederberg and Prezbindowski (2000) summarized the literature on the interactions of mothers who could hear with their babies who were deaf and found that the mothers missed their children's signals or cues. When a mother misses these, she misses a prime opportunity to provide language stimulation. Although mothers with normal hearing tend to lack natural skills in visual communication, mothers who are deaf understand how to maintain their child's attention. Communication development is based on shared attention, which in turn depends upon the responsiveness of a caring adult with whom the child routinely interacts (Sass-Lehrer, 1999). Reilly and Bellugi (1996) noted that mothers who are deaf clarify communication for their preschoolers who are deaf and willingly produce ungrammatical (i.e., baby talk) utterances in an effort to make their messages clear.

Of great concern in the instruction of children with hearing loss is the need to provide a coherent, consistent model of natural language as rapidly as possible. However, this rarely occurs because families tend to change communication modes over time (Lederberg & Spencer, 2001). Typically, families choose an oral approach, and then switch to a signing approach at a later date (Stredler-Brown, 1998). Fathers who can hear tend to have poorer signing skills than do mothers who can hear (Gregory, 1995), further limiting and confusing communication availability in the home. How and when intervention begins is more important in determining communication outcomes than whether or not the parents use a spoken language or a signed language option. Although there are few studies of large numbers of children with hearing impairment comparing signed to spoken vocabulary development, the case and small-group studies available consistently report positive benefits for signed vocabulary development. (Daniels, 1993; Notoya, Suzuki, & Furukawa, 1994; Preisler & Ahlstroem, 1997). Whether a hearing loss is mild or profound, it has a significant impact on the language learning process.

> For children with hearing loss, how and when intervention begins is more important to the child's communicative abilities than whether or not the parents use spoken language or signed language.

Vision Loss

Studies of the language of children with vision losses show that structurally their language is not significantly different from that of sighted children (Matsuda, 1984). However, differences are found in how their language is acquired. Impairment in vision results in an absence of the early gestural language that occurs between a mother and an infant. Further, a child with a vision impairment lacks mobility, resulting in fewer experiences with the environment. Limiting direct experiences results in a child's forming concepts based on insufficient or incomplete perceptual clues that, in turn, result in only partial understanding of experiences (Warren, 1984). According to Santin and Simmons (1977), the "early language of the blind child does not seem to mirror his developing knowledge of the world, but rather his knowledge of the language of others" (p. 427).

The preschool teacher must assume a number of roles in relation to the developing language of a child who is visually impaired. In particular, the teacher must be aware of helping the child overcome **verbalisms.** First, the teacher must make words as richly meaningful as possible so that they hold semantic loads as close as possible to normal. Second, the teacher must help keep the child in touch with the environment. Because much communication is gestural, children who are blind miss out on many aspects of a daily routine. For example, children who are sighted see the teacher putting away his materials and know it is time to go to the music circle. They see the juice tray rolled into the room and know it is snack time. Children who are visually impaired must be told that these events are occurring. The teacher must maintain a running dialogue with a child who is blind, describing each event that occurs in the room to give the child an opportunity to interact more naturally with the environment. Keeping a running commentary going can be very tiring, but it is absolutely essential. If aides or parents

> Verbalisms are words used for which the speaker has no experiential base.

are in the classroom, rotating turns will keep the child in touch while giving the speaker a rest.

Cerebral Palsy

The language of a young child with cerebral palsy may be restricted by neuromuscular involvement. As many as 50% of babies with cerebral palsy have speech and language problems associated with CP or that are in conjunction with an associated secondary disability (Wilson, 1973). There are multiple challenges to serving a preschooler with cerebral palsy who also has language deficits. Olswang and Pinder (1995) found that as children with cerebral palsy improved in their ability to engage in coordinated looking, or joint attending, with an adult to an object, their sophistication in play behaviors increased. Restricted mobility may limit a child's interaction with the environment, resulting in a sparser meaning to the language that the child understands and produces. Pragmatically, the child may not have the opportunity to interact with the world in the same fashion as her peers with no motor problems; hence, some of the functions of language may be overused whereas others are delayed in developing. Children with cerebral palsy must learn to compensate for structural differences.

Other Health Impairments and Neurological Problems

The category of other health impairments and neurological problems is so extensive that it cannot be treated adequately in this chapter. Several of the more pervasive problems, however, are described briefly.

Substance Abuse. Maternal ingestion of chemical substances such as alcohol, tobacco, tranquilizers, cocaine, and marijuana can cause disabilities in newborns. Ingestion of a chemical often is taking place before a mother knows she is pregnant (Sparks, 1993), and within the drug culture, trips to the doctor are often infrequent (Kronstadt, 1991). As noted in Chapter 2, infants with fetal alcohol syndrome (FAS) have distinct physical features and behavior manifestations, including characteristics of attention-deficit disorder, memory problems, and language delays. Children with FAS can be difficult to manage because they are unresponsive to verbal cautions (Olson, Burgess, & Streissguth, 1992), exhibit poor impulse control, have difficulty relating behavior to consequences, possess poor short-term memory, have an inconsistent knowledge base, have difficulty grasping abstract concepts, have difficulty managing anger, and possess poor judgment (McCreight, 1997). These problems interfere with language acquisition as well as with social interactions.

AIDS/HIV. Approximately 75% of children who are infected with HIV are born to mothers who are intravenous drug users or who were infected through sexual activity (Crites, Fischer, McNeish-Stengel, & Seigel, 1992). Children born with

HIV/AIDS have multiple insults associated not only with the disease, but also with the drug used, the poor nutrition usually found in drug users, and the prematurity of infants born to drug users. Prematurity and poor nutrition influence all aspects of a child's development, including the development of communication.

Autism Spectrum Disorder

Among the most challenging of preschool children are those with autism spectrum disorder (ASD), which occurs in 1 in 500 children (Maugh, 2000). Disorders along the continuum include autism, Asperger's disorder, pervasive developmental disorder (PDD), childhood disintegrative disorder, and Rett syndrome (American Psychiatric Association, 1995). The absence or delay of speech and language is a common characteristic of children along the autism spectrum and is a diagnostic criterion of ASD (Autism Society of America, 1996). Since ASD exists along a spectrum, communication intervention must be highly individualized (Schreibman, Koegel, Charlop, & Egel, 1990). Moore-Brown and Montgomery (2001) reported the existence of a variety of methods for communication intervention, and the decision regarding which method to use is best made by teams including the parents (Greenspan & Wieder, 1999).

> Communication problems represent critical components in the diagnosis of ASD.

The perspective on language often associated with ASD is that individuals are unable to achieve intersubjectivity (Kasari, Sigman, Yirmiya, & Mundy, 1993), which requires the ability to focus on the same thing as the communicative partner. Language development may be impaired because joint attending (intersubjectivity) is a key component to language development.

Bernard-Opitz (1982) discovered that the pragmatic behavior of her subjects varied across communicative settings and partners, but was stable within settings and with partners. Communicative intent is difficult to understand in children with autism. Even individuals who are very familiar with a child may have difficulty understanding what various actions mean (Donovan, 1993); however, pragmatic study may prove to be useful in elucidating the needs of this population. Such information suggests that there may be a base of abilities from which to work with children who have autism.

Attention-Deficit Hyperactivity Disorder

Many of the characteristics of children with **central auditory processing disorders** (CAPD)—that is, difficulties in perceiving and understanding language not associated with hearing loss, intelligence, or specific language impairment—are similar in nature to the characteristics of children who have attention-deficit hyperactivity disorder (ADHD), although assessment and intervention for these two disorders differ (Tillery & Smoski, 1994). Some of these shared characteristics include inappropriate verbal responses, distraction in the presence of background noise, difficulty in sustaining attention for verbal instruction over a period, inattention, and difficulty completing multistep tasks. An evaluation of a child with ADHD should include information about her auditory processing skills. This includes assessment of the child's ability to make fine auditory discriminations, to retain and recall auditory sequences, and to focus on an auditory figure against a distracting background.

Children from Culturally and Linguistically Diverse Backgrounds

A survey conducted by the American Speech-Language-Hearing Association (ASHA, 1998) revealed that approximately one-third of the students on the caseload of speech-language pathologists nationwide were comprised of children from culturally and linguistically diverse (CLD) backgrounds, and the percentage of CLD students is on the rise. This means that a large portion of the early interventionist's caseload will consist of families who are nonspeakers or new learners of English.

Moore-Brown and Montgomery (2001) identified several factors that must be considered in designing services for CLD children. These include:

- Selecting a language of instruction
- Knowledge of the child's facility with each language
- Knowledge of when and how to use interpreters, or not to use interpreters
- Awareness of accents and dialects within languages
- Cultural factors that must be taken into consideration prior to intervention

This population will continue to change the face of instruction over the next several decades.

Speech and Language Assessment

Assessing speech and language is an intensive and time-consuming process. Numerous test instruments provide a quick survey of skills; however, quick surveys offer little direction for formulating the necessary remediation strategies.

Communication assessment should be ongoing. A variety of strategies should be used, from language sampling and formal tests to observations of the child's behaviors in natural settings. All areas of development should be considered as they relate to communication acquisition. Parents and primary caregivers should be involved actively in the process. Assessment should be tailored to specific communication objectives rather than being determined by a score, and application to intervention should always be considered (Prizant & Bailey, 1992). Screening assessments and diagnostic assessments must be conducted on young children, and information from these assessments must be shared at a multidisciplinary team meeting.

A few particularly noteworthy tests for preschoolers are presented in Table 10.3. Because new tests appear on the market often and because of the unique needs of young children, it is wise to consult a speech-language pathologist to determine how best to assess current communication skills. Further, a strong knowledge base in the development of speech and language skills will make the evaluator or interventionist a more astute consumer.

Test	Author/Publisher	Description
Receptive-Expressive Emergent Language Test–Second Edition	Bzoch, K., & League, R. (1991). Austin, TX: PRO-ED.	The REEL-2 is a revision of an earlier tool. Designed for use in early intervention programs, it assesses both receptive and expressive language via parent interviews of infants and toddlers.
Boehm Test of Basic Concepts 3–Preschool Version	Boehm, A. (2001). New York: Psychological Corporation.	The Boehm Preschool Version assesses the knowledge in children aged 3 to 5 years of 26 basic relational concepts necessary to begin school.
Sequenced Inventory of Communication Development–Revised Edition	Hendrick, D., Prather, E., & Tobin, A. (1984). Austin, TX: PRO-ED.	The SICD-R is a diagnostic battery useful with children whose functional levels range from 4 months to 4 years. The kit comes complete with engaging materials designed to hold even the youngest child's attention.
Test of Early Language Development–Third Edition	Hresko, W., Reid, D. K., & Hammill, D. (1999). New York: Psychological Corporation.	The TELD-3 is a diagnostic language test for use with children from 2.0 to 7.11 years in age. It provides data on receptive and expressive language systems and syntactic/semantic language features.
Preschool Language Scale–Fourth Edition and Preschool Language Scale–Spanish Edition	Zimmerman, I., Steiner, V., & Pond, R. (2002). New York: Psychological Corporation.	The PLS-4 assesses auditory comprehension and expressive communication in children from 2 weeks of age to 6 years 11 months. Conducting a conversation, although seemingly effortless, actually requires a complex set of practical skills.
Assessment of Phonological Processes–Revised	Hodson, B. W. (1986). New York: Psychological Corporation.	Designed to provide a tool for evaluating the phonological processes in highly unintelligible children. Children are provided with a series of objects they that must name. Results that are obtained provide an indication of the severity of the disorder and provide a direction for planning remediation.
Clinical Evaluation of Language–Preschool Fundamentals	Wiig, E.H., Secord, W., & Semel, E. (1992). New York: Psychological Corporation.	Measures a broad range of receptive and expressive language skills in children aged 3 to 6.

TABLE 10.3 Commonly Used Tests of Preschool Communication Development

Assistive Technology and Augmentative and Alternative Communication

IDEA defines **assistive technology** (AT) as "any item, piece of equipment, or product system, whether acquired commercially off the shelf, modified, or customized, that is used to increase, maintain, or improve functional capabilities of a child with a disability" (34 C.F.D. Sec. 300.5) and includes such things as hearing aids, other assistive listening devices, tape recorders, closed-circuit televisions, and computer programs. **Augmentative** and **alternative communication** (AAC) devices are AT tools that assist students specifically in the area of communication. For children with severe mental and motor impairments, oral communication may not be a realistic goal; yet, given appropriate tools, these children may be able to communicate their needs and wishes.

McCormick and Shane (1990) defined **augmentative communication** as "the total arrangement for supplementing and enhancing an individual's communication. The arrangement includes (a) the communication device or technique, (b) the representational symbol set or system, and (c) the communication skills necessary for effective use of the system" (p. 429). They include such products as communication boards, picture exchange communication systems, speech-to-speech telephone access, speech output augmentation devices, and assistive listening devices (Moore-Brown & Montgomery, 2001).

When determining which AT or AAC option to choose, team members should take several factors into account. First, an evaluation of the student's communication skills and needs must be conducted. Second, training and technical assistance for the device must be secured. Third, procedures for acquiring and using the device must be undertaken. Fourth, procedures for maintaining and troubleshooting the device must be established. In addition, there must be procedures in place to coordinate training for users and managers of the device (Moore-Brown & Montgomery, 2001). The use of AT and ACC devices is a dynamic process, not a static one, and continued monitoring of the child's skills is essential. Finally, although AT and AAC devices can be of significant value, they are useless if no one knows how to fix them when they break or whom to turn to for assistance.

An alternative communication system that has been used successfully with a wide array of communication problems is **sign language.** It has been used with such disabilities as autism (Bondy & Frost, 2002), mental retardation (Grove & Dockrell, 2000), and multiple disabilities (Creedon, 1975). Sign language is an appropriate tool because it can be used by individuals at very young mental ages. Schlesinger and Meadow (1972) reported a case of an 8-month-old child with a hearing impairment whose communication environment and mode consisted of signs. In fact, in typical development, babies of about 9 to 13 months of age rely heavily on communicative gesturing (Bates et al., 1975) and develop a pseudosign system to express their wishes and needs. This tool allows them to communicate long before they are developmentally ready to utter their first words. Therefore, until a child with a disability is developmentally ready to produce words orally, the use of signs may provide the same kind of bridge between understanding and orally communicating as does communicative gesturing in the typically developing child.

Issues and Principles of Communication Intervention

As we saw in chapters 1 and 6, the efficacy of early intervention programs cannot be overlooked. Report after report support the impact of early programs on development (Calderon & Naidu, 2000; Guralnik, 1997; Talay-Ongan, 2001; Yoshinaga-Itano, 1999). The age at which intervention begins has such a critical impact on a child's development that IDEA requires states to provide preschool services to all children with disabilities. Early intervention encourages family members to incorporate appropriate interactions into their daily routines and develop a supportive communication environment without which a child's communication development may be permanently delayed. Lack of early intervention significantly limits the influence of later education.

Intervention approaches and practices have changed over the years to reflect the changes in linguistic theory described earlier in this chapter. A discussion of general theories of intervention and some guiding principles for intervention follow.

Collaboration

Early interventionists are required to understand a variety of intervention procedures across an array of service options to meet the needs of a diverse population. In order to bring into play the best expertise, **collaboration** is often necessary. "Collaboration is a style in which two co-equal parties engage voluntarily in shared decision making as they work toward a common goal. It involves shared participation, resources ownership, accountability, and rewards" (Secord, 1999, p. 7). Sharing problems, resources, and solutions to enhance outcomes for children is the key to this approach (West & Idol, 1990). Collaboration must occur during every facet of intervention, from identification and assessment through goal and objective setting to service provision.

> Collaboration entails calling upon the expertise of a variety of individuals to understand and provide for the needs of an individual child.

With regard to the youngest children, the early interventionist, the parents, and related personnel become the collaborators. Because the parents have such a central role in the application of information, they must by necessity become the focal point. Parents should be recognized for their expertise. They know their children better than anyone else does, and they know their family's lifestyle better than anyone else does. Mutual respect fosters trust, and trust is the key to involvement. The only way to make a real impact on the life of a child within the context of the family is to be involved with that family. A spirit of openness, sharing of information, and a mutual effort to bring about positive change and growth are the hallmarks of collaborative consultation.

Didactic and Child-Directed Approaches

Didactic approaches are those that involve direct teaching of a communication goal in a highly structured manner (McCormick & Schiefelbusch, 1990). Techniques such as reinforcement, shaping, chaining, fading, and prompting are used as well as modeling, imitation, and expansion (Yoder & Warren, 1993).

Caregiver-Child Interactions and Naturalistic Environments

Naturalistic environments are those in which the child routinely interacts with an important adult or caregiver.

Parents are a child's first language teachers. When a child has an obvious disability or when language is not developing, some parents begin to doubt their effectiveness in guiding their youngsters through the communication environment, but parents *can* learn strategies to develop communication in their children (Alpert & Kaiser, 1992). Instruction for the parents in the home, or for caregivers in a child-care environment outside the home, can build confidence in both the parent or caregiver and child (Kaiser, Hemmeter, Ostrosky, Alpert, & Hancock, 1995).

Influence of Preschool Inclusion on Language Intervention

Inclusion means educating a learner with a disability in the same environment in which she would be included if she did not have a disability, and includes the actions required to maximize the experience.

The early education classroom can be an excellent environment for assisting children in developing communication skills. For a young child with even the most severe disability, the social environment of a preschool can provide opportunities to learn new ways to communicate and to practice developing skills. Interaction is the key ingredient to communication development, and most children are often full of ideas and desires that they can share more easily with their peers.

Principles of Intervention

It is a rewarding challenge to help young children learn to communicate. Consider the following principles and practices when designing communication interventions:

1. *Use comprehensive assessment results.* Interventionists should base language goals and objectives on a sound assessment of a child's current and unique status. Assessment based on a good understanding of developmental sequences in form, content, and use of language is essential. Chronological and mental ages can give only gross approximations of a child's needs and abilities.

2. *Develop activities that focus on interaction within a social context.* This means that language should be worked on in the context of communication with others. Computer-assisted instruction, picture cards, and sentence-building cards are useful for reinforcement, but they cannot take the place of human interaction while new forms and uses of language are developing.

3. *Make activities purposeful.* Language must be meaningful and purposeful, not rote and sterile, if a child is to achieve maximum gains. Involving teachers, classmates, parents, siblings, and all possible intervention agents in the interactive process is essential. Create the need to communicate.

4. *Use natural situations.* Language should be taught naturally. Asking the child to repeat "The spoon is in the box" is unrealistic because one rarely places a spoon in a shoe box in real life. Encouraging language in naturalistic settings does not, however, mean that the choice of skills to be taught should be left up to chance occurrence in the communicative exchange. Specific language goals should

Age	What You Can Do
Birth to 3 months	Sing. Talk, talk, talk. Listen to music. Imitate baby's cooing sounds back to him.
3 to 6 months	Get eye contact, then talk, smile, and sing. Imitate baby's precanonical babblings back to him. Touch baby and move his arms and legs rhythmically to a sing-songy voice. Talk, talk, talk.
6 to 9 months	Move baby's hands to play peek-a-boo and pat-a-cake. Play silly voice games. Present child with a variety of toys and other familiar objects. Describe these. Use lots of intonation and inflection. Play "Where's the _____? There's the _____." Point out the location of the object in question. Play with baby's name. Search around and say "Where's _____? There you are. I see _____!" Play same game in front of mirror. Look at what child is looking at and label it. Talk, talk, talk. Show your child picture books that he can chew and touch. Describe the objects.
9 to 12 months	Sing. Talk, talk, talk. Wave baby's hand "bye-bye" when someone leaves. Start other scripting activities. Play "Where's your nose? There's your nose. Where's Mommy's nose? There's Mommy's nose." Attach a familiar sound to a set of objects, such as *brrrr-brrrr-brrr* to a toy car, *wooo-wooo* to a toy train, and *mooooo* to a toy cow. Roll balls back and forth saying "Roll the ball." Engage in repetitive activities where you say a word multiple times, such as *rock-rock, rock-rock* or *washy-wash, washy-wash*. Imitate his babblings. Show your child picture books that he can manipulate. Watch what child is pointing to and comment about it.
12 to 15 months	Label objects in the environment and describe them. Read stories to your child and talk about the pictures. Ask child to label familiar objects in the pictures. Engage in fingerplays. Sing. Script interactions such as, "Say, 'Please.' Say, 'Thank you.' Say 'Night-night Daddy.'" Tell your child nursery rhymes. Express great enthusiasm when your child produces words. Do activities over and over again. This age loves repetition and familiarity.

Continued

TABLE 10.4 *Continued*

Age	What You Can Do
	When child gives you an object, talk about it.
	Label objects and actions associated with daily routines.
15 to 18 months	Allow child time to express himself.
	When he pulls you somewhere, go along and talk about what he has led you to.
	Ask questions about objects and actions associated with daily routines, such as "Which cup do you want today? The blue cup or the red cup?"
	Introduce "sabotage" where you place an object in an unusual situation. For example, put child's sock on your head and say, "Sock, sock, where are you sock?" or give him a serving spoon to eat with then say "Uh-oh. That's too big. You need a smaller spoon."
	Engage in pretend play with dolls, cars, stuffed animals, etc.
	Expand scripting to social routines, such as, "Say, 'Don't hit me.'" Or "Say, 'I want some.'"
	Expand on your child's language. Repeat what he has said, then add a little bit more grammar or a little bit more information.
	Read stories with evident sequences. Reread, then reread.
18 to 24 months	Encourage child to do activities where he must follow directions such as bringing his shoe or throwing away her napkin.
	Read, read, read.
	Teach your child lots of nursery rhymes.
	Expand your pretend play to include actions that occur outside the home.
	Expand scripting to community routines such as, "Tell the mailman, 'Here's a letter.'" Or "Tell the grocery store lady, 'See you tomorrow.'"
2 to 3 years	Language is growing by leaps and bounds. Continue to provide a model of good grammar, good speech, and good manners.
	Continue to model and expand child's language.
	Engage in imaginary play extensively.
	Teach child his first and last name.
	Expand your descriptions of objects and actions in the environment by using descriptive adjectives.
	Read and reread favorite books. Go to storytime at the local library. Be sure that Dad reads to child as well.
	Continue to develop a repertoire of nursery rhymes and fingerplays.
	Ask lots of questions about everything. Answer all his questions.
	Set aside some quiet time where you and child can sing, read, talk, or just be quiet with each other.

Sources: Adapted from Estabrooks, 1994; Hulit & Howard, 2001; Morrisset-Huebner & Lines, 1994.

be outlined, and appropriate situations that allow for the development of these should be fostered.

5. *Allow for variability of development*. Language does not develop in a linear fashion. Some processes develop rapidly whereas others develop more slowly;

growth in one area affects growth in another. Children tend to learn language in spurts. The early interventionist must account for this and pace intervention to a child's rhythm, not to what a particular checklist or convention dictates.

6. *Take advantage of spontaneous opportunities.* Although programming decisions must be based on a firm knowledge of the developmental processes, this does not preclude the need to take advantage of vicarious, incidental, and spontaneous learning experiences.

7. *Develop new information within the context of old information.* Children need a means of classifying and categorizing what they are learning. They accomplish this most easily when interventionists attach new information to old. New syntax structure should develop within the context of known experiences and known vocabulary. New vocabulary should develop within the context of known syntax. Children need to have their auditory environment organized and consistent in order for it to make sense.

8. *Teach vocabulary in depth.* Teach all contexts and meanings of a word. Using one word in all its contexts and functions is better than using a number of words in a limited context and more closely approximates natural language development. Initially children put most of their efforts into labeling objects and actions, but they rapidly try them out in new situations as if they were testing their hypotheses about language. If interventionists are too concerned about adding greater numbers of words to children's vocabularies, children may stay at the labeling stage far longer than is natural. This does not give children the opportunity to test and expand the language skills that they have acquired. Conversely, a core lexicon of 50 vocabulary items is required for fast-mapping (see p. 381), which is an important gateway into multiword use.

9. *Make language experiences fun.* Often, what an adult thinks is fun is entirely different from what a child thinks is fun. Knowledge of what children find enjoyable at different ages is essential.

10. *Be aware of developmentally appropriate intervention.* There are significant differences between how a baby learns and how a toddler learns. Intervene as is developmentally appropriate (see Table 10.4).

Summary

The acquisition of a system of communication is an achievement of monumental proportion; yet, good communication is so central to our existence that we are barely aware of it. Only when communication is delayed does the complexity of its nature become apparent. This chapter discussed development, assessment, disorders, and intervention within the domain of communication. Current communication theory points to the need on the part of interventionists to understand the complex nature of communication.

Communication is multifaceted and tends to develop in a common sequence; however, it does not develop in a linear fashion. Different processes undergo spurts at different times. Delays or growth in one area affect delays or growth in another. By 4 years of age, the average youngster has mastered the basics of adult language. If remediation is not available to children with communication problems before they reach school age, they may never completely catch up on all their delayed skills.

Assessment of communication in children is the first step toward remediation. Depending upon the cause of the deficit, different intervention strategies may be appropriate. In some cases, alternative communication devices may be recommended for a child. Collaboration among professionals and caregivers is always an essential ingredient. The importance of communication in our society demands that its development be a high priority in programs for young children with special needs.

Review Questions and Discussion Points

1. What are the important features of development around the one-word stage that lead to a child's acquisition of word combinations?
2. Why is newborn hearing screening so important?
3. Describe how the following impact language development: hearing loss; vision loss; diminished intellectual capacity; and linguistic and cultural diversity.
4. Reread the opening vignette. How would you relate the issue of naturalistic environment to Ian's case?
5. Language develops within a cultural context. Explain what this means.

Recommended Resources

Recommended Reading

Journal of Early Intervention

Young Exceptional Children

Hemmeter, M. L., Joseph, G. E., Smith, B. J., & Sandall, S. (Eds.). (2001). *DEC recommended practices program assessment: Improving practices for young children with special needs and their families.* Denver, CO: Division for Early Childhood. Order online at **http://www.sopriswest.com**

Sandall, S., McLean, M., Smith, B. (Eds.). (2000). *DEC recommended practices in early intervention/early childhood special education.* Denver, CO: Division for Early Childhood. Order online at **http://sopriswest.com**

Professional Associations

American Association of Homebased Early Interventionists (AAHBEI).

AAHBEI serves parents and those who work in the field of early home intervention with infants, toddlers, and preschoolers with special needs. (www.aahbei.org).

Division for Communicative Disabilities and Deafness (DCDD).

DCDD is the division of the Council for Exceptional Children that focuses on issues pertaining to communication. Its Constituent Committee on Infants, Toddlers, and Preschoolers addresses early intervention (www.gsu.edu/dcdd).

Division for Early Childhood (DEC) of the Council for Exceptional Children (CEC).

The DEC is a nonprofit organization advocating for individuals who work with or on behalf of children with special needs, birth through age 8 and their families. Founded in 1973, the Division is dedicated to promoting policies and practices that support families and enhance the optimal development of children. Children with special needs include those who have disabilities or developmental delays, are gifted or talented, and are at risk of future developmental problems (www.dec-sped.org).

Web Sites

American Speech-Language-Hearing Association **http://www.asha.org**

Boystown National Research Hospital **http://www.babyhearing.org**

Head Start Bureau
http://www.acf.dhhs.gov/programs/hsb/

National Center for Hearing Assessment Management
http://www.infanthearing.org

National Childcare Information Center
http://ericps.crc.uiuc.edu/nccic/

National Association for the Education of Young Children (NAEYC)
http://www.naeyc.org.

Zero to Three National Training Institute
http://www.zerotothree.org/

References

Abbeduto, L., & Rosenberg, S. (1980). The communicative competence of mildly retarded adults. *Applied Psycholinguistics, 1,* 405–426.

Abbeduto, L., & Rosenberg, S. (1992). Linguistic communication in persons with mental retardation. In S. Warren & J. Reichle (Eds.), *Causes and effects in communication and language intervention* (p. 131). Baltimore: Brookes.

Adler, D. A., & King, D. A. (1994). *Oral communication problems in children and adolescents* (2nd ed.). Boston: Allyn & Bacon.

Alberto, P. A., & Troutman, A. C. (1999). *Applied behavior analysis for teachers* (5th ed.). Upper Saddle River, NJ: Merrill/Prentice Hall.

Alpert, C. L., & Kaiser, A. P. (1992). Training parents as milieu language teachers. *Journal of Early Intervention, 16,* 31–52.

Altman, G., & Steedman, M. (1988). Interaction with context during human sentence processing. *Cognition, 30,* 191–238.

American Psychiatric Association. (1995). *Diagnostic and statistical manual of mental disorders* (4th ed.). Washington, DC: Author.

American Speech-Language-Hearing Association. (1998). *Survey of speech-language pathology services in school-based settings* [Final report]. Rockville, MD: Author.

Arehole, S. (1995). Middle latency response in children with learning disabilities: Preliminary findings. *Journal of Communication Disorders, 28,* 21–38.

Austin, J. L. (1962). *How to do things with words.* London: Oxford University Press.

Autism Society of America. (1996). Definition of autism. *Advocate, 3,* 1.

Bates, E. (1976). *Language and context: The acquisition of pragmatics.* New York: Academic Press.

Bates, E., Camaioni, L., & Volterra, V. (1975). The acquisition of performatives prior to speech. *Merrill-Palmer Quarterly, 21,* 205–226.

Bates, E., & Johnston (1977). *Pragmatics in normal and deficient child language.* Paper presented at the annual meeting of the American Speech-Language-Hearing Association, Chicago, IL.

Baum, D. D., Odom, M., & Boatman, R. (1975). Environment-based language training with mentally retarded children. *Education and Training of the Mentally Retarded, 10,* 68–73.

Berko, J. (1958). The child's learning of English morphology. *Word, 14,* 150–177.

Bernard-Opitz, V. (1982). Pragmatic analysis of the communicative behavior of an autistic child. *Journal of Speech and Hearing Disorders, 47,* 96–99.

Bloom, L. (1970). *Language development: Form and function in emerging grammars.* Cambridge, MA: MIT Press.

Bloom, L. (1973). *One word at a time: The use of single-word utterances before syntax.* The Hague, Netherlands: Mouton.

Bloom, L., & Lahey, M. (1978). *Language development and language disorders.* New York: Wiley.

Boehm, A. (2001). *Boehm Test of Basic Concepts–Preschool Version.* New York: Psychological Corporation.

Bondy, A., & Frost, L. (2002). *A picture's worth: PECS and other visual communication strategies in autism. Topics in autism.* Bethesda, MD: Woodbine House.

Brown, R. (1973). *A first language: The early stages.* Cambridge, MA: Harvard University Press.

Brownlee, S. (1998, June 15). Baby talk. *U.S. News & World Report, 124*(23), 48–50.

Bruner, J. (1981). The social context of language acquisition. *Language and Communication, 1,* 155–178.

Bruner, J., Goodnow, J., & Austin, G. (1956). *A study of thinking.* New York: Wiley.

Bzoch, K., & League, R. (1991). *Receptive-Expressive Emergent Language Test* (2nd ed.). Austin, TX: PRO-ED.

Calderon, R., & Naidu, S. (2000). Further support of the benefits of early identification and intervention with children with hearing loss. *The Volta Review, 100,* 53–84.

Chomsky, N. (1957). *Syntactic structures.* The Hague, Netherlands: Mouton.

Chomsky, N., & Halle, M. (1968). *The sound pattern of English.* New York: Harper and Row.

Clark, E. V. (1974). Some aspects of the conceptual bases for first language acquisition. In R. L. Schiefelbusch & L. L. Lloyd (Eds.), *Language perspectives, acquisition, and retardation.* Baltimore: University Park Press.

Clark, E. V. (2001). Emergent categories in first language acquisition. In M. Bowerman & S. Levinson (Eds.), *Language acquisition and conceptual development* (pp. 379–405). Cambridge, UK: Cambridge University Press.

Clark, H., & Clark, E. (1977). *Psychology and language.* New York: Harcourt Brace Jovanovich.

Clark, H. H. (1973). Space, time, semantics and the child. In T. E. Moore (Ed.), *Cognitive development and the acquisition of language.* New York: Academic Press.

Coggins, R., & Carpenter, R. (1981). The Communicative Intention Inventory: A system for coding children's early intentional communication. *Applied Psycholinguistics, 2,* 235–252.

Crago, M. B., & Gopnik, M. (1994). From families to phenotypes: Theoretical and clinical implications of research into the genetic basis of specific language impairment. In R. Watkins & M. Rice (Eds.), *Specific language impairment in children.* Baltimore: Brookes.

Craig, H. K. (1991) Pragmatic character of the child with SLI: an interactionist perspective. In T. Gallagher (Ed.), *Pragmatics of language: Clinical practice issues* (pp. 163–198). San Diego, CA: Singular

Creedon, M. P. (Ed.). (1975). *Appropriate behavior through communication: A new program in simultaneous language.* Chicago: Dysfunctioning Child Center.

Crites, L., Fischer, K., McNeish-Stengel, M., & Seigel, C. (1992). Working with families of drug-exposed children: Three model programs. In L. Rosetti (Ed.), *Developmental problems of drug-exposed infants.* San Diego, CA: Singular.

Cunningham, C. E., Reuler, E., Blackwell, J., & Deck, J. (1981). Behavioral and linguistic developments in the interaction of normal and retarded children with their mothers. *Child Development, 52,* 62–70.

Dale, P., Simonoff, E., Bishop, D., Eley, T., Oliver, B., Price, T., Purcell, S., Stevenson, J., et al. (1998). Genetic influence on language delay in two-year-old children. *Nature Neuroscience, 1,* 324–328.

Daniels, M. (1993). ASL as a factor in acquiring English. *Sign Language Studies, 78,* 23–29.

deBoysson-Bardies, B., Sagart, L., & Durand, C. (1984). Discernible differences in the babbling of infants according to target language. *Journal of Child Language, 11,* 1–15.

Dever, R. B. (1972). A comparison of the results of a revised version of Berko's Test of Morphology with the free speech of mentally retarded children. *Journal of Speech and Hearing Research, 15,* 169–178.

deVilliers, J., & deVilliers, P. (1978). *Language acquisition.* Cambridge, MA: Harvard University Press.

Donovan, E. (1993). "I NO I NOT EASY TO HELP BUT KEEP HELPING ME." Facilitated communication and behavior management. In D. Smukler (Ed.), *First words: Facilitated communication and the inclusion of young children* (2nd ed.). Syracuse, NY: Jowonio School.

Dore, J. (1974). A pragmatic description of early development. *Journal of Psycholinguistic Research, 3,* 343–350.

Dore, J. (1975). Holophrases, speech acts, and language universals. *Journal of Child Language, 2,* 21–40.

Dromi, E. (1999). Early lexical development. In M. Barrett (Ed.), *The development of language: Studies in developmental psychology* (pp. 99–131). Philadelphia: Psychology Press.

Dunn, L. M. (Ed.). (1973). *Exceptional children in the schools.* New York: Holt, Rinehart & Winston.

Durand, V. M., & Merges, E. (2001). Functional communication training: A contemporary behavior analytic intervention for problem behaviors. *Focus on Autism and Other Developmental Disabilities, 16,* 110–119.

Ervin-Tripp, S. (1964). Imitation and structural change in children's language. In E. H. Lennenberg (Ed.), *New directions in the study of language* (pp. 163–189). Cambridge, MA: MIT Press.

Ervin-Tripp, S. (1978). Some features of early child-adult dialogues. *Language in Society, 7,* 357–373.

Estabrooks, W. (1994). *Auditory-verbal therapy for parents and professionals.* Washington, DC: AG Bell Association.

Facon, B., Facon-Bollengier, T., & Grubar, J. (2002). Chronological age, receptive vocabulary, and syntax comprehension in children and adolescents with mental retardation. *American Journal on Mental Retardation, 107,* 91–98.

Fenson, L., Dale, P. S., Reznick, J. S., Bates, E., Thal, D. J., & Pethick, S. J. (1994). Variability in early communicative development. *Monographs of the Society for Research in Child Development, 59*(5, Serial No. 242), 1–189.

Fey, M. E., & Leonard, L. G. (1983). Pragmatic skills of children with specific language impairment. In T. M. Gallagher & C. A. Prutting (Eds.), *Pragmatic assessment and intervention issues in language.* San Diego, CA: College-Hill Press.

Flexor, C. (1995). Auditory disorders in school children. In R. J. Roeser & M. P. Downs (Eds.), *Auditory disorders in school children: The law, identification and remediation* (pp. 235–257). New York: Thiene Medical Publications.

Frazier, L. (1993). Processing Dutch sentence structure. *Journal of Psycholinguistic Research, 22,* 85–108.

Gallagher, T. (1977). Revision behavior in the speech of normal children developing language. *Journal of Speech and Hearing Research, 20,* 303–318.

Garvey, C. (1975). *Contingent queries.* Unpublished master's thesis, Johns Hopkins University, Baltimore.

Greenspan, S. I., & Wieder, S. (1999). A functional developmental approach to autism spectrum disorders. *Journal of the Association of Persons with Severe Handicaps, 24,* 147–161.

Gregory, S. (1995). Deaf children and their families. Cambridge, England: Cambridge University Press.

Grove, N., & Dockrell, J. (2000). Multisign combinations by children with intellectual impairments: An analysis of language skills. *Journal of Speech, Language, and Hearing Research, 43,* 309–323.

Guralnik, M. J. (Ed.). (1997). *The effectiveness of early intervention.* Baltimore: Brookes.

Halliday, M. (1975). *Learning how to mean: Explorations in the development of language.* London: Edward Arnold.

Hendrick, D., Prather, E., & Tobin, A. (1984). *Sequenced Inventory of Communication Development* (Rev. ed.). Austin, TX: PRO-ED.

Hodson, B.W. (2001). Assessment of Phonological Processes (APP-R). New York: Psychological Corporation.

Hresko, W., Reid, D. K., & Hammill, D. (1999). *Test of Early Language Development* (3rd ed.). Austin, TX: PRO-ED.

Hulit, L. M., & Howard, M. R. (2001). *Born to talk* (3rd ed.). Upper Saddle River, NJ: Merrill/Prentice Hall.

Iverson, J., Volterra, V., Pizzuto, E., & Capirci, O. (1994, June). *The role of communicative gestures in the transition to the two-word stage.* Poster presented at International Conference of Infant Development, Paris, France.

Jakobson, R. (1968). *Child language, aphasia, and phonological universals.* The Hague, Netherlands: Mouton.

Johnson, R., Liddell, S., & Erting, C. (1989). *Unlocking the Curriculum: Principles for achieving access in deaf education.* Gallaudet Research Institute Working Paper 89-3. Washington, DC: Gallaudet University Press.

Kaiser, A. P., Hemmeter, M. L., Ostrosky, M. M., Alpert, C. L., & Hancock, T. B. (1995). The effects of group training and individual feedback on parent use of milieu teaching. *Journal of Childhood Communication Disorders, 16,* 39–48.

Kamhi, A. G., & Johnston, J. R. (1982). Towards an understanding of retarded children's linguistic deficiency. *Journal of Speech and Hearing Research, 25*(3), 435–445.

Kasari, C., Sigman, M., Yirmiya, N., & Mundy, P. (1993). Affective development and communication in young children with autism. In A. Kaiser & D. Gray (Eds.), *Enhancing children's communication.* Baltimore: Brookes.

Krivcher-Winestone, J. (1980). Limits of syntactical development of educable mentally retarded children (Doctoral dissertation, Yeshiva University, 1979). *Dissertation Abstracts International, 40,* 6230A. (University Microfilms No. 8012676)

Kronstadt, D. (1991). Complex developmental issues of prenatal drug exposure. *The Future of Children, 1,* 36–49.

Lederberg, A. R., & Prezbindowski, A. K. (2000). Impact of child deafness on mother-toddler interaction: Strengths and weaknesses. In P. Spencer, C., Erting, and M. Marschark (Eds.), *The deaf child in the family and at school: Essays in honor of Kathryn P. Meadow-Orlans* (pp. 73–92). Mahwah, NJ: Lawrence Erlbaum Associates.

Lederberg, A. R., & Spencer, P. E. (2001). Vocabulary development of young deaf and hard of hearing children. In M. D. Clark, M. Marschark, & M. Karchmer (Eds). *Context, cognition, and deafness* (pp. 88–112) Washington, D.C.: Gallaudet University Press.

Lenneberg, E. (1967). *Biological foundations of language.* New York: Wiley.

Ling, D. (1972). Rehabilitation of cases with deafness secondary to otitis media. In A. Glorig & I. K. Gerwin (Eds.), *Otitis Media Proceedings of the National Conference, Collier Hearing and Speech Center Dallas.* Springfield, IL: Charles C. Thomas.

Lucas, E. V. (1980). *Semantic and pragmatic language: Assessment and remediation.* Rockville, MD: Aspen.

Luria, A. R. (1961). *Speech and the regulation of behavior.* New York: Liveright.

Lyytinen, P., Poikkeus, A., Laaks, M., Eklund, K., & Lyytinen, H. (2001). Language development and symbolic play in children with and without familial risk for dyslexia. *Journal of Speech, Language, and Hearing Research, 44,* 873–885.

Maugh, T. H. (2000, May 4). Test identifies newborns likely to have autism. *Los Angeles Times,* p. 4.

Mar, H. H., & Sall, N. (1999). Profiles of the expressive communication skills of children and adolescents with severe cognitive disabilities. *Education and Training in Mental Retardation and Developmental Disabilities, 34,* 77–89.

Matsuda, M. M. (1984). Comparative analysis of blind and sighted children's communication skills. *Journal of Visual Impairment and Blindness, 78,* 1–5.

McCormick, L., & Schiefelbusch, R. L. (1990). *Early language intervention: An introduction* (2nd ed.). Upper Saddle River, NJ: Merrill/Prentice Hall.

McCormick, L., & Shane, H. (1990). Communication system options for students who are nonspeaking. In L. McCormick & R. Schiefelbusch (Eds.), *Early language intervention.* Upper Saddle River, NJ: Merrill/Prentice Hall.

McCreight, B. (1997). *Recognizing and managing children with fetal alcohol syndrome/fetal alcohol effects: A guidebook.* Washington, DC: Child Welfare League of America, Inc.

McLean, J., & Snyder, L. K. (1977). *A transactional approach to early language training: Derivation of model system. Final report.* Washington, DC: U.S. Department of Health, Education, and Welfare.

Mervis, C. B., & Bertrand, J. (1997). Developmental relations between cognition and language. In L. B. Adamson & M. A. Romski (Eds.), *Communication and language acquisition: Discoveries from atypical development* (pp. 75–106). Baltimore: Brookes.

Montgomery, J. (2000). Verbal working memory and sentence comprehension in children with specific language impairment. *Journal of Speech, Language, and Hearing Research, 43,* 293–308.

Moore-Brown, B. J., & Montgomery, J. (2001). *Making a difference for America's children: Speech-language pathologists in public schools.* Eau Claire, WI: Thinking Publications.

Morgan, J. L. (1996). Prosody and the roots of parsing. *Language and Cognitive Processes, 11,* 69–106.

Morrisset-Huebner, C. E., & Lines, P. (1994). *Learning link: Helping your baby learn to talk.* Washington, DC: U.S. Department of Education, Office of Educational Research and Improvement.

Muma, J. R. (1998). *Effective speech-language pathology: A cognitive socialization approach.* Mahwah, NJ: Erlbaum.

National Center for Hearing Assessment & Management. (2002). *Early hearing detection and intervention information & resource center.* Retrieved September 1, 2002, from http://www.infanthearing.org/ehdi.html

National Institutes of Health. (1993). Early identification of hearing impairment in infants and young children. *NIH Consensus Statement, 11,* 1–24.

Nelson, I. (1973). Structure and strategy in learning to talk. *Monographs of the Society for Research in Child Development, 38,* (Serial No. 149).

Noonan, M. J., & McCormack, L. (1993). *Early intervention in natural environments: Methods and procedures.* Florence, KY: Wadsworth.

Notoya, M., Suzuk, S. & Furukawa, M. (1994). Effects of early manual instruction on the oral-language development of two deaf children. *American Annals of the Deaf, 139* (3), 348–351.

Ogletree, B. T., & Oren, T. (2001). Application of ABA principles to general communication instruction. *Focus on Autism and Other Developmental Disabilities, 16,* 102–109.

Oller, K. D. (1980). The emergence of the sounds of speech in infancy. In G. Yeni-Komshian, J. Kavanaugh, & C. Ferguson (Eds.), *Child phonology* (pp. 93–112). New York: Academic Press.

Olson, H., Burgess, D., & Streissguth, A. (1992). Fetal alcohol syndrome (FAS) and fetal alcohol effects (FAE): A lifespan view, with implications for early intervention. *Zero to Three, 13,* 29–33.

Olswang, L. B., & Pinder, G. L. (1995). Preverbal functional communication and the role of object play in children with cerebral palsy. *Infant-Toddler Intervention: The Transdisciplinary Journal, 5,* 277–299.

Owens, R. (1996). *Language development: An introduction* (4th ed.). Boston: Allyn & Bacon.

Piaget, J. (1952). *The origins of intelligence in children* (M. Cook, Trans.). New York: International University Press.

Prather, E. M., Hedrick, D., & Kern, A. (1972). Articulation development in children aged two to four years. *Journal of Speech and Hearing Disorders, 37*, 55–63.

Preisler, G. M., & Ahlstroem, M. (1997). Sign language for hard of hearing children: A hidrance or a benefit for their development? *European Journal of Psychology and Education, 12* (4), 465–477.

Prizant, B., & Bailey, D. (1992). Facilitating acquisition and use of communication skills. In D. B. Bailey & M. Wolery (Eds.), *Teaching infants and preschoolers with disabilities* (pp. 299–361). Upper Saddle River, NJ: Merrill/Prentice Hall.

Prutting, C. (1979). Process: The action of moving forward progressively from one point to another on the way to completion. *Journal of Speech and Hearing Disorders, 44*, 1–20.

Ratner, V., & Harris, L. (1994). *Understanding language disorders.* Eau Claire, WI: Thinking Publications.

Reichle, J., Mirenda, P., Locke, P., Piche, L., & Johnson, S. (1992). Beginning augmentative communication systems. In S. Wairer & J. Reichle (Eds.), *Causes and effects in communication and language* (pp. 132–156). Baltimore: Brookes.

Reilly, J. S., & Bellugi, U. (1996). Competition on the face: Affect and language in ASL motherese. *Journal of Child Language, 23*(1), 219–39.

Rice, M. L., Buhr, J. C., & Nemeth, M. (1990). Fast mapping word learning abilities of language-delayed preschoolers. *Journal of Speech and Hearing Research, 55*, 33–42.

Sachs, J., & Devin, J. (1976). Young children's use of age-appropriate speech styles. *Journal of Child Language, 3*, 81–98.

Santin, S., & Simmons, J. N. (1977). Problems in the construction of reality in congenitally blind children. *Journal of Visual Impairment or Blindness, 71*, 425–429.

Sarff, L. S. (1981). An innovative use of free field amplification in regular classrooms. In R. Roeser & M. Downs (Eds.), *Auditory disorders in school children* (pp. 263–272). New York: Thieme-Stratton.

Sass-Lehrer, M. (1999). Techniques for infants and toddlers who are deaf or hard of hearing. In S. Raver (Ed.), *Strategies for infants and toddlers with special needs: A team approach.* (2nd ed., pp. 259–297). New York: Prentice Hall.

Sattler, J. (2001). *Assessment of children: Cognitive applications* (4th ed.). San Diego: Author.

Schlesinger, H., & Meadow, K. (1972). *Sound and sign.* Los Angeles: University of California Press.

Schreibman, L., Koegel, R. L., Charlop, M. H., & Egel, A. L. (1990). Infantile autism. In A. S. Bellack, M. Hersen, & A. E. Kaxdin (Eds.), *International handbook of behavior modification and therapy* (pp. 763–789). New York: Plenum Press.

Searle, J. R. (1969). *Speech acts: An essay in the philosophy of language.* Cambridge, England: Cambridge University Press.

Secord, W. A. (1999). *School consultation: Concepts, models, and procedures.* Flagstaff: Northern Arizona University.

Selman, R. (1971). The relation of role-taking to the development of moral judgment in children. *Child Development, 42*, 79–92.

Sharf, D. (1972). Some relationships between measures of early language development. *Journal of Speech and Hearing Disorders, 37*, 64–74.

Shulman, B. (1985). *Using play behavior to describe young children's conversational abilities.* Paper presented at the Annual Meeting of the National Association for the Education of Young Children, Los Angeles, CA.

Skinner, B. (1957). *Verbal behavior.* New York: Appleton-Century-Croft.

Snow, C. (1972). Mother's speech to children learning language. *Child Development, 43*, 549–565.

Sparks, S. (1993). *Children of prenatal substance abuse.* San Diego, CA: Singular.

Spencer, P. (1993). Communication behaviors of infants with hearing loss and their hearing mothers. *Journal of Speech and Hearing Research, 36*, 311–321.

Spencer, P., & Lederberg, A. (1997). Different modes, different models: Communication and language of young deaf children and their mothers. In L. B. Adamson & M. A. Romski (Eds.), *Communication and language acquisition: Discoveries from atypical development* (pp. 203–230). Baltimore: Brookes.

Stoel-Gammon, C. (1998). Role of babbling and phonology in early linguistic development. In A. M. Wetherby, S. F. Warren, & J. Reichle (Eds.), *Transitions in prelinguistic communication.* (pp. 87–110). Baltimore: Brookes.

Stredler-Brown, A. (1998). Early intervention for infants and toddlers who are deaf and hard of hearing:

New perspectives. *Journal of Educational Audiology, 6,* 45–49.

Stremel, K., & Wilson, R. M. (1998). Communication interactions: It takes two; Receptive communication: How children understand your messages to them; Expressive communication: How children send their messages to you. *DB-Link Fact Sheets (Revised)* (The National Information Clearinghouse on Children Who Are Deaf-Blind). Washington, DC: Office of Special Education and Rehabilitative Services. (ED 395 445).

Talay-Ongan, A. (2001). Early intervention: Critical roles of early childhood service providers. *International Journal of Early Years Education, 9,* 221–228.

Tallal, P., Hirsch, L. S., Realpe-Bonilla, T., Miller, S., Brzustowicz, L. M., Bartlett, C., et al. (2001). Familial aggregation in specific language impairment. *Journal of Speech, Language, and Hearing Research, 44,* 1172–1182.

Templin, M. (1957). *Certain language skills in children.* Minneapolis: University of Minnesota Press.

Tillery, K. L., & Smosky, W. J. (1994). Clinical implications of the auditory processing abilities of children with attention deficit-hyperactivity disorder. *Central Auditory Processing: Consensus Development Conference.* Rockville, MD: American Speech-Language-Hearing Association.

Tomasello, M. (1992). *First verbs: A case study of early grammatical development.* New York: Cambridge University Press.

Trantham, C. R., & Pedersen, J. K. (1976). *Normal language development.* Baltimore: Williams & Wilkins.

Veneziano, E., Sinclair, H., & Berthoud, I. (1990). From one to two words: Repetition patterns on the way to structured speech. *Journal of Child Language, 17,* 633–650.

Vygotsky, L. (1962). *Thought and language.* Cambridge, MA: MIT Press.

Warner-Rogers, J., Taylor, A., Taylor, E., & Sandberg, S. (2000). Inattentive behavior in childhood: Epidemiology and implications for development. *Journal of Learning Disabilities, 33,* 520–536.

Warren, D. H. (1984). *Blindness and early childhood development* (2nd ed.). New York: American Foundation for the Blind.

Watkins, R. (1997). The linguistic profile of SLI. In L. B. Adamson & M. A. Romski (Eds.), *Communication and language acquisition: Discoveries from atypical development* (pp. 161–185). Baltimore: Brookes.

West, J. T., & Idol, L. (1990). Collaborative consultation in the education of mentally retarded and at-risk students. *Remedial and Special Education, 11,* 22–31.

Wiig, E. H., & Semel, E. M. (1984). *Language assessment and intervention for the learning disabled* (2nd ed.). Upper Saddle River, NJ: Merrill/Prentice Hall.

Wiig, E. H., Secord, W. & Semel, E. M., (1992). *Clinical evaluation of language fundamentals–Preschool (CELF–Preschool).* New York: Psychological Corporation.

Wilson, M. I. (1973). Children with crippling and health disabilities. In L. M. Dunn (Ed.), *Exceptional children in the schools.* New York: Holt, Rinehart & Winston.

Yoder, D. W., & Miller, J. F. (1972). What we know and what we can do: Input toward a system. In J. E. McLean, D. E. Yoder, & R. L. Schiefelbusch (Eds.), *Language intervention with the retarded* (pp. 89–110). Baltimore: University Park Press.

Yoder, P. J., & Warren, S. F. (1993). Can developmentally delayed children's language development be enhanced through prelinguistic intervention? In A. Kaiser & D. Gray (Eds.), *Enhancing children's communication: Research foundations for intervention* (pp. 35–62). Baltimore: Brookes.

Yoshinaga-Itano, C. (1999). Development of audition and speech: Implications for early intervention with infants who are deaf or hard of hearing. *Volta Review, 100* (5), 213–34.

Yoshinaga-Itano, C., & Apuzzo, M. L. (1998). Identification of hearing loss after 18 months is not early enough. *American Annals of the Deaf, 143* (5), 380–87.

Zimmerman, I., Steiner, V., & Pond, R. (2002). *Preschool Language Scale–4.* New York: Psychological Corporation.

11

Social and Emotional Development

Joan Lieber and Warren Umansky

Chapter Outline

Adam

*M*rs. Glenn is a teacher at Brookfield, an inclusive child-care program. She has 15 children in her classroom ranging in age from 3 to almost 5. About a month ago, a new child, Adam, started the program. He has Down syndrome and he's having a hard time getting used to the classroom routine, particularly to the other children. When Adam's mom brought him to the program on his first day, he had a hard time separating from her. He clung to her and was beginning to get teary-eyed. But Mrs. Glenn knew that Adam really liked trains, so she had asked Adam's mom to make sure Adam brought his favorite engine with him. When Adam noticed the train track that was on the floor in the block area, he brought his engine over and added it to the trains on the track. At that point, Adam's mom was able to leave.

In the month that Adam has been at Brookfield, Mrs. Glenn has spent some time observing Adam as he participates in the daily routine. Although Adam now engages in most of the teacher-led activities, Mrs. Glenn has noticed that Adam doesn't pay much attention to the other children. There are many times during the day when children have the opportunity to interact: circle time, choice time, snack time, and outside time. The 45-minute choice time gives him the opportunity to initiate whatever activity he wants and to be with other children. But Mrs. Glenn has observed that Adam spends his time wandering around the room, taking toys off the shelves, and watching other children. If another child approaches him, Adam might smile, but he hasn't joined the play of the other children. Mrs. Glenn knows that Adam has been at Brookfield only a month, but she's concerned that he doesn't have even one friend. Mrs. Glenn has concerns about Adam's social and emotional development.

Social and emotional development in children is a particularly rich and complex topic. These areas not only encompass the development of abilities in the individual himself, but how he uses these abilities to engage others. Emotions evolve from simple physiological responses to more complex responses. These include a cognitive component that is necessary to understand one's own emotions as well as those of others. Social behavior also starts out simply, with overtures toward others that can be as straightforward as a smile. Social responses quickly become more complex and soon children are engaged in friendships.

When we study social and emotional behavior, partner and setting are important considerations. Children interact quite differently with different partners such as their parents, teachers, and peers. Children's behaviors vary in different settings as well: at home, at school, and on the playground, for example.

Our understanding of social and emotional behaviors is influenced by many researchers and research traditions. Each presents us with a slightly different view of how these important skills develop.

Stages of Typical Emotional and Social Development

Emotional Development

> Emotion is defined as the expression of feelings, needs, and desires and involves the organism as a whole.

Emotion involves the expression of feelings, needs, and desires accompanied by specific physiological responses. Because emotions are biologically based, they are "one of the most ancient and enduring features of human functioning" (Shonkoff & Phillips, 2000, pp. 106–107). Newborns' emotions are limited to states such as hunger and sleepiness. Their ability to express their feelings is also limited and involves vocalizing or crying. In as short a time as 2 years, however, children have an almost complete repertoire of emotional expressions.

As children grow, they develop **emotional competence.** According to Denham (1998), emotional competence has three components: expression, understanding, and regulation.

> The three growth areas leading to emotional competence are expression, understanding, and regulation.

Emotional Expression.   According to Denham, the basic emotions of happiness, sadness, anger, and fear are evident before children are 2 years old. As children get older, they learn adaptive behaviors in response to their emotions. For example, if a child is confronted by a snarling dog and he experiences fear, he will avoid dogs with bared teeth in the future.

During early childhood, the ways that children express their emotions change, becoming "more flexible, complex, and differentiated" (Denham, 1998, p. 28). For example, depending on the context a child might display his happiness by smiling at a friend during a shared story experience, or by running, jumping, and laughing out loud during an outdoor activity.

Children's repertoire of emotional expression expands significantly during the preschool years. As children become more self-aware, pride, shame, and guilt emerge (Denham, 1998, p. 30). Children also experience emotions that include another's perspective, like empathy.

Emotional Understanding.   As children become preschoolers, their cognitive and language abilities mature and they become better equipped to understand their own emotions and those of others. Denham (1998) lists nine areas of growth in emotional understanding for young children. They range from simply having words to label emotions, to a basic knowledge that their feelings can differ from others' feelings, through some understanding of complex emotions such as pride and embarrassment. Given the complexity of the skills required for emotional understanding, it is not surprising that by the end of the preschool period, these understandings are just emerging.

Emotional Regulation.   It is difficult to separate children's emotional development from their ability to regulate emotions so that they can function adequately in social interactions (Shonkoff & Phillips, 2000). Emotional regulation is needed when "the experience and expression of emotion become too strong or too long-lasting for the child and/or his social partners" (Denham, 1998, p. 149). For example, children spend 15 minutes chasing each other on the playground during outside time at their preschool. They grow more and more excited, but then their teacher abruptly tells them it is time to come in and get ready for story time. They need to use emotional regulation to switch their expressions of excitement and hilarity to calmness for both themselves and their teacher. At another time during the preschool day, a child learns to regulate his anger at a peer who knocks down an elaborately constructed block structure. He expresses his anger through words rather than hitting or having a tantrum.

Denham (1998) suggests that children go through three steps when confronted with an emotion that needs regulation. In the first step, they take notice of their emotion. Second, they consider what the emotion means to them. Finally, they choose a specific response: "Given this feeling what can I *do* about it?" (Denham, 1998, p. 154). The response isn't necessarily an overt behavior. Children can cope emotionally, cognitively, or behaviorally. Here are some examples:

- ***Emotional coping.*** The child who gets angry because someone knocks down the block structure he was building might glare at his peer rather than hitting him. He's coping by modulating his response.
- ***Cognitive coping.*** The child whose mom won't take him to the movies might cope by saying to himself, "I didn't want to go anyway."
- ***Behavioral coping.*** The child who's confronted with a snarling dog might cope by seeking protection from his mother.

So, for young children, the emotions that begin as mere feelings during infancy combine with growing cognitive and language development during early childhood to become quite sophisticated.

Social Development with Peers

We know that children are interested in other children very early in life because we can monitor their physiological changes. The heart rates of 3-month-old infants increase when they see other infants (Field, 1979). They also are more likely to smile, reach, and vocalize when they see other infants than when they see their own reflection in a mirror. According to Rubin, Bukowski, and Parker (1998), important social

Emotional understanding is just beginning to emerge at the end of the preschool period.

Children regulate their emotions by becoming aware of the emotion, considering how the emotion affects them, and then responding.

behaviors emerge during infancy as they (1) direct smiles, frowns, and gestures at play partners; (2) show an interest in peers by carefully observing them; and (3) respond to their peers' overtures.

Toddlers engage in increasingly complex social interactions. During the second year, there is a steady increase in turn-taking behavior, and toddlers use imitation as their predominant strategy to coordinate their social behavior with that of a partner. Additionally, toddlers begin to incorporate objects into their social exchanges through joint attention or manipulation (Eckerman, Davis, & Didow, 1989).

Social coordination has another element that emerges between 20 and 24 months: **complementary play.** In complementary play both partners have specific roles to play (Howes, 1987). If one child initiates a social interchange, his partner must reciprocate with an act matched to the initiator's act. For example, in a game that toddlers might create, one child runs to the middle of the room and looks back at his partner invitingly; then the other child runs to the middle of the room to join him. This game, involving a leader and a follower, might continue for several turns. The game may seem simple, but it requires being finely attuned to a partner, at least until the game abruptly ends.

During the preschool years, children interact with their peers with greater frequency and complexity. In an influential study conducted over 7 decades ago, Parten (1932) proposed categories to describe how children's social participation changes over the preschool years. Her categories included the following:

- unoccupied behavior
- solitary play
- onlooker behavior
- parallel play in which children play next to each other but don't interact
- associative play in which children play and share with others
- cooperative play in which children coordinate their efforts

Based on her limited sample of 40 children, Parten concluded that between the ages of 2 and 5, children showed more associative and cooperative play and less unoccupied, solitary and onlooker behavior.

Rubin et al. (1998), however, argue that Parten's conclusions were too simplistic. They suggest that earlier developing behaviors don't disappear as children get older, but that all of the behaviors that Parten observed are exhibited by children throughout the preschool years because they are useful under a variety of circumstances. For example, 5-year-olds may continue to use onlooker and parallel play as effective ways to join in the play of other children.

Preschool children also are able to combine social play with pretend play (Howes, 1987). Children may play together in the "housekeeping" area of a classroom, with one child assuming the role of mother and the other the role of father. The ability to coordinate pretend play with another child is more difficult and occurs later than solitary pretend play. **Social pretend play** is considered more complex than other forms of social play because the child must not only be able to engage in pretense and interact with others but must also coordinate these two activities.

Socially competent preschool children can also organize their play and the play of others. Goncu (1987) describes four phases of social play and the ways that children maintain their play activity through different phases.

As toddlers grow, their social skills increase and become more sophisticated.

Preschool-aged children begin to establish peer relationships.

- *Entering the play group.* Preschool children make *indirect* attempts to enter, such as standing and watching others play, and more *direct* attempts, such as asking if they can join the play. Indirect attempts are usually more successful than direct ones (Lieber, 1993).
- *Initiating the play itself.* Children may accomplish this by simply beginning to play or by discussing the play in advance, including which child might play which role.
- *Maintaining and extending play.* In order for play to continue smoothly, partners must express and negotiate a shared plan. This collaboration is evident for children between 3 and 5, but usually only older children compromise their plans based on the wishes of others.
- *Terminating the play.* For preschoolers, this often occurs by simply leaving the play area.

> For young children, social and emotional development is shaped through much of their play activities.

In summary, the complexity and sophistication of children's social interactions with peers changes substantially from infancy to the end of the preschool years. The progression is from awareness of and interest in peers to simple act-react interchanges to play episodes that involve entering into the play of a group of children, initiating play with them, expanding and extending play through negotiation, and finally terminating the play. Children's social and emotional development is shaped through the context of play in the early childhood years.

Friendship

Friendships are special social relationships. Children can engage in both positive and negative social interactions without having friends (Rubin et al., 1998).

> Friendships are special social relationships.

First, friendships are *reciprocal*. Both partners must share the feeling. Second, the partners feel *affection* toward one another. They seek out each other, not because of what they can do for each other, but rather because of what they feel for each other. Third, friendship is *voluntary;* friendships cannot be mandated.

Children as young as 2 years old form friendships. These young children are considered to have friendships with others whom they specifically seek out for positive social interactions (Vandell & Mueller, 1980). So, although toddlers' friendships differ significantly in form from those of older children, the roots of friendship can be found in very young children.

Children's preferences for some children over others continue into the preschool years. Children select friends who are similar to them in age, gender, or behavior; once they select these friends, their social interactions with them are different from social interactions with nonfriends. Play with friends is more positive, and more complex. Friends also have more conflicts with each other, but once these conflicts are resolved they continue to play near each other and engage in interactions (Rubin et al., 1998).

Theories of Social and Emotional Development

Many theories have contributed to our understanding of how children develop emotionally and socially in their first 5 years. Some theories emphasize the role of nature and suggest that children are born with particular emotional and social tendencies, whereas others emphasize nurture. In these theories, the environment plays the more important role in children's social and emotional development. Some of those theories and the research traditions that have developed from them are discussed below.

Attachment Theory

The connection between caregiver and child influences the child's relationships with peers.

Attachment theory is one of the most well-known and well-researched theories to explain children's relationships with their caregivers. Children's attachment to their caregivers not only explains that primary relationship, but it also influences children's relationships with their peers.

Attachment theory was first described by John Bowlby in the 1940s and 1950s. Mary Ainsworth, who worked with Bowlby, was also a major contributor to the theory (Cassidy, 1999). According to Bowlby, **attachment** is an evolutionary process through which infants form bonds with their caregivers so that they have a secure base from which to explore their environment (Weinfield, Sroufe, Egeland, & Carlson, 1999). Infants exhibit attachment behaviors, like approaching, crying, and seeking contact, when they want comfort and reassurance. Depending on the infant's perception of how the caregiver responds to these behaviors, an attachment relationship is formed. These relationships have been divided into two categories: *secure* and *anxious* or *insecure*. In a secure relationship, the caregiver reacts to an infant's attachment behaviors with warmth, sensitivity, and responsiveness. An infant who is securely attached feels confident in new social situations with a variety of partners. In contrast, in insecure relationships the caregiver is unresponsive to an infant's overtures. The infant learns to expect inaccessibility and a lack of responsiveness in future relationships as well (Rubin et al., 1998).

The infant-caregiver relationship is classified as secure, avoidant, or ambivalent or resistant.

Ainsworth developed the **"Strange Situation" procedure** to assess the quality of the attachment relationship between the infant and his caregiver. Solomon and George (1999) explain that during this assessment, which takes about 20 minutes, a parent and an infant (between 12 and 20 months) are put into a room. After the infant has had a few minutes to explore, a stranger enters the room and attempts to play with the infant. Then both the parent and the stranger leave the room. The parent returns, then leaves again. Next, the stranger enters the room. Finally, the parent returns and the stranger leaves. During all these comings and goings, the infant's reactions are observed. Based on his responses, the infant's attachment with his caregiver is categorized into one of three groups:

- *Secure.* These children use the mother as a secure base for exploration. They are upset when the mother leaves and, when the mother returns, they greet her happily. When they are upset, they turn to their mothers for comfort, then return to exploring.
- *Avoidant.* These children explore readily, and don't appear to miss their mother when she leaves. If the mother attempts to comfort the child, he avoids her.
- *Ambivalent or resistant.* These children don't explore the new environment. When the mother leaves, they are very upset. When the mother returns, they may have a tantrum or be passive. The mother is not a source of comfort for these children.

This theory has spawned hundreds of empirical studies on topics from how attachment changes from infancy through adulthood; to how children who are avoidant or ambivalent may become hostile, aggressive, and antisocial; to cross-cultural studies of attachment.

There also have been a series of studies of attachment with children with disabilities including Down syndrome (Atkinson et al., 1999), cerebral palsy, and autism (Pipp-Siegel, Siegel, & Dean, 1999). These studies reveal that children with severe disabilities may show atypical attachment patterns. In interpreting these findings, Barnett, Butler, and Vondra (1999) conclude that children with Down syndrome may be delayed in their ability to exhibit attachment-related behaviors (e.g., smiling, approaching, vocalizations), and their mothers may have difficulty in interpreting their signals. On the other hand, children with cerebral palsy may have difficulty because they have "damage to the systems that underlie movement" (Barnett et al., 1999, p. 176). Barnett et al. suggest that children with disabilities may behave differently than typically developing children in the "Strange Situation" procedure, but that difference may be one of form rather than function.

Emotional Intelligence

Along with a renewed interest in the physiology of emotions, the concept of emotional intelligence has been proposed. The model was first proposed by Salovey and Mayer (1990). In Salovey and Mayer's view, intelligence includes more than the cognitive and linguistic components measured by standardized IQ tests. They suggest that intelligence includes an emotional component that is part of social intelligence. It is the "ability to monitor one's own and others' feelings and emotions, to discriminate among them and to use this information to guide one's thinking and actions" (Salovey & Mayer, 1990, p. 189). Emotional intelligence allows people to live and work well with others. According to Salovey and Mayer emotional intelligence has several distinct components:

> Emotionally intelligent people are cognizant of their own and others' feelings.

- Knowing and expressing emotions
- Regulating emotions
- Recognizing emotions in others and responding to them in empathetic ways
- Using emotions in adaptive ways

Psychosocial Theory

Erikson (1950) described milestones of development in terms of emotional conflicts that a child must resolve to become a socialized individual. He identified three such conflicts during the child's first 5 years: trust versus mistrust, autonomy versus shame and doubt, and initiative versus guilt.

> Erikson's developmental milestones consist of emotional conflicts that an individual must resolve to become socialized.

Trust Versus Mistrust. The physical closeness of an infant with his caregiver facilitates the formation of a very strong bond. Consistency of caregiving and physical comfort allows the child to trust the caregiver. This prepares him to deal confidently with the experiences that his environment will present. Inconsistent caregiving, which leads to frustration and discomfort for the child, may interfere with typical development. The child, in this case, may mistrust new experiences and relationships. In most children, this conflict is resolved within the first 18 months of life. Although Erikson's theory and attachment theory arose from different research traditions, they are similar in the importance they place on a secure bond between child and caregiver.

Autonomy Versus Shame and Doubt.   Society has certain expectations for a toddler. Now that he can move about freely, he must adhere to certain social mores. He will be prepared for encounters with new situations if he has been given the freedom to explore the environment and to initiate interactions (White, 1975). This contributes to development of self-control and feelings of independence and autonomy. Poor caregiving, on the other hand, causes the child to doubt his ability to control his own actions and to feel shame at being so powerless. Most children achieve self-regulation when they resolve this conflict by 3 years of age.

Initiative Versus Guilt.   As a child develops, he becomes aware of his power as an initiator of activity. He is more able to control his environment as he gains mastery over his own body. The child understands that people have different motivations and perceptions, and he delights in his ability to figure things out. However, some actions that display initiative lead to feelings of guilt. For example, a child might climb up high on a jungle gym, then fall down and break his arm. If he climbed in spite of his mother's warnings, he might feel guilty about what happened. Such feelings can be inhibiting, contributing to a later lack of initiative. When a child resolves this conflict, usually by age 6, he perceives himself as distinctly separate from his parents and free to explore his world.

Social Learning Theory

Learning theory emphasizes the role of the environment on the development of personality and specific behaviors. Bijou and Baer (1979) place great emphasis on interpreting a child's current behaviors based on his history of interactions with the environment. **Socialization,** then, is viewed as a child's range of experiences from which he develops his personality and learns appropriate behaviors.

A child acquires his personal identity through the process of socialization.

Bandura (1977) provided the foundation for explaining social learning theory and for distinguishing it from behavioral theory. Whereas the latter emphasizes the role of reinforcement in maintaining or halting certain behaviors, Bandura proposed that most learning occurs when children observe, model, and imitate people in their environment. Consequently, an organized and carefully structured environment helps children achieve desired goals. As applied to development of social and emotional skills, sound models and situations that encourage the display of prosocial behaviors are those that facilitate the most typical development.

Factors Affecting Social and Emotional Development

Young children often show unique behaviors in their interactions with others or when they're confronted with overwhelming emotions. Yet, the range of typical behavior is broad. Children's behaviors and reactions can be attributed to factors that are within and outside themselves.

Temperament

Theorists and researchers who emphasize the role of nature in development believe that every child is born with a set of personality characteristics that Thomas and Chess (1977) call **temperament.** These characteristics play an important role in shaping the responses of a child's caregivers and, ultimately, in molding the child's future personality. There has been enormous interest in temperament since researchers first studied it in the 1920s. Since those early investigations, the concept of temperament has evolved. For example, Thomas and Chess originally identified 9 dimensions of temperament. Because their dimensions were not independent, other researchers combined them into a smaller number of dimensions. One dimension, negative affect, includes fearful distress and irritable distress. In the former, the child has difficulty adjusting to a new situation; in the latter, the child is fussy or difficult to soothe. Another dimension is positive affect, which characterizes children who generally respond with smiles and laughter. Other dimensions are activity level and attention span/persistence. Children's rhythmicity also is rated. Rhythmicity is related to whether the infant's states of hunger, sleepiness, and distress are predictable (Rothbart & Bates, 1998).

These attributes of temperament combine to characterize differences between children and how they respond to their caregivers. The **easy child,** for example, is very adaptable, playful, and responsive to adults. This type of child is likely to receive a great deal of adult attention during the early years because interactions are so pleasant and reinforcing. The **difficult child,** on the other hand, provides little positive feedback to adults. He is fussy, difficult to soothe, and has problems sleeping and eating. This type of child is likely to get less positive attention from adults (van den Boom & Hoeksma, 1994). Finally, the temperament of the **slow-to-warm-up child** is characterized by slow adaptability. Adults who sustain contact with this type of child are usually rewarded by the positive behaviors found in the easy child, but it takes considerably longer to elicit them. Some qualities of temperament are more stable over time than others. For example, infants who are irritable and prone to distress are more likely to show these qualities as they get older, as well (Rothbart & Bates, 1998). It is important to note, however, that although some aspects of temperament are relatively stable, temperament influences a child's experiences, and it is also influenced by these experiences.

> Temperament attributes have a major impact on the way a child develops and interacts with caregivers.

Gender

One of the more widely reported gender differences in social and emotional development is that boys exhibit more aggression than girls. Although there seems to be little difference in the rate of aggression in infancy, by the time children enter preschool, boys engage in more conflict and in more verbally and physically aggressive acts than girls. According to Coie and Dodge (1998), this gender difference holds across socioeconomic groups and across cultures.

> Boys tend to exhibit more verbal and physical aggression than girls during the preschool years.

Males tend to be more vulnerable to family and life stresses than females (Walker, Cudeck, Mednick, & Schulsinger, 1981; Wolkind & Rutter, 1973). It has been postulated, however, that males are reinforced for more aggressive and competitive behavior by family members and peers, which accounts for increasing differences in their social patterns as they develop (Block, 1982; Serbin, O'Leary, Kent, & Tonick, 1973).

Although the rate of overt aggression is much higher among boys, **relational aggression** is higher among girls. Relational aggression "harms others through damage to peer relationships" (Crick, Casas, & Mosher, 1997). Crick and her colleagues designed teacher and peer rating scales to measure relational aggression in preschool children. Behaviors that reflected relational aggression included children who don't invite someone to their birthday party, children who don't let someone play in the group, and children who don't listen to someone if they're mad at them. These behaviors contrasted with those that reflected overt aggression such as children who push and shove, and children who throw things at other children if they don't get their way. Crick et al. found that teachers particularly rated girls as more relationally aggressive and less overtly aggressive than preschool boys. They also found that children who showed either type of aggression were rejected more often than those who weren't aggressive.

> Children who behave aggressively typically experience more peer rejection than do less aggressive children.

Stress

> A secure attachment with one parent may shield a child from later psychosocial problems.

The formation of a child's personality is closely related to the types of stress to which he is subjected in his early years and to how he deals with the stress. A child who lives in poverty, has multiple hospital stays, or comes from a dysfunctional home is at risk for long-lasting psychosocial disorder. Still, some children handle stress better than others do, and many progress through adverse early years relatively undamaged (Quinton & Rutter, 1976). Some emerge better able to cope with later stresses, whereas others are more vulnerable (Rutter, 1980). Rutter (1971, 1978) has indicated that a secure attachment with one parent during the stressful early years may shield a child from later psychosocial disorders.

Sibling Relationships

> A close sibling relationship may compensate for a lack of socialization skills with peers.

Researchers have speculated that children's social interactions with peers are affected by the relationships they have with their siblings. This makes intuitive sense for a number of reasons. First, children spend a lot of time with siblings—more time than they spend with either their parents or, when they are young, with their peers. Second, siblings give children the opportunity to practice social skills. They have the opportunity to engage in positive social exchanges and to resolve conflict with partners who, unlike parents, have a similar level of sophistication. So, although researchers have hypothesized that there would be a link between children's interactions with siblings and with peers, there isn't much evidence for that link. According to Parke and Buriel (1998), "there doesn't seem to be a straightforward carryover of interaction styles between children's relationships" (p. 485).

There is one area of social relationships in which siblings do seem to have a strong influence. Siblings may compensate when children have difficulty forming

Siblings can affect children's relationships with their peers.

peer relationships. Parke and Buriel (1998) note that having a favorite sibling may buffer adjustment problems for socially isolated children.

Parental Style

Baumrind (1973) speculated that parents' style of interacting with their child would have an impact on that child's later development. She described parents as authoritative, authoritarian, or permissive.

The **authoritative parent** is firm and willing to set limits, but not intrusive. Authoritative parents encourage their children to explore their environments and gain interpersonal competence. In contrast, the **authoritarian parent** is harsh, unresponsive to her children, and has a rigid style. The third type of parent, the **permissive parent,** is affectionate toward her children but lax and inconsistent with her discipline. As a consequence, her children are uncontrolled and may show impulsive behavior (Parke & Buriel, 1998).

Parke and Buriel (1998) found a number of problems with Baumrind's conceptualization of parental style. First, a distinction can be drawn between style (or parental attitudes) and parental practices. Second, as noted by Sameroff and his colleagues (Sameroff & Chandler, 1975; Sameroff & Fiese, 1990), the direction of effects is as likely to be from the child to the parent as the reverse. Finally, the scheme may not be universal; that is, it may not apply to parents from different socioeconomic backgrounds or to parents from diverse cultures.

According to Parke and Buriel, parents do indeed affect their children's social and emotional development through three different routes: (1) they interact directly with their children; (2) they instruct, teaching their children about what constitutes important social behavior; and (3) they provide their children with opportunities for social experiences.

Parents can enhance their children's opportunities for social interaction.

Citing Bronfenbrenner's ecological theory (1979), Parke and Buriel note that children's social relationships extend beyond the immediate family, to the extended family, the neighborhood and school, and places of worship. Because children have so many chances to interact with others and form relationships, parents can enhance children's relationships by actively managing these opportunities. For example, parents can supervise their children's choices of activities and friends, they can initiate and arrange play dates for their children, and they can enroll their child in organized activities like religious school.

Mothers and fathers affect their children's social and emotional development in different ways.

Both mothers and fathers influence social and emotional development, but they appear to have distinctive styles of interaction. Fathers, who typically spend less time with their children than mothers, spend much of the time they do have in play activities. Fathers engage in more physical play, whereas mothers' play tends to involve objects. Research does show that, regardless of the gender of the parent, parents who are responsive, warm, and engaging are more likely to have children who are more socially competent; parents who are hostile and controlling have children who have more difficulty with their peers (Parke & Buriel, 1998).

Social and Emotional Development in Children with Special Needs

Many children, particularly children with special needs, find it difficult to develop friendships.

There are a variety of disabilities that affect children's development in the areas of emotion and emotional regulation, social skills, social competence, and friendship formation. Establishing successful relationships with peers is a complex process that proves difficult for many children. Asher (1990) noted that as many as 10% of children in elementary school are rejected by their peers. These numbers are even higher for some groups of children, particularly those with disabilities.

Children with Autism

Children with autism tend to be self-focused and often express their emotions inappropriately.

Children with autism display emotions at inappropriate times and in inappropriate ways. For example, children with autism smile, but they may direct their smiles at toys rather than to other children. Further, whereas typically developing children might show pride when accomplishing a particularly difficult task by glancing at an adult for acknowledgement, that self-consciousness is missing in children with autism (Denham, 1998). This interpersonal sharing depends on joint attention, which is a particular area of deficit among children with autism (Sigman & Ruskin, 1999). According to Sigman and Ruskin, children with autism "fail to attend jointly, show objects to others, point to objects and people, and track the pointing and eye gaze of others" (p. 49).

The majority of children with autism show differences in emotional understanding as well. Sigman and her colleagues (Sigman, Kasari, Kwon, & Yirmiya, 1992; Sigman & Ruskin, 1999) found that children with autism were less responsive to adults who pretended to injure themselves. They spent less time looking at the injured adult, and were rated as showing less empathy than either typically developing children or children with Down syndrome. Sigman and Ruskin (1999) concluded that children with autism generally show a lack of social attention, and they tend to avoid looking directly at the faces of other people.

Children with autism have particular difficulty in their social relationships with peers. Sigman and Ruskin (1999) found, when they compared children with autism to children with developmental delays, that the children with autism played in isolation significantly more. When they were at recess, much of their time was spent in self-stimulatory activities rather than in play with others. Although they sometimes attempted to interact with other children, they initiated and responded less frequently than children with other disabilities. When children with autism did participate in social activities with other children, and did make social bids, those bids were accepted as frequently as those of other children. Once they began social interchanges, they lasted as long as those of other children.

Children with Developmental Delays

Sigman and Ruskin (1999) did a series of studies examining the emotional development of children with Down syndrome and other developmental delays. In contrast to the children with autism, when confronted with an experimenter who showed distress, the children with developmental delays looked frequently at the experimenter's face. They also were rated as showing greater empathy than the children with autism, and were rated similarly to the typically developing children in the sample.

Substantial research has documented the social interactions and social competence of young children with developmental delays. Guralnick and his colleagues found that, in comparison to typically developing peers, these children generally show more solitary play, are more negative with their partners during play, and have less success with peers when they make social bids (Guralnick, 2001). Hestenes and Carroll (2000) found similar results; the preschool children with disabilities that they studied spent more of their time in solitary and onlooker play than their peers (see the story of Adam in the opening vignette). They did, however, spend about 30% of their play time in cooperative play.

Children with Communication Disabilities

As noted in chapter 10, it might be expected that children with communication disabilities would have difficulty developing successful relationships with their peers. These children may have difficulty with any of a number of areas of communication including articulation, and the development of syntax, semantics, or pragmatics. These disabilities may affect children's expressive abilities, which in turn may influence their ability to be understood by their peers, and their peers' subsequent willingness to participate in a social interchange.

Guralnick, Connor, Hammond, Gottman, and Kinnish (1996) used play groups of children with communication disabilities and typically developing children to evaluate the social interactions and the social competence of both groups of children. They evaluated children's play for the proportion of solitary, parallel, and group play, as well as the amount of time spent unoccupied, as onlookers, and in other activities such as reading and interacting with an adult. They also observed children's peer-related behavior in other categories such as using peers as resources, expressing affection, imitating a peer, joining a peer's play, and expressing hostility. Finally, each child was rated by the other children as someone they really liked to play with, someone they "kinda" liked to play with, or someone they don't like to play with—a measure of popularity.

Children with communication disorders were similar to their typically developing peers in a number of areas. Neither group of children had much unoccupied time, and there were no differences in acceptance in the two groups. However, there were some differences. Children with communication disorders engaged in fewer conversations, had lower rates of positive social behavior, and were less successful when they made social overtures to their peers.

> Communication disorders impact a child's ability to converse and interact socially with peers.

Children with Sensory Impairments

Visual Impairments.   Limited research has been conducted on how young children with limited sight interact with their peers. There are a number of reasons why research has been so limited. Children with vision impairments make up a diverse group. There are children who are completely blind, and those with functional vision. In addition, children with vision impairments often have other disabilities as well, so it is difficult to attribute results to the visual impairment alone. Finally, visual impairments are a very low incidence disability; the number of children who are affected is small (Crocker & Orr, 1996). In spite of these limitations, we do know something about the social development of children who are blind.

> Vision plays a critical role in developing social competence.

It is logical to assume that the social development of children with visual impairments would be affected by their loss of sight. Vision is important in our social interchanges because a major part of these interchanges involves the observation of others. Emotional understanding for children who are blind is affected as well. Children recognize others' emotions through facial expression; however, that avenue is not open to children who can't see those expressions. Thus, for children who are blind, all learning about others relies on their use of other senses (Farrenkopf, Howze, & Sowell, 1995).

Farrenkopf and her colleagues (1995) describe other limitations encountered by children who are blind as they engage in social interchange. Some of these limitations are difficulty in maintaining eye contact, noticing gestures and other context cues, and initiating and maintaining social interaction. Children with visual impairments may exhibit behaviors that limit the willingness of their peers to interact with them. These behaviors are called **"blindisms"** or **"mannerisms"** and are "behaviors that are repetitive, usually involving such things as eye rubbing, head turning, hand gestures, finger flicking, and body rocking or swaying" (Farrenkopf et al., 1995, p. 15). For young children, whose understanding of others' behaviors is limited, these different behaviors may discourage involvement.

Children who are typically developing provide challenges to children who are blind too. Young children—particularly those who play without using much language—may be unpredictable in their movements around children who are blind (Zanandra, 1998). They may expect quick responses to their social overtures, and may move quickly from one activity to another. Expectations for a quick response, and transitions from one play activity to another present problems for children who are blind (Zanandra, 1998).

Crocker and Orr (1996) compared the social behaviors of preschoolers with visual impairments to those without in a variety of preschool classrooms. They found variability among children with visual impairments in their involvement in the classrooms, which they attributed to the amount of vision the children had as well as their mobility. Crocker and Orr also found that the children tended to play alone, but in proximity to children who could see. They also explored toys repetitively. When several of the children made overtures to join the play of peers, those overtures were ignored. They found that the children with visual impairments did initiate social interactions; however, those initiations were directed more often to teachers in the classrooms than to their peers.

Hearing Impairments.   Children who have limited hearing share the problems and frustrations in social interaction experienced by children with other sensory impairments. This disability limits children's social experiences and feelings of social competence (Brown, Remine, Prescott, & Rickards, 2000). On the other hand, Vandell and George (1981) reported examples of consistent social competence by children with hearing impairments in their interactions with hearing children. They were persistent initiators of interactions and, in the absence of language, developed alternate communication strategies. Hearing children did not do as well in modifying their communication strategies (i.e., they still used verbal modes), but their social interactions were positive. The implications of these findings support the position that children with hearing impairments can benefit from opportunities for independence and interactions with their environment at an early age.

Other researchers have investigated how children who are deaf or hard of hearing enter and maintain play episodes with their peers (Brown et al., 2000; Messenheimer-Young & Kretschmer, 1994; Roberts, Brown, & Rickards, 1996). Findings from these researchers have varied. Using a case study of one child, Messenheimer-Young and Kretschmer (1994) noted that the child with a hearing impairment used a range of behaviors to enter a play group; however, the strategy used most frequently was to directly request access. Direct strategies result in successful entry less frequently than indirect approaches (Lieber, 1993). Roberts et al. (1996) found that the entry behaviors of children with hearing impairments they observed were similar to a matched group of children with normal hearing.

Brown and her colleagues (2000) compared entry strategies to dramatic play and nonplay activities of kindergarteners with profound hearing losses and those with normal hearing. They found both similarities and differences between these two

> All children with sensory impairments experience a degree of frustration in interacting socially.

groups. Both groups used utterances or actions that were related to the group activity to gain entry to sociodramatic play and nonplay activities. Both groups were equally successful in gaining entry to the group. However, children with normal hearing showed a greater range of entry behaviors. For example, these children were more likely than children with hearing loss to survey the ongoing play activity and then choose an entry behavior that was related to the play. Children with normal hearing also used entry behaviors that brought attention to themselves and that provided information about themselves to the other play partners.

Children with Challenging Behaviors

Many different terms are used to describe and categorize children who exhibit problematic behavior. However, it remains unclear how the available classification systems apply to young children, particularly when typical developmental variations are taken into consideration. There are no norms to help us determine, for example, what constitutes normal activity level, patience, or attention during the preschool years. Additionally, children who have difficulty expressing themselves with words may attempt to resolve their conflicts physically. There is agreement, however, that "it's not the presence of specific problem behaviors that differentiates 'normal' from 'abnormal' but their frequency, intensity, chronicity, constellation, and social context" (Campbell, 1988, p. 60).

> What constitutes normative behavior for preschoolers remains unclear.

Despite the relative lack of data on their application to preschool children, a number of classification systems exist and have been used to diagnose and describe specific emotional and behavioral problems in children. It is important for professionals working with young children with special needs to be familiar with these systems, particularly because some of these systems have measurement devices that may need to be completed by teachers as part of the diagnostic evaluation process.

One of the most commonly recognized systems for classifying child psychopathology is the *Diagnostic and Statistical Manual* (DSM) of the American Psychiatric Association (1994). Now in its fourth edition *(DSM–IV),* this system provides a multidimensional framework for conceptualizing problem behaviors. The current version of the *DSM* has more specific diagnoses for children than any previous version, and it requires greater specification for a professional to assign a specific diagnosis. This is the diagnostic system that typically is used by most mental health professionals in the United States.

Regardless of the classification system used, there is a very high prevalence of young children whose parents and teachers report that they show challenging behaviors. According to Webster-Stratton (1997), between 7% and 25% of preschool children in the United States fit the criteria for a clinical diagnosis of **oppositional defiant disorder** (ODD). Among the behaviors that these children exhibit are noncompliance, poor self-control, overactivity, aggression, and disruptiveness. The term *ODD* is most frequently applied to young children. **Conduct disorder** is the term used with older children and adolescents (Coie & Dodge, 1998).

> Challenging behaviors can be classified as externalizing or internalizing.

One way of classifying challenging behaviors is by considering those children who have problems with externalizing versus internalizing behaviors. Children who exhibit **externalizing behaviors** show high rates of hyperactivity, impulsivity, aggression, defiance, and noncompliance. These children show *undercontrol;* they are behaviors that adults find annoying and are behaviors that can hurt other people (Campbell, 1990). Externalizing behaviors are directed outwardly toward people or objects.

In contrast, children who have **internalizing behaviors** are fearful, depressed, and withdrawn (Webster-Stratton, 1997). Internalizing behaviors are directed inward by the child. Both parents and teachers have more difficulty with children with externalizing behaviors, and those behaviors are remarkably stable over time. Campbell (1991) found that over half of the children who had moderate to severe externalizing behaviors in preschool still showed those behaviors in elementary school, and 67% of these children were diagnosed as having attention-deficit hyperactivity disorder, oppositional defiant disorder, or a conduct disorder at age 9.

It is not clear what causes children to have behavior problems at such an early age, but researchers have suggested that both organic and environmental factors may put them at risk. For example, children with delays in social, communication, or cognitive development, and children who experience poor home or school environments, are more likely to exhibit challenging behaviors (Conroy & Davis, 2000).

> Children who experience cognitive, social, and communicative developmental delays and who lack a healthy environment are more at risk for behavioral problems.

Children with Attention-Deficit Hyperactivity Disorders

Attention-deficit hyperactivity disorders (ADHD) refer to neurologically based problems wherein a child manifests inattention, distractibility, and impulsivity, and may be hyperactive as well. In fact, it is often the hyperactivity component that contributes to earlier identification of the problem in young children. For children who do not exhibit the hyperactivity component, diagnosis frequently is delayed until the child is in an academic setting.

Alienation from peers, uncompleted school tasks, poor self-esteem, and family conflicts are typical consequences of these children's behaviors. Peer problems result from the young children's impulsiveness and inability to read social cues. Poor self-esteem may result from continuous negative feedback from adults, not being able to meet others' expectations, and an inability to complete tasks or to get along with other children. Family conflicts persist as a result of the stress of a noncompliant young child who rarely sits still, runs off in public places, engages in dangerous activities, won't stay in bed at night, and demands constant attention and supervision. Unfortunately, the child has little voluntary control over these behaviors (Umansky & Smalley, 2003).

In most cases, these problems can be attenuated through a combination of behavior management and medication. With early treatment, the social and academic outcomes can be very positive. However, ADHD often coexists with other impairments, which makes effective treatment more challenging (Ingersoll, 1995). The teacher often is part of a team consisting of a physician, therapists, the child's parents, and other professionals to help decide on the best course of treatment and intervention.

> Most behavioral problems stemming from ADHD can be managed by behavior therapy and medication.

Children with Physical Impairments

A child who is limited in movement, has poor control of voluntary motor acts, and has atypical physical features or other physical impairments suffers the same social and emotional risks as children with other disabilities. For example, they show lower levels of persistence on problem-solving tasks than do children without disabilities (Jennings, Conners, & Stegman, 1988). In addition, Graham and Rutter (1968) reported psychiatric disorders in 37.5% of children with brain lesions but without epilepsy, and in 58.3% of children with epilepsy. More than 1 in 10 children that they studied who had a physical disability exclusive of central nervous system damage displayed an emotional disorder. These findings support the belief that environmental factors, such as the caregiver's expectation for a child and level of acceptance of the child, also contribute to disturbance in the child's social and emotional development. For example, the level of spontaneous play of infants with cerebral palsy can be predicted by the extent to which mothers make necessary adaptations when interacting with their children (Blasco, Hrncir, & Blasco, 1990).

Similar conclusions were reached for a large group of children with physical disabilities in a British study (Seidel, Chadwick, & Rutter, 1975). It appears that the influence of the environment on a child with a physical impairment can be at least as powerful as that of the impairment itself. This is consistent with information presented about other impairments.

Social Acceptance and Rejection

Although there is agreement that children without disabilities interact more often with others without disabilities than they do with children with disabilities (Guralnick, 1999; Hestenes & Carroll, 2000), there are clearly children with disabilities who have successful social relationships with other children. Odom et al. (2002) suggest that if we look only at the frequency of interactions for children with disabilities we are not getting a complete view of their social relationships. They suggest that we should broaden our perspective and use a multimethod approach. In their work, Odom et al. combined observations of children's interactions with peers, peers' ratings of how much they like to play with others in their classrooms, and teachers' and parents' descriptions of friendships to develop indices of children who were socially accepted and socially rejected. Although children with disabilities were rejected more than their typically developing peers, about one-third of the children in their sample of 80 were well accepted by their peers. Those well-accepted children had a number of common characteristics and abilities. They had effective social skills, had a least one friend, could communicate with and show affection to others, could engage in pretend play, and were interested in interacting with their peers. Children who were rejected had a number of characteristics in common as well. These children lacked effective communication and social skills, they were disruptive, came into conflict with other children, and were often physically aggressive.

> Children with disabilities can have satisfactory relationships with their typically developing peers.

Friendship and Children with Disabilities

Although the social behaviors and social interactions of young children with disabilities have been widely studied, fewer researchers have specifically examined friendship. Having at least one friend is important for children with disabilities for several reasons. According to Buysse (2002), friendship provides children with the potential for enhanced cognitive and language development as well as social and emotional benefits. These benefits are "an increased capacity for understanding another's perspective, the ability to regulate one's emotions, and a general feeling of well-being and happiness" (Buysse, 2002, p. 18).

Buysse, Goldman, and Skinner (2002) investigated the friendships of 120 children with disabilities who attended either inclusive child-care programs, where a majority of children were typically developing, or specialized programs, where a majority of children had disabilities. Children had a variety of disabilities; about 40% had severe disabilities. They found that as a group, 28% of the children with disabilities had no friends according to their teachers. However, children with disabilities in the inclusive child-care programs were almost twice as likely to have at least one friend than the children in specialized programs. In addition they found that, in child-care settings, the children with disabilities were more likely to have a friend who was typically developing.

Friendship helps children develop their cognitive and language skills as well as their social and emotional skills.

Specific Strategies for Social and Emotional Assessment

Social skills and emotions are perhaps the most difficult areas of human development to understand. They are situational in nature; a child may be aggressive in one situation and passive in another. He may cry when confronted with some strangers and befriend others. He may engage in complex imaginary play at the babysitter's house but not at home. How, then, is one to gain an understanding of this complex array of behaviors? Systematic assessment of the child may provide some answers.

Issues in Assessment

Multimethod Assessment.   The behavior of young children is extremely variable depending upon the setting, the time of day, who is present, and other factors. As a result, there has been a shift away from using a single instrument or observation to document a child's behavior. Thus, it is important to evaluate children's behavior over time, and in a variety of settings. A multimethod approach uses a combination of strategies for collecting information and may include systematic observations in various settings, interviews, and rating scales (see chapter 5).

Effective assessment requires using a multimethod approach.

Direct observation of a child in different settings may be the most desirable means to evaluate developmental characteristics, because the farther one strays from direct measurements of behavior, the less reliable the results are likely to be. However, in considering the behavior of young children, observations can be enhanced by both parent and teacher reports.

There are plusses and minuses when adult reports are used. Yarrow (1963), for example, examined the value of the interview as an assessment technique and found that information gathered by interviewing parents tends to follow a pattern of idealized expectations and cultural stereotypes. Parents may confuse a child with siblings or feel obligated to respond to questions in spite of vague recollections.

Others, however, have found parental reports to be quite valid. Rothbart and Bates (1998) noted that researchers have determined the accuracy of parental reports by correlating parent ratings with those of an independent rater. When correlations are low, people assume that it is the parents who are less accurate than independent raters. In contrast, it may actually be the independent raters who are not accurate. They may not be familiar with the child, and may not see all the behaviors that the parent sees. Additionally, the parents are likely to be aware of children's behaviors that occur infrequently, but may greatly influence ratings.

The skill of the interviewer also affects parents' responses. Parents may not understand exactly what information the interviewer wants. The validity of information gathered in this way may be improved when the parent is requested to recall recent events, when the behaviors to be recalled are clearly defined, and when response choices are specific and easily quantified.

Interviews with children—a technique that Piaget used to discover how they process information—are limited by a child's verbal skills; however, the technique does offer an opportunity for the evaluator to establish a relationship with the child that can be helpful throughout the assessment process. With older and typically developing children, interviews may indeed provide valuable information about social and emotional development.

What Is Normal or Typical?   A basic problem arises with the issue of assessment of social and emotional development. Although we have discussed characteristics of normal, or typical, development in these areas, it is difficult to assign expected ages to significant social and emotional milestones. There appears to be some consensus about what abnormal behavior is, so that an observer can identify a child exhibiting inappropriate behavior. It is considerably more difficult to be precise about what behaviors children should be displaying in various situations and at different ages. Newer assessment instruments have increased our ability to make comparisons among children and among different situations for a single child.

Types of Assessment Instruments

Systematic Observation.   The most reliable information about a child can be gathered by observing him in a familiar setting. For most children, that setting can be his home or classroom. Several principles guide this type of assessment. Observations across many settings may be necessary to get a complete impression of how a child interacts with others, how he interacts with objects, and how he deals with challenging situations or conflicts. Furthermore, behaviors may change if the child is aware of being observed. This phenomenon has been well documented in adults (Moustakas, Sigel, & Schalock, 1956; Zegoib, Arnold, & Forehand, 1975), but less so with children. However, it can be expected that a child will not behave typically in a setting that is not one he is used to. Moreover, if the child is not familiar with the observer, it is important to establish rapport with the child before the observation begins.

Finally, the assessor must have defined specific behaviors to observe and have an objective way of recording the observations. Many electronic coding devices have been developed to record time and frequency data, but some sophistication is necessary to record information reflecting a child's abilities.

Direct observation is valuable to document the frequency of individual social behaviors as well as social interactions among groups of children. When a child's social behaviors are observed, the assessor typically notes the frequency of particular behaviors, and whether they are positive or negative. It is also important to capture whether the child initiated or responded to a social overture (Odom & Munson, 1996). One observation system that can be used is the Individual Social Behavior Scale designed by Guralnick et al. (1996). With this scale, the frequency of 19 different behaviors a child directs toward a peer is recorded. Behaviors include: seeks attention, uses peer as a resource, leads in peer activities, imitates a peer, observes a peer, joins a peer, shows pride, competes with peer for adult attention, expresses affection, shows empathy, shows hostility, takes unoffered object, defends property, and seeks agreement. Given that this is a complicated system, it requires a lot of practice to observe all these behaviors reliably. However, once proficiency is achieved with this system, a great deal of information about a child's social behavior with peers is known.

Other observational measures go beyond the individual social behaviors of a child, and capture the child's participation within a group. One measure that is used extensively was initially described by Parten (1932) and was adapted by Rubin and his colleagues. Observers decide if the target child is engaging in solitary, parallel, or group play as well as determining if there is functional, constructive, or sociodramatic play. Rubin, Coplan, Fox, and Calkins (1995) expanded this system even further to capture behaviors of extremely withdrawn or extremely aggressive children.

These observational systems give teachers valuable information that can be used to make decisions about children's eligibility for special education services, to plan interventions, and to evaluate children's progress. They do have a downside, however, in that they require a great deal of time to use.

There are other general developmental assessments that include measures of social and emotional development, and rely on observation or a combination of observation and interviews with parent. The AEPS Test–Birth to Three Years and Three to Six Years (Bricker, Capt, & Pretti-Frontczak, 2002) includes a social domain among other developmental domains. The assessor uses a combination of observation, parent report, and direct testing to measure children's interactions with others, with the environment, and knowledge of self and others.

Another popular assessment that is appropriate for children from birth through age 6 is the Transdisciplinary Play-Based Assessment (Linder, 1993). A child's social-emotional development is assessed primarily through observation. This assessment is unique in that each child is systematically observed with a variety of partners including the parent, the facilitator, and peers. In addition, observers rate a child's temperament, mastery motivation, humor, and use of social conventions.

Interviews and Questionnaires.   Most assessment batteries now include a social and family history in the form of an interview or questionnaire protocol. For example, The DIAL3 (Mardell-Czudnowski & Goldenberg, 1998), a developmental screening, includes a questionnaire that the parent completes before the child's motor, concepts, and language abilities are screened. The questionnaire includes items about :.·ild's social development and behavior.

A child's social behavior may be assessed through direct observation.

Both parents and teachers can use a questionnaire to assess children's friendships. In the Early Childhood Friendship Survey (Buysse, 1991), parents and teachers list children's reciprocal friends, how those friendships began, and the kinds of activities the friends pursue together.

Squires, Bricker, and Twombly (2002) developed the Ages and Stages Questionnaires: Social-Emotional specifically to identify young children who may need further assessment and intervention to address their social-emotional problems. The questionnaire uses parent-report to identify children's social-emotional competence as well as problem behaviors. Parents report on their child's behavior in the areas of self-regulation, compliance, communication, adaptive behaviors, autonomy, affect, and interactions with people. Some of the questions that parents respond to are: "When upset, can your child calm down within 15 minutes?" and "Does your child try to hurt other children, adults, or animals?" It's appropriate for children from 3 to 63 months.

Rating Scales. O'Leary and Johnson (1979) indicate that rating scales are popular for assessing social development. They suggest four strategies to maximize the reliability and validity of a scale: Use raters who know the child very well, use as many raters as possible, use clearly defined points on the scale, and use scales that have several response alternatives. For example, yes-no responses offer little information in assessing a child's aggressiveness, whereas a range of 5 to 7 points along the scale makes the rating more meaningful. Lorr and McNair (1965) also suggest that a rating for a single characteristic should range from "no appearance of the behavior" to "maximum appearance."

There are a number of rating scales that parents and teachers can use to evaluate a child's emotional and social development. Some rating scales cover all developmental domains, and some target only social and emotional development.

One rating scale that specifically targets social and emotional development is the Devereux Early Childhood Assessment (LeBuffe & Naglieri, 1998). This scale is one of the few norm-referenced instruments with a focus on social and emotional development. It can be used by both parents and teachers, and it asks them to rate a child's behavior over the past month. It has three scales that rate a child's initiative, self-control, and attachment. Those ratings are then used to evaluate behavioral concerns as well as protective factors.

Another widely used measure is the Child Behavior Checklist (CBC; Achenbach, 2000) whose scales combine to define children with externalizing and internalizing behaviors. The CBC has numerous other scales that help raters identify children who are emotionally reactive, anxious or depressed, withdrawn, and have somatic complaints, aggressive behaviors, or attention problems. These scales are appropriate for children from 1½ to 5 years old.

Sociometric measures gauge a child's popularity and acceptability by his peers.

Sociometric Measures. Children's popularity and how well they are accepted by their peers are measured using sociometric measures. One example of this measure is a peer rating measure developed by Asher, Singleton, Tinsley, and Hymel (1979). A child is shown a picture of every other child in his class. He then puts each picture into a box. One box is for children with whom he likes to play a lot, one for children he likes to play with a little, and a third box for children with whom he doesn't like to play. Average peer ratings are then computed for each child. Children who receive ratings close to 3 ("play with a lot") are considered well accepted by their peers; those who receive ratings close to 1 ("don't like to play with") are considered rejected by their peers. These measures have been used reliably with preschool children who have first been trained in the sorting procedure using pictures of toys and food.

In summary, the state of the art in assessment of social and emotional development emphasizes systematic observation of quantifiable behaviors. It is not sufficient to say that "the child is very active." One should be able to specify a relative level of activity. In addition, information from parents and other good reporters should be integrated with observational data to identify the child's needs in terms of his interactions with others and his responses to various new and challenging situations.

Technology in Social and Emotional Assessment and Intervention

As early as the 1980s, computers were found to facilitate social interactions for young children with disabilities. Spiegel-McGill, Zippiroli, and Mistrett (1989) observed four young children with disabilities and four children without disabilities paired in three different conditions: a typical free-play condition, a computer condition in which pairs of children had the opportunity to work together using a variety of programs, and a condition in which the children could activate a remote-controlled robot. They found that the children with disabilities, particularly those with more significant impairments, showed more socially directed behaviors when they were working at the computer.

Using a larger sample of children, Howard, Greyrose, Kehr, Espinosa, and Beckwith (1996) found similar results. The social behaviors of groups of two to three toddlers and preschoolers with disabilities who participated in computer activities were compared to those who used toys. Both toddlers and preschoolers on the computer showed more positive affect (e.g., laughter and positive vocalizations) and engaged in more parallel play in which they were aware of the play of other children than those in the noncomputer group.

Although some early childhood educators have expressed concern about the effect of technology use on the social skills of children, these concerns seem unwarranted. Hutinger and Johanson (2000) note that technology that is integrated into a developmentally appropriate curriculum fosters children's development in a variety of areas including communication, sharing, turn taking, and positive social interactions. When Hutinger and Johanson evaluated their Early Childhood Comprehensive Technology System (ECCTS) they found that children made progress in all areas of development, but gains were particularly impressive in the social-emotional area. Children's growth rate in this area more than doubled in comparison to growth before the classrooms instituted the technology system.

> Technology can enhance children's social skills such as communicating, sharing, and turn taking.

Intervention Strategies to Promote Social and Emotional Development

The need for external controls is important for maintaining order in one's life and in society. That is the fundamental reason for having laws and rules that govern society and its institutions. But external controls do not obviate each individual's need to control his impulses and make independent decisions about his own behavior. Children with special needs often have a particularly difficult time with this responsibility. However, whether they have a cognitive deficit that limits problem-solving and decision-making skills or a sensory or physical impairment that limits the quality of their interactions with the environment, children can learn to be more socially and emotionally competent individuals.

McEvoy and Odom (1996) recommended ways to promote social interaction and emotional development for young children with special needs and their families. They suggest that interventions for infants and toddlers should focus on supporting positive interactions between the children and their caregivers and on developing secure relationships. The focus of interventions for preschoolers should be social interaction with peers, development of secure peer relationships, and specific social skills.

> A positive relationship between infant or toddler and caregiver is critical to the child's social-emotional development.

Family-Focused Interventions

For infants and toddlers with disabilities, IDEA stipulates that interventions take place in the children's natural environment. Further, interventions for these youngest children should be family- rather than child-focused. According to Bailey et al. (1998), focusing on the family optimizes outcomes for children for a number of reasons. First, outcomes for children are affected by the quality of the interactions they have with their parents. Second, because infants and toddlers are with their parents more than any other adults, parents have the greatest influence on young children's development. Finally, parents often face special challenges as caregivers of children with disabilities. If interventionists can help parents with these challenges, the children will benefit.

Skills of the Caregiver

Consistency of Care.   A very young child develops trust in a relationship when his needs are met and he gains satisfaction. Subsequently, he begins to feel secure enough to explore the environment and take small risks with new experiences. Caregivers who are consistent in meeting a child's biological needs (e.g., feeding, changing diapers, and attending to scrapes) and subsequent needs for support in his explorations (e.g., through confidence-building hugs and positive words) are likely to find the child becoming confident in his own abilities and secure in relationships with new people.

With a child who has disabilities, the caregiver may require help in determining the child's needs, and how to meet them. The interventionist may find that enhancing the confidence and observation skills of the caregiver are of primary importance. Some caregivers overrespond to a child's cues, never giving the child an opportunity to respond or causing the child to become overstimulated and withdrawn (Marfo, 1991). The child may be expressing his needs plainly, but the caregiver expects something different from a child with special needs. When interactions between caregiver and child are not fun or at least reinforcing, the caregiver may become less responsive to the child. The interventionist may choose to spend considerable time with the caregiver, at least initially, observing the child and helping the caregiver interpret the different ways the child expresses his wants and feelings.

Providing High-Quality Interactions.　The ways in which caregivers and children interact have been the subject of extensive study (Haney & Klein, 1993; Wasserman, Lennon, Allen, & Shilansky, 1987), and the importance of verbal and nonverbal communication between the two is universally acknowledged. Face-to-face interaction helps to establish eye contact and attentional skills in a young child. When tied to supportive verbalizations by the caregiver (e.g., "What a nice smile!" and "I'm going to kiss you on the nose"), the child is encouraged to experiment with vocal play. Later, the caregiver provides words for feelings and for important objects in the child's environment. The child is then better able to communicate his own thoughts and feelings without being totally dependent upon adult interpretation. The interventionist should model appropriate ways to interact with a child, observe the caregiver doing it, and provide feedback. For a child with disabilities, assistance may be needed to identify the child's signaling system or to help the child develop a consistent way to communicate (Hussey-Gardner, 1992; 1996). Principles of behavior theory (e.g., shaping of successive approximations, prompting, reinforcement) may be used to shape the responses of a child with a severe disability so that the caregiver can more easily interpret the messages that the child is conveying.

Providing Diverse Learning Experiences.　As Dunst and his colleagues note, "children's everyday lives include many different kinds of learning experiences and opportunities" (Dunst, Bruder, Trivette, Raab, & McLean, 2001, p. 19).

The interventionist may be able to help a caregiver plan a way to take a child along to the grocery store rather than leave him home with an older child. The local park may not have been used before by the family, but the interventionist can show the caregiver how the child and family can enjoy and benefit from a periodic outing. She may also be in a position to bring a group of caregivers and children together regularly for play groups. The interventionist need not be present at these and, in fact, may choose to be absent in order to facilitate spontaneous sharing by the caregivers.

The interventionist can help the family see the neighborhood and the larger community as places where the young child can learn to interact socially with a variety of partners.

Dunst et al. (2001) suggest that the interventionist help the child's parents to identify appropriate learning environments in the community by asking the following questions:

- What gets the child excited?
- What makes the child laugh and smile?
- What does the child especially work hard at doing?

- What activities does the child enjoy doing?
- What gets and keeps the child's attention?

For a child who likes water, a good learning environment might be the community pool; for a child who likes the feel of sand, the local school playground might provide both a sandbox and other toddlers. Dunst et al. (1998) list a wide variety of other locations that may be available to parents and children including shopping malls, the library story hour, a church Sunday school, the beach, a local recreation center, and even the post office.

Skills of the Interventionist

Effective interventionists use a family-centered approach.

Early intervention has changed since its advent with the passage of P.L. 99-457 in 1986. Our field has come a long way from "the initial notion of parent involvement, which said that parents should participate in the activities that professionals deemed important" (McWilliam, Tocci, & Harbin, 1998, p. 206). Now interventionists seek to establish a collaborative relationship with families (Dinnebeil, Hale, & Rule, 1999).

Working in a home setting demands that an interventionist be able to modify strategies quickly, be sensitive to and an excellent observer of family dynamics, and know how to suggest and model, while letting the caregiver assume responsibility for interactions with the child. Little is gained from working with a child in the home if the interventionist is not absolutely sure that the caregiver has benefited and that the child will receive those benefits in her absence.

McWilliam et al. (1998) found additional qualities in service providers who epitomized a family-centered approach.

- A family orientation
- Thinking the best of families
- Sensitivity
- Responsiveness
- Friendliness
- Having child-level skills

Child-Focused Interventions

The classroom provides its own challenges to the teacher of young children with special needs. Not the least of these is attempting to meet the individual needs of children in a group setting. The classroom provides the teacher with an opportunity to guide a child's interactions in a minisociety. Although it may be unlike life on the outside, it does offer the child opportunities to learn and practice skills that are transferable to real-world situations and that relate to his success in later school and life experiences (Chandler, Lubek, & Fowler, 1992).

The Classroom Setting

Providing **inclusive classrooms** in which young children with disabilities learn alongside their typically developing peers has been advocated as a way to improve social outcomes for the children with disabilities. Teachers and parents believe that children with disabilities improve their cognitive, linguistic, as well as their social skills through observing, modeling, and interacting with more competent peers (Lieber et al., 1998; Paul-Brown & Caperton, 2001). Researchers have found, however, that just providing access to inclusive classrooms is not always sufficient to improve children's outcomes (Odom, 2000), so it is important for teachers to be familiar with a range of interventions to foster social and emotional development. Providing access to inclusive classrooms alone is not always sufficient to improve children's outcomes.

> Teachers must offer a variety of options, in addition to inclusive classrooms, to meet the needs of young children with disabilities.

Strategies to Improve Social Relationships

Brown, Odom, and Conroy (2001) outline an intervention hierarchy that classroom teachers can use to foster children's social relationships and friendships (see Figure 11.1). What is valuable about the interventions that they include in their hierarchy is that teachers can implement them easily, and that researchers have shown them to be effective in improving social outcomes. The base of their hierarchy consists of two foundational approaches that can be used with all children. If those basic approaches do not result in improved social outcomes for children with disabilities, then Brown et al. offer two naturalistic interventions. However, teachers should be prepared to move up the hierarchy to direct interventions with individual children.

Foundation One: Have a High-Quality Preschool Program.   High-quality programs use developmentally appropriate practices. Teachers in these programs plan for activities that are interesting and engaging to children, and offer them physical and emotional security (Sandall & Schwartz, 2002). In high-quality programs, teachers ensure that children have plenty of social opportunities. For example, teachers can provide materials that encourage participation by more than one child—like ball games, some outdoor equipment, and learning centers such as housekeeping and blocks. Teachers can provide extended time periods that allow children to engage in complex pretend play (Dickinson, 1994) with other children. In addition, teachers are available to offer encouragement, model play and social behaviors, and provide feedback to children.

Foundation Two: Promote Positive Attitudes.   Teachers can provide a variety of activities in their classroom that promote positive attitudes toward children with disabilities. Favazza and Odom (1997) recommend that teachers use a number of activities including the following:

- Read positive and realistic stories about children with disabilities.
- Talk about people with disabilities.
- Have materials that include pictures of people with disabilities.
- Group children heterogeneously for activities.

According to Favazza and Odom, the first three activities are good suggestions for parents to implement at home, as well.

Naturalistic Approach One: Teach Social Behaviors Incidentally.   Incidental teaching opportunities occur when children are involved in an activity and the teacher uses that involvement as an opportunity to zero in on a child's objectives. For example, if a child spends his time in the sandbox playing next to other children, the

FIGURE 11.1 Intervention hierarchy to foster children's social relationships.

Source: From "An Intervention Hierarchy for Promoting Young Children's Peer Interactions in Natural Environments," by W. H. Brown, S. L. Odom, and M. A. Conroy, 2001, *Topics in Early Childhood Special Education: Enhancing Professional Development for Providers of Early Care and Intervention, 21,* p. 164. Reprinted with permission by PRO-ED, Inc.

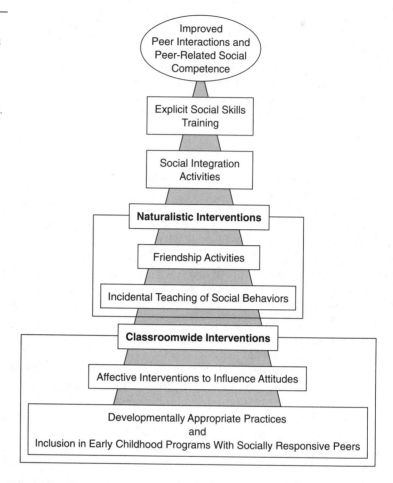

teacher might purposely provide only a few materials then help the target child ask his peers to share the shovel, or the dump truck, thus helping him initiate a social interchange. In this case, the opportunity to target a child's social skills emerged from the ongoing activity.

Naturalistic Approach Two: Plan Friendship Activities.   Another set of activities that have been widely used and are easy for teachers to implement are friendship activities (McEvoy et al., 1988). Teachers take early childhood songs, games, and other activities and transform them into positive, supportive experiences. They can be as easy as having children exchange "high fives" at the end of circle time (Sandall & Schwartz, 2002).

Individual Intervention One: Social Integration Activities.   At the next level of the hierarchy, teachers need to provide more direct opportunities for children to learn social skills and participate in successful social interactions. Brown et al. (2001) describe one way of implementing these activities:

Some materials are designed to help children work together.

- Teachers select children who have problems with social interactions, and they also select responsive peers.
- Teachers select an area of the room for the activity. It might be the block area one day and the housekeeping area another day.
- Children stay and play within that area for 5–15 minutes.
- Teachers plan activities to promote specific social behaviors like sharing, talking, and helping each other.
- Teachers organize and introduce the activity, then monitor to be sure the children are interacting. If they are not, the teacher might suggest an idea, comment on the play, or directly prompt the child to interact.

Chandler (1998) suggests that teachers implement this approach by setting up a **peer interaction play center** (PALS center) in their classroom. The PALS center then becomes one of the options available to children during free-play time.

Individual Intervention Two: Explicit Social Skills Instruction. Some children need explicit instruction in social skills to learn how to interact successfully with their peers. Researchers have explored a number of different approaches to help these children. One example is the buddy-skills training program (English, Goldstein, Shafer, & Kaczmarek, 1997). In this program:

- Teachers coach buddies to "stay with your friend, play with your friend, and talk with your friend" through modeling, guided practice, and independent practice with feedback.

- Teachers set up free play, snack, and large-group activities.
- Children with interaction problems are also taught to stay and play.

Interventions for Emotional Development

Some children's difficulties lie with their inabilities to understand others' emotions and to regulate their own emotions. Denham and Burton (1996) developed a social-emotional prevention program for day-care providers to use with preschoolers at risk both for developing conduct disorders and for those who were withdrawn. Their program has four parts:

- *Relationship building*—teachers use "floor time" to build a supportive relationship with the children. During this time, teachers observe the children, and follow their lead in play.
- *Emotion understanding*—day-care providers teach children words to understand their emotions, and to use the words to label how they're feeling.
- *Emotion regulation*—children learn the "turtle technique" to retreat into their "turtle shell" when they feel hurt or angry.
- *Social problem solving*—children learn to deal with conflicts by generating different ways to proceed and evaluating the effects of their choices. (Denham, 1998, pp. 216–218)

Interventions for Challenging Behaviors

There are a number of long-term interventions to improve children's emotional and social relationships with adults and with their peers. Sometimes, however, children exhibit behaviors that interfere with their learning, are dangerous, or are of tremendous concern to their families. These challenging behaviors often respond well to **positive behavior support** that have been used successfully by parents and teachers (Boulware, Schwartz, & McBride, 1999).

The key to this approach is to assume that the behavior exhibited by the child fills a communicative function; that is, they are used to gain attention, to escape an unpleasant situation, to get or keep an object, or to have a sensory experience. Identifying the function of the behavior is part of a behavior support plan that has five steps. Those steps include:

- *Identifying the problem*—What is the child doing?
- *Brainstorming*—What function is the behavior serving?
- *Making a plan*—What can we do to meet the child's needs in a more appropriate way?
- *Implementing the plan*—How can we implement our plan consistently across a variety of settings?
- *Evaluating the outcomes*—Did the plan work? Is everyone satisfied? What do we do next? (Boulware et al., 1999, p. 31)

Summary

A child's concept of himself and of the world around him is constantly being shaped by every event in his life. For all children, social and emotional development benefits from being in a loving and secure relationship with caregivers, and by having the opportunity to interact and develop relationships with a variety of peers and adults outside the family.

The ability of children with disabilities to form satisfying social and emotional relationships may be affected by aspects of their impairment. Parents, in collaboration with interventionists and teachers, can take steps to mediate the effect of those disabilities.

Social skills and emotions are perhaps the most elusive areas of human development to comprehend. Maladaptive behaviors evolve over many years, yet they change from day to day and from situation to situation. They may contribute to great success in life or to misery and frustration. In this chapter, substantial evidence has been provided that reveals the critical components of social and emotional development in young children with special needs. Interventionists can be optimistic that many of the factors that contribute most to a child's outcome can be influenced by their approach. By including both child and caregiver in the positive educational process, a socially competent and emotionally mature young person can develop.

Review Questions and Discussion Points

1. Spend time observing pairs of infants, toddlers, and preschoolers. What differences in behavior do you see as they interact with each other?

2. Identify four emotions that you might see in young children. Describe how the ways in which children express these emotions change from infancy to preschool.

3. How do disabilities affect young children's social competence? Are there particular disabilities that have greater effects than others?

4. You are a day-care provider and are concerned about the behavior of one of the children in your classroom. What assessment methods can you use to evaluate that behavior? What are the strengths and weaknesses of each of these methods?

5. Interview a teacher in an inclusive preschool classroom. Ask the teacher what strategies she uses to encourage social relationships among the children with and without disabilities in the classroom.

Recommended Resources

Intervention Ideas

For more information about:

Buddy Skills-Training Program

English, K., Goldstein, H., Shafer, K., & Kaczmarek, L. (1997). Promoting interactions among preschoolers with and without disabilities: Effects of a buddy-skills training program. *Exceptional Children, 63,* 229–243.

A Cognitive-Social Learning Curriculum

Mize, J. (1995). Coaching preschool children in social skills: A cognitive-social learning curriculum. In G. Cartledge & J. F. Milburn (Eds.), *Teaching social skills to children and youth: Innovative approaches* (3rd ed., pp. 237–261). Boston: Allyn & Bacon.

The PALS Center (peer interaction play center)

Chandler, L. (1998). Promoting positive interaction between preschool age children during free play: The PALS center. *Young Exceptional Children, 1,* 14–19.

Floor Time

Greenspan, S. I. (1992). *Infancy and early childhood: The practice of clinical assessment and intervention with emotional and developmental challenges.* Madison, CT: International Universities Press.

Attachment

Honig, A. S. (2002). *Secure relationships: Nurturing infant/toddler attachment in early care settings.* Washington, DC: National Association for the Education of Young Children.

Web Sites

Child Trends DataBank
http://www.childtrendsdatabank.org/

Children and Adults with Attention-Deficit/Hyperactivity Disorder
http://chadd.org

Early Childhood Technical Assistance Center
http://www.ectac.org

National Information Center for Children and Youth with Disabilities
http://nichcy.org

References

Achenbach, T. M. (2000). *The Child Behavior Checklist.* Burlington, VT: Achenbach System of Empirically Based Assessment.

American Psychiatric Association. (1994). *Diagnostic and statistical manual of mental disorders* (4th ed.). Washington, DC: Author.

Asher, S. R. (1990). Recent advances in the study of peer rejection. In S. R. Asher & J. D. Coie (Eds.), *Peer rejection in childhood* (pp. 3–14). New York: Cambridge University Press.

Asher, S. R., Singleton, L. C., Tinsley, B. R., & Hymel, S. (1979). A reliable sociometric measure for preschool children. *Developmental Psychology, 15,* 443–444.

Atkinson, L., Chisolm, V. C., Scott, B., Goldberg, S., Vaughn, B. E., Blackwell, J., et al. (1999). Maternal sensitivity, child functional level, and attachment in Down syndrome. In J. I. Vondra & D. Barnett (Eds.), *Atypical attachment in infancy and early childhood among children at developmental risk* (pp. 45–66). *Monographs of the Society for Research in Child Development, 64* (3, Serial No. 258).

Bailey, D. B., McWilliam, R. A., Darkes, L. A., Hebbeler, K., Simeonsson, R. J., Spiker, D., et al. (1998). Family outcomes in early intervention: A framework for program evaluation and efficacy research. *Exceptional Children, 64,* 313–328.

Bandura, A. (1977). *Social learning theory.* Upper Saddle River, NJ: Prentice Hall.

Barnett, D., Butler, C. M., & Vondra, J. I. (1999). Atypical patterns of early attachment: Discussion and future directions. In J. I. Vondra & D. Barnett (Eds.), *Atypical attachment in infancy and early childhood among children at developmental risk* (pp. 172–192). *Monographs of the Society for Research in Child Development, 64* (3, Serial No. 258).

Baumrind, D. (1973). The development of instrumental competence through socialization. In A. D. Pick (Ed.), *Minnesota Symposium on Child Psychology* (Vol. 7, pp. 3–46). Minneapolis: University of Minnesota Press.

Bijou, W. W., & Baer, D. M, (1979). Child development I: A systematic and empirical theory. In B. G. Suran & V. Rizzo (Eds.), *Special children: An integrative approach.* Glenview, IL: Scott Foresman.

Blasco, P. M., Hrncir, E. J., & Blasco, P. A. (1990). The contribution of maternal involvement to mastery performance in infants with cerebral palsy. *Journal of Early Intervention, 14,* 161–174.

Block, J. H. (1982). Gender differences in the nature of premises developed about the world. In E. K. Shapiro & E. Weber (Eds.), *Cognitive and affective growth: Developmental interaction.* Hillsdale, NJ: Erlbaum.

Boulware, G., Schwartz, I., & McBride, B. (1999). Addressing challenging behaviors at home: Working with families to find solutions. *Young exceptional children monograph series: Practical ideas for addressing challenging behaviors.* Washington, DC: Division for Early Childhood.

Bricker, D., Capt, B., & Pretti-Frontczak, K. (2002). *AEPS test birth to three years and three to six years* (2nd ed.). Baltimore: Brookes.

Bronfenbrenner, U. (1979). *The ecology of human development: Experiments by nature and design.* Cambridge, MA: Harvard University Press.

Brown, P. M., Remine, M. D., Prescott, S. J., & Rickards, F. W. (2000). Social interactions of preschoolers with and without impaired hearing in integrated kindergarten. *Journal of Early Intervention, 23,* 200–211.

Brown, W. H., Odom, S. L., & Conroy, M. A. (2001). An intervention hierarchy for promoting young children's peer interactions in natural environments. *Topics in Early Childhood Special Education, 21,* 162–175.

Buysse, V. (1991). *Early Childhood Friendship Survey.* Chapel Hill: Frank Porter Graham Center, University of North Carolina.

Buysse, V. (2002, Winter). Friendship formation. *Early Developments, 6,* 18–19.

Buysse, V., Goldman, B. D., & Skinner, M. L. (2002). Setting effects on friendship formation among young children with and without disabilities. *Exceptional Children, 68,* 503–517.

Campbell, S. B. (1988). Longitudinal studies of active and aggressive preschoolers: Individual differences in early behavior and outcome. In D. Cicchetti & S. L. Toth (Eds.), *Internalizing and externalizing expressions of dysfunction: Rochester symposium on developmental psychopathology* (Vol. 2, pp. 57–89). Hillsdale, NJ: Erlbaum.

Campbell, S. B. (1990). *Behavior problems in preschool children.* New York: Guilford Press.

Campbell, S. B. (1991). Longitudinal studies of active and aggressive preschoolers: Individual differences in early behavior in early behavior and outcome. In D. Cicchetti & S. L. Toth (Eds.), *Rochester symposium on developmental psychopathology.* Vol. 2: *Internalizing and externalizing expressions of dysfunction* (pp. 57–90). Hillsdale, NJ: Erlbaum.

Cassidy, J. (1999). The nature of the child's ties. In J. Cassidy & P. R. Shaver (Eds.), *Handbook of attachment* (pp. 3–20). New York: Guilford Press.

Chandler, L. (1998). Promoting positive interaction between preschool-age children during free play: The PALS center. *Young Exceptional Children, 1,* 14–19.

Chandler, L. K., Lubek, R. C., & Fowler, S. A. (1992). Generalization and maintenance of preschool children's social skills: A critical review and analysis. *Journal of Applied Behavior Analysis, 25,* 415–428.

Coie, J. D., & Dodge, K. A. (1998). Aggression and antisocial behavior. In W. Damon (Series Ed.) & N. Eisenberg (Vol. Ed.), *Handbook of child psychology.* Vol. 3: *Social, emotional and personality development* (5th ed., pp. 779–862). New York: Wiley.

Conroy, M. A., & Davis, C. A. (2000). Early elementary-aged children with challenging behaviors: Legal and educational issues related to IDEA and assessment. *Preventing School Failure, 44,* 163–171.

Crick, N. R., Casas, J. F., & Mosher, M. (1997). Relational and overt aggression in preschool. *Developmental Psychology, 33,* 579–588.

Crocker, A. D., & Orr, R. R. (1996). Social behaviors of children with visual impairments enrolled in preschool programs. *Exceptional Children, 62,* 451–462.

Denham, S. A. (1998). *Emotional development in young children.* New York: Guilford Press.

Denham, S. A., & Burton, R. (1996). A social-emotional intervention program for at risk four-year-olds. *Journal of School Psychology, 34,* 225–245.

Dickinson, D. K. (1994). Features of early childhood classroom environments that support development of language and literacy. In J. F. Duchan, L. E. Hewitt, & R. M. Sonnenmeier (Eds.), *Pragmatics: From theory to practice* (pp. 185–201). Upper Saddle River, NJ: Prentice Hall.

Dinnebeil, L. A., Hale, L., & Rule, S. (1999). Early intervention program practices that support collaboration. *Topics in Early Childhood Special Education, 19,* 225–235.

Dunst, C. J., Bruder, M. B., Trivette, C. M., Raab, M., & McLean, M. (2001). Natural learning opportunities for infants, toddlers, and preschoolers. *Young Exceptional Children, 4,* 18–25.

Eckerman, C. O., Davis, C. C., & Didow, S. M. (1989). Toddlers' emerging ways of achieving social coordination with a peer. *Child Development, 60,* 440–453.

English, K., Goldstein, H., Shafer, K., & Kaczmarek, L. (1997). Promoting interactions among preschoolers with and without disabilities: Effects of a buddy-skills training program. *Exceptional Children, 63,* 229–243.

Erikson, E. (1950). *Childhood and society.* New York: Norton.

Farrenkopf, C., Howze, Y., & Sowell, V. (1995, April). Social skills development for preschool children with visual impairments. Paper presented at the Annual International Convention of the Council for Exceptional Children, Indianapolis, IN.

Favazza, P. C., & Odom, S. L. (1997). Promoting positive attitudes of kindergarten-age children toward people with disabilities. *Exceptional Children, 63,* 405–418.

Field, T. (1979). Differential behavior and cardiac responses of three-month-old infants to a mirror and to a peer. *Infant Behavior and Development, 2,* 179–184.

Goncu, A. (1987). Toward an interactional model of developmental changes in social pretend play. In L. G. Katz (Ed.), *Current topics in early childhood education* (Vol. 7, pp. 108–125). Norwood, NJ: Ablex.

Graham, P., & Rutter, M. (1968). Organic brain dysfunction and child psychiatric disorder. *British Medical Journal, 2,* 695–700.

Guralnick, M. J. (1999). The nature and meaning of social integration for young children with mild developmental delays in inclusive settings. *Journal of Early Intervention, 22,* 70–86.

Guralnick, M. J. (2001). Social competence with peers and early childhood inclusion. In M. J. Guralnick (Ed.), *Early childhood inclusion: Focus on change* (pp. 481–502). Baltimore: Brookes.

Guralnick, M. J., Connor, R. T., Hammond, M. A., Gottman, J. M., & Kinnish, K. (1996). The peer relations of preschool children with communication disorders. *Child Development, 67,* 471–489.

Haney, M., & Klein, D. M. (1993). Impact of a program to facilitate mother-infant communication in high-risk families of high-risk infants. *Journal of Communication Disorders, 15,* 15–22.

Hestenes, L. L., & Carroll, D. E. (2000). The play interactions of young children with and without disabilities: Individual and environmental influences. *Early Childhood Research Quarterly, 15,* 229–246.

Howard, J., Greyrose, E., Kehr, K. Espinosa, M., & Beckwith, L. (1996). Teacher-facilitated microcomputer activities: Enhancing social play and affect in young children with disabilities. *Journal of Special Education Technology, 13,* 36–47.

Howes, C. (1987). Social competence with peers in young children: Developmental sequences. *Developmental Review, 7,* 252–272.

Hussey-Gardner, B. (1992). *Parenting to make a difference: one to four years.* Palo Alto, CA: VORT Corporation.

Hussey-Gardner, B. (1996). *Understanding my signals: Help for parents of premature infants* (2nd ed.). Palo Alto, CA: VORT Corporation.

Hutinger, P. L., & Johanson, J. (2000). Implementing and maintaining an effective early childhood comprehensive technology system. *Topics in Early Childhood Special Education, 20,* 159–173.

Ingersoll, B. (1995). ADD: Not just another fad. *Attention, 2,* 17–19.

Jennings, K. D., Conners, R. E., & Stegman, C. E. (1988). Does a physical handicap alter the development of mastery motivation during the preschool years? *Journal of the American Academy of Child & Adolescent Psychiatry, 27,* 312–317.

LeBuffe, P. A., & Naglieri, J. A. (1998). *The Devereux Early Childhood Assessment.* Villanova, PA: Devereux Foundation.

Lieber, J. (1993). A comparison of social pretend play in young children with and without disabilities. *Early Education and Development, 4,* 148–161.

Lieber, J., Capell, K., Sandall, S. R., Wolfberg, P., Horn, E., Beckman, P. (1998). Inclusive preschool programs: Teachers' beliefs and practices. *Early Childhood Research Quarterly, 13,* 87–105.

Linder, T. W. (1993). *The transdisciplinary play-based assessment* (Rev. ed.). Baltimore: Brookes.

Lorr, M., & McNair, D. M. (1965). Expansion of the interpersonal behavior circle. *Journal of Personality and Social Psychology, 2,* 823–830.

Mardell-Czudnowski, C., & Goldenberg, D. S. (1998). *DIAL3: Developmental Indicators for the Assessment of Learning* (3rd ed.). Circle Pines, MN: American Guidance Service.

Marfo, K. (1991). The maternal directiveness theme in mother-child interaction research: Implication for early intervention. In K. Marfo (Ed.), *Early intervention in transition: Current perspectives on programs for handicapped infants* (pp. 177–203). New York: Praeger.

McEvoy, M. A., Nordquist, V. M., Twardosz, S., Heckaman, K., Wehby, J. H., & Denny, R. K. (1988). Promoting autistic children's peer interaction in an integrated early childhood setting using affection activities. *Journal of Applied Behavior Analysis, 21,* 193–200.

McEvoy, M. A., & Odom, S. L. (1996). Strategies for promoting social interaction and emotional development of infants and young children with disabilities and their families, In S. L. Odom & M. E. McLean (Eds.), *Early intervention/early childhood special education: Recommended practices.* Austin, TX: PRO-ED.

McWilliam, R. A., Tocci, L., & Harbin, G. (1998). Family-centered services: Service providers' discourse and behavior. *Topics in Early Childhood Special Education, 18,* 206–221.

Messenheimer-Young, T., & Kretschmer, R. R. (1994). Can I play? A hearing impaired preschooler's requests to access maintained social interaction. *The Volta Review, 96,* 5–18.

Moustakas, C. E., Sigel, I. E., & Schalock, N. D. (1956). An objective method for the measurement and analysis of child-adult interaction. *Child Development, 27,* 109–134.

Odom, S. L. (2000). Preschool inclusion: What we know and where we go from here. *Topics in Early Childhood Special Education, 20,* 20–27.

Odom, S. L., & Munson, L. J. (1996). Assessing social performance. In M. McLean, D. B. Bailey, & M. Wolery (Eds.), *Assessing infants and preschoolers with special needs* (2nd ed., pp. 398–434). Upper Saddle River, NJ: Merrill/Prentice Hall.

Odom, S. L., Zercher, C., Marquart, J., Li, S., Sandall, S. R., & Wolfberg, P. (2002). Social relationships of children with disabilities and their peers in inclusive preschool classrooms. In S. L. Odom (Ed.), *Widening the circle: Including children with disabilities in preschool programs* (pp. 61–80). New York: Teachers College Press.

O'Leary, K. D., & Johnson, S. B. (1979). Psychological assessment. In H. C. Quay & J. S. Werry (Eds.), *Psychopathological disorders of childhood* (pp. 210–246). New York: Wiley.

Parke, R. D., & Buriel, R. (1998) Socialization in the family: Ethnic and ecological perspectives. In W. Damon (Series Ed.) & N. Eisenberg (Vol. Ed.), *Handbook of child psychology.* Vol. 3: *Social, emotional and personality development* (5th ed., pp. 463–552). New York: Wiley.

Parten, M. (1932). Social participation among preschool children. *Journal of Abnormal and Social Psychology, 27,* 243–269.

Paul-Brown, D., & Caperton, C. J. (2001). Inclusive practices for preschool-age children with specific language impairments. In M. J. Guralnick (Ed.), *Early childhood inclusion: Focus on change* (pp. 433–463). Baltimore: Brookes.

Pipp-Siegel, S., Siegel, C. H., & Dean, J. (1999). Neurological aspects of the disorganized/disoriented attachment classification system: Differentiating quality of the attachment relationship from neurological impairment. In J. I. Vondra & D. Barnett (Eds.), *Atypical attachment in infancy and early childhood among children at developmental risk* (pp. 25–44). *Monographs of the Society for Research in Child Development, 64* (3, Serial No. 258).

Quinton, D., & Rutter, M. (1976). Early hospital admissions and later disturbances of behavior: An attempted replication of Douglas's findings. *Developmental Medicine and Child Neurology, 18,* 447–459.

Roberts, S. B., Brown, P. M., & Rickards, F. W. (1996). Social pretend play entry behavior of preschoolers with and without impaired hearing. *Journal of Early Intervention, 20,* 52–83.

Rothbart, M. K., & Bates, J. E. (1998). Temperament. In W. Damon (Series Ed.) & N. Eisenberg (Vol. Ed.), *Handbook of child psychology.* Vol. 3: *Social, emotional and personality development* (5th ed., pp. 105–176). New York: Wiley.

Rubin, K. H., Bukowski, W., & Parker, J. G. (1998). Peer interactions, relationships, and groups. In W. Damon (Series Ed.) & N. Eisenberg (Vol. Ed.), *Handbook of child psychology.* Vol. 3: *Social, emotional and personality development* (5th ed., pp. 619–700). New York: Wiley.

Rubin, K. H., Coplan, R. J., Fox, N. A., & Calkins, S. (1995). Emotionality, emotion regulation, and preschoolers' social adaptation. *Development and Psychopathology, 7,* 49–62.

Rutter, M. (1971). Parent-child separation: Psychological effects on children. *Journal of Psychology and Psychiatry, 12,* 233–260.

Rutter, M. (1978). Early sources of security and competence. In J. S. Bruner & A. Garton (Eds.), *Human growth and development.* London: Oxford University Press.

Rutter, M. (1980). The long-term effects of early experience. *Developmental Medicine and Child Neurology, 22,* 800–813.

Salovey, P., & Mayer, J. D. (1990). Emotional intelligence. *Imagination, Cognition, and Personality, 9,* 185–211.

Sameroff, A. J., & Chandler, M. J. (1975). Reproductive risk and the continuum of caretaking casualty. In F. D. Horowitz, E. M. Hetherington, S. Scarr-Salapatek, & G. W. Siegel (Eds.), *Review of child development research* (Vol. 4), Chicago: University of Chicago Press.

Sameroff, A. J., & Fiese, B. H. (1990). Transactional regulation and early intervention. In S. J. Meisels & J. P. Shonkoff (Eds.), *Handbook of early childhood intervention* (pp. 119–149). New York: Cambridge University Press.

Sandall, S. R., & Schwartz, I. S. (2002). *Building blocks for teaching preschoolers with special needs.* Baltimore: Brookes.

Seidel, V. P., Chadwick, O., & Rutter, M. (1975). Psychological disorder in crippled children. *Developmental Medicine and Child Neurology, 27,* 563–573.

Serbin, L. A., O'Leary, D. K., Kent, R. N., & Tonick, I. J. (1973). A comparison of teacher response to pre-academic and problem behavior of boys and girls. *Child Development, 44,* 796–804.

Shonkoff, J. P., & Phillips, D. A. (Eds.). (2000). *From neurons to neighborhoods: The science of early childhood development.* Washington, DC: National Academy Press.

Sigman, M. D., Kasari, C., Kwon, J. H., & Yirmiya, N. (1992). Responses to the negative emotions of others by autistic, mentally retarded, and normal children. *Child Development, 63,* 796–807.

Sigman, M. D., & Ruskin, E. (1999). Continuity and change in the social competence of children with autism, Down syndrome, and developmental delays. *Monographs of the Society for Research in Child Development, 64* (1, Serial No. 256).

Solomon, J., & George, C. (1999). The measurement of attachment security in infancy and childhood. In J. Cassidy & P. R. Shaver (Eds.), *Handbook of attachment* (pp. 287–316). New York: Guilford Press.

Spiegel-McGill, P., Zippiroli, S. M., & Mistrett, S. G. (1989). Microcomputers as social facilitators in integrated preschools. *Journal of Early Intervention, 13,* 249–260.

Squires, J., Bricker, D., & Twombly, E. (2002). *Ages and Stages Questionnaires: Social-Emotional.* Baltimore: Brookes.

Thomas, A., & Chess, S. (1977). *Temperament and development.* New York: Bruner/Mazel.

Thomas, E. B., Liederman, P. H., & Olson, J. P. (1972). Neonate-mother interaction during breast feeding. *Developmental Psychology, 6,* 110–118.

Umansky. W., & Smalley, B. S. (2003). *ADHD: Helping your child: A comprehensive program to treat attention-deficit/hyperactivity disorder at home and in school.* New York: Warner Books.

Vandell, D. L., & George. L. B. (1981). Social interactions in hearing and deaf preschoolers. Successes and failures in initiations. *Child Development, 52,* 627–635.

Vandell, D. L., & Mueller, E. (1980). Peer play and friends during the first two years. In H. Foot, A. Chapman, & J. Smith (Eds.), *Friendship and social relations in children* (pp. 181–208). New York: Wiley.

van den Boom, D. C., & Hoeksma, J. B. (1994). The effects of infant irritability on mother-infant interaction: A growth curve analysis. *Developmental Psychology, 30,* 581–590.

Walker, E. F., Cudeck, R., Mednick, S. A., & Schulsinger, F. (1981). Effects of parental absence and institutionalization on the development of clinical symptoms in high-risk children. *Acta Psychiatrica Scandanavica, 63,* 65–109.

Wasserman, G. A., Lennon, M. C., Allen, R., & Shilansky, M. (1987). Contributors to attachment in normal and physically handicapped infants. *Journal of the American Academy of Child & Adolescent Psychiatry, 26,* 9–15.

Webster-Stratton, C. (1997). Early intervention for families of preschool children with conduct problems. In M. J. Guralnick (Ed.), *The effectiveness of early intervention* (pp. 429–453). Baltimore: Brookes.

Weinfield, N. S., Sroufe, L. A., Egeland, B., & Carlson, E. A. (1999). The nature of individual differences in infant-caregiver attachment. In J. Cassidy & P. R. Shaver (Eds.), *Handbook of attachment* (pp. 68–88). New York: Guilford Press.

White, B. (1975). *The first three years of life.* Upper Saddle River, NJ: Prentice Hall.

Wolkind, S., & Rutter, M. (1973). Children who have been "in care": An epidemiological study. *Journal of Child Psychology and Psychiatry, 14,* 97–105.

Yarrow, M. R. (1963). Problems of methods in parent-child research. *Child Development, 34,* 215–226.

Zanandra, M. (1998). Play, social interaction, and motor development: Practical activities for preschoolers with visual impairments. *Journal of Visual Impairment & Blindness, 92,* 176–188.

Zegoib, L. H., Arnold, S., & Forehand, R. (1975). An examination of observer effects in parent-child interactions. *Child Development, 27,* 109–134.

PART IV

Epilogue

CHAPTER 12
Issues and Directions

12

Issues and Directions

Stephen R. Hooper and Warren Umansky

Chapter Outline

Alex and Margie

*A*lex and Margie (in the opening vignette in Chapter 1) were on their way to the obstetrician's office for the 16-week amniocentesis. Alex and Margie shared a number of fears and worries regarding their pending parenthood. Although they talked with each other about many of their hopes and dreams for their unborn child (e.g., college aspirations), as well as some of their trepidations (e.g., would they be good parents, would they have a good relationship with their son or daughter), they kept many of their fears and worries to themselves. Given the family history of developmental disabilities on each side of the family, they both knew that the chances of having a child with some type of problem was higher than most—not to mention that they had waited until their mid-30s to begin a family. These were topics that were not discussed.

For the most part, Margie's pregnancy had progressed in a rather uneventful fashion. She experienced the initial phases of pregnancy without undue difficulty; she could have done without the frequent morning sickness shortly after finding out about the pregnancy, but she gained the expected amount of weight and participated in all of her prenatal care visits. Given her age, she was classified as a high-risk pregnancy and knew that she was going to have a number of prenatal screening tests. At about 10 weeks gestation, Margie had chorionic villi sampling performed. Several weeks later the doctor invited Alex and Margie in for a conference. A positive finding for Down syndrome was reported. Although they were initially devastated, they knew about how well Margie's older brother was doing as a young adult and they were aware from their nephew's experiences that the early intervention services seemed to be better than ever. Would it be so bad? Their obstetrician also had informed them that the false positive rate for this prenatal screening procedure was unusually high, and that Margie would undergo the more reliable amniocentesis prenatal screening procedures at about 16 weeks' gestation.

As they drove to the appointment, they were quietly supportive of each other and tried to be as positive as possible. Again, there were many unspoken questions that Alex and Margie unknowingly shared—many of which involved the future of their child and family. If they had a child with Down syndrome, would he or she be retarded? What kind of label or terminology would be used to identify their child? Would that label hold potential harm, or would it open up

possible service options, or both? Could their child play and go to school with typically develop-
ing children, or would the child have to stay with children with disabilities? Which one would
be better? Regardless of the setting, would their child be happy and accepted or constantly teased
because of the disabilities? How would having a child with special needs affect their family, par-
ticularly their marriage or the desire for other children?

Alex and Margie had discussed having several children, but now what? What if the medical
care or special services exceeded their financial resources? How would they cope? Are there any
medical procedures or medical technologies that could lessen the possible degree of disability that
might be present? From their family experiences they knew that knowledgeable professionals
existed in their community, but who were they and where did they need to begin to get possible
services? How would they know if someone was a well-trained professional or knowledgeable
about their child and family's needs? How much would they have to fight for services and
resources for their child to address potential needs? Do parents with typically developing children
have to do all of this? Do they experience all of these worries and concerns? How would their lives
be different? These questions were swirling in their heads as they reached the doctor's office. As
they got out of their car, they each took a deep breath and realized that their lives were going to
change forever—regardless of the outcome of the amniocentesis procedure.

In this text we have sought to provide a thorough overview of early childhood issues that are pertinent to infants, toddlers, and preschoolers with special developmental needs. Early childhood special education has witnessed an explosion in knowledge since the first edition of this text was published. Although the direct application of new knowledge generally lags behind **best clinical practices** and **evidence-based strategies** (i.e., those actually supported by research findings) in most fields of study, we have tried to provide current information in a form that we hope encourages rapid application with children and families. We hope that students and professionals working in the field of early childhood special education will strive for evidence-based best practices and that the information provided in this text will facilitate those efforts. As we close, there are many remaining questions, issues, and trends that confront professionals in this field. A brief discussion of the most important of these follows.

Striving to provide best practices, particularly those that are evidence-based, will better serve professionals, children, and their families.

Terminology

We have attempted to standardize the terminology used in this text from one chapter to the next; this was a compromise of semantics and principles. For example, in a world that attaches status and importance to titles, what title best characterizes what we do? What title or titles are more appropriate and desirable? We decided to use the term *early interventionist* or *interventionist* in most cases rather than *early childhood special educator, teacher, educator,* or *therapist.* Although all these terms refer to professionals who work with infants, toddlers, and preschoolers, not all have special education training, college degrees, or training in specialized aspects of intervention (e.g., feeding, play, and positioning). We settled on a term that appears to encompass all professionals who offer early intervention programming.

We also struggled with the terms used to describe children who have special needs. *Handicapped children, mentally retarded children,* and similar terms have been out of favor for several years. We also avoided using the term *developmentally delayed* because, although federal and state legislators endorse the use of this term, the concept of delay suggests that these children will "catch up." In fact, as illustrated by many of the chapters in this text, most children will continue to show a wide range of developmental problems throughout their life spans. We opted for the terms *children with disabilities* and *children with special needs* for clarity and consistency; however, do other terms define the population as clearly or more clearly? Outside of accessing special services, does a single label accurately describe all of the characteristics of a young child with special needs?

The terms *children with disabilities* and *children with special needs* are currently the most appropriate for this population.

There also are a number of issues inherent in how children with special needs are classified. Although it appears that the terminology employed in IDEA will continue to be used to identify children for special education services, what happens when a field moves ahead of definitional standards? For example, with the AAMR's (2002) new definition of *mental retardation* in place, many of the current clinical and research conventions will need to be modified or adapted. This will involve training of early interventionists not only in the new knowledge base, but also in any new measurement, assessment-treatment linkages, and program or system change issues. A change in the definition and associated terminology also will contribute to an ever-changing research base on this special education classification. Keeping up with the current terminology is important for clinical services as well as what might be "politically correct" for the families and the larger group of community service providers.

Inclusion

Some advocates for children with disabilities believe that all children with special needs should be educated in integrated settings with their regular peers. This was a theme echoed across many of the chapters in this text. The logistics of this approach pose one dilemma; the benefits pose another. It is relatively easy to integrate school-aged children into classes within a school building; however, given that early childhood programs are rarely conducted in "school" buildings and more typically done in community-based settings (i.e., the home), particularly for children under 4 years of age, finding "typical" programs in which young children with special needs can be included poses a challenge.

Finding "typical" programs in which young children with special needs can be included continues to pose a challenge for professionals and families.

Another concern is the training of staff who work in programs that include children with special needs and the availability of specialized staff to provide support at times when such support is most needed. Also, should all young children with special needs be included in regular classes without regard to the type or intensity of their disabilities? Should consideration be given to the effects of such children's inclusion on the learning of children without disabilities in the class? Is the inclusion strategy supported by research data? Is inclusion more beneficial for children with certain types or degrees of disabilities than others? The resolution for many of these issues and questions is being studied by researchers. Hopefully, guidance will be forthcoming to help parents and early interventionists make sound decisions.

Families

Related to the concept of inclusion is the involvement of families. In fact, we propose extending the definition of *inclusion* to encompass the involvement of families in the entire early childhood special education process. Indeed, family matters and issues have been discussed in nearly every chapter of this text. Although the inclusion of families in this process has been discussed for years, it has been only recently that models have attempted to incorporate a family perspective. Family thoughts, feelings, ideas, and observations have been addressed relative to their importance to assessment; they also are critical to intervention, to developmental monitoring, and ultimately, to increasing the chance of positive developmental outcomes. Recent findings (see Chapter 3) suggest that a parent's responsiveness to her child represents one of the best predictors of a positive developmental outcome!

Family involvement, however, is not a program component with which many professionals in the field feel secure and comfortable. Indeed, most early interventionists are not well prepared to work with mothers, fathers, or other family members. Consequently, it will remain an ongoing challenge for professionals who work with young children with special needs to keep other family members appropriately involved *and to do so in a sensitive, appropriate fashion.* What role, for example, should parents have in their child's program? How prepared are professionals now entering the field of early intervention to analyze family needs and to work productively with family members who show very diverse characteristics?

A strong family component needs to be incorporated into all early childhood training programs.

Extended family involvement can be critical to the on-going development of children.

Cultural Diversity

Related to the important considerations surrounding families is the broad concept of diversity. As nicely described in Chapter 5, diversity comes in many different packages and with many different associated ideas for the same terms. In order to work with children with special needs and their families it will become increasingly important, given the changing demography in the United States, that professionals improve their understanding of a wide range of cultures. The American family has become increasingly diverse over the past 2 decades with notable increases, for example, in Hispanic families, families who are economically disadvantaged, and families who are homeless. The finding reported in Chapter 3 indicating that 42% of homeless children are under the age of 5 years is striking. This diversity will impact on nearly every aspect of early childhood education including assessment, treatment, community-based programs, involvement of schools, how service delivery occurs, and training. How prepared are you to deal with the increasing diversity of your community, state, or region? How should we approach cultural diversity issues in our communities? In our homes? What does this mean for you and how you will work with children and families from various cultural backgrounds? Should specific training in this broad area be required of all early interventionists and others working with young children with special needs?

> Diversity will have an impact on nearly every aspect of early childhood education.

Training

The primary emphasis of this text has been on understanding child development and applying it within the context of the individual needs of a child and family. We believe strongly that a firm grounding in the concepts of development are critical to how competent professionals will be in the field, and we affirm the use of the Council for Exceptional Children Division for Early Childhood's recommended practices in early intervention and early childhood special education described in the chapters on assessment (Chapter 4) and intervention (Chapter 5).

> A firm foundation in development will facilitate how professionals work with children with special needs and their families.

Further, those who have observed their own children or younger siblings growing up begin their formal training with an enriched perspective of how children develop. We cannot overstate the importance of the best practices and evidence-based practices models, which are built on a sound knowledge of what makes children tick. At the same time, training programs should orient early interventionists to a team approach to assessment and intervention, preferably an interdisciplinary or transdisciplinary team approach, with special time and consideration being given to matters of family, culture, and diversity more generally (e.g., socioeconomic status).

Still, questions remain. Should training programs in early childhood special education reflect a single philosophical orientation or should they be more eclectic in their makeup? How can diverse training needs, such as how to work within a wide variety of different ecologies or learn various assistive technologies, be integrated into a time-limited college-based training program? What other training components might be needed? How should state certifications work to ensure minimum training competencies in their credentialing process? Is there a credentialing process in place?

One thing is certain: Working with children with special needs requires familiarity with many different disciplines. Training programs for early interventionists must address the interdisciplinary and transdisciplinary facets of assessment and treatment. Such training improves the quality of services that these professionals provide to young children with special needs and their families.

Technology

These are great times in which to live. Computers, microwave ovens, compact disc players, and computer-chip-based toys all make life easier, but only because we know what we want and buy what we can. When a technological aid is recommended as being of benefit to a young child with special needs, the child's caregivers must appreciate the importance of the aid, know how to use it, understand when to use it, and get support to continue to use it with or for the child. In addition, the need for the technological aid must be evaluated regularly to determine whether the approach is working and the child has progressed, or whether the child has regressed and a new approach or different technological aid is required. Computers have improved certain aspects of assessment and intervention for children with special needs (e.g., by offering other vehicles for play), and they have contributed to the dissemination of information in a more rapid and thorough fashion. The "information superhighway" is now a reality and can be used by nearly anyone.

Medical technology has shared in an abundance of significant advances that will continue to have a dramatic impact on early childhood special education. For example, more infants are surviving birth trauma and very low birth weight than ever before, which may add to the population of children who need early intervention. On the other hand, prenatal surgery holds promise for correcting problems even before infants are born. Since the last edition of this text, these prospects have expanded even further. In addition, new medications and surgical treatments can cure, correct, or lessen problems that otherwise would cause serious, lifelong impairments.

As noted in Chapter 6, technology undoubtedly will continue to expand, and the types of technology available will continue to proliferate. It is not possible for a textbook to keep pace with the rapid rate at which advances are evolving, but suffice it to say that technology is here to stay and it likely will be an ever-growing component in the early childhood domain with which interventionists must keep pace. It is unproductive, however, for technology to be dumped on caregivers without the support necessary to help make it successful. Technology creates questions as well as solutions: Should technology be withheld from a child or family if a program cannot provide the necessary ongoing support? Should more efforts be made to enlist the most sophisticated technological approaches with children regardless of cost? How can ongoing training be provided to teachers so that they can stay on top of technology? How does a program keep from relying too heavily on instructional technology to the detriment of person-to-person instruction?

> Early interventionists must be aware of a variety of technologies or they need to know where to ask for help.

Public Policy

Although most early interventionists will focus their time and energy on working with children and their families, or on systemic or administrative issues within a program, it is critical for them to be keenly aware that public policy can shape how they focus their time and energy. It is important for early interventionists to remain aware of the rapidly changing information base related to new clinical findings and scientific breakthroughs, and that these findings can influence legislative activities. Indeed, legislative mandates will change how the early interventionists will perform their services. As noted in Chapter 1, a clear research base and a strong child advocacy mission shaped how early intervention is conducted today. Although these efforts have created a strong basis from which to move the field of early childhood forward, public sentiment can be swayed by non-evidence-based conjectures and political winds that have other important issues to address. Consequently, it remains critical for those working in the field to be cognizant of just how fragile this support base is, and to work diligently to press for the evolving needs of children with special needs and their families.

But, what resources are available to help early interventionists keep up with scientific, legislative, and other relevant events in the field? What vehicles are available for interventionists to have an impact on decision making in their communities and states? Given the fiscal pressures at all governmental levels, funding for early intervention services may determine what progress is made in the field. Logical, rational, and informed professionals can tilt the legislative and fiscal scales in favor of necessary support for programs and, subsequently, influence public policy in their communities. Staying abreast of public policy issues and related political matters important to early childhood will be important to continue progress in the field. Liberally using state and federal resources devoted to early childhood, such as those offered by the Maternal and Child Health Bureau (http://www.mchb.gov), the Administration on Developmental Disabilities (http://www.aucd.org), and state Title V agencies all should facilitate the ongoing importance of public policy to the field of early childhood and early childhood special education.

Staying abreast of public policy issues in early childhood will be critical to positive growth and movement in the field.

Learning about the many resources available through state and federal agencies will support the ongoing importance and awareness of public policy in the broad area of early childhood.

Keeping Pace

An obvious theme of this text is the need to keep pace with advancing knowledge in the field. There have been significant changes in legislation regarding how services are provided and to which constituents these services are offered. Further, as noted earlier, the continued research base to support early intervention remains strong, with new developments seemingly occurring on a daily basis. This is good news in that more children from birth to age 5 are being served than ever before, although as the vignettes in each of the chapters wonderfully illustrate, these cases are becoming more complex and surely require the assistance of early childhood services. The field is making new advances in the areas of assessment and intervention, and the linkages to new scientific knowledge are increasing as well (e.g., the brain differences noted in children who are abused and neglected). The prenatal,

How we work with children with special needs will certainly have an impact on our future!

perinatal, and postnatal factors that have an impact on development also are being better understood, with these findings being translated into public policy and clinical practice with greater speed than ever before.

To the Future

We hope that this text has provided professionals and students interested in early intervention with a clearer picture of the current state of the field. Just as this fourth edition reflects the marked changes that have occurred in the progress of early childhood special education since the publication of the first three editions, we look forward to reporting on future significant changes in the next edition—changes in which the reader well may have played a role. It should be exciting to see how the field will change in the next 5 years!

Name Index

Subject Index